Moreton Morrell Site

WARWICKSHIRE
COLLEGE
LIBRARY

KT-142-360

You may

You may have this book requested for a further
by another reader.

The
Sport Management

www.pearsoned.co.uk

WITHDRAWN

00090016

PEARSON

Education

We work with leading authors to develop the
strongest educational materials in business and finance,
bringing cutting-edge thinking and best learning
practice to a global market.

Under a range of well-known imprints, including
Financial Times Prentice Hall, we craft high-quality print
and electronic publications which help readers to
understand and apply their content, whether studying
or at work.

To find out more about the complete range of our
publishing please visit us on the World Wide Web at:
www.pearsoned.co.uk

The Business of Sport Management

Edited by

John Beech
Coventry Business School

and

Simon Chadwick
Leeds University Business School

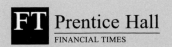
796.06 BEE

Acc. No:
0090016

Date: April 04

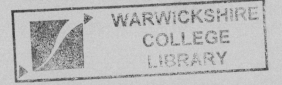
WARWICKSHIRE
COLLEGE
LIBRARY

FT Prentice Hall
FINANCIAL TIMES

An imprint of **Pearson Education**
Harlow, England • London • New York • Boston • San Francisco • Toronto • Sydney • Singapore • Hong Kong
Tokyo • Seoul • Taipei • New Delhi • Cape Town • Madrid • Mexico City • Amsterdam • Munich • Paris • Milan

Pearson Education Limited

Edinburgh Gate
Harlow
Essex CM20 2JE
England

and Associated Companies throughout the world

Visit us on the World Wide Web at:
www.pearsoned.co.uk

First published 2004
© Pearson Education Limited 2004

All rights reserved. No part of this publication may be reproduced, stored in a retrieval system, or transmitted in any form or by any means, electronic, mechanical, photocopying, recording or otherwise, without either the prior written permission of the Publishers or a licence permitting restricted copying in the United Kingdom issued by the Copyright Licensing Agency Ltd, 90 Tottenham Court Road, London W1T 4LP.

All trademarks used herein are the property of their respective owners. The use of any trademark in this text does not vest in the author or publisher any trademark ownership rights in such trademarks, nor does the use of such trademarks imply any affiliation with or endorsement of this book by such owners.

ISBN 0 273 68268 7

British Library Cataloguing-in-Publication Data
A catalogue record for this book is available from the British Library.

10 9 8 7 6 5 4 3 2 1
08 07 06 05 04

Typeset in 10/12.5 pt Sabon by 3.
Printed and bound by Ashford Colour Press, Gosport.

The publisher's policy is to use paper manufactured from sustainable forests.

Brief contents

Contents

19 The future for sport businesses

Simon Chadwick

Figures

Tables

Exhibits

Case studies

About the authors

Dave Arthur

Dave is Senior Lecturer in sport management at Southern Cross University. His current research interests include strategic sport marketing and corporate sponsorship. He has worked extensively with industry and has been involved in the management and promotion of many major events.

Alan Barnard

Alan is a marketing and communications consultant. He was heavily involved with modernising both the Labour Party in the 1990s and then the Football Association. He lives in London and is a life-long Chelsea fan.

John Beech (co-editor)

John is the Head of Leisure, Sport and Tourism Management at Coventry Business School. He teaches on both the MBA (Sport Management) and BA Sport Management degrees and has published widely on the use of internet marketing by soccer clubs. He is a committee member of SPRIG.

Karen Bill

Karen is Senior Lecturer at University College Worcester, where her main role is 'New Curriculum Development Coordinator'. She is currently completing the Post-Graduate Diploma in Legal Studies (CPE) and has published in the *Legal Executive Journal*.

Terrence Wendell Brathwaite

Terry is Senior Lecturer in International Human Resource Management and Employment Law at Coventry Business School. A former Lecturer on Human Relations in Sport at the University of the West Indies, he has also served as Sports Marketing Manager for the Ontario Amateur Football Association in Canada. Terry is a member of various professional bodies including ILAM, CIM and IoD.

Terri Byers

Terri is Field Chair for Sport and Recreation at Buckinghamshire Chilterns University College, where she is also Senior Lecturer in Sport and Leisure Management, and Book Review Editor for *European Sport Management Quarterly*. Her research interests include control in voluntary sport organisations, strategic decision-making and small firms in the sport and leisure industry.

Simon Chadwick (co-editor)

Simon lectures in Marketing at Leeds University Business School and is Programme Director for the MA in Advertising and Marketing. He has published work on sport marketing and strategic collaboration in sport, and has recently worked with the Premier League and the Institute of Football Management and Administration.

Dominic Elliott

Dominic is Professor of Business Continuity and Strategic Management at the University of Liverpool Management School, and is also Editor of *Risk Management: An International Journal*. His research interests include risk management in sport, and the regulatory nature of behaviour in football.

Bill Gerrard

Bill is Professor of Sport Management and Finance, Leeds University Business School, and the Editor of *European Sport Management Quarterly*. He is a specialist in the economics and finance of professional team sports and consultant to several football clubs.

Ian Henry

Ian is Professor of Leisure Policy and Management, and Director of the Institute of Sport and Leisure Policy at Loughborough University. His research interests include comparative and transnational analysis of sports policy, and Olympic policy and politics.

Ping Chao Lee

Ping is a doctoral student in the Institute of Sport and Leisure Policy at Loughborough University. His principal research interest is in the field of the governance of professional sport in Taiwan.

David Morris

David is Dean of Coventry Business School. He lectures on sports betting on undergraduate and MBA programmes and has advised a number of organisations in the horseracing industry.

Cameron O'Beirne

Cameron is Lecturer in eBusiness at Edith Cowan University and a consultant in eCommerce and sport management, specialising in aquatics. He was the project manager for the world's first artificial surfing reef at Cables, in Western Australia.

John Old

John is Principal Lecturer at Coventry Business School, where he teaches economics and organisational management. His research and consultancy interests include sports organisations, organisational economics and the management of small businesses.

Chris Parker

Chris is Senior Lecturer in Sport and Leisure Management at The Nottingham Trent University. He is an experienced management consultant, trainer and author and the co-author of *Developing Management Skills for Leadership*. He is a licensed Master Practitioner of NLP.

Harry Arne Solberg

Harry Arne is Associate Professor at Trondheim Business School, Sør-Trøndelag University College, where his teaching covers sports, micro, and welfare economics. Harry's research interests include the economic impacts of various sport activities.

Susan Stoney

Susan works at Edith Cowan University where her role entails leading pedagogic developments in the Faculty of Business and Public Management. Her interests embrace eSport and online learning strategies.

Malcolm Sullivan

Malcolm is Principal Lecturer in Marketing and Director of MBA Programmes at The Nottingham Trent University. His research interests lie predominantly in the field of Applied Consumer Psychology within the retail environment.

Alan Tapp

Alan is Senior Lecturer at Bristol Business School, where he specialises in direct and database marketing. He is a former international athlete who has numerous publications in sports marketing.

Des Thwaites

Des is a Senior Lecturer in Marketing and a former Director of Studies in Management at Leeds University Business School. His sports research focuses on aspects of marketing, sponsorship and tourism.

Preface

The two co-editors of *The Business of Sport Management* have each been teaching sport management for over a decade, in various universities in the United Kingdom. During that time there have been tremendous advances in the extent and nature of both teaching and learning in this area. A decade ago, sport management was an area that a few academics were beginning to enter from the perspective of business and management. Others were also entering the area from the worlds of sociology and sports science. While today there are large numbers of students graduating with degrees in sport management, few senior academics can claim to have spent their working life exclusively in that area. As a result, core texts tend to have a subtext that betrays the author's 'home' discipline. It became clear to the co-editors that no core text existed which they felt they could whole-heartedly recommend to students. That is not to say that there was nothing available that they felt they could recommend, merely that the available texts were either too lacking in basic management theory, or were too restricted in the business theory that they covered. The underlying aim of this book is to fill that gap.

The main objective of this book is to provide an introduction to key aspects of sport management for both undergraduate and postgraduate students. The book will also serve as a useful resource for staff involved in teaching on sport-related modules and programmes, and for practitioners working as managers of sport businesses.

The book consists of nineteen chapters which are split into three parts: context, business functions and management issues. The rationale for this structure is a reflection of the underlying aim outlined above. Part I – context – explains how sport management exists within the worlds of both business and sport. It shows how professional sport has evolved, and how sport businesses operate within a broader context of governing bodies and state involvement. It is essential when approaching the subject to be familiar with this context; otherwise the more advanced areas of study are not realistically accessible.

Once an understanding of the context of sport management has been achieved, the student can begin to assimilate the basics of business management theory, the subject of Part II. Part II is divided into chapters whose titles would not be unfamiliar to the general business studies student. The content of each chapter is, however, presented with particular reference to sport businesses. It thus concentrates on functions of business, which are generic but presented from a sport business perspective.

While it is generally accepted that any business needs to be customer-focused, a number of sectors have faced the difficulty of equating their 'customers' with the generic view of 'customers'. Examples are the health sector, the education sector and even the transport sector, where 'patients', 'students' and 'passengers' are more complex notions than simply 'customers'. In the sport business sector, many organisations face difficulties with matching the notions of 'customers' and 'fans'. As a result, a number of management issues have to be addressed that are unique to sport businesses. These issues are covered in the first seven chapters of Part III, which then concludes with a consideration of the future prospects for sport businesses.

Each of the chapters in this book contains the following:

- a statement of learning outcomes;
- a chapter overview;
- subject content appropriate to one of the parts mentioned above;
- case studies, including one extended case;
- a conclusion;
- guided reading;
- recommended websites;
- keywords;
- a bibliography.

At the time of writing, all recommended websites were live. However, it may be the case that sites become inaccessible.

Support Materials

Material for further study, including relevant annotated weblinks, is available at www.booksites.net/chadwickbeech. Lecturers can also visit this site to download additional support material, including PowerPoint slides.

Acknowledgements

The editors would like to thank each of the chapter authors for their hard work and commitment in getting the book written. Each author has written the chapter under their name with the exception of the final, longer case study. These have been added by the editors to enhance the cross-chapter coherence of the book. Special thanks are extended to those chapter authors who worked under especially tight time constraints.

Thanks are also due to the following organisations that have allowed us to use case material relating to their work in the sport industry: Cadability, and James Chapman and Co.

Respect is due to the patient staff at FT–Prentice Hall. After years of trying to get us to write this book, they finally succeeded and gave us a level of support for which we are grateful. Jacqueline, Nicola, Janey and Camilla deserve a special mention.

Both the editors reserve a special mention for Sue and her excellent proofreading.

John dedicates his work on the book to Sue, who has tolerated a considerable amount of displacement activity. He promises to return to the serious business of painting the house.

Simon dedicates his work on the book to Barbara and Tomasz, who have put up for months with his incessant tales about books and publishing. Thanks are also given to Joan, Hania, Harry and Tadek for their support.

Publisher's acknowledgements

Figure 6.2 from 'Planned versus impulse purchase behaviour', *Journal of Retailing*, Vol. 62, No. 4, pp. 384–409 (Cobb, C.J. and Hoyer, W.D. 1986) used by permission, copyright New York University, Stern School of Business; Table 8.2 from www.businesslink.org; Figure 10.3 from *Operations Management* by Russell/Taylor, © reprinted by permission of Pearson Education, Inc. Upper Saddle River, NJ; Figure 10.4 adapted from 'A conceptual model of service quality', *International Journal of Operations and Production Management*, Vol. 8 , No. 6, p. 25 (Haywood-Farmer, J. 1988); Figures 11.1 and 11.3 reprinted by permission of Cadability Pty Ltd; Table 12.2 from www.thefa.com reproduced by kind permission of The Football Association; Figure 13.1 from 'Risk management: a tool for park and recreation administrators', *Parks and Recreation*, August, pp. 34–7 (Nilson, R. and Edginton, C. 1982).

Case 6.4 Design's great leap forward from *The Financial Times Limited*, 3 December 2002, © Michael Exon; Case 10.4 Hired to be fired from *The Financial Times Limited*, 12 October 2002, © Michael Steinberger.

We are grateful to the Financial Times Limited for permission to reprint the following material:

Case 1.4 A game with no team players, © *Financial Times*, 28 May 2002, Case 2.3 Formula 1 looks for an alternative escape route, © *Financial Times*, 6 July 2002, Case 3.4 The Olympic sport of book-balancing, © *Financial Times*, 8 August 2002; Case 4.2 Chinese golfers wait for the game to tee off, © *Financial Times*, 4 September 2001; Case 5.6 Putting their personal best foot forward, © *Financial Times*, 16 July 2002; Case 7.2 Clubs in crisis as losses mount, © *Financial Times*, 1 March 2002; Case 8.5 Real tennis, © *Financial Times*, 30 March 2002; Case 9.4 Tennis stars light way ahead for Argentina, © *Financial Times*, 31 May 2003; Case 11.6 Clubs get smart by marking fans' cards, © *Financial Times*, 6 November 2002; Case 12.6 A middleman on top of his game, © *Financial Times*, 25 March 2002; Case 13.5 A great race goes steadily downhill, © *Financial Times*, 16 May 2003; Case 14.6 Charting a course to fraternité, © *Financial Times*, 20 November 2002; Case 15.2 Sport broadcasting in the European Union, © *Financial Times*, 1 June 2001; Case 15.3 Football's TV-run gravy train grinds to a sharp halt, © *Financial Times*, 9 March 2002; Case 16.5 Pukka Chukkas out of Africa, © *Financial Times*, 18 May 2002; Case 17.3 Cricket World Cup a mere rehearsal for football, © *Financial Times*, 22 March 2003; Case 19.4 Power, but not enough glory, © *Financial Times*, 4 August 2001.

In some instances we have been unable to trace the owners of copyright material and we would appreciate any information that would enable us to do so.

Abbreviations

AIS	Australian Institute of Sport
ASP	Association of Surfing Professionals
BBC	British Broadcasting Corporation (UK public service broadcaster)
BSkyB	British Sky Broadcasting (part of Rupert Murdoch's News International group; commercial satellite broadcaster)
CAD	Computer-aided design
CAE	Computer-aided engineering
CAM	Computer-aided manufacturing
CCC	County Cricket Club
CCT	Compulsory Competitive Tendering
DCMS	UK's Department of Culture, Media and Sport
EFQM	The European Foundation for Quality Management
EU	European Union
FA	(English) Football Association
FIA	Fédération Internationale de l'Automobile
FIFPRO	Fédération Internationale des Footballeurs Professionnels
FIFA	Fédération Internationale de Football Association
FMCG	Fast-moving consumer goods
FOA	Formula 1 Administration
FOCA	Formula 1 Constructors Association
GAIF	General Association of International Sport Federations
IDTV	Interactive digital television
IF	International Sporting Federations
ILAM	Institute of Leisure and Amenity Management
IOC	International Olympic Committee
ISO	International Organization for Standardization; used to refer to the numbered documents they issue, e.g. ISO9000
ITV	Independent Television (UK commercial broadcaster)
MCC	Marylebone Cricket Club (responsible for cricket in England)
MUTV	Manchester United Television
NBC	National Broadcasting Corporation (US commercial broadcaster)
NOC	National Olympic Committee
NPSO	Not-for-profit Sport Organisation
PFA	Professional Footballers Association
RYA	Royal Yachting Association
SME	Small- to Medium-Size Enterprise
SPRIG	UK organisation which promotes information sources in leisure, tourism and sport
TOP	The Olympic Programme
UEFA	Union of European Football Associations

UK	United Kingdom (comprises England, Scotland, Wales and Northern Ireland)
WADA	World Anti-Doping Agency
WCPP	World Class Performance Programme

Useful websites

Academic Associations
European Association for Sport Management: http://www.easm.org
North American Association of Sport Management: http://www.nassm.com
Sport Management Association of Australia and New Zealand:
     http://www.gu.edu.au/school/lst/services/smaanz

Academic Journals
Culture, Sport and Society: http://www.frankcass.com/jnls/css.htm
European Sport Management Quarterly: http://www.meyer-meyer-sports.com
International Journal of Sport Marketing and Sponsorship:
     http://www.winthrop-publications.co.uk/SMSFrontpage.htm
Journal of Sport and Social Issues: http://www.swetswise.com
Journal of Sport Management: http://www.humankinetics.com/products/
journals
Managing Leisure: http://www.tandf.co.uk/journals
Sociology of Sport Journal: http://www.humankinetics.com/products/journals
Sport Marketing Quarterly: http://www.smqonline.com
Sports Management Review:
     http://www.gu.edu.au/school/lst/services/smaanz/content3.html
The Sport Journal: http://www.thesportjournal.org
Villanova Sports & Entertainment Law Journal:
     http://vls.law.vill.edu/students/orgs/sports/index.html

Government bodies
European Union Sport Unit: http://europa.eu.int/comm/sport
The Australian Sports Commission: http://www.ausport.gov.au
The Olympic Movement: http://www.olympic.org
UK Sport: http://www.uksport.gov.uk

Links to these websites and other chapter specific websites are available at:
www.booksites.net/chadwickbeech.

Part I

The context of sport

- This section sets the context for the book. Given the main focus of the book – that of private sport businesses – the section charts a path to the start of sport in the twenty-first century. The section nevertheless acknowledges that sport businesses must still adhere to certain morally acceptable practices, and that the state still has a big role to play in influencing sport.

- The purpose of the section is to examine the development of sport from amateurism to professionalism to commercialism. As a counterpoint to the model of private, profit-oriented sport businesses that this book implies, the section also considers the role of the state in sport and details the importance of ethics and governance for sport businesses. As such, the section establishes an agenda within which the rest of book is written.

- The section contains chapters on the evolution of business and commerce in sport, governance and ethics, and the role of the State.

- Cases included in this section are the professionalisation and commercial development of rugby, the promotion of women sport leaders in the Olympic movement and the problems of redeveloping a national stadium.

Chapter 1

Introduction

John Beech
Coventry Business School, Coventry University

'I can remember the day when, as a goalkeeper playing for Reading against Millwall in a reserve match at the Den in 1951, I collected nine pence in old pennies which had bounced off my skull. We needed the money in those days.'

Edward Bird in a letter to the *Daily Telegraph*, 31 January 2002

Upon completion of this chapter the reader should be able to:

■ outline the various processes which take place as a sport moves from a pure sport activity to a sport business;

■ identify the scope of the business of sport and of sport businesses;

■ identify the main business factors that are relevant to the management of sports organisations;

■ explain the facets of sport that make it different from conventional businesses;

■ identify the main contents of this book.

Overview

This introductory chapter sets out the three basic elements of the book.

The main focus of this book

This is a perspective driven by management theory but recognising the uniqueness of the sport industry. This perspective is implicit in the various chapters, written by a variety of authors from a variety of educational institutions in the United Kingdom, continental Europe and Australia.

The development of professional sports and their subsequent commercialisation

A two-part case study which looks at the split between Rugby Union and Rugby League is used as an example of this, and explores the continuing paradox of these two sports, which split over the issue of payments to players but are now both amateur and professional. This leads to an exploration of basic themes – professional and amateur sport, professional and amateur players, the processes of professionalisation and commercialisation in sport, sport as competitive event-based activity and the limits of the book in terms of what is within and what is outwith the limits of 'sport business'.

Its content on a chapter-by-chapter basis

The contents of the book are introduced in terms of business functions applied to sport and management issues specific to sport businesses.

The two-part case study is presented with discussion questions, and more general discussion questions are offered at the end of the chapter, a method used throughout the book.

The main focus of the book

The concept of sport and the ideals it encompasses are often seen as emerging from amateur and altruistic principles in a historical perspective. This approach to sport as one of activity exemplifying 'muscular Christianity' – a nineteenth-century public school approach to sport – has been a popular one, and a rich source of research by sports sociologists. Similarly, sports scientists have brought their academic expertise to bear on the analysis of sport activity, considerably expanding our understanding of sport in general and of particular sports.

It is only in recent years that sport management has begun to emerge as a study with its own particular characteristics. This is perhaps surprising as the notion of sport as inherently amateur and altruistic is misguided even in its origins, athletes at the original Olympic Games being known to have received payment. A moment's reflection makes clear that it is difficult to generalise in this respect, some sports more clearly being identifiable with an Olympian ideal, while others have no historical connection with that ethos, or indeed with the Games themselves.

Although professional sport has been with us in the United Kingdom for over a century, it has generally attracted little academic interest other than from social historians. This has changed very noticeably as professional sport has moved from a long-standing and fairly steady state of 'professional' to a rapidly evolving process of large-scale 'commercialisation', a distinction which is discussed below. In general, commercialisation has happened to sports that had already reached the 'professional' stage in their development. Some sports, however, have progressed directly from 'amateur' to 'commercial' and, in this respect, this book generally restricts itself to sports that have moved beyond 'amateur'.[1]

---

[1] 'Amateur' sports are not excluded from consideration as amateur clubs still need to be managed, to promote themselves in a marketing sense, to control their finances etc.

The development of a sport as business

Sports vary considerably in the extent to which they have become 'big business'. Those that have have generally followed a similar sequence (summarised in Figure 1.1). This sequence is best understood by distinguishing between *evolutionary* phases, where change is slow and incremental, and *revolutionary* phases, where change is rapid and the phase is characterised by high levels of uncertainty. These phases are:

Foundation (Evolutionary) The sport emerges through ancient folk tradition (e.g. soccer).

Codification (Revolutionary) Codification may take place as a formalisation of practice (e.g. cricket), as the outcome of an organisational breakaway (e.g. rugby league) or through the need to define the game at the time of invention (e.g. snooker). In cases like rugby league, the sport may in fact see its foundation as coincident with codification; in cases like snooker, they are coincident.

Stratification (Evolutionary) As a sport grows, the body responsible for codification sets up or administers through merger a variety of leagues, typically with an element of promotion and relegation, and normally characterised by a regional dimension, especially at lower levels. In this phase, the sport remains amateur. The changes in the governance of the game may be considered revolutionary, but the effects of these changes have relatively little impact on the overall stability of the game, and growth is slow but steady.

Professionalisation (Revolutionary) As a sport gains a popular appeal, the willingness of spectators to pay to watch, and the willingness of investors to support clubs, for altruistic reasons as well as commercial ones, allow the payment of players. Initially payment is in terms of expenses. This may extend to payment for loss of earnings. At this point the distinction between amateur and professional status may become blurred. Where full-blown professionalisation occurs, the elite players are able to play sport as a full-time job.

Post-professionalisation (Evolutionary) During this phase, a senior game which is professionalised typically sits alongside an amateur junior game.

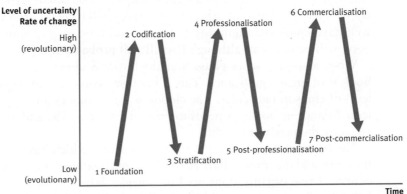

Figure 1.1 **Framework: the development of a sport as business**

Commercialisation (Revolutionary) As the sport develops an overtly business context, external organisations see the opportunity of using the sport for their own purposes, typically marketing in the forms of sponsorship – involving governing bodies, leagues and clubs – and endorsement – involving players. If the sport organisations, leagues and clubs are inept in their management of the greatly increased financial revenues which become available, they will come under pressure to the extent that some professional clubs in particular may be forced out of existence.

Post-commercialisation (Evolutionary/Revolutionary) Outside the 'Big Four' North American sports, few major sports can claim to have reached this phase. European soccer is entering this phase, and certainly F1 motor racing has been in this phase for a number of years. The phase may often appear to be evolutionary – a period of stability and growth following the commercialisation phase – but, because major revenues derive from outside the sport, sudden dramatic change (i.e. revolutionary change) may be thrust upon the sport since the sport has a reduced level of control over the steadiness and predictability of its income.

The terms 'evolutionary' and 'revolutionary' should not necessarily be taken to imply long and short phases respectively. Table 1.1 is an application of the framework to English soccer which shows the timescale of the phases. It should be noted that the evolutionary stratification phase in fact lasted for a shorter time than the revolutionary commercialisation phase. The table also includes examples of the iterative nature of the process – the recent creation of the Premiership and the current review of the structure of leagues at a lower level. This highlights a further important dimension to the model – the level within the sport. In sports that are large enough to support a 'tall' structure of leagues, development through the various phases is more rapid at higher (professionalised) levels, with lower levels remaining at the earlier stratification (amateur) level.

The progression from each phase to the next is not necessarily a process which has been completed by every sport. Sports which have not progressed beyond phase two are generally outside the scope of this book. The significance of phase two is that it defines the governing body of the sport, and the role of the governing body in the management of the sport becomes clear as the sport progresses to higher phases.

Those at phase three are certainly within its scope, as the sport 'as organisation' has emerged, and there will be financial, marketing and human resource dimensions to the operation of the business. Although the sport will have no professional players, it may well have employed administrators on a full-time or part-time basis. Part II of this book will be relevant, although Part III will probably not.

When a sport reaches phase four the business dimension covered in Part II of the book is of great significance. This is because people are employed in the sport at the level of clubs in particular. The club now has revenues and expenditures – it must at least balance its books, it needs to promote its activities, and as an employer it has to consider the needs of its staff.

The business dimension is to the fore in sports which have reached phase six. Now the clubs and the leagues have strong business relations with sponsors and with broadcasters. These organisations need to consider how they will manage risk, what legal liabilities they may incur, and how they might maximise the revenues generated by their main physical asset – their stadium or ground.

Table 1.1 An example of the application of the framework: English soccer

Phase	Commentary
1. Foundation	The game emerged from various forms of two teams kicking a ball around with a view to scoring by reaching a goal.
2. Codification	Codification by the (English) Football Association (FA) in 1863 – the first codification of 'football', and the basis of the English claim to have 'invented' the game, standardised the game as one between two teams of eleven players and defined the characteristics of the 'goals'.
3. Stratification	The game grew rapidly and a range of leagues, national and local, became affiliated to the Football Association.
4. Professionalisation	By the mid-1870s, some clubs had begun to employ semi-professional and even professional players, and in 1885 such practices were authorised by the FA.
5. Post-professionalisation	The game entered a steady state, with a structure of leagues surmounted by three national leagues, ultimately developed into four national leagues. The players in these top leagues were professionals.
6. Commercialisation	A commercial dimension began to enter the game in the late 1960s. Early examples are the sponsorship of cups by Texaco (an oil company) and Watneys (a brewery), and the emergence of shirt sponsorship, a practice initially banned by the FA but which Jimmy Hill's Coventry FC attempted to circumvent.

The major event in this phase was the formation of a new Premiership (league), driven by the clubs in the existing 'top flight' who sought to gain a larger share of the newly available funding from broadcasting rights.

By the end of the 1990s commercialisation had become firmly embedded across the whole of the top four leagues as well as the FA, with sponsorship of a range of events and facilities, including individual stadia, common practice. Club websites had become integrated with betting companies, mobile phone companies and other external organisations, typically offering directly soccer-related services. Weaker (in terms of financial success) clubs have faced major pressures such as being forced into administration. |
| 7. Post-commercialisation | As we move into the first decade of the twenty-first century, a case can be made that English soccer has reached this phase. The involvement with external bodies seems to have reached a natural limit, with further expansion by sponsors generally being limited to becoming involved with the lower levels of the game. However, it is still perhaps too early to judge, and further restructuring may yet happen – in particular, the relationship between soccer and sports broadcasters can be seen as still potentially 'revolutionary'. |

The further the organisation progresses through the phases, the greater the tendency for iteration – the revisiting of previous steps. The best examples of this lie in English and Scottish soccer. Clubs at the phase of commercialisation revisited stratification in the sense that their developing relationship with sports broadcasters influenced the way in which the games were structured – the English Premiership and the Scottish Premier League emerged in the process of strengthening the sport's links with broadcasters.

Table 1.2 Stakeholder phases in the commercialisation of sport

The amateur game) (Phases 1 to 3	The professional game (Phases 4 and 5)	The commercial game (Phases 6 and 7)
Players are unpaid.	Players are paid, although a strong supporting amateur structure persists.	Players at the highest level are very highly paid. Other players are paid, and still an amateur structure persists.
Stakeholders consist progressively of players, fans, clubs, and governing bodies.	Stakeholders now include investors.	Stakeholders now go well beyond players, fans, clubs, governing bodies and investors; they include external sponsors with only contractual loyalty, and broadcasters.

Clearly there are implications for players and stakeholders which derive from the steady-state phase that the sport has reached. These are set out in Table 1.2 above.

Great attention has been paid by academics to the business of soccer in the past five years, no doubt because it is in this sport that the largest sums of money have been invested. This coverage has frequently shown a censorial tone, implicitly protesting at the loss of control of the game to the external paymasters – sponsors and broadcasters – (but less often protesting at the loss of control to the particular sport's highly-paid elite participants) and frequently has lacked analysis using management theory. This book has been written to provide a source which:

- sets the management of sport businesses in theoretical frameworks from a range of management disciplines;
- reflects the growing range of sports that have clear commercial dimensions.

The book focuses on sports which are familiar in the United Kingdom and Europe, and hence there is relatively little coverage of North American sports, although they are not ignored.

How significant is the scale to which many sports have become commercialised? Exhibit 1.1 gives some indications for a range of stakeholders.

Exhibit 1.1   How significant is the commercialisation of sport?

When it comes to who is involved in the commercialisation of sport, what is spent and who benefits, there are too many examples to mention. However, here is a brief selection of recent events that help to illustrate just how commercial the world of sport has become:

The performer
'Musicians, sports stars and actors are rapidly overhauling established business tycoons as some of America's wealthiest young people.'

The gambler
'Merrill Lynch has revealed that the online gambling industry in total will be worth an estimated £123bn by 2015, while online sports betting will be valued at £100bn.'

The spectator
'Since it began 14 years ago, the sport [World Superbikes] has become ever more popular with over 1m spectators in 2001, double that of 1996.'

The club
'A report published by Deloitte & Touche and Sport-Business Group has revealed that Manchester United heads football's rich list with a turnover of £117m. It is based upon turnover for the season 1999–2000. In 2nd place is Real Madrid with turnover of £103.7m.'

The consumer
'The Sport Industry Research Centre at Sheffield Hallam University, in a report entitled "Sport Market Forecasts 2001–2005", revealed that UK spending on sport in 2000 was £15.2 billion. This ensures that sport accounts for approximately 3% of consumer spending. In the 1990s this market has grown by more than 70%, an estimated 64% of which is spent on sports services, while 20% goes on clothing and footware.'

The corporation
'Over the past 4 years the corporate hospitality industry has experienced huge growth. The sector is now worth more than £100m a year. A major investment and service-driven approach adopted by many sporting venues has not only served the hospitality industry, it has also opened the floodgates for conference opportunities.'

The sponsor
'Kellogg has signed its biggest ever UK sports sponsorship deal. It is linking its Nutri-Grain brand with the Rugby League's Challenge Cup. Kellogg will invest more than £1 million into the sponsorship.'

The governing body
'World Snooker, the governing body of professional snooker, is to invest £100m to promote the sport. World Snooker is expected to unveil details of a five-year plan to spark greater interest in the game next month.'

The merchandiser
'Hays and Robertson is planning a two-way split, by floating International Brands Licensing, the Admiral and Mountain Equipment brand business on Aim in June 2002, in an attempt to raise its market value to £11.5m. Hays and Robertson will then join with Sky in a deal to sell England kits and other football kits later on in the year and focus on purchasing licenses for other brands for UK distribution.'

The venue
'According to Wembley, the events company, a good performance from its 6 greyhound tracks in the UK helped to boost interim profits 12.5% to £16.2m.'

The rights owner
'Formula 1 Administration (FOA), the company which owns the rights to Formula 1 motor racing, posted an 8% increase in profits in 2001. FOA's pre-tax profits rose to $180m, up from $165m in the previous year. Turnover jumped to $594m, up from $538m in 2000.'

Sources: 'Wealthiest men and women under 40', *Evening Standard*, 5 September 2001, p. 3; 'Online sports gambling', *Sport Business*, 1 October 2001, p. 2; 'The World Superbike Championships', *Sport Business*, 1 March 2002, p. 8; 'Richest football clubs report', *Financial Times*, 1 December 2001, p. 2; 'Consumer spending on sports increases', *Leisure Management*, 10 August 2001, p. 10; 'Corporate hospitality industry has experienced massive growth over the past 4 years', *Marketing*, 20 September, 2001, p. 47; 'Kellogg signs its biggest ever UK sports sponsorship deal', *Marketing*, 6 December 2001, p. 4; 'World Snooker to invest £100m to promote the sport', *Sunday Business*, 7 October 2001, p. 7; 'Hays and Robertson to float IBL', *Daily Express*, 20 May 2002, p. 54; 'Income from greyhound tracks boosts Wembley', *BBC News Online*, 16 August 2001, www.bbc.co.uk; 'FOA posts 8% rise in profits', *The Business*, 21 April 2002, p. 5

The development of professional sport and professional players

There are sports in which it is clear when an individual 'turns professional'. This act may have two distinct aspects, although the two aspects may be irrevocably entwined:

- the decision to seek to make a living by earning money from participating in the sport;
- the changing of status with respect to membership of sport governing bodies.

These two aspects lie at the core of Case Study 1.1a 'The development of rugby'. The sport of rugby has been chosen because of its interesting extra dimension – the emergence of two varieties of the sport, arising out of the differing views held at the time on whether professionalisation was an appropriate way forward for the then single sport, and the similar ways the two varieties faced up to commercialisation at a much later date, albeit from different starting points.

CASE 1.1a   The development of rugby

The Rugby Football Union was founded in 1871 on a strictly amateur basis. In 1893 the Union received reports that a Yorkshire Club had made a financial offer to induce a player to leave another club and join them. Payment to cover 'broken time' – pay that was lost through being absent from work in order to play rugby – was not unknown.

The Union was warned that the chief clubs in Lancashire and Yorkshire would react by breaking away, no insignificant threat as many of the national team came from these clubs. The particular club was suspended. In August 1895 twenty-two clubs made the threatened break and formed the splinter Northern Union. Within two years a total of 80 clubs were members of the Northern Union. In 1922 the Northern Union changed its name to the Rugby Football League.

As an entity quite separate from the Rugby Football Union, the Northern Union was responsible for the laws of the game its members played. In the early days a number of changes were made, including the reduction in the number of players in a team from fifteen to thirteen.

Thus began a clear divide between the amateur Union and the professional League.

As the League game quickly became distinct from Union, it required an amateur base from which to draw its professional players. However, control of Rugby League remained completely in the hands of the professional clubs. In 1973 the amateur League clubs, fed up with lack of democracy, formed the British Amateur Rugby League Association, a move that initially was contested vigorously but unsuccessfully by the League. Within a few years the League relented, giving the amateur League Association its blessing.

Discussion questions

1. Why do you think the northern clubs were willing to force their case through?

2. Why do you think the League introduced new rules of play?

In the case of rugby, differences over payment led to the emergence of two distinct sports – Rugby Union and Rugby League. In other sports, such as boxing, two sports, one amateur and one professional, coexist with essentially the same rules, any differences being relatively minor and insufficient for the two sports to be seen as 'different sports'.

Some sports have sought to allow the two statuses, 'amateur' and 'professional', to coexist. Cricket maintained the two categories of 'Gentleman' and 'Player' (amateur and professional respectively) until 1963. This distinction had by the end of its life become both blurred and absurd. It was not uncommon for County Cricket clubs to find patrons who would offer token jobs to a cricketer to ensure that he could retain his amateur status, or even to employ them as club officials. This allowed the club to continue with the myth that the team captain was a 'Gentleman' and not a 'Player'. The absurdity of the distinction is best illustrated by the story Fred Titmus tells of the announcement over the PA system at Lords which sought to clarify that he was a professional rather than an amateur: 'We apologise for the error on your scorecards – "F.J. Titmus" should read "Titmus, F.J."' Clearly the earning status of the sportsman was of vital importance, and had to be reflected in the way his name was on the scorecards!

Whatever the attitude that the governing body of a particular sport had taken to the issue of 'professionalism', by the end of the twentieth century it might well, depending on the sport, have found itself under pressure to accept money from broadcasters and sponsors. The former sought a ready-made and familiar product to sell its customers; the latter sought to align their particular brands with the lifestyle surrounding the sport, and hence to gain an enhanced public perception of their products. While normally working well in terms of synergy, the matching of team and sponsor can seem incongruous – the sponsorship of the England soccer team by a Danish lager manufacturer, for example, arguably working rather better for the sponsor than for the sponsee. Not infrequently some sponsors have sought marketing outlets that were needed to replace ones that were blocked through restrictive legislation, cigarette and spirits manufacturers being good examples.

Rugby, is of course, untypical in that the early conflict between 'amateurism' and 'professionalism' led to the divergence of a splinter group to found a new and distinct sport. This schism was not however to remain as clear cut as the steady state of the first half of the century was to suggest.

CASE 1.1b The development of rugby

Throughout the twentieth century, there had continued to be a total schism between the Union and the League, the Union debarring for life anyone who dared to cross to the League. The climate within Union began to change in the late 1980s amid isolated reports of Union players compromising their totally amateur status by accepting unreasonably high expenses which amounted to appearance money. In 1987 two-way movement of players between Union and amateur League was allowed by both parties. In the early 1990s, for the first time since the original rift, a significant number of senior players 'defected' from Union to League.

The Union game as far as the vast majority of its participants was concerned remained thoroughly amateur. The world of sport was changing fast nevertheless, and in 1987 the Union negotiated a £1.6 million sponsorship deal with the brewers Courage. In 1995 the International Board announced that the Union game would be opened up to the payment of players. In a move prompting comparisons with the formation of soccer's Premiership in 1992 as well as with the events of almost a hundred years previously, in 1997 the top two Union leagues in England (a total of twenty-four clubs) received a £7.5 million sponsorship package over three years from Allied Dunbar, the financial services organisation. The attraction to Allied Dunbar was the televising of these clubs by Sky Sports, a deal worth £87.5 million, negotiated jointly through the auspices of English Professional Rugby Union Clubs, subsequently replaced by the English First Division Rugby body.

Discussion questions

3. Given the context of history, is it an absurdity that there is a British Amateur Rugby League Association and, recently, there has been a body called English Professional Rugby Union Clubs?

4. As a Rugby Union club manager in the early 1990s (i.e. before the permitting of payment to players), how might you have addressed the problem of stopping players moving to the paid world of Rugby League?

5. Compare the distribution of wealth between particular clubs and players in the two games, noting where the balance has changed over time.

6. Why do you think there was a rapprochement between the two amateur 'wings' and yet not between the two games as a whole?

This two-part case study together with some significant dates from a business perspective in the development of sport, as shown in Table 1.3, provides a basis from which we can identify the features of this book:

■ key themes that underpin the book's contents and which are implicit throughout the chapters;

- key topics that consist of business functions which are applied to the particular context of sport businesses;
- key issues that are specific to 'sport' as 'business' and which determine the uniqueness of applying management theory to sport businesses.

Key themes

▣ 'Professional sport' and 'amateur sport'

This book is not about the difference between 'professional sport' and 'amateur sport'. It *is* about 'professional sport' and 'sport businesses'. This distinction has clear implications for which sports are covered and what aspects of sport are covered.

'Professional sport' is taken broadly to mean sport which derives income from non-participants and which is dependent on that income to survive in the form that it currently has. Such income may come from one or more of a variety of sources which the

Table 1.3 Some significant dates in the development of sport as business

1806	First 'Gentleman' v. 'Players' match organised by the MCC.
1863	Foundation of the (English) Football Association (FA) (and the myth that the English invented soccer) on an amateur basis.
1880s	Widespread rumours of illegal cash payments to soccer players, succeeded by clubs openly admitting it. Leads to . . .
1885	FA approval of professionalism.
1888	Foundation of (English) Football League and league match system.
1890	(English) Football League imposes transfer restraints on players changing clubs.
1900	Introduction of Maximum Wage Rule for soccer players (£4 per week).
1901	Professional Golfers Association founded; first sponsored tournament follows in 1903.
1907	Foundation of soccer Players' Union.
1909	Soccer players' strike. Advances prove more psychological than tangible.
1937	First sports broadcast by BBC – 25 minutes of tennis from Wimbledon.
1948	Foundation of Pegasus Football Club to champion the ideal of amateur soccer and sport in general.
1961	Professional Footballers Association achieves the abolition of the maximum wage.
1963	Abolition of distinction between 'Gentleman' and 'Player' in cricket. Transfer restrictions in amateur soccer introduced to curtail the unauthorised transfer market.
1968	Lawn Tennis Association accepts professionals and prize money at Wimbledon.
1981	International Amateur Athletics Federation relaxation of rules on amateur status.
1992	Senior English soccer clubs form breakaway Premier League. BSkyB acquires the broadcasting rights.
1995	The International Rugby Board removes the ban on payments to players. Rupert Murdoch's News Corporation begins multinational negotiations for the rights to broadcast Rugby Union.
1996	Rugby League introduces 'video referees'.
1998	First women's boxing bout sanctioned in the UK. BSkyB introduces UK's first digital broadcasting allowing interactive programming.
2001	EU Directive bans sponsorship by tobacco companies.
2002	Collapse of ITV Digital. British Horseracing Board sells major bookmakers rights for use of data in betting shops and internet betting operations.

sport organisations – governing bodies, clubs, events organisers – have control over. These might include gate revenue, broadcasting rights, branding and merchandising.

It will be helpful if you start to see any particular sport as part professional and part amateur. It is not difficult, for example, to see that the world of Sunday morning soccer in the local park is a very different world from that of Manchester United. The causes of the emergence of the latter from the former is the domain of sport sociologists and sport historians, and is an important area of academia. It is not the domain of this book, although it provides an interesting background to it. This book is about the management of the Celtics, the Ferrari Teams and the Wigan Warriors of sport.

'Professional players' and 'amateur players'

The distinction between amateurs and professionals has been the subject of more soul searching and debate by the governing bodies of all the major sports than any other issue. The distinction received particular attention in two eras. In the last twenty years of the nineteenth century, the governing bodies of many sports, dominated as they were by Oxbridge 'gentlemen', resisted the realities of payment to players by clubs that were run by local businessmen seeking to make a profit as well as to promote local sporting pride. How they handled this perceived issue varied from sport to sport. We have seen how rugby was split into two sports; soccer accommodated professionals, and within twenty years only clubs who employed professionals made any significant contribution at the highest level of the sport; athletics ignored the problem in reality, although maintaining a total opposition to commercial athletic activity as practised, for example, in parts of Scotland.

Whatever the matters of 'ideal' were, it became clear in every sport that the only chance of achieving excellence was by a total time commitment to sport. The 'amateur' road could not lead to such excellence as the norm. The distinction matters less and less, and in this book we will be looking at the David Beckhams, the Tim Henmans, the Colin Montgomeries and the Lennox Lewises of sport, and their less well-known professional colleagues.

Professionalisation and commercialisation

The professionalisation of a sport – the appearance of money-earning players – became, as noted above, an issue in many sports in the late Victorian era. The existence of professional players became, in many but not all sports, an acceptable modus operandi, a means to a healthy and vibrant set of sporting competitors who offered a clear focus to Saturday afternoon leisure activity. 'Professionalisation' was thus a practical measure, and a sacrifice most sports were prepared to make.

In the last decade of the twentieth century however, a different process took place in the major sports: the emergence of satellite broadcasting and the opportunities for sports, and hence the top players, to earn previously unimagined sums. With the potential to earn much larger sums, players began to make use of professional agents. When, in 1961, the Professional Footballers Association (PFA) managed to get the maximum wage for professional soccer players abolished, that maximum wage stood at £20 per week.[2] In 2002, David Beckham was rumoured to be seeking a wage of £100,000 per week from Manchester United, on the grounds that he would be paid that by other clubs eager to sign him up. The previous ten or so years had seen the injection of vast sums of money into the game through television rights and sponsorship deals. Typically these sums had gone straight through 'the game' and to the players. This process is the 'commercialisation' of sport and has attracted much academic interest, especially with respect to soccer. It should be noted that for some sports – Rugby Union, for example – 'professionalisation' has been driven through alongside 'commercialisation', the latter making the former irresistible. Case Study 1.2 gives some indication of the scale which commercialisation can reach and the consequences for a select few individuals.

CASE 1.2   Who is the richest person in sport?

The answer is either Philip H. Knight or Eitaro Itoyama, depending on definitions.

Forbes, the US magazine, publishes a list of the world's billionaires. If we ignore the billionaires who can attribute only part of their wealth to sport – the media moguls, the cable TV and satellite broadcasting giants, and the kings of the gaming world, in 2001 there were only four people on the list who attributed their billionaire status entirely to sport.

Poorest of the four, at a ranking of 421, was David Bromilow ('Mr Adidas', with $1.2 billion). The UK's Bernie Ecclestone, the Formula 1 Czar, was third, ranked 182, with a net worth of $2.5 billion. At no. 2 was Eitaro Itoyama, a developer of golf courses in Japan, worth $3.3 billion, and ranked 130. Top sports person, if indeed you accept being 'Mr Nike' as counting, was Philip H. Knight, ranked 92 and worth $4.3 billion.

If the English footballer David Beckham earns £100,000 a week, he is only on a salary of just over $7.3 million a year. The top US sportsmen can earn up to ten times this sum when endorsements are included.

Discussion questions

7. Do you think business men and women, who are not and may never have been players, count as persons 'in sport'?

8. Alan Sugar, erstwhile Chairman of Tottenham Hotspur FC, has said of the way that the massive incomes of English soccer clubs seem to flow through the clubs and into players' pockets that it was 'like drinking prune juice while eating figs'. Is this inevitable? Why is it difficult in today's Europe to stop this from happening?

---

[2] In very broad terms, this wage equated roughly to the earnings achievable by someone newly graduated from university, or to a manual worker such as a dustman (the author worked as a dustman during summer vacations while studying in the 1960s). In today's world, allowing for the inflation which has taken place since 1961, a comparable figure would be a salary of roughly £30,000 per year. The fact that a comparison is made between a footballer's *wages* in the 1960s and a footballer's *salary* today reflects a change in the way that society sees their job, as, of course, does the marked difference in level between payment over forty-plus years.

Written in the current era, it follows that this book is interested in both professionalisation and commercialisation.

Sport as competitive event-based activity

In applying management principles to sport businesses it is inevitable that the unique nature of sport makes for interesting problems. Unlike other businesses, sport businesses have the following particular characteristics:

- Each organisation has no meaningful existence without direct competitors with which it must literally compete. On the other hand, competition cannot take place without coordination and collaboration with those competitors.
- The organisation of competition is controlled by governing bodies which operate like a cartel, in a way that would be considered illegal in other more conventional businesses where their trade associations wield far less power.
- The focus of this activity is an event, sometimes held on the organisation's own premises, sometimes on its immediate competitor's premises, or, rarely, on neutral ground. An event carries with it the factors of fixed place, fixed time and fixed duration.
- The set of competitors is defined in terms of 'leagues', and changes annually as a result of performance in the sport during the year. These changes impact on income but not on costs. (It is costly being relegated, in other words!)
- Direct income from such competition is usually seasonal.
- The essence of sport is thus competitive, seasonal, event-based activity, and, as a direct result, organisations seek indirect and more regular income streams through activities such as merchandising. With more and more commercialisation, direct revenue forms a smaller and smaller percentage of total revenue.
- The uncertainty of outcome in matches forms the basis of a sport's attractiveness.

Rogan Taylor, the sports sociologist, has famously remarked about the passion and commitment of soccer fans, in comparison with brand loyalty to supermarkets, that 'nobody ever wanted to get married in their local supermarket', unlike the albeit limited, but nonetheless real, appeal of home football grounds for this purpose, and this contrast helps when looking at the business aspect of sport. Supermarkets can seek sites where they have local monopolies, they do not operate other than in their own premises, they compete in a relatively free market, uncontrolled in any formal sense by their fellow supermarket chains, they are never 'promoted' or 'relegated', and they do not get serious income from television sponsorship. Their customers do not buy branded shirts to wear provocatively when visiting their competitors. The business of sport *is* different from most business, but in practical operational aspects, not just in emotive, sociological ways. In this book, having explored the context of sport business, we explore first the similarities with which business functions can be applied to sport businesses, see Chapters 4 to 11, and then the distinctive characteristics, the management issues that are specific to sport businesses, see Chapters 12 to 18.

■ The broader sport industry

Sport businesses are not confined to professionalised sports clubs and players. The following are all participants in the sport industry:

Players	Players' agents
Clubs and their teams	Stadia owners and operators
Leagues	Tournament and event organisers
Governing bodies	Sports equipment manufacturers
Players' associations	Sponsors of players, clubs, leagues, events etc.

Beyond these organisations, it becomes less clear where the boundary lies. Certainly organisations such as MUTV, the television subsidiary of Manchester United, are within the industry, but few would include the manufacturers of the branded merchandise that all major organisations sell to maintain revenue streams. This indicates the general boundaries adopted by this book. The main criterion for inclusion is that the organisation is essentially based in or around sport – Sky Sports therefore qualifies, but the parent Sky Television does not.

Sponsors generally fall into one of two categories:

- those that qualify by virtue of their core business – Nike qualifies as a manufacturer of sports footwear, for example, irrespective of its sponsorship activity;
- those that qualify with respect to their sponsorship role – the sponsorship activities of Benson & Hedges, for example, are within the sport industry, whereas their core business clearly is not.

See Case Study 1.3 'The changing Olympics' for an idea of the role of sponsorship in a sports tournament.

CASE 1.3   The changing Olympics

The summer Olympics take place every four years and last sixteen days. The right to host the event is always fiercely contested. In the past this was an issue of city and/or national pride rather than any commercial aspect. Until the 1984 Games in Los Angeles, the outcome was a considerable financial deficit – the citizens of Montreal are still paying for the 1976 Games.

The trend for a more commercialised Olympics is epitomised by the centennial Games, held in Atlanta in 1996. Only 26% of the income for these games came from direct sales of tickets. The largest income stream was from television rights (34%), followed closely by corporate sponsorship (32%). A further 8% derived from retailing and product licensing. NBC, the Games' host broadcaster, supplied 3,000 hours of broadcasting, which compares with the 100 hours provided by the previous soccer World Cup. They guaranteed to earn the International Olympic Committee $500 million through selling the broadcasts, and still expected to make $70 million from the deal.

Since 1986 the International Olympic Committee has offered sponsors the opportunity to be a member of The Olympic Programme (TOP), restricted to ten members and costing the member \$40–\$50 million. For the Atlanta Games the TOP sponsors were Bausch & Lomb (manufacturers of Ray-Ban sunglasses), Coca Cola, John Hancoc (US insurance group), Kodak, IBM, Panasonic, Rank Xerox, Sports Illustrated (US magazine), UPS (parcel delivery service), and Visa. As well as exposing their logos in an Olympic context, sponsors expose the Olympic logo in their own advertisements. Sponsors also sponsor individual athletes, and their success offers another opportunity to advertise.

During the Atlanta Games, Nike ran a series of advertisements which included the Games-oriented strap-lines 'You don't win silver. You lose gold.' and 'If you are not here to win, you're a tourist.'

Success in the Olympics leads to individual sponsorship deals, and those successful in high-profile sports can negotiate very favourable deals. The self-sustaining nature of personal promotion by sports individuals is well illustrated by the Xerox presence at the Atlanta Games. They recruited a team of 100 ex-sports stars to promote Xerox, led by Mark Spitz, the winner of a record-breaking seven gold medals at the 1972 Munich Olympics.

Sources include *The Independent, Independent on Sunday* and *The Sunday Business*

Discussion questions

9. To what extent is it possible to view the Atlanta Games as representing an Olympian ideal?

10. How do individuals in team sports rise above their team-mates in securing sponsorship deals?

11. Review the ways in which Olympic sponsorship enhances the brands of each of the ten TOP sponsors.

Key topics and issues

At the heart of any understanding of sports management is a common core of management theory. It is in the application of this theory that there is a need for a book such as this one. We have already seen that the various sectors of sport have distinctivenesses which prompt characteristic behaviour. This phenomenon is by no means confined to sport – it is certainly not being argued that sport is unique in being different, only that sport is uniquely different. John Spender (1989) argued:

> Having worked in several different industries before I began my research work, I already suspected that managers often deal with the problems that uncertainty creates in ways that are characteristic of that industry ... the industry recipe is the business-specific world-view of a definable 'tribe' of industry experts, and is often visibly articulated into its rituals, rites of professional passage, local jargon and dress ... [Practising managers and industry analysts] could use [the industry recipe], for instance, to diagnose corporate performance, measure the fitness of the firm for its industry, guide strategic thinking and evaluate the appropriateness of mergers

... I see the industry recipe as part of a particular firm's response to the varying competitive conditions, work practices, technologies, public policies, legislation, and so forth prevailing at the time. (pp. 6–8)

It is with these notions of 'industry recipe' that we are concerned, and which the following chapters focus on.

The remaining chapters in this first part continue to develop an understanding of the context of sport business. Chapter 2 considers the *governance and ethics* of sports, how the playing of a sport is organised. Issues raised include who controls sport, who should control sport and whether there is any place for 'fan power'. Chapter 3 explores the *role of the State* in sport with particular reference to the United Kingdom.

Part II, on business functions, opens with Chapter 4, on *organisational behaviour*, the study of how people behave individually and collectively within organisations, how they communicate, how they are motivated and how they exercise and react to different forms of leadership. The issues which concern us are the 'off-the-pitch' commercial and professional dimensions, rather than the 'on-the-pitch' ones, which would be appropriate in a textbook on Sports Coaching rather than Sport Management.

A closely related field is that of *human resource management*, the subject of Chapter 5. This explores further the notions of motivation and looks at the problematic area of reward systems, systems which in professional sport have shot off at a tangent from the reward systems of conventional businesses. The disparity between the top players and the lowest professional players has become extreme in the last ten years. The employment of professional sportsmen and sportswomen has been contentious and confrontational in many areas – soccer, rugby, tennis, and golf, for example – and has attracted more than its fair share of case law, such as soccer's Bosman Ruling. *Law* and its particular application to sport are the subject of Chapter 12.

After its players, a club's greatest tangible asset is usually its stadium, and by the nature of sport it is often a greatly under-utilised asset. *Events and facility management* forms the subject of Chapter 13, which includes a look at the phenomenon of fans travelling to away matches – sport tourism and its impact.

As the product of a sport business is essentially different from conventional businesses (see above: Sport as competitive event-based activity), it follows that their *marketing* will have essentially different characteristics. Chapter 6 outlines basic marketing principles as applied to the world of sport. It looks at the segmentation of fans in particular – who are sports fans in business rather than sociological terms. The specialist areas so important to the marketing of sport businesses – *eManaging sport customers* – are covered in Chapter 16, and in Chapter 14 which looks at *sponsorship and endorsement*.

Since money is the fundamental issue that separates professional from amateur sport, it comes as no surprise that *finance* merits a chapter of its own, Chapter 7. Here, the distinctive characteristics of sport accounting are considered. For example, the greatest assets of any team are its players, yet they do not appear in the financial accounts. In terms of managerial accounting, the most obvious aspects of most professional sports organisations are that (a) they are not financially viable in terms of direct revenue and (b) they are vulnerable to changing fortunes arising from poor team performance or players' injury. *Risk management* is investigated in Chapter 17, and a significant industry in its own right, the *sports betting industry*, is explained in Chapter 18.

Such problems are obviously not unique to the big names of sport, and even the smallest amateur club has to worry about risk, finance, marketing and so on. The particular issues of *managing small and not-for-profit sports organisations* are analysed in Chapter 8. Similarly, all clubs have to worry about the business environment they operate in, at the mercy of political, economic, social and technological changes and developments. Chapter 9 explains *strategy and environmental analysis*. The smaller clubs are the ones who most often need the support of the public sector. Both quangoes which promote sport and the National Lottery play significant roles in sports development.

Today's businesses have been quick to take advantage of the possibilities which new technology has presented. Chapter 11 covers *information technology and management information systems*. *Managing operations, quality and performance* is also an area that managers must be familiar with if their businesses are to be successful, and is considered in Chapter 10.

Broadcasting has had the most amazing impact on the top levels of sport. The technological innovation of colour television made snooker a national sport for the first time. The advent of satellite television and the escalating rates being paid for the rights to broadcast sports events are investigated in Chapter 15.

The book concludes with a look at *the future of sport businesses* (Chapter 19).

Conclusion

Studying the business of sport management can be challenging. If you come to this book with a background of sports studies, it will be hard to take on board that management is at the core of sport business – the sociology of sport will help to explain the social environment which influences the development of sport business, but will in itself prove totally inadequate to explain sport business strategy, for example. If you come from a sports sciences background, this book will offer an entirely different set of analytical tools to apply in a fundamentally different dimension.

If on the other hand you approach this book with a basic understanding of business principles, you may feel that you come with a flying start. Be careful! While the idea that sport management is the application of general management to sport underpins this book (Chapters 4 to 11), it is also clear that the *distinctiveness* of sport business – the 'industry recipe' – is also at the core (Chapters 12 to 18).

Although the majority of research into sport management, at least from the European perspective, has been into soccer, the examples and case studies have been chosen from a wide variety of sports, including, albeit on a small scale, from North American sports. By developing a range of business skills which you will have developed in a range of applications, this book should help you not only with Sport Management Studies, but with your personal development regarding a career in Sport Management. Such careers should span a working lifetime and are more realistic in terms of opportunity for most students.

CASE 1.4   A game with no team players

FT

Ever since professional sports hit their stride in the late 19th century, sport has also been a business that generates billions of dollars in revenues: through tickets, broadcasting, sponsorship and merchandise.

Which poses a mystery: where does all the money go? After all, professional sports teams have singularly failed to generate profits on the scale that their social impact might suggest. Manchester United, the most professionally managed of the big football teams, and one of the few with a genuinely international appeal, has a market capitalisation of little more than £300 million, roughly half the value of Capital Radio, the radio group.

In the US, Major League Baseball, one of the few sporting organisations to have achieved legal immunity for a formal monopoly, had revenues of $3.5 billion (£2.4 billion) in 2001 and a collective operating loss among the two leagues' 30 clubs of $232 million. These figures may understate baseball's true profitability, since they were issued as part of its interminable pay wrangle with its players. But there is no doubt that baseball is in poor financial shape.

Some people have made money from sport, of course. Bernie Ecclestone raised $1 billion by selling chunks of Formula 1 motor racing. British Sky Broadcasting used Premier League football matches to create a business now valued at nearly £14 billion.

But for every winner there is a substantial loser. The Kirch media empire – which ended up with control of Formula 1 and the rights to Germany's Bundesliga football matches – went bankrupt. So did ITV Digital, when it attempted to use less glamorous Football League matches to copy Sky's strategy. Many of the smaller Football League clubs that had relied on the promised ITV Digital money are teetering on the brink of insolvency. And even handling the rights to a global game is no guarantee of financial success – as testified by last year's collapse of ISMM/ISL, sports marketing partner of Fifa, the world football federation.

In truth, the bulk of the money in sport accrues to its star players. Clubs are able to prevent this only if they impose collusive restrictions on the amount they pay their teams. But competition authorities have gradually closed off this option, allowing players to exploit their negotiating power to the full during their brief playing lives.

For individuals, these high payments will last only a short time. For the clubs they are permanent, since each generation of players will seek to match or improve on the pay of its predecessor.

As the Ecclestone and Sky stories show, there is one other way of making very large sums of money from sport: opportunism, the art of spotting an undervalued sports asset and exploiting it. This can come about either from taking an essentially amateur sport and turning it into a serious business, or from acquiring rights cheaply and using them to build a broadcasting franchise. Yet both are risky and likely to be short-lived.

Attempts to create new professional sports fail more often than they succeed, as the limited commercial success of rugby, soccer in the US and American football in Europe proves. And broadcasting rights remain ultimately in the hands of the originating sports bodies, which eventually understand their true value and drive a hard bargain. In time, the broadcasters have to pay a real price for the sports rights – even, as the ITV Digital/Football League story shows, an inflated one. The teams are unable to hold on to this money themselves, since the internal dynamics of sport ensure that it eventually accrues to the players.

So the real money in sport goes to two sets of recipients with limited time horizons: players and opportunists. Both of them know that the period for which they can exploit their access to riches is limited. For the players, the limit is imposed by the frailty of the body; for the opportunists, it is imposed by the inevitable reversion of power to the star talent.

Others can make a longer-lasting living – intermediaries, advisers, agents and professional managers can all hope for many years of lucrative employment. But they are unlikely to earn the scale of returns earned by the very best players and the most successful opportunists.

There are some general lessons for business from this story. The first is that businesses that depend on unique talents are inherently unattractive for all but the owners of those skills. The rewards will accrue to the talent; everyone else will lose out, unless they can erect anti-competitive barriers to protect themselves.

The second is that businesses in which ego and the desire to mingle with celebrities are powerful motivating factors are commercially dangerous, since many participants will have motives other than the search for profit. This makes them undesirable competitors, lacking the normal discipline in bidding for resources.

And the third is that businesses where there are many tiers of intermediaries – rights brokers, agents and so on – are both inefficient and non-transparent. They provide scope for allegations of misbehaviour such as those currently enmeshing the Fifa leadership; and they siphon off revenues in ways that do not necessarily add economic value.

The last lesson is that where participants believe they have only a limited time to make money, they will grab all they can get. Sometimes this belief is externally created; there is little that can be done about the ageing process. But sometimes it is created by the industry itself. There is no particular reason, for example, why investment bankers should be past their best at 40, yet the industry is increasingly forcing its most talented people to grab their rewards early, then get out.

Talent, ego, intermediaries, haste. Hollywood, the record industry and investment banking all possess most of these characteristics. The talent and the opportunists make the real money and one company's profits are offset by its rivals' losses. In short, like football, they are zero sum games.

Source: Peter Martin, *Financial Times*, 28 May 2002

Discussion questions

12. To what extent do you agree that the continuing commercialisation of sport is both necessary and desirable?

13. As either a student, or the manager of a sport business, what is your view of the impact this is having on sport and how do you feel that sport businesses are responding and should respond?

Discussion questions

14. 'As businesses go, the sport industry is like the music industry.' Explore this statement by comparing and contrasting the two industries.
15. 'Sport Management and the Sociology of Sport are irrevocably inter-connected.' Discuss.
16. In the 1880s, Preston North End regularly fielded teams with up to nine 'imported' Scottish players. How, if at all, is this different from today's Chelsea fielding a team of eleven overseas non-home nationals?

Guided reading

For further information on professionalism in the original Olympic Games, see Slack (1998). The early professionalisation of soccer in England is well covered by Tischler (1981).

Hill (1998) provides some interesting personal insight into the final fight for the abolition of the maximum wage for soccer players, and also into the commercial development of a soccer club. See also Douglas (1973) for an insight into English soccer as it began to progress from the post-professionalisation phase to the commercialisation phase.

Smith and Porter (2000) gives excellent coverage of the recent amateur/professional issue in soccer, cricket, golf, athletics, horse racing and rugby union, and is highly recommended.

Quirk and Fort (1992) provides a good example of the commercialisation of sport in North America. For the commercialisation of English soccer, see, for example, Conn (1997) or Hamil, Michie and Oughton (1999). There are many texts on the commercialisation of soccer but very little on the professionalisation or commercialisation of other sports in the United Kingdom.

The impact of broadcasting on professional soccer is comprehensively covered by Hamil *et al.* (2000), but the contributions to this collection need to be read selectively. Lee (1999) is particularly relevant, giving a clear picture of how modern professional sport is developing from a management perspective.

As a basis for Chapters 4 to 11, students will find it useful to have access to standard texts in organisational behaviour, human resource management, finance, marketing and corporate strategy. Suitable texts are recommended in the appropriate sections of these chapters. For someone with no prior knowledge of business studies, Lynch (1997) is recommended.

Recommended websites

Websites which are relevant to the case studies include the following:

Rugby Union: http://www.irfb.com
Rugby League: http://www.rfl.uk.com
Forbes Magazine: http://www.forbes.com
Olympic Games: http://www.olympic.org

Visit www.booksites.net/chadwickbeech for links to these and other relevant websites.

Keywords

Business; commercialisation; management; organisation; professional.

Bibliography

Conn, D. (1997) *The Football Business*, Mainstream, Edinburgh.

Douglas, P. (1973) *The Football Industry*, George Allen and Unwin, London.

Hamil, S., Michie, J. and Oughton, C. (eds) (1999) *The Business of Football – A Game of Two Halves?*, Mainstream, Edinburgh.

Hamil, S., Michie, J., Oughton, C. and Warby, S. (eds) (2000) *Football in the Digital Age: Whose Game is it Anyway?* Mainstream, Edinburgh.

Hill, J. (1998) *The Jimmy Hill Story*, Hodder & Stoughton, London.

Lee, S. (1999) 'The BSkyB bid for Manchester United plc', in *The Business of Football – A Game of Two Halves?*, S. Hamil, J. Michie and C. Oughton (eds), Mainstream, Edinburgh, pp. 82–111.

Lynch, R. (1997) *Corporate Strategy*, Pitman, London.

Quirk, J. and Fort, R.D. (1992) *Pay Dirt*, Princeton University Press, Princeton.

Slack, T. (1998) 'Studying the commercialisation of sport: The need for critical analysis', *Sociology of Sport On-Line*, 1(1), (physed.otago.ac.n2/sosol).

Smith, A. and Porter, D. (2000) *Amateurs and Professionals in Post-War British Sport*, Frank Cass, London.

Spender, J.-C. (1989) *Industry Recipes: The Nature and Sources of Managerial Judgement*, Basil Blackwell, Oxford.

Tischler, S. (1981) *Footballers and Businessmen*, Holmes & Meier, London.

Chapter 2

Governance and ethics in sport

Ian Henry and Ping Chao Lee
Institute of Sport and Leisure Policy, Loughborough University

Upon completion of this chapter the reader should be able to:

- differentiate three concepts of governance, systemic governance, corporate, organisational or good governance, and political governance, and explain the relevance of these concepts to management in the sports industries;

- clarify changes in the nature of systemic governance in terms of the environment, and skills demanded, of managers in sports systems;

- identify and apply criteria for the evaluation of good governance and related ethical practices in sport management contexts;

- clarify the nature of the relationship between normative governance concerns and ethical business practices in the context of the commercialisation and professionalisation of sport;

- highlight the nature of political governance of sport and the implications for managers in the delivery of services and the implementation of policies.

Overview

The chapter focuses on the relationship between governance and ethical management practices in the business of sport. It is structured around elucidating three key approaches to governance. These approaches or concepts of governance are *systemic governance*, which is concerned with the competition, cooperation and mutual adjustment between organisations in business and/or policy systems; *organisational or 'good' governance*, which is concerned with normative, ethically-informed standards of managerial behaviour; and *political governance* which is concerned with how governments or governing bodies in sport 'steer', rather than directly control, the behaviour of organisations.

Introduction

In recent years sport has been subject to a whole series of high-profile difficulties that have threatened the credibility or legitimacy of key sporting bodies. Among the most highly publicised of these has been the Salt Lake City Olympic bribery scandal (Jennings and Sambrook, 2000); the uncovering of widespread drugs abuse in the Tour de France cycling race; and accusations of malpractice surrounding the election to the presidency of FIFA (Sugden and Tomlinson, 1998).

Such problems are neither new, nor are they restricted to the activities of international sporting organisations (witness for example the Enron collapse in the United States). However, together these failings represent a failure of governance in world sporting organisations. By a failure in governance we mean some or all of the following: a failure of coordination between sporting and other relevant bodies; a failure of governments to regulate or control potentially harmful activities; and a failure to establish decision-making, or to control procedures, which are fairly, transparently and efficiently implemented. In order to elucidate the nature of these problems and their implications for managers, we will first of all clarify what we mean by the term governance by introducing a brief discussion of the three main approaches to governance (systemic, political and organisational governance) in the academic and policy literature. Secondly we want to illustrate each of these three approaches, and their application in the field of sports policy. In using this three-part distinction[1] we mean to tease out the relationship between analytic/explanatory uses of the concept of governance and prescriptive/normative accounts of how a governance system ought to be operated.

As Figure 2.1 illustrates, the three concepts of governance we employ are inter-related, and we offer here a brief definition of each of the three, before going on to more detailed discussion below. Beginning with the notion of *systemic governance* – academic and policy-related interest in governance has grown with the increase in complexity of business and policy environments. Most such environments are characterised by the interaction of organisations and of groups working within and across organisations. Sport is no exception here. If we think about the role of media interests, major sponsors, players' agents, the major clubs and their shareholders in professional sport, we see an ever more complex field of activity. *Systemic governance* is concerned with the competition, cooperation and mutual adjustment between organisations in such systems.

Corporate governance, or 'good organisational governance', refers to the accepted norms or values for the just means of allocation of resources, and profits or losses (financial or other) and for the conduct of processes involved in the management and direction of organisations in the sports business.

Political governance relates to the processes by which governments or governing bodies seek to steer the sports system to achieve desired outcomes by moral pressure,

---

[1]   The three-part typology of governance concepts we have adapted elsewhere (Henry, 2001a, 2003) from Leftwich's work in the field of social policy/political economy (Leftwich, 1994), for application to the sports field.

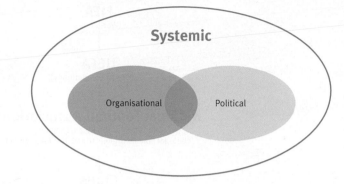

Figure 2.1 **Three interrelated approaches to governance**

use of financial or other incentives, or by licensing, regulation and control to influence other parties to act in ways consistent with desired outcomes.

Systemic governance

The notion of systemic governance underlines the nature of a key shift in the way that sport is organised and controlled – a shift that is away from the *government*, or direct control, of sport. This shift is in part a reflection of the globalising trends in sport. We will use two examples here to illustrate what we mean by this shift, from the fields of soccer and from the Olympic movement.

One of the most effective examples of the shift from government to governance is that of soccer, and Figures 2.2 and 2.3 relate to the example of European football. In the days before multimillion sponsorship deals, media packages, the European Union's Bosman ruling, and the emergence of the G14 clubs (see Appendix 1), including Manchester United, Liverpool, Arsenal, Barcelona, Real Madrid, Inter Milan, AC Milan etc. as a pressure group, it was possible to conceptualise the control of soccer as a hierarchy from FIFA as the ultimate authority in world soccer with responsibility for the premier competition, the World Cup, and with UEFA and national Football Associations occupying lower tiers in the authority structure. In this model of power, clubs and then players lay at the bottom of the decision-making hierarchy (see Figure 2.2). This is, of course, a simplified model and it was never the case that the system operated in isolation without reference to other actors in the system, but nevertheless this model captures something of the structure and functioning of the government of sport up to perhaps the early 1970s.

In the contemporary setting, however, it has become impossible to think in terms of a national or international governing body as being the sole author of its own sport's destiny. The G14 clubs (see Appendix 1) have, for example, become so powerful that they can use the threat of a breakaway competition as a lever by which to obtain virtually guaranteed access to the European Champions League for the big and powerful clubs, providing them with, in effect, a built-in revenue stream and thus a strategic advantage over less affluent clubs. Satellite broadcasters are able to construct alliances with (and gain ownership rights in) clubs, giving them privileged access to sports broadcasting opportunities. National and European governments, and particularly the

FIFA
(World Cup)

UEFA
(European competitions)

National Football Associations
(National competitions/Leagues;
National players organisations; National teams)

Clubs

Players

Figure 2.2 **Traditional hierarchical model of the government of football**

European Union, are able to regulate contractual frameworks for players, clubs and media. Professional players, associations, agents, and even sponsors are able to apply pressure to have their own interests met. Nike as sponsor has been able to influence the fixture list of the Brazilian football team (Advanced Marketing Services Inc., 1997), and has even had to deny publicly claims of influence over player selection (CNN and Sports Illustrated, 1998). Thus the old, hierarchical model of the government of sport, the top-down system, has given way to a complex web of interrelationships between stakeholders in which different groups exert power in different ways and in different contexts by drawing on alliances with other stakeholders. Figure 2.3 illustrates this networked model of governance. This new set of circumstances which

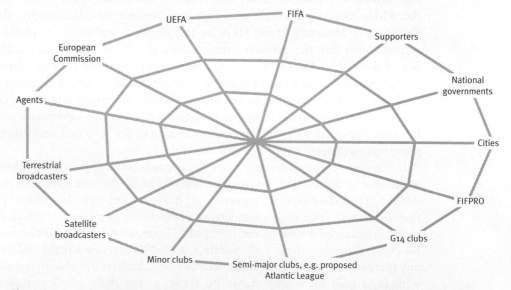

Figure 2.3 **Systemic governance of sport: football – a web of interaction between stakeholders**

is prominent in professionalised sports is also evident in the second example we will use of the Olympic movement. The traditional model of hierarchical control (see Figure 2.4) is one which the International Olympic Committee (IOC) fought long and hard to defend, with the IOC as a sovereign body and IOC members being representatives of the IOC in their respective countries rather than representatives of their countries on the IOC (defending IOC interests in their respective countries rather than promoting national interests in the IOC), and with National Olympic Committees (NOCs) independent of their governments. This model has now been replaced.

Figure 2.5 illustrates the network model of systemic governance in operation in relation to the Olympic movement (Houlihan, 1999). The IOC's reliance on media funds, and on its Top Sponsors, and its need of the cooperation of the NOCs, of the International Sports Federations, and of athletes are clearly evident. Nor are governments any longer content to allow the IOC and sporting authorities freedom to self-regulate in terms, for example, of drugs in sport. The IOC in its 2000 Commission, which introduced reforms in the make-up and conduct of the IOC, has sought to 'manage' this network of relations principally in two ways.

The first is by 'incorporation' of interest groups which might challenge its authority into membership of the IOC (there are seats for International Federations, for athletes, and for NOC representatives in the new make-up of the IOC). The second is by contract (the Top Sponsors scheme and media contracts for the Games) where the nature of contractual obligations allows the IOC to control to some extent the activities of sponsors and media.

Thus the emergence of these new forms of *systemic governance* has at least three major policy implications. First, it is clear that in such a context, significant policy change can only be achieved by negotiation and/or trade-off between various parties in the network. Second, governing bodies of sport in such contexts no longer govern, or wholly control, their sport, or at least if they do, they do so by virtue of their ability to negotiate outcomes rather than by dictating those outcomes to passive recipients of their message. Third, this has implications not only for the organisations but also for the skills required of the people who work within them. The skills are much more those of negotiation and mutual adjustment than of rational, ordered planning and control.

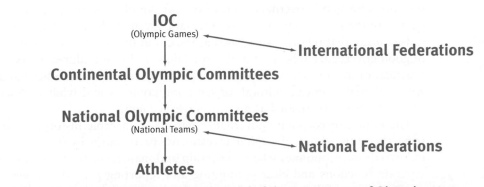

Figure 2.4 **Traditional hierarchical model of the government of Olympic sport**

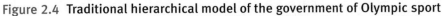

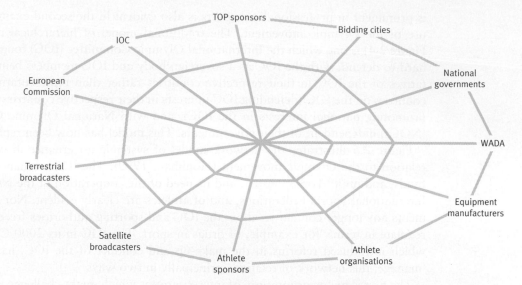

Figure 2.5 **The governance of sport – the Olympic movement**

Organisational governance and the ethics of governance

The notion of organisational governance and business ethics are clearly interrelated. Principles of corporate or good governance are in effect normative ethical principles on how organisations should operate. Approaches to business ethics can be normative (spelling out the 'rules of right conduct') or descriptive (analysing how moral principles are, or are not, evident in the actual operation of organisations or systems). This section of the chapter adopts a mixture of the two approaches, identifying key principles and then evaluating whether or not they are evident in the actual management of exemplar sports organisations. It is worth emphasising what this section does not do. Our account does not consider the basis in ethical theory for the adoption of such principles. Although the defence of the principles of good governance in terms of consequentialist, utilitarian or situationist ethics is neglected here, these are legitimate concerns in philosophical approaches to business ethics (see, for example, Chryssides and Kaler, 1993). In this section in discussing corporate or good organisational governance we limit ourselves to those principles which are evident in contemporary prescriptions for good governance. However, we should acknowledge that though such neglect of the philosophical base is pragmatic given the focus and size of this chapter, it does mean that related issues, such as the culturally relative nature of the principles of good governance rehearsed in this section, are also not addressed. Notions of, and practical means of achieving, democracy, accountability, and other values will vary with different political, cultural, or temporal contexts and what is described below should therefore be treated as a Eurocentric account.

The notion of corporate governance has a considerable history. Its origins derive from the early stages of capital investment, particularly in the nineteenth-century industrialising economies when ownership and management of organisations became separate functions and clear accounting and reporting procedures were required to give owners confidence that their resources were being well managed. In the context of sporting organisations we prefer to use the term organisational governance, since it infers a wider set of tasks and responsibilities than traditional notions of corporate governance.

This expanded notion of good organisational governance might be said to be founded on seven key principles for the management of sporting and other public-welfare-oriented organisations (though the list is not intended to be exhaustive) and these are the types of principles which tend to be cited when criticisms are levelled at the international sporting world.

These principles are:

Transparency: clarity in procedures and decision-making, particularly in resource allocation. Organisations charged with care of a public good such as sport have a particular obligation not simply to act in a fair and consistent manner but also to be seen to do so. Thus their inner workings should as far as possible be open to public scrutiny.

Accountability: sporting organisations are not only responsible to financial investors through financial reporting procedures, but also to those who invest other resources in the organisation – athletes, coaches, parents, supporters, sponsors and so on, even where that investment is largely emotional rather than material.

Democracy: access to representation in decision-making should be available to those who make up the organisation's 'internal constituencies' – with for example representation on boards of such organisations for constituencies such as players, supporters, and managers as well as owners.

Responsibility: for the sustainable development of the organisation and its sport, and stewardship of their resources and those of the community served.

Equity: in treatment of constituencies – for example gender equity in treatment of sports participants and in terms of positions within the organisation; and equity in treatment of sports participants (and employees) with disabilities.

Effectiveness: the establishing and monitoring of measures of effectiveness with measurable and attainable targets.

Efficiency: the achievement of such goals with the most efficient use of resources.

If we take these principles as a sort of checklist, as Sunder Katwala (2000) points out in the excellent report *Democratising Global Sport*, international sports organisations are perhaps best known for their failure to reflect them. With reference to the example of the IOC, in relation to *democracy*, the constitution of the IOC, as a group whose members are appointed by the votes of existing members, represents a force for conservatism and inertia. From 1896 to 2003 there had been only 7 IOC Presidents as compared with, for example, 21 British Prime Ministers or 19 US Presidents (Katwala, 2000) and all of the IOC Presidents had been from western Europe except the American, Avery Brundage, and a number including Juan Antonio Samaranch carried aristocratic titles. One proposal to combat this self-perpetuating oligarchic tendency is to have members nominated by their NOCs, though this was a proposal explicitly rejected by the IOC's own 2000 Reform Commission. In relation to *financial accountability* and *transparency*, apart from the need for clearly detailed and audited accounts, there is a need to ensure that business and commercial relationships are properly regulated with fair and open competition and disclosure of information. Allegations of inappropriate behaviour by members of FIFA, the world soccer body, during the election won by Sepp Blatter and the defence of cash payments as advances on subsidies for national associations might thus be avoided (Sugden and Tomlinson, 1998).

Fair treatment of stakeholders is required whether such stakeholders are commercial entities or non-commercial stakeholders such as athletes or coaches. An example of a body which has been under criticism (and legal pressure from the European Union) for failing to treat stakeholders fairly and for attempting to abuse its dominant position in the market for staging motor races, is the Fédération Internationale de l'Automobile (FIA) – the Formula 1 motor racing Grand Prix governing body. The FIA used to incorporate into its contracts with media companies exclusion clauses forbidding the broadcasting of any car racing other than that recognised by the FIA. Thus, if a television company wanted to win the contract to broadcast a Grand Prix it had to agree not to broadcast any other motor races other than those sanctioned by the FIA. This type of contract was ruled as anti-competitive in business terms by the European Commission and the FIA has subsequently had to abandon this practice (European Commission, 2001).

Failure to consult such stakeholders increases the potential for splits in sporting governance. The Formula 1 Constructors Association (FOCA) for example threatened to establish a rival Grand Prix series because it felt that the FIA was imposing rules and conditions on them in an unreasonable manner and with little consultation, and although this may have been posturing, the prospect of having more than one 'grand prix' world championship was not appealing (van Damme, 2003). The boxing situation, in which there is a proliferation of competing world championships, demonstrates how the notion of a world champion in a given sport can be devalued by having multiple governing bodies and multiple world titles, and can dilute the public's interest.

The need for efficient and professional administration of sport is illustrated aptly by the International Rugby Board, which as a governing body dealing with the transformation of Rugby Union to a professional sport had only a single full-time administrator until the late 1990s, and it is not surprising therefore that there were problems such as players being able to claim false national qualifications, playing for countries to which they had no affiliation. This had the potential both to demean the experience of fans of national teams, and thus to subvert what had become a major professional world sport.

As Sunder Katwala (2000) points out, formal and established codes of practice need to be developed in relation to issues such as sponsorship or the rights to host major events. A code of practice for sports sponsors is required to protect both the sponsors' interests and the interests of the sport. Any suggestion of sponsor influence in areas such as selection or fixture setting should be avoided, while sponsors should be guaranteed fair and open competition for contracts.

Sponsors should also be encouraged to consult and involve fans or community groups in decisions, so that mutualism can be fostered.

Katwala gives the further example of a need for clear rules for the allocation of the right to host major tournaments with, for example, some form of geographic rotation;

clear specification of criteria for selection of a city or site; audited accounts and limits to budgets spent on campaigns; use of, for example, junior tournaments to promote interest and expertise on the part of emerging sporting powers (e.g. Trinidad and Tobago hosting the U-17 world soccer cup and Chile the U-19 World Rugby Cup in 2001). There is also a strong argument to be made in relation to denying rights to host events where malpractice has been identified, as some have argued in the case of Salt Lake City and the 2002 Winter Olympics (Jennings and Sambrook, 2000).

Similarly, as the European Union has argued in relation to sport and television there is a need for clear rules for the award of broadcasting contracts which guarantee some access via free-to-air, terrestrial television, including the broadcasting of all 'decisive' international matches in tournaments such as the World Cup (Reding, 2000).

Equity issues have been raised within a number of international sporting bodies. Equity in relation to gender, disability sport, ethnicity, age, religious practices and other variables have been the subject of policy developments in a range of sporting bodies, both commercial and voluntary sector in orientation. The FA's 'Kick Racism out of Football' campaign, the promotion of the Paralympic movement by the IOC, and the promotion of female participation by bodies such as the Rugby Football Union (RFU) provide good examples as does the IOC's campaign to promote women in the administration of Olympic sport described in Case Study 2.1. However, it seems unlikely that progress will be made in these and other areas of concern without explicit codes of ethics and indeed sanctions for those situations in which such ethical requirements are ignored.

CASE 2.1   Principles of good governance: equity – the promotion of women sports leaders in the Olympic movement

The first two women members of the International Olympic Committee were co-opted in 1981. Following the recommendations of a Study Commission of the IOC Centennial Olympic Congress in 1994, a Women and Sport Working Group was established in 1995 by the IOC President to advise the IOC Executive Board on suitable policies to be developed in this field. It meets once a year. On the basis of its recommendations, an action programme is developed and implemented by the IOC through its Section for Women's Advancement.

The IOC in 1997 adopted a target of 10% minimum female membership for the Executive Boards of National Olympic Committees (NOCs) and for International Sporting Federations (IFs) by 31 December 2000, and a target of at least 20% by the end of 2005. By 2003 66% of NOCs and 43% of IFs had met the first target but there were only 2 women as members of the continental NOC umbrella organisations in 2003, and only 2 of the 15 members of the IOC's own Executive were women. Thus the legitimacy of the IOC's targets for organisations in the Olympic family such as NOCs and IFs may be subject to question given its own performance in respect of its targets. Nevertheless the adoption of a formal policy at least engenders public internal and external debate about this aspect of good governance.

Political governance

When questions are asked about 'good governance' it is usually in respect of good organisational governance, but one might ask similar questions in respect of good political governance. Political governance relates to the achievement of goals through strategies such as regulation and inducement rather than through direct action and control. The notion of governments steering (rather than commanding) change is helpful here (Pierre, 2000), and governments (including the EU here as a quasi-government) do seek to influence and steer the sports system, even if the resources which are brought to bear in sport are a mixture of public, voluntary and commercial sector resources rather than solely public resources.

The role of national governments and/or the European Union is in part related to seeing that 'sport's goals' are not 'subverted' by commercial abuse, while also ensuring that governmental goals are pursued in the sports field. Governments have open to them a range of tools such as the use of funding leverage, of moral pressure, or the threat of regulation, with which to achieve policy aims. There are perhaps two principal types of question concerning political governance in relation to the activities of governments (and the EU). These refer to the questions of whether such governmental activities are legitimate and effective. We can consider these questions first in respect of commercial sport. The EU has involved itself in a number of high-profile interventions in sport in recent years, perhaps the most spectacular being the Bosman ruling and the subsequent development of a professional football transfer system agreement brokered with FIFA and UEFA. In the Bosman ruling the EU's message was clear, that sport was to be regarded as an area of trade like any other. Thus restraint on out-of-contract players, or national quotas on European players in national leagues, were deemed to be illegal. Similarly, as we have discussed, the Grand Prix Governing Body, the FIA, was deemed to be abusing its dominant power in the control of Grand Prix racing and the European Commission acted to force the FIA to amend its operation specifically in relation to broadcasting contracts. Both of these examples show how professional sport as big business is subject to government control as are any other areas of trade and industry. By contrast the European Union ruling introduced with the revising of its directive *TV without Frontiers* in 1997 argued that sport was a special commodity and that European citizens' access to selected sports events on television should be protected, giving national governments the right to reserve selected sports events for free-to-air, terrestrial television. The key issue here was whether sport is like any other product, and whether consumers are like any other consumers. In fact there is, most of us would argue, a substantive difference between sports production and consumption and those of other products and services. Consumption of sport as spectators, particularly of events involving national teams, is regarded by many as part of one's national identity – a cultural heritage which forms an element in the cultural citizenship of any nation. To deny access to all such events to those who cannot afford, or have no access to, pay television is to place limits on their ability to participate in the cultural life of the nation in important ways. Thus one might argue that the EU's role here is essential and pivotal.

CASE 2.2 Political governance in sport: the role of the State in professional soccer in England

The case of government policy in relation to professional football illustrates the use of three major tools of political governance in sport. These are moral persuasion, the use of financial incentives and the use of direct regulation.

In 1998 the UK Government established the Football Task Force, which brought together a range of stakeholders (fans, club management, players' union, club owners etc.) to try to establish voluntary agreements about ticket pricing, pricing of club shirts, access to matches for disabled groups, and problems such as racism in sport. In the recommendations made by the Task Force was the implicit notion that football clubs should not simply act like any other commercial service provider.

For most supporters there is no substitutability of service, since fans do not switch loyalty from the club they support because of normal economic criteria such as increases in the cost of tickets. Clubs are thus in effect monopoly providers. It is also the case that fans themselves are part producers of their own experience, and they add value to a club by their support (televised games are, for example, given atmosphere and thereby value through enthusiastic live support). In these circumstances the Football Task Force and the government-assisted movement Supporters Direct have been able to argue strongly for the supporters' voice to have a legitimate place in the governance decisions of 'their' clubs and as with the case of the Task Force in wider forums relating to the football industry (Hamil, Michie, Oughton and Shailer, 2001; Hamil, Michie, Oughton and Warby, 2001).

While the establishment of the Football Task Force involved voluntary agreement, the government also uses financial incentive and/or regulates sporting markets directly. Funding leverage was, for example, employed in implementing the recommendations of the Taylor report when government agreed to reduce the tax on football pools and gave the substantial savings to the Football Trust to provide financial aid to clubs to rebuild their stadia in line with the required safety standards (Conn, 1997). By contrast, direct regulation or governmental control may also be employed, as in the case of the British government's rejection of the BSkyB takeover bid for Manchester United. This was rejected on the grounds that media companies which would be bidding for the rights to broadcast football matches should not be allowed to gain market advantage by controlling those who make the decisions about which bids should be accepted. Thus government regulation limits media company ownership of football clubs to 10%.

These examples of the use of a mixture of regulation, voluntary agreement and legislation thus provide evidence of the exercise of influence on sport – its political governance – by means other than direct provision of sporting opportunities funded from the public purse.

Systemic, organisational and political governance and sports policy in the United Kingdom

In the United Kingdom over the last 25 years there has been a series of key shifts in sports policy. Many of these changes were associated with decline of a welfare state orientation on the part particularly of the Conservative governments of Margaret Thatcher and John Major. In the area of sports policy this was reflected in the decline of programmes to promote 'sport for all', sporting access through publicly funded facilities and services (Henry, 2001b) to ones in which the government interest in sports provision was targeted on elite sport and sport for young people to be increasingly funded through the National Lottery rather than through the public purse (Department of National Heritage, 1995). The Conservatives also introduced a system of Compulsory Competitive Tendering (CCT) to local authority sport and leisure facilities in the Local Government Act 1988, which required that contracts to manage local authority facilities be drawn up and that these be subject to competition between the public and the private sector. Although the commercial sector did not gain a majority of such contracts, the process of competition rendered public sector management more commercial as public sector managers sought to ensure that they were not undercut in submitting bids to win management contracts for sports facilities.

When the New Labour government of Tony Blair came to power it maintained the policy focus and the system of funding of elite sport and sport for the young through income from the National Lottery (Department of Culture Media and Sport, 2000) and as part of its Modernisation Programme also introduced a system of Best Value to replace CCT (Stoker, 2002). Both the Lottery-funded initiatives and the Best Value system represent aspects of a governance approach to replace what had formerly been policy areas of direct government provision.

The funding of elite sport in the United Kingdom received major investment with the advent of the National Lottery. More than £1.4 billion has been invested in sport in England alone on community projects from 1993 to 2003 and £100 million on elite sport from 1997 to 2003 from Lottery sources. Sports coaching and athlete services as well as the athletes themselves have professionalised in this period and UK performance in the Sydney Olympics is said to have reflected this approach. The new professionalised era of elite performance administration and the shift from amateurism has reinforced aspects of corporate governance procedures.

In the first two decades of the Sports Council's grant aiding of governing bodies (1973–93) although grant recipients were required to bid for funding and submit accounts to audit, concerns with effectiveness, efficiency and other aspects of corporate governance were not required or emphasised. However, in the 1990s good organisational governance procedures were both adopted by UK Sport (which took over administration of elite sport Lottery funding in 1997) and were required of the various sports national governing bodies (NGBs) themselves by UK Sport. UK Sport required NGBs to provide detailed, transparent, costed business plans with clear output measures (in terms of medals and performance improvements) as well as evidence of consultation with appropriate stakeholders. UK Sport itself adopted a 'transparent' system for allocation of Lottery Funds. Its goal was for Britain to be in the top 15 medal-winning nations in Sydney for the Olympics and 3rd in the Paralympics (it was ranked 10th and 2nd respectively) and UK Sport adopted the target of 10th to 8th in the medal table for the Olympics and 1st for the Paralympics in Athens in 2004. Money for elite performance was thus to be allocated with these and related goals in mind, and many national governing bodies therefore were not to be funded at all if they were unlikely to contribute to these overall goals. The implication here is that effectiveness is to be measured in the numbers of medals won, and efficiency is measured in medals per pound (Nichol, 2001). There are some obvious but unfortunate consequences which flow from this approach. For example, team sports which only have the potential to gain a single medal are relegated in terms of priority behind individual disciplines with many medals, and some non-Olympic sports are also neglected. In striving for open, accountable, and transparent resource allocation policies the funding system therefore clearly works against the interests of some sports even though the principles are inspired by the wish to promote good governance practices.

In relation to local government provision of community sports services, the New Labour government's advocacy of the Best Value system has also been motivated in part by adherence to principles of good governance. The system was premised on the requirement to consult local people about the nature of the services they required (democratic involvement), to compare performance of management by benchmarking against like local authorities (defining efficiency in performance assessment), to compete with commercial or voluntary sector providers or potential providers of services (transparency in selection of the most appropriate means of delivering policy goals), and thus to challenge local authorities to improve performance in service delivery whether such delivery was directly by the local authority itself or through appropriate partnerships. By using the commercial and voluntary sectors as both partners and competitors, and by abandoning the monolithic system of delivering policy through direct provision of services by public sector bodies alone, the Modernisation Programme in local government is seen by many commentators as having improved provision, or at least value for money, through the development of enhanced governance procedures (Stoker, 2002).

However, despite squeezing efficiency savings out of the system of provision through Best Value, it is suggested that state provision of sporting opportunities for all has declined in real terms as the budgets of local governments (the major providers of public sector sports facilities) have been squeezed, and while it is true that commercial sports and health and fitness provision has grown to meet the needs of those who can afford to pay commercial prices, and that public facilities are becoming more competitive in terms of service quality with commercial sector providers, those reliant on subsidised services may be less well served. There is thus a danger that a two-tier system has emerged in terms of sports provision in some localities, with those affluent enough to pay being able to take advantage of generally high-quality private facilities or high-quality public facilities delivering services at the market rate, contrasting with those relying on an under-funded and residual set of public sector facilities. This is obviously an unintended consequence of the shift from direct provision of facilities and opportunities to what we have described as a political governance approach.

Conclusion

What this chapter has sought to argue is that a profound shift has taken place in the way that sport is managed in the national and international context. This shift is encapsulated in the move from direct control or government of sport, to a governance of sport approach. The chapter has described governance as incorporating three dimensions, and each of these three dimensions places requirements on the policy-making system if it is to be effective. Systemic governance emphasises the need for mutual adjustment between the various parties or organisations involved in the production of sport. Governing bodies of sport, for example, can no longer simply impose their will without negotiation with the other interested parties and organisations. Corporate or organisational governance is a normative approach which requires sporting organisations to conform to wider societal expectations of good practice, and this in turn has implications for managers of such organisations. Finally, political governance places emphasis on governments 'steering' rather than commanding change such that key policy skills in defining policy goals and identifying policy incentives or forms of regulation which will achieve those goals have become much more significant. Each of the three types of governance therefore implies challenges to traditional forms of the management and politics of the sports industries requiring flexibility in organisational responses to changing environments and implying also a greater range of skills and competences in respect of sport managers.

CASE 2.3   Formula 1 looks for an alternative escape route   FT

As the grid prepares to line up for tomorrow's British Grand Prix at Silverstone, a mix of bankers, big carmakers, independent team principals and F1 promoter, Bernie Ecclestone, will be eyeing each other warily.

Each is looking for an acceptable exit from the trap in which F1, as a business, has become stuck. That trap is what even Mr Ecclestone now says was a flawed decision to sell his family trust's commercial control of F1 to the now collapsed German media group Kirch.

The creditor banks of Kirch – Bayerische Landesbank, Lehman Brothers and JP Morgan – are seeking to recoup the $1.8 billion lent to Kirch to buy its 75 per cent stake in SLEC, the formerly exclusively Ecclestone family trust-owned company holding the commercial rights to F1.

Most of the carmakers taking part in F1 – notably Ford (through Jaguar), Fiat (Ferrari), DaimlerChrysler and Renault – want control of the stake themselves.

But they have no intention of paying anything like what the banks think it is worth. And with informal talks with the banks having gone nowhere fast, they are pressing on with their declared intent to create their own alternative championship to F1, the Grand Prix World Championship (GPWC), from 2008. That is when the current agreement between SLEC and the team's and the sport's governing body, the Fédération Internationale de l'Automobile (FIA), runs out.

Caught in the middle are the independent teams, increasingly cash-strapped by F1's soaring costs and alarmed at the threat to their incomes, mainly derived from a share of media broadcasting rights payments to SLEC.

One team, Prost, has already collapsed. Another, Tom Walkinshaw's Arrows, was yesterday facing exclusion from tomorrow's race if it cannot hand $5 million to its engine suppliers. At least two others are in dire financial straits.

Crucially, the popular belief is that Mr Ecclestone still runs everything through SLEC and that a new owner of SLEC would therefore be in charge. But control of SLEC does not, in fact, mean control of F1.

The reality is that F1's governance is a lot more complex and no one group has more than partial control.

As one senior F1 figure puts it: 'Bernie has great personal influence. He is listened to and respected. But he and SLEC share power – with the teams, the race promoters and the FIA.'

In fact, everything concerning the F1 championship is decided by the FIA Formula 1 Commission, set up by the FIA under the terms of the Concorde Agreement, which specifies what SLEC must pay the teams and sets out the mechanisms for governing the championship.

The Commission has 26 voting members – eight for individual race promoters, two for sponsors' representatives, one each for tyre and engine suppliers, and one each for the FIA and SLEC. The other 12 votes belong to the teams. The Commission's decisions go to the FIA's governing World Motor Sport Council for approval.

The system has operated successfully since 1981. But no one from Kirch, its creditor banks or the carmakers in F1 has as yet been exposed to it.

This is because in practice many day-to-day management decisions which are nominally within the power of the Commission are left to Mr Ecclestone.

The possibility of a rival GPWC championship has been received by the seven independent teams politely in public, but with near-hostility behind the scenes. To lure them into a new, untried series with unknown management, they have indicated, would require large financial guarantees and secure engine supplies for many years to come.

Such a commitment would run into billions of dollars – to possible shareholder disapproval.

One possible outcome could leave the carmakers out of the loop. That is, if the Kirch banks come to an agreement with the independent teams instead, together with the Ecclestone family trust, leaving the teams and trust holding a majority in SLEC.

A new long-term Concorde Agreement could then be negotiated, retaining F1's current structure.

After a suitable period of stability, SLEC itself could then be prepared for a float.

Then, the Kirch banks and bondholders might recover much more of their money than a fire sale might now.

Source: John Griffiths, *Financial Times*, 6 July 2002

Discussion questions

1. It is sometimes argued that the practice of governance and ethics in Formula 1 is unsatisfactory. Discuss this view, noting arguments for and against the current arrangements in the sport.

2. In response to your answer to the first part of the question, what, if any, changes would you propose to the practice of governance and ethics in Formula 1?

Discussion questions

3. Professional soccer is a business like any other and as such the principles of good governance should be those applying to any business. Supporters are paying customers and clubs should be no more accountable to them than a supermarket is to its customers. Discuss.

4. What kinds of contemporary sports in your country might be said to be governed by traditional hierarchical structures and which to networked forms of systemic governance? Will this distinction hold true for other countries?

5. Evaluate the claim that major transnational sporting organisations are undemocratic in their workings and therefore less effective than they might otherwise be.

Guided reading

A useful review of governance of sport is provided by Hindley (2003).

Materials specifically relating to the governance of sport include Caiger and Gardiner (2000) and Katwala (2000). The papers associated with a conference on the governance of sport in Europe which focuses predominantly on the role of the European Union are available at http://www.governance-in-sport.com/. A number of the sources cited in this chapter are useful including Hamil, Michie, Oughton and Shailer (2001) and Hamil, Michie, Oughton and Warby (2001). For a discussion of systemic governance in relation to sport and leisure see Henry (1999).

Sources dealing with the generic aspects of good governance are provided by Agere (2000) and Keasey, Thompson and Wright (1997), and with generic features of political governance by Kooiman (1993) and Pierre (2000).

Finally for material dealing with aspects of business ethics the reader by Castro (1996) and the introductory text of Chryssides and Kaler (1993) provide accessible sources.

Recommended websites

See David Hindley's LTSN Resource Guide in Governance and Sport http://www.hlst.ltsm.ac.uk/resources/governance.html.
A series of publications in relation to the governance of football in Britain has been published by the research group at Birkbeck College, London and these can be viewed on http://www.football-research.org.

Visit www.booksites.net/chadwickbeech for links to these and other relevant websites.

Keywords

Equity; ethics; governance; stakeholder.

Bibliography

Advanced Marketing Services Inc. (1997) *Nike Brasil World Tour 1997*, Advanced Marketing Services Inc., http://www.admksv.com/proj_4/brasil.html.

Agere, S. (2000) *Promoting Good Governance: Principles, Practices and Perspectives*, Commonwealth Secretariat, London.

Caiger, A., and Gardiner, S. (eds) (2000), *Professional Sport in the European Union: Regulation and Re-regulation*, Time Asser, The Hague.

Castro, B. (ed.) (1996) *Business and Society: A Reader in the History, Sociology and Ethics of Business*, Oxford University Press, Oxford.

Chryssides, G. and Kaler, J. (1993) *An Introduction to Business Ethics*, International Thompson Business Press, London.

CNN & Sports Illustrated (1998, Monday July 13) *Nike denies forcing Ronaldo onto field*, CNN & Sports Illustrated, http://sportsillustrated.cnn.com/soccer/world/events/1998/world-cup/news/1998/07/13/nike_ronaldo/.

Conn, D. (1997) *The Football Business*, Mainstream Sport, London.

Department of Culture Media and Sport (2000) *A Sporting Future for All*, DCMS, London.

Department of National Heritage (1995) *Sport: Raising the Game*, DNH, London.

European Commission (2001, 30/10/2001) *Commission closes its investigation into Formula One and other four-wheel motor sports*, European Commission, http://europa.eu.int/comm/sport/key_files/comp/a_comp_en.html.

Hamil, S., Michie, J., Oughton, C. and Shailer, L. (2001) *The State of the Game: The Corporate Governance of Football Clubs 2001*, The Football Governance Research Centre, Birkbeck, University of London, London.

Hamil, S., Michie, J., Oughton, C. and Warby, S. (eds) (2001) *The Changing Face of the Football Business: Supporters Direct*, Frank Cass, London.

Henry, I. (1999) 'Globalisation and the governance of leisure: the roles of the nation-state, the European Union and the city in leisure policy in Britain', *Loisir et Société/Society and Leisure*, 22(2), pp. 355–79.

Henry, I. (2001a) 'Good Governance in Sport'. Paper presented at the Paper to the Irish Sports Council/Sports Council of Northern Ireland Conference on Sports Development, 1–2 November 2001.

Henry, I. (2001b) *The Politics of Leisure Policy* (2nd edn), Palgrave, London.

Henry, I. (2003) 'The Changing Nature of the Governance and Management of International Sports Systems – Oman 24 February, 2003'. Paper presented at the Toward a more considerable role for physical education and sport in Arabian Gulf Countries Conference, Oman.

Hindley, D. (2003, March 2003) *Sport and Governance: A Resource Guide*, Learning and Teaching Support Network: Hospitality. Leisure, Sport and Tourism, Oxford Brookes University, http://www.hlst.ltsn.ac.uk/resources/governance.html.

Houlihan, B. (1999) 'Anti-doping policy in sport: the politics of international policy co-ordination', *Public Administration*, 77(2), pp. 311–34.

Jennings, A. and Sambrook, C. (2000) *The Great Olympic Swindle: When the World Wanted its Games Back*, Simon & Schuster, London.

Katwala, S. (2000) *Democratising Global Sport*, The Foreign Policy Centre, London.

Keasey, J., Thompson, S. and Wright, M. (eds) (1997) *Corporate Governance: Economic and Financial Issues*, Oxford University Press, Oxford.

Kooiman, J. (ed.) (1993) *Modern Governance: New Government-society Interactions*, Sage, London.

Leftwich, A. (1994) 'Governance, the state and the politics of development', *Development and Change*, 25, pp. 363–86.

Nichol, E. (2001, November) 'Investing in High Performance Sport': The UK Experience'. Paper presented at the Sports Development Conference, Dublin.

Pierre, J. (ed.) (2000) *Debating Governance: Authority, Steering and Democracy*, Oxford University Press, Oxford.

Reding, V. (2000) *Discours de Madame Viviane Reding, Membre de la Commission européenne, chargée de l'Education et de la Culture: Les politiques européennes de l'audiovisuel et du sport quelles orientations?*, Commission des Affaires Culturelles du Sénat Français, Paris.

Stoker, G. (2002, Thursday April 25, 2002) 'Five years of New Labour: local government: could do better'. Guardian Unlimited, http://politics.guardian.co.uk/fiveyears/comment/0,11899,690946,00.htm.

Sugden, J. and Tomlinson, A. (1998) *FIFA and the Contest for World Football: Who Rules the Peoples' Game?*, Polity, Oxford.

van Damme, S. (2003, 01/03) 'Les accords de la Concorde', Histomobile, http://www.histomobile.com/histomob/concorde.asp.

Chapter 3

The role of the State in sport

Chris Parker
The Nottingham Trent University with Alan Barnard, Communications and Marketing
Consultant

Upon completion of this chapter the reader should be able to:

■ identify pathways highlighting the State's influence and role in sport;

■ understand how government funding and attitudes determine the profile and perceived value of specific sports;

■ recognise how and why sport bodies and businesses respond to government initiatives;

■ understand the relationship between State and sport from a number of perspectives;

■ place this relationship in a historical context.

Overview

This chapter focuses on the role of the State on the development of sport at all levels, in particular within the United Kingdom. It asks the question 'What role should the State play – and why?' and considers several different answers. It explores current government initiatives and the implications of these for sport bodies and their potential impact on the development of particular sports. Throughout the chapter the reader is encouraged to examine the relationship between State and sport from a number of perspectives, particularly those of the government, major sporting bodies, education, sport businesses and what might be termed minority sports. Specific case studies are provided although, in one sense, the discussion of the current situation can be seen as an extended case in its own right: by placing it in a historical context and exploring the pathways of influence that derive from the government's Stated vision and aims, the reader will be encouraged to consider possible – or likely – future roles of the State and associated changes in the performing, supporting, selling, sharing and teaching of sport at all levels.

Progression through the chapter is as follows:

■ a historical overview of the role of the State;
■ current government aims, initiatives and influences;
■ a consideration of the future role of the State.

Essentially, this chapter argues that, in order to understand fully the role of the State on the business of sport management, it is necessary to identify the degree and expressions of the State's influence at all levels of sport, including those beyond the pure context of business, to recognise the relationships that exist between these levels and to understand what drives the State to adopt the role that it does.

A historical overview of the UK

'I went skiing and broke a leg. Fortunately it wasn't mine.'

(Anon.)

Sport influences us as individuals and as a society in myriad ways, irrespective of whether or not we are sportsmen or women. It is impossible to be on the mountain and not be influenced by the skiers, although the influence need not be a negative one, as in the case referred to above. In the same way, it is impossible to be involved in the business of sport management and not be influenced explicitly or implicitly by the role the State plays in shaping the industry.

Sport fulfils a number of important functions in society: it provides employment, entertainment and escapism; it improves physical and mental well-being; it creates a sense of belonging and sharing on a local and national level. Sport itself is transient, subjective and immediate. For some, their sporting involvement defines their personal identity. For others, it is simply the way they make their living. The sport industry in the United Kingdom is growing rapidly and, whilst the industry has not always been so large, sport has always played an important role in society on a variety of levels; which is why, to some extent, the argument can be made that those who control the nature, practices and development of sport wield considerable national power. Whannel, writing in 1983, argued that, 'Only in the last 20 years has the State played much of a role' (Whannel, cited in Critcher, Bramham and Tomlinson, 2001: 222). In the eighteenth century, for example, sport was influenced significantly – if not controlled – by aristocratic patronage. However, in the nineteenth century, concern for the physical condition of the working class led to legislation that included the Public Baths and Washroom Act of 1846 (which was actually intended to encourage the working class to bathe in disinfected water rather than take up swimming) and the Education Act of 1870 (which introduced physical education into the curriculum). These concerns, however, were not to go away and were not simply the result of governments moving philosophically towards the creation of a welfare State. As Haywood *et al.* (1995) report:

> The impetus for the introduction of school meals came from the Report of the Interdepartmental Committee on Physical Deterioration in 1904, which expressed concern about fitness for military service. The Boer War and a recognition of the need for readiness to defend the Empire did much to stimulate support for this apparently altruistic concern.

(Haywood *et al.*, 1995: 173)

By the end of the nineteenth century aristocratic patronage had been replaced by the rise of sport institutions controlled predominantly by sections of what Whannel described as 'the upper-middle class …These predominantly amateur-paternal sport organisations dominated English sport until the post-war era' (Whannel, cited in Critcher, Bramham and Tomlinson, 2001: 222).

By the 1930s an increased sense of the value of physical culture expressed by members of the medical and physical education professions helped spur the many voluntary bodies who felt the need for a coordinating body to organise their activities into action. In 1935 the Central Council for Recreation and Training was formed. The Council enjoyed royal patronage as well as support from the Board of Education. Its Stated aim was: 'to help improve the physical and mental health of the community through physical recreation by developing existing facilities for recreative physical activities of all kinds and also by making provision for the thousands not yet associated with any organisation'.

The government demonstrated its concern with the nation's fitness by creating a National Fitness Council. It did not last long. The outbreak of the Second World War turned concerns away from physical fitness towards matters of far more immediate importance. With the war over, the Council focused on the provision of facilities; an initiative that led to the development of seven National Recreation Centres, serving as residential centres for elite performers in a variety of sports. The aim now was to increase Britain's chances of success in international competition.

In the 1950s, the increasing internationalisation of sport and the growth of media coverage – particularly the effects of television – and associated sponsorship led to an increasingly marked difference between the worlds of amateur and professional sport, and the need for governments to recognise and manage the social, national and international values of a growing industry. In 1957, the Council established the Wolfenden Committee. Its task was to suggest how statutory bodies could assist in promoting the general welfare of the community in sport and leisure. The twin needs of developing a sporting elite and encouraging and enabling sporting participation amongst the general public were now clearly visible.

In 1960, the Wolfenden Committee produced the 'Sport and the Community' report, in which it argued for statutory funding of sport and the development of a sports council made up of six to ten people to control expenditure of approximately five million pounds per year. When a Labour government was formed in 1964, it expressed its commitment to the creation of a sports council and, as an initial step, set up an advisory council. By 1969 sport funding was removed from the education budget and consequently gained greater status. One year later, the Conservative government determined to establish a statutory sports council with the power to disburse funding and, in 1971, the Sports Council, with a Royal Charter giving it control over its own budget, finally came into being.

The Sports Council's brief reflected the twin needs identified previously. It had to work with sports governing bodies to help develop the highest possible levels of performance and skill, whilst simultaneously developing knowledge of, and participation in, all forms of physical recreation in the interests of social welfare. Haywood *et al.* write:

These extrinsic rationales (supporting provision because of its side-effects) and intrinsic rationale (supporting provision as worthwhile in its own right) were echoed in both the House of Lords Select Committee Report Sport and Leisure and the subsequent White Paper Sport and Recreation. Indeed, the latter document argues that leisure provision is a need and, therefore, constitutes a necessary welfare service.

(Haywood *et al.*, 1995: 191)

This latter argument was not and – as will be demonstrated shortly – has not been accepted, even though the political perception at the time was that leisure time would increase and, commensurate with it, levels of participation would grow. It was also acknowledged that provisions to meet this expected increase in sport and recreational pursuits were seriously lacking. Whannel reported, 'In 1964 there was just one purpose-built sport centre in the whole of England and Wales. By 1972 there were still only 30. By 1978 there were 350.' (Whannel, cited in Critcher, Bramham and Tomlinson, 2001: 225).

In the 1970s the rationale for leisure provision – and particularly sport – changed from one emphasising the State's role in ensuring social equality by providing access for all (an example being 'Sport for All') to one of economic benefit. From the mid-1970s the Sports Council provided funding for 'Football in the Community' and 'Action Sport' amongst other initiatives intended, in part at least, to alleviate the costs of policing inner cities and repairing vandalised properties by targeting the energy and relieving the boredom and frustration of the young and unemployed. However, user surveys of sport facilities carried out throughout the 1970s indicated that usage was dominated by groups other than disadvantaged inner-city dwellers. (These groups were predominantly middle-class users, the young, those with cars and white males.) The Sports Council, with encouragement from the government, came to the conclusion that the provision of facilities alone was not sufficient; there was a need also to invest in personnel who could stimulate awareness, interest and participation within target groups.

As the State's rationale for involvement in sport and other forms of recreation changed during the decade, so too did the Sports Council's clearly defined independence from central government. The provision of a Royal Charter had been intended to ensure no direct government involvement in the Council's policy-making; the principle had been that the government would allocate a sum of money, but would not attempt to influence how it was spent. In 1978, though, the Labour government gave over £800,000 to the Sports Council to be spent specifically on alleviating urban deprivation, and a further £1.7 million for schemes linking football clubs more fully with their local communities. Haywood *et al.* argue that 'The Council, in accepting these funds and agreeing to implement policies decided by the government, assisted the breaching of their own independent status. Since the election of the Conservative government in 1979, this erosion of independence has continued.' (Haywood *et al.*, 1995: 193). Certainly this rationale and relationship continued in the early years of the Thatcher government until, according to Bull, Hoose and Weed:

the government began to squeeze the funding given to the leisure quangos as it attempted to take more direct control over many areas of policy ... During this period both the Arts Council and the Sports Council were being encouraged to raise more private sponsorship (Treasury 1988, 1990), and were increasingly having to justify their claims for grant aid in terms of the externalities that might accrue, rather than intrinsic value.

(Bull, Hoose and Weed, 2003: 173)

After John Major's election win in 1992, another shift occurred. A new department was created – the Department of National Heritage (to be renamed the Department for Culture, Media and Sport five years later) – with responsibility for sport, tourism, broadcasting, heritage and the arts. David Mellor was its first minister and the main emphasis was, once again, on the intrinsic value of these activities. Indeed, in his introduction to *Sport: Raising the Game*, the Conservative government's sports policy Statement (DNH, 1995), John Major wrote, 'I have never believed that the quality of life in Britain should revolve simply around material success. Of equal importance, for most people, is the availability of those things that can enrich and elevate daily life in the worlds of arts, leisure and sport.'

The Sports Council was subsequently restructured. It became less independent of the government, but its role and capabilities increased.

In 1997, Tony Blair's Labour government, the first Labour government for seventeen years, swept to victory and, according to Bull, Hoose and Weed, their:

> more recent initiatives ... appear to indicate that the brief flirtation with intrinsic rationales for provision is at an end ... both sport and the arts have played a significant part in the Blair government's social policy agenda. This has been made possible as a result of the revised directions regarding the National Lottery in 1998. These directions allowed agencies such as Sport England and the Arts Council to be strategic in their distribution of funds within guidelines laid down by the Department for Culture, Media and Sport. Such guidelines directed Lottery funding, particularly in the sports sector where programmes are now almost exclusively based on the Lottery Sports Fund Strategy (Sport England, 1998), towards initiatives such as social inclusion and the delivery of Best Value.
>
> (Bull, Hoose and Weed, 2003: 174)

In the Thatcher era leisure policy was viewed as relatively insignificant; in subsequent years its profile has risen markedly, helped, in part at least, by the work of high-profile politicians such as Chris Smith and Tony Banks.

Only three influences?

The prediction of increased participation and diversity has proved true. Some (e.g. Whannel, 1983) argue that despite this growth and diversification, the State influences sport in three essential ways. Firstly, it works to ban certain activities. Examples cited could include attempts to ban football in the seventeenth century, anti-cruel-sport legislation in the nineteenth century, and current debates regarding the future of fox hunting and boxing. Secondly, the State regulates and licences activities. One obvious example of this is the 1960 Betting and Gaming Act, which led to the creation of the off-course betting shop. In London in 1953 police made four thousand arrests because of street betting. The fact that they made only three arrests for the same offence in 1967 indicates clearly that a new industry had been developed. Thirdly, as discussed, the State provides required facilities. At local authority level, the degree of funding available for this is determined by the ways in which services are categorised. Wilson and Game (with Leach and Stoker) provide the following categorisation:

Need services, provided for all, regardless of means ... Education and Social Services are the main examples.

Protective services, provided for the security of the people, to national guidelines ... Police and fire services are examples.

Amenity services, provided largely to locally-determined standards to meet the needs of each local community. Cleaning and lighting of streets ... are examples.

Facility services, for people to draw upon if they wish. (1994: 86)

Sport facilities fit into this last category and, as need services receive the greatest percentage expenditure, facility services invariably receive the least. According to Haywood *et al.*, 'Sports provision might seem to represent the "luxury" end of welfare and therefore to be most likely to suffer cuts when central government is looking to reduce public expenditure.' (1995: 192)

Wilson and Game (1994: 27) also note that, 'In many cases the local authority is the regulator and monitor of the activities of other agencies and organisations.' This includes '... the certification of sports ground safety, as the public became acutely aware following the Bradford and Hillsborough football disasters'.

Whilst the above is undoubtedly true, the State's pathways of influence are more complex and far-reaching than is suggested by the three broad influences outlined.

Discussion question

1. Before reading any further, identify ways in which the State influences sport by considering the following sectors:

   - Education
   - Health
   - Business
   - Amateur sport
   - Professional sport

Explore the relationships that exist between these sectors; identify ways in which influences on one sector impact upon the others.

Whatever the precise nature and reach of the State's pathways of influence on sport, one fact that is beyond discussion is that in England the State does now play a significant role. The essential questions to be asked in this regard are:

   - Why is the State involved?
   - Is the State's role appropriate?
   - Who is in charge of policy-making?

Why is the State involved? A modern perspective

Sport matters. From 73,000 spectators packed into Wembley Stadium and roaring their support for England to a girl hitting a tennis ball for hour after hour against a wall, sport inspires a passion and a dedication which plays a central part in many people's lives. Whether it is watching some of our great sportsmen and women strive at the very edge of their ability or the rest of us working hard in a Sunday morning local league team, whether it is supporting our children in sport at school or swimming lengths in the local pool to get fit, sport matters to us all – to individuals, to families and in bringing people together for a common aim, to communities at every level.

Tony Blair (Blair, 2000)

The Prime Minister's foreword to the Labour government's paper 'A Sporting Future For All' provides one answer to the question posed. The State has a role to play because 'sport matters' in a variety of ways. But what is that role? According to Blair, it is not to control sport. In the same foreword, he States:

> The Government does not and should not run sport. Sport is for individuals, striving to succeed – either on their own or in teams. However those individuals, together or alone, need the help of others – to provide the facilities, the equipment, the opportunities. So there is a key role to play for those who organise and manage sport – local authorities, sports clubs, governing bodies, the Sports Councils and the Government ... We need to see new thinking and new action about ways to improve sport in our country.

A study of the ways the State currently impacts upon sport reveals three areas of focus different in many regards to the three influences suggested earlier. These are:

- the provision of funding;
- sporting bodies: Sport England, UK Sport, SportsScotland, the Sports Council for Wales and the Sports Council of Northern Ireland;
- sport in education.

Before we explore each of these in more detail, consider the following discussion question.

Discussion question

2. 'The Government does not and should not run sport.' Do you agree with Tony Blair's Statement? What should the government's role be?

Funding

The most obvious source of funding in the United Kingdom is the National Lottery. At the time of writing this is approximately £200 million per annum, with an additional £100 million approximately by way of Exchequer grants. This latter sum was increased from £50 million by Gordon Brown at the request of Chris Smith, then Minister of Culture, Media and Sport. Lottery money to fund sporting activities is also available through other avenues, one example being the new Opportunities Fund.

Lottery grants have caused some controversy, with debates arising over the identity of the recipients and the nature of the grants. The majority of the grants, however, are spent on facilities – the most noticeable examples being the Millennium Stadium in Cardiff and the Hampden Stadium in Glasgow, both of which were acclaimed successes. At the time of writing, the English national stadium project at Wembley is ongoing. It is a project worthy of further inspection as it draws together many of the key elements of this chapter, namely: the role of the government; sport bodies and sport funding; facility development; the relationship between the public and private sectors; sports education. It is the contention of the writers of this chapter that, to understand the role of the State fully, it is necessary to explore and clarify the interaction between these various elements; they should be viewed as a system rather than independent parts, with developments or changes to one element inevitably influencing (some of) the others to a greater or lesser degree.

CASE 3.1   Wembley stadium

The introduction of the National Lottery in 1994 encouraged a number of English cities to apply to the Sports Council for Great Britain (now Sport England) for Lottery funding to build major new stadiums. Consequently the Council decided to create a national stadium competition, with the expressed aim of developing a stadium that would accommodate three sports: football, rugby league and athletics. In keeping with Lottery requirements, the project would be financed by a mixture of Lottery funding and 'partnership funding' drawn from a variety of sources; profits generated by the new stadium would be spent for the benefit of sport.

In December 1996 Sport England chose Wembley as the home for this grand development and, in November 1998, awarded £120 million to the project – the majority of which was used to purchase the existing stadium and associated business. The project was to be run by Wembley National Stadium Ltd, a wholly owned subsidiary of the Football Association (FA). In December 1999, in response to expressed concerns regarding the viability of the proposed design, the Secretary of State for Culture, Media and Sport announced that athletics provision was no longer part of the plan. (This decision was reversed later in the project.) It was agreed that, in the light of this change, £20 million of Lottery funding would be repaid over a five-year period beginning in December 2000. However, Wembley National Stadium Ltd had not signed the revised Lottery funding agreement and consequently the expected first repayment was not forthcoming. In December 2000 it also became clear that Wembley National Stadium Ltd was unable to raise the required level of partnership funding and the possibility arose that the project would not continue. Had that been the case, Sport England would have been entitled to ask for its £120 million to be returned. However, Wembley National Stadium Ltd had only limited funds available and the FA had not provided a parent company guarantee which would have underwritten the grant. Sport England, would, therefore, in all likelihood have found it difficult to reclaim their money.

In April 2001 the FA requested further public funding from the government for the project to the tune of £350 million! The government rejected this point-blank and in June 2001 the new Secretary of State, Tessa Jowell, commissioned Patrick Carter to determine whether the project could be funded and managed successfully at Wembley. His conclusion was that it could, dependent on a number of key issues being resolved. In September 2002, after the FA and Wembley National Stadium Ltd had passed a series of additional government tests, the Department for Culture, Media and Sport committed £20 million of government funding for non-stadium infrastructure costs – the majority of which was to improve transport links – making it clear whilst doing so that the project could expect no additional funding in the future.

Key facts:
- The stadium is scheduled for completion in 2006.
- The total cost is expected to be £757 million.
- The FA is contributing £148 million; commercial lenders have provided debt facilities of over £400 million.
- Sport England provided £120 million of Lottery funding, the Department for Culture, Media and Sport provided £20 million and the London Development Agency provided £21 million.
- The stadium will host football, rugby league and, after adaptation, international athletics events.
- The stadium will be owned and operated by Wembley National Stadium Ltd, a subsidiary of the FA.
- Profits will be spent by the FA for the benefit of football.
- Five years after the stadium opens, Wembley National Stadium Ltd will donate 1% of its yearly turnover to sports education and additional projects.

Discussion question
See Case 3.3 'Stade de France: the French approach' for the discussion question relating to this case.

Such big stadia high-profile projects are supported by hundreds of smaller projects – sports halls, tennis courts, swimming pools, football pitches, changing rooms etc. – intended to improve sporting facilities throughout the country.

A smaller amount of Lottery money is spent on supporting sporting activity, particularly elite performers. The most obvious example of this is the World Class Performance Programme (WCPP), delivered via UK Sport. The rationale for this focus appears to be twofold:

1. The notion that elite sportsmen and women are good role models who encourage others into sport and a healthy lifestyle;
2. The many social and economic benefits from top-class sporting competition and, particularly, success on the international stage.

The WCPP is aimed at Olympic sports in the broadest sense, with the intention of funding the training and development of potential Olympic competitors and, ultimately, an increase in the number of medals won.

The Sport England Lottery Fund Strategy, 1999–2009, identifies eleven principles against which applications for funding will be assessed. These are:

- Young people, recreationally deprived communities and people with disabilities will be high priorities.
- Projects promoting partnerships and improving coaching at all levels will be a key priority.
- At least two-thirds of funding will be invested in community facilities or activities.
- At least 50% of the funding for community projects will be invested in areas of greatest need.
- Decision-making will be open and accessible.
- Local projects will respond to local priorities.
- Improving and upgrading existing facilities will be as important as building new ones.
- Proposals will strive to ensure equality of access for all.
- Sport facilities will be of the highest quality.
- Strategies, policies and budget allocations will be significantly amended only after consultation.
- Funding will be provided to promote and maintain success at international level.

(*Source*: Sport England Lottery Fund Strategy, 1999–2009)

There are no assistance programmes within the EU specifically for sports. There are, however, some EU structural funds for promoting employment and regeneration in areas of industrial or rural decline, which could support those sport projects that contribute towards social and economic regeneration. Local authorities in England have similar funds offering similar opportunities for sports that show (how) they are meeting specific criteria. One example of such a fund is the Single Regeneration Budget. This focuses on creating change within local communities and can assist a variety of capital schemes. Regional Development Agencies have the authority to allocate grants to projects that promote sustainable economic development; again, sports seeking sources of additional funding would need to demonstrate the value of their particular projects in terms of politically pre-determined needs.

Some funding is also provided to increase activity in areas of low participation by supporting existing club structures. In this regard, the current policy is to provide relatively small amounts of money to nurture involvement rather than giving significantly larger amounts to the governing bodies. It could be argued that the government could play a far greater role in encouraging and/or creating opportunities for people to play sport at all levels, thus helping to produce the raw talent needed for the elite State-funded programmes. If England's approach is compared to that of, say, Australia, France or Sweden, it falls short. The extent to which readers view this as a failure on the government's part is linked directly to the answers elicited by the previous discussion questions regarding the level of involvement government should have in sport – a topic we will return to again as we consider sporting bodies.

Interestingly, the response to the question 'To what extent should the government involve itself, and influence, sport?' varies from country to country. As previously

Stated in Australia, Sweden and France the State's involvement is significant and welcomed by many. In America, however, there is a general view amongst senior sport administrators that the government should stay far removed from sport administration. One senior American sport administrator said, 'We don't even have a Minister for Sport – or if we do, I don't even know his name.' The British approach would appear to be mid-way between these two extremes.

CASE 3.2 — Sport strategies for ensuring funding: the case of the Royal Yachting Association and funding for sailing

From 1994 to 1999 the Royal Yachting Association (RYA) received over £20 million from the Sports Lottery Fund towards the improvement and/or development of facilities. Not content with this the RYA has established a team, funded largely by Sport England, to work on ensuring that at least this degree of funding continues. They do this by ensuring that their bids fit within the wider government agenda.

Sailing clubs are encouraged to ensure that Lottery or other public funding invested in facilities meets three criteria:

1. benefit local, area, regional or national needs;

2. benefit the community;

3. encourage new people into the sport.

RYA staff encourage and enable successful bids in a variety of ways. They:

- discuss projects with clubs;
- advise on the various sources of funding available;
- encourage new projects.

The sport's Olympic success at Sydney, 2002, led to both Sport England and the United Kingdom Sports Institute (UKSI) selecting it as eligible for World Class Funding. However, compared to the ever-improving quality of overseas racing venues, England still lacks quality sailing facilities and so has difficulty attracting prestigious international championships and providing appropriate training facilities for elite performers. The RYA's response is to develop a regional network of Sailing Academies that will provide sailing conditions comparable to those found at the top event sites around the world and comprehensive shore facilities. The Academies will also enable the training year to be extended and help potential medal-winners make an easy transition from youth to senior sailing.

The RYA's strategy also addresses issues of social inclusion, having published and adopted a Statement of Equal Opportunity. RYA Sailability, for example, is an independent charitable organisation that provides opportunities for disabled people to experience and enjoy sailing. The use of ambassadors to promote the sport within currently under-represented sections of society, such as black and Asian communities, is also part of the strategic plan.

The RYA understands the various roles the sport of sailing must play – the different political and social needs it must meet – if it is to receive the level of funding aimed for. Indirectly, at least, the government is influencing the behaviour, strategies and growth of sailing by setting funding criteria. The RYA appears to be happy with this trade-off. The implications for those sports without this level of awareness and resultant strategic intent are clear.

Sporting bodies and international sporting achievement

UK Sport focuses on international excellence and effectively removes the need to have agreements brokered between governing bodies and home countries' bodies. It receives limited government funding and negotiates the remainder directly from sports governing bodies. The perceived benefits of international sporting success are worthy of mention providing another insight into why 'sport matters' and, by extension, why many governments feel they have a role to play. These benefits are identified as:

■ the 'feel-good factor';
■ a heightened sense of national pride and identity;
■ an increased positive image of the country.

The 'feel-good factor', a euphoria in society, is usually created by victory or a performance that exceeds expectation. Such a benefit is difficult to measure and has attracted very little academic research. This sense of 'feel-good' has been linked, though, to the concept of 'social capital' which, in turn, has been defined as 'the relationships and norms that shape the quality and quantity of a society's social interactions' (Prime Minister's Strategy Unit, 2003).

The suggestion has been made that social capital increases with the 'feel-good factor', resulting in a decrease in crime and an increase in social bonding and, possibly, GDP. While it is possible, therefore, that the 'feel-good factor' might have positive long-term benefits beyond the immediate euphoria of success, the case has not been proven.

National pride is also associated with the 'feel-good factor'. Bairner (1996) suggests that an increased sense of national pride, spawned by great sporting achievement, may enhance social inclusion and help unite a nation.

Clearly, though, the extent to which the nation feels good is linked directly to the amount of media coverage a particular sporting event receives. In June 2002, for example, the British men's athletics team won the European Cup and yet received only limited media attention. Consequently, there was little evidence of increased public euphoria.

Sport can create a positive image of a country on the international stage. In research carried out by the British Council, people in a variety of countries aged 25–34 were asked which images best summed up the home countries. Eleven per cent of respondents associated soccer with England and 6 per cent associated rugby with Wales. When the same people were presented with a list of famous Britons and asked to identify them, 33 per cent recognised Linford Christie and 13 per cent Tim Henman. (It should be noted, though, that musicians, models and actors were more widely recognised than sports stars.)

The argument can also be made, however, that these benefits can be reversed. If a national team is perceived to under-perform, there is a likelihood of a 'feel-bad' factor and a diminishing of national pride. If such a performance also leads to outbreaks of hooliganism a negative image is created.

Despite these potential risks many governments seek out opportunities to host major sporting events, acknowledging this as one of the key goals of their national sports policy. In France, for example, this approach is justified on several levels, including foreign policy grounds. Major events, it is argued, ensure the recognition of France internationally, aid in the development of sport within France and can play a significant role in urban regeneration.

CASE 3.3   Stade de France: the French approach

Stade de France was built as the flagship stadium for the soccer World Cup hosted by France in 1998. The overall cost of the stadium was 2.67 billion francs, of which the French government paid 47%; a move widely supported by the French public and media. The French government also promised to pay compensation of 50 million francs a year (rising over time) if no football tenant could be found. Overtures were made to Paris St Germain to move from Parc des Princes, but these fell on deaf ears and, at the time of writing, the search goes on.

The stadium is also used for rugby, with the French Rugby Federation signing a fifteen-year deal to hold four events at the stadium, albeit at a fee four times higher than it previously paid for the use of Parc des Princes. An athletics track was added in 1999, facilitated by rolling back the first level of seats to expose the track. This retractable seating takes up a lot of concourse space, whether retracted or not, and limits the potential for revenue raising at events held at the stadium. However, in France, success is not measured solely by box office receipts and income generated by the stadium. The construction of the Stade de France was the centrepiece of the regeneration and urban renewal of the St Denis area of north Paris, which previously had over 18% unemployment. New jobs have been created and new industries attracted as well, increasing civic pride.

Whereas in France there is public and media support for these large-scale projects, something happened in the twentieth century to change the notion that the State can embark upon big projects in this country. However much cheaper Stade de France was than the proposed costs of the new Wembley Stadium, it's still millions more than the government would ever pay over here.

(Mark Sudbury, Head of Policy at the FA in conversation with the authors, 1 April 2003)

Discussion question

3. Compare the French government's approach to the Stade de France with that of the English government's approach to the new Wembley stadium. How do you explain the differences? Which do you support – and why? Is regeneration and urban renewal an appropriate justification for investing so heavily in sport facilities and major sporting events? (Read the 'five benefits' listed in the main text before discussing this final question)

The five benefits that are most frequently cited for investing in major sporting events are:

■ tourism and image benefits;
■ wider economic benefits;
■ urban regeneration benefits;
■ sporting legacy benefits;
■ social and cultural benefits.

Hosting a major event may well increase revenues from tourism and international recognition for the host city – particularly if it was not already well known globally. However, as tourism is influenced by so many other factors, the long-term benefits are not so clear. Tourist visits to Sydney, for example, have decreased since the 2000 Olympics, but this could be due primarily to the effects of the September 11th terrorist attacks. The potential downsides of bidding for and/or hosting a major event are:

■ increasing costs of bidding for an event;
■ the negative 'fall-out' following an unsuccessful bid (e.g. England's bid to hold the 2006 Football World Cup);
■ the negative image created if the event is not a great success;
■ the potential financial loss if the event is mismanaged or unsuccessful.

Wider economic benefits are also difficult to quantify. Although economic growth is often put forward as a justification for hosting an event, Jeanrenaud warns:

> Not only are the results of many economic impact studies misinterpreted ... in order to support ... policy beliefs, but the results themselves are often miscalculated by economists, sometimes deliberately to please the sponsors of the research project, sometimes unintentionally, the number of pitfalls in estimating the net benefits of a public investment being numerous.
>
> (Jeanrenaud, 2000)

Similarly, some economists are sceptical of the claimed urban regeneration benefits of hosting major events. Clearly, some regeneration takes place but, to date, there is minimal statistical or economic evidence of significant impacts in this regard. Barcelona, host city of the 1992 Olympics, experienced significant regeneration in its downtown area as a result of the Games. However, this has to be set against the estimated $12 billion it cost to host the event, leaving one to wonder if the same benefits could have been achieved at less cost? In the United Kingdom, Manchester City Council – host of the 2002 Commonwealth Games – began work after the Games developing a framework for the long-term evaluation of benefits. For Manchester, the Games were one significant aspect of a wider vision for regeneration with the City highlighting sustainable after-use of venues as a clear priority. Given the above it would seem that economic justifications for bids to host major sporting events need to be assessed rigorously. Perhaps the best argument that can be made is that these events act primarily as a catalyst for leveraging funding for regeneration.

The case is often put that the sporting legacy benefits of hosting a major event are new facilities, increased mass participation and sustained levels of international success. Again, the case is not as simple as it might first appear. Compare Olympic hosts Sydney and Barcelona, both left with a legacy of under-used facilities and stadia, with

Manchester, which built new facilities for the Commonwealth Games that were designed to have long-term viability. (Examples would be the swimming facilities, which were criticised for inadequate seating during the Games, but have met all subsequent needs and – by way of comparison with Stade de France – the athletics stadium, which was conceived and built on the agreement that it would become the home of Manchester City Football Club.) The message would seem to be to plan facilities for the long term, not just the event.

There is also limited data available to support the increased participation and international success claims. Certainly, many sports claim increased participation and interest following significant international success – especially if it was televised – but how long such increases last and their impact on future international achievement is not clear. For example, the number of people playing curling does not appear to have increased greatly despite Britain's success in the recent winter Olympics.

Social and cultural benefits – the so-called 'feel-good' factor discussed earlier – are also difficult to measure and impossible to ignore. Szymanski (2002) moves away from the economic debate by arguing that the primary reason for hosting an event is celebration and reward. This argument alone might be sufficient reason for governments to encourage such events. As Szymanski argues: 'Rather than thinking of an event as investment in generating an economic return, it should be considered a form of public consumption – a reward for past efforts.' (pp. 169–78)

■ The United Kingdom

UK Sport, Sport England, SportsScotland, the Sports Council for Wales and the Sports Council of Northern Ireland have myriad problems to manage, including interacting with all of the different sports governing bodies. This problem alone is magnified because some sports are organised on a country basis, some are organised on a UK basis, whilst others are a mixture, being organised on a country basis and competing on a UK basis, or vice versa.

Sport England experienced internal and external difficulties throughout the late 1990s and into the new millennium, having been criticised for, amongst other things, their levels of spending on self-publicity and administration; even the appointment of a new chair, Sir Patrick Carter, in 2003 failed to silence those with concerns regarding Sport England's distribution of funds. Kate Hoey, for example, former Minister for Sport, writing in the *Daily Telegraph* (22 March 2003) decried the allocation of £9.4 million each out of a total of £60 million to UK sport's 'big four' – soccer, rugby union, cricket and tennis – leaving only £12 million to be shared amongst the rest. Her conclusion that sport 'cannot be treated as a business' is clearly worthy of debate.

These sporting bodies tend to focus on the top end – elite athletes – or on the bottom end – schools – and pay little attention to creating pathways of opportunity for people who simply want to play sport socially and recreationally once they have left school.

Currently, the rules for playing individual sports are determined by each sport's governing body. The government does provide legislation regarding health and safety, racial hatred, crowd violence etc., but legislation does not apply automatically to a footballer who assaults another player by, for example, head-butting him during a match, or a rugby player who deliberately punches a member of an opposing team.

Governments also occasionally apply a 'carrot and stick' approach. For example, in 2003 the Labour government threatened to withhold funding from sport governing bodies that had not signed up to international standards for doping regulations. The question is: should it? Beyond that, how far should the principle of State involvement in sport be applied in the geo-political sphere? The sporting boycott of South Africa, President Carter's decision to withdraw the US team from the 1980 Moscow Olympics and, far more recently, the decision that the English cricket team would not play against Zimbabwe in the cricket World Cup of 2003 remind us of the seemingly blurred line that, according to individual perspective, either separates or connects sport and politics.

Sport in education

Whilst there is more organised sport than ever before, it is not based primarily in schools. School-based sport is now secondary to club- and community-based sport. Although 18,000 primary schools feed 3,000 secondary schools in England there is limited opportunity to play team sports at secondary level, as the schools simply do not have the staff to run sufficient teams. The reason for this is twofold:

1. schools are judged on their national curriculum results, not the quality of their sports teams;
2. a great amount of teachers' goodwill – upon which after-school PE activities are dependent – was lost during the teachers' industrial action in the 1980s.

The understandable focus on national curriculum results in secondary schools has meant that, for the most part, only a limited number of teachers can devote time to extra-curricular sport; many of those who might once have assisted with the running of sports teams now concentrate solely on their subject specialism and the need for ever-improved exam results. The development of literacy and numeracy hours magnified this effect. So, too, did political attitudes towards the potential value of school playing fields. Pre-1997 playing fields were being sold at, what seemed to be, an ever increasing rate. When the Labour party came into power in 1997, sales had reached an average of forty per month – a figure which did not reflect the new government's expressed commitment to the nation's increased health and well-being through either active participation in sport or through the 'feel-good' factor of sporting success.

Chris Smith introduced two conditions designed to reduce sales of school playing fields and ensure the 'appropriateness' of any agreed sales. These were:

1. Playing fields larger than the specified minimum size had to have authorisation explicitly from the Secretary of State for Education before sales procedures could take place.
2. If Sport England objected, the case was automatically referred to the Secretary of State for the Environment, who could not only judge the merits of the case, but also determine future planning conditions – specifying, for example, that the land sold could only be used for sport and/or leisure use.

Interestingly, Sport England rarely objected and local authorities sought to minimise the first condition by securing planning gain that would benefit schools generally as a result of the sale of playing fields. Often, however, this benefit was expressed through general improvements in schools other than increased sport provision. Despite this, sales of playing fields reduced greatly.

In response to the lack of teaching staff involvement, Chris Smith invested £750 million over a three-year period employing school sports coordinators who linked groups of schools and facilitated after-school activities. This initiative, linked with the development of specialist Sports Colleges (see below), is intended to create a national infrastructure for providing PE and sport in schools, with an initial focus on disadvantaged areas.

Sports Colleges were included in the specialist schools programme in 1997 and by September 2002 161 schools had achieved Sports College status. This initiative has drawn some controversy because specialist schools attract extra funding and can select up to 10 per cent of children according to aptitude. Specialist schools also have to gain funding from the private sector, which is then matched by the government. Critics of this approach claim that it:

- creates a two-tier education system;
- is socially divisive;
- works against ordinary State schools.

The government's argument is that specialist schools:

- raise standards;
- increase diversity;
- build on improvements made in primary schools;
- enable schools to build on their unique character and strengths.

The government's aim is for 50 per cent of all comprehensives in England to become specialist centres. The network of Specialist Sports Colleges will focus explicitly on elite sport. According to *A Sporting Future for All*:

> The main thrust of these centres will be:
>   A commitment to the hightest academic standards;
>   A fast track route to Lottery funds, to ensure they have world-class facilities;
>   Access to facilities for other schools and the community;
>   Access to specialist coaching for pupils from other schools and the community;
>   A flexible day that allows time for high quality training and learning;
>   A link to the United Kingdom Sports Institute (UKSI) network centres so that talented youngsters can have access to the best sports science, sports medicine and coaching.

And the government's rationale for creating schools that specialise in sport? 'We know that excellent physical education and school sport are a key part of an effective school. Sporting achievement and academic standards go hand in hand.' (Blair, 2000)

Whilst there are few – if any – who would debate the fact that schools and, indeed, educational establishments in general are important and obvious places in which people can learn sport and engage in physical activity, the actual relationship between sporting achievement and academic standards is worthy of more consideration.

Current sociological research into the links between sport participation and educational achievement focuses on three specific mechanisms:

1. Pre-existing conditions: Athletic performance does not influence academic perform-ance and those sportsmen and women who do well academically do so only because of pre-existing conditions such as personality traits.
2. Zero-sum theory: As students have a finite amount of time and energy, those who participate in sport have fewer reserves to apply to their academic studies.
3. Developmental theory: Through involvement in sport, students can develop a var-iety of skills and attitudes, like time management, self-discipline and interpersonal skills, which can improve academic performance.

The results of research carried out in the USA appear to support the developmental theory, and there is case-study evidence from the UK which suggests that:

1. Playing sport may impact positively on emotional and cognitive development and thus lead to improved academic performance.
2. Sports can encourage students who under-achieve academically to pursue edu-cational programmes.

In support of the above, an Ofsted evaluation report (*Specialist Schools: An evalu-ation of progress*, 2001) talked positively about the broad impact of Sports Colleges on youngsters' development.

However, the following observations need to be born in mind. Much of the early American research has been criticised, as the samples chosen made it difficult to deter-mine causality (i.e., whether participation in sport led to improved educational per-formance or whether those who do well academically are more likely to play sport). Coakley (1997) argues that academic improvements are the result of a variety of adults paying particular attention to sporting youngsters, rather than the actual play-ing of sport itself.

It would appear, therefore, that whilst it is reasonable to claim that 'sporting achievement and academic standards go hand in hand', the actual nature of the relationship and the key influences operating within it are still open to debate.

There is also an increased focus on sport-related programmes in Higher Education, with many universities offering sports science and/or sport management courses and some making the quality of their sport facilities an integral part of their 'sales pitch' to prospective students. It should be noted, too, that the Football Association has established a women's centre of excellence at Loughborough.

The future role of the State

The role of the State in sport changes from country to country and, perhaps even more significantly, from government to government. Those sport businesses or sport bodies wanting to determine, or influence, the future role of the State need to:

- set a specific time-frame;
- predict election results within that time-frame;
- determine the future government's attitudes to: the economic value of the sport industry; the educational, social, health and national benefits of sport from ama-teur to elite level;
- determine the way(s) the government will express these attitudes;

- determine the likelihood of a public demand for the State to play a particular role;
- predict the most significant changes in sport itself;
- predict likely future social trends.

Scenario planning is a useful tool in helping determine and plan for the future. There are three levels of scenario. According to Sondhi: 'PESTEL factors[1] are projected into future scenarios of the world ... these are then cascaded down to the industry level, thus giving a view of the external environment. At the company level, we will develop options to address the scenarios that we have projected.' (Sondhi, 1999: 180)

Scenarios enable a sport business to consider a variety of possible futures and ensure the business monitors the key variables that influence the industry. On a strategic level, the most proactive sport businesses and/or bodies will carry out the above activities with a view to creating aspects of the future rather than simply fitting in with changes created by others. The key questions both sport businesses and sport bodies need to ask themselves are:

- How will we change within a specific time-span?
- How will these changes be of benefit to us and will they influence others?
- How will we communicate and campaign for these changes and associated benefits?
- How can we influence public and media attitudes and involvement?
- How, through, the above, will we influence the role of the State?

Ultimately, the most successful sport businesses and sport bodies will be:

- adaptable – able to fit in to the agenda of the State;
- influential – able to create, lead and set the agenda of the State.

Conclusion

The aim should be that in five years time every child at school should have the chance to play the sport of their choice, every local neighbourhood and eState should offer youngsters the opportunity to engage in sport outside school, and there should be a real effort to encourage adults to continue active participation in sport for many years afterwards. Government can't dictate a sporting life to anyone, but can help to provide the facilities, the opportunity and the encouragement. And as government becomes more serious about promoting sport, so it will ensure that other sports clubs and providers across the country have the chance to do more too.

(Rt Hon. Chris Smith MP, Secretary of State for Culture, Media and Sport 1997–2001, in conversation with the authors)

Sport matters because it fulfils a variety of important functions at a variety of levels. It can have both positive and negative effects, raise ethical and moral questions and influence public feeling and perception. For that reason, those who play roles in managing, shaping and delivering sport have significant power and responsibility. In the last fifty years the internationalisation of sport has combined with increased media

---

[1] For an understanding of PESTEL factors read Chapter 9 'Strategy and environmental analysis in sport'.

coverage and sponsorship to raise the profile – and, therefore, significance – of elite sport and mark a difference between amateur and professional sport. Subsequent English governments have brought their own philosophies and approaches to address the twin needs of developing a sporting elite and encouraging sporting participation amongst the general public.

The many claims and assertions made by governments about the positive benefits of sport do not always have the validity of extensive academic research to support them, but they are compelling for all that. As fans and/or participants many people have experienced – *do* experience – the emotional, social and physical benefits of sporting involvement. On the economic level, sport is providing those benefits associated with rapidly growing industries.

Chris Smith summarises the government's role in the quote above; it is, he believes, to provide the facilities, the opportunity and the encouragement for all in society to participate actively in sport. This chapter has highlighted the ways in which recent British governments have approached this role, placed this in a historical context, and provided some comparisons with governmental approaches in other countries.

The State can influence sport in a variety of explicit ways. These include:

- banning certain activities;
- regulating and licensing;
- providing facilities (or supporting facility provision);
- encouraging and supporting major sporting events;
- providing funding;
- through education (including health education);
- interacting with sporting bodies.

The extent to which the above provide 'opportunities' and 'encouragement' – and to whom – is determined by myriad factors and is inevitably open to interpretation and debate. As has been discussed previously, the State's involvement through these activities creates, at the very least, ripples of influence throughout all aspects of sport: from sport development and amateur sport to professional sport and international competition; from sport in schools to the many businesses dependent on sport; from improving the nation's health (and all associated savings) to improving infrastructure, national pride and even global recognition. It is the complexity of these interactions that makes the role of the State – whatever role it chooses – of such importance. It is because of this importance that one vital aspect of the business of sport management is understanding and influencing that role.

> The futility of arguing whether sport is good or bad has been observed by several authors. Sport, like most activities, is not *a priori* good or bad, but has the potential of producing both positive and negative outcomes . . . Questions like 'What conditions are necessary for sport to have beneficial outcomes?' must be asked more often.
>
> (Patriksson, 1995)

CASE 3.4 The Olympic sport of book-balancing FT

The half-built amphitheatre in a quarry on the western edge of Athens could be the set for a sword-and-sandals epic. But the House of the Weightlifters – its official name – is designed to help Greece's sporting heroes win more medals at the 2004 Olympics.

Across town, Albanian immigrant workers toil under the hot August sun to complete the foundations of an indoor stadium for wrestling – also a sport at which Balkan athletes excel.

Athens is the first Olympic host city to spend lavishly on permanent venues for weightlifting and wrestling. While these events are considered of marginal interest in some parts of the world, they pull big crowds in Greece. Pyrros Dimas, a weightlifter who won gold medals at the last three Olympics, is the country's most famous athlete.

Officials at Athoc 2004, the organising body for the games, make clear no expense will be spared. One official said: 'It's not just about providing world-class facilities for two sports that have a high profile in Greece. These locations were chosen because the presence of an Olympic complex would upgrade people's surroundings and lifestyles.'

But deep cuts are planned at less high-profile venues. Greece is the smallest country to stage a summer Olympics since Finland in 1952 and the Socialist government faces a daunting challenge to deliver all the facilities on time and to the required standards. According to finance ministry estimates, the Games budget has soared from Euros 2.5 billion to Euros 4.4 billion (£2.8 billion), in spite of cuts in transport projects and road improvements aimed at easing traffic congestion.

Budget concerns are the latest in a series of problems that have plagued the Athens Games. After the Sydney Olympics in 2000, Greece faced threats that the Athens Games could be moved to Seoul because of delays in launching construction projects.

Cabinet infighting over Games-related projects and the sacking of several senior managers at Athoc triggered tension with the International Olympic Committee (IOC).

The cost-cutting plan has already threatened to end in a collision with the IOC. Last month, Denis Oswald, head of the coordinating commission for 2004, complained that the government had announced specific changes without consulting the international sports federations concerned.

Evangelos Venizelos, the culture minister, hastily promised that nothing would be implemented without the sports officials' approval.

Athoc officials say most cost overruns are the result of construction delays. For example, contractors building the Olympic village, intended to house 16,000 athletes, have managed to make up lost time but only by hiring extra workers and operating up to 24 hours a day.

Athens had already built more than 70 per cent of the sports facilities needed for an Olympics when it was awarded the 2004 games. But the main sports complex north of the city centre had been operating for two decades and the government under-estimated the refurbishment required to meet the IOC's technical criteria.

Yannis Pyrgiotis, Athoc's head of construction, says the aim is to trim up to Euros 500 million from the budget by eliminating some training facilities, reducing seats and transferring some events to existing sports stadia instead of building new venues.

Mr Pyrgiotis says: 'We worked with the government to find imaginative solutions using existing resources.'

Boxing contests will be held in an indoor city stadium fitted with extra seats rather than a specially constructed pavilion. Aircraft hangars at the city's former inter-national airport are to be converted for basketball and softball.

Jacques Rogge, president of the IOC and a strong supporter of giving less well-off countries the opportunity to stage a summer Olympics, has backed the government's decision to opt for a less ambitious games.

And Athoc is already promoting a theme of informality, with Athens billed as an Olympics 'on a human scale'.

Source: Kerin Hope, *Financial Times*, 8 August 2002

Discussion questions

4. Given the financial demands associated with bidding for and staging the Olympic Games, examine whether the Greek State or private corporations should have covered the costs of the event.

5. In establishing the costs of staging such an event, what calculations might the Greek government have made and how should they have sought to successfully fund the bidding for and staging of the event?

Discussion questions

6. Should UK Sport, Sport England, SportsScotland, the Sports Council for Wales and the Sports Council of Northern Ireland be agents of government policy or independent agents of sport?

7. Consider Chris Smith's comment 'The aim should be that in five years time every child at school should have the chance to play the sport of their choice' in the light of governments' attitudes to certain sports, for example boxing and some martial arts. To what extent does the State determine the nature and extent of sporting opportunities for youth?

8. What are the conditions necessary for sport to have beneficial outcomes?

Guided reading

The Labour government's Game Plan document published by the Strategy Unit at 10 Downing Street gives a clear insight into the State's rationale for the role it currently plays, discussing many of the topics contained in this chapter.

In *An Introduction to Leisure Studies*, Bull, Hoose and Weed (2003) provide a number of chapters that explore the role of the State from different perspectives. The most obvious of these discuss: the historical development of leisure (and the influences of a variety of political, economic and social factors); the economic and political significance of leisure; the political framework for leisure provision and leisure and local government.

Wolsey and Abrams (2001) include two chapters of particular interest in *Understanding the Leisure and Sport Industry*. These are: 'The UK and International Sports Organisations', which considers the different perspectives of the various sectors, the range of organisations involved and the impact of the market place; and 'Globalisation', which identifies six dimensions of globalisation and discusses global firms and responses to globalisation.

Scase's book *Britain in 2010* (2000) is a useful read not only for this chapter but also for 'Strategy and Environmental Analysis'; sport managers need to be managing not only (for) today but (for) the future, and Scase provides insights and raises questions in an entertaining and, in some ways, challenging book.

Recommended websites

The Department of Culture, Media and Sport: www.culture.gov.uk
The Game Plan: www.strategy.gov.uk/2002/sport/report.shtml
World Class programme: http://archive.sportengland.org/whatwedo/world_class/class.html
UK Sport: www.uksport.gov.uk
Sport England: www.sportengland.org
SportScotland: www.sportsscotland.org.uk
Sports Council for Wales: www.sports-council-wales.co.uk
Sports Council of Northern Ireland: www.sportni.net

Visit www.booksites.net/chadwickbeech for links to these and other relevant websites.

Keywords

Amenity services; Central Council for Recreation and Training; Facility services; National Recreation Centres; Need services; protective services; The Sports Council; Wolfenden Committee.

Bibliography

Bairner, A. (1996) 'A sportive nationalism and nationalist politics: a comparative analysis of Scotland, the Republic of Ireland, and Sweden,' *Journal of Sport and Social Issues*, 23, pp. 314–34.

Blair, T. (2000) *A Sporting Future for All*, DCMS.

Bull, C., Hoose, J. and Weed, M. (2003) *An Introduction to Leisure Studies*, FT/Prentice Hall, Harlow, Essex.

Coakley, J. (1997) *Sport in Society: Issues and Controversies*, Mosley, London.

Critcher, C., Bramham, P. and Tomlinson, A. (2001) *Sociology of Leisure: A Reader,* Spon, London.

Department of National Heritage (1995) *Sport: Raising the Game*, HMSO, London.

Haywood, L., Francis, K., Bramham, P., Spink, J., Caperhurst, J. and Henry, I. (1995) *Understanding Leisure*, Nelson Thomas, Cheltenham.

Investing in our Sporting Future: Sport England Lottery Fund Strategy 1999–2009, Sport England Publications.

Jeanrenaud, C. (ed.) (2000) *The Economic Impact of Sports Events.*

Ofsted (2001) *Specialist Schools: An Evaluation of Progress.*

Patriksson, G. (1995) *The Significance of Sport for Society – Health, Socialisation, Economy: A Scientific Review*, Scientific Review Part 2, Council of Europe Press.

Prime Minister's Strategy Unit (2003) 'Game plan: Government's strategy for sport'.

Scase, R. (2000) *Britain in 2010*, Capstone Publishing, Oxford.

Sondhi, R. (1999) *Total Strategy*, Airworthy Publications, Bury, Lancashire.

Szymanski, S. (2002) 'The economic impact of the World Cup', *World Economics*, 3(1), pp. 169–78.

Treasury 88 *The Government's Expenditure Plans 1989/90–1991/92*, HMSO, London.

Treasury 90 *The Government's Expenditure Plans 1991/92–1993/94*, HMSO, London.

Whannel, G. (1983) *Blowing the Whistle*, Pluto Press, London.

Wilson, D., Game, C. with Leach, S. and Stoker, G. (1994) *Local Government in the United Kingdom*, Macmillan, Hampshire.

Wolsey, C. and Abrams, J. (eds) (2001) *Understanding the Leisure and Sport Industry*, Pearson Higher Education, Harlow, Essex.

Part II

Business functions applied to sport

- This section examines sport businesses from a functional perspective, considering the roles, operations and challenges facing a range of departments typically found in a sport business. The reader should note that all of these departments will be found inside every sport business. Even in cases where sport business managers are involved in activities that can be characterised by the chapters in this section, a single designated person may be involved in a number of activities that overlap what is presented.

- The purpose of the section is to help the reader become familiar with business functions, and to ensure that the importance of managing the organisation, human resources, marketing, finance, information, quality and performance are all recognised. The section also embraces a longer-term perspective and considers a range of strategic challenges facing sport businesses.

- The section contains chapters on organisational behaviour, human resource management, marketing, finance, managing small and not-for-profit sports organisations, strategy and environmental analysis, managing performance and quality, and information technology and management information systems.

- Some of the cases included in the section are: the organisation of a Formula 1 motor racing team, equal opportunities in sports organisations, marketing a horse-racing venue, the financial problems of a major soccer club, running a small real tennis business, building strategy in karate and diving, and the use of information technology in Australian surfing.

Chapter 4

Organisational behaviour in sport organisations

John Old
Coventry Business School, Coventry University

Upon completion of this chapter the reader should be able to:

■ identify the internal aspects, functions and processes of organisations;

■ examine different group behaviours;

■ examine individual behaviours within a group;

■ explain different models which classify organisational culture;

■ recognise the features of different communications systems.

Overview

It is probably not an exaggeration to say that the ability to organise themselves is one of the key factors that has made the human race so successful as a species. Other creatures may have more spectacular physical attributes, or even larger brains, but none appear to have the ability consciously to coordinate the activities of a large number of individuals to achieve collectively what is impossible for them working alone. The word 'consciously' is central to the above statement: 'eusocial' insects such as ants and bees can produce fantastic collective work in their nests and hives, while many other animals appear to have complex organisational structures that help them achieve certain ends, but only human beings appear to have the ability continuously to organise and re-organise themselves towards any number of goals. In this chapter we examine the nature of organisations, how they are structured, key processes that take place inside organisations, and how people behave inside organisations.

Organising and organisations

■ Organising is not the same as organisation

Human activity can be organised in all sorts of ways. For example, what we do, and how we relate to each other, are also governed by laws, traditions, customs and family relations. Managers of organisations need to note that *markets* are another way of coordinating activity. For example, instead of having our own departments for cleaning or transport, we can simply contract these out to other agencies, and save ourselves the problems of having to run and coordinate these activities 'in-house'. Instead of having to recruit, direct, motivate and control the people undertaking these functions directly, the task of management becomes one of agreeing with an outside supplier the service to be provided (a 'service level agreement'), negotiating a contract based upon this, and then monitoring the performance of the contract.

The important point here is that simply because something has to be 'organised' does not mean that it has to be done inside the organisation. An alternative is to buy it in from outside suppliers. Many organisations have come to see this in recent years, and sports-based organisations are no exceptions. For example, many professional soccer and rugby clubs have contracted out the advance sales and distribution of tickets to specialist firms such as Ticketmaster. Nike, the sportswear manufacturer, effectively outsources all the manufacture of its athletic shoes to partners, and concentrates on research, design, and marketing.

Like the managers of any organisation, the managers of sport organisations have to ask themselves of any activity: is this one we should organise for ourselves? Or one that we should buy in? Even the committee of a village cricket club must consider whether ground maintenance can be safely entrusted to volunteer members, or whether it should be contracted out. The answer to these questions will be strongly affected by the relative ease with which a function or activity can be organised in house, compared with how easily it can be contracted out.

One other very important practical implication of recognising that organising through organisations and organising through markets are distinctly different alternatives is that organisations and markets require managing in quite different ways. For example, if work is put out to a contractor, the manager's skill will lie in negotiating the contract, and then monitoring its performance. If instead the work is done 'in-house', the relationship between the manager and the employees is very different. It is rare that one can specify precisely in advance exactly what the employee is required to do (and it probably would not be very efficient to do so). Instead, at least up to a point, the employee is a resource at the disposal of the organisation, and it becomes the manager's responsibility to use that resource effectively. As an example, managers sometimes wonder why they cannot 'motivate' their employees simply by offering them more money for more, or 'better', work – after all this is the way things work in markets. But inside organisations it is much more complex. Do we know in advance what 'better' work will be? Who will say whether it is 'better'? Can the manager monitor precisely what has been done, and will they be judged by the employee to assess it impartially? To what extent is the performance of the employee under their control, and to what extent is it affected by the performance of others – including, crucially, the manager? None of these questions arise when we buy something in, whether it be cleaning services or a ground maintenance contract. The specific issue of how organisations manage their 'Human Resources', especially individual employees, is covered in the next chapter. In this chapter we examine some of the other unique characteristics of organisations, and issues that these raise for managing them.

■ So what is an organisation?

An organisation is a deliberate arrangement of people to achieve a particular end. If we are members of an organisation, then our behaviour is not explained by custom, law, tradition, or some market arrangement, but by our membership of that organi-sation.

Crucially, an organisation may be said to comprise three elements:

- Members
- 'Rules'
- Purpose

Members

Organisations are made up of people, and managing organisations is first and fore-most about managing people. But an organisation is more than simply a collection of people, even if they share the same purpose. People watching a professional sports event, or in the club's bar, or store, share a common purpose, but they are not mem-bers of the organisation. Membership of the organisation implies that to some extent at least your behaviour is governed by its 'rules'.

'Rules'

By 'rules' we mean all the structures and procedures that determine who does what inside the organisation, and the way they interact with each other. These 'rules' may be formally laid down, or emerge informally, but either way they determine:

- *tasks, roles, and responsibilities* – who is responsible for what. One of the great advantages of organisations is that they get the benefits of the division of labour by creating a number of specialised jobs. Formal *job descriptions* will often specify exactly what the responsibilities of each person are – for example, at a cricket club, who has the final say on the type of grass that is used and the pitch that is produced – the cricket manager, the groundsman, or the stadium manager?
- *patterns of communication* – is important information communicated verbally or in writing? Can people communicate freely with anyone they wish to within the organisation? Or, at the other extreme, must everything go through a formal 'chain of command' – up through one manager, across to another, and then back down? This is related to:
- *authority relationships* – in simple terms, who is whose boss; who can give orders to whom? More formally, we talk of 'superior–subordinate' relationships, or 'reporting lines'. Is the organisation one with many layers of management, so that communication tends to be *vertical*, or is it very flat, with few layers of manage-ment? If the latter, then clearly each manager becomes responsible for more people and more activities – the '*span of control*' is larger. It becomes more difficult for the manager to be involved with the detail of work, and there must be more *delegation* and *lateral* communication (directly, between people at the same level of the organ-isation, rather than through their superiors).

It is possible to distinguish between members and non-members of an organisation in terms of the extent to which they accept these 'rules'. Those who operate within this framework are members. Those who do not – for example customers and suppliers – are not. Managers need to recognise this when they deal with non-members – these latter are not bound by the rules of the organisation. There are few more effective ways of antagonising suppliers, and especially customers, than to insist that they behave in a certain way that suits the internal workings of the organisation, for example by insisting that they can only purchase from the organisation in a certain way, or that they join excessively long queues at turnstiles because it does not suit the organisation to open more. Organisations should also recognise that, to the outsider, internal distinctions of rank and authority mean nothing. To a customer, the person they deal with at the gate or over the phone represents the organisation just as much as – probably much more than – the chief executive.

Purpose

All these rules and structures exist for a purpose, and it is the responsibility of managers to ensure that the efforts of all the members contribute to the achievement of that purpose. This may be particularly problematic for sports organisations. On the face of it, the purpose of a sports club may appear to be straightforward – to be successful in that sport – but in reality it is much more complex. If the objective were simply 'to win' then by the nature of the business, only a very few professional sports organisations achieve their purpose, as most rarely if ever win trophies. The founders of the Football League recognised from the outset that their primary purpose was to provide a form of entertainment. At a local level, amateur clubs have as a primary purpose the provision of opportunities for individuals to engage in sport and other recreation. A cricket club such as Warwickshire CCC not only wishes to produce a successful county side, but also supports the development of local cricket. In addition, it has a major asset, in the form of its stadium at Edgbaston, that it can look to use for other, non-cricketing uses. Many professional sports clubs are also subsidiaries of larger commercial organisations, and success on the field may have to take second place to financial requirements to make profits, or at least reduce losses. In 2003 Leeds United, a major English Premiership soccer club, had to transfer out a number of its leading players in order to both reduce its salary bill, and realise cash in the form of transfer fees. This contributed to significantly poorer playing results. Reconciling these perhaps conflicting objectives is a major task of management.

Types of organisation

It is beyond the scope of this book to examine the different types of structure that organisations may employ, but a useful distinction can be made between those that are more and less bureaucratic.

■ Bureaucracy

To most people, the term 'bureaucracy' conjures up pictures of red tape, narrow-mindedness, timidity, and buck-passing. But it is probably true that *all* organisations are bureaucratic to a greater or lesser extent. 'Bureaucracy' in itself is neither 'good' nor 'bad', but simply a description of an organisation which has the following features:

- *Precise definition of jobs and responsibilities* – which means that everyone knows exactly what is expected of them, and full use can be made of specialised skills.

■ *A hierarchy of subordinate–superior relations and communications* – everyone knows whom they report to, and which subordinates they are responsible for. Communication within the organisation tends to be formal, in the sense that important communications are written down, and records kept; and it tends to take place vertically – information flowing upwards to superiors, and information and instructions flowing downwards to subordinates.

■ *An impersonal approach to work* – epitomised by the use of set *procedures* to solve problems and *rules* to govern what people do. The use of such rules and procedures can speed up decision-making. It also increases the predictability of everyone's behaviour in the organisation, which has major advantages for management. It is a mistake to think of bureaucracies as organisations in which 'bosses' are forever giving instructions to subordinates. On the contrary, in a well organised bureaucracy, people's job descriptions, along with the use of plans, routines, rules and set procedures, mean that people can work unsupervised for long periods, and yet management can be confident that work is proceeding as planned. It is a form of *control* that does not require constant intervention by managers to tell people what to do.

Defined like this, many familiar work patterns and processes can be described as 'bureaucratic', from the work of the finance office, to a refreshment bar having to dispense large quantities of food and drink in a short period of time at a major stadium. In the latter, speed is essential – every customer unserved may mean the loss of several pounds' worth of revenue. Reducing the production and sale of tea, coffee, and a few other basic refreshments to a routine speeds customer throughput and maximises efficiency.

Bureaucratic structures and systems can clearly aid organisational efficiency, which is why they are so widely used. They allow the maximum use of the division of labour. They give management confidence that the work of the organisation is being carried out as intended. Because people have to concentrate only on a fairly narrow range of activities, in which they may develop specialised skills, they may develop greater confidence in their work. If they leave, then the tight job descriptions and the structure of the organisation allow them to be replaced without widespread disruption. 'Fundamentally, good organisational design is about a clear chain of command and identification of specific responsibilities – such structures make organisations very much more effective when compared to agencies in which everybody wanders around wondering what exactly their specific roles and tasks are.' (Watt, 1998: 125) However, it is true that bureaucracies can be frustrating places to work, and frustrating organisations to deal with. Their procedures may slow down activities, as information is processed 'through channels' and passed between individuals and departments; decisions sometimes appear narrow-minded or arbitrary, and people working within them can feel that new ideas are discouraged or ignored. Efforts are sometimes made to cut out or at least reduce bureaucracy, but it is important to recognise that the advantages and disadvantages of bureaucracy are often two sides of the same coin. For example, specialisation allows people to develop and use particular skills, but it also tends to make people lose sight of 'the big picture', and concentrate only on their own work, sometimes to the detriment of the organisation as a whole. (Some leading sportsmen have sometimes been accused of being poor 'team players', as they appear to be too concerned with their own performance – for example, Test Cricket batsmen who appear to be more concerned with preserving their wicket, and therefore their average, rather than taking a chance and speeding up their scoring for the benefit of the team.) The use of rules helps speed up decision-making, and ensures that everyone is treated 'fairly', that is, the same, but it can also lead to arbitrary and sometimes bizarre decisions. You cannot solve this problem by rewriting the rules, or by telling people to ignore the rules when they do not seem to apply – because then they are no longer rules. You have to decide whether to use rules, or instead to rely on people using their own judgement. (This is an insoluble dilemma that underpins the constant calls for soccer referees on the one hand to be consistent, and on the other to 'use their common sense'. The latter implies that the referee will *not* apply the 'letter of the law', and therefore conflicts with the demand that every instance be treated the same way.)

Whether or not a bureaucratic approach is best for an organisation depends on a number of factors, for example:

■ Is the work *routine*, or is each job that comes along different, requiring a different approach? For example, processing ticket enquiries, or handling sales at a till, are jobs that are probably best reduced to best-practice routines, whereas planning a new clubhouse, devising a new advertising campaign, or negotiating a new sponsorship contract, are one-off tasks that may require novel and creative approaches.

■ How fast-moving, changeable or unpredictable is the *environment* within which different sections of the organisation operate? The more settled this is, the easier it is to plan and control things centrally. If individual people, or departments, need to be very responsive to changes 'on the ground', or to grasp opportunities, then they need more freedom and flexibility to adapt their working methods to these changes.

■ How *large* is the organisation? Bureaucratic procedures, including standardised ways of working, clear responsibilities, and clearly laid down rules for communication, can help ensure that all the different parts of the business are working towards the same end, or that the customer receives the same (hopefully high!) standard of service from everyone in the organisation.

■ What sort of structure suits the *people* – both managers and subordinates – within the organisation? For example, if we have a large number of part-time employees, employed to do particular jobs at particular times, a more bureaucratic structure which defines and schedules their work may be preferable. Many 'sport organisations' change dramatically in size and structure at certain times of the year – for example staging a major golf or tennis tournament. Many employees are brought in, as marshals, programme sellers, or whatever, for a brief period. It is important that their duties and responsibilities are carefully planned and communicated to them before the event begins. Younger or inexperienced workers may also work better in a more 'settled' way than more experienced employees who can make better use of a situation where they are empowered to make their own decisions.

It is a mistake to think that one way of structuring and organising work is always more effective than another – it depends on the type of work to be done.

Alternatives to bureaucracy

It is often said that it is not a question of whether an organisation is to be bureau-cratic, but *how* bureaucratic it is to be. In other words, it is difficult to imagine an organisation that did not make at least some use of specialisation, routines, and so on, but there are other ways in which management can control the organisation. It is important in this respect to understand the meaning of management control. It does not mean direct physical control of everything and everyone inside the organisation – among other things this would be enormously inefficient, if not impossible. (This is one reason why prisons are so expensive to run, and why it is so exhausting to 'con-trol' young children!)

Instead, it is 'control' in the sense that a thermostat controls a central heating system – it monitors performance, and then makes adjustments accordingly. Bureaucracies emphasise *control of process*. Through specialisation, plans, rules and routines, management determines *how* activities must be conducted. If all is designed, and works as planned, the desired outcome is produced. If it does not, then manage-ment reviews and redesigns the procedures, etc. The analogy is with trying to produce a well-designed and efficient machine, or with the design of the many new sorts of stadia built in the 1990s and early twenty-first century. Careful attention to planning how people enter the stadium, find their seat, and leave at the end should ensure that the aims of reduced congestion and increased safety are met.

An alternative is *control of outcome* – management sets targets, against which per-formance is measured, and intervention is focused on where significant deviations occur. However, rather than try to 'mastermind' or re-engineer all the processes in the problem area, a review will take place of whether the targets are realistic, or whether support – training, resources, etc. – are required – or even whether the personnel should be replaced. Much greater freedom is allowed to people inside the organisation as to how they do their work, how they communicate with each other, and so on.

You might note that whether the emphasis is on control of process or control of outcome, senior management should not be continuously involved in directing day-to-day operations. Not least, this would mean that they had insufficient time to focus on their own jobs – setting and overseeing the overall strategy of the business, reviewing the performance of its various parts, negotiating with major outside investors, cus-tomers and suppliers, and so on. This is the major value of *delegation* in any situation – it frees up your time to do what only you can do. It may have other advantages – for example, people may feel more motivated, or trusted, if work is delegated to them, and they do not waste time waiting for the boss to make a decision. But the big gain is the time liberated for the delegator to do their own job more effectively. The man-ager of a Premiership soccer club will be concerned to discover new talent, but cannot afford to spend all his time with the youth and reserve teams, or 'scouting' at other clubs' games. So these tasks – of coaching the reserves and juniors, and watching other games – are likely to be delegated to others who are both competent and trusted by the manager. The last point – *trust* – is essential. Having set out what needs to be done, the delegator must have the confidence to trust the work and judgement of the subordinate. If they do not, not only are they likely to waste their own time 'checking up', but they are likely to undermine the confidence and motivation, and hence the performance, of the subordinate.

Examples of non-bureaucratic approaches to organising work

■ *Project teams*: groups of workers with a variety of skills are drawn together for a particular purpose. Workers may be members of several project teams simultaneously. The project usually has a defined object; when this is achieved the workers move to new projects. In some organisations project teams are combined with specialised departments in *matrix structures*. While workers are 'based' in specialist departments, they join project teams as and when required. We have already referred to the new stadia built in the 1990s: typically the planning of these involved not just architects, but also financial experts, representatives from the sporting side of the organisation, grounds maintenance staff, and even representatives of supporters.

■ *Self-managing teams*: instead of work being done by a group in which each worker specialises in a particular task, a group has responsibility for a whole activity – they organise the work between themselves, rather than be directed by a manager or supervisor. We have already noted that 'organisations' and 'markets' are two ways of organising human activity: a third is 'self-organisation'. Thousands of people can be relied upon to make their way to and from a sporting event without colliding with each other: it should be possible for them to organise aspects of their work without having to rely on rules and procedures laid down by someone else. If this can work with thousands of people, there is a good chance it will work with a few.

■ *Network communication*: in bureaucracies, communication tends to take place vertically, between manager and subordinate, and be in written form (or at least permanent electronic records). Instead, workers can be encouraged to communicate with whoever they need and want to, whether in writing, verbally, or electronically.

■ *Autonomous units*: different parts of the business are structured and run in ways that are different, according to their purpose. Typically they are set targets and budgets, and their managers are given a high degree of discretion as to how they are organised – performance is measured not in terms of how well they carry out processes laid down by senior management, but how well they achieve their objects. (Recall that an alternative to carrying out a function 'in-house' is to contract it out to an independent supplier. The use of 'autonomous units' can be seen as a 'halfway house' – the activity is still carried out by the organisation itself, but by a unit which is semi-independent from the rest of the organisation.) Stadium catering is often organised this way.

These alternative methods of working often appeal to both managers and workers. They appear to offer more flexibility and freedom; they can be stimulating and motivating ways in which to work; and they appear to free people from some of the restrictions of bureaucracy. However, we should not lose sight of the advantages of bureaucratic ways of working. There is the danger that these alternative methods of working can give rise to inefficiency in a number of ways, for example:

■ If the same activity is being carried out in a number of different project teams, autonomous units, or whatever, there is a danger that the economies of scale associated with *specialisation* will be lost. Put simply, a lot of effort may be wasted in duplicated effort.

■ It may be unrealistic to expect people to master the range of skills necessary to make this sort of system work. This can be a source of *stress*, and lead to *demotivation*. People may be happier doing one job and feeling that they are doing it well.

■ *Information* flows round a bureaucracy on a 'need to know' basis, and the use of standard ways of reporting means that the meaning of information should be fairly unambiguous. If, in contrast, everyone can communicate with everyone else, and in any way they like, there is a danger that people will be swamped with information, and in the end unable to cope with it all. (It is sometimes said that if you tell everybody everything, you end up telling nobody anything – they simply cannot process it all.) Managers who practise an 'open door' policy often find that they end up working very long hours, but achieve disappointingly little, as they are continually taking queries from subordinates. In turn the latter sometimes feel that they have to 'run things past other people' – especially the boss – before acting, and the whole organisation slows down.

The point is: bureaucratic systems suit some situations, and non-bureaucratic systems others.

A recent article (Suutari, 2001) demonstrates the difference between bureaucratic and other ways of working through a rather striking sporting parallel. American football is a game made up of a succession of set plays. On each play someone (usually the coach) determines the tactics. Players each have their specialist roles to perform during the play – in professional American football specialist players come on to the field for different tactics – for example, whether the team is in offensive or defensive mode. Once the play is complete, the coach reappraises the situation, and draws up the plan, and designates the roles for the next play.

In rugby (especially Rugby League, but increasingly Rugby Union), while there may be superficial parallels with American football, play is much more continuous. For example, players may have to switch from offensive to defensive mode and back again in the same passage of play. It is impossible to determine in advance the details of the play. Instead the coach can only give broad directions, and then rely upon players with a variety of skills to interpret these as play unfolds.

In terms of the discussion of this chapter so far, American football is more 'bureaucratic' than rugby. Suutari (2001) asks 'Are you playing American football when you should be playing rugby?' with the implication that in business, rugby is a better metaphor for how things should be organised. But this is an oversimplification. The tight control of process, specialisation, and planning of American football suit the type of game which is being played – and, as we have seen, bureaucratic systems are appropriate for some business situations, but not for others.

Managing groups and teams

'Every manager is a manager of people'. This is heard so often that it has become a cliché (one that is ignored, for example, by every manager who tries to pass off 'people problems' to their human resources specialists). But it encapsulates a profound truth: that managers only achieve what they do through the efforts of other people. So managers of organisations have to be aware of how to produce the best from other people.

In the next chapter we look in depth at aspects of managing people as individuals: here we concentrate on looking at their behaviour in groups. Managers need to understand that people may behave differently when working in groups or teams – a group is more than simply a collection of individuals. Knowledge of some of the forces which shape group behaviour is invaluable as a management tool. For example, we often talk of 'peer group pressure' – influences that may have a profound effect on the behaviour of people when they work collectively rather than on their own. Sometimes these effects may be positive for the organisation – for example, schoolteachers and army officers use them to help enforce discipline. The success of many leading sports teams has been ascribed to this, rather than the individual skills of their members. Sometimes they can be negative – for example, an individual may feel inhibited from giving as much effort as they could for fear of being thought to be 'sucking up' to management. Or a group may have established its own *norms* which are below those wanted by the organisation, and group members adhere to these norms for fear of retribution from the group. Some soccer clubs have in the past allowed or even encouraged players to socialise in heavy drinking sessions – initially it was thought this would help to build 'team spirit', but later the damaging effects on performance became obvious and were difficult to eradicate. (Group norms are standards of behaviour and performance that develop from the interaction of the group. Although they emerge informally, they can often influence people as much as, or even more than, the formal standards laid down by management.)

When managing people as a group, and even more so when considering whether to establish a group to perform a task, managers need to consider the likely balance of these *process gains* – the positive effects – and *process losses* – the negative effects – likely to flow from group working. Both are likely to be greater, the more *interdependent* are the members of the group – in other words, to what extent does the work of one person depend on the work of another?

The simplest form of interdependence is '*pooled*' *interdependence* (see Thompson, 1967 for the original work on interdependence). Here each individual can work on their own, and at their own pace, but the outcome depends upon them all performing their own work satisfactorily when it is all brought together. Here, of course, people may not even have to work together as a group at all, but there may be process gains if having them work together – for example, in an open plan office – helps encourage performance, or monitor slacking. However, there may also be losses if their working together encourages wasteful social interaction, or the development of inefficient group norms. On the other hand, if interaction between people is deliberately suppressed, this can reduce efficiency. For example, unbeknown to each other, they may be duplicating the same work; and often 'social interaction' is not wasteful at all, but helps remove feelings of isolation, can satisfy the very human need for social contact, and can build positive *esprit de corps*. Remember that group norms can have positive as well as negative effects – a group may take pride in its performance that leads it to exceed what is expected by management.

All of the preceding also applies to *sequential* interdependence. Here one person's work depends on another's being done first. This is epitomised in manufacturing industry by the assembly line, but also affects all sorts of other work – for example a sports team's performance when on tour could be affected by the efficiency with which those responsible for travel arrangements, hotel bookings, etc., have done their job. (In 2003 the planning for Arsenal FC's European Champions League trip to Valencia had to take into account that it coincided with a local festival, and accommodation needed to be arranged away from street parties, firework displays, etc.) There are many gains to be had from this type of interdependence – for example, the ability of people to specialise – but a potential loss is that everyone can only proceed at the speed of the slowest; and that the whole 'chain' is only as strong as its weakest link.

The greatest interdependence is *'reciprocal' interdependence* – I cannot do my job unless you do yours, and vice versa. This is where it really makes sense to talk of a 'team', and the best examples are in team sports, where success depends on the performance of everybody, and not least on their willingness to support and cover for colleagues who are underperforming. Here it makes sense to redefine your own job along the following lines: 'My job is to help *us* perform well'. The potential process gains are the greatest, but so are the potential losses. For example, any member of the team may reason that as long as the others are performing, they can take it easy; and if the others are not performing, why should they try anyway? The opportunities for 'social loafing' of this sort are at their greatest, not least because in a team situation, it is very difficult to detect. And other members of the team may rapidly grow frustrated, and demotivated, if they feel they are being required to 'carry' other people who are not pulling their weight.

Table 4.1 summarises these different types of interdependence.

Effective management of groups and teams also requires attention to the type of people in the group – for example their age, skills, background, and personality. If group members are very similar, the group is likely to be more *cohesive* – that is, more willing to work together and contribute to group goals. Other factors that are likely to contribute to cohesiveness include the size of the group (large groups are likely to be less cohesive), past successes, and a sense of exclusivity, and outside groups with which one is in rivalry. Managers can build more cohesive groups by manipulating these factors – for example, by 'bringing through' a group of young players from the youth to the first team, most of the conditions for high cohesiveness are likely to be met – but beware! Cohesive groups can be a major source of process gains, and increased productivity, as long as the goals of the group are well aligned with those of the organisation. If they are not, they may be a positive hindrance.

Table 4.1 Types of interdependence in a group

Type of interdependence	Examples of process gains	Examples of process losses
Pooled (all work separately, pool the results)	Division of labour 'Audience' and 'co-action' effects ('peer group pressure!')	Wasteful duplication of effort Coordination costs
Sequential (my work depends on you doing yours first)	Economies of scale Specialisation, 'assembly line' effects	Governed by the slowest, or 'weakest link'!
Reciprocal (we are continually dependent on each other)	Motivation Positive support and help from other team members	Opportunities for free riding

Another factor that contributes to the effective functioning of groups is a balance of roles that people play within it. A well-balanced group requires a number of roles to be undertaken – for example, not everyone can be a leader, and there is a place both for those who can plan what has to be done, and those who can make sure it is finished on time. The group may need someone who can contribute creative ideas, and someone who can be 'practical', and check that ideas are feasible and can be resourced. There is a role for people who can keep the group working together happily, and also for those who can make sure it does not lose sight of the job to be done.

Recognition of the different roles to be played within a group gives an insight into effective leadership. Being a 'leader' is best viewed as fulfilling a particular *group role*, as it is possible to conceive of a group functioning without a leader, but a leader without followers is meaningless. In this context, effective leaders are likely to be those who identify the greatest need in their followers – whether it be for guidance, training, motivation, or whatever – and provide it. Some followers – for example, young and inexperienced members of the organisation – probably require a rather authoritarian leader who can tell them what to do, and how to do it. More experienced members, who probably have useful ideas to contribute, probably appreciate a leader who takes a more 'participative' approach, and puts more effort into building harmony and motivation.

In recent years there has been a fashion for promoting 'teams' in the workplace, as if these were always the best basis on which to organise. In practice, some work is best organised on an individual basis. The manager must first ask: what is it that needs to be done, and if I form a group to do it, what is the likely balance of process gains and losses? If a group is to be formed, how cohesive should it be, and how can I affect this? What roles have to be carried out within it – do I have the people who are suited to these roles? Last but not least, do people have the necessary skills to work in teams? Not everyone is naturally suited to this – for example, are they prepared to trust other people? – do they have the necessary communication skills? – and extensive training may be required. In professional team sports there are such obvious advantages to be gained from effective teamwork in the actual playing of the game that it is tempting to believe that the rest of the organisation must benefit from being run on the same lines, but this is not necessarily the case – for example a better playing surface may be produced where it is the unambiguous responsibility of a single individual.

Communication

Inside organisations, we have many options as to how we communicate with each other – verbally, in writing, over the phone or by email; face-to-face, individually, or in groups. Yet many organisational failures, large and small, are often put down to a 'failure of communication'. Why is this?

It is important to remember that there are three key elements to communication:

- the sender
- the message
- the recipient

If you 'send' a 'message' you presumably have some purpose. For example, if you ask someone to 'check if the mail has come', what do you expect them to do? Report back to you? Bring the mail with them? Open the mail and respond to it? If it has not come, and you are expecting a confirmation from a customer or supplier, phone them up and find out what's going on? The important point is, does the recipient know what you want them to do? (See also Chapter 6.)

As the sender, you must always try to imagine the *context* in which the recipient receives your message, because this will govern how they respond to it. The 'bureaucratic' approach to this problem is to write messages in a standard, unambiguous way, and send them to people whose job description and/or expertise will mean they know exactly what they are supposed to do with it. So a secretary may know that it is their job, on collecting the mail, to open it, arrange standard responses to routine enquiries, and take the rest to the manager for action. In Rugby Union, at a line out, the hooker will call out a coded instruction to his forwards so that they know where he intends to throw the ball and therefore what they should do.

If it is not possible to standardise communication in this way, then we need other ways to clarify the context. Alternatives include:

- *Include the context in the message*, for example 'Please check the mail – I'm looking out for that confirmation from the bus company – if it's not there please phone them and ask what is going on.'
- *Allow two-way communication*. Allow the recipient to check back with you what you want them to do, and why – do not be tempted to say 'Just do it!' Quite apart from anything else, they might impart useful information to you, for example that the bus company has just phoned to confirm the booking.
- *Consider face-to-face communication*. We do not only communicate with what we say, but also how we say it, through our body language, etc. For example, the recipient will get a much clearer idea of how important the message is if they see that you are agitated about it.
- *Use group meetings*. Communicating to a group allows them to see the context of the message. ('If Baljit would check the mail, and let Les know if the confirmation is through, we can get the team together, and I'll confirm our arrival time.') It also allows members of the group to share ideas and discuss problems.

Organisational culture

We often talk of an organisation exhibiting or being pervaded by a particular type of culture – for example, 'a blame culture', 'an innovative culture' or 'a culture of fear'. Management 'guru' Tom Peters (Peters, 1992) has claimed that he can assess an organisation by a few minutes in its reception area, as it exudes and demonstrates the organisation's culture.

What do we mean by 'culture'?

There are a large number of definitions of culture, but it is generally agreed it is *not* simply a question of 'how things are done around here', though this may be the most notable element. The notion of 'culture' goes deeper: it also refers to similar ways of thinking, and, at a deeper level still, our subconscious or unconscious psychological frameworks for ordering our experiences and perceptions. 'How things are done' both *reflects* these, and *reinforces* them. For example, in a particular organisation, people may wear business suits to work. Why? Because that is what they believe is the norm. And everybody does it, so that belief is reinforced.

When observing cultures we may notice what Geert Hofstede (1980) calls '*practices*' – for example the 'rituals' – how people behave, the language they use, the stories they tell which reinforce the culture – for example, what the group has achieved in the past, or what was done to it, even the 'heroes' – the present or past members admired and held up as examples – but it is the *values* of the culture which give these practices meaning, and are the most deep-rooted parts of the culture.

The significance of this 'psychological' aspect of culture (as opposed to the observable practices) can be seen when considering how an organisation tackles a totally new problem. If there is a 'team culture' there will be an immediate tendency to involve people collectively – if individualistic, then emphasis may be placed upon the efforts of people working on their own to come up with ideas, and to tackle 'their part' of the problem. Again, in either scenario, how much emphasis is placed on building consensus? – 'a lot' will mean that a solution will be sought (however arrived at) that commands widespread support, 'not much' means that 'consensus' will not be regarded as an important factor in deciding what is the 'best' course of action.

Importance of culture

Particular cultures are compatible with other aspects of management and organisation. For example, a culture which encourages concern for detail, stability, and adherence to process will fit better with a bureaucratic rather than non-bureaucratic system. An organisation which seeks to pursue a strategy of growth through innovation will find it easier to do so if it has a culture which puts a high value on creativity, and a low value on stability. Human resource management policies which emphasise teamwork and/or personal development are more likely to flourish in a supportive culture.

Subcultures

Within a dominant culture there may be a number of subcultures – for example, the sales and research departments of an organisation may have distinctive cultures. To the designers of a new sports kit and to the people whose job it is to sell it the simple word 'urgent' may have a totally different meaning. To one group it may mean 'in the next couple of months', to the other 'by 3:30 this afternoon'. It is worth noting that sometimes this 'clash of cultures' may be so great that a major problem for the organisation – its management – may be to find ways to keep the different sections 'pulling together'. The managers of the different sections may need to be particularly skilled in appreciating the differences in the different cultures, and in negotiating methods of working together that keep the different parts 'pulling in the same direction', rather than trying to impose a culture which is appropriate for one on another.

Impact of culture on behaviour

The effect of a culture, or subculture, on its members depends not just on the *extent* to which it is shared, but the *intensity* with which it is shared. We may all (in a group) be comfortable doing things the way they are, but does that matter that much to us? – compared with say, the survival of the firm, or our own job prospects, or a pay rise? An issue for a globalised business can be: what will have the strongest impact on how a particular national branch of the company performs and behaves – the 'organisational' culture, or the national culture of the host country?

Some famous 'models' of culture

The Harrison/Handy model

Charles Handy (1991) has popularised the idea (originally put forward by Harrison) that organisational cultures can be typified as:

Power (e.g. the small entrepreneurial firm) – there is little emphasis on formal procedures and job descriptions; the organisation revolves around one or a few people who control all its resources. Tasks tend to be undertaken on the basis of direct instructions from the 'power-holders', or, in their absence, on the basis of what subordinates know, or believe, the power-holders would want. Jobs are ill-defined; decisions are made quickly. Speed is often possible as people are often able to decide what to do on their knowledge of 'the boss' and what s/he wants, so formal communication and instructions are not necessary. This type of culture is typical both of small businesses – but also of some political dictatorships. Some long-serving and successful soccer managers have successfully created this type of culture revolving around themselves; but problems can arise if this causes clashes with other types of culture – for example if the soccer club is only part of a larger organisation with a different culture.

Role (e.g. the classic bureaucracy) – there is an emphasis on rationality, order and predictability. Emphasis is put on doing your own job, in the correct way, following the laid-down procedures of the organisation. This culture fits well with 'bureaucratic' structures and procedures.

Task (e.g. emphasis on new technologies, project teams) – the emphasis is on problem solution, and harnessing human and other resources to tackling a succession of new and unpredictable challenges. You do not expect to concentrate on simply your own role, but to bring your skills to bear wherever they help solve the problems of the organisation. This culture is often found in organisations where teamwork and project based operations are common.

Person (where individuals have a high degree of autonomy). In the first three cultures the individual is subordinate to the organisation. Here the picture is reversed – the organisation is there to support the work of (typically highly-skilled) individuals. Examples include medical general practices and some university departments. Some sports agencies may also reflect this culture, as their only purpose is to further the interest of their star clients.

Exhibit 4.1   A party game – what does someone do for a living?

Ask someone what they do for a living. Suppose they work for Lord Chadwick on the Beech estate as a gamekeeper. How do they reply to your question?

'I work for Lord Chadwick' = Power Culture

'I work for the Beech Estate' = Role Culture

'I work in gamekeeping' = Task Culture

'I'm a gamekeeper, and a ****** good one' = Person Culture

The Deal and Kennedy model – risks and feedback

Deal and Kennedy (1982) identify two key factors that shape culture: the *types of risks* assumed – high or low – and the *speed of feedback from decisions* – fast or slow – and on the basis of this identify four main organisational cultural types:

Tough Guy/Macho cultures (high risk, fast feedback) tend to be characterised by rapid 'gut instinct' decision-making, high individualism, competitiveness, even superstition. Examples include television, advertising, many professional sport organisations.

Bet Your Company cultures (high risk, slow feedback) may exhibit high regard for expertise, meticulous planning, and mentoring of younger by older staff. Examples include investment banking, the armed forces.

Work Hard, Play Hard cultures (low risk, rapid feedback) – high volume activities such as mass retailers and many (particularly amateur) sports teams. An emphasis on hard work, teams, and dynamism.

Process cultures (low risk, slow feedback) – employees find it difficult to measure directly the success of what they do (at least in the short run), but unlike in a 'Bet Your Company' culture are unlikely to make decisions that could be catastrophic for the organisation. Hence an emphasis on 'doing things right', rather than on the long-term outcome, and the value placed on mastering and maintaining the internal systems. Examples include national sports administration bodies, retail banking and public administration.

Exhibit 4.2   Another party game

Deal and Kennedy believe that certain types of physical recreation appeal to people in different types of culture. So what type of physical activity do you and your friends take part in?

'Tough Guy/Macho' types like highly competitive individual games – such as squash.

'Work Hard, Play Hard' types like team sports.

'Bet Your Company' types like games where the outcome remains in doubt as long as possible – such as golf.

'Process' types like activities where the emphasis is more on the participation than the outcome – such as swimming, aerobics, or jogging.

Structure, behaviour, communications and culture – bringing them all together

It should by now be clear that these four aspects of organisations cannot be dealt with in isolation from each other. For example, a bureaucratic structure tends to go with a 'role' or 'process' culture; communication is likely to be hierarchical, and be written, in a standardised form; and there is probably more emphasis on individual specialised work. Team-based organisations, in contrast, may have 'task' or 'work hard/play hard' cultures, be flatter and less hierarchical, and encourage networking, verbal communication and meetings. This can extend to other aspects of management and organisations that we have not considered here. For example, in making *decisions*, should managers consult their subordinates, or even delegate decisions to them? In a bureaucratic hierarchy, subordinates may be used to the manager making decisions at one level, but leaving lower level decisions to them to take, as they fall within their area of competence and responsibility. What is seen as 'excessive' communication and consultation about decisions may be viewed as unnecessary, unexpected, and disruptive. In contrast, in another organisation, where it is felt that subordinates have vital inputs to make into decisions, or where it is felt that commitment by subordinates to decisions is vital (so they need to feel that their views, ideas, and fears have been taken into account), consultative decision-making, built round meetings and verbal communication, may be the norm.

Managers need to be aware of how these organisational and work practices link together for organisational efficiency. At any one time there are always fads and fashions in management, whether it be for teamwork, electronic communication, 'culture change' or whatever. It is important to recognise that, while there is no 'magic formula' for success, it is more likely to come if management recognises that organisational structure, communications, culture, people-management methods and decision-making are part of a single 'system', one part of which affects all the others, and no part of which can be treated or altered in isolation.

CASE 4.1 A Formula 1 team, *c.* 2001

This study is based upon the Arrows team, but the general structure and points made would hold for most F1 teams.

A Formula 1 'team' typically employs between 140 and 450 people. These range from business specialists such as accountants and secretaries, who could, and often have, worked in quite different types of business, through specialist engineers to race drivers on seven-figure contracts.

As with most sporting organisations, while the team may have aspirations to win its tournament – in this case the F1 World Championship – this is not a realistic business goal for the medium term, as in the last decade only four teams (Benneton [now known as Renault], Williams, McLaren, and Ferrari) have achieved this. Realistically, success is measured in terms of achieving top eight finishes in races.

Business planning and activities therefore work in a series of cycles of decreasing length. There is a long-term objective, achievable only over several seasons, to develop better technology, and better cars, that will increase the likelihood of podium finishes. On an annual basis, there is the need to generate sufficient revenues (at least £40 million) to maintain the team, largely through sponsorship and marketing, and negotiate supplies of competitive key components such as engines and tyres. During the season, there is a two-weekly cycle of competing in the current race and preparing for the following one.

Figure 4.1 is a chart representing the organisational structure of the team. In reality, this comprises a number of groups, whose work interacts and overlaps. In addition, there are intricate relations with outside firms (the 'boundaries' of the team are shown by broken lines). Tyre and engine suppliers in particular are keen that their products are seen to perform well, and will work intimately with members of the F1 team to improve performance (shown on the chart by the interaction between the Chief Engineer of the engine supplier and the team Technical Director, and between the team R&D and the engine supplier's Race Engineering group). Indeed, at times, employees of the supplier may be based with the team – for example with the specialist groups – and working alongside them in a way that would make it difficult for an outsider to distinguish the difference between them. The chart also illustrates that this interaction may link back to the suppliers of the suppliers – for example, from the team's R&D, to the engine supplier's Race Engineering group, to the latter's R&D section, and then back to their suppliers.

The different business horizons of the firm are reflected in the working patterns of the various groups within the organisation. For example, the Race team is involved in intensive bursts of preparation for the races, when all-night working may not be uncommon, while the R&D team is working on a more regular pattern towards longer-term objectives – though even they may find themselves diverted to a short-term problem such as a cure for a 'grenading' gearbox or failing crankshaft. The Test team serves both the Race, Design and R&D teams, and their work patterns may therefore reflect whatever is the greatest imperative. While the specialist work groups have the most regular work patterns, at any time these may have to be adjusted to meet urgent requirements of the Race, Test, Design or R&D teams.

In-factory activities are typically organised with managers and section heads reporting back and up. Race and Test teams mechanics are organised via the chief mechanic, who liases with (and receives instructions from) the Technical Director, the senior chassis race engineer, and the senior engine race engineer. He passes on instructions to the no. 1 mechanic on each car (no. 1 mechanic is responsible for the preparation of the car), who in turn is aided by the no. 2 mechanic, and then the front end and rear end lead mechanics.

The engine and chassis race engineers then also liaise with the no. 1s for their relevant car. The senior race engineer (in both chassis and engine areas) give instructions to and receive information from their subordinate engineers. At any time boundaries can be crossed as needs dictate. It is not uncommon for senior race engineers to join in with working on a chassis or to be found preparing a race

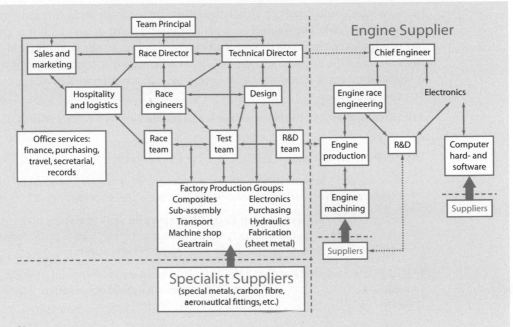

Notes:

In many respects, apart from size the Test and Race teams are identical – although the Test team will be 30%–40% the size of the Race team they do have their own transport facilities and drivers. Work will often be shared between these two areas in times of great stress.

Production is 'factory-based', working what would be considered normal hours, unless urgent parts are required due to crashes, parts failure, or new designs.

Design is again 'factory-based', but may attend test sessions with the Test team, and also work closely with the R&D department.

Office services is the sort of organisation one would expect to find in any place of manufacturing, with the exception of sales and marketing who will attend test sessions and races to provide hospitality support to sponsors and sponsors' guests.

Figure 4.1 **Organisation of a Formula 1 team, *c.* 2000**

engine. In these circumstances they will be told what to do by the engine dresser! (A specialised mechanic whose function is to fit the engine to the chassis. Interestingly, the engine dresser could be employed either by the team itself, or by the engine supplier.)

The intricacies of this structure, and its links with suppliers, place particular demands on the organisation. There is network rather than vertical communication. Post-race Monday meetings of all employees (the 'prayer meetings') help set priorities. Employees must be prepared to work flexibly, and be comfortable with joining *ad hoc* project teams. Managers must be able to negotiate their requirements, rather than rely upon being able to command what they need. For example, at any one time, the immediate orientation of the business – which tasks take priority – must be negotiated by the Race and Technical (and even Sales and Marketing) Directors. There is obviously a danger that one or other of these could prevail on a consistent basis, which could result in either the short- or medium-term interests of the team being overlooked. The Team Principal can intervene to arbitrate, but if this were to happen on a regular basis it would represent a failure in the organisation. Similarly, at the level of the engineers in the specialist groups, while specialist skills are valued, it is also important that individuals recognise and are prepared to adapt to the needs of other sections.

Source: compiled by John Old based on information provided by Martin Smith, Arrows

Discussion questions

1. Why does an F1 team have such an intricate structure? Would this be appropriate or necessary in other sport organisations, for example a soccer or rugby club?

2. Managers in F1 teams must often deal with people who work elsewhere in the automobile industry, where organisation structures are often much more 'bureaucratic' in the sense described in the text. What 'culture clashes' might this give rise to?

3. In the Case Study it states that if the Team Principal were to have to intervene on a regular basis to arbitrate disputes, this would represent a failure of organisation. Why, and in what sense?

Conclusion

Organisations are deliberate arrangements of people to achieve a particular purpose. The way an organisation is structured sets out what is expected of its members, in terms of job descriptions, communication patterns, and general rules. The more formal these are, and the more the organisation depends for its efficiency on hierarchy, control of process, standardisation and written communication and record keeping, the more 'bureaucratic' we say that it is. All organisations rely on bureaucratic methods to some extent, but the degree of bureaucracy will vary according to the purpose of the organisation, the tasks it has to perform, its size, and the environment within which it operates. Different parts of the same organisation may well be structured and run in quite different ways.

The structure of the organisation affects, and is affected by, the behaviour of the people working within it, the way they communicate with each other, and the 'culture' of the organisation. The behaviour of people working in groups is likely to be affected by the nature of the group task, the size and cohesiveness of the group, and the group norms. The 'culture' of an organisation, or the subcultures of parts of it, provides members of the organisation with a common psychological framework through which they interpret what is happening and how they should respond to it. Communication within the organisation can take a number of forms; which is appropriate depends on the information to be shared, and its purpose, the structure and culture of the organisation, and the extent to which the context of the message needs clarification.

CASE 4.2   Chinese golfers wait for the game to tee off   **FT**

A year after he had paid Rmb250,000 (£20,800) for membership of a golf course near Shanghai, a young Chinese businessman was surprised to see the club offering a similar deal for less than half the price. When he complained, the Binhai club bosses had a ready explanation – his 'gold' membership entitled him to play all of the club's planned 54 holes, whereas the new Rmb98,000 deal covered only one 18-hole course. There was just one problem: Binhai, so far, has only one 18-hole course – though it says that construction has started on a second. The evident devaluation of his membership left the golfer dismayed. 'They have no understanding of a golf membership,' he says.

If Asia is any guide, golf should be enormously successful in China, just as it is in places such as Japan and Taiwan, where it has become an essential and expensive lubricant in the top levels of business and politics.

The sport has long been promoted as a natural match for the stereotypical Asian character, rewarding patience and discipline in a framework centred on ethics and etiquette. The Chinese, like many Asians, also enjoy a wager, with some hackers employing an extra 'ethics' caddie to keep an eye on their opponents' observance of the rules.

Sure enough, China now has a bunker-full of new golf courses. There are more than 100 in the country, most of them in southern China where businessmen from Hong Kong and Taiwan first invested. Shanghai alone has about 15 courses, compared with one before the arrival of the communists in 1949.

And yet, as Binhai's growing pains show, golf is struggling to establish itself in China as a business, a pastime and a sport. 'Some courses are making money but it's only a minority,' says Stephen Allen, of the Australia-based Golf World Management. 'The fundamental problem is that they over-estimated the number of golfers who were willing to pay expensive, US dollar-equivalent membership fees.'

Another barrier is the game's arcane rules and its lengthy, sometimes pretentious traditions. These had no roots when golf reappeared with the market economy in China 20 years ago.

The government's attitude – always crucial for new businesses in China – has not helped. On the one hand, the authorities have encouraged the sport, handpicking young golfers for training scholarships to ensure that China can compete in top tournaments.

At the same time, however, other arms of government have periodically cracked down on golf and issued edicts urging executives not to play what is considered an elite sport.

'There's a view that playing golf is a sign of corruption and that membership fees are a form of bribery but this is wrong,' says Sun Ge, who produces a golf programme for cable television in Shanghai.

The manager of one Shanghai golf course says that Chinese bankers received a circular this year warning them off the sport for a few months.

'The government attitude is not clear, like most things in this country,' the manager says. 'One day they will say "let's promote this" and on the next they will send out little red letters discouraging people from playing.'

The government's concern about course construction had some merit. In a country concerned about the depletion of arable land and water resources, officials had questioned the building of some links.

'Courses used to use expensive arable land, which helps explain the high price of memberships,' says Mr Sun. 'Now developers are using deserted land, so the price will go down.'

The sport's difficult birth in China is reflected in the absence of a secondary market in memberships. Unlike in Japan, where the cost of memberships became a barometer of asset prices during the bubble economy, Shanghai's property inflation of recent years has not flowed through to golf.

A businessman with Shimizu, the Japanese construction company, recently advertised two memberships bought seven years ago for $125,000 (£86,200). He was asking only $80,000. 'But no one wants to buy at this price,' he says.

The Binhai club in Shanghai explains that it has two memberships on offer, one with a 40-year maturity and the other lasting only 20 years. But if there is no market to sell into, that is cold comfort for a holder of the more expensive membership.

The optimists are unbowed. Mr Allen, who says he has five Chinese courses on his books looking for buyers, reckons the market will start 'a rapid climb of profitability (return on investment) from mid-2004'.

As well as a revival in the world economy, he expects corporate leisure pursuits such as golf to get a psychological boost in the lengthy lead-up to Beijing's 2008 Olympics.

Rudi Butt, of the Shanghai West Golf Club, which has 200 members, of whom only 10 are locals, also senses a turnaround. 'Golf is now definitely being considered as a medium for entertainment,' he says. 'You go to a driving range in the city and there are more locals than expats.'

Mr Sun has his own litmus test for the game's rising popularity. Once he used to hear only foreign languages on Shanghai's golf courses. 'Now,' he says, 'I hear more and more of the Shanghai dialect because the locals are taking it up too.'

Among such players, the Japanese influence is detectable. The young caddies in Shanghai encourage players whose shots land on the green with the perky compliment of 'nice on!' – a Japanese adaptation of an English phrase. Likewise, the pitching wedge is offered to you as a 'pitchi'.

In golf etiquette, however, an area in which the Japanese are well schooled, the Chinese are still learning. 'They don't understand the spirit or the tradition of the game,' complains one course manager. 'They only want to know how far they can whack the ball.'

One course manager said it was hard to enforce rules that ensured that bunkers were raked and balls marked on the green. 'We had lots of complaints,' he says. 'People said: "Why do we have to do it this way?".'

Source: Richard McGregor, *Financial Times*, 4 September 2001

Discussion questions

4. To what extent are the 'members' of commercial golf clubs 'members' in the sense described in the text? Is this likely to be different in different national cultures? How is this likely to affect members' attitudes to the rules of the club?

5. In the light of this, might it be better for golf clubs in China to be organised differently from those in other parts of the world?

Guided reading

Robbins (2003) gives a very readable introduction to all of the topics covered in this chapter. Mullins (2002) and Robbins and Coulter (2002) give more depth, explanations of relevant research, and a wealth of examples. For an expanded view of the issues and topics in this chapter, particularly organisational design and culture, set in a sports context, see Slack (1997). Chapter 6 of Parks, Zanger and Quarterman (1998) is a brief but rather intense overview of organisational behaviour in a sports context, and shows how different aspects of organisational design and behaviour work together as a single 'system'.

For a really in-depth view of modern thinking about organisations, see Morgan (1997). This is a deliberately challenging book, but for someone who wants to study organisations it provides a stimulating variety of different perspectives on what organisations are, and how they work.

For further reading on corporate culture, see Deal and Kennedy (1982) and especially Handy (1991). The latter uses a metaphor (which has become quite famous) of four Greek Gods to represent the four cultures, and explores what the 'worship' of these four gods means for an organisation.

Smith and Stewart (1999) includes chapters on organisational structure and culture. Parkhouse (2001) has chapters on organisational design and group decision-making.

Recommended websites

The website 'businessballs.com' (http://www.businessballs.com) contains a wealth of short, punchy definitions, articles, and activities on business topics, many of which are relevant to this chapter. A more conventional source of material is to be found at 'theworkingmanager.com'; while for in-depth reading and research, the Social Science Information Gateway links to articles, case studies, biographies of management writers, and so on. Especially worthwhile for this chapter are the pages for organisational management: http//www.sosig.ac.uk/roads/subject-listing/world-cat/orgman.html and organisational behaviour: http://www.sosig.ac.uk/roads/subject-listing/world-cat/orgbehav.html

Visit www.booksites.net/chadwickbeech for links to these and other relevant websites.

Keywords

Bureaucracy; control; culture; group norms; leadership; organisation.

Bibliography

Deal, T. and Kennedy A. (1982) *Corporate Cultures: The Rites and Rituals of Corporate Life*, Addison-Wesley, Reading MA.

Handy, C. (1991) *Gods of Management* (3rd edn), Business Books, London.

Hofstede, G. (1980) *Culture's Consequences: International Differences in Work-Related Values*, Sage, Beverly Hills.

Morgan, G. (1997) *Images of Organization* (2nd edn), Sage, London.

Mullins, L.J. (2002), *Management and Organisational Behaviour* (6th edn), FT Prentice Hall, Harlow, Essex.

Parkhouse, B.L. (ed.) (2001) *The Management of Sport* (3rd edn), McGraw Hill, New York.

Parks, J.B., Zanger, B.R.K. and Quarterman, J. (eds) (1998) *Contemporary Sport Management*, Human Kinetics, Champaign IL.

Peters, T. (1992) 'Hot times call for hot words', available from http://www.tompeters.com/toms_world/t1992/121192-hot.asp.

Robbins, S. (2002) *Organizational Behavior* (10th edn), Prentice Hall, Upper Saddle River NJ.

Robbins, S. (2003) *Essentials of Organizational Behavior* (7th edn), Prentice Hall, Upper Saddle River NJ.

Robbins, S. and Coulter, M. (2002) *Management* (7th edn), Prentice Hall, Upper Saddle River NJ.

Slack, T. (1997) *Understanding Sports Organizations*, Human Kinetics, Champaign IL.

Smith, A. and Stewart, B. (1999) *Sports Management: A Guide to Professional Practice*, Allen & Unwin, St Leonards NSW.

Suutari, R. (2001) 'Organizing for the New Economy', *CMA Management*, April.

Thompson, J.D. (1967) *Organizations in Action*, McGraw-Hill, New York.

Watt, D.C. (1998) *Sports Management and Administration*, E & FN Spon, London.

Chapter 5

Human resource management in sport

Terrence Wendell Brathwaite
Coventry Business School, Coventry University

Upon completion of this chapter the reader should be able to:

■ explain the main theories of motivation;

■ apply them to different professional sports scenarios;

■ assess the importance of Human Resource (HR) to the overall strategic position of an organisation;

■ explain the key functions of HR within an organisation;

■ explain and assess the key HR processes within an organisation;

■ explain the factors of Human Resource Management (HRM) which are particular to professional sports.

Overview

In this chapter[1] we explore the essence of managing the human capital in sports organisations. The people factor in sports can be essentially placed into the following categories: technicians (i.e. amateurs, self-employed professionals, employed professionals); technical specialists (including operatives and support staff); and managers (who may be either volunteers or paid administrators). In its contextual crisscrossing of each category, this chapter's trajectory will be threefold and based on a voyage of discovery not in seeking new landscapes, but in having new eyes for responding quickly to market forces in this generation of uncompromising global competition. First of all, we shall consider the nature and dynamics of psychological motivation in people management and leadership performance within the sports industry. At this juncture, the discussion will centre on the function of people management and leadership as being further determined from a triad of ancillary fundamental aspects:

---

[1] Dedicated to Caribbean sport pioneers and family icons, Trinidad's road cyclist of the century George Terry, Jamaican-British boxer and 1968 Olympic finalist Edwin Stanley, Grenadian sports scholar Alma Thomson and the memory of the late Dr Bryce Taylor, founder of the Sports Administration Programme, York University (Toronto, Canada).

- a system of *interaction* –
  that is, the basic nature of any interpersonal relations;

- a system of *influence* –
  in other words, a system of reciprocal impact between a sports organisation's situational factors, the human resources manager or leader (coach), and the subordinates (employees, athletes or team) upon each other;

- and a system of *empowerment* –
  within the employer–employee relationship, human resource managers or leaders have a greater potential for exerting influence, due to the intrinsic power of their position.

Savants in management science have suggested that the main underlying dispositional attribute which correlates this threesome to managerial leadership is *intelligence*, which is generally acknowledged as the ability to cope with uncertainties in a discerning fashion via planning, organising, coordinating, and evaluating various options of action using innate cognitive abilities (or 'common sense'). But while the twentieth century has witnessed a continuous review of intelligence as an oversimplified notion,[2] the advent of the millennium has ushered in a modernistic model of multiple intelligences that is more reflective of the phenomenal matrix of personal diversity and excellence in sports management today. The chapter thus commences by exploring the reality that there is more than one way of being a discerning motivator and manager of people in the sports industry, where, like all places of work, there can be found any and every emotion – affirmation, rejection, love, anger, envy, jealousy, sense of well-being, and a sense of emotional patterns revisited – that together make up part of the human experience.

Within this context, the chapter also asserts that the key to understanding the motivational and multiple intelligence theories of human experience in sports management is the fact that the workplace is not a mechanised apparatus, because those who inhabit it are not mechanical appliances. To help explain by example the many social and emotional aspects of motivational relationships within the sports industry, consideration will be given to a poignant case study featuring the British Olympic Athletics Team captaincy and an anthropomaximological (AML) approach to inspirational leadership, which deems powerlessness as the root cause of many human relations problems in the workplace today, where physical and mental potential are sometimes squandered or not fully discovered. The AML approach embraces the analysis of the reserve potential of the physical motor system and the psychofunctional system of a healthy employee (or sports competitor), and the broad beliefs controlling their performance under extreme stress conditions.

---

[2] Cross-cultural psychologists (see Segall, Dasen, Berry and Poortinga, 1990) have challenged the stereotypical idea of intelligence by advocating that just because a test is identified as an intelligence test does not guarantee that it actually measures intelligence. The line of reasoning has been made, perhaps most convincingly, by earlier empirical studies which establish that benchmark IQ intelligence tests measure only the current aptitude of individuals to partake efficiently in western (Euro-American and Australian) schools (see LeVine, 1970: 581). Therefore, it is established within a hard-core scientific context that this is all IQ tests do measure and whether they measure anything else is quite dubious indeed.

Supported by a second case study which signifies the advantage of positive feedback loops at work in the Rugby League, the chapter will then move on to explore the key dimensions of a sports organisation and the importance of developing a 'Yenza' (proactive and synchronous) strategy for managing employees. Within this context, consideration will be given to the historical constitution of the HR Manager's influential authority, and the current need to develop a more focused, coherent but flexible people strategy in a rapidly changing sports environment. By acknowledging the development of such a human resource strategy the chapter will also address the questions of (a) quality staffing (b) people programmes and initiatives and (c) the key seven corporate dimensions of sports organisations.

To conclude, the chapter will address the logistics of managing social and technological change while transforming people performance in professional sports, and volunteer groups through effective communications, 'emotional intelligence' (EQ) and an equitable rewards determination process. Employing the principles of a third case study that focuses on the changes in current employment legislation, particular emphasis will be placed on the importance of dispute procedures, the energies of organisation and change in building bridges within the sports company as a learning milieu.

The 'impact of expectancy' and managing people in sport

In a world where the scheme of work, infrastructure and corporate spirit of contemporary sports have been radically influenced and institutionalised by the globalisation of capitalism and its protestant work ethic, HRM in general terms has been charged with becoming too insular as a function and in need of broadening its aspirations transculturally and from an interdisciplinary perspective. Originally instituted in the USA and concerned with the human aspect of enterprise management and employees' relations with their companies, HRM is underpinned by the findings of industrial psychology and applies consolidated systems and strategies commonly accepted as personnel management (PM) in the UK.

As a significant part of the HRM panorama PM deals with the more practical, utilitarian and instrumental application of policies and management techniques including employee resourcing, appraisal, employee training and development, business to employee relations and employment law. However, with businesses across the planet recognising that a competitive advantage and sustained customer contentment are heavily dependent on creating employee satisfaction, corporate strategists are now ensuring that the customer's needs, the company's brands and the commitment of employees are all synchronous. Therefore, as we venture further into this digital age, we see the empowerment of human capital becoming even more of a strategic imperative, while chief executives look for HR functions to move beyond a legalistic 'commitment to the people mantra' and play a greater integral role in getting more out of the minds of employees by really understanding how they learn, create and perform best. In sports, as in other areas, this motivational (rather than aptitudinal) approach to managing human (and intellectual) capital is geared towards delivering value to different parts of the business and making a contribution to improving productivity levels.

To advance their roles and address the monetary and pecuniary rewards synonymous with the 'bottom line', it is important that HR professionals in sports better understand why people behave the way they do and the organisational practices for the optimum utilisation of all human resources. This involves managers, coaches and trainers acknowledging the importance of internal forces and those external to a person that stimulate enthusiasm and devotion to persevere along a particular course of action towards the accomplishment of goals and the accrual of rewards. With reference to sports and other business enterprises, the rewards for an individual's drive to take initiative are both intrinsic and extrinsic. The intrinsic rewards refer to the inner satisfaction one derives from performing and completing a challenging task, while the extrinsic motivating forces are normally the more substantial earnings such as promotion and 'hard currency'. However, while professional sports performers and aspirant professionals are without a doubt animated by money, there are other components which also account for their expectancy of motivation.

Throughout the twentieth century sports psychologists have provided a number of different phenomena and various conceptual perspectives to interpret energising, directing and stopping human behaviour. These include:

- *The drive theory*: In terms of sport and physical activity research, drive is the energiser for behaviour while habits (or learned behaviours) account for the direction and pattern of an individual's preferred initiatives during certain stages of the decision-making process (see Hull, 1952 and Spence, 1956).
- *The optimal level theory*: This model is summarised by the proposal that a congruous relationship exists between the intensity of arousal and the effectiveness of performance during individual decision-making processes (see Landers, 1978).
- *The attribution theory*: This is viewed as a 'common sense' model individuals use in everyday situations to account for behaviour. Thus they see the result of an action or outcome as being attributed to (a) cultural and socio-environmental contexts, (b) specific properties of the situation, (c) the nature of the activity and (d) the personal traits of the participants/competitors (see Heider, 1958).

When these models of motivation are applied to the sports organisational context, we see them as the inducement factor of an employee's thoughts and actions through appeals to that individual's specific needs and personality to work toward organisational goals. The expectation is that the employee will be able to see that she or he can achieve personal objectives by achieving the company's goals, while the employer can be able to tap the deepest levels of intellectual creativity and the highest levels of productivity of that worker. However, motivation is convoluted by the fact that we are addressing people and their attitudes – both tremendously complex factors in their own right. The employee in the office who has entered into or works under a contract of employment is therefore no different to the employee out of the office, or the athlete on the track, who is working towards a better intuitive understanding of the general AML principles governing normal regulation of his or her functioning of physiological systems in circumstances of ultra-intense activity. In the same vein, the coach in the gym can be juxtaposed to the employer who seeks to know more about the true potential of the employee as a healthy organism who is socially active and emotionally inspired, while engaged in activities that involve strict occupational selection. On a daily basis she or he transfers to the work environment those attitudes, prejudices, feelings, tensions and emotions developed by his or her total life pattern of preferred initiatives.

In some way the employer also has to communicate to the employee(s) a sense of mission and organisational vision which focuses on:

■ Why is the sports organisation in business?
■ What is/should be our purpose?
■ What values does it offer to users, community?
■ What are the constituency needs?
■ What activities should we undertake/avoid?
■ How unique or special is the sports organisation?
■ What do we stand for (style, relationship)?

As such, the sports organisation's vision must be systematically checked (see Case 5.1 below) and objectives recognised at multiple levels, along with the cultivation of a feeling of commitment to these objectives which can only be accomplished via a consistent communication programme based not just on lip-service, but through deeds. Furthermore, for the employees to believe in and be committed to their management, they must be provided with very clear objectives and know that their achievements would finally be given recognition. It is only in a climate such as this that management can expect their staff to be truly motivated, because the integration of human resources and overall company objectives safely establishes the workforce as a supportive or facilitating function, constructing a milieu and a culture within which valuable contributions can be provided by all employees. This is the crux of the 'HRM' concept and forms a key part of the sports industry's organisational re-orientation for 'employee resourcing' in its widest context. It can thus be argued that HRM in sports and other industries today represents a shift in the pragmatics of traditional personnel management, from that of an 'odd job' to being a strategic contribution which focuses not only on obtaining skilled healthy people who are in short supply, but in making the best use of the employees' reserve potential in the mental, psychological and physical spheres of their occupational activity, for the purpose of increasing instruction levels, working capacity and creative longevity. The Sports HR Manager's input to this AML approach can be consolidated through training and development, rewards, organisational culture, strategic planning and checking that the vision is shared (see Senge, 1990: 205–32).

CASE 5.1   Motivation and the sports HR manager as a visionary

Diagnose the present state of your chosen sport as you perceive it.

Checking the vision of the sports organisation

	Strongly agree				*Strongly disagree*
■ There is a clear understanding in our sports organisation of the fundamental reasons why we are in business.	1	2	3	4	5

- We know what particular values we intend to provide to the users we serve.

  1 2 3 4 5

- We know what particular values are provided to those who serve in the organisation (volunteers, staff).

  1 2 3 4 5

- We clearly know the needs of the constituencies that we hope to address.

  1 2 3 4 5

- We have defined the programmes and services that we will undertake.

  1 2 3 4 5

- We have dealt with and stated the activities and temptations that we will avoid.

  1 2 3 4 5

- In general, we know what distinguishes us as unique or special in the community we serve.

  1 2 3 4 5

- In particular, we know what advantages we have over our competition (other organisations offering programmes in the same sport, other sports, other recreational time pursuits, etc.).

  1 2 3 4 5

- We are clear about the values and principles we stand for as an organisation.

  1 2 3 4 5

- We are clear about how we intend to operate externally, i.e., with the public and users.

  1 2 3 4 5

Motivation as theory and praxis in HRM

Notably, we have the benefit of recent neurobiological findings that (at least on the atomic level) our human consciousness observes and creates its own 'reality'. This has led to the exciting suggestion from both neuroscientists and management psychologists that human behaviour is motivated by what we observe as our 'reality of needs' (see Pert, 1997; Lucas, 2001). This principle also represents the driving force behind all activities in one or more of our personal unfulfilled needs. The 'reality of needs' here can therefore be easily correlated with the work of Abraham Maslow the noted behavioural scientist.

Maslow (1943) theorised that human needs are hierarchical in nature and while it is often stated that *Man does not live by bread alone*, the crux of the matter is that this is only 'a reality' for the man who has bread. Maslow's construct on a hierarchy of needs is perhaps the most widely-known model which has offered formulae to account for what animates people. He contends that those personal needs which are not satisfied will operate as motivators within the contextual framework of physiological needs being the most basic, followed by psychological and social needs and ultimately the crowning AML need for self-actualisation (see Figure 5.1).

Within the sports industry we will find individuals (whether technicians, technical specialists or managers) repositioning up and down the hierarchy of needs, with class, age, gender, ethnic origin and other psycho-cultural variables impinging on the defi-

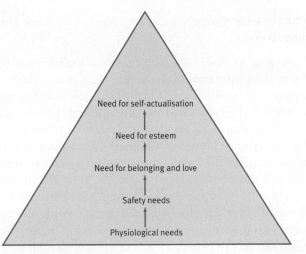

Figure 5.1 Maslow's hierarchy of needs
Source: Maslow (1943)

nition of needs at the upper levels. At the lower levels, the individual whose tummy is unfilled will tend to be quite obsessed with thoughts about 'bread'. Thus the need to find a meal as soon as possible will be the motivational force behind his behaviour. On the other hand, once that meal has been obtained and the tummy filled, the motivation to find food will no longer be of significance and a higher need will emerge until the individual reaches that AML point of self-actualisation. This is a point where the normal that lies hidden in the pathological becomes manifest (Pavlov, in Kuznetsov, 1982: 282), and she or he simply feels the need to be what she or he must be, in the same way dolphins have the natural urge to swim and humming birds must fly. This behavioural construct of 'what a wo/man can be s/he would be' is well illustrated in the Case 5.2 which features the former England athletics coach Linford Christie.

CASE 5.2 Motivation and true potentialities

When British sports journalist Richard Williams read that Linford Christie had refused an offer to actively seek election for the UK athletics presidency in October, 2002, it made him reflect on an emotional reply he received two years earlier from the athlete Katherine Merry, when she was asked about the influence of Christie as her coach in preparing her to compete at the Olympic Games in Sydney. As Merry celebrated her winning of a silver medal, she confessed that if she tried to talk about what Linford Christie had done for her, she would start crying.

Williams also deliberated on a discussion he had with Christie during the summer of 2001, as the final night fell on the Commonwealth Games track and field event. Christie had a big smile on his face, since four of the five athletes he coached for the competition had won. When asked to sum up the feats of the athletes from the home nations, and what their achievements meant for the British athletics team in the future, Christie explained that when one considers the success of the team as a whole, there were those athletes who had not received medals but ran personal bests. He emphasised that this is what it was all about, and since the majority of the athletes were young, he envisaged that they were going to be competing for some time to come.

According to Williams, such honest demonstration of this sense of gratification in the accomplishments of the whole team was a clear reminder of the time when, as captain of the British athletics squad, Christie brought a touch of real importance to what many critics had initially deemed 'a nothing job'. He had been offered the captaincy almost by accident and with no other raison d'être than to comply with the regulations. However, although Christie was not the first choice of many people at the time, Williams noted that, as far as he can recall, no other British team captain ever did very much to validate the title. The arrival of Linford Christie – a black athlete who was rapidly increasing his achievements at the international level – altered all that. He was by now a notable symbol of appeal to the collective of black runners and jumpers and throwers working their path up the British ranks. As such, when the team's captaincy was bestowed on him, his worth increased exponentially with each title he earned.

Williams acknowledged how privileged the British team was to be able to gain from the morale-boosting effect of having a team leader who retained at the same time both the Olympic and world titles in the sport's most spectacular event. Thus, in Barcelona 1992 and Stuttgart during 1993, Christie emerged as a distinguished, invincible and inspirational sight. But, observed Williams, there was still something more extraordinary about him than that. While the high-speed American sprinters of the Santa Monica Track Club opted to stay in five-star hotels, Christie chose to bivouac in the athletes' villages. His decision meant that in Barcelona he and his athletes had to share accommodation in a cluster of basic, crowded (but not unpleasant) purpose-built apartments near the waterfront. Moreover, in Stuttgart they had to settle for an old US army barracks in the middle of nowhere.

The fact that Christie never protested, but rather revelled in these conditions impressed Williams. He describes how Christie loved getting in line to get his food in the athletes' restaurant alongside his team-mates, whilst encouraging the younger ones and sharing his insights on the Games. Of particular interest to the journalist though, was the piece of motivational magic he achieved in Barcelona, which Williams firmly believes ought to have a mention in every higher-education sports psychology textbook. In his commentary, he points out that Christie had already won his Olympic gold medal when his colleague and captain of the women's team Sally Gunnell, demonstrated signs of unexpected anxiety while preparing to run in the final of the 400-metres hurdles. Christie's reaction reflected concern, yet his words to her were profound: 'Look, just imagine arriving back at Heathrow with the team. I'll have my medal to show the photographers. Now go out and get yours.'

Williams appreciates that there are people currently involved in athletics who continue to despise Christie, and are hardly ever averse to raising the subject of his positive drug test for nandrolone three years ago, or the question of his use of ginseng in Seoul during 1988. He, along with the UK Athletics Association, duly contended that they found it extremely difficult to accept as true that a 40-year-old male athlete, with plainly nothing to be won or lost, would attempt to improve his performance via synthetic means. The UK Athletics Association even went so far as to advocate the lifting of his two-year ban from competition, only to have its pronouncement quite properly annulled by the International Association of Athletics Federations (IAAF) which dictated that the convention had to be observed, notwithstanding the doubts surrounding the whole affair of nandrolone.

Williams thus conceded that most of Christie's enemies will be elated that he is not seeking election to a position that would have made him a mere figurehead of British athletics. He even weighs up Christie's preference to concentrate on his coaching career with the view that there must be a suspicion Christie looked at the panorama of a distasteful campaign and concluded that he had more constructive things to do. He therefore wraps up his article by admitting that, in his opinion, he thinks Christie's decision 'says more about the rest of us than it does about him'.

Source: Based on Richard Williams in *The Guardian*, 30 October 2002, p. 32

After having won an Olympic 100m gold medal prior to embarking on his successful coaching tenure, Christie was deemed to have a most inspiring effect on his team mates and the many younger athletes he eventually opted to train. In Case 5.2, his message was quite a poignant one, when he observed that those athletes who did not acquire medals (a tangible reward in sports) were instead quite satisfied to run 'personal bests' (which can be juxtaposed to aspiring towards their highest AML need or potential). Of great significance was his uncompromising suggestion to Sally Gunnell. He asserted that as team captain for the male athletes he had his gold medal (highest tangible reward) and in her role as team captain for the females, it was only natural that she fulfil that 'highest AML need' by acquiring her own gold medal for public presentation upon returning home. In doing so, she would not only be affirming her leadership 'expectations', but she would also fortify her self-image of sovereignty in the process. Here we must acknowledge the importance of self-image to motivation and the 'impact of expectancy' when managing people in sports.

Self-image is a person's own view of him or herself. It is:

- learned (acquired through important life experiences);
- moulded by the reactions of others (e.g. parents, peers, coaches);
- susceptible to change;
- extremely important both on and off the sport's field.

Self-image also affects:

- motivation (drive to pursue some goal);
- learning (acquisition of new knowledge or new skills);
- athletic performance (as well as performance in other areas);
- personal relationships (liking for others and acceptance by others);
- life satisfaction (realisation of personal goals);
- personal satisfaction (how a person feels about themselves).

It can be argued that Christie therefore encouraged Gunnell towards cultivating a positive self-image, by:

- showing acceptance;
- offering specific praise;
- giving her personal attention;
- emphasising her self-responsibility as a team leader.

Christie also demonstrated a level of interpersonal competence deficient in many non-self-actualised individuals. He showed himself to be a sports leader with an 'emotionally intelligent'[3] as opposed to a scientific management style. The latter is a classical approach to workplace organisation and job design associated with the American engineer F.W. Taylor. It is based on the principle of giving as much initiative as possible to managerial experts about how tasks are done. These experts then define exactly how each meticulous aspect of every job is to be carried out (see Watson, 1995).

Christie showed he had the ability to give to others, as well as receive from them. This is particularly important in the sphere of human resource management theory, which regards the organisation's human resources as potential 'talent' or investments that can benefit both the firm and the worker if properly managed. We can therefore see the functioning of HRM philosophy in this case study as Christie signposts Gunnell to her personal growth opportunity. Off the track and in the traditional sports organisation office, where so few managers reach their capacity for 'emotional intelligence' (EQ), implementation of the HRM theory not only establishes personal growth prospects and planned career experiences for employees. Indeed, such activities also result in greater self-actualisation for everyone by capitalising on employee personnel needs, their capability for career enhancement, and overall organisational effectiveness.

By accepting Gunnell for what 'she must be' Christie therefore *interacted* with her as a person. And as a human being, he *influenced* her own positive view of herself by his show of respect for her capacity,[4] potentiality[5] and reserve,[6] and *empowered* her

---

[3] In his text, *Working With Emotional Intelligence*, Daniel Goleman (1998) contends that the world of work has essentially neglected an extremely important array of skills and abilities – those which deal with human relations and emotions. Goleman focused specifically on the need to have appreciation for one's own emotional life, adapting one's own feelings, and understanding the emotions of others, while being able to work with and have empathy for other people. He wrote of various methods to improve our emotional competence (especially where children are concerned), while he averred that the business world in particular would be a more convivial environment if employers and employees nurtured emotional intelligence as conscientiously as they now endorsed cognitive intelligence or the IQ (see also Gardner, 1999). Goleman's stance on the limitations of cognitive intelligence and such related tests is supported quite robustly by Segall, *et al.*, (1990: 59) in their earlier publication *Human Behaviour in Global Perspective*.

[4] Christie did not just perceive Gunnell as merely a person with knowledge, skills or know-how in the art of running. He considered her as possessing a distinctive personality characteristic for the successful performance of her special athletic feat. Her AML capacity was therefore revealed in the speed intensity and soundness of her mastery of the technique and procedures relevant to her sporting activity.

[5] It can be argued that Christie recognised in Gunnell an objective trend of personality development that was 'real' when everything needed for her AML point of self-realisation was present.

[6] With Christie's support, Gunnell was able to tap into her reserve or 'standby supply'. This is an intuitive source from which the fresh forces of all human organisms are drawn, without any irreparable damage to the said organism. By accessing such a 'standby supply' Gunnell's energy depletion was made good during her AML process of self-regulation and she realised her dream of winning an Olympic gold medal – a tangible reward.

towards self-actualisation through a demonstration of concern while providing a major source of specific but reassuring and informative feedback. This AML approach to HRM contrasts significantly with the scientific management style mentioned above, in which managers perceive their employees mainly as a 'cog in the wheel' of production and planned work to be as uncomplicated and repetitive as possible to assume the highest output. Furthermore, the essential lesson one can extrapolate from Case Study 5.2 is that if sports managers were more competent in 'giving' to their staff through an alliance of *interaction*, *influence* and *empowerment*, they would also receive more from these employees and thus facilitate their own AML need for self-actualisation. This lesson however cannot be learnt properly without first acknowledging the underlying competencies or intelligences which correlate the triad of *interaction*, *influence* and *empowerment* to effective HR leadership in the sports industry.

Multiple intelligence and motivation in HRM

In a modern business mileau where managers do not hesitate to tell their staff lies to boost morale (see Goleman, 1997; Winstanley and Woodall, 2000), Christie's level of interpersonal competence enabled him to fulfil both his need for self-actualisation and demonstrate a greater cross-gender understanding, caring and concern for trainees and peers alike. In his text, *Intelligence Reframed: Multiple Intelligences for the 21st Century* (1999), Harvard University Professor Howard Gardner concluded that interpersonal competence is one of seven different kinds of minds or multiple intelligences. An adaptation of these seven intelligences is as follows:

1. *Linguistic Intelligence* – the ability to think in words and to use language to express and appreciate complex meanings. Linguistic intelligence allows us to understand the order and meaning of words, and to apply metalinguistic skills to reflect on our use of language.
2. *Musical Intelligence* – the capacity to discern pitch, rhythm, timbre, and tone. This intelligence enables one to recognise, create, reproduce, and reflect on music, as demonstrated by composers, conductors, musicians, vocalists, and sensitive listeners. Interestingly, there is often an affective connection between music, and the emotions, and mathematical and musical intelligences may share common thinking processes.
3. *Bodily-kinesthetic Intelligence* – the capacity to manipulate objects and use a variety of physical skills. This intelligence also involves a sense of timing, and the perfection of skills through mind–body union.
4. *Logical-mathematical Intelligence* – the ability to calculate, quantify, consider propositions and hypotheses, and carry out complex mathematical operations. It enables us to perceive relationships and connections, to use abstract, symbolic thought, sequential reasoning skills, and inductive and deductive thinking processes.
5. *Spatial Intelligence* – the ability to think in three dimensions. Core capacities of this intelligence include mental imagery, spatial reasoning, image manipulation, graphic and artistic skills, and an active imagination.

6. *Interpersonal Intelligence* – the ability to understand and interact effectively with others. It involves effective verbal and non-verbal communication, the ability to note distinctions among others, a sensitivity to the moods and temperaments of others, and the ability to entertain multiple perspectives.

7. *Intrapersonal Intelligence* – the capacity to understand oneself – one's intelligence and feelings – and to use such knowledge in planning and directing one's life, and the human condition in general.

Like Goleman's 'emotional intelligence' construct, Gardner's theory has been applauded as a meaningful way to account for the knowledge that we are culturally different and do not all have the same psychological conditioning. It infers that managing human capital will be more effective if human cultural differences are taken seriously, and people can learn to bolster their 'weaknesses' through their strengths and share their expertise. This way, they can be appreciated for the gifts they possess and can in turn appreciate others for their gifts they bring to share. Such an assertion not only gives further credence to Maslow's initial model of human needs, but also suggests that as humans we were not born with these hierarchical needs. Instead they are acquired through our cultural experiences or interrelationship with out external environment. For example, we can see both Maslow's and Gardner's theories at their strongest in the following case study where an attempt is being made to account for why individuals perform optimally at some Changing Management of Volunteer Sports Systems times and below par at other times. Here, we note that a more radical and fundamental AML approach to managing human capital needs to be considered, so that particularly within the business of sports, neither players nor employees would continue to remain under-valued, under-trained and under-utilised.

CASE 5.3 Interplaying anthropomaximology with people strategy

British psychologists have concluded that psychological superiority alone could account for why the Australian rugby league team has won every World Cup since 1975, and why northern hemispheric teams are lagging so far behind. This is asserted in view of the fact that previous research has found no real difference in physical or tactical preparation between players from either the northern and southern hemisphere. Thus Michael Sheard at Teeside University in the United Kingdom suspects that psychological differences could be solely responsible for the success of the Australians. Using questionnaires Sheard and his colleagues systematically studied seventy players from the English, Welsh, French and Irish teams, and although the Australian and New Zealand teams refused to take part, he reasoned that Australian nationals with Welsh ancestry do play for Wales and therefore it was a legitimate approach to include them.

Sheard realised that those players who had learned to play rugby league in Australia, and currently compete mostly in Australia, retained the highest levels of self-confidence. However, when nationality alone was acknowledged, the Welsh emerged as leading in 'mental toughness' – a measure of motivation. They also achieved the highest score for 'hardiness', which was a measure of the ability to view a potentially tense situation as challenging. The results of the experiment further showed that Wales was the only team that ever led against Australia in the 2000 tournament, and this to Sheard was quite an interesting development.

As such, Sheard extrapolates that self-confidence alone could explain Australia's continuing domination of the sport. He argues that the Australian team ventures on to the field physically powerful and firm in the belief that they're going to win the game. He also acknowledges that there is a positive feedback loop at work, with winning leading to soaring confidence and leading back to more victories. However, the positive news for the northern hemispheric teams is that their self-confidence can be boosted. According to Sheard, mental processes can be transformed, and one can build self-confidence through activities such as role-playing situations, where players are encouraged to visualise certain situations which eventually influence the outcome of their game.

Source: Based on *The New Scientist*, 29 March 2001

The results of the research highlighted in the case study confirm that to be successful in any business venture, whether in the northern or southern hemisphere, we must understand how the brain works and how to apply it in our working life. The gist of the study is that our effort to satisfy needs will depend on our belief that we can expect such efforts to be followed by a certain result which will bring required rewards. Furthermore, the study suggests that the more appealing an employee considers a particular incentive and the higher the likelihood that the physical and mental exertion of effort will lead to that incentive, then the more positive will be the mental feedback loop and resultant physical energy the individual will put into his or her work. Therefore we can acknowledge that within the AML process, an employer or employee's behaviour and psychological superiority is influenced by:

- what she or he wants to take place;
- his or her educated guess of the likelihood of the thing occurring;
- how strongly she or he believes that the experience will satisfy a higher need.

For the purpose of this chapter, we can also postulate that, based on the behavioural approach of the sports employer or employee during this AML process, the following implications should be considered:

- The HR manager should be unambiguous with employees when explaining what exactly is expected from modern working practices.
- Employees should be able to see a direct link between their labour output and the rewards such hard work generates.
- Rewards (psychological and fiscal) should fulfil workers' needs for security; esteem; independence and personal self-development.
- Complex reward or bonus systems are unlikely to increase the effort of workers because employees cannot relate harder work to higher wages.

Such implications forge the relationship between effort, satisfying reward and performance (see Porter and Lawler, in Graham and Bennett, 1995: 17) in a world where research has shown that the aspirations and values of management tiers are varying

(Cashmore, 2002). Emerging from the twentieth century is a new breed of sports manager who seek a career that mirrors his or her own personal/emotional values and frames of mental faculties (human multiple intelligences) rather than those of the sports organisation. Thus while managers in general are admitting serious dissatisfaction with existing organisational life and the pressures being exerted on them to do 'more with less', the motivational force driving enlightened HR leaders is the opportunity to seek greater self-determination and sovereignty in a corporate milieu where stress costs the sporting and other industries over £370 million a year (*ILAM Leisure News*, 2002: 1). Such open-minded HR managers clearly understand the magnitude of an employee's reserve biopsychological potential (intelligence) to sort out information which can be stimulated in a cultural locale, to resolve a crisis or generate products that are of value within that particular culture (Gardner, 1999). Moreover, it is argued that within the sporting business, the liberal HR managers who, in adopting the AML approach, offer more comprehensive occupational health-support services which address these reserve biopsychological potentials (multiple intelligences) and socio-physical needs of their employees can better boost worker performance and cut health-care risks and costs (Attridge, 1999).

The sports HR manager as a Yenza strategist

As I live in a multicultural United Kingdom where foreigners play a most important role in sports, I can safely admit that my initial introduction to the value of HR strategic decision-making was from my mother and life mentor Helena Brathwaite,[7] who fondly reminded me many times in the Caribbean rhythmical dialect of an expression that says 'Only a fool see ting in day time and tek firestick to look for it in de nite.' When translated for the benefit of the Euro-American reader, the proverb simply means 'Only a fool will know something and yet act as if he is ignorant of it.' This is a very meaningful thought, which can be equated with the popular 'Acres of Diamonds' story I have heard so many western management gurus rework in their public speeches on both sides of the Atlantic. Such speeches tell of a man who left his large estate in Africa unexplored for years and years to seek riches all over the world, until one day he returned home to find diamonds in his own backyard. The thread of both proverbs is the same. When thinking about a human resource or people strategy, dig deep for the diamonds (driving force) in your own backyard.

Yenza, a popular Zulu word in Southern Africa which means 'do it' signifies the 'dig deep' principle, which revolves around strategic action (i.e. doing things). According to organisational sociologist Dr Piet Human (1998), the *Yenza* trajectory dictates that until policies and strategies developed on a theoretical level are moved beyond the paralysing comfort zones of debate, planning or further research, they will always remain imperfect. The concepts must be tested or manifested in the real world. Therefore, instead of waiting until everyone is totally happy with each strategic element before implementation, the concepts must be actualised while being tested,

---

[7] A retired secondary-school teacher who also taught the 1976 Montreal Olympic Games 100 metres gold medallist, Haseley Crawford, at primary school level in the Republic of Trinidad and Tobago.

cultured and improved during the process. This means that the sports HR manager transforms his organisation from a mere bureaucracy to what Human characterises as a 'revocracy' or institution which can fulfil a 'revolutionary role' within the community it serves. In this context, the sports HR manager graduates from being a mentally-paralysed 'bureaucrat' to become the *Yenza* strategist or 'revocrat' who proactively reshapes and recreates the organisational 'revocracy' via a three-prong approach:

- Attention: initially finding out or determining 'what' needs to be accomplished in a 'real world' context;
- Intention: thinking about and framing an appropriate strategy which specifically outlines 'how' the HR problem will be tackled;
- Commitment: eventually 'doing it', that is, taking the necessary action by executing the said strategy.

When developing such a 'cutting edge' *Yenza* HR strategy towards creating a 'revocracy', a number of critical factors must be addressed in determining the 'driving force' of a sports organisation. As highlighted in Figure 5.2, we see nine elements which range from *natural resources* to *return/profit (cash and kind)* being featured. For the sports HR manager or revocrat each of these requisites is important, but the first, that is, *natural resources* is obviously the 'catalyst' through which the other eight can be realised. The term *natural resources* refers to people skills level, staff capacity, biopsychological potential and reserve, and management capability. The *natural resources* are also postulated to epitomise the energy and consciousness of organisation and change.

Therefore in utilising the *Yenza* approach to construct a proactive sports HR strategy based on such subrequisites, two critical questions must be addressed:

- What kinds of human capital are needed to manage and run the sports organisation and to meet the strategic business objectives?
- What people-oriented programmes and initiatives must be planned and employed to invite, improve and hold on to skilled staff so that the sports organisation can compete resourcefully?

In order to respond properly to these questions, we must address the seven key dimensions of organisational consciousness (see also Barrett, 1998). This construct of organ-

What should the scope of our sports services and market constituencies be?

Driving force

1 Natural resources: human capital
2 Sports services offered
3 Market needs
4 Special technology and training
5 Production capability
6 Method of sales
7 Method of distribution
8 Size/growth of organisation
9 Return/profit: cash and kind

Sports
— Market needs
— Services offered

Figure 5.2 Fundamental HR strategic decision-making

isational consciousness is based on the premise that employee fulfilment, social responsibility and environmental stewardship are the recipe for increased productivity and creativity in the future. It also implies that the revocracy ideals which a sport organisation embraces have been more and more of an influence in its ability to recruit the best talent and market its services.

A macro-derivative of Maslow's hierarchy of micro-needs comprises seven dimensions of organisational consciousness (see Figure 5.3) include:

- **Society:** Input to improvement of public conditions from a long-term perspective.
- **Constituencies:** Considered partnership with consumers, providers and the local population. Also involves ecological awareness and worker fulfilment.
- **Culture:** Concrete affirmative organisational culture established on 'shared vision' and principles, conviction, honesty and corporate cohesion.
- **Growth:** Corporate innovation and development based on cooperative learning, worker involvement and improvement of sports services and natural resources.
- **Self-image:** Corporate change for the better with regards to provision and quality of services, staff competence, systematic designs and procedures.
- **Rapport:** Highlighting exchange of ideas and interaction with employees, consumers and suppliers.
- **Staying power:** Focus on economic security, production output and corporate growth.

When applied to managing the people element in sports, it is fair to assume that senior business executives may well focus on maybe one or two of the above dimensions while neglecting the rest. However, what is needed is an HR stratagem directed at

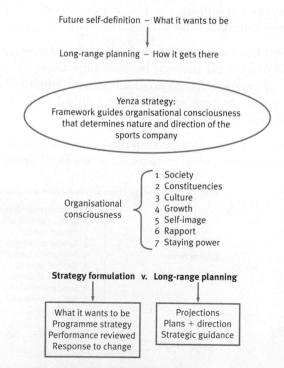

Figure 5.3 **Organisational revocracy driving force**

bonding the relationship between all seven dimensions at the organisational level (as illustrated in Figure 5.4). In this context, we see the benefit of proactively consolidating both the sports organisational 'Vision' and 'Driving force'. In reality this *Yenza* approach means that emphasis must be placed on not only retraining staff, but also on:

- considering the business strategy, accentuating the main driving forces and the implications of these driving forces for the human side of the sports business;
- developing a mission statement relating to the human capital constituent of the business;
- conducting a SWOT (strength, weaknesses, opportunities and threats) analysis of the sports management system, the PESTEL (political, economics, social, technological, environmental and legal) impact of the external and business market milieu and the human resources capability;
- carrying out a meticulous HR review with emphasis on the sports organisation's culture, organisation, and people/HR systems (COPS);
- revisiting the business strategy and juxtaposing it against the SWOT and the COPS analyses, while identifying and prioritising the critical people issues;
- accentuating the decisive options/consequences for managerial action regarding each critical HR issue and translating them into an action plan based on wider objectives linked to the following specialist HR matrix:
    wo/manpower planning;
    recruitment and selection;
    training and development;
    management development;
    organisation development;
    performance appraisal;
    pay and reward;
    communication.

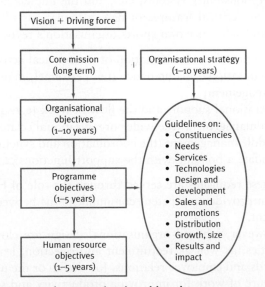

Figure 5.4 **HR stratagem at the organisational level**

Once the revocracy action plan has been developed around the critical issues and the targets/dates for achieving the essential objectives linked to the HR areas above have been set, execution and appraisal of the said action plans must proceed.

Thus the effectual development of a *Yenza* HR strategy in sports ensures that the aims and objectives which have been set are reciprocally supportive so that the appropriate reward and payment mechanisms are incorporated with relevant training and career development plans. However, it cannot go without denotation that the management of a sports organisation gains little advantage in training its human capital, only to then put a damper on things by failing to make available any adequate professional and personal improvement prospects. As such, it is important that we now gain some insight into the logistics of the HRM revocracy matrix as it relates to the sports industry.

Functions of the HRM matrix in sports

Having explored the motivational and strategic dimension of HRM, we can now examine the revolutionary mechanics of the modern HRM matrix, which can be broken down into the following departmental functions:

- organisational and job design;
- employee resourcing;
- employee development;
- performance management;
- managing the employment relations and legal dynamics.

Organisational and job design

The adequacy of a sports company's structures, communication networks, authority and responsibility systems, etc., and the implementation of measures for improving them are critical features of new formulations of HRM. Therefore the operational sum and substance of a sports organisation's revocracy must be concerned with:

- the immediate manifestation of its technical activities;
- organisational maintenance (i.e. personnel, management accounting and facilities management;
- operational support and the flow of work (e.g. quality control);
- top management (the wider organisational strategic direction and policies);
- middle management (the coordination and synchronicity of activities which accommodate a bonding with the support functions).

All these requisites are served through the role of HR, which ensures that the organisation provides competent communications between each activity, whilst remaining resilient.

However, job and organisational design are closely interrelated to all key HRM activities, as well as recruitment and selection, learning and development, pay and rewards and employee relations. Job design or the use of motivational rationale to the structure of work for improving productivity and satisfaction, is also essential to the recruitment and selection function. Thus, a sports company that provides a range of high-value added consultancy services using skilled workers within a team-based organisational grouping will definitely have more rigorous resourcing priorities than a sports firm which specialises in large-scale project-oriented activities operated by unskilled volunteers, who are superintended in the classical pyramid-shaped organisational order of ranking (see Bratton and Gold, 2003).

Approaches to job design are normally classified as:

- Job simplification – a job design whose intention is to emend task efficacy by cutting the number of tasks a single employee must carry out.
- Job rotation – a job design that methodically transfers employees from one job to another to replenish them with diversity and stimulation.
- Job enlargement – a job design which blends a sequence of assignments into a fresh and more comprehensive job to give employees variety and challenge.
- Job enrichment – a job design that consolidates accomplishments, recognition, and other high-level motivators into the work to help the sports employee achieve a sense of self-commitment, self-planning, self-motivation, self-discipline, self-management and, with such self-development, to enable influencing his or her own reward through participation.

So in order to situate the intent and outputs of jobs, along with the mode by which such job outputs will be determined, and the medium or assignments by which these outputs will be attained, it is meaningful that in the job analysis (or formulation) and design function, the sports HR revocrat must pay careful attention to motivation and job satisfaction, as discussed earlier in this chapter.

The result of the job analysis is normally a job specification or calculated statement of the mental and physical activities involved in a job, and other germane factors in the socio-physical milieu. Such a record of the requirements of each task is essentially an assessment of the relative importance of identified duties along with those which take up significant proportions of time and are problematic. The job specification also quantifies data on the scale of activities of each employee or section(s) controlled by employee(s) and sets frequencies of tasks and duties, while listing the management processes to be carried out, along with reforming the group main tasks into ordered structure. Consequently, sports HR revocrats may use both the job analysis and the resulting specifications for wo/man power planning, or for assessing and developing an operational plan that focuses on hiring the right HR for a job and training them to be productive (see Figure 5.5). From this HR planning, further blueprints can be developed for:

- recruitment and selection based on a comprehensive classification of the vacant job;
- appraisal so that an assessment can be made of how well an employee has completed the mandates of the job;
- the creating of training and development programmes which help to appraise the knowledge and skills needed in a job;
- in constituting rates of pay connected with job evaluation;
- in eliminating risks and identifying hazards in the job;
- in re-formulating the organisational framework by reappraising the design, importance and interrelationships of various jobs.

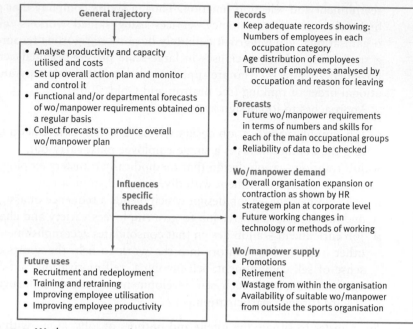

Figure 5.5 Wo/manpower planning

■ Employee resourcing

Judging from the 'tug-of-war' between the UK soccer club Manchester United and its counterparts in Spain (Barcelona and Real Madrid) and Italy (AC Milan) over the favoured player David Beckham, it is clear that the only major demarcation between the sports organisation and its competitors is the sum total and class of human resources that it can lure and retain. Therefore, with vacancies identified from the wo/manpower plan and person specifications drawn up in tandem with a knowledge of the responsibilities from job descriptions, it is only then that the sports HR revocrat can decide on the trajectory to find the most appropriate candidates. This proactive approach must obviously consider the socio-legislative and politico-cultural framework within which the recruitment and selection is taking place.

A case in point, illustrating the ongoing variations on the theme of racial differences and the related explanations, would be the recent medical declaration by Dr Roger Bannister (who on 6 May 1954 ran the first recorded sub-four-minute mile) that black athletes have tendons that are superior in development due to climatical determinants (see Gardiner, Felix, James, Welch and O'Leary, 1998: 135). When it comes to recruitment and selection within a wo/manpower plan, the question can then be advanced that once the sports HR revocrat chooses the media, sets the recruitment campaign in train, arranges the necessary interviews and assessment centres and categorises each candidate into a short-list for final selection, would the HR department then decide to favour a black professional or volunteer over candidates of other ethnic origins based on the stereotypes which would inevitably result from this type of corroborated bio-scientific pronouncement? Following such a unilateral track or the reverse approach, where a European athlete is chosen over a non-European in view of corresponding racial ideals, would certainly be a legally risky decision on the part of the sport HR selectors. Moreover, such an example provides a realistic point of reference for the need to have sports HR staff and the managers responsible for interviewing applicants properly trained in structured cross-cultural interviewing techniques, as well as the use of valid, reliable EQ/Multiple Intelligence versus IQ-based selection tests, which will reflect the company's commitment to diversity and the type of applicant sought.

CASE 5.4   Equal opportunities within the resourcing process

While recruiting sufficient numbers of potentially qualified applicants, all employers in sports and other UK industries must keep legal considerations in mind and practise equal opportunities at each juncture of the employee resourcing process, so that the candidates chosen are adequately matched to the job descriptions and wo/man power specifications.

Discuss how a chosen sports company can make sure that the personnel staff and managers, responsible for recruitment and selection, adopt the corporate Equal Opportunities policy or code of conduct.

Many companies, and not least those in the sports industry, experience problems in recruiting the required number and quality of employees required for the posts. The reason may well be that not all possible sources of recruits have been thoroughly explored, including universities, technical colleges, recruitment agencies or even volunteers, which over the years have proved to be a most vital resource within the sports milieu. People volunteer to work in sports for diverse reasons:

- a love of the particular sport activity;
- obtaining job skills or a desire to gain experience in the area of sport with a view to working professionally in the field later on;
- a desire to make a contribution to the community;
- a need to fill leisure time with useful work.

Volunteer supporters in sports can be organised in one or two ways: *integrated* or *autonomous*. If the sports organisation prefers to integrate volunteers into the company, then volunteers become like additional staff members working in individual departments. This system is an uncomplicated one, and is normally used by smaller and medium-sized firms. Because it is integrated, it requires no special liaison, but its success usually depends on the volunteer skills of individual department heads, and these are, naturally, quite variable. A strengthening of this system has been to have a part-time staff person recruiting and liaising with volunteers. On the other hand, larger sports companies often have an *autonomous* organisation that has its own officers, meetings and plans, although it exists solely to support the work of that one sports organisation. As with professional graduate workers within the traditional corporate context, working in such an *autonomous* framework with volunteers who may be either multi-skilled technicians or unskilled amateurs enthusiastic about the development of their sporting interest can be particularly rewarding or very frustrating. It all depends on whether the interview (one-to-one or panel type) and subsequent induction programme has provided the new recruits with adequate information about the job they are required to carry out. They should include a job description:

■ job title;
■ job title of immediate supervisor to whom volunteer/job holder reports;
■ job tile of each person reporting to the job holder;
■ overall responsibility;
■ summary for each immediate subordinate volunteer of the overall purpose of the job or the main functions or activities that are carried out or for which his or her responsibility is attached;
■ details and full picture of the organisational structure and subordinate organisational structure including the number and type of staff.

With particular reference to consultants who work with volunteers, managers who use volunteer labour, and chairpersons of voluntary groups, the voluntary group may include several informal organisational structures. For example, there are:

■ the totally voluntary community group;
■ the funded organisation dependent on volunteers to function;
■ committees or groups within institutions (especially universities and sports clubs) established for a specific purpose.

During the induction, the sports HR staff should be mindful of and prepare to address the potential problems which such organisational structures may share. These issues along with their recommended solutions include:

1. *Too many goals* – Most volunteer groups attempt more than they can actually accomplish. Their goals are so broad and ambiguous that the effort often fails, thus creating dissatisfaction in volunteers, leading to rapid turnover.
   Solution: One method, based on consensus and group decision-making, is for volunteer groups to set aside a block of time to devote totally to a planning workshop design session, during which brainstorming, priority-setting, individual programme objective charts and the execution of these objectives may be set in train.
2. *Lack of an adequate contract between the group and its membership* – This is one of the broadest and most fundamental problems facing volunteer groups. Moreover most groups do not allow the members to indicate their resources, experience and backgrounds during an interview or even during induction. Hence, a specific agreement between members and the organisation regarding what each person can and will do is quite rare. Moreover, discovering members' resources and establishing members' time commitments usually occurs informally and haphazardly, costing the group much maintenance time. As such under-utilisation of volunteer skills and experiences is often the result.
   Solution: There are a number of methods for developing this contract. The use of group meetings to share individual resources and group expectations is useful, along with the provision of specific, written statements of expectation for each volunteer to help clarify individual responsibilities. Moreover, the creation of a permanent agenda item where one asks questions at each meeting can legitimise explicit discussion about the HR manager's and the volunteers' mutual expectations.

3. *Lack of leadership and accountability* – Unwillingness to confront the problem of leadership liability is common in volunteer groups. Since most sports volunteers are not paid, this issue is especially uncomfortable. Failure to establish adequate leadership structures and to make the leaders (and even volunteers) accountable for their responsibilities can be extremely serious.

   Solution: An effort can be made to select project leaders for each major programme attempted – a task which can be assumed by an active sport volunteer. If money is available, a full-time volunteer can also be useful in maximising the contribution of volunteers through regular volunteer staff meetings and orientation sessions, which can help examine progress toward objectives, create group cohesiveness and a climate of support.

4. *Lack of rewards or recognition* – Volunteers are known to quietly assist a sports organisation, but not receive due recognition for their contributions.

   Solution: It is important that qualified staff receive first consideration for full-time staff training programmes, which could help make them more employable. Such training sessions can include decision-making methods and other group-process activities, along with workshops on process issues such as structured experiences, role-plays, and discussions which may help the group generate process objectives for improved functioning.

5. *Lack of attention to group process* – Within the framework of the protestant work ethic, volunteer groups are usually left to 'get on with the job' and not much attention is paid to group dynamics, the problems that hinder group effectiveness or the possible preventative actions.

   Solution: Examples of preventative actions would be assigning a process observer whose existence would make group dynamics a legitimate discussion item. She or he would also be able to persuade the group to pursue the subject or prevent certain members from dominating. The role of the process observer can then revolve so that all members become accustomed to observing process. A check-list of process objectives can also be an important aid for the observer.

The resourcing of full-time staff and volunteers can therefore be a rewarding experience for a sports HR revocrat especially when all participants in the relationship have a mutual respect and desire to cooperate in meeting designated needs. However, it can be even more of a positive initiative when the HR revocrat ensures that everyone concerned is provided with a clearer view of his or her role, and the responsibilities and rights of the volunteer within the organisation she or he is associated with and of the people whom the volunteer's effort endeavours to assist are properly identified.

Employee development

With a significant dual function of application and motivation, employee training and developing the ability to improve leadership within a wo/manpower plan also serves to enhance the subordinates' ability to perform the tasks required by the sports organisation. This therefore leads to overall organisational efficiency and maximises the job satisfaction of both employers and employees (including volunteers). But it is not unusual for sports organisations to function without clearly defined training policies which involve:

- the objectives of training;
- the range or scope of the training schemes;
- the limitations of expenditure on training;
- the commitment of management.

The sports organisation's methodology for training its leaders and subordinate can be uneconomical and wasteful if the approach is not a systematic one based on:

- Assessment of the job;
- Performance levels for quality and codes of ethics;
- Performance accomplishments;
- Requirements of the training and development programme;
- Origination of the training as course of action;
- Administering of the training programme;
- Checking of the training results;
- How the training can be improved next time.

(adapted from Graham and Bennett, 1995: 228)

Moreover, such a systematic approach must also demonstrate the long-term training needs of the sports employer/employee/volunteer, which can be assessed on the basis of the organisation's wo/manpower forecasts, job analyses and performance reviews. These long-term training needs can then be used to prepare training plans which set out:

- problem areas of the sports organisation;
- proposed action by the HR department;
- the personnel responsible for such action;
- costs of the training proposals;
- future benefits (including who are the beneficiaries) of such training.

Once the training needs have been identified and the training plan designed, the sports HR revocrat must then ensure that each of the main groupings of employees are fully taken into account by the said plan and the current training proposal, which must be flexible in nature. Accordingly, due regard must be given to the internal training programmes and courses, which also need to be based on a proper appraisal of collective and individual training needs, so as to ensure that the overall objectives of such courses are clearly defined in terms of the standards of performance which must be attained for the good of the organisation. It is therefore expected that the syllabus of the internal training programmes and courses should be logically planned and properly linked to the overall HR and organisation's revocracy objectives, while the individuals responsible for delivering the training must be adequately trained and skilful in conducting the courses with a balanced mix of informal instruction, discussion, projects, case studies and functional practice where necessary. Upon completion of the training courses, an evaluation of and (if necessary) adjustments to the programme must be made, in the light of follow-up action after training so as to make sure that what has been taught is in effect being implemented by the recruits.

Performance management

Incorporating the employee development process with results-based performance assessment is the next step in ensuring that individual group accountability is increased and innovation encouraged within the sports organisation. Such integration includes:

- performance appraisal;
- goal-setting for individuals and departments;
- suitable training programmes;
- performance-related pay and rewards.

Whether a written *performance review* from the sports HR revocrat, with separate comments on past successes/failures for future improvement, or a *potential review* which assesses the employee's suitability for promotion and/or further training, or even a *rewards review* for determining pay rises, there are various types of performance appraisal schemes. They include variations on the following:

- Grading – employees are designated into pre-determined merit groupings such as outstanding, fair, or poor standards on guideline judgements with regard to specific points (e.g. industry and application, loyalty and integrity, cooperation, accuracy and reliability etc.).
- Merit rating – here numerical points are allotted on guideline judgements to give an overall score.
- Results-oriented – targets are set and results jointly agreed between the sports HR manager and employee.
- Target setting and reward – in this context, bonuses are linked with achievement.

Particularly in the world of sports, the appraisal mechanism does subject managers and administrators to a discipline of performance standards not unlike those continually experienced by athletes. During the organisation appraisal process, comparisons are made between actual performance and agreed standards and targets, which do not assess undefined personality traits of the person being appraised. The performance review results are normally made available to employees and, where appropriate, counselling meetings after the performance review are held to further discuss the appraisee's strengths and weaknesses. From this point, review reports are analysed, training and development needs are agreed and promotion potential established based on the appraisee's career interests and ambition. Furthermore, and like many traditional organisations the appraisal process can be linked to pay reviews, although some companies may claim the performance review results are not just salary incremental and that associating appraisal and pay reviews creates chaos and discord during what is supposed to be a holistic process.

An alternative to such an argument is the use of a skills-based system of rewarding staff for their exhibited skills and knowledge and their capability in undertaking a set of tasks at some benchmark level. For instance, a member of staff responsible for the planning and administration of a sports conference or regional track and field games has opted to pursue an e-learning programme in computerised database management. She or he eventually used those skills not only to update the company's sponsorship portfolio but also provide the marketing department with access to a wider network of sponsors which resulted in increased funding. It is appropriate that the productivity growth which resulted should be used to provide a pay rise, since the skills-based system has been linked directly to achievements and a more enhanced sales pitch and through creativity. Sports HR revocrats should also note that such organisational rewards for creativity can be given both *extrinsically* (i.e. via annual performance appraisals or the assignment of bonuses) or assigned on *intrinsic* motivation – in this context we can see the HR manager as custodian of Maslow's 'motivators' and Gardner's 'multiple intelligences' discussed earlier – by recognising the important value of creative efforts as well as the skill and perseverance required to generate creative solutions to organisational issues. Moreover, to amplify the impact of such 'compensation' in promoting personal creativity, it is imperative that sports HR revocrats themselves be creativity role models. As role models, they can therefore consistently focus their and the employees' attention on engendering creative ideas to resolve complex organisational issues.

Managing the employment relations and legal dynamics

The quality of employment relationship in all organisations determines whether employees will feel they are either a valued member of the company or a mere 'chattel labourer'. Sports HR revocrats are also aware that during the last half of the twentieth century, conflict management and resolution have emerged as a very important competency of organisational leadership. As a matter of fact, recent studies for the American Society of Human Resource Management (SHRM) have rated conflict management as a topic of equal or slightly higher importance than planning, communication, motivation and decision-making (Grensing-Pophal, 2003). Thus HR managers in general are becoming more interested in the sources of conflict management, which emphasises psychological factors such as misunderstanding, communication failure, personality clashes and value differences. As highlighted in Case 5.5, many managers look upon conflict as a negative experience. These managers just want to 'manage'. The obvious retort here would be to 'manage' what? This is the key to their problem, since such managers fail to realise that it is people they are managing and without these people, the corporation or sports organisation will fail to exist. However, to the managers who maintain a dim view of conflict, they firmly believe that it:

- diverts energy from the real task;
- destroys morale;
- polarises individuals and groups;
- deepens differences;
- obstructs cooperative action;
- produces irresponsible behaviour;
- creates suspicion and distrust;
- decreases productivity.

On the other hand, there are those corporate and sports organisational leaders who understand the positive and creative values intrinsic to conflict. Conflict also:

- opens up an issue in a confronting manner;
- develops clarification of an issue;

- improves the quality of organisational problem-solving;
- increases employee involvement;
- provides more spontaneity in communication;
- initiates growth;
- strengthens a relationship when creatively resolved;
- helps increase productivity.

Therefore, ensuring a working climate of trust and solidarity is crucial to good people management, and, particularly in the case of sports, the understanding that conflict is also a creative and positive occurrence is helpful in monitoring and developing a non-violent organisational culture. As such, five principal methods of interpersonal conflict resolution are identified for consideration by sports HR revocrats. These include:

- Withdrawal: avoiding or retreating from an actual or potential situation;
- Smoothing: defusion by emphasising areas of agreement and de-emphasising areas of difference over conflictual areas;
- Compromising: searching for solutions through negotiations which bring some degree of satisfaction for conflicting areas;
- Forcing: where appropriate, exerting one's viewpoint at the potential expense of another, thus leading to an often open competition and a win–lose situation;
- Confrontation: addressing a disagreement directly and in a problem-solving mode, allowing both parties to work through their disagreement.

In managing the employment relationship at work, the 'psychological contract' has also become a 'front burner' issue as more employees consider their quality of working life and their personal beliefs as influenced by the company, with particular reference to agreed terms and conditions exchanged between each employee and the organisation. The postulate of the 'psychological contract' provides a challenge for the organisation where managers fail to communicate with one voice, make promises they cannot keep and render null and void the ethical essence of the written contract, which dictates that all employers are legally bound to a 'duty of care' as far as their employees are concerned. Moreover, employees have recently gained additional rights under the Human Rights Act 1998, which was enforced from 2 October 2000, and gave 'further effect to rights and freedoms guaranteed under the European Convention on Human Rights' (cited in Ewing, 2000: 5; see also *Council of Civil Service Unions v. Minister of State for the Civil Service* [1985] AC 374). Included in the extensive menu of new rights which are now in keeping with the grain of UK law, is the unequivocal prohibition of 'torture' and 'inhuman or degrading treatment or punishment' (article 3) and 'slavery or servitude' and 'forced or compulsory labour' (article 4). This ensures that even volunteers in the sports milieu are protected to a considerable degree from 'bullish' or 'abusive' supervisors and do have rights to freedom from discrimination (article 14) in the execution of their responsibility.

However, while the employee does have the benefit of being galvanised under the EU's macro-legal umbrella, of especial importance within the micro-framework of the employment relationship are the rights inherent in his/her contract of terms and conditions for service. The problematic of the contract in the sports industry is well addressed in Case 5.5, which features the small sports firm 'Sports Tours International'. The contract is a written statement of terms which includes:

- the name of the employer and employee;
- date and details of start of continuous employment;
- information on previous service towards the candidate's length of service;
- pay intervals, rates of pay or pay scales;
- hours of work;
- holiday entitlement and related pay;
- public holidays;
- sickness procedures and sick pay;
- pension and pension schemes;
- notice period from both sides (employer/employee);
- job title;
- disciplinary rules in detail;
- person who administers discipline procedures.

CASE 5.5   The impact of changing employment legislation in sports

Former international marathon runner Vince Regan is used to tenacity. Having successfully completed a total of 38 marathons and represented Ireland on three of those occasions, he transferred his passion for sport to the field of sports management sixteen years ago when he set up the small business enterprise Sports Tours International. This Manchester-based company coordinates overseas excursions for sports teams involved in training programmes, competitions and the development of a database along with entries for marathons in a number of countries worldwide. However, despite touring extensively and providing a support system for notable international sporting heroes, Vince continues to manage his small company which employs sixteen people. And he is also confronted by identical issues to those which the majority of UK managers are now addressing, as they try to come to terms with the government's zeal for modernising employment legislation.

Vince admits he has spent a lot of time analysing the Employment Act 2002, but had serious difficulty understanding any aspect of it. He therefore gave up and, rather than ignore the newly-introduced legislations, he instead paid an employment-law firm to provide helpline services and to keep him apprised of any new developments. On the surface this seemed to be an extravagant approach. However, Vince knew it was worth his while, because last year a female employee at his company complained that she was being sexually discriminated against. She was distressed that Vince always selected the men to travel abroad with the clients. Vince only heard about her grievance when he received a letter from her lawyer. He had always felt that his employees were a small but contented team, so receiving the letter proved to be a really shocking experience for him. Vince argued that the company was expected to send accomplished athletes on the excursions with his clients and it happened that in the company they were all men. However, Vince did not take the letter's warning for granted. He quickly pursued expert advice on the appropriate method of response and closely followed such instructions when replying to the legal correspondence. He explained his predicament and arranged a number of meetings with the female employee. Once the situation had been sorted, he acknowledged how fortunate it was that he chose the route that he did, because, if he had approached the problem differently, his company would have been penalised heavily and forced to pay a large fine.

Vince represents one of the few examples of sensible managerial practice within the United Kingdom, where there are a lot of sports executives who may not have been as mindful. However, employment law veterans say they should be. The Employment Act of 2002 in the United Kingdom is this Labour government's most important intervention in the equilibrium between managers and their workers and, within the near future, additional sanctions will be introduced to alter the majority of the national working relationship. However, recent statistics show that over 80 per cent of UK owner-managers are not aware of the legislation's content. And especially since the number of employment tribunals brought against employers has quadrupled since the early 1990s (128,000 were filed in 2002 and the maximum award limit has risen from £12,000 to £50,000), employee relations advisers contend that bosses are taking a big gamble if they disregard the Act and especially the major changes, which will affect small business enterprises.

These changes include the legislation on the resolution of disputes, which, from April 2003, requires employers to implement lawful dismissal and grievances procedures as part of every worker's contract. Currently, there are many small firms which do not issue comprehensive contracts, and such malpractice needs to be revisited by the employers in question, who must develop a dispute procedure which both they and their employee will agree to respect in the event that a problem arises in the workplace. Such regulations now give tribunals supplementary powers to fine either party if they have not adhered to the contractual protocol on procedure.

Interestingly, the Employment Act 2002 has also modified maternity and paternity rights. In the case of the former, leave will increase from 40 to 52 weeks and mothers will qualify for full pay over the initial six months and £100 a week after that. As far as the latter is concerned, new fathers and adoptive parents will be entitled to paid leave for a period of two weeks. Employers will be able to reclaim the parental-leave payments from the State; however, the functional ramifications of these family-friendly policies may most likely be a major worry for managers of small firms like Sports Tours International, who will find it increasingly difficult to acquire temporary employee cover for expanded intervals, particularly as temps now have additional rights too.

The third main area of change concerns fixed-term workers. This aspect of the legislation, instituted in October 2002, means that fixed-term workers must have the equal pay and pension rights to permanent staff. This is a law which analysts believe will have a harsher impact on small businesses since they quite often depend on fixed-term workers to do particular jobs instead of hiring new permanent employees. Moreover, temps will be more costly and more of a hassle to recruit. So all in all, the Employment Act will undoubtedly be a major encumbrance for small businesses, which will only be eased if managers come to terms with it early in the game, along with running their business.

(*Source:* Adapted from 'Don't trip up on employment red tape' by Armistead, L. in *The Sunday Times*, 24 November 2002: 17)

The underlying logic of the contract is to ensure that both parties must act reasonably and not undermine each other during the execution of their duties. This is essential for the contract to be binding. The employer further requires that the employee must be fit and competent, ready to work in good faith and to obey 'reasonable' instructions. However, the rights of the employee must also be well understood by the employer in his or her effort to maintain a 'duty of care' towards all subordinates. The employee must receive:

■ payment even if service is not produced to defined limits;
■ itemised pay statements;
■ access to a trade union and permission to engage in the activities of the trade union, which normally interfaces with HR over matters of employee grievance, discipline, pay bargaining and general negotiations on employment conditions;
■ time off with pay for activities such as trade union or public duties, and (if made redundant) the opportunity to seek employment or retraining.

Conclusion

In this chapter an attempt has been made to cover a wider range of complex issues and to offer some meaningful insight into the key elements of the HR function within the sports industry. In essence, the emphasis has been placed on the fundamentals of anthropomaximology, motivation and the neurodevelopmental intelligences within the HRM context. We have established that to maintain the competitive advantage and understand the nature of human capital in the sports milieu, managers must be revocrats and acknowledge the biopsychosocial needs of their subordinates on the micro level, while appreciating the *Yenza* strategic imperatives of the organisation and its customers on the macrocosmic stage. These two paradigms in effect are influenced by new technology and creative processes which cascade down and impact in diverse ways on the employees and their work, as well as on the overall HRM function and process within the sports organisation.

We therefore end on a philosophical note, and it is to say that in view of the current UK Labour government's support for the EU's Social Charter and as far as Employment and Sport Law are concerned, the dynamic matrix of HRM will continue to act as a compelling force which drives sports managers to place more emphasis on the problematics of employee rights along with the motivational advantages of maintaining a multicultural workforce that increasingly embraces volunteers of diverse skills and backgrounds. As such, it is to the greater benefit of European sports HR managers to understand the importance of creating an environment not only of adequate physical facilities/equipment and finances, but one in which employees can do their best work to serve a supportive public, who loyally invest in the sports industry.

CASE 5.6   Putting their personal best foot forward   **FT**

On 25 July, 11,000 volunteers will arrive for their first day of work at the 17th Commonwealth Games, in Manchester. Some will have taken time off from their full-time jobs to work as VIP lounge attendants, security marshals, public-relations executives, catering assistants or one of the hundreds of other roles the Games have created. Others are out of work and see the Games as a chance to beef up their CVs.

Managing this large and disparate group of people will not be easy. Volunteers are by definition enthusiastic and motivated but they are not easy to discipline if, for example, they do not show up on day two. When they are mixed with paid staff, as they will be at the Commonwealth Games, there is a temptation to treat volunteers as second-class workers and give them the duller jobs.

And, when the event is over – in Manchester's case on 4 August – there is the danger that the volunteers will be demoralised and demotivated and that their new skills will go to waste.

To deal with these concerns, the Games' organisers – with Manchester City Council and Adecco, the recruitment consultancy that sponsors the Games – have developed a twofold approach: first, a healthy recognition of volunteers' work and value during the event; second, programmes to help them build on their skills and experience once the Games are over.

'Managing volunteers is obviously different from managing in an office setting,' says Amy Parrish-Rett, the Games' volunteer programme manager. 'In an office we expect people to do what we say – if they don't, they lose their job. With volunteers, the rewards are less tangible: things like feeling good about yourself, expanding your network of contacts, taking part in a successful event and giving something back to the community.

'From a management side, volunteers need to be given interesting things to do – it's no use palming off the boring jobs on them. They need recognition for what they have achieved. And they need to feel they are as much part of the team as their paid colleagues.'

Volunteers will be managed by a team leader but a bottom-up approach to management is being encouraged, with power and responsibility devolved as far as possible down the hierarchy.

'If people feel needed, they will go the extra mile,' she says. 'If you see the results of your hard work, you will come back the next day even if you are tired. What this requires is individual relationships, with one team leader managing at most 5 to 10 volunteers, helping them, monitoring them and giving them feedback. We are also encouraging competitiveness between volunteers – which PR runner can get news and results to journalists most quickly, for example – and rewarding this with prizes.'

Although some volunteers will pick up technical and process-based skills during the Games, most skill-learning will be of the softer sort, such as teamwork, listening and communication. According to Manchester's Chamber of Commerce, this is just what the region needs.

'Softer skills are exactly what employers are looking for,' says Angie Robinson, the chamber's chief executive. 'Teamwork is crucial for every business. Work is no longer just about turning up and operating a machine or pushing some papers around. It's about working with customers, with people you don't know, listening, communicating, giving and finding information. The most important skill for the region is exemplary customer service and volunteers on the games will learn a lot about this during the event.'

Once the Games are over, all volunteers, and those who applied to be a volunteer but were unsuccessful, will be invited for an interview with Adecco, with a view to further training or job placement.

Katie Brazier, Adecco's director of marketing, is frank about the opportunity this presents to expand the company's client database: 24,000 people applied to the games and filled in extensive forms, to which Adecco has access, about their skills and experience.

But she also believes many people will find new jobs on the back of their experience of volunteering. This month Asda, the supermarket chain, has opened a new super-store next to the City of Manchester Stadium, creating 1,000 new jobs, and KPMG, the consultants, estimates that 30,000 '10-year' (relatively permanent) jobs will be created by the Games in the long term.

Alberta Barton, who works behind the counter in the Games' shop, is one of a small group of volunteers who have already begun working for the Games. She will be looking for work when the event is over and says volunteering has already given her skills she would not have found elsewhere.

'I have learnt so much about retail, licensing, computers, dealing with customers, interviewing, making presentations – none of which I would have been able to learn in the normal market,' she says. 'After the games I shall be looking for a job and I feel very confident about that.'

As well as employment, Manchester City Council is hoping the event will encourage further volunteering. The council is launching a £450,000, 18-month programme of recruitment fairs, publications and a website highlighting opportunities for volunteering in the area and targeting both those who are interested in volunteering in purely altruistic way and those who see such work as a means to finding a new job.

Richard Leese, leader of the council, says the programme will not only help boost volunteering in the region but also 'address the government's interest in volunteering generally'.

Further afield, the international nature of the Games will, according to Ms Robinson, help to create a workforce ideally suited to inward investment.

'Working on the games,' she says, 'will give everyone a better understanding of cultures different from their own. This is extremely important to people in the North

West. Recognising diversity, working with people from different backgrounds, is, I believe, going to add enormously to the economy of the region.'

Source: David Baker, *Financial Times*, 16 July 2002

Discussion questions

1. Evaluate the view that voluntary workers are more highly motivated than other groups of worker, highlighting what their motives might be for working 'free of charge'.

2. What are likely to be the major challenges in managing voluntary workers and how can a sport business ensure that it continues to attract appropriately-qualified and high-quality voluntary workers?

Discussion questions

3. Using an appropriate theoretical model, compare and contrast what you think are, or might have been, the motivating factors for tennis player Serena Williams, former racing driver Eddie Irvine, and the paralympian Tanni Grey-Thompson. How might this influence how you would manage each of them?

4. Select a successful sports professional such as Marcello Lippi, the manager of Juventus, Cathy Freeman, the Australian athlete, or Phil Knight, the CEO of Nike. To what extent do you think this person displays the characteristics of multiple intelligence noted earlier in the chapter? How has this enabled them to become successful sports professionals?

5. If you were the manager or strategist for Fiorentina, the Italian football club, Jan Ulrich, the German cyclist, or Andrzej Golota, the Polish heavyweight boxer, what would you do to improve their performances and why?

6. You are the manager of a sports team that is bottom of the league, struggling, and set for relegation. How would you use wo/manpower planning to help overcome your problems, and what proposals would you include in such a plan?

7. 'Being successful in sport is all about harnessing aggression, power and skill, and has nothing to do with the theory and practice of human resource management techniques.' Discuss.

Guided reading

For a useful general HRM textbook the reader is referred to Bratton and Gold (2003). Lewis *et al.* (2003) provide good coverage of employee relations, while Ewing (2000) covers the more specific area of human rights in the workplace. The inter-relationships of work, stress and health are explored by Attridge (1999). Lucas (2001) offers a practical approach to personal self-development. Managing employee needs is explored by Attridge (1999)

For sports law, Gardiner *et al.* (1998) is recommended, and sports culture is explored by Cashmore (2002).

The concepts of anthropomaximology and *Yenza* are fully developed by Kuznetsov (1982) and Human (1998) respectively.

Recommended websites

Reward Management: www.rewardstrategies.com
Legal Resources in Europe: www.jura.uni-sb.de
Economic, political and collective bargaining developments in the EU:
www.eiro.eurofound.ie
Multiple Intelligence Test: http://www.nedprod.com/niall_stuff/intelligence_test.html
UK Trade Unions: http://www.tuc.org.uk/tuc/unions_main.cfm
Bullying in the Work Place: http://www.bullyonline.org

Visit www.booksites.net/chadwickbeech for links to these and other relevant
websites.

Keywords

Anthropomaximology; impact of expectancy; motivation; multiple intelligences;
Yenza.

Bibliography

Attridge, M. (1999) 'The business response to biopsychosocial needs of employees: a national
survey of benefits managers'. Study presented at the American Psychological Association
Conference: *Work, Stress and Health: Organisation of Work in a Global Economy* in
Washington. Retrieved from http://www.apa.org/pi/wpo/niosh/thursday2.html]

Barret, R. (1998) *Liberating the Corporate Soul: A Values Driven Approach to Building a
Visionary Organisation*, Butterworth Heinemann, New York.

Bratton, J. and Gold, J. (2003) *Human Resource Management, Theory and Practice* (3rd edn),
Palgrave Macmillan, New York.

Cashmore, E. (2002) *Sports Culture*, Routledge, London.

Ewing, K.D. (ed.) (2000) *Human Rights At Work*, The Institute of Employment Rights,
London.

Gardiner, S., Felix, A., James, M., Welch, R. and O'Leary, J. (1998) *Sports Law*, Cavendish
Publishing Ltd, London.

Gardner, H. (1999) *Intelligences Reframed: Multiple Intelligences for the 21st Century*, Basic
Books, New York.

Goleman, D. (1997) *Vital Lies, Simple Truths: The Psychology of Self Deception*, Bloomsbury
Publishing, London.

Goleman, D. (1998) *Working With Emotional Intelligence*, Bloomsbury Publishing,
London.

Graham, H. and Bennett, R. (1995) *Human Resource Management*, Pitman Publishing Ltd,
London.

Grensing-Pophal, L. (2003) 'Should you offer self-defense training?: consider the message
you're sending – and the potential liability you're taking on – by teaching employees to
defend themselves', *SHRMagazine*, June, p. 80.

Heider, F. (1958) *The Psychology of Interpersonal Relations*, Wiley, New York.

Hull, C.L. (1952) *A Behavior System: An Introduction to Behavior Theory Concerning the
Individual Organism*, Yale University Press.

Human, P. (1998) *Yenza: A Blueprint For Transformation*, Oxford University Press, Cape Town.

Kuznetsov, V.V. (1982) 'The potentialities of man and anthropomaximology', *Journal of International Social Science*, 34(2), pp. 277–89.

ILAM, *Leisure News* (2002), September 5–11, p. 1.

Landers, D.M. (1978) 'Motivation and performance: the role of arousal and attentional factors', in W.F. Straub (ed.), *Sport Psychology: An Analysis of Athlete Behaviour*, Movement Publications.

LeVine, R.A. (1970) 'Cross-cultural study in child psychology', in P. Mussen (ed.), *Carmichael's Manual Of Child Psychology*, vol. 2 (3rd edn) (pp. 559–612), John Wiley, New York, pp. 559–612.

Lewis, P., Thornhill, A. and Saunders, M. (2003) *Employee Relations: Understanding The Employment Relationship*, FT Prentice Hall, London.

Lucas, B. (2001) *Power Up Your Mind: Learn Faster, Work Harder*, Nicholas Brealey Publishers, London.

Maslow, A. (1943) 'A Theory of Human Motivation', *Psychological Review,* 50, pp. 370–96.

Pert, C. (1997) *Molecules of Emotion*, Simon & Schuster, London.

Segall, M.H., Dasen, P.R., Berry, J.W. and Poortinga, Y.H. (eds) (1990) *Human behavior in global perspective: An introduction to cross-cultural psychology*, Pergamon Press, New York.

Senge, P. (1990) *The Fifth Discipline*, Double Day Currency Publishers, London.

Spence, K.W. (1956) *Behavior Theory and Conditioning*, Yale University Press.

Watson, T. (1995), *Sociology, Work and Industry*, Routledge & Kegan Paul Ltd, London.

Winstanley, D. and Woodall, J. (eds) (2000) *Ethical Issues in Contemporary Human Resource Management*, Macmillan Press, London.

Chapter 6

Sport marketing

Malcolm Sullivan
The Nottingham Trent University

Upon completion of this chapter the reader should be able to:

■ explain the development and operation of markets for sports;

■ identify the factors which influence the behaviour of sports consumers;

■ demonstrate the elements of marketing tactics (marketing mix) in a sports context, and explain how they are interrelated;

■ assess operational marketing plans for sports organisations.

Overview

This chapter aims to provide a comprehensive introduction to sport marketing. In essence, sport marketing comprises all aspects of the marketing function within sport businesses and thus includes a number of interrelated elements such as product development and management, promotion, pricing, and (customer) relationship management. A working definition that will form the basis of this chapter is:

> *The fundamental aim of the sport marketing activity is to satisfy the right sport customer needs with sport products or services that offer benefits in excess of all other competitor offerings whilst making the maximum sustainable profit.*

This definition highlights the key areas that will be covered in this chapter. The opening section will provide a more detailed coverage of the sport marketing activity exploring the key tasks. This will then be followed by an analysis of sport customers to highlight and explain essential factors such as motivation, behaviour and individual characteristics. The final section, operational sport marketing, seeks to address the critical factors associated with the planning and implementation of sport marketing activities.

The nature of sport marketing

This section will briefly explore the definition of sport marketing given at the start of the chapter by explaining both the key terms and the processes involved. Looking at the definition again allows a number of key areas to be highlighted:

> The fundamental aim of the sport marketing activity is to satisfy the right sport customer needs with sport products or services that offer benefits in excess of all other competitor offerings whilst making the maximum sustainable profit.

Satisfying customer needs is at the heart of marketing in any context, as is the notion of finding the right customers. Needs (the reasons why people buy) are satisfied by the benefits (what the product or service does for the person) offered by the sport provider. If a fan is to maximise his or her satisfaction gained from watching a sport, team or player, the benefits offered by that sport, team or player must be greater than any other activity that competes for that person's time and money. As an example, if a person has the option of watching rugby union, soccer, ice hockey or basketball on a given day, that person will choose the sport that offers the greatest benefits. Table 6.1 gives examples of sport fans' needs and benefits.

Finding the right customers is important, as it is rare for one sport, team or player to appeal to all. Many sports have a strong gender preference for example, with more male-dominated sports, such as boxing, being contrasted with more female-dominated sports, such as netball. Other reasons could include geography (e.g. supporting the local team or player), demographics (e.g. social-class associations) or interest value. A key task, therefore, is to analyse all actual and potential sports fans that are right for a given sport, team or player. The first part of this analysis should cover, amongst other things, needs and benefits sought. The second key area concerns the building of a fan profile.

The needs of sports fans are ultimately satisfied by the sport product and services (or marketing offering). The term 'product' is often mistakenly used to cover everything offered to the customer but it is more correct to consider tangible and intangible elements. Tangible elements are those things that can be seen and touched, and include elements like the stadium, hospitality, merchandise and programmes. Intangible elements are those things experienced by the individual and include the experience inside the arena (or the spectator experience in general), the service offered by the arena personnel, branding and the actual game itself. An appropriate combination of tangible and intangible elements provides the benefits that satisfy customer needs. It should be noted, however, that there may be other spectator opportunities

Table 6.1 Typical sport fans, needs and benefits

Needs	Benefits
Excitement, being part of a group, filling leisure time, wanting a shared activity with family and friends, the instinct for competition (survival), success and achievement, appreciation of sport prowess and security and safety.	Atmosphere of the game, camaraderie with other fans, rivalry with opposing fans, reflected glory, seeing the technical skills of the players, arena facilities, opposing teams/players both trying to win.

that could satisfy the sports fan's needs, hence it is necessary to ensure that the fan gets more, that is, greater benefits = greater satisfaction. Another key part of sport marketing is, therefore, analysis of the competition.

The final key element relates to the need to make the maximum sustainable profit, meaning that sport providers should not be seen by sports fans as taking advantage of their loyalty to make excessive profits. There are many examples of sports where this has been seen to happen (e.g. English soccer) but there is little the fan can do except stop supporting. The converse is also true, however, not making enough profit can lead to revenue problems that may impact on results, hence it is important that the sport marketer gets the balance right.

CASE 6.1   Why sport?

Why is sport important to people? Clearly, the reasons lie in its appeal to the population or, more specifically, the benefits that it can offer. To understand this further, a survey of a random sample of 200 adults in the UK was made and the findings presented below.

Sports interest survey

Why do participant rates differ from spectator rates?

Sport	Spectator		Participant
	On TV	At the stadium	
Soccer	35%	10%	5%
Cricket	26%	3%	5%
Snooker	25%	2%	1%
F1 Motor racing	20%	1%	0%
Tennis	18%	2%	3%
Golf	17%	1%	15%
Cycling	8%	0%	15%
Swimming	5%	1%	35%

Source: Sullivan (2003)
Note: Figures refer to % of the sample.

Discussion questions

1. What benefits does sport offer to people?

2. Why do people watch sport on television rather than attend the game?

3. Why do participant rates differ from spectator rates?

Sports customers

This section will seek to gain an understanding of the sports customer by addressing issues such as why do they watch, how often do they watch, do they prefer to go to the arena itself or watch on the television? Sports customers differ quite markedly, hence the sports marketer needs to be able to identify, locate and communicate with different types of customer in a personalised way. This personalisation accounts for differences in the way that the sport product offering is consumed (experienced) and the reasons underlying that consumption. As an example, would it be correct to assume that the two golf customers in Exhibit 6.1 were the same, and therefore could be marketed to in the same way?

Exhibit 6.1	Sport customer differences

Customer A – Eighteen years old, never really tried to actually play golf, admires Tiger Woods and got into the sport recently when watching the Ryder cup on television. Tends to only watch the major events and dips in and out of the coverage, that is, does not watch for long periods of time. Has no real interest in attending an event because holds the belief that 'you get a better view on the TV anyway'.

Customer B – Thirty-six years old, keen golf player (handicap of 13.1) and member of a golf club. Has always watched golf on television and started playing the game at a young age. Has no particular favourite player but takes the opportunity to watch as much golf on television as possible. A regular visitor to golf events because 'it's only when you get up close to a pro that you appreciate just how awesome they are'.

The answers are clearly 'no' and 'no'. This section will address this issue in more depth.

Understanding the sports fan

When considering customers in a sport context, the term 'fan' is most commonly used. This term is misleading in the sense that it derives from *fanatic*, hence would tend to imply that all sports fans are highly loyal (almost addictively so). This clearly is not the case as sport customers, like those in any other business sector, exhibit different levels of attachment (loyalty). For this reason, the term fan will be used in its broadest sense and will, therefore, imply a range of attachment levels.

A further point concerns the way that fans spectate. Market data (as illustrated by Case 6.1) shows that a significant proportion of fans prefer to (or are only able to) follow a given sport on the television, radio or online rather than going to the arena. This point highlights another aspect of the term 'fan', namely that a fan does not necessarily consume the sport product at the point of production, that is, sport fans do not necessarily go to the sport arena; their participation can be much less direct but often no less involving.

The profiling of sports fans can be based on three key sets of factors (see Table 6.2).

Geographic and demographic factors

A prime influence in an individual's 'decision' to become a fan is residency; the place or environment where that individual spends, or has spent, a proportion of their time. The reason for the influence of this geographic factor is the importance of local affiliation. Fans often support their home-town side or players irrespective of where they

Table 6.2 **Key factors in profiling sports fans**

Factor	Details
Geographic	Current residency (domestic, work), birthplace, other places of residency (domestic, work)
Demographic	Age, gender, occupation, level of education, family status, social class, income
Behavioural	Benefits sought, attitudes, perception, motivation (and involvement), learning, personality, culture, lifestyle, reference groups, behavioural type

now happen to live. Even individuals that become fans later in life may choose to support a team or individual associated with their current or past place of residency or work. Understanding a fan's pattern of residency is, therefore, a key part of understanding that fan's behaviour.

Demographics describe the fan using personal characteristics such as age, gender, social class, level of education, occupation and family status. These personal characteristics (or demographic factors) can have an effect on the behaviour with many sports being predominantly watched by a given gender (rugby union versus netball) or social class (soccer was traditionally a working-class game). Occupation and level of education will have a less obvious effect although both have an influence on lifestyle. Family status, or the composition of an individual's family unit over time, can have a marked effect on behaviour (see Table 6.3).

Behavioural factors

Behavioural factors can be broken down into those that relate to the individual (benefits sought, attitudes, perception, motivation and involvement, learning, personality), to how that individual lives or has lived (culture, lifestyle, reference groups) and to how that individual actually behaves (purchase behaviour).

Amongst the individual factors, perhaps the most important is *benefits sought*. As discussed earlier in this chapter, benefits are what the fan wants to get from consuming the sport product and can be quite diverse, hard to uncover and complex. *Attitudes* are thought-based knowledge, opinion and faith, and influence the way fans react to the world (see perception below). Attitudes are enduring (that is, can be firmly held and, hence, take a long time to change) and thus can lead fans to behave in a fairly consistent way. *Perception* is important as it relates to how individuals make sense of the things that they sense. For example, if a fan hears negative comments about their team or player they react in a way that is personal to them. In more detail, perception relates to what we choose to sense, think about and remember. Ask fans of opposing teams for their view on the game and you would probably get very different interpretations, for example, what was clearly an act of foul play to one may be perfectly acceptable to the other and judgements of which team was lucky or unlucky could also vary.

Motivation is based on motives, or needs that are sufficiently pressing to drive the individual to act. Biogenic motives relate to physiological states of tension such as hunger, thirst, and discomfort whilst psychogenic relate to psychological states of tension such as pride, esteem, love and belonging. Maslow's hierarchy of needs (1943, 1968, 1970) states that motives or needs can be divided into groups and ranked in order of importance. The basic survival needs such as hunger and thirst are the most

Table 6.3 **The family life cycle**

Stage in cycle	Behaviour pattern
1. Singles: young, single, not living at home	Few financial burdens, recreational spending high. Has time and sufficient money to be a keen spectator.
2. Childless couples: young couples, no children	Quite well off, high purchase rate, practical spending plus recreational. Influence of partner may encourage or discourage watching sport.
3. Full nest I: youngest child under six	Home buying, little money, buys practical things and children's products. Time and money constraints may limit sport involvement.
4. Full nest II: youngest child six or over	Financial position better, buys practical goods in large-pack sizes plus children's products. Children become possible sports spectators hence watching sport may become a family activity.
5. Full nest III: older couples with dependant children	More money still, some wives work, buys better household goods and more recreational spending. More time and money to watch sport either individually or in family groups.
6. Empty nest I: older couples, children moved out	Home ownership at peak, money situation good, recreational spend increases, home improvements and luxuries bought. Circumstances most conducive to watching sports.
7. Empty nest II: older couples, head of household retired	Drastic cut in income, spending reduced to replacement only. If retired, plenty of time available to watch sport, though money may be a problem.
8. Solitary survivor I: one partner left, still working	Income steady, likely to sell home, spending much more limited. Time and money constraints make spectating difficult.
9. Solitary survivor II: one partner left, retired	Drastic cut in income, spending for attention, affection and security. May have more time and sufficient money to spectate.

important and always have top priority. The remaining needs (typically psychogenic) can then be ranked in importance forming a total of five levels (see Figure 6.1). Maslow stated that an individual would be motivated by the most basic need that remained unsatisfied, only moving to a higher level when satisfaction had occurred. In a sport context, basic survival needs are not relevant although some obsessive fans may view their team or player in a life or death context.

The concept of *involvement*, or the degree of interest an individual has about something, can be used to assess the relative importance of motives. Involvement depends mainly on perceived risk, or the negative factors associated with the decision to support. Risk can be physical (actual bodily harm), financial (loss of money) or psychological (lack of satisfaction and self-image issues such as self-esteem). As perceived risk increases, so involvement increases and the fan attaches increasing importance to the

Figure 6.1 Maslow's hierarchy of needs
Source: Maslow (1943)

supporting activity. In the sport context, psychological risk is usually the most important although a number of high-profile sports disasters would imply that physical risk is also an issue.

Learning relates to the way that individuals build up a memory bank of perceptions and associated responses. The process allows fans to learn a way of supporting their team or individual and may include interactions with other fans (for example, the Mexican wave), accepted behaviour before, during and after the game and, at the most basic level, the intricacies of the particular sport in question. *Personality* is important as 'everything we buy helps us to convey to others the kind of people we are, helps us identify ourselves to the world at large' (Martineau, 1958). Personality traits are identifiable personality characteristics that relate directly to response, are relatively stable and are assumed to influence behaviour. A fan's self-concept is an individual's mental picture of himself or herself based on the traits that the individual thinks he or she has. If supporting a sport, team or player fits this mental picture, purchase likelihood increases, that is, fans want to be associated with something or someone that fits with the sort of person they believe they are.

Factors relating to a fan's pattern of living seek to explain all the social interactions that may have an effect on behaviour. *Culture* is the pattern of life adopted by people to help them interpret, evaluate and communicate as members of society. Behaviour, both inside and outside the arena, is strongly influenced by culture as the 'pattern of life' and also usually determines the boundaries of acceptable behaviour. A social-class cluster is a distinctive part of culture (a subculture), is relatively homogenous and enduring, is hierarchically ordered, and contains members who share similar values, interests, and behaviour. Many sports have a definite social class heritage, for example, in the United Kingdom, soccer was traditionally working class whilst rugby union was more middle to upper class. *Lifestyle* is an individual's pattern of living in the world as expressed by activities, interests and opinions. Activities and interests detail how the fan spends time both in an active and a passive sense. This distinction is important as only a small proportion of fans are also participants. Opinions are linked to attitudes (discussed earlier in this section).

A *reference group* is a group of individuals (also a subculture) that has a direct or indirect influence on a person's attitudes or behaviour. Membership groups are those to which the individual belongs either automatically (ascribed groups) or has sought membership of (acquired groups). Individuals may wish to join other aspirational groups or not be associated with dissociative groups. Formal groups have clear operating rules whilst informal groups are more casual. Groups with close emotional contact and face-to-face communication are primary groups whilst secondary groups are more impersonal and often larger. In a sport context, fans usually want to be associated with the body of supporters for a given team or player (an acquired, aspirational, informal and secondary reference group), may have friends or family that also support (ascribed or acquired, possibly aspirational, more formal and primary) and may actively seek to avoid fans of opposing teams or players (dissociative). The family is a strong reference group and is one that often shapes the supporting habits of a given fan, that is, many children support the same team or players as their parents or actively not conform by supporting another team or player.

The actual way that the purchase is made, or *purchase behaviour*, can provide valuable insight. Extremes of purchase behaviour can be identified as impulse and planned or largely unconsidered and largely considered acts respectively. Cobb and Hoyer (1986) classify such purchase types using intent to buy the product category (for example, watch a soccer match) and intent to buy the specific brand or product type (for example, watch a specific soccer team's match). *Impulse* behaviour would indicate that the fan had not considered either what sport or what team/game to watch whilst *planned* would show thought about both the sport and the specific team/game. The intermediate type, *semi-impulse*, implies a decision had been made about the sport but not about the team/game to watch (see Figure 6.2).

Building the profile

After considering the four key factors discussed above, it is possible to build a profile of sports fans that will be invaluable to the sports marketer. A useful model, developed by Hunt *et al.* (1999), identifies five types of fan: the temporary fan, the local fan, the devoted fan, the fanatical fan and the dysfunctional fan, as shown in Table 6.4.

Table 6.4 shows that fans can be categorised depending on the degree of importance attached to the object of their support and the resulting behaviour. At one end of the scale, the *temporary fan* shows only a limited engagement that will not lead to high levels of loyalty or particularly fan-like behaviour. Indeed, supporting the team or individual is only a peripheral part of this fan's life. Conversely, the *dysfunctional fan* has little else in their life apart from supporting the team or individual. Loyalty is taken to the extreme and quite obsessive, often anti-social, behaviour results. Success 'on the

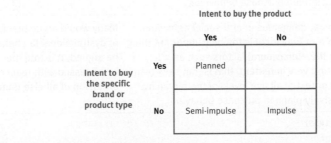

Figure 6.2 Cobb and Hoyer's classifications
Source: Cobb and Hoyer (1986)

Table 6.4 **Five types of fan**

Fan type	Characteristics	Examples
Temporary	Interested for a specific time period (e.g. special event, specific sports personality, influence of others). Geographic and demographic factors not important (depending on the sport), behavioural factors (e.g. reference groups) may be reason for interest. Typically impulse or semi-impulse purchase behaviour.	A fan that supports the national athletics team during the Olympic Games but not at any other time. A female fan that supports motor racing due to the influence of a male partner but only does this when in that partner's presence. A fan that supports golf due to an admiration of Tiger Woods but will not continue to support golf when Tiger stops playing.
Local	Identifies with particular geographic area (e.g. place of birth or current location). Geographic factors very important, demographic may also be important for certain sports. Behavioural factors important (e.g. reference groups, culture, motivation), being part of a local group is key. Typically planned or semi-impulse purchase behaviour.	A French skiing fan, born in Albertville, now lives in Paris but supports the alpine skiers that grew up in the Albertville area. A cricket fan who lives in the county of Nottinghamshire (in the UK) and always checks out the results of Nottinghamshire County Cricket club and watches any games that are televised.
Devoted	Strong association. Tends to be more team-based but can also be personality-based. Geographic and demographic factors may be important but social factors (reference group, culture, motivation, learning, etc.) very important. Usually planned purchase behaviour.	A tennis fan that follows a particular professional and will attend tournaments as often as possible. Views his/her support of the player as a very important part of his/her social life but still finds time for other activities and people. A rugby union fan that holds a season ticket for his/her club and also attends as many home games as possible. Rugby is the only thing that matters on match days but other matters (family, work, etc.) are more important for the rest of the week.
Fanatical	Quite addictive but controlled behaviour. The object (team or individual) is a key, but not the most important, part of the fan's existence. A more extreme version of the devoted fan, hence geographic and demographic factors may be important but social factors (reference group, culture, motivation, learning, etc.) very important. Always planned purchase behaviour.	The soccer fan that attends every game both home and away, has their house painted in the team colours and may even have named a child after a player, manager or other name associated with the team.
Dysfunctional	Obsessive, dangerous or anti-social behaviour. The team or individual is the *only* important thing in their life. Behavioural factors such as motivation very important, that is, fan sees team in the context of all five levels of the hierarchy. Obsessively planned purchase behaviour.	Many would argue that hooliganism is an example of dysfunctional fan behaviour. Whilst this could be argued, it is true that the dysfunctional fan will be obsessed with team or individual to the exclusion of all else (family, work, etc.).

Source: Based on Hunt *et al.* (1999)

Table 6.5 Marketing approaches to different types of fan

Fan type	Key marketing tasks
Temporary	Timing crucial. Link event to social activity. Give reasons to watch other than just to watch the game. Give information about sport and event.
Local	Give fans a stake in their local team. Stage community events. Build and maintain a local identity.
Devoted	Give detailed team/player information. Offer branded products and services. Maintain and augment the event experience.
Fanatical	Give ways for fan to demonstrate loyalty and identify with the team or individual. Personalised marketing with events, facilities, products and services only available to 'true' fans.
Dysfunctional	Demarketing important to curb and modify socially unacceptable behaviour. Education programmes. Segregation.

pitch' leads to increased self-worth whilst failure has an opposite and often devastating effect. Between these two extremes, fans can be seen to be increasingly loyal, have an increasing long-term and emotional attachment, and engage in behaviour that could be seen as increasingly obsessive. Showing the percentage of fans that fall into a given type would be difficult and probably inaccurate, as each particular sporting situation would have quite different characteristics. However, the model can be used to give some idea of how to market to the various fan types (see Table 6.5 above).

CASE 6.2 Survey data on the F1 motor racing fan

A detailed study of 40 self-confessed Formula 1 motor racing fans produced the following findings.

Survey findings

Whilst all were spectators, only 2 actually went to F1 race meetings and none actually participated.

The main reasons for non-attendance were convenience (getting to the circuit), cost (admission prices) and attending other sports.

The average TV viewing time last season was 9 hours.

Of the 40, 9 were women, 31 were men.

The main reasons why men watched on the TV were excitement, identification with the drivers (usually British), appreciation of the skill involved and the fact that it was seen as a family event on a Sunday.

The main reasons why women watched on the TV were excitement, identification and the fact that it was seen as an event to watch with their partner.

The differences between reasons for TV viewing and attendance for both men and women were atmosphere and the closeness to the cars.

The age groups of the fans were quite evenly spread although 18–25 was the largest category.

Fans tended to come more from families without children although the difference was not large.

The majority of the fans had been watching F1 for more than 3 years.

The vast majority of fans had a favourite driver or team.

A majority of the fans planned to watch races on the TV well in advance.

Men were more likely to complain about a lack of action in races than women.

Source: Sullivan, 2003

Discussion questions

4. What can be deduced about the profile of F1 motor sport fans?

5. How could this profile be used to improve F1 marketing?

Operational sport marketing

Operational sport marketing deals with the execution of sport marketing and involves research, analysis, planning, implementation and control. Environmental analysis seeks to gather the essential data on the sport environment then analyse this to gain a clear understanding of the sport market(s) and the key determinants of success. Planning can then take place to set objectives, develop strategies to achieve those objectives and consider the actions required for successful implementation and control of marketing efforts (sport marketing plans).

Environmental analysis

As discussed above, environmental analysis is a two-stage process: data collection and data analysis. Data collection is achieved through the sport marketing audit that aims to systematically address all the key areas of the sport environment: macro-environment, customers, competitors, market(s) and company (internal). The audit specifies certain key data that is required (see Table 6.6) if a full understanding of the environment is to be gained. The importance of this 'full understanding' lies in the fact that key determinants for successful operation come from the environment. Once the full data set has been collected, analysis is necessary in order to gain a clear understanding of the influential factors. There are many approaches to this analysis but here only two of the most common will be discussed.

SWOT analysis aims to organise audit data under internal factors (strengths and weaknesses) and external factors (opportunities and threats) so that an analysis of the company's position can be considered by a balanced assessment of the relative strengths or weaknesses. Add to this an assessment of market opportunities and threats, and the sport marketer should have a clear picture of the factors that will lead to successful operations (see Exhibit 6.2). On a simple level, matching an opportunity with the strength required to capitalise on that opportunity highlights possible areas of success whilst matching a threat with a weakness highlights the potential problems. Issue–Impact analysis is a more flexible approach that seeks to analyse audit data (issues) by assessing influence (impact) on the environment. The process requires all

Table 6.6 **Key data required for the sport marketing audit**

Audit area	Key data
Macro-environment	Political, social, technological, economic and physical
Customers	Needs, benefits, profile, behaviour
Competitors	Profile, success (market share), strengths and weaknesses, objectives, strategy and future performance
Market(s)	Size and growth rate, tactical situation (products offered, prices charged, distribution used, promotion undertaken, relationships), critical success factors
Internal	Customer profile, success (market share, profit), strengths and weaknesses

key issues to be gathered from the marketing audit with each assessed individually for any impact. Next, an overall assessment of impact is made by considering the issues (and associated impacts) collectively.

Exhibit 6.2   Examples of SWOT and issue–impact analysis

Marketing audit extracts
'Skiing shares many characteristics with golf. Both sports were traditionally restricted to a limited part of the population, usually those with money and influence. In recent years, both have seen an expansion of participation due the increased availability of affordable holidays or courses. Figures for the ski market show that between 1988/9 and 1997/8 the numbers of ski holidays taken decreased from 705,000 to 655,000 although the amount of money spent on those holidays increased from £210m to £255m . . .'

'. . .80% of holidays are sold by the very powerful top five companies with a large cost advantage over the smaller specialist operators that account for the remaining 20%. Company X, a small specialist operator can offer unique service elements such as multi-resort holidays, heliskiing, personal service in the resort, luxury accommodation and ski guiding (on- and off-piste)'.

Issue–impact analysis

Skiing shares many characteristics with golf
Development of ski holiday market may follow that of golf

Previously restricted, now expanding (holiday availability)
Potential demand should increase

Number of holidays fell by 7.1%, money spent increased by 21.4%
Fewer holidays but 30.7% increase in average price

80% of market controlled by top 5 and top 5 powerful with cost advantage

SWOT analysis

Strengths of company X:
■ Ability to offer unique service elements

Weaknesses of company X:
■ Cost disadvantage compared to large operators

Opportunities in the market:
■ Strong future growth potential
■ Move to higher price holidays may mean more demand for additional features such as unique service elements

> *Sales potential limited for small companies and price competition difficult*
>
> **Threats** in the market:
> - Dominance of major operators
> - Fall in number of holidays taken
>
> Unique service elements can be offered by company X
> *Company X has a means of competing with the top 5*
>
> *Overall impact: like golf, the ski holiday market is expanding in value terms and further potential for growth is likely to exist. Company X can use its unique service elements to compete successfully.*

Objective setting

Once the sport marketer has a clear understanding of the environment, it is necessary to map out what the given organisation wishes to achieve in the future. This process of objective setting sets the parameters for all the operational marketing processes that follow (e.g. strategy development, implementation and control). If the objectives that are formulated at this stage are to be useful, there are a number of key criteria that must be adhered to. A useful mnemonic is SMART (see Table 6.7):

Specific – an objective must relate to an identifiable part of the business
Measurable – an objective must be assessable by measurement
Actionable – an objective must be capable of being operationalised
Realistic – an objective must be achievable and appropriate for the market situation
Time framed – an objective must have a 'completion' date

Developing operational strategy

Operational strategy outlines the set of marketing tactics that will make the step(s) from the current situation (sport marketing audit analysis) to the desired future position (objectives). The term 'marketing mix' is often used interchangeably with marketing tactics; the latter will be the preferred term for this chapter. Sport marketing

Table 6.7 'Smart' and 'Not so smart' objectives

*S*mart	*Not so smart*
Achieve a market share of 2.5% on a value basis in market A by March 2005	Improve the performance of the business
Achieve a customer satisfaction rating of 97% in market B by January 2004	Ensure that spectators are satisfied
Achieve an increase of 5% in match ticket sales volume by the end of the 2004/5 season	Improve the returns from match ticket sales
Achieve merchandise sales of £10m by the end of the 2006/7 season	Gain significant sales from new merchandise lines

tactics relate to both products and services (largely tangible and intangible respectively) and hence will comprise product, service, pricing, distribution, promotional and customer relationship tactics. It is important to note that these areas are interconnected and therefore must be consistent, that is, operational strategy is not simply a collection of individual tactical areas, it is an integrated solution made up of a number of component parts – the product must fit the price (and vice versa), distribution must be appropriate for the product and price, promotion must communicate the right message that includes the product, price and distribution, and an appropriate relationship must be built for that combination of product, price, distribution and promotion.

Product tactics

The sport product will incorporate both tangible (facilities, players etc.) and intangible elements (spectator experience, services offered, etc.), and can be considered to have a multi-layer structure (see Figure 6.3).

When considering what product to offer, it is important to remember that the product must provide the benefits that will meet sport customer needs. At the basic product level, the product must be seen by customers to offer the core benefit. This core benefit is usually quite simple and could, for example, be the excitement gained from watching the game. In the vast majority of cases, however, this core benefit does not explain why a given customer chooses to watch a given sport, team or player. Indeed, the basic product is usually considered to be an 'order qualifier', that is, a benefit that has to be given but one that will not make the difference between one product and another. The order winners, or those facets of a product that do make the difference, would usually be associated with the real and total product levels. The real product covers all the features of the product (stadium, league or ranking position, team colours, merchandise, etc.). A difference can be made at this level, e.g. customers may choose a team or player due to perceptions of success or stadium quality. The total product covers all those parts of a product that are intangible and are judged by each customer in a quite unique way. To give an example, two different customers may see the same team in completely different ways due to differences in, for example, their attitudes about that team. One may love the team, the other may hate it.

As mentioned above, intangible elements of the product such as service are often the source of important and valued customer benefits. Services are different to products in five key ways.

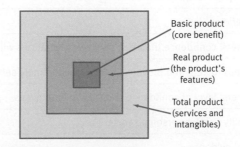

Figure 6.3 **The composition of a sport product**

- Firstly, services are largely intangible and hence are much harder to measure by both sports businesses and customers alike. This means that sports services are much harder to market to customers as it is quite unclear what is actually being marketed.
- Secondly, customers do not actually own the service, they merely experience it for a certain amount of time.
- This fact also implies the third difference: once a match has finished, that service experience has also finished, hence, unlike products, it is not possible to put unsold items in stock to be sold at a later date. The revenue from any unused seat, for example, can never be recouped.
- The fourth difference relates to the fact that services are effectively consumed by customers at the same time that they are produced, hence, there is no opportunity to produce extra services in advance to meet demand. All service providers have a maximum capacity at any given time and so must maximise profit under these constraints.
- The fifth difference is that services tend to be unique each time they are delivered due to the involvement of employees as service providers and the inherent intangibility, that is, there is no standardisation and hence service quality may vary markedly.

These differences mean that services must be marketed in a different way to pure products. The key factors to manage are the people, the process and physical evidence. People refers to the contact employees that actually deliver the service, for example, ticket sellers, stewards, catering staff, etc. These contact points are crucial as they affect the level of satisfaction or dissatisfaction and thus are often referred to as 'moments of truth' and must be optimised by staff training and empowerment. Process concerns the way that the service is delivered whilst physical evidence relates to the more tangible parts of the service such as hospitality arrangements, the quality of the seating, retail activities and the match programme. Table 6.8 adds more detail to these points by identifying the five key sport services marketing tasks.

Pricing tactics

Pricing is a key factor for sport businesses, as it is for any business, due to its impact on profitability and, in some cases, demand. When setting price, three broad options exist relating to the focus taken. *Internally centred methods* look at the organisation's

Table 6.8 The five key sport services marketing tasks

Task	Explanation
Reliability	Customers' confidence that their service expectations will be met every time
Responsiveness	Readiness to help and provide customers with timely service
Assurance	Customers' level of confidence and trust in employees
Empathy	The ability to offer personalised service
Tangibles	Physical evidence

costs and seek to price in such a way that a certain profit is made. This method is often known as cost-plus pricing. In contrast, *externally centred methods* are based on an analysis of the sport marketing environment and seek to set a price that is right for that company's product in that particular market. This method is often known as market-based pricing. The final broad option is simply a *hybrid of internally and externally centred methods*, and in practice is the method that many sport businesses use. Table 6.9 lists the main factors that must be considered when setting a price.

Once the main factors have been analysed, it is possible to select the actual pricing approach from a number of basic options. The basis of the options is the price/reference price comparison and price/quality assessment made by customers. In essence, an individual assesses a price by comparing it to a reference price. This reference price may be an actual price of a competing product, the market price or a price seen by that individual as being fair. The price/quality assessment requires the customer to weigh up the quality of the product being offered (perceived quality) with the price being charged. Price and perceived quality can either be balanced (value-for-money) or imbalanced (either superior or inferior value-for-money). Combining price/quality assessment with value-for-money considerations produces four pricing approaches (see Figure 6.4).

■ Distribution tactics

Distribution, or the delivery of products from supplier (sport business) to customer (sports fan) relates to the sports arena or, in the case of merchandising, the outlets where products can be purchased. In the case of the arena, this can often be to the home stadium of a given team, hence, distribution is less of an issue. Distribution is important, however, in sports where matches are played at a number of different locations (e.g. golf, tennis, motor racing, etc.). In these cases, decisions need to be made on the number and location of venues used in a given season. In the case of merchandising, distribution would relate to the outlets and channels through which merchandise is made available (note: a distribution channel is any means by which

Table 6.9 **Factors to consider when setting price**

Factor	Explanation
Company	Minimum required profit levels, attitudes to risk, company/brand image
Costs	Sets the baseline for pricing decisions
Strategy	Pricing must fit other elements such as the product, distribution, etc.
Product	The nature of the product (newness, perceived quality) is important
Market	Market price levels set reference price points (points of comparison)
Competition	Pricing in relation to other companies that a customer may buy from
Customers	Ultimate assessors of price. Price sensitivity and price perceptions important
Value	The result of customer judgements about price and product quality

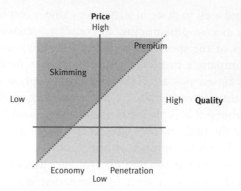

Figure 6.4 Pricing approaches

products are 'transferred' from the sport business to the sport customer). In both the cases mentioned above (multiple venues and merchandising), the sport marketer needs to consider the best combination of venues or outlets (market coverage) that would make the sport product available to all the fans that have an interest. The three broad options in this respect are intensive distribution (maximum availability), selective distribution (more restricted availability) and exclusive distribution (limited availability).

An additional consideration is the relative cost of any distribution approach compared to the degree of control exercised. Sanctioning events in areas outside the control of the governing organisation could lead to problems that affect the sport as a whole, whilst many clubs and players seek to control their merchandising activities tightly to ensure that the club's or player's name is protected. The typical options are third party (low cost, low control) and in-house (high cost, high control). An example of the former would be using a merchandising company whilst the latter would be control of merchandising by the sport business itself.

◼ Promotional tactics

A sport business needs to communicate with its customers (fans) in order to ensure that existing (and new) customers are aware of the sport, team or player, hold positive attitudes, have extensive and appropriate knowledge of the sport offering, and provide a source of revenue. Three broad groups of communication objectives can be identified, namely informing, persuading and reinforcing:

- Informing involves giving information to build awareness that a sport, team or player exists and explain what is being offered.
- Persuading concerns creating a favourable attitude thus giving reasons why one particular sport, team or player should be supported.
- Reinforcing relates to the dispelling of doubts about the decision to support, building loyalty and ensuring that sales continue into the future.

Achieving these communication objectives requires knowledge of the communication process, the spectators, the content of the communication, the delivery method and a number of other factors that will be discussed below.

The basic communication process (see Figure 6.5) involves a message being sent from the sender (sport business) to the receiver (spectator) that has been designed to achieve one or more of the three objectives mentioned above. The message may either be informational (facts and figures) or symbolic (image-related) depending on what is most appropriate to convey the message successfully to the recipients. If the spectator has the opportunity to reply (e.g. telephone communication) this is known as feedback. The method used to deliver the message is called the 'promotional tool' (e.g. advertising, direct marketing, etc.) whilst the term 'medium' relates to the message carrier (e.g. national radio, newspapers, etc.). Any factor interfering with this communication process is known as 'noise' (e.g. conflicting promotional messages from competitors).

The elements of the basic communication process show that effective promotion is based on knowledge of the customer and the environment. Sport marketers must be aware of what messages are more likely to be understood, what promotional methods are more likely to be effective (see Table 6.10), what media will be the most appropriate and what external factors could be the cause of noise.

■ Customer relationship tactics

Customer relationships are becoming increasingly important due to the benefits that a successful relationship can give. Firstly, more loyal customers have been found to spend more, hence, successful relationships can build and maintain income. Secondly, the costs associated with keeping a customer are lower than those associated with gaining a new one, hence, overall costs can be reduced. Thirdly, customers that have a good relationship with a company are more likely to spread positive word of mouth (say good things to others about that company), hence, the company's image can benefit. The three key elements of a customer relationship approach are the building and maintenance of the relationship, the retention of the customer (loyalty) and the recovery from any problems that could affect the relationship. In reality, relationships are managed by effective retention and recovery strategies, and so these two areas will be discussed here.

The key retention strategy is to maintain customer satisfaction, as satisfied customers have no good reason to be disloyal. Sports customers form a number of expectations about what they want out of the spectator experience (excitement, comfort, security, etc.) and compare this with their perceptions of what they actually experienced. Satisfaction exists when perceptions equal or exceed expectations. Other ways of building retention include simple financial approaches (price incentives such as loyalty

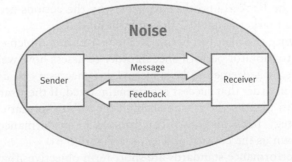

Figure 6.5 **The communication process**

Table 6.10 **Methods of sport promotion**

Promotional method	Characteristics
Merchandise display	Presentation of products to customers
Personal selling	Interaction with personnel (team/player or stadium)
Sales promotion	Inducements to purchase
Advertising	Messages to customers
Direct marketing	Direct contact with customers
Sponsorship	Link to related event, individual or company
Public relations	Information management via 'news' sources

schemes), personalised approaches (personal treatment such as tailored spectator packages) and emotional approaches (making the sport, team or player part of the fan's life).

Recovery strategies seek to anticipate, recognise and quickly and effectively solve customer problems. Anticipation of potential problems requires customer research to uncover all the potential failure points. Recognising problems when they arise requires close customer contact and hence a useful strategy is the implementation of a service guarantee that 'rewards' customers for bringing problems to the attention of the sport business with financial or non-financial compensation. Swift action is essential to lessen the impact of any negative experiences, whilst solving problems effectively requires the empowerment of the front-line worker to take appropriate action.

Implementation and control

Once the operational strategy has been formulated, the sport marketer must consider how the strategy will be turned into reality (that is, implemented). This necessitates the development of a set of appropriate sequential actions that need to be specified, costed, scheduled and assigned to an individual or group if implementation is to be successful. Furthermore, those charged with executing a specific action need to be aware of the reasons behind the action if they are to be truly motivated, that is, understanding why the action is necessary usually gives employees more of a shared sense of purpose. The sport marketing plan is the means by which all these tasks are achieved, in that it specifies, costs, schedules and assigns actions whilst also presenting the background that explains why the actions are necessary. The typical format for a marketing plan is shown in Exhibit 6.3.

Once the plan has been developed and the implementation completed, it is necessary to monitor performance in order to assess how well the strategy is working. If the strategy is deemed to be a success, it is necessary to uncover the reasons for this success in order that success can be maintained. If the strategy is not a success, it is necessary to identify the reasons behind the failure so that changes can be made to put the strategy back on track. This process of performance measurement and analysis is known as the control process (see Figure 6.6).

Performance standards are short-term objectives that allow success to be measured. Just like any objectives, performance standards must be SMART. The most basic per-

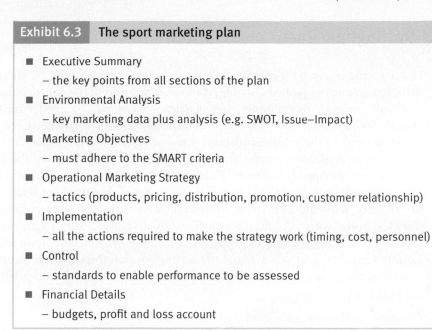

Exhibit 6.3	The sport marketing plan

- Executive Summary
  - the key points from all sections of the plan
- Environmental Analysis
  - key marketing data plus analysis (e.g. SWOT, Issue–Impact)
- Marketing Objectives
  - must adhere to the SMART criteria
- Operational Marketing Strategy
  - tactics (products, pricing, distribution, promotion, customer relationship)
- Implementation
  - all the actions required to make the strategy work (timing, cost, personnel)
- Control
  - standards to enable performance to be assessed
- Financial Details
  - budgets, profit and loss account

formance standards relate to financial performance such as market share, sales and profit although these would only allow the sport marketer to measure success or failure not the reasons behind the performance that are crucial in planning future actions. This extra level of sensitivity is achieved by setting further performance standards that relate to the product (e.g. customer acceptability), price (e.g. customer value-for-money judgements), distribution (e.g. % coverage), promotion (e.g. customer awareness) and the customer relationship (e.g. customer satisfaction).

Once performance has been evaluated and the reasons for success or failure identified, corrective action can be taken either to maintain success or to produce success in the future. These actions would usually see a change in the strategy but could also relate to any element of the operational marketing process (e.g. revised objectives). Once corrective action has been taken, a new set of performance standards are produced and the control process begins again.

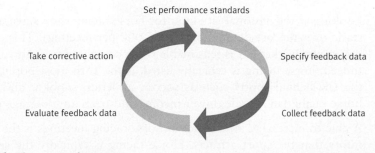

Figure 6.6 **The control process**

CASE 6.3   Nottingham Race Course (NRC)

Horse racing began on the Colwick Park course in Nottingham, UK, in 1892. Since then, the course has gained a strong, if modest, position in the sports industry in the midlands area. In recent times, new facilities have been opened (the Centenary Stand), the first ever listed flat race was held and in the current year the £750,000 refurbishment of the main grandstand was completed. Despite these developments, the course struggles to compete with other sports in the area during the key time in the season from April to October. The nature of this season means that horse racing competes with both winter and summer sports, hence, Nottingham Race Course has to compete with the two main soccer clubs (Nottingham Forest Football Club (NFFC) and Notts County Football Club (NCFC)), the rugby union club (Nottingham Rugby Football Club (NRFC)), the cricket club (Nottinghamshire County Cricket Club (NCCC)) and the ice hockey club (Nottingham Panthers (NP)) as well as more marginal sports. The table below outlines their competitor market-ing packages.

Company and competitor data (typical average figures):

Club	Admission price range (£)		Event duration (hours)	Hospitality packages	
	Adults	Children		Offered	Cost (£)
NRC	10–15	<16 years free over 16 years 7–12	3	Yes	14–97
NFFC	15–25	6–13	2	Yes	50–90
NCFC	11–16	0–12 years free 12–15 years 5	2	Yes	30
NRFC	7	3.50		No	–
NCCC					
■ One-day international	30–48	15	~7	Yes	250–350
■ County championship	10	5	~7	No	–
NP	13–15	7–15	1½	INA	INA

Source: Club websites and ticket offices (data correct at 28 February 2003)
Note: INA = information not available

Looking at the national situation for horse racing shows average crowds relatively static over the last decade (approx. 5,000 per meeting). This compares badly with soccer and cricket but is reasonable when compared to rugby union and ice hockey. Indeed, horse racing is typically listed as the 15th most popular spectator sport in the UK behind sports such as soccer, athletics, snooker and cricket. The typical horse racing fan is male, lower income and from an older age group.

A clue to increasing attendance at horse racing meetings is the number of TV spec-tators that the sport attracts. Horse racing is typically the second most televised sport in the UK with over 3,500 hours of coverage per year (the number 1 is soccer with significantly more hours than this figure). Looking at the UK population as a whole, shows that in the region of 15% of the population attend race meetings, about half this figure watch the sport regularly on TV and almost 25% watch the sport occasionally on TV. The question for courses such as Nottingham is, how can the occasional TV spectator be persuaded to attend race meetings?

Discussion questions

6. What are the key factors affecting NRC and horse racing in general?

7. What approaches could NRC consider to build its attendance and sales?

8. How could occasional TV spectators of horse racing be persuaded to attend race meetings?

9. Construct a reasoned sport marketing plan for NRC.

Conclusion

This chapter has shown that sport marketing fundamentally concerns the satisfaction of sport customer needs with sport offerings that provide benefits in excess of all other sports or pastimes that compete for the customer's time and money. Sport fans' needs and benefits were identified as being quite diverse and hence, customer satisfaction can only realistically be achieved amongst a subset of the market, that is, only certain customers will be predisposed towards a given sport, team or player. In order to achieve customer satisfaction it is necessary for the sport marketer to carry out a detailed analysis of the customer and broader marketing environment to allow for all the key issues to be screened and analysed. The data gathered in the customer audit allows a detailed profile of fans to be compiled and the resultant profile to provide general guidance on the key marketing tasks. Key parts of this profile include geographic, demographic and behavioural factors, all of which allow the marketer to understand the customer and, hence, to design a marketing offering that should be acceptable.

Once the marketer has researched and analysed the operating environment, it is necessary for an approach to that environment to be formulated. Formulation of this approach requires the sport marketer to adopt the operational marketing planning process including further analysis of the audit data such that the marketer (and company) can select the most appropriate and realistic objectives. Given that objectives set the framework for strategy development, it is vitally important that they are correct. The SMART mnemonic is a useful one in this respect as it details the criteria for successful objective setting. Of these five criteria, it can be argued that 'realistic' is the most important to the marketer, as an unrealistic objective will either be very difficult to achieve and hence will demotivate employees or will be too easy to achieve and so will also demotivate.

On completion of the objectives development, the marketer must plan out the actions required to take the company from its current position to that detailed by the objectives. These actions include tactics that can be individually formulated, but must be collectively considered, as consistency is vital. Implementation, or the act of turning thinking and analysis into reality, is the next stage and it is here that the marketer really earns his or her money. This move from thought into reality brings with it uncertainty and hence it is necessary to consider the control process or a series of short-term targets against which performance is assessed. Collection of data to test performance against these targets leads to a detailed knowledge of the reasons for success or failure, which can be used to take the appropriate corrective action to ensure success in the future.

As a final thought, it is essential that the sport marketer is always aware of what he or she is trying to do. Numerous marketing failures can be traced back to a lack of consideration of the core function of sport marketing, namely:

> The fundamental aim of the sport marketing activity is to satisfy the right sport customer needs with sport products or services that offer benefits in excess of all other competitor offerings whilst making the maximum sustainable profit.

CASE 6.4 Design's great leap forward FT

If the words 'Nike' and 'brand' are virtually inseparable, it is down to one man, Phil Knight. But while he may not have run his last race for the company he set up 30 years ago, the signs are that Knight could soon join the bench. In March last year he anointed two co-presidents who now effectively call the shots day-to-day. And if having two 'number twos' is not unusual enough, one of them is a creative.

As president, Nike brand, Mark Parker is now in charge of the entire global product and brand management of Nike – a fitting promotion for a man who spent his formative years as a footwear designer. While his counterpart, Charlie Denson, focuses on distribution, Parker runs product development, his new status testament to the growing importance played by design in Nike's fortunes.

Parker, the man that invented the cross-trainer, is leading a charge to secure Nike's future by going back to basics. While Nike has long had a reputation for its design, it was accused of losing its way by focusing on marketing and treating its product as a commodity.

During the mid-1980s, Knight turned Nike into what he dubbed a 'marketing-oriented company'. The novel idea was to focus on the promotion of wares, rather than on their production; design was somewhat relegated in all the euphoria.

The move into marketing enabled Nike to shrug off its revenue stall of 1987 and achieve meteoric gains. But after racking up record sales of $9.5 billion for its 1998 fiscal year, revenues fell to $8.8 billion in the next. Knight spent millions on Michael Jordan endorsements, but once Jordan's stardom faded, Nike was left wondering what it could do next.

Finding growth since has not been easy, particularly in its domestic market, and Parker's role is to do just that.

'Phil Knight once said "we are a marketing company and our greatest marketing tool is our product",' says Parker. 'But I would say we are as much a design and product-led company as we are anything. The way we work is that marketing comes into design and asks, "what's going on, what's interesting?" Design leads the company. I think that's incredibly rare, not just in our business, but in any business.'

Many businesses might find it hard to employ a 'creative' in such a top role, but the word in Nike's hometown of Portland, Oregon, is that there is definitely a sense that Parker can deliver for Nike.

'When the announcement about Mark Parker's promotion was made over a year ago, the reaction was very favourable,' says Teresa Meyer, analyst at DA Davidson in Portland. 'The buzz is certainly that this is a very positive step for Nike.'

Parker was born in Poughkeepsie, New York, in 1955. He graduated in political science from Pennsylvania State University, and joined Nike's design division in 1979. He rose through the ranks to become director of footwear design and then general manager for global footwear.

Under his auspices, the marketing-led company of old is now celebrating design again with creations such as the Kukini triathlon shoe (out next year), and the Portable Sport Audio MP3 player. It is probably no coincidence that the creatives at Nike headquarters recently regrouped under a single roof.

Outsiders agree that there has been a visible shift to design at Nike, something traced back to the demise of the Air Jordan 'marketing juggernaut'.

'The trend back towards design has probably been the more critical issue (for the brand) in the last few years. Nike has always been a marketing powerhouse first and foremost, but the last three or four years have been different,' says RBC Capital Markets equity research analyst, Bob Toomey. Under Parker, Nike is putting its innovation expertise to work not just for today's footwear, apparel and equipment businesses, but also for its categories of the future. He knows that the challenge facing Nike is to keep applying its skills of re-invention to the way the brand is perceived by its public, creating new connections and extending its reach.

The strategy, he says, is not simply about selling more and more units, it is about inventing new products and finding new places to take the brand: 'The future for us isn't going to be, hey, here's better shoes, better apparel, better product. Its going to be a lot more dimensionalised than that.'

One potential new dimension is selling services. Parker says Nike is beginning to explore the viability of selling on-brand services in areas like sports coaching or information. Such a move would not only fit Nike's brand position but, given its access to the top minds and methodologies in sport, it could make solid strategic sense for the business, too.

'We are definitely looking at (selling services), but we need to pace ourselves to the point where we do what we do well. The worst thing that we can do is to get into something new and not commit,' he says.

Then there are brand extensions like events. Not long ago, Nike was tipped to be extending its sponsorship of athletes into event sponsorship. But while small initiatives like its successful 'Run London' race have promoted the brand in a more emotional context, it remains to be seen whether the Nike marque will be applied to major sporting events. 'We're not going to launch heavily into the events business, but I think we will definitely scour that service area as another way for Nike to help people to experience athletics or be active,' Parker says.

And then there is the personalisation of products. 'One of the things I've been dealing with a lot lately is the growth of customisation and the personalisation of products and services,' Parkers says. 'This is going to be a bigger and bigger part of our future. It's currently one of the higher priority items of our advanced research and development area.'

Aside from developing concepts to rejuvenate existing lines such as shoes, equipment and clothing, Parker's aim now is to devote time and resources to tomorrow's game plan. For this he has set up a crack team called the 'explore group'.

'The explore group is way out there in what we call "deep space". It's a small group of Green Beret–Navy Seal-type operatives who are really big thinkers. And they are supported by a network of some of the most leading-edge technology specialists out there. We don't talk a lot about this, but it's a big deal,' Parker says.

'Together with the Massachusetts Institute of Technology, Nasa and digital companies like Philips, they are exploring things like smart products that can feed into networks,' he continues. 'One of the biggest items on their agenda is customisation and personalisation.'

Parker sees a future for Nike in which, through personalisation, customisation and service, Nike's product becomes more dynamic and more integrated with technology. And though the question of Phil Knight's succession is not clear, maybe it takes a creative to believe that there are places the brand can go that have not yet even been imagined.

Source: Michael Exon, *Financial Times*, 3 December 2002

Discussion questions

10. What does Nike contribute to the sport industry, should the company be seen as a marketing friend or a marketing foe, and what lessons can sport managers learn about marketing from the company?

11. If Nike becomes involved in selling services such as sports coaching, would you, as the manager of another business in the sport industry, see this as the inevitable development of a powerful global brand signalling the end of your business? Or would you be more optimistic and see this as an opportunity for the development of your business? Discuss, indicating how different sport businesses might respond to the commercial challenges this might pose.

Guided reading

For further details on the content covered in this chapter read the following books:

Adcock, D., Halborg, A. and Ross, C. (2001), 4th edn, *Marketing Principles and Practice*, Financial Times Management, Harlow.

Blackwell, R.D., Miniard, P.W. and Engel, J.F. (2001) *Consumer Behaviour*, Harcourt, Orlando.

Jobber, D. (2001) *Principles and Practice of Marketing*, McGraw-Hill, Maidenhead.
The following articles add extra detail in specific areas:

Bradish, C. and Lathrop, A.H. (2001) 'Girl power: examining the female pre-teen as a distinct segment of the sport marketplace', *Sport Marketing Quarterly*, 10(1), pp. 19–25.

Fink, J.S., Galen, T.T. and Anderson, D.F. (2002) 'Environmental factors associated with spectator attendance and sport consumption behaviour: gender and team differences', *Sport Marketing Quarterly*, 11(1), pp. 8–19.

Hopkinson, G.C. and Pujari, D. (1999), 'A factor analytic study of the sources of meaning in hedonic consumption', *European Journal of Marketing*, 33(3/4), pp. 273–90.

Kwon, H.H. and Armstrong, K.L. (2002) 'Factors influencing impulse buying of sport team licensed merchandise', *Sport Marketing Quarterly*, 11(3), pp. 151–63.

Mason, D.S. (1999) 'What is it the sports product and who buys it? The marketing of professional sports leagues', *European Journal of Marketing*, 33(3/4), pp. 402–18.

McDonald, M.A., Milne, G.R. and Hong, J. (2002) 'Motivational factors for evaluating sport spectator and participant markets', *Sports Marketing Quarterly*, 11(2), pp. 100–13.

Real, M.R. and Mechikoff, R.A. (1992) 'Deep fan: mythic identification, technology and advertising to spectator sports', *Sociology of Sport Journal*, 9, pp. 323–39.

Recommended websites

The Olympic Marketing Structure: http://www.olympic.org/uk/organisation/facts/structure/index_uk.asp

The *Sports Journal* (published by the United States Sports Academy: http://www.thesportjournal.org

The Australian Sports Commission's website on Sports Administration, Marketing and Sponsorship: http://www.ausport.gov.au/info/administration.htm

Visit www.booksites.net/chadwickbeech for links to these and other relevant websites.

Keywords

Behavioural factors; benefits; demographic factors; devoted fan; dysfunctional fan; fanatical fan; geographic factors; local fan; needs; operational sport marketing; quality; sport marketing plan; temporary fan.

Bibliography

Cobb, C.J. and Hoyer, W.D. (1986) 'Planned versus impulse purchase behavior', *Journal of Retailing*, 62(4), pp. 384–409.

Hunt, K.D., Bristol, T. and Bashaw, R.E. (1999) 'A conceptual approach to classifying sports fans', *Journal of Services Marketing*, 13(6), pp. 439–52.

Martineau, P. (1958) 'The Personality of the retail store', *Harvard Business Review*, 36, pp. 47–55.

Maslow, A.H. (1943) 'A theory of human motivation', *Psychological Review*, July, pp. 370–96.

Maslow, A.H. (1968) *Toward a Psychology of Being* (2nd edn), Van Nostrand, New York.

Maslow, A.H. (1970) *Motivation and personality*, Harper and Row, New York

Sullivan, M. (2003) 'Consumer attitudes towards sport marketing', unpublished paper.

Chapter 7

Sports finance

Bill Gerrard
Leeds University Business School

Upon completion of this chapter the reader should be able to:

■ interpret the behaviour of sports organisations as value creators;

■ understand the relevance of the study of financial management for sports organisations;

■ calculate financial value as the present value of expected future cash flows;

■ use company accounts to analyse the financial performance of sports organisations;

■ apply discounted cash flow (DCF) analysis to investment decisions in sports organisations;

■ estimate the corporate value of sports businesses;

■ determine the appropriate mix of debt and equity for the long-term financing of sports businesses;

■ understand the key drivers of share prices of publicly-traded sports businesses.

Overview

This chapter provides an introduction to the use of financial management techniques within sports organisations, broadly defined to include all organisations involved in the provision of participant and spectator sports. The chapter begins with a definition of the subject matter of sports finance leading on to the notion of sports organisations as engaged in the creation of value. The concept of financial value as the present value of expected future cash flows is introduced. The structure of financial statements is explained with the emphasis on how to use company accounts to analyse the financial performance of sports organisations. Attention then focuses on two particular valuation problems: how sports organisations should use DCF analysis to value potential investment projects; and how corporate valuation techniques can be applied to determine the value of sports businesses. This is followed by an examination of the factors influencing the optimal mix of long-term financing for sports businesses. This leads on to a discussion of how stock markets determine the values of publicly-traded sports businesses. A case study on the recent financial performance of a leading English football club, Leeds United, is developed to illustrate the application of financial analysis to a sports organisation in crisis. The chapter concludes with some suggested future directions for sports finance.

Introduction: the study of sports finance

There is a huge variety of sports (and sports-related) organisations operating within the sports industry. Sports organisations include the direct providers of participation or spectator sports opportunities as well as the support providers supplying the multitude of ancillary goods and services required by sports organisations and their users/customers. Sports organisations may be large profit-seeking businesses or publicly-funded bodies or member clubs. Whatever their size, structure and function, all sports organisations require financial management. The aim of this chapter is to provide a basic understanding of financial management and its application to sports and sports-related organisations.

The subject of sports finance can be defined as *the study of the effective management of cash flows by sports organisations in pursuit of their organisational objectives*. This definition of sports finance highlights the four key aspects of the subject.

First, it is a management subject concerned with the effective operation of sports organisations. As such it is a sub-field of sport management, an inter-disciplinary subject that draws on a variety of parent disciplines such as organisational behaviour, corporate strategy, marketing, human resource management, economics and finance in order to understand the behaviour of sports organisations.

Second, the focus on effective management implies that the subject has both positive and normative aspects dealing with not only 'what is' but also 'what ought to be'. Sports finance is *descriptive* of the financial behaviour of sports organisations. Sports finance is also *explanatory*, seeking to understand the causal processes determining the financial behaviour of sports organisations through the application of the scientific method of proposing theoretical hypotheses and testing their validity through confrontation with empirical evidence. But, importantly, sports finance is also *prescriptive* in that it should provide an important input into the decision-making process within sports organisations, helping to identify the most appropriate course of action in any decision situation.

The third key aspect of sports finance is its concern with cash flows. Sports finance is the study of cash flows in sports organisations. 'Cash is king.' Whether the sports organisation is a large-scale profit-seeking business or a small community-based not-for-profit user group, its activities will involve the flow of cash into and out of the organisation. The survival of any sports organisation ultimately depends on ensuring that it can maintain positive net cash flows.

The final key aspect of sports finance is its coverage. Sports finance deals with financial management in all types of sports organisations. Inevitably sports finance has tended to concentrate on professional team sports as the most high-profile and most commercialised aspect of the sports industry. But sports finance is relevant to all forms of sports organisations. All sports organisations have organisational objectives and must manage their cash flows effectively in pursuit of these objectives. Knowledge of financial management techniques is essential for managers in all sports organisations, not just those engaged in the running of elite spectator sports. Sound finance is a necessary prerequisite for the successful operation of all sports organisations.

The financial structure of all sports organisations can be broken down into four components: capital employed, assets, operating cash flows and return to capital employed.

1. *Capital employed*: All sports organisations require capital to provide long-term financing to support the asset base of the organisation. There are two broad types of long-term financing: debt and equity. Debt includes bank loans and other borrowings. Equity is the capital provided by the owners of the organisation and confers rights to any residual income after all other financial obligations have been met in full.
2. *Assets*: Sports organisations use their capital employed to purchase the assets required for their operating activities. The assets of an organisation may include tangible assets such as land and buildings as well as machinery and equipment. In addition sports organisations may have intangible assets such as, for example, player registrations that give a professional sports team exclusive rights to the use of a player's playing talent.
3. *Operating cash flows*: Operating cash flows are the revenues and cash expenses generated by a sports organisation's operating activities. Revenues will be generated by the sale of goods and services to the organisation's users/customers. Cash expenses are the running costs of the organisation's operations, and include the purchase of raw materials, intermediate goods and other supplies, as well as the payroll costs of the organisation's employees.
4. *Return to capital employed*: Providers of long-term finance require to be compensated for the use of their capital. The return paid to capital providers must reflect the *opportunity cost* of the forgone alternative investment opportunities. Return to capital employed will include a risk premium as compensation for any risk of loss faced by the capital providers. Debt providers receive a return in the form of interest payments. Equity providers in profit-seeking organisations will receive a return in the form of dividend payments and, possibly, through appreciation of the capital value of their equity investment.

The overall cash flow of a sports organisation can be separated into six constituent cash flows linked to the different components of the organisation's financial structure:

1. *Operating activities*: As discussed above, a sports organisation's operating activities generate operating cash flows consisting of revenues and cash expenses.
2. *Non-operating investments*: As well as investing in real assets to support its own operating activities, a sports organisation may have financial investments in other businesses in the form of equity and commercial bonds that generate cash returns but do not involve any direct operating responsibilities.
3. *Financing*: A sports organisation may require periodically to raise new debt and equity for a variety of purposes including the provision of finance for further investment in real assets. In addition, existing debt will become due for repayment. Cash flows associated with new issues and retirement of debt and equity constitute financing cash flows.

4. *Investment*: Cash flows generated by the purchase and sale of fixed and financial assets are referred to as investment cash flows.
5. *Taxation*: Profit-making sports businesses are liable for the payment of corporate taxes on any net profits earned.
6. *Servicing of finance*: A sports organisation is required to service its debt and equity. Servicing (or distribution) cash flows include interest payments on debt and, in the case of profit-making sports businesses, dividends paid to shareholders.

Effective financial management of a sports organisation's cash flows in order to attain the organisational objectives has two distinct functions.

First, there is a *planning* function based on expected future cash flows. Financial planning involves investment (and divestment) decisions on the optimal composition of the organisation's portfolio of real assets along with the consequent financing decisions. Planning is necessarily forward-looking and requires valuation of alternative investment opportunities.

The second function of financial management is *reporting*. A sports organisation must record and communicate its financial performance. In addition, the organisation must evaluate its financial performance using appropriate internal targets and external benchmarks. The evaluation of its performance may in turn lead to revisions of its future investment plans.

Value in sports organisations

The basic behavioural hypothesis in sports finance is that the fundamental objective of a sports organisation is to maximise organisational value. This organisational objective encompasses both profit-seeking sports businesses and not-for-profit sports organisations. All sports organisations should be attempting to maximise their *potential value surplus* defined as *total user value net of resource cost*. Total user value is measured as the total private willingness to pay (WTP) by the users/customers for the goods and services provided by a sports organisation. However, from the perspective of society as a whole, total user value should also include the value of any positive externalities (benefits) to non-users/customers. Resource cost is measured as the private organisational costs of producing the goods and services including the costs of raw materials and other intermediate goods, wages, overheads and the cost of capital. Again, from the perspective of society as a whole, resource cost should also include any negative externalities to non-users/customers.

The operational definition of organisational value depends on the specific objectives of a sports organisation. Organisational objectives depend on the nature of the organisation's governance structures and processes. Ownership and control in sports organisations vary from member clubs to publicly-funded bodies and privately-owned corporate businesses. Publicly-funded sports bodies tend to have a very wide definition of user value and resource cost that includes the private and social, as well as financial and non-financial costs and benefits of their activities. Sports businesses, on the other hand, are likely to be concerned primarily with revenues and financial costs, with social costs and benefits given only secondary consideration, often as a result of regulatory requirements to recognise corporate social responsibility.

Profit-seeking sports businesses are assumed to be attempting to maximise corporate value defined as the *present value of expected future surplus cash flows*. Value creation (generating a potential value surplus) is a necessary but not sufficient condition for the creation of corporate value. The sport business must capture a share of the potential value surplus. This requires a *sustainable competitive advantage* that allows the sports business to appropriate exclusive or principal benefit of the created value. There are two principal sources of competitive advantage. The *external* source of competitive advantage is the market structure within which the business operates. Strategic analysis frameworks such as the structure–conduct–performance paradigm and Porter's five-forces model focus on the external context, highlighting the determinants of market power and the positioning of the business relative to its competitors. By contrast, the resource-based view and operational effectiveness approaches concentrate on the *internal* context as the source of competitive advantage, emphasising the capabilities of the business.

The conventional view of sports businesses is that their fundamental corporate objective is the *maximisation of shareholder value*. Shareholder value is defined as the *present value of the expected future dividend stream*. From this perspective, sports businesses are viewed as seeking to generate value for their owners, the shareholders, by maximising profits after tax that are either distributed by dividend payments or retained within the business to finance further value-creating growth. The conventional view is closely associated with *the principal–agent theory of the firm*. In the modern firm there is a separation between ownership and control. The shareholders own but management controls the day-to-day operations of the firm. The principal–agent theory views the shareholders as the principal and the management as the agents. Inevitably the separation of ownership and control creates a potential problem if there is goal divergence between the management and shareholders. The principal–agent problem relates to how the principals can ensure goal congruence such that their agents pursue appropriate objectives. In the case of shareholders, the principal–agent problem is how to ensure that the firm's management seeks to maximise shareholder value. This principal–agent problem is exacerbated by an *asymmetric information problem* in that the management has much more detailed information about the firm's performance than the shareholders and, indeed, the management controls the public disclosure of information. Firms can attempt to resolve the principal–agent problem by better monitoring of firm performance and/or improved incentives to maximise shareholder value through performance-related pay, such as share options and bonuses based on share-price performance. Financial reporting and corporate governance regulations are also intended to improve the relationship between shareholders and management by setting standards for the disclosure of financial information and good governance practice. The discretion for management to pursue goals other than the maximisation of shareholder value is limited by the ultimate shareholder sanction of replacing the current management team. Shareholders can exercise this sanction either directly through their power to elect and dismiss the board of directors or indirectly by the threat of takeover through their right to sell shares to another, potentially hostile, party.

An alternative perspective on the behaviour of sports businesses is provided by *stakeholder theory of the firm*. From this perspective, the firm is seen as managing a set of stakeholder relationships involving users/customers, owners, employees, suppliers and the wider community. The distribution of corporate value becomes a crucial strategic-political decision. This creates a possible divergence between shareholder value and corporate value to the extent to which some of the captured value surplus is distributed to stakeholders other than the shareholders.

It is important to remember that corporate value is always relative. The business process is necessarily relative in that competitive advantage exists relative to other competing businesses. Shareholder value, as will be shown later, is measured relative to an appropriate cost-of-capital benchmark. It is the marginal firm in a contestable market earning just enough profit to survive that provides the benchmark for measuring competitive advantage and corporate/shareholder value.

The valuation of assets depends on the expected future stream of returns. Hence valuation is always forward-looking. Information about past returns only affects valuations indirectly by influencing expectations of future returns. Valuations are always dependent on the underlying assumptions about an uncertain future. It is, therefore, important to engage in 'assumption-busting' to test the sensitivity of valuations and business/financial decisions to specific assumptions. This is the role of risk management techniques such as scenario analysis and Monte Carlo simulations. Sports organisations must avoid a passive approach to management often engendered by financial analysis. Performance must be continually monitored with feedback into future planning cycles. In a very fundamental sense, *finance should be largely irrelevant.* Organisational value ultimately depends on an organisation's decisions to acquire a particular set of assets and to undertake particular operating activities. The financial structure of a sports organisation is a secondary consideration with no fundamental impact on organisational value. In the context of profit-seeking sports businesses, the financing decision on the appropriate mix of debt and equity has only a second-order impact on corporate value arising from tax effects and information problems. The corporate value of a sports business primarily depends on its business model and investment decisions. Indeed, it is often the case that when financial matters take precedence in a sports organisation it is indicative of a serious organisational failure. Hence it is always important to keep financial matters in a proper perspective. Sound finance has a necessary supporting role for any successful sports organisation but sound finance alone cannot generate organisational value.

Measuring financial value

The financial value of an asset is the *present value of the expected future net cash flows* to be generated by holding or using that asset. In order to calculate the financial value of an asset, future cash flows have to be projected and discounted by the time value of money. This valuation procedure is known as discounted cash flow (DCF) analysis. DCF analysis is applicable to financial assets such as bonds and annuities, and real assets, both individual investment projects as well as the corporate valuation of a complete company portfolio of assets.

Apart from magnitude, the net cash flows generated by different assets vary in their time profile and riskiness. Some assets, such as Treasury Bills, may generate returns over a relatively short period with little risk attached. Other assets, such as shares in new start-up ventures, may be very high risk with little or no dividend payments expected in the foreseeable future. Hence, in order to compare alternative asset investment opportunities, it is necessary to use a standardised valuation metric that takes account of differences in time profile and riskiness. This standardised metric is provided by *present value* defined as cash flow discounted by the *time value of money*. The time value of money represents the minimum return required by the asset holder in order to continue holding or using the asset. The asset holder requires to be compensated for delay, risk and inflation. The required return for delay is known as the *'pure' time value of money* or the risk-free rate of return and reflects the compensation required for having to wait for a future cash flow. The required return for risk is known as the *risk premium* and represents the compensation to risk-averse investors for the risk that future cash flows may be less than expected. The time value of money must also include an *inflation premium* to compensate asset holders for any loss in the purchasing power of future cash flows if there is a general rise in prices in the intervening period.

The concept of present value is best understood as the inverse of future value. The future value of an asset is the value at some specified future date calculated on the basis that returns are reinvested and earn the same rate of return. Formally, future value is defined as:

$$FV = C_0(1 + r)^t \tag{7.1}$$

The future value, FV, is defined as the value of an initial cash investment, C_0, after t periods at a compound interest rate, r.

Present value is the inverse of future value. Whereas future value is compounding value forward to a future date, present value is discounting value backward to the current date. Formally, present value is defined as:

$$PV = \frac{C_t}{(1 + r)^t} \tag{7.2}$$

The present value, PV, is defined as the value of a future cash flow, C_t, to be received after t periods discounted using a discount rate, r. The term, $1/(1 + r)^t$, is often referred to as the *discount factor*.

Present value can be easily extended to allow for multiple future cash flows.

$$PV = \frac{C_1}{1 + r} + \frac{C_2}{(1 + r)^2} + \dots + \frac{C_n}{(1 + r)^n} \tag{7.3}$$

The present value of a set of multiple future cash flows is the summation of the present value of each component cash flow, C_1, C_2, ..., up to the time horizon, n.

For simplicity, it is assumed that the discount rate is constant over the whole time period. However, it is quite straightforward to extend the definition of present value to allow for period-specific discount rates, r_1, r_2, ..., and so on.

$$PV = \frac{C_1}{1 + r_1} + \frac{C_2}{(1 + r_1)(1 + r_2)} + \dots + \frac{C_n}{(1 + r_1)(1 + r_2)\dots(1 + r_n)} \tag{7.4}$$

Exhibit 7.1	Worked example 1: Purchasing new equipment

Suppose that a sports club wishes to purchase new equipment costing £7,750. As an alternative to immediate full cash payment, the supplier offers a deferred payment schedule over the next two years with an immediate payment of £4,000 followed by two end-of-year payments of £2,000.

If the sports club uses an annual discount rate of 8 per cent, should it accept the supplier's offer of deferred payment?

Solution

PV(Deferred Payment) $= PV(C_0) + PV(C_1) + PV(C_2)$

$PV(C_0) = £4,000$

$PV(C_1) = £2,000/(1 + 0.08)^1 = £1,851.85$

$PV(C_2) = £2,000/(1 + 0.08)^2 = £1,714.68$

PV(Deferred Payment) $= £7,566.53$

Decision: The sports club should accept the supplier's offer of deferred payment since the present value of deferred payment is less than the immediate full cash payment.

Rationale: If the sports club has a cash sum of £7,750, it would better off paying £4,000 to the supplier and investing the balance to earn an annual return of 8 per cent. After paying the two further end-of-year instalments, the sports club would have earned a surplus of £214. (Note: the surplus after two years is calculated as the future value of the difference between the present values of the two alternative payment options.)

The present value methodology of DCF analysis can be applied to the valuation of any individual financial or real asset or portfolio of such assets. The calculation is very straightforward. The practical difficulties arise in projecting future cash flows, and/or determining the appropriate discount rate to use, to reflect delay, risk and inflation. There are two very widely used present value formulae for valuing perpetuities and annuities with applications beyond just valuing specific types of financial assets. A perpetuity is an asset that provides a regular stream of fixed cash flows in perpetuity. An annuity is an asset that provides a regular stream of fixed cash flows for a limited period of time. The present value of a perpetuity is defined as:

$$PV \ (Perpetuity) = \frac{C}{r} \tag{7.5}$$

where C is the fixed cash flow received at the end of the first period onwards in perpetuity and r is the constant discount rate.

The present value of an annuity is defined as:

$$PV \ (Annuity) = C\left[\frac{1}{r} - \frac{1}{r(1+r)^t}\right] \tag{7.6}$$

where C is the fixed cash flow to be received at the end of the first period onwards for t periods of time, and r is the constant discount rate.

Evaluating financial performance

The evaluation of financial performance requires the proper understanding and careful interpretation of *accounting information*. There are three roles for accounting within a sports organisation:

- *identifying* the key financial information in the organisation;
- *measuring* financial values in a true and fair manner;
- *communicating* financial information to allow informed judgements by users both within and outside the organisation.

There are two broad types of accounting information. *Financial accounting* is concerned with the recording and reporting of financial transactions for external needs. *Management accounting* involves the provision of financial information for internal planning and decision-making. It is important to recognise the differences between the type of information produced by financial accounting and that required for financial management. Financial accounting is a backward-looking process of recording and reporting known financial outcomes. The emphasis is on profit with assets and liabilities measured in terms of book value based on historic costs. By contrast, financial management is a forward-looking process of planned and uncertain future resource allocation. Financial management emphasises cash flows, not profits, and measures the current market value, not book value, of assets and liabilities on the basis of the present value of expected future net cash flows. Financial management necessarily utilises financial accounting information but only inasmuch as past outcomes provide a starting point for future expectations.

Financial statements

Financial statements consist of three components: the *profit and loss account* (or income statement), the *balance sheet* and the *cash flow statement*.

The profit and loss account reports the calculation of an organisation's profit for a specified reporting period. The basic format of the profit and loss account is given in Exhibit 7.2, where operating profit is defined as profit before interest, tax, depreciation and amortisation (PBITDA) and net profit is defined as profit before interest and tax (PBIT).

Exhibit 7.2	Profit and loss account
	Sales revenue
minus	Cost of sales
equals	Gross profit
minus	Operating expenses
equals	Operating profit (or PBITDA)
minus	Depreciation and amortisation
equals	Net profit (or PBIT)
minus	Net interest paid
equals	Profit before tax
minus	Tax
equals	Profit after tax (PAT)
minus	Dividends
equals	Retained profit

The balance sheet provides a statement of the assets and liabilities of an organisation at the end of the reporting period. The basic balance-sheet identities can be stated formally as:

Total Assets = Current Assets + Fixed Assets   (7.7a)

Total Liabilities = Current Liabilities + Long-term Liabilities   (7.7b)

Total Assets = Total Liabilities + Shareholders' Funds   (7.7c)

Current assets include stocks of unsold goods, trade debtors, cash and short-term financial instruments. Fixed assets include both *tangible assets* such as land, buildings and equipment, as well as *intangible (i.e. non-physical) assets* such as goodwill, trademarks, and player registrations. Current liabilities include trade creditors, short-term debt and tax liabilities due within the next 12 months. Long-term liabilities include bank loans and other borrowings and long-term obligations that are repayable in more than 12 months. Shareholders' funds consist of the funds raised from the initial and subsequent sales of equity plus cumulative retained profits (or losses) plus any profit from any upward revaluation of the organisation's assets.

The balance-sheet identities can be rearranged as:

Net Current Assets = Current Assets – Current Liabilities   (7.8a)

Capital Employed = Long-term Liabilities + Shareholders' Funds   (7.8b)

Net Current Assets + Fixed Assets = Capital Employed   (7.8c)

The cash flow statement shows the cash flows during the reporting period. As previously discussed, an organisation's net cash flow can be separated into six constituent cash flows:

- Net cash flow from operating activities (or operating cash flow, OCF)
- Net cash flow from non-operating activities
- Net cash flow from investment activities
- Net cash flow from financing
- Net cash flow from taxation
- Net cash flow from servicing of finance

The cash flow statement also typically includes a reconciliation of the cash flow statement with the profit and loss account. This reconciliation is required because the net profit generated from operating activities (i.e. PBIT) differs from the OCF. The profit and loss account is calculated on an 'accruals' or 'matching' basis. The profit and loss account reports sales (rather than cash receipts) and matching costs (not cash payments) that are properly attributed to the reported sales. One example of this matching principle is the *depreciation* charge. Depreciation is a non-cash charge allocating the net cash cost of a fixed asset over its economic life. Hence, in the profit and loss account, the cost of purchasing a new machine is spread over the whole useful life of the machine. In the cash flow statement the cash payment for the new machine shows up as part of the net cash flow from investing activities at the time the machine is purchased. Formally:

OCF = PBIT + Non-cash Expenses – Changes in Working Capital   (7.9a)

Working Capital = Stocks + Trade Debtors − Trade Creditors   (7.9b)

Care must be exercised when analysing the balance sheet of an organisation. The balance sheet records the book values of assets and liabilities, not their current market values. Book values are backward-looking based on the value at the time of acquisition. The book value of fixed assets shows the historic cost of the assets net of the cumulative depreciation charge. By contrast, market values are forward-looking with current sell-on values based on expected future returns.

Financial ratio analysis

Financial ratio analysis involves the calculation of selected ratios using the financial information provided in financial statements. It is a very convenient means of summarising and evaluating a large volume of information. Financial ratio analysis is useful for both external and internal evaluation of organisational performance as well as for setting targets for future performance. But financial ratio analysis is only a starting point that often helps ask the right questions by highlighting key aspects of organisational performance. Financial ratio analysis is largely descriptive. On its own it offers little by the way of explanatory or prescriptive content.

There is a very wide range of financial ratios covering all aspects of an organisation's financial performance. These financial ratios can be usefully categorised into five groups: profitability, asset efficiency, liquidity, financing and market value. The most frequently used financial ratios are defined and calculated in the worked example later in this section (Exhibit 7.3). For profit-seeking sports businesses, profitability ratios are a key set of financial ratios. Profitability ratios are calculated either as profit margins on sales revenue or as asset rates of return:

Gross Profit Margin = Gross Profit/Revenue   (7.10a)

Operating Profit Margin = PBITDA/Revenue   (7.10b)

Net Profit Margin = PBIT/Revenue   (7.10c)

Return on Assets (ROA) = PBIT/Total Assets   (7.10d)

Return on Capital Employed (ROCE) = PBIT/Capital Employed   (7.10e)

Return on Equity = PAT/Shareholders' Funds   (7.10f)

It should be noted that it is quite common to calculate net profit margin, ROA and ROCE using PBIT net of tax.

Financial ratios can be decomposed into constituent components as a guide for further analysis. For example, ROCE can be decomposed into two constituent ratios: the net profit margin and asset turnover:

$$\text{ROCE} = \frac{\text{PBIT}}{\text{Capital Employed}} = \frac{\text{PBIT}}{\text{Revenue}} \times \frac{\text{Revenue}}{\text{Capital Employed}}$$

$$\text{where } \frac{\text{PBIT}}{\text{Revenue}} \equiv \text{Net Profit Margin}$$

$$\text{and } \frac{\text{Revenue}}{\text{Capital Employed}} \equiv \text{Asset Turnover} \qquad (7.11)$$

The net profit margin can be interpreted as an indicator of operating-cost efficiency (i.e. the ability to generate net profit from sales revenue). Asset turnover is an indicator of marketing efficiency (i.e. the ability to generate sales revenue from the asset base). Using this decomposition of ROCE, it is possible to begin to identify the possible causes of any change in the profitability of a business.

Several important points must be borne in mind when calculating and interpreting financial ratios. First, financial ratios are meaningless in isolation and must always be benchmarked against pre-determined targets, previous years, similar organisations and/or industry/sector norms. Second, the specific definitions of the quoted ratios should be clarified in order to allow meaningful comparisons. Third, care should be taken to minimise the effects of differences in accounting policies over time and between organisations. Finally, financial ratios in any single year may be distorted by one-off extraordinary items. It is important to be aware of such distortions.

Exhibit 7.3   **Worked example 2: Sporting Apparatus plc**

The following financial information has been extracted from the company accounts of Sporting Apparatus plc, a medium-sized, publicly-listed sports equipment manufacturer based in the United Kingdom.

Using relevant financial ratios, comment on the financial performance of Sporting Apparatus in 2001 and 2002.

Profit and loss account for year ended December 31

	2002 (£000)	2001 (£000)
Revenue	5,700	5,300
Cost of sales	4,330	4,000
Gross profit	1,370	1,300
Operating expenses	520	420
Operating profit	850	880
Depreciation	215	200
Net profit	635	680
Interest	220	190
Profit before tax	415	490
Tax	175	125
Profit after tax	240	365
Preference dividends	90	90
Ordinary dividends	140	140
Retained profits	10	135

Balance sheet as at December 31

	2002 (£000)	2001 (£000)
Fixed assets	5,405	4,880
Current assets:		
Stock	900	880
Debtors	460	460
Cash	5	60
	1,365	1,400

Creditors due within one year:		
Trade creditors	425	190
Bank	0	800
Taxation	155	110
Dividends	<u>230</u>	<u>230</u>
	810	1,330
Creditors due after one year:		
Debentures	1,100	1,100
Bank loan	<u>1,000</u>	<u>0</u>
	2,100	1,100
Capital and reserves:		
Share capital:		
Ordinary, 100 pence	1,500	1,500
Preference, 100 pence	1,000	1,000
Share premium	500	500
Reserves	<u>860</u>	<u>850</u>
	3,860	3,850
Ordinary share price (pence):	135	220

Solution

Ratios	Definition	2002	2001
<u>Profitability Ratios</u>			
Gross profit margin	Gross Profit/Revenue	24.04%	24.53%
Net profit margin	Net Profit/Revenue	11.14%	12.83%
ROA	Net Profit/Total Assets	9.38%	10.83%
ROCE	Net Profit/Capital Employed	10.65%	13.74%
ROE	(Profit After Tax − Preference Dividends)/ (Shareholders' Funds − Preference Shares)	5.24%	9.65%
<u>Liquidity Ratios</u>			
Current ratio	Current Assets/Current Liabilities	1.69	1.05
Quick ratio	(Current Assets − Stocks)/Current Liabilities	0.57	0.39
<u>Activity Ratios</u>			
Total asset turnover	Revenue/Total Assets	0.96	1.07
Fixed asset turnover	Revenue/Fixed Assets	1.05	1.09
Revenue/ net working capital	Revenue/ (Stocks + Debtors − Trade Creditors)	6.10	4.61
Revenue/ net current assets	Revenue/Net Current Assets	10.27	75.71
Debtors' ratio	365 × Debtors/Revenue	29.46 days	31.68 days
Creditors' ratio	365 × Trade Creditors/Cost of Sales	35.83 days	17.34 days
Stock turnover	365 × Stocks/Cost of Sales	75.87 days	80.30 days
Cash conversion cycle	Debtors' Ratio + Stock Turnover − Creditor's Ratio	69.50 days	94.64 days
<u>Capital Structure</u>			
Capital gearing ratio	Long-Term Liabilities/Capital Employed	35.23%	22.22%

Debt/equity ratio	Long-term Liabilities/Shareholders' Funds	0.54	0.29
Interest cover	Net Profit/Interest	2.89	3.58
Income gearing ratio	Interest/Net Profit	34.65%	27.94%
Shareholder Ratios			
Dividend per share	Ordinary Dividends/No. of Ordinary Shares	9.33p	9.33p
Earnings per share	(Profit After Tax − Preference Dividends)/ No. of Ordinary Shares	10.00p	18.33p
Dividend cover	Ordinary Dividends/ (Profit After Tax − Preference Dividends)	1.07	1.96
Price/earnings ratio	Share Price/Earnings Per Share	13.50	12.00
Payout ratio	Ordinary Dividends/ (Profit After Tax − Preference Dividends)	93.33%	50.91%
Dividend yield	Dividend Per Share/Share Price	6.91%	4.24%

Interpretation of financial ratios

Profitability

ROCE has fallen despite increased revenue. The fall in ROCE reflects a deterioration in both net profit margin (due to operating expenses growing faster than revenue) and asset turnover. The deterioration in asset turnover is partly due to the increase in capital employed as a result of the financing decision to replace a short-term bank overdraft with a longer-term bank loan.

Activity and liquidity ratios

The replacement of the bank overdraft with a bank loan has improved both the current and quick ratios. The creditors' ratio has doubled implying a greater reliance on trade creditors for short-term finance.

Gearing and financial risk

Long-term gearing has increased as a consequence of the new bank loan. Interest cover has fallen due to a combination of lower net profit and higher net interest payments.

Shareholder ratios

Sporting Apparatus has maintained the level of dividend payments despite the fall in profit after tax. Dividend yield has increased due to the fall in the share price. The high price–earnings ratio may reflect increased investor confidence about the company's future prospects.

DCF analysis

The fundamental requirement for an investment decision rule is that it leads to the acceptance of only those investment projects that are expected to contribute towards the maximisation of organisational value. The investment decision rule should ensure the rejection of all projects that are expected to reduce organisational value. In the context of a profit-making sports business, an investment decision rule must distinguish between those investment projects that create shareholder value and those that destroy it. Such a decision rule has three necessary characteristics:

- First, it must involve consideration of all project cash flows since shareholder value depends on all expected future cash flows.
- Second, the investment decision rule must make proper allowance for the time value of money. Investment projects must be evaluated with appropriate recognition of the returns required to compensate for delay, risk and inflation.
- Finally, the investment decision rule must distinguish between investment projects in terms of expected returns irrespective of the method of financing any specific project.

The investment decision (i.e. the appropriate mix of the firm's portfolio of real assets) should be independent of the financing decision (i.e. the appropriate mix of the firm's financial liabilities).

There are two broad types of investment decision rules: rules of thumb and discounted cash flow (DCF) rules. Rules of thumb have no theoretical justification but are useful as relatively simple guides to action. The two most frequently used investment rules of thumb are the *payback rule* and the *accounting rate of return*.

The *payback rule* is to only accept those investment projects in which the initial capital outlay is expected to be recovered within a specified period of time. It is a simple rule for a risk-averse organisation seeking a fairly immediate return on investment with a minimum exposure to changing market conditions. It inevitably implies a bias against longer-term projects with large initial outlays and delayed cash flows. The payback rule does not imply maximisation of corporate/shareholder value since it ignores cash flows beyond the payback period and makes no allowance for the time value of money.

The other frequently used investment rule is the *accounting rate of return* (ARR). The ARR is defined as the average profit after tax as a percentage of average book value calculated over the length of the project. The ARR provides an indicator of the accounting impact of the project. However, there is no necessary connection between the ARR and corporate/shareholder value since the ARR uses accounting profits not cash flows and ignores the time value of money.

Theoretically the optimal investment decision rule must be based on *DCF analysis* to ensure consistency with the maximisation of corporate/shareholder value. DCF analysis, properly applied, includes all incremental cash flows attributable to an investment project and allows for the time value of money through discounting. There are two alternative methods of applying DCF analysis to the investment decision: the *net present value* (NPV) method and the *internal rate of return* (IRR) method.

Project NPV is defined as project value net of the initial capital outlay. Project value equals the present value of expected future project net cash flows. Project NPV represents the expected incremental impact of an investment project on shareholder value. A sports business maximises its corporate value by accepting all projects with positive NPV.

The IRR is defined as the discount rate consistent with zero project NPV (i.e. the discounted value of future project net cash flows is just equal to the initial capital outlay). The IRR investment decision rule is to accept only those projects with IRR in excess of a minimum required rate of return (known as the *hurdle rate*) reflecting the opportunity cost of capital. However, the IRR decision rule is not necessarily consistent with maximising corporate value. Achieving a high IRR is not an end in itself. Project IRR provides only an imperfect operational guide to maximising corporate value. It may be indicative of positive NPV projects (i.e. projects creating shareholder value). But in choosing between mutually exclusive projects there is no necessity that the project with the highest IRR has the highest NPV. Projects with good rates of return may have higher NPV than shorter-term projects with better rates of return. A further complication with the IRR method is that the IRR may not be unique and may even be non-existent for projects with irregular cash flows, resulting in periods of negative net cash flows. Given the theoretical difficulties with the IRR method, the NPV method emerges as the only DCF method of investment appraisal that is fully consistent with the maximisation of corporate value.

When applying DCF analysis to investment decisions, there are four key principles that must be observed:

Investment principle 1: Discount project cash flows not profits

For the purposes of investment appraisal, the concern is to estimate the present value of the net future cash flows expected to be generated by the investment project. There are three types of project cash flows: operating cash flow (net of tax), investment (i.e. capital expenditure) cash flow, and cash flow due to changes in working capital (i.e. stocks, debtors and trade creditors). Project operating cash flow is defined as revenue minus cash expenses and taxes. The tax liability on project profit is calculated as if the project is all-equity financed. It should be remembered that depreciation is not a cash expense. Depreciation has only an indirect impact on project cash flows through the effects on the tax liability. Allowance should be made for any cash flows generated at the start of the project by the sale of existing assets that are rendered obsolete by the new investment. In addition, end-of-project cash flows from the sale of assets and recovery of working capital should be included. It should also be noted that if the realised scrap value from the sale of assets differs from the book value, there is a profit or loss that will affect the tax liability.

Investment principle 2: Ensure that project cash flows are properly attributed

It is vital that project cash flows include all and only expected incremental future cash flows arising from the investment project. These project cash flows should include all likely indirect effects of the project on the company's other cash flows. The opportunity cost (i.e. the value of alternative uses) of all resources utilised by the project should be included. Sunk costs should be excluded from the DCF analysis. These represent past cash flows that are the outcome of past decisions and, therefore, are irrelevant to the current decision about current capital expenditures and future cash flows.

Care must also be taken in attributing to the project only those additional overhead costs that would be incurred as a consequence of the project.

Investment principle 3: Separate the investment decision from the financing decision
DCF analysis should ignore how an investment project is to be financed. Project net cash flows should be calculated excluding financing cash flows, interest payments and tax effects. The cost of capital is allowed for in the discount rate. To include the effects of financing project cash flows would imply double-counting. Effectively the project should be treated as generating cash flows directly to and from shareholders. A project should be accepted if it is expected to generate positive NPV. A subsequent decision should then be made on the optimal financing method.

Investment principle 4: Be consistent in the treatment of inflation effects
DCF analysis requires a consistent treatment of inflation effects. If inflation effects are included in the project cash flows, the discount rate should also include expected inflation as a component of the time value of money. This is known as the nominal (or monetary) discount rate. If inflation effects have been excluded from the project cash flows, consistency requires the use of a real discount rate that excludes expected inflation from the time value of money. The real discount rate can be calculated using the Fisher definition.

$$1 + \text{real discount rate} = \frac{1 + \text{nominal discount rate}}{1 + \text{expected inflation}} \qquad (7.12a)$$

As a rough approximation

$$\text{real discount rate} = \text{nominal discount rate} - \text{expected inflation} \qquad (7.12b)$$

Exhibit 7.4   Worked example 3: Performancewear International

Performancewear International Inc. is a US-based manufacturer of sportswear specialising in running shoes and athletic apparel. Performancewear International operates on a five-yearly planning cycle. The company's financial director has been asked to prepare a recommendation on two alternative investment options for the next planning period: (1) build a new expanded production facility for the manufacture of running shoes; or (2) retain and update the existing production facility.

If Performancewear International expands, the initial capital cost is $450,000 to be financed by fixed-interest debt, repayable in five equal instalments at the end of each year. Sales revenue in the first year is expected to be $865,000 and to grow annually by 8% thereafter. Direct production costs in the first year will be $264,000 and fixed costs (excluding depreciation charges) will be $150,000. It is expected that both direct production costs and fixed costs will grow at 7% per annum.

Updating the existing production facility will cost $250,000. Sales revenue in the first year will be $504,000 with expected annual growth of 5%. Direct production costs in the first year will be $156,000 and fixed costs will be $62,000. Direct production costs and fixed costs are both expected to grow annually at 7%. The capital cost would also be financed by fixed-interest debt repayable in five equal year-end instalments.

Performancewear International can raise sufficient fixed-interest debt for either investment option at an annual interest rate of 10%. Performancewear International uses straight-line depreciation over a five-year period with expected scrap value equal to 20% of the original cost. It is assumed that the end-of-project scrap value will be realised at the end of year 5. The existing production facility has a book value of $10,000 but the market scrap value is $28,000. If the existing production facility is updated, the remaining book value will be charged as depreciation in the first year. The tax rate on company profits is 35%. Performancewear International uses a discount rate of 12% in its investment decisions.

Discussion questions
1. Construct project income statements to determine profit after tax for both options.
2. Construct project cash flow statements to determine the net cash flow (before financing) for both options.
3. Calculate the NPV of the incremental project cash flows if Performancewear International expands rather than updates its existing production facility.
4. Should Performancewear International's financial director recommend expansion? Why?

Solution

Option 1: Expansion
Project income statement

	Year 1	Year 2	Year 3	Year 4	Year 5
Sales revenue	865	934	1,009	1,090	1,177
Direct production costs	264	282	302	323	346
Fixed costs	150	161	172	184	197
Depreciation	72	72	72	72	72
Profit from sales of assets	18	0	0	0	0
PBIT	397	419	463	510	562
Interest	45	36	27	18	9
Profit before tax	352	383	436	492	553
Tax	123	134	153	172	194
Profit after tax	229	249	283	320	360

Project cash flow statement

	Year 0	Year 1	Year 2	Year 3	Year 4	Year 5
Capital outlay	450					
Proceeds from sale of assets	28					90
Sales revenue		865	934	1,009	1,090	1,177
Direct production costs		264	282	302	323	346
Fixed costs		150	161	172	184	197
Operating cash flow		451	491	535	582	634
Tax		139	147	162	179	197
Net cash flow	−422	312	344	373	404	527

Option 2: Update existing production facility
Project income statement

	Year 1	Year 2	Year 3	Year 4	Year 5
Sales revenue	504	529	556	583	613
Direct production costs	156	167	179	191	204
Fixed costs	62	66	71	76	81
Depreciation	50	40	40	40	40
Profit from sales of assets	0	0	0	0	0
PBIT	236	256	266	276	287
Interest	25	20	15	10	5
Profit before tax	211	236	251	266	282

Tax		74	83	88	93	99
Profit after tax		137	153	163	173	183

Project cash flow statement

	Year 0	Year 1	Year 2	Year 3	Year 4	Year 5
Capital outlay	250					
Proceeds from sale of assets	0					50
Sales revenue		504	529	556	583	613
Direct production costs		156	167	179	191	204
Fixed costs		62	66	71	76	81
Operating cash flow		286	296	306	316	327
Tax		83	90	93	97	100
Net cash flow	−250	203	206	213	220	276

NPV of incremental change in cash flows

Year	NCF: Option 1 Expansion	NCF: Option 2 Update	Incremental Change in NCF	Discount Factor (12%)	Present Value
0	−422	−250	−172	1.000	−172
1	312	203	109	0.893	97
2	344	206	138	0.797	110
3	373	213	160	0.712	114
4	404	220	184	0.636	117
5	527	276	251	0.567	142
				NPV = 408	

Conclusion: Performancewear International's financial director should recommend expansion since this is expected to generate additional shareholder value of $408,000 compared to the updating option.

Note: The tax payments differ between the project income and cash flow statements. In the project income statement the tax calculation includes the effects of project financing (i.e. interest payments). The project cash flow statement is constructed as if the project is all-equity financed with no interest payments. The cost of capital (including the tax advantages of debt finance) is allowed for in the discount rate.

Valuing sports businesses

When valuing a sports business, it is vital to recognise that there are alternative concepts of value and methods of calculation. From the perspective of the shareholders (i.e. owners) of a business, there are three different definitions of the value of a sport business:

- *Book value*: net asset value (i.e. assets minus liabilities) calculated using balance sheet data.
- *Liquidation (or break-up) value*: the realisable proceeds, net of obligations, from a quick sale (i.e. a distress or 'fire' sale) of assets.
- *Market value*: the current market value of the business as a going concern.

As discussed previously, the book value of a business may be very misleading as a guide to the value that could actually be realised from the sale of a business's assets net of outstanding obligations. Book value is based on historic costs not current sell-on value. In addition the balance sheet may not include all of the intangible assets of a business, such as goodwill and brand value.

Liquidation value represents sell-on value if the business stops trading and its assets are sold off individually. Liquidation value is likely to be significantly lower than the sell-on value of the business as a going concern for two main reasons. First, 'fire' sales create a buyers' market in which buyers know that there is an imperative to dispose of assets at almost any price. Hence, unless there is an active auction between rival buyers, prices are likely to be relatively low. Second, many forms of intangible assets cannot be sold off individually. For example, the value of a company based on the human capital of its employees cannot be sold. If a company is liquidated, the contracts of its employees will be terminated and the value of the human capital will be entirely lost.

The market value of a sports business to its shareholders represents the total value of the equity invested in the business if the business is sold as a going concern to a new set of owners. The total market value of the equity equals the share price multiplied by the total number of shares issued.

A key principle in corporate valuation is the equivalence proposition. The equivalence proposition states that the total market value of a company to all of its investors (i.e. debt providers and sharcholders) can be measured in three equivalent ways:

1. the present value of expected future free cash flows (i.e. the DCF valuation method);
2. the current market value of debt and equity;
3. the current going-concern value of the company's assets.

The total market value of a company should equal all of the project cash flows expected to be generated (i.e. after-tax operating cash flows plus investment and working-capital cash flows). By definition, the total market value of a company can be measured either by the market value of its assets or the market value of its debt and equity.

There are three principle methods of calculating the value of a sports business:

■ DCF analysis;
■ the dividend discount model (DDM);
■ valuation ratios.

DCF analysis

The total market value of a sports business is the present value of the expected *future free cash flow* (FCF). FCF is defined as the after-tax operating cash flow minus investment expenditure. Thus the DCF analysis of company value involves projecting future revenues, cash expenses, tax and investment expenditures. The equity value of the company is calculated as the present value of expected FCF minus the present value of the company's debt obligations.

It is usual to undertake a detailed DCF analysis for a defined planning period, usually between 5 and 10 years. The present value of expected FCF beyond the planning horizon is estimated by multiplying the present value of the expected FCF in the horizon year by a terminal multiple (often the price–earnings ratio).

The DCF method of company valuation can be summarised as follows:

Company Value = PV(FCF)   (7.13a)

Equity Value = PV(FCF) − PV(Debt)   (7.13b)

FCF = Operating Cash Flow − Investment   (7.13c)

$PV(FCF) = PV(FCF_1) + \ldots + PV(FCF_H) + PV(\text{Terminal Value})$ (7.13d)

$PV(\text{Terminal Value}) = PV(FCF_H) \times \text{Terminal Multiple}$ (7.13e)

The dividend discount model (DDM)

The DDM is based on the proposition that the current equity value of a company equals the present value of the expected future stream of dividends to be paid to shareholders. The DDM simplifies the calculation of the present value of the expected future dividend stream by treating equity as a perpetuity. There are two forms of the DDM:

(i) Fixed dividend payment

Suppose that a company pays out all of its profit after tax as dividends (i.e. no retained profit). Suppose also that the company undertakes replacement investment expenditure equal to the depreciation charge to maintain the current economic value of the fixed assets. In this case, profit after tax equals the expected FCF and the expected dividend payment. It follows that the equity value of the company can be modelled as a fixed perpetuity:

$$\text{Equity Value} = \frac{DIV_1}{r}$$

where $DIV_1 \equiv$ total dividend payment, end of Year 1   (7.14)

and $r \equiv$ discount rate

(ii) Constant-growth dividend payment

Suppose that the dividend payment is expected to grow at a constant rate, g, indefinitely. It follows that the equity value of the company can be modelled as a growth perpetuity with a growth-adjusted discount rate, $(r - g)$.

$$\text{Equity Value} = \frac{DIV_1}{r - g}$$ (7.15)

Valuation ratios

Valuation ratios are benchmark ratios derived from similar companies that are listed on the stock market and, hence, their *market capitalisation* (i.e. the market value of equity) is continually observable. Two of the most widely used valuation ratios are the market-to-book ratio and the price–earnings ratio.

$$\text{Market-to-Book Ratio} = \frac{\text{Market Capitalisation}}{\text{Net Asset Value}}$$ (7.16)

$$\text{Price–Earnings Ratio} = \frac{\text{Market Capitalisation}}{\text{Profit After Tax}} \qquad (7.17)$$

The valuation of a non-listed company can be inferred by multiplying its net asset value or profit after tax (or some other performance indicator) by the appropriate benchmark ratio for similar listed companies.

Although there are several alternative valuation methods, they are theoretically consistent. It is useful to apply a variety of valuation methods to check the robustness of the estimated values. It is also important to test the sensitivity of valuations to key assumptions about the future, for example future growth rates. Corporate valuation is both an art and a science, requiring both calculation and judgement based on experience.

Exhibit 7.5   Worked example 4: FitVital Ltd

FitVital Ltd is a privately-owned health and fitness business that has been trading for fifteen years. The following summary of financial information is available covering the last three years:

£000	2002	2001	2000
Turnover	17,510	15,985	14,650
Operating profit	5,643	5,299	4,980
Profit after tax	3,254	3,064	2,890
Dividends	1,653	1,545	1,445

Currently, the company has fixed assets consisting of freehold land (current market value = £1.8 million), buildings (original cost = £3.6 million), equipment (original cost = £6.8 million), and fixtures and fittings (original cost = £0.6 million). The company applies straight-line depreciation to all of its fixed assets except the freehold land. The current buildings were acquired five years ago and have an estimated remaining working life of 15 years. Equipment and fixtures and fittings have an estimated working life of 10 years with an average remaining working life of 5 years. The company has net current assets of £1 million. There is a long-term bank loan of £3.5 million secured against the company's assets currently repayable in 2020. The company's existing equity consists of ten million ordinary £1 shares. FitVital Ltd plans to seek a stock market listing. It is envisaged that the initial public offering (IPO) will consist of seven million newly-issued ordinary £1 shares plus the existing shares.

Discussion questions

5. Determine what might be a reasonable current (i.e. prior to the IPO) estimate of the net asset value per share for FitVital.
6. Using the estimate of current net asset value per share and an average industry market-to-book value ratio of 1.5, determine a possible flotation share price for FitVital.
7. Derive a possible flotation share price for FitLife using the dividend discount model (DDM) with a required shareholder rate of return of 15% and assuming that the company can maintain its recent financial performance. How sensitive is the flotation share price to changes in the growth assumption and/or the required rate of return?
8. Using the average price–earnings (p/e) ratio for the engineering industry of 16.5, derive a possible flotation share price for FitVital.

Solutions

5. Net asset value

Fixed Assets	Cost	Cumulative Depreciation	Book Value
Land	£1,800,000	−	£1,800,000
Buildings	£3,600,000	£900,000	£2,700,000
Equipment	£6,800,000	£3,400,000	£3,400,000
Fixtures and fittings	£600,000	£300,000	£300,000
Total	£12,800,000	£4,600,000	£8,200,000

Net asset value = fixed assets + net current assets − long-term debt

Net asset value (cost) = £12,800,000 + £1,000,000 − £3,500,000 = £10,300,000

Number of shares = 10,000,000

Net asset value (cost) per share = 103 pence

Net asset value (book) = £8,200,000 + £1,000,000 − £3,500,000 = £5,700,000

Number of shares = 10,000,000

Net asset value (book) per share = 57 pence

6. Flotation share price: market-to-book ratio

Market-to-book ratio = 1.5

Number of shares at flotation = 17,000,000

Net asset value (book) per share = net asset value (book)/number of shares = 33.5 pence

Flotation share price = net asset value (book) per share × market-to-book ratio = 50.3 pence

7. Flotation share price: DDM

Dividend growth, $g = (DIV_{2002}/DIV_{2000})^{1/2} = 6.96\%$

Expected dividends, $DIV_{2003} = DIV_{2002} \times (1 + \text{growth rate}) = £1,767,972$

Expected dividend per share, $dps_{2003} = DIV_{2003}/\text{number of shares} = 10.4$ pence

Discount rate, $r = 15\%$

Flotation share price = $dps_{2003}/(r - g) = 129.3$ pence

Flotation share price, alternative growth rates and discount rates

	g = 4%	g = 5%	g = 6%	g = 7%	g = 8%
r = 10%	168.5p	204.2p	257.7p	346.8p	525.1p
r = 12%	126.4p	145.9p	171.8p	208.1p	262.5p
r = 15%	91.9p	102.1p	114.5p	130.1p	150.2p
r = 18%	72.2p	78.5p	85.9p	94.6p	105.0p

8. Flotation share price: price–earnings ratio

Industry p/e ratio = 16.5

Profit after tax = £3,254,000

Estimated market capitalisation = profit after tax × p/e ratio = £53,691,000

Flotation share price = market capitalisation/number of shares = 315.8 pence

Commentary

The market-to-book value ratio indicates a relatively low flotation price of 50 pence per share. However, given that most of the assets are relatively young, it may be more appropriate to use net asset value based on cost. This yields a flotation share price of 91 pence. This is closer to the DDM estimate of 129 pence. But the DDM estimate assumes that dividend pay-out ratio post-flotation will remain unchanged. If dividend growth fell to around 4%, this would give a flotation price of 92 pence in line with the market-to-book value ratio (using cost). However, the industry p/e ratio of 16.5 suggests a much higher level of valuation. Indeed the industry p/e ratio would imply a discount rate of around 11% with a 7% growth rate. Overall the flotation share price is likely to be set in the range 80–150 pence depending on the general market conditions and specific market sentiment towards the company.

Financing decisions in sports organisations

There are two main types of long-term financing available to sports organisations – debt and equity. Debt providers receive interest payments but have little direct control over the organisation. Shareholders have only residual income claims but are the ultimate owners. In deciding the appropriate mix of debt and equity, a sports organisation must evaluate the different costs of the alternative types of long-term financing. The explicit cost of debt is generally lower than that for equity for three reasons. First, there is lower investor risk to debt providers due to the priority of their income and liquidation claims. Second, interest charges are a tax-deductible expense. Finally, the transaction costs involved in the arrangement of debt provision are typically lower than those associated with the issue of new equity. But debt finance has implicit costs because it increases the financial risk of the organisation. Interest obligations are invariant to changes in the organisation's cash flows. As a consequence, the financial performance of organisations that are highly geared (i.e. high levels of debt relative to equity) is much more sensitive to changes in operating performance.

The cost of capital

The overall cost of long-term financing to an organisation is measured by the weighted average cost of capital (WACC). The WACC is defined as follows:

$$\text{WACC} = \left[(1 - T_C) k_{debt} \frac{D}{V} \right] + \left[k_{equity} \frac{E}{V} \right] \tag{7.18}$$

where $T_C \equiv$ corporate tax rate; $k_{debt} \equiv$ cost of debt; $k_{equity} \equiv$ cost of equity; $D \equiv$ market value of long-term debt; $E =$ market value of equity; $V = D + E$.

The definition of the WACC can be extended to all different types of debt and equity with different costs.

The WACC represents the investor's required rate of return on the complete portfolio of the organisation's securities (i.e. debt and equity). The WACC provides the benchmark discount rate for evaluating 'average-risk' projects.

One of the main issues in calculating the WACC is how to determine the cost of equity, which, unlike interest payments, is not directly observable. There are two principal methods of inferring the cost of equity. One method is to use the DDM model to determine the implied discount rate (i.e. cost of equity) given the observed market capitalisation, dividend payments and expected growth rate.

$$\text{Market Capitalisation} = \frac{DIV_1}{r - g}$$

$$\Rightarrow r = \frac{DIV_1}{\text{Market Capitalisation}} + g \tag{7.19}$$

The cost of equity is the required dividend yield plus the expected growth rate.

An alternative approach is to use the capital asset pricing model (CAPM). The CAPM postulates that the required rate of return on equity depends primarily on the sensitivity of the equity to general market movements. The basic CAPM equation (known as the *security market line*) states that:

$$r_i = r_f + \beta_i(r_m - r_f) \tag{7.20}$$

The expected return for the ith asset, r_i, consists of two components: (i) the pure time value of money as measured by the rate of return on risk-free assets, r_f; and (ii) the risk premium, $\beta_i(r_m - r_f)$. The risk premium for the ith asset is calculated as the product of the market risk premium, $(r_m - r_f)$, where r_m is the market rate of return, and the asset beta, β_i. The asset beta measures the degree of sensitivity of the returns of an asset to general market movements. The asset beta is defined as follows:

$$\beta_i = \frac{\text{cov}(r_j, r_m)}{\sigma^2_m} \tag{7.21}$$

where $\text{cov}(r_j, r_m) \equiv$ covariance of asset and market returns
and $\sigma^2_m \equiv$ variance of market returns.

■ The optimal capital structure for a sports business

A key proposition in finance is the debt irrelevance proposition. It can be shown theoretically under ideal conditions of well-functioning capital markets in which individuals and companies can borrow and lend at a common interest rate, and, importantly there are no taxes and no bankruptcy or financial distress costs, the total value of a company is unaffected by the gearing ratio (i.e. the proportion of debt in the company's capital structure). This implies that any gains to gearing from the lower explicit cost of debt are exactly offset by the increased cost of capital due to higher financial risk. It follows, therefore, that the level of debt is irrelevant to the value of the company. Although the debt irrelevance proposition is a theoretical result derived under very unrealistic assumptions, it does represent a fundamental principle of corporate valuation. Ultimately the value of a company depends primarily on its business model (i.e. real assets and operating activities) not its financial structure.

The optimal capital structure for any sports business will depend on at least four important considerations:

- *Taxes*: Interest payments on debt are a tax-deductible expense. Hence borrowing creates an *interest tax shield* that is valuable to tax-liable companies. It follows that company value increases with the gearing ratio, creating a preference for debt over equity.

- *Business risk*: If a company operates in a sector characterised by high business risk, there is a high risk of financial distress. Such companies are likely to prefer equity over debt in order to minimise any additional financial risk. This will be exacerbated by the high and increasing costs of debt charged by investors.

- *Asset type*: Companies that are highly dependent on intangible assets are likely to find debt finance to be unavailable or prohibitively expensive. In such circumstances debt providers are unable to obtain much in the way of security in the form of fixed tangible assets with significant resale value in the event of liquidation.

■ *Incentive effects*: Companies operating with a high degree of financial slack in the form of surplus cash and ready access to debt finance are able to finance investment projects largely from internal sources. This may lead to acceptance of projects with marginal prospects on generating shareholder value. Financial slack can foster slack management. It is argued that returning surplus cash to shareholders combined with high levels of debt can create effective incentives for greater managerial efficiency because of the increased threat of financial distress and bankruptcy.

It follows, therefore, that there is likely to be an optimal capital structure that maximises the company value. The returns from higher gearing, due to tax and incentive effects, must be balanced against the costs of higher financial risk. However, it may be difficult to identify precisely the optimal mix of debt and equity for any individual sports business. And, crucially, company value depends fundamentally on investment and operating decisions, not financing decisions.

Exhibit 7.6	Worked example 5: Operation Stadia plc

Operation Stadia plc is a UK-listed company that owns and operates several sports stadia. Operation Stadia proposes to build a new stadium. Operation Stadia currently has a long-term debt of £240 million with a rate of interest of 8 per cent. The current market capitalisation of the company is £320 million. Operation Stadia expects to pay dividends to shareholders of £9.6 million in the next year. The expected company growth rate is 9 per cent per annum. A leading credit agency has recently assessed the company beta as 1.25. The average rate of return in the equity market is currently 10 per cent. Treasury bills are currently paying an interest rate of 4 per cent. The tax rate on profits is 35 per cent.

Discussion question

9. What is the appropriate discount rate for assessing whether or not to proceed with the new stadium project?

Solution

Provided the new stadium project is average risk relative to the rest of the company's operations, the appropriate discount rate is the WACC.

To determine the company WACC, it is necessary to calculate the after-tax cost of debt and the cost of equity.

After-tax cost of debt   = (1 – tax rate) × interest rate
         = (1 – 35%) × 8%
         = 5.2%

Cost of equity
Method 1: DDM
Cost of equity   = dividend yield + growth rate
       = (dividends/market capitalisation) + growth rate
       = (6.4/320) + 6%
       = 12%

Method 2: CAPM
Cost of equity   = risk-free rate + (company beta × market risk premium)
       = 4% + [1.25 × (10% – 4%)]
       = 11.5%

Estimated average cost of equity = 11.75%
Total capital   = long-term debt + equity
                  = £240m + £320m
                  = £560m
Share of long-term debt   = long-term debt/total capital
                          = £240m/£560m
                          = 42.9%
Share of equity   = equity/total capital
                  = £320m/£560m
                  = 57.1%
WACC   = (after-tax cost of debt × share of debt) + (cost of equity × share of equity)
       = (5.2% × 42.9%) + (11.75% × 57.1%)
       = 8.9%

Sport and the stock market

The shares of many sport businesses are traded on stock markets. Indeed, an interesting phenomenon over the last decade has been the public listing of several professional sports team organisations particularly leading British football clubs. Companies that are listed on the stock market tend to have better access to capital markets to raise new debt and equity finance at more preferential rates than similar privately-owned companies. Companies with their shares traded publicly on the stock market are continuously being valued by market traders. Share prices are news-driven. Share-price movements are caused by new information that affects the market's expectations about the company's future cash flows. There are three types of information that can influence a company's share price: general economic information, sector information, and company-specific information.

Another key proposition in finance is the efficient market hypothesis (EMH). The EMH states that an asset market is information (or price) efficient if asset prices fully reflect all information on future asset returns currently available to market participants. An important implication is that new information (i.e. 'news') is incorporated quickly and correctly into asset prices. Thus if market news suggests a downward revision in the expected future returns of a particular asset, the price of the asset will tend to fall as the consequence of increased selling. A corollary of the EMH is that a company's share price will only change if the news is truly unexpected and leads to a change in future expectations. This means that it is not news per se that affects share prices but news relative to what is currently expected. The public announcement of poor financial results need not necessarily depress a company's share price if the market had already correctly anticipated these results.

The EMH implies that share prices should follow a *random walk* in the sense that future share price movements cannot be predicted from past share price movements. All currently available information will be fully reflected in current share prices so that future share-price movements will be caused only by new, unpredictable information.

The EMH is remarkably well supported by the empirical evidence. Asset prices do tend to adjust rapidly to significant information events. However the claim that stock markets are information-efficient does not exclude the possibility of stock market bubbles and crashes (i.e. periods of explosive growth in share prices followed by rapid decline). Current share prices are always being benchmarked against previous prices and the current prices of other comparable shares. Market efficiency implies that *relative* share prices rapidly adjust to new information. Stock market crashes reflect a loss of general market confidence in the correctness of the *absolute* level of share prices.

Market efficiency has important implications for the financial management of all companies. Financial managers should focus on the long-term fundamentals of the business rather than engaging in short-term financial manoeuvres. Efficient markets are able to correctly interpret all available information and, as a consequence, will not be fooled by 'creative accounting'. The EMH also provides support for the use of the WACC as the appropriate discount rate for investment appraisal. If capital markets are efficient, investors are able to correctly evaluate the degree of business and financial risk of a company and this will be reflected in the cost of capital. Hence the WACC represents the market assessment of the appropriate time value of money for any individual company to be used in determining whether or not potential investment projects will create shareholder value.

Conclusion

This chapter has introduced some of the basic principles of financial management and demonstrated their relevance to sports organisations. The subject of sports finance is in its infancy. Most of the focus of research to date in sports finance has been on the financial management of professional sports teams and sports businesses. Further research is required on the concept of organisational value in not-for-profit sports organisations. This in turn will lead to further developments in the financial management techniques available to such organisations.

The basic principles of financial management discussed in this chapter should provide a starting point for the analysis of a wide range of financial issues in sport including the financing of new stadium developments (e.g. the redevelopment of Wembley Stadium) and mega-events (e.g. the Olympic Games). Whatever the scale or function of a sports organisation, sound financial management is a necessary prerequisite for its successful operation.

CASE 7.1   Leeds United

Background

Leeds United is one of the leading professional football clubs in England. Founded in 1919, Leeds United came to prominence in the 1960s and 1970s when, under the management of Don Revie, the club won the league championship (twice), the FA Cup, the League Cup and the UEFA Inter-Cities Fairs Cup (twice). Leeds United spent much of the 1980s in the Second Division but, following promotion in 1989–90, went on to win the league championship again in 1991/92. Leeds United has been an ever-present member of the FA Premier League since its formation in 1992. The club was listed on the London Stock Exchange in 1996 following its acquisition by Caspian, a small media company. The appointment of David O'Leary as team manager in 1998 coincided with the emergence of an outstanding crop of young players from the club's football youth academy. In addition O'Leary spent heavily in the transfer market to produce a team that reached the semi-finals of the UEFA Cup in 2000 and the semi-finals of the UEFA Champions League in 2001. However, failure to qualify for the Champions League in subsequent seasons has resulted in a severe financial crisis that has forced the sale of several top players. As a consequence, Leeds United just avoided relegation from the Premier League in 2003. At the time of writing, further player sales have been announced. Leeds United provides a salutary lesson on the potential impact on sporting performance of imprudent financial management.

Profit and Loss Account, Leeds United, 1998–2002

£000	1998	1999	2000	2001	2002
Turnover	28,512	36,971	57,064	86,252	81,503
Staff costs	15,858	18,551	27,794	43,329	53,612
Net profit before player trading	4,372	6,436	5,582	8,650	−7,930
Player amortisation	5,143	6,791	8,463	14,335	20,576
Profit/loss on disposal of players	2,032	2,518	5,891	1,657	296
Profit/loss before interest and tax	1,321	2,163	3,010	−4,118	−28,210
Net interest paid	993	1,452	1,766	3,561	5,665
Profit/loss after tax	307	607	777	−7,042	−33,875

Turnover grew rapidly over the period largely driven by European success and increased media revenues. Turnover peaked in 2001 when Leeds United reached the semi-finals of the UEFA Champions League. Although Leeds failed to qualify for the Champions League the following year, most of the loss of revenue was offset by increased media revenues from the new FA Premier League TV deal. Despite the rapid revenue growth, the growth in net profit before player trading was only modest, largely due to the rapid growth in staff costs. Staff costs grew by over £10 million in 2002 despite the fall in turnover. This resulted in net losses before player trading of just under £8 million.

Player amortisation charges represent a straight-line allocation of transfer costs over the whole length of a player's contract. The quadrupling of player amortisation charges from £5.1 million in 1998 to £20.6 million in 2002 reflects heavy investment in new players acquired in the transfer market particularly in the last two years. By contrast Leeds earned just over £12 million profit (i.e. excess over book value) over the five-year period through the sale of players.

Net interest payments also increased significantly over the period from under £1 million in 1998 to £5.7 million in 2002 due to the reliance on fund investment and transfer expenditures.

Overall the financial performance of Leeds United deteriorated dramatically in 2001 and 2002. Whereas a small profit after tax was earned in the previous years, large losses were recorded in the last two years. Large operating losses combined with large transfer expenditures and an increasing debt burden resulted in an overall loss of £33.9 million in 2002. Such huge losses are not sustainable and represent a company in very severe financial distress.

Balance Sheet, Leeds United, 1998–2002

£000	1998	1999	2000	2001	2002
Tangible fixed assets	30,764	32,549	35,894	39,583	42,537
Purchased player registrations	15,152	16,669	28,569	63,490	66,469
Net current assets	−7,102	−7,641	−2,428	−24,684	−25,267
Capital employed	38,828	41,591	62,285	78,389	83,739
Long-term liabilities	11,573	13,729	22,774	43,120	82,345
Net asset value	27,255	27,862	38,861	35,269	1,394

The financial position of Leeds United over the period is captured very succinctly in the balance sheet. The investment in tangible fixed assets (principally the Thorpe Arch training facility) plus large transfer expenditures to acquire players saw the total fixed assets increase from £45.9 million in 1998 to £109 million in 2002. However, overall capital employed increased more slowly due to the large increase in current liabilities in the last two years (£51.9 million in 2001 and £57.0 million in 2002), reflecting the increased use of short-term finance to fund the expansion of the asset base.

Long-term financing of fixed assets was principally provided by debt. Long-term liabilities increased from £11.6 million in 1998 to £82.3 million in 2002. The largest component of the debt is a 25-year *securitisation* loan of £60 million secured over the club's Elland Road stadium with a priority claim over ticket revenues.

The net asset value (i.e. the book value of shareholders' funds) rose to a peak of £38.9 million in 2000 but fell to only £1.4 million in 2002 as a consequence of the large losses posted in the last two years. With virtually no shareholders' funds remaining in the business by June 2002, the club was on the brink of financial insolvency and urgently required restructuring and a new injection of funds.

Key Financial Ratios, Leeds United, 1998 – 2002

	1998	1999	2000	2001	2002
Wage–turnover ratio	56.1%	50.2%	48.7%	50.2%	65.8%
Net profit margin	4.5%	5.9%	5.3%	−4.7%	−34.6%
Asset turnover	0.73	0.89	0.92	1.10	0.97
ROCE	3.3%	5.2%	4.8%	−5.1%	−33.7%
Current ratio	0.62	0.59	0.88	0.46	0.56
Capital gearing	29.8%	33.0%	36.6%	55.0%	98.3%

The financial performance of Leeds United over the period can be summarised by some key financial ratios. Leeds earned a small return on capital employed in 1998–2000 but thereafter ROCE declined sharply. Asset turnover tended to increase over the period, implying that the fall in ROCE was largely due to declining profit margins caused by high wage costs. The wage–turnover ratio rose to nearly 66% in 2002. The current ratio also fell in the last two years as current liabilities rose relatively faster than current assets. The rise in the capital gearing ratio shows that Leeds United is now almost entirely debt-financed with only a minimal equity investment. This is in sharp contrast to the position in 1998–2000 when long-term liabilities accounted for only around one-third of the capital employed.

Financial Ratios, Leading Premiership Clubs, 2002

	Arsenal	Chelsea	Leeds Utd	Liverpool	Man Utd
Wage–turnover ratio	67.6%	49.7%	65.8%	56.8%	47.9%
Net profit margin	−25.5%	−6.7%	−34.6%	10.6%	22.1%
Asset turnover	0.96	0.59	0.97	1.34	0.76
ROCE	−24.4%	−4.0%	−33.7%	14.2%	16.8%
Current ratio	0.93	0.31	0.56	0.45	0.62
Capital gearing	19.8%	55.1%	98.3%	25.5%	0.5%

Comparing the financial performance of Leeds United with other leading Premiership clubs in 2002 is very revealing. Arsenal's financial performance was closest to that of Leeds United, with high losses largely as a consequence of an excessively high wage–turnover ratio. By comparison, Liverpool and Manchester United achieved significant positive ROCE. Both of these clubs operated with wage–turnover ratios significantly below Arsenal and Leeds. The current ratio of Leeds United was similar to that of Liverpool and Manchester United. However, Leeds United is unique in the extent of its capital gearing. Chelsea is the only other club in the sample with long-term liabilities exceeding shareholders' funds (and only just) but Chelsea has invested extensively in a hotel and leisure complex so that a much higher proportion of its debt is backed by tangible fixed assets.

Cash Flow Statement, Leeds United, 1998–2002

£000	1998	1999	2000	2001	2002
Operating cash flow	3,837	4,997	3,372	15,741	−5,716
Tax	−510	0	−76	0	0
Net sales/purchases, tangible fixed assets	−3,204	−2,569	−5,783	−3,651	−3,545
Player trading	−6,200	−3,418	−16,156	−28,189	−25,470
Free cash flow	−6,077	−990	−18,893	−16,099	−34,731
Net interest receipts/payments	−993	−1,452	−1,619	−3,525	−3,212
Net increase in borrowing	−2,648	1,753	12,080	18,227	48,837
Net share issues	12	0	8,987	1,235	0
Other financing activities	2,785	2,025	0	0	0
Net cash flow	−6,921	1,336	555	−162	10,894

The cash flow statement shows the true extent of Leeds United's financial crisis in 2002. Despite positive operating cash flows until 2002, Leeds United generated no positive free cash flows (FCF = operating cash flow + tax + net sales/purchases of tangible fixed assets + player trading). In 2002 the free cash outflow grew to £34.7 million, largely as a result of the £20 million reversal in the operating cash flow between 2001 and 2002. With increasing net interest payments, the growing demand for financing cash flows was primarily met by increases in net borrowing. Sustained negative FCFs over a period of time are not necessarily an indicator of a financial crisis provided the company is investing in asset growth that will ultimately improve operating cash flows. However, in the case of Leeds United there has been no sustained improvement in operating performance. Indeed, Leeds suffered a net operating cash outflow of £5.7 million in 2002.

Annual Share Price Changes, Selected Listed Clubs, 1997–2003

Date	Chelsea Utd	Leeds Utd	Man Utd	Newcastle	Spurs	FTSE All-Share
May 1998	−29.6%	−31.4%	−23.0%	−23.7%	−33.2%	31.5%
May 1999	−16.5%	4.2%	50.2%	−22.3%	−13.1%	5.5%
May 2000	−12.4%	14.7%	93.7%	−21.0%	7.9%	0.1%
May 2001	−33.3%	−39.5%	−51.9%	−26.6%	−28.7%	−4.8%
May 2002	−53.8%	−48.1%	−32.8%	−41.0%	−40.2%	−10.7%
May 2003	−10.8%	−49.9%	15.1%	22.5%	−39.7%	−24.7%

Football club shares generally performed very poorly over these six years relative to the stock market as a whole (as measured by the FTSE All-Share index). However, Leeds United bucked the trend in 1999 and 2000, and, in fact, Leeds United shares outperformed the market as a whole between May 1999 and May 2000. In part this was a knock-on effect of the rapid growth in the equity value of Manchester United following BSkyB's bid to acquire the club. This sparked general speculation of further media bids for other leading clubs with Leeds as an obvious target. The rise in the Leeds share price also reflected the improved sporting performance with a belief that eventually this would generate significant shareholder returns. However, with successive failures to qualify for the Champions League and the onset of a severe financial crisis, the Leeds share price collapsed as investor confidence evaporated. The Leeds share price closed on 5 May 2003 at 3.5 pence compared to 26.25 pence on 5 May 1997. A share price of 3.5 pence implies a market capitalisation of Leeds United of around £12.2 million. (Note that there were 348 million issued shares at this time.) In other words, with little expectation of positive future FCFs and a very high level of debt, there was little equity value left in Leeds United in its then financial position.

Recent developments

The crisis at Leeds United has continued to deepen. The club has changed its football manager twice since June 2002 and sold six top international players with further sales imminent. Sporting performance inevitably declined, with Leeds avoiding relegation with one match remaining. The six-month interim financial statement for the period July–December 2002 was horrendous, reporting net losses before player trading of £10.1 million and overall losses before tax of £17.2 million. Net asset value by 31 December 2002 had dropped to −£15.8 million. The executive directors have all been removed and a new executive chairman appointed. A team of business recovery specialists has been appointed to advise on restructuring and refinancing the club. The club's short-term prospects look bleak and the twin threats of insolvency and relegation remain very real.

CASE 7.2   Clubs in crisis as losses mount   FT

One of Italy's most prized historic possessions was granted a temporary preservation order yesterday when a judge in Florence granted the city's debt-ridden football club a stay of execution until next Wednesday in its attempts to avoid being placed in receivership.

But Fiorentina's parlous financial state – at one time it faced reported debts of approaching £100 million – is merely the worst case in an industry that many suggest is facing financial meltdown.

Players in Serie A are routinely paid late, loan deals are increasingly replacing cash transfers and even the richest clubs are voicing concern over wage costs that have doubled over three seasons. Furthermore Lazio has admitted that it is late in paying the second instalment of the £16 million transfer fee for Dutch defender Jaap Stam from Manchester United last summer.

'Action is urgently needed,' says an executive at one leading Serie A club. 'Why should teams go bankrupt to create billionaires? There's no reason why one player should be paid Euros 5 million (£3 million) a year when his club loses more than Euros 30 million a year."

The crunch is likely to come, as in England and other European leagues, with the re-negotiation of television contracts – especially the pay-per-view deals – that have largely funded the clubs' spending sprees.

Several are anxious about what happens if the television money is reduced or remains static while spending continues to soar. Lazio president Sergio Cragnotti, among others, has openly discussed introducing a salary cap at his club. Adriano Galliani, vice-president of AC Milan, is leading discussions on domestic salary controls, which are also taking place at a European level with fellow members of G14, the lobby group of the continent's leading clubs.

Milan is a leading member of G14, which includes the likes of Real Madrid, Manchester United and Barcelona. Galliani is keen that self-imposed wage controls are adopted across Europe, and has received the support of other G14 members.

One proposal is that rather than introduce a salary cap, clubs impose an agreed limit on squad sizes. 'What you do is bring down the squad size to 25 – the minimum level for entry to Uefa competitions,' says one Italian football insider. 'Trimming squads by three or four players could reduce salary spending by 10 per cent,' he adds. 'We really feel that Real Madrid, Barcelona and Manchester United are on the same wavelength with us about this.'

The financial health of Italian football will play a prominent role in a meeting of the country's 38 league chairmen today in Milan. The gathering is ostensibly to elect a new president but for many the choice between Roma president Franco Sensi and his counterpart at Parma, Stefano Tanzi, will come down to a vote on future funding. The split will not be clean cut between the rich and poor because the traditional north–south allegiances will come into play.

At present an away team receives 18 per cent of the ticket and television income from a league game. The larger clubs want to 'restructure' the financial split and the smaller ones, coalescing around Sensi, are accusing them of trying to reduce their share.

Serie A, like its English Premier League counterpart, realised its value to the TV companies in the late 1990s. But many clubs now fear a drastic drop in TV revenues as viewing figures fall. Gate receipts from 'real' fans clicking through the turnstiles comprise only 15–20 per cent of bigger clubs' income, leaving many clubs nowhere to hide if the next round of TV contracts brings, as some fear, huge cuts.

Clubs individually negotiated pay-per-view deals – the latest of which end in 2005 – worth a total of Euros 428 million last time round, with the Italian Football League, hauling in another Euros 94 million for cup coverage. Yet despite that, Serie A's 18 clubs ended last season with a combined operating loss of Euros 740 million. Once players' transfers had been taken into account, the loss amounted to Euros 152 million.

A spokesman for Cragnotti this week admitted that the Rome club is two months behind in paying its players salaries: 'Most clubs are the same these days. Italian football is in crisis. But we ourselves are paid three or four months late by Stream (the satellite broadcaster).'

Vittorio Cecchi Gori, Fiorentina's beleagured owner, has also publicly blamed much of his club's financial problems on late payment from satellite broadcasters.

But Lucia Morselli, who negotiated some of the television deals for Stream, says: 'It's absolutely not true (that payments are late). We are well within the payment windows in the contracts.'

More worryingly, it has emerged that Lazio has failed to make the second of four instalments on its £16 million purchase of Stam. Lazio cite 'a difference in the interpretation of the dates of the payment schedule' for the delay. But as one of the three Italian clubs quoted on the Rome stock market, such news is symptomatic of the problems of Italian football.

'There is no dispute with Manchester,' says Cragnotti's spokesman. 'They know all about it. Fifa have also been informed. We are having meetings with Manchester in March, and the second and third instalments will be merged.'

Generally, matters are made worse by the lost income caused by the widespread 'pirating' of pay-per-view games. Antonio Marchesi, football industry analyst at Deloitte Touche in Milan, says: 'Pirating, by an estimated 1.5–2 million people, is one of the main things that the football industry in Italy needs to confront.'

He also insists that clubs need to reduce their wage bills. He does not, however, share the widespread pessimism over future TV deals. 'It is too early to predict what the next round of TV rights may bring. It's not definite that clubs' TV incomes will drop.'

Lucia Morselli at Stream goes even further: 'I believe that the next round of TV deals (Stream's run until 2005) will probably not see a reduced offer to the football industry. I believe that the football sector still is not fully exploiting its potential income as a whole.'

But clubs are already making losses despite the income from the biggest TV contracts in Italian football's history. It is a similar picture in England and Spain where clubs are girding themselves for less income.

At perennial southern strugglers Lecce, vice-president Ricco Semeraro is pessimistic: 'I'd say that the condition of Italian football is probably even worse than people think.'

Source: Kevin Buckley, Matthew Garrahan and Thilo Schafer, *Financial Times*, 1 March 2002

The case studies of both Leeds United and the Italian Serie A illustrate problems common to professional sports leagues around the world – uncertainty of future TV revenues, excessively high levels of player wages, high working capital requirements and onerous debt burdens. It is very difficult for teams individually to break out of the 'arms race' dynamic in player wages. If teams do not offer wages as high as their rivals, they will find it difficult to recruit and retain the top players and inevitably their sporting performance will tend to decline. Professional sports leagues have an important role to play in helping to secure the financial viability of teams as well as maintaining a reasonable degree of competitive balance. As discussed in the Italian Serie A case study, salary caps and limits on squad size are two possible solutions actively under consideration.

Discussion questions

10. To what extent are the current financial problems in professional team sports, as typified by Leeds United and the Italian Serie A, due largely to the failure of individual teams to control player wage costs?

11. You have just been appointed finance director of a troubled professional sports team with large operating losses and a substantial debt burden. Your task is to construct a financial plan to achieve financial stability for the team over the next three years. Outline your proposed financial plan and discuss the difficulties of trying to refinance the team by issuing new equity.

Guided reading

There are two specialist textbooks on sports finance written for sport management students, Howard and Crompton (1995) and Fried, Shapiro and DeSchriver (2003). The two textbooks provide alternative but complementary approaches. Howard and Crompton focus on the acquisition of financial resources by sports organisations. Topics covered are the public-sector funding of sports facilities, revenue streams and sponsorship. There is no coverage of budgeting and financial analysis. In contrast, Fried *et al.* adopt a much more standard corporate finance approach, similar to that of this chapter, covering a range of topics in financial analysis, capital structure and financial management as applied in the sports context. Topics are illustrated with reference to four case studies that run throughout the book.

Students of sports finance are also advised to consult Brealey, Myers and Marcus (2004) and Broyles (2003) on corporate finance. Brealey *et al.* is one of the leading undergraduate texts on corporate finance providing a comprehensive and detailed introduction to all of the topics covered in this chapter. Broyles provides similar coverage but with an emphasis on real option analysis as a method of investment appraisal.

On the topic of corporate valuation methods, students are recommended the detailed treatments by Barker (2001) and Ferris and Pécherot Petit (2002). In addition, an interesting and entertaining account of stock market valuation methods is to be found in Malkiel (1996).

Much useful material on the financial aspects of professional team sports can be found in the literature of the economics of sports. Examples include Quirk and Fort (1992), Scully (1995) and Dobson and Goddard (2001). Quirk and Fort cover topics such as the market for sports franchises, tax, stadia and arenas, and player wages. Scully also covers the market for sports franchises and player wages. Both Quirk and Fort and Scully focus on the North American major leagues. Dobson and Goddard focus on the economics of (association) football principally in England. Their book includes chapters on the historical development of club revenue streams, player wages and transfer fees, and the impact of team performance on share prices.

Finally, students will also find informative discussions of issues in sports finance in the leading academic sport management journals such as *Journal of Sport Management*, *European Sport Management Quarterly* and *Journal of Sports Economics*, trade journals such as *SportBusiness International*, *Street & Smith's SportsBusiness Journal* and *Soccer Investor*, and newspapers and magazines such as the *Financial Times*, the *Sunday Times*, the *Economist* and *BusinessWeek*.

Recommended websites

www.corporateinformation.com: A website providing individual company information with worldwide coverage.

www.hemscott.com/equities/compindx.htm: A useful source of summary information for listed UK companies.

www.londonstockexchange.com: The official website of the London Stock Exchange with extensive information including individual companies, share prices, new issues and company announcements.

www.uk-wire.com: This website provides an alternative source for all company announcements on the London Stock Exchange.

www.bloomberg.com: Another very widely used general financial website with market news, company information and share prices.

finance.uk.yahoo.com: Yahoo's finance website providing a wide range of financial information and resources.

www.updata.co.uk/directory/uk.asp: An excellent listing of links to websites with UK company information.

www.carol.co.uk: An excellent source of annual reports for UK companies.

www.ft.com: The website of the leading European financial newspaper containing information on the sports industry and individual companies.

sport.telegraph.co.uk: The *Daily Telegraph*'s website provides comprehensive coverage of all sports news including one of the most reliable listings of football transfer fees.

www.sportbusiness.com: An excellent source of general sport business news available to subscribers to *SportBusiness International*.

www.soccerbase.com: A useful source for general player and club information covering the UK and other leading European leagues including transfer fees.

www.pullman.com/rodfort: An excellent source of sports business data for the North American major leagues compiled by one of the leading sports economists.

www1.ncaa.org/finance/index.html: Detailed financial data on US collegiate athletics provided on the NCAA official website.

www.olympic.org/uk/organisation/facts: A wide range of financial information on the Olympic Games provided on the official IOC website.

Visit www.booksites.net/chadwickbeech for links to these and other relevant websites.

Keywords

Capital asset price model (CAPM); debt irrelevance proposition; discounted cash flow (DCF) analysis; dividend discount model (DDM); efficient market hypothesis; equivalence proposition; financial statement; financial ratio analysis; return on capital employed (ROCE); shareholder value; weighted average cost of capital (WACC).

Bibliography

Barker, R. (2001) *Determining Value: Valuation Models and Financial Statements*, Pearson Education, Harlow.

Brealey, R.A., Myers, S.C. and Marcus, A.J. (2004) *Fundamentals of Corporate Finance*, 4th edn, McGraw-Hill, Boston.

Broyles, J. (2003) *Financial Management and Real Options*, John Wiley & Sons, Chichester.

Dobson, S. and Goddard, J. (2001) *The Economics of Football*, Cambridge University Press, Cambridge.

Ferris, K.R. and Pécherot Petitt, B.S. (2002) *Valuation: Avoiding the Winner's Curse*, Prentice Hall, Upper Saddle River, NJ.

Fried, G., Shapiro, S.J. and DeSchriver T.D. (2003) *Sport Finance*, Human Kinetics, Champaign, IL.

Howard, D.R. and Crompton J.L. (1995) *Financing Sport*, Fitness Information Technology Inc., Morgantown, WV.

Malkiel, B.G. (1996) *A Random Walk Down Wall Street*, 6th edn, W.W. Norton & Co., New York.

Quirk, J. and Fort, R.D. (1992) *Pay Dirt: The Business of Professional Team Sports*, Princeton University Press, Princeton, NJ.

Scully, G.W. (1995) *The Market Structure of Sports*, Chicago University Press, Chicago.

Chapter 8

Managing small and not-for-profit sport organisations

Cameron O'Beirne
Edith Cowan University

Upon completion of this chapter the reader should be able to:

■ identify a range of operational issues that facilitate the effective management of small and medium sport enterprises;

■ have developed an awareness and appreciation of the components of small and medium sport enterprises;

■ demonstrate the characteristics of the not-for-profit sport organisation;

■ outline the strategic issues facing not-for-profit sport organisations.

Overview

This chapter provides a general overview of the management of two types of sport business; the small- to medium-size enterprise (sometimes called an SME), and the not-for-profit sport organisation. Issues that influence the activities of both types of sport business will be identified and reviewed including the task of operations, strategic planning, financial activities, and the role of customer or participant interactions. Later in this chapter we examine the differences between types of sport businesses and how they differ in management.

Introduction

■ The small- to medium-size sport enterprise

The SME as a sport organisation can be as diverse as a retail sports merchandiser, a sports information service, commercial sports medicine and sports science providers, tourism and recreation providers, and event managers. Table 8.1 provides a description of the types of SME sport business that may exist. The sport SME has been identified as a key contributor to the growth of the leisure industry (Berrett, Burton and Slack, 1993), not only in the United Kingdom but globally as well. The changing nature of participation in, and consumption of, sport influences the types of business function that occur and, consequently, the types of sport SMEs that exist. Trends in

Table 8.1 Examples of sport SMEs

Sector	Example
Professional services	Fitness centre operations, professional coaches and athletes, sports medicine and sports science, tourism
Venue and events	Planning, construction, management, amusement parks, parks and gardens, tourism
Goods and equipment	Livestock, manufacturing and retailing
Media	Print, TV, cable, satellite and internet

sport participation away from formal club and association membership to a more unstructured fee-for-service arrangement is becoming increasingly prevalent. Changes at the social and cultural levels are linked to the growth of new, commercially-operated sport and recreational activities such as indoor cricket, workplace-based sports, touch football, leisure centres and gymnasiums, and swimming centres.

Sport SMEs interact with other sport businesses, particularly those involved in the not-for-profit and participatory type activities which include sport and recreation clubs. There is also considerable overlap as many not-for-profit sporting organisations attempt to develop commercial arms to their operations.

Characteristics of the sport SME

Not withstanding the large variation in the type of sport business that sport SMEs are engaged in, most sport SMEs have certain characteristics that define them as SMEs. These include:

- providing goods or services to a market;
- focus on making a profit;
- small management structures;
- few employees;
- privately or independently owned.

Internationally, SMEs may be considered differently. In the United Kingdom, Section 248 of the Companies Act of 1985 provides the following criteria for evaluating companies' categories:

Small enterprise	Medium enterprise
A turnover not greater than £2.8 million	A turnover not greater than £11.2 million
A balance sheet total not greater than £1.4 million	A balance sheet total not greater than £5.6 million
50 employees or fewer	250 employees or fewer

SMEs are sometimes categorised by the number of employees they may have. The Small Business Service (2003) describes these categories thus:

- micro-businesses are those with 0–9 employees;
- small businesses have 10–49 employees;

- medium-sized businesses have 50–249 employees;
- large businesses 250+ employees.

Similarly, the European Commission has adopted a single definition of SMEs which uses the figures shown in Table 8.2.

Issues for the sport SME

Like other SMEs, the sport SME faces a number of issues that will affect the viability, and ultimately the profitability, of the business. Four key areas need to be addressed:

- developing a customer focused business strategy;
- building a competitive edge;
- operational planning;
- cash flow management.

Developing a business strategy

The key element to success in any business is that of possessing a clear strategy designed to minimise wasted effort and maximise results. Devising a business strategy is a process of exploring opportunities, identifying and evaluating options and determining a plan of action to achieve realistic results. The business strategy will establish the way in which the business will operate and ultimately succeed. A business strategy could start with a simple analysis using the SWOT technique that is discussed in detail in Chapter 9. SWOT is an acronym for Strengths, Opportunities, Weaknesses and Threats, where the 'SW' are internal factors affecting the business, and the 'OT' are external influences. Each of these descriptive categories is used to look at the business from an objective perspective.

A customer focus

A key component in developing a business strategy is the need to understand customers. What motivates customers to purchase your products or services? Importantly, remember that customers do not buy goods or services; they buy

Table 8.2 **European Commission definitions of SMEs**

Criterion	Micro	Small	Medium
Maximum number of employees	9	49	249
Maximum annual turnover	–	7m euros	40m euros
Maximum annual balance sheet total	–	5m euros	27m euros
Maximum % owned by one, or jointly by several, enterprise(s) not satisfying the same criteria	–	25%	25%

Source: www.businesslink.org

benefits. For example, when people join a health club, some are buying a lifestyle, some are buying social interaction, and others may be buying fitness. The products and services offered in the marketplace are constantly changing but basic buying motives such as health, beauty, safety, comfort, convenience, enjoyment and economy change very slowly.

Using the health club example, what can be offered to people who only have time to work out in the evenings or have children to look after? The business may open at times that are *convenient* for them, and perhaps organise a crèche facility, thereby offering a *benefit* that appeals to their basic buying motives.

As well as understanding customers' buying motives, we can ascertain more information using a simple form of market intelligence. Using certain questions we can uncover vital information to assist in the growth of the business by understanding our customer demographics:

Who	uses the product or service?
	decides to make the purchase?
	actually makes the purchase?
	buys from me?
	buys from the competitor?
Where	is the product or service used?
	do customers find information?
	do customers decide to buy?
	do customers actually buy?
	are the potential customers located?
What	benefits does the customer want?
	is the basis of comparison with other products or services?
	is the rate of usage?
	price are customers willing to pay?
	is the potential market for the product or service?

CASE 8.1   Hooking new customers: Pro-Angler Fishing Tackle Direct

Pro-Angler Fishing Tackle Direct (PAFT) was established in 1993 as a mail-order fishing equipment, clothing and accessory retailer. Targeting the 30–50-year-old demographic in the fly-fishing industry, Pro-Angler also offers courses on tying flies and casting in addition to product demonstration nights. Based in the state of Victoria, Australia, Pro-Angler employs three full-time staff as well as several freelance distributors in Australia and New Zealand.

As part of its business strategy to understand its customers better, and increase sales, PAFT developed a company website in 1999. As the majority of the company's business was generated through mail and telephone order, the expansion to an online medium was a relatively smooth process. The website reduced the burden of producing costly hard-copy catalogues to be mailed Australia-wide. With new products being introduced frequently the catalogues were often out of date before they were sent. The website incorporated software that assisted Pro-Angler to maintain customer information relevant to future marketing opportunities and enhance product placement.

For example, when new customers register their details on the website, the company database is automatically updated with this information. Using this information, the company sends out newsletters to target groups bi-monthly with the latest specials and new products.

In addition to becoming an additional point of sale, Pro-Angler's website provides information about the products available for sale, course information and a list of regional distributors. Links are available to fly-fishing guide sites, guides, tours and educational courses. The website allows customers to conveniently research the company, its products, and other external information before making online purchases. Pro-Angler also uses the internet to conduct supplier research and, where available, order products online. Market research on competitors and potential suppliers both domestically and internationally is performed and the owner uses the internet to contact international suppliers with the aim of becoming an Australian distributor.

As well as providing an easier way to communicate with customers, there were also a number of financial benefits. Additional revenue was generated by the website, and cost savings were also seen, through reductions in postage and printing and staff time required to compile, fold and send the catalogues.

The internet also provided Pro-Angler with non-financial benefits such as a tool enabling online marketing, point of sale, and communication. The company's brand has been promoted far beyond the narrow focus of magazine advertising and mail-outs, and the website has enabled it to accurately target promotional material to existing customers. The convenience and time saved with electronic ordering compared to phone or mail ordering has benefited both Pro-Angler staff and its customers. Visit the Pro-Angler website (*www.proangler.com.au*).

Small-business life cycle

The nature of businesses changes over time, as societal, environment and consumer demands and pressures change. As a result, the sport SME needs to be agile enough to be able to respond to changes in the environment in which it operates. It is useful to identify different stages of the small-business life cycle, each of which places different demands upon the business and management of such. Table 8.3 illustrates the sport SME life cycle, the different phases of growth (or decline) and the goals of each phase. In addition, the role of the owner of the business is described. It is important to note that in most sport SMEs, the owner plays a number of roles, from marketing, to leadership, through sales and even cleaner!

Research in the area of sport SMEs (Byers and Slack, 2001) has suggested that owners of small leisure businesses typically engage in adaptive decision-making based upon a number of factors such as the size of the business, limited human and financial

Table 8.3 Small-business life cycle

Phase	Start up	Take off	Harvest	Renewal
Goal	Survival	Sales	Profits	Revival
Role of owner	Initiator	Developer	Administrator	Successor
	Innovator	Implementer	Manager	Reorganiser
		Delegator	Leader	
Typical Crises	Confidence	Cash flow	Leadership	Inertia
	Cash flow	Delegation	Complacency	Succession

resources, and the person's own involvement in the leisure or sport as his or her primary hobby.

Discussion question

1. Looking at the typical crises that can occur in the small-business life cycle in Table 8.3, how do you think the sport SME owner can overcome these issues?

Start-up phase

This initial phase can be best characterised by enormous uncertainty. Typically, the owner lacks confidence in the business and has all-consuming thoughts of failure; will it be profitable? What will happen if it does not work? The fledgling business will almost certainly face a cash crisis caused by a large amount of initial capital and inertia before sales occur.

Discussion question

2. A large proportion of SMEs fail in this critical time. What do you think are some of the reasons this occurs?

The successful sport SME owner needs to be a good initiator, innovator and organiser during the start-up phase. An idea has to be transformed into a viable and realistic enterprise through generating enthusiasm, sound business strategy, planning and working towards creating a strong competitive advantage.

Take-off phase

The take-off phase is characterised by a sharp increase in sales volume, with the priority being to capitalise on your competitive advantage. At this time the business is growing quickly and more resources in infrastructure, staff and other items may be required to support the increased sales volume. The additional investment though can cause more cash flow problems that need to be monitored and allowed for. Planning for cash flow is a key component and is discussed later in this chapter.

During this time the business is growing too quickly for one person to handle and overwork and stress can start to have negative influence if not managed. A delegation crisis will occur unless the owner makes the transition from being just an owner, to an owner-manager. Accompanying this shift, management and operational policies need to be developed and implemented, 'the what to do and how to do it', so that the owner can focus on more strategic activities of the business. Learning how to delegate responsibilities to others, whilst exercising sufficient control to keep the business on track, is a key aspect of this phase.

Harvest phase

Following the rapid growth in sales the business begins to stabilise and enters what is termed the harvest phase, which is typified by a prolonged period whereby making profits is the primary goal; you are reaping what you have sown. However, accompanying this time of continual profits and 'business as usual', the focus can become more internal, with cost efficiencies, accounting and management policies taking up a lot of the business time. Administration detail and paperwork may become all-consuming, and enthusiasm may decline in the business. Complacency on the part of the business owner may lead to a vacuum in strategy and leadership within the business, and the business may start a gradual decline.

Renewal phase

This phase begins with the recognition and awareness that the business's competitive advantage has eroded. If this phase is not recognised, the business will typically continue to decline, lose staff and sales, and ultimately close. The goal is revive the business's competitive advantage and restore its ability to harvest. In this phase the successful sport SME operator will be a reorganiser and revitaliser. The objective is to breathe new life into the business by reasserting or defining a new competitive edge for the business. A reversal in declining sales, profits and cash flow occurs as the enterprise's assets begin to pay their way once again.

Building a competitive edge

Like any other business, the sport SME needs an edge or advantage over other similar businesses and competitors. This competitive edge will differentiate the business from competitors, and assist customers in selecting which products or service to purchase. Research into the factors of success in sport SMEs (Department of Industry, Science and Resources, 2001) has suggested key factors of accomplishment for the sport SME:

- strategic alliances for growth and new markets through enhancing efficiency through effective management of supply, production and distribution;
- operation changes to ecommerce systems and procedures including the establishment of a website and raising revenue through the promotion of the internet as an additional sales channel;

- part ownership offers to secure funds for growth;
- decision to change banks because of service dissatisfaction;
- expansion being assisted by an accountant or other professional.

Another key component to building and maintaining a competitive edge, especially in the take-off and harvest phases of the small-business life cycle, where staff become paramount to the success of the business, is the ability of management to keep staff motivated and rewarded for their efforts. This can be achieved through a number of means including:

- keeping staff informed and providing them with ownership of aspects of the business;
- properly remunerating staff;
- offering profit-sharing arrangements, bonuses, commissions and the like;
- providing an exciting and interesting environment in which to work,
- providing career development and training;
- keeping the management structure flat and encouraging open communications.

CASE 8.2   Flytxt: Sport Relief

Flytxt is a marketing and media company based in London that helps companies create interactions with customers using mobile and digital channels. Flytxt has a range of clients including TV, radio, publishing, consumer goods, retail, entertainment, financial services, leisure, charity, government, transport, B2B and pharmaceutical companies.

Flytxt wanted to create a competitive advantage over other providers of text-messaging services. Sport Relief was developed as a new fundraising venture in conjunction with Comic Relief and BBC Sport to raise money for children and young people. Using SMS as the medium for the fundraising campaign, Flytxt provided 'premium-rate' or 'reverse-billed' SMS using mobile phones across all four UK network operators to raise funds for the Sport Relief cause.

Three varying campaigns were used by Flytxt in the programme:

1. *Total Ticket* invited sports fans to answer a multiple-choice sport-related question for the chance to win season tickets to major sporting events in 2003 in the UK and overseas. The quiz was heavily publicised on television as well as the Sport Relief websites.

2. The *Wimbledon competition* coincided with the start of the Wimbledon Tennis Championships. Tennis fans watching TV coverage were shown a series of archive Wimbledon clips and were invited to enter a competition by texting to a short-code or calling a premium-rate phone line with the year it took place. At the end of each day one winner was picked to receive a Sport Relief Wimbledon goody bag and then entered into a prize draw for the chance to win a week's holiday for two at the Lawn Tennis Association's winter training base in Spain.

3. *World Cup Alerts* provided football fans with SMS updates on the World Cup games and at the same time raised money via a reverse-billed SMS mechanism.

Subscribers to the service paid 20 pence per message to receive the latest news, scores and opinions from TV and radio pundits during the World Cup tournament.

In total, entries for Sport Relief's text and phone competitions raised over £220,000, half of which came from SMS activity. The Total Ticket competition received over 230,000 entries, raising almost £150,000 for Sport Relief, with over 50% generated from text messages. The Wimbledon competition brought in more than 90,000 entries, raising over £55,000, with almost 50% of this amount raised by texting.

The campaign marked several significant firsts for the wireless marketing industry, as it was the first time a UK charity has ever involved SMS as part of its fundraising activity. It was also the largest reverse-billed SMS service to be executed across all four major UK network operators, using one common short-code. Flytxt developed a number of strategic alliances by providing the SMS fundraising service for the Sport Relief competitions, managing the IT infrastructure and enabling the connectivity to mobile operators in the UK.

For more information about Sport Relief visit their website (*www.sportrelief.com*).

Operational planning

The operational plan for the sport SME is concerned with day-to-day processes of the business, procedures, workflow and efficiency. The main purpose of the operational plan is to assist the business owner to work smarter rather than harder. The process of completing an operational plan enables the owner to determine what commitment is required to make the business a success. Planning significantly increases the chance for survival and prosperity by focusing attention on areas in which SMEs sometimes get lost.

Formalising the plan

The most important aspect with any plan is to formalise it. This means writing it down in a format that is easy to read and can be referred to when necessary, or used by external parties such as financial institutions if support is required in the future. The plan provides a way to examine the consequences of different strategies and to determine what resources are required to launch or expand the business. Components of the plan need to include those shown in Table 8.4.

Cash flow management

Cash flow management is one of the most important aspects for operations within the sport SME. Financial accounting systems measure profit by matching revenues (what you earn) and expenses (your costs). Unfortunately, commonly-used accounting processes do not distinguish between financial transactions and cash transactions. Consequently, cash flowing into the business is not profit as it may be used in areas of the business such as expenses, stock or operating costs. Case 8.3 explains why profits are not cash.

Table 8.4 Components of a business plan

Heading	*Detail*
Introduction	State the objectives of the plan as simply as possible, i.e. what is it you want to do?
The industry	Indicate the present status and opportunities for the industry in which the business will operate. Discuss any new products, new markets and customers. Identify any national, regional or economic trends that could have an impact on the business.
The business	Briefly describe what type of business is to be engaged in. Indicate its name, how it is organised and its main activities (retailing, service provision, manufacturing, wholesaling or some combination). Identify the status of the business such as start up, expansion, or purchase of an existing enterprise. Describe its location and facilities.
The offering	Describe exactly what is going to be sold or offered as a service. Emphasise those factors that make the product or service unique or superior to those already on the market. Discuss any opportunities for the expansion of the product/service or the development of related products/services. If the product processes or services require design or development before they are ready to be placed into the market the nature and extent of work should be included.
The market	Identify your customer profile. Determine the size of the market. Assess the competition. Estimate sales.
Marketing strategy	Based on the assessment of the market, explain pricing policies, and tactics for advertising and promotions.
Management and staffing	Describe the skills and abilities of the management and explain roles within the business. State duties and responsibilities of all staff. What will be the costs of staffing?
Financial forecasts	Provide forecasted profit and loss cash flows and balance sheets that indicate the projected financial status of the enterprise. If the business already exists, show its current financial position before proceeding to a forecast.

CASE 8.3   Dolphin Surfcraft: cash flow and profits

Dolphin Surfcraft manufactures surfboards for surfers worldwide. They have customers in Australia, the UK, Japan and the USA. International customers are given 30 days credit on their purchases, which enables more sales to be made as international wholesalers can then move stock and sell it on without the capital outlay. This has resulted in sales of $10,000 in the first month, which doubled every month after that. However, Dolphin pays for raw materials in cash, which is 50% of the retail price. Operating expenses are 10% of sales revenue and must also be paid for in cash. The result is a net profit margin of 40% and after four months of trading a profit of $60,000 is seen.

	Month 1	Month 2	Month 3	Month 4	Total
Sales revenue	$10,000	$20,000	$40,000	$80,000	$150,000
Expenses					
Stock	$5,000	$1,000	$10,000	$2,000	$20,000
Operating	$4,000	$40,000	$8,000	$75,000	$15,000
Profit	$4,000	$8,000	$16,000	$32,000	$60,000

However, on closer inspection of these figures, some discrepancies occur in the cash flow. Because the international wholesalers do not have to pay for purchases for 30 days (receipts), and expenses must be paid for immediately (payments), the actual cash flow of the business is in reality in overdraft by $20,000 as $80,000 from month 4 sales revenue is tied up with what are called trade debtors (the international wholesalers). Subsequently without cash flow planning this business could run out of cash and go out of business.

	Month 1	Month 2	Month 3	Month 4	Total
Receipts	$0	$10,000	$20,000	$40,000	$70,000
Payments	$6,000	$12,000	$24,000	$48,000	$90,000
Cash flow	($6,000)	($2,000)	($4,000)	($8,000)	($20,000)

In determining cash flow budgeting a number of steps need to be put in place that act as controls in the sport SME operation. These include:

1. Forecasting sales: a physical forecast in terms of units sold or services provided, or the number of transactions completed can be translated into dollar figures based upon your schedule of prices. Actual sales will ultimately be different from the forecast; however the forecast provides a range of possible outcomes that will assist in determining the cash flow options for the business.
2. Identifying cash receipts: is divided into two categories: operating cash receipts and non-operating cash receipts. The non-operating cash receipts are associated with one-off transactions such as borrowing money, obtaining new equity capital or selling an asset. Operating cash receipts are directly related to operating the business as described in the Dolphin case (Case 8.3) and may include the cost of purchasing raw materials, paying freight, and selling on to wholesalers using credit.
3. Identifying cash disbursements: can also be categorised as operating and non-operating disbursements. Operating disbursements are those costs which occur in operating the business; they can be variable, such as stock purchases, wages, marketing, or fixed, such as interest payments, plant and equipment, and building rent. Non-operating disbursements are usually one-off transactions of initial stock, plant and equipment.
4. Determining net cash flow and future cash position: is achieved by summarising the cash receipts and the cash disbursements to determine their net effect. This will provide a surplus or deficit for each month. That can then be related to the bank balance to determine the future cash position of the enterprise and used to further manipulate forecast sales or change projections of cash receipts and disbursements.

Section summary

This section has provided an overview of the characteristics of the sport SME, and the types of goods and services that may be provided by such a business. Key issues for the sport SME were identified, and the small-business life cycle discussed relative to the sport SME. The next section of this chapter focuses on a different type of sport organisation; the not-for-profit sport organisation.

Managing the not-for-profit sport organisation

The not-for-profit sport sector plays a vital role in the overall model of sport business and it has been suggested that the importance of not-for-profit sport should not be underestimated in its ability to deliver health, societal and other outcomes for the community (Australian Sports Commission, 1999). The not-for-profit sport organisation (NPSO) typically involves volunteer management structures and a large participation base.

Not-for-profit sport organisations can range in size from a local darts club with limited resources, to a bigger, financially secure Olympic sport. Since the early 1980s, the not-for-profit sport system in countries such as Australia (Shaping Up, 1999), Canada (Kikulis, Slack and Hinings, 1992) and the UK (Sport England, 2003) has undergone radical change, with a shift away from volunteer administration and structures, to more of a professional way of administering and controlling sport activities. This transition is illustrated in Table 8.5. Moreover, these changing paradigms have assisted in determining the management of the NPSO so as to provide value to members and supporters alike.

Table 8.5 **Changing management of volunteer sport systems**

Level of involvement	Traditional sport structure	Contemporary sport structure
Club	Volunteer committees and boards	Volunteer councils and boards. Some clubs may have a paid administrator.
Regions/State/Counties	Volunteer councils and boards	Volunteer board that oversees function and determines policy. Professional management and paid staff with defined roles and duties.
National	Volunteer councils and boards determine key decisions. May have had a paid administrator.	Volunteer board that oversees function and determines policy. Professional management and paid staff with defined roles and duties.

What features determine a not-for-profit sport organisation

The not-for-profit sport organisation can be categorised in a number of ways. Kikulis (2000) provides two useful definitions for the not-for-profit sport organisation based upon certain criteria. One is that of the straightforward, simple sport organisation, the 'kitchen table' sport organisation. 'Kitchen table' sport organisations are so named as most decision-making in the organisation and administration typically occurs around the kitchen table or something similar. These sport organisations are typically characterised by the following attributes:

- an absence of a central office location, paid staff, and strategic plans;
- heavy reliance placed on volunteers who hold a number of different roles within the organisation;
- the structure has few hierarchical levels;
- the sport organisation is governed by few formal rules, little specialisation of volunteer roles or tasks;
- decision-making is centralised with a few volunteers.

Contrastingly, the more sophisticated so-called 'executive office' sport organisation can be defined by the following characteristics:

- an organisational design defined by structures and systems;
- a number of professional staff with specialised roles;
- specialised roles for volunteers;
- comprehensive plans, policies, and programmes;
- a decision-making structure that is decentralised to professional staff with reduced volunteer involvement.

Strategic issues for the not-for-profit sport organisation

With increasing demands placed on the not-for-profit sport organisation (NPSO), a range of issues emerge that shape and form the functions, structure and policies of the typical NPSO. Broadly speaking they include, but are not limited to, the following:

- stakeholder relationships;
- governance and control;
- strategic direction;
- processes and policies.

Stakeholder relationships

As with any organisation, the NPSO has a range of stakeholders, all with levels of accountability, reporting and influence within the organisation. Not-for-profit sport organisations characteristically have three key groups of stakeholders with varying levels of involvement, as shown in Table 8.6.

Table 8.6 Key stakeholders in NPSOs

Stakeholder relationship	Description
Legal	Legal owners are usually those bodies or persons identified in an organisation's constitution or articles of association who own the NPSO. They may be affiliated clubs or regional associations that form the umbrella body that controls the sport. Legal owners have the right to make changes to the NPSO constitution or articles of association, appoint or elect members to various boards and control the finances of the NPSO.
Moral	These stakeholders are usually more difficult to define as they may have no definitive constituted role within the organisation but nevertheless influence the way that the NPSO operates. This group can include players, coaches, officials, and fans or spectators of the sport.
Business	Stakeholders in this category include all entities and individuals with which the NPSO has a business or contractual relationship. These can include staff of the NPSO, sponsors and suppliers of goods and services, and in some cases the general public as paying customers.

Governance and control

Chapter 2 introduced governance issues for sport businesses and provided an appreciation of ethics and the regulatory framework within which sport businesses need to operate. The governance structure of the NPSO creates systems that enable stakeholders of the organisation to interact with and contribute to the operations of the NPSO. Most governance structures include:

- formal documentation that defines the rules and regulations of the NPSO, usually through a constitution or articles of association;
- a board or committee of directors whose duty is to govern the NPSO on behalf of the members and stakeholders;
- a board committee structure with defined portfolios of responsibilities within the NPSO that control the operations of the organisation on a day-to-day basis. This may include paid staff who may have the delegated authority to control the NPSO on a day-to-day basis.

With greater responsibility now required of NPSOs, including increased financial accountability and duty of care to participants, a key concern surrounding a conflict of values between volunteer boards and paid professionals can and does occur. Work by Kikulis, Slack and Hinings (1992), and more recently O'Beirne (2001), highlighted that with increasing bureaucratisation of volunteer not-for-profit sporting organisations, tensions arose and paid professionals conducted duties and made decisions that were once the preserve of volunteer participants.

Why does conflict occur? One suggestion is that due to the nature of the rich traditions and deeply-embedded values prevalent in most sport organisations (Kikulis, Slack and Hinings, 1995), a reluctance of volunteer board members to 'let go' of governance and decision-making occurs. Consequently, the involvement of a paid sport executive can be characterised by disagreements, conflict, and negotiation to ensure the traditional role of the board and other volunteers in governance, operations and decision-making is maintained to some level. A vital step in negating conflict is the need for strategic direction, coupled with policy formulation and implementation, within the NPSO, as discussed next in this chapter.

■ Strategic direction

The strategic direction of the NPSO, outlined within the organisation's strategic plan, will typically include the board's vision for the NPSO, accompanied by clearly articulated results to be achieved (sometimes called KRAs – key results areas or variation thereof), with each KRA having broadly stated objectives and outcomes with related strategies. Strategic direction is characteristically developed by the NPSO through a consultative process driven by the board and staff, with key stakeholders having representation and input where necessary. Importantly, the strategic direction of the NPSO must be dynamic, so that continual refinement and updating can occur in response to factors in the NPSO's environment that can and will affect the sport growth.

As well as being internally driven, Bryson (1995: 29) suggests that the influence of an organisation's external stakeholders is critical in determining a strategy, although confusion can occur in measuring the performance of the organisation, as the external stakeholder (such as a sponsor or the media) 'judge the organisation according to the criteria they choose, which are not necessarily the same criteria the organisation would choose'. This argument has been supported by Slack (2000: 4), who suggested that corporate sponsors who fund sport organisations expect a 'significant degree of commitment from athletes whose interests in terms of their competition become subordinate to the sponsor's desire'. Notwithstanding these comments, the NPSO must be mindful of the need to ensure the organisation has clearly established goals, as well as objectives and strategies for achieving them, and that they have ownership by all stakeholders.

CASE 8.4 Surfing Western Australia: formalising and organising a 'freedom' sport

Globally the sport and lifestyle of surfing is driven by a $40 billion industry. As the peak body, representing the sport in Western Australia, Surfing WA does not own any of its 'playing facilities'; the natural environment of the ocean provides the venue and 'players' typically do not engage in organised sport activities. Surfers prefer to pursue the recreational and lifestyle options associated with the sport and rarely involve themselves in the formalised part of the sport business that is surfing competition. Whilst statistics indicated that over 80% of the Australian population surf or were involved in ocean or other aquatic pursuits, Surfing WA had few members in the organisation. To entice new members to the organisation, Surfing WA devised strategies to change the sport that included changing the structure and changing the product offering.

Surfing WA was previously known as the West Australian Surfriders Association (WASRA) and was formed in 1964 by members of various boardriding clubs that existed at the time. For this reason the role of the Association was to basically form higher levels of State and National competition. An overview of surfing in the mid-1980s determined that various performance levels of the sport were controlled and conducted by a variety of groups. By the mid-1980s surfing in WA was not only run by WASRA – club and state level – but also by the Australian School Surfing Association (ASSA) – school-level competition – Australian Pro Surfing Association (APSA) – national-level events – and the Association of Surfing Professionals (ASP) – international surfing events. Through strategic change, stakeholder input and constitutional change, all groups were brought under one umbrella to create Surfing WA which now conducts all the business of the sport. One of the key questions that surfing asked itself was: Are we a sport or a business or both? Do we continue to provide state-level competition and basic membership benefits? Or do we recreate the concept of what our Association stands for?

Discussion question

3. What sort of products do you think surfing developed? Ask yourself these questions in determining the type of product that participants would be receptive to: Do they compliment the sport? Do they provide an income stream? Can we sell them to a sponsor?

Processes and policies

Policy has previously been described as 'an expression of the values and perspectives that underlie organisational actions' (Carver, 1991). Generally policies describe the course or general plan of action adopted by the NPSO. Policy writing is very particular; words are used carefully in order to ensure precise meaning or intent, as well as aiming to convey the most meaning without verboseness. Importantly, when NPSOs develop and then apply policy, care needs to be taken that users of the policy are able to adequately interpret the policy in order to achieve the outcome intended. Policy is only worthwhile if it is applied, and the NPSO needs to then ensure that a process is in place to see to this.

Within the NPSO's environment, the growth of contemporary policies that reflect wider societal values has been at the forefront of sport organisation development in recent years. Specific policies and procedures for dealing with a wide range of issues that affect the NPSO can be developed. These may include policies and processes for risk management within the organisation, child protection, the use of drugs in sport, special populations, as well as event management and the conduct of international events (O'Beirne and Broadbridge, 1999). An example of a specific policy concept is outlined in Case 8.5.

CASE 8.5   Development of child protection policy for sport

In April 1998, the Australian Government's Standing Committee on Recreation and Sport (SCORS) established a working party to examine issues pertaining to the prevention of child abuse in sport and recreation. This was based upon the principle that children should be free to take part in sport and recreation without undue exposure to the risk of child abuse. Furthermore, legislation enshrines the principle and supports the child's right by prohibiting specific forms of behaviour that a child or young person may find intimidating and offensive and that may impose restrictions upon their participation in sport.

The Western Australian State Department of Sport and Recreation took a lead role in influencing the prevention and reporting of child abuse in sport and recreation. This was achieved by developing a policy based on several key issues:

- Intimidating and offensive behaviour is not acceptable in any sport and recreation setting and is also against the law.
- From a risk management perspective, organisations need to be aware of responsibilities to their members and the public and the resultant duty of care.
- There is an increase in the number of organisations requiring a police clearance for those who will be involved in the operations of the organisation. This is a step being taken to try and avoid inappropriate situations arising from another person's behaviour. These clearances have become particularly important for those in positions where there is unsupervised access to children, or access to the records of children.
- There is a cost to the individual or the organisation: the cost of police screening/clearances of employees and/or volunteers.
- Identification of child abuse is not easy and care needs to be taken not to misrepresent the situation, hence resulting in false accusations. Sport and recreation personnel need to be trained with the necessary skills to assist them to identify potential illegal situations and to report instances in an appropriate manner.
- The establishment of confidential reporting procedures for child abuse cases need to be done and maintained as there are no legislative or mandatory reporting requirements.
- Adequate and appropriate monitoring is needed of the number of sport and recreation specific incidences of child abuse.

Importantly, after the policy was developed, the working party responsible produced a range of policy-based and education awareness strategies to address these principles. These initiatives included:

1. Two resources for the sport and recreation industry: Child Protection – Procedure: (June 2000) and Child Protection – Policy (June 2000).

2. Organisations funded through the Department of Sport and Recreation will be encouraged to develop and adopt a child protection policy.

3. The Department of Sport and Recreation will conduct education and awareness raising forums for staff and those involved in the administration of community sport and recreation.

4. The issue will be raised with local governments and information provided, so that they are in a position to assist local sport and recreation groups to manage child protection issues appropriately.

For further information and copies of the procedure and policy visit *http://www.dsr.wa.gov.au/organisations/childprotection.asp.*

Conclusion

This chapter has provided a wide-ranging overview of the management of two types of sport business; the sport SME and the not-for-profit sport organisation. Characteristics of both categories of sport business were identified and discussed in the context of the business they are engaged in. The sport SME is a diverse provider of goods and services across a wide range of business types. We have identified the changing nature of participation in sport and the accompanying growth of commercially-operated sport and recreational activities, goods and services. A number of issues related to operating the sport SME were discussed that focused on developing a clear business strategy, building a competitive edge, completing operational planning and proving cash flow management, all with the aim of making the business successful and profitable.

Conversely, the not-for-profit sport organisation provides a contrasting model of sport business. Two different types of NPSO were identified: the 'kitchen table' sport organisation and the 'executive office' sport organisation, and the changing management of the NPSO in a contemporary environment was explained. A number of strategic issues were identified that included stakeholder relationships, governance and control, strategic direction and policy formulation and processes.

CASE 8.6 Real tennis   FT

Not so very long ago, the ancient and venerable game of real tennis was dying. Courts in the 1970s had fallen out of use, no new facilities had been built for 50 years, and the magisterial sports journalist John Arlott predicted in his Oxford Companion to Sports and Games that none would be built again. The sport of renaissance kings and Victorian gentlemen – and of peasants, townsfolk and monks before them – had apparently had its day.

How things have changed. Real tennis entered the new millennium with a spring in its step, enjoying the umpteenth revival of its 1,000-year history. New courts have been built from Bristol to Sydney in the past decade and others are planned. Old clubs and courts have been resuscitated. Professional players enjoy a thriving international tournament circuit – even if the rewards pale by comparison with professional football, golf or lawn tennis – while at club level, M&G, the fund management group, sponsors a UK national league with 48 teams in eight divisions.

So how does a minority sport with an elitist image generate interest in a sporting world dominated by the mass-entertainment games such as football, cricket and rugby? How does it recruit participants when more modern racket games – lawn tennis, squash and badminton – are so easily and cheaply available?

Chris Ronaldson, a former world champion who has been head professional at the Hampton Court real tennis club for 21 years, has been at the centre of the sport's revitalisation since becoming assistant pro at the Oxford University court in 1971.

He was a gifted all-round sportsman who, on graduating from university, originally set out to become a lawn tennis pro. But, as the next season was not due to begin for six months, he decided to apply for the job advertised at the Oxford real tennis club. Nobody else applied and so he became a pro at a sport he had never seen.

Ronaldson soon became entranced with the game, but saw no future in the traditional pro's role of court retainer, sewing balls all day, and with little interest in widening access to the court. Amateur players were another obstacle, former public schoolboys who liked to phone their club pro on a whim and have a game that afternoon. 'It was very convenient for them' says Ronaldson, 'but they wanted to keep the game just for themselves. It had to end.'

The new popularity of the game, says Ronaldson, has come from a reaction against 'the era of cheap mass production – people wanted to do things differently'.

Real tennis balls are still made by hand. The pro winds string and cloth around a small piece cut from a wine-bottle cork. The asymmetrical racket produced only by Grays of Cambridge has also defied modernity: the alloys developed by the US space agency, NASA, and used in lawn tennis and squash rackets have been banned from real tennis.

Many of the game's converts – there are now more than 4,000 players in the UK, twice as many as 30 years ago – tend to be in the Ronaldson mould; experienced, talented racket-ball players with a cerebral approach. They talk of the game's tactical elements, comparing it to chess or backgammon, and see themselves as the intellectual elite of sportsmen. Some switch from tennis or squash as they reach middle age because they can no longer serve with power or run the ball down; in real tennis, you can go on improving even when in physical decline, such is the advantage of experience.

Mike Gooding, a Scottish-born pro ranked no. 4 in the world, explained that lawn tennis champions such as Pete Sampras achieve greatness by simplifying their game as far as possible. 'In most sports, you hear of top players aiming to get into "the zone", a trance-like state where you barely think. Well, you just can't do that in real tennis – you have to keep thinking all the time.'

History also plays its part in the appeal. The court has visual reminders of the medieval streets on which the game originated, including sloping penthouse roofs along three of the four walls, once medieval shop-fronts, and the tambour, a buttress that juts into the court.

At Hampton Court Palace, today's players use a court built for his own use by Charles I and refurbished by Charles II. At Falkland Palace in Fyfe, a hardy band of players use an outdoor court built by Mary Queen of Scots' father, James V, in 1528.

Real tennis is a sort of genetic link between medieval games of field, street and palace and modern tennis: the name itself comes from the old French 'tenez', alerting the receiver to get ready, while the term 'service' comes from the former custom of having a servant put the ball into play for each rally.

The odd but familiar tennis scores – 15, 30, 40, game – come from the sexagesimal counting system, with 60 meaning a whole (as in minutes and hours); 45 had been contracted for convenience to 40 by about 1800.

Access to the sport is only restricted by the limited number of courts, says Ronaldson. There is a waiting list to join the Hampton Court club, but the annual cost to a regular player, including membership subscription, rackets, balls and court hire, is about £700 – less than many golfers pay, or those thousands of lawn tennis players who join a smart club and take a winter week's coaching in Spain.

An attempt to widen access was launched two years ago with the building of a state-of-the-art court at Middlesex University's campus in Hendon, off London's North Circular Road. The court was built with a donation from real tennis devotee Peter Luck-Hille, and is open to students, free for beginners and then at a low subsidised rate, as well as to paying members of the public.

Interest from the students has been disappointing, although this perhaps reflects the make-up of the student body, a third of whom are from overseas. Also, sports-minded UK students are more likely to apply to universities outside London with a reputation for good facilities.

A recent midweek visit found retired investment banker David Lowden on court. Already a member and player at Lord's and Hatfield House, Lowden welcomed the new court as more convenient and cheaper; but he hardly represents new blood. He was followed by Lieschen Pogue, a 21-year-old drama student who had stumbled on the court while visiting the university gym next door.

'I fell about laughing when they told me it's a mix of tennis and squash,' she said. 'But it was fun – I'll definitely give it another go.'

Source: The *Financial Times*, 30 March 2002

Discussion questions

4. Evaluate the view that real tennis will always essentially be a small and not-for-profit sport, noting where you think there might be opportunities for its development.

5. What do you think are the main differences between managing the development of real tennis and managing the development of a grand slam tennis event such as the French Open or a squash tournament such as the World Masters, and how will this influence what you do as a sport manager?

Discussion questions

6. Using the definitions provided for categories of not-for-profit sport organisations, provide a snapshot of two sport organisations that illustrate both the executive office type and the kitchen table type. List the features related to the typology definitions for both sports. How do they differ? What are the key resources that the kitchen table sport lacks?

7. Determine where in the small-business life cycle a local sport SME is. How would they move to the next level and continue to grow the business? What resources are required to allow the business to be further developed?
8. Using the operational plan guidelines, write an operational plan for a local sport SME.
9. Provide an example of a 'kitchen table' sport you know of? Why have you defined it as a kitchen table sport organisation?

Guided reading

Further information on the application of organisation theory within sport business is available in the book *Understanding Sport Organizations* (1997) by Trevor Slack. This book provides a comprehensive overview of the sport organisation within a contemporary framework

Recommended websites

The following websites may provide useful starting points for further knowledge on the management of SME sport business:

The small business research portal at http://www.smallbusinessportal.co.uk

The UK Government small business website at http://www.sbs.gov.uk

Businesslink.org is the website of Business Link, the UK national business advice service at http://www.businesslink.org

The Department of Sport and Recreation of the Western Australian Government has a comprehensive list of online resources for not-for-profit sport associations at http://www.dsr.wa.gov.au/pubs/listpubs.asp. These include templates for conducting club meetings, draft constitutions, strategic planning information and guides, member protection policies, insurance guides and job descriptions for office bearers.

A comprehensive guide to codes of conduct for players, spectators, parents, coaches and officials is available at the same website at http://www.dsr.wa.gov.au/organisations/codeofconduct.asp.

The Sport England website also has a comprehensive publications page at http://www.sportenglandpublications.org.uk, which outlines a number of publications available free online or by mail order. These include information facilities management, general sport club development, volunteer investment and sport and the environment.

Visit www.booksites.net/chadwickbeech for links to these and other relevant websites.

Keywords

Not-for-profit sport organisation (NPSO); small- to medium-size enterprise (SME); SWOT analysis.

Bibliography

Australian Sports Commission (1999) *Active Australia – A National Plan, 2000–2003*, Ausinfo, Canberra, ACT.

Berrett, T., Burton, T.L. and Slack, T. (1993) 'Quality products, quality services: factors leading to entrepreneurial success in the sport and leisure industry', *Leisure Studies*, 12(2), 93–106.

Bryson, J.M. (1995) *Strategic Planning for Public and Non Profit Organisations: A Guide to Strengthening and Sustaining Organisational Achievement*, Jossey-Bass, San Francisco.

Byers, T. and Slack, T. (2001) 'Strategic decision making in small business within the leisure industry', *Journal of Leisure Research*, 33(2), pp. 121–36.

Carver, J. (1991) *Boards that Make a Difference*, Jossey-Bass, San Francisco.

Department of Industry, Science and Resources (2001) *Game Plan 2006: Sport and Leisure Industry Strategic National Plan*, Commonwealth of Australia, Canberra, ACT.

Kikulis, L. (2000) 'Continuity and change in governance and decision making in national sport organisations: institutional explanations' *Journal of Sport Management*, 14(4), pp. 293–320.

Kikulis, L.M., Slack, T. and Hinings, B. (1992) 'Institutionally specific design archetypes: a framework for understanding change in national sport organizations', *International Review for the Sociology of Sport*, 27(4), pp. 343–70.

Kikulis, L.M., Slack, T. and Hinings, B. (1995) 'Towards an understanding of the role of agency and choice in the changing structure of Canada's national sport organizations', *Journal of Sport Management*, 9(2), pp. 135–52.

O'Beirne, C. (2001) 'Exploring the on-line sports organisation: the need for critical analysis', *Cyber Journal of Sports Views and Issues*, June 2001. Available: http://sptmgt.tamu.edu/

O'Beirne, C. and Broadbridge, M. (1999) *Developing Sport Through Hosting International or Major Events: A Resource for Sport*, Ministry of Sport and Recreation, State publishers, Perth.

Shaping Up (1999) *Shaping Up: A Review of Commonwealth Involvement in Sport*, a report to the Federal Government, Canberra, Ausinfo.

Slack, T. (1997) *Understanding Sport Organizations*, Human Kinetics, Champaign, IL.

Slack, T. (2000) 'Studying the commercialisation of sport: the need for critical analysis', *Sociology of Sport*, 1 (1). Available: http://physed.otago.ac.nz/sosol/v1i1/v1i1a6.htm.

Small Business Service (2003) *Business Link. What is the Definition of a Small Business or SME?* Available: http://www.businesslink.org/cgi-bin/bv1/detail.jsp

Sport England (2003) 'Delivering best value through sport', Sport England website. Available: http://www.sportengland.org/whatwedo/best_value/bestval.htm.

Chapter 9

Strategy and environmental analysis in sport

Chris Parker
The Nottingham Trent University

Upon completion of this chapter the reader should be able to:

- define strategy;
- understand the difference and relationship between strategic planning and strategic thinking;
- explain the need for, and value of, the strategic process in the business of sport management;
- analyse the sport industry and associated environments using a variety of methods and frameworks;
- identify and justify the key skills sport managers need to perform successfully as strategists and environmental analysts.

Overview

This chapter focuses on the sport manager's role as a business strategist and explains the relationship between environmental analysis and strategy development. It explains and justifies the centrality of the strategist's role within the sport management context and considers the key skills needed to be a successful sport management strategist.

Progression through the chapter is as follows:

1. Understanding strategy: strategic planning and thinking; strategic stretch and fit; the importance of vision.
2. Identifying, understanding and analysing environments: global/social; industry; internal.
3. The core skills of the sport management strategist.

The chapter highlights the practical ongoing nature of the strategic approach and argues that it provides the foundation upon which all other business functions operate, irrespective of the focus and/or nature of the sport business. This point is reinforced through the inclusion of three case studies based on the following sports and businesses:

- Martial Arts (the Colne Valley Black Belt Academy);
- Diving (Triton Diving Ltd);
- Soccer (the Football Association).

Understanding strategy

> I look at a fight like a chess game or a maths problem – I've got to work out my strategy and tactics. I've got to weigh up my assets and his assets, and work out how my strengths are going to attack his weakness … He could never beat me as long as I had a good strategy. Lennox Lewis, World Heavyweight Boxing Champion, (quoted in Gorman, 1997: 152.)

Sport is inherently competitive in nature. To be successful over a period of time sportsmen and women need to:

- determine the nature of the environments within which the competition is taking place, ensuring they have the resources and, by extension, the capabilities to move successfully through those environments;
- understand the competition: their strengths, weaknesses, goals, capabilities, preferred and possible strategies and tactics;
- have a clear, detailed vision of what they need to accomplish – in what timescale and in what manner;
- use the above to create a suitable strategy;
- implement that strategy;
- evaluate its success and adapt it as and when appropriate.

Lennox Lewis has been accused by some of being a boring performer. This accusation has never been levelled at him by the competitors he has met (and often levelled!). Lewis understands and applies the six steps outlined above as comprehensively as any sport business strategist.

Business, like sport, is inherently competitive. Those sport businesses which do not develop and implement appropriate strategies and tactics consistently in response to the needs of changing environments and competitors risk stagnation, defeat and possible demise. However, the nature of competition within the sport industry is arguably changing faster than the nature of competition in any sport! Chris Wolsey refers to Prahalad (1997) when he writes: '… the traditional assumptions that underpin competition are no longer valid. No longer do industries have clear boundaries with distinct characteristics. Moreover, the assumption that you can plan for the future is considered misguided.' (Wolsey and Abrams, 2001: 91) This is not an isolated view. According to Hamel and Heene (1994): 'The task of coming to an agreement on what strategy is, or should be, is complicated by the fact that the phenomena under study are changing faster than they can be described.' Sondhi is clear about what strategy is, and about its value in changing, competitive environments:

> The strategy is a form of communication that allows people to share and achieve common goals and objectives … Strategy also ensures that these goals are achieved through optimal use of resources, such as financial, physical and human, that are generally treated as being quite scarce. (Sondhi, 1999: 12)

Given the above, it can be argued that the sport manager assuming the strategist's role is facing a series of challenges that will test her/him and his/her organisation in ways never before experienced. Unlike the sport management strategist, Lennox Lewis is sure of the competition he is facing, the nature of the environment in which he will perform, the deadline towards which he is working, the absolute reward for success and the rules of the game!

To be a successful strategist in the business of sport management, then, requires the development of appropriate resources applied with a mixture of:

- analysis
- passion
- courage
- adaptability
- creativity

combined with high-level communication skills – after all, once formulated, the strategy has to be 'sold' to stakeholders – and an overpowering need to create a valuable new reality.

The primary requirement, however, is that sport managers understand the nature of strategy, the difference between strategic planning and strategic thinking, and its value in gaining competitive advantage.

Strategy: planning and thinking

The word strategy has its origins in the field of military planning, stemming from the Greek word 'stratos' meaning 'army'. the fact that the strategic process is at the heart of the most demanding, complex and challenging competition known to humanity – that experienced in the theatre of war – is in itself a powerful argument for its value in dynamic, complex and competitive industries like sport. It is a reminder also that when resources and/or opportunities appear equally matched, great strategic thinkers determine the outcome.

Mintzberg and Quinn (1991) state that: '... strategy is a plan – some sort of consciously intended course of action, guideline (or set of guidelines) to deal with a situation'. Whilst Sondhi (1999: 7) writes: 'Strategy is a broad and general plan developed to reach long term objectives, focusing on actions for each of the functional areas.' He goes on to observe: 'Strategy can be expressed in terms of the visions, missions, objectives and tactics. This is the translation of the strategy into meaningful terms for the benefit of employees, customers and all other stakeholders.'

Strategy, then, is a plan that sport managers create and hold based on their knowledge of the culture, resources, capabilities and purpose of their own organisation, the nature and needs of the external environments within which they operate or by which they are influenced, and the current, or likely, behaviours of their competitors. The strategic purpose is the same in the business of sport management as it is in any other competitive endeavour: to 'win'.

Although sport managers need to create and hold strategies, they must also be willing and able to adapt their strategy in response to unexpected environmental changes. Simply put, sport organisations exist to meet the needs of the market in ways that differentiate them from their competitors. As these needs, or the ways in which they can be satisfied, change so too must the organisation's strategy. The business of sport management, therefore, requires strategic thinkers, not simply strategic planners.

> Strategic planning is seen by many to reflect the conventional view of strategy, where the future is relatively stable and planning activities merely represent the linear extrapolation of future scenarios based on historical precedent ... However, the increasing dynamism and complexity of the business environment militates against relatively prescriptive approaches in favour of more progressive ways to understand and develop strategic praxis. (Wolsey and Abrams, 2001: 82)

And, as Mintzberg (1994) observes: '... strategic planning is not strategic thinking. Indeed, strategic planning often spoils strategic thinking, causing managers to confuse real vision with the manipulation of numbers.' (Cited in Wolsey and Abrams 2001: 94) Further, Mintzberg differentiates between 'deliberate' and 'emergent' strategies, observing that emergent strategies grow out of the original, deliberate strategy. It is essential that the strategy that a sport organisation espouses is, in reality, the one being put into action. As illustrated in Figure 9.1, the strategic journey might include the occasional change in direction. This change needs to be intentional: the result of ongoing strategic awareness, analysis and thought, rather than a gradual, unintended organisational shift. Strategic intent precedes strategic means. The former is the willingness to create an agreed valuable new reality; the latter the processes and goals that need to be implemented and achieved in order to create that reality. Strategic intent is clearly defined at the outset. Strategic means are often determined as the plan is progressed.

Sport management strategists need to answer clearly the questions:

■ what elements of our operation and associated relationships have to change? (why, how and by when?)
■ what can remain the same?

if they are to establish a coherent strategic approach.

Strategies have two broad approaches. Strategic *fit* describes the deliberate matching of the sport organisation's activities to the demands of the environments in which it operates. Strategic *stretch* describes the process of identifying those existing organisational resources or capabilities that can be used to create new opportunities.

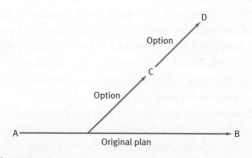

Figure 9.1 **Strategic change**

◼ Examples of strategic fit and strategic stretch

Triton Diving Ltd, a scuba-diving business based in Islington, London (Case 9.2) is an example of a business creating strategic fit; despite the absence of open water in London there is a significant community of divers with very specific needs, which Triton seeks to meet.

The Colne Valley Black Belt Academy (Case 9.1) based in Huddersfield, Yorkshire, is an example of a business utilising strategic stretch; the attitudes inherent within the martial arts of self-discipline, respect, social responsibility and hard work have been highlighted in an original way and 'sold' to a community concerned with teenage crime, underachievement at school and diminishing family values.

What these two very different sport businesses do have in common is a very clear vision of what they intend to achieve and how their business will grow, based on their understanding of the environments they function in and the changing nature of the sport industry.

Vision

A sport manager on holiday in Devon some years ago was struggling to find his way to a hostelry of fine repute. Stopping to ask a local person for directions, he was told: 'Yes I do know where that pub is, but if I was going there I wouldn't start from here!'

Sport management strategists must determine the direction in which their organisation should go and have a clear sense of where they are 'starting' from. The truth, as all strategists and travel writers know, is:

- If you do not know where you are going, any road will take you there.
- You cannot know where you are going if you do not have a vision.

So what exactly is a vision?

David Kirk, former New Zealand All Blacks captain, described it thus: 'Visions must be rational, but they must be emotional. They are often distant. They must engage and frighten. They must be big. Leaders of potential world class teams ask for sacrifices that are immense. There has to be a reason for asking. Only a vision can unite and invoke at the highest level.' (Quoted by Sondhi, 1999: 9)

Discussion question

1. What are the key words in the above quote? What challenges do they present for sport management strategists operating in dynamic, complex environments?

CASE 9.1   The Colne Valley Black Belt Academy: business built on vision

Bob Sykes is a 6th degree karate black belt, the editor of the UK's leading martial arts magazine, *Martial Arts Illustrated*, and the owner of the Colne Valley Black Belt Academy in Huddersfield, England. Throughout the 1980s he ran what he describes as a 'kick and spit' gym with a reputation for hard-core training and attitudes.

'In those days', he says 'students had to meet my demands. I had no regard for what the local community needed, or what the martial arts could offer anyone who didn't want to train in the way that I did and for the same reasons.' (Bob was a competitive kickboxer.) 'If you wanted to train it was, quite literally, my way or the highway.'

Not surprisingly, student turnover was significant. In 1995 a disillusioned Bob Sykes gave up teaching completely. 'I couldn't see the point in continuing,' he explains. 'My business was going nowhere. We were doing what we had always done and I couldn't see a future in it.'

In 1999 Bob came into contact with the Educational Funding Company (EFC), an American company providing consultancy and information back-up to full-time martial arts schools. Four key elements of their process excited Bob immediately. They were:

1. Monthly agreements

Students paid by direct debit. According to Bob, 'It's an extra sign of commitment on the students' part. Also it makes the Academy seem more professional – private leisure clubs always ask for monthly agreements.'

2. The student creed

The years outside the martial arts world had given Bob a new perspective. 'I became increasingly aware of the community's problems – particularly those associated with disaffected youth and teenage crime. Youth Clubs had effectively disappeared. The Scouts and Guides didn't operate. Local cricket clubs had closed. There was no way for youngsters to develop their self esteem, develop positive friendships, learn new skills and gain a respect for family and society.'

Bob had an increasingly clear vision. He says, 'I saw for the first time the significant role a martial arts school could play in meeting these needs. The EFC's student creed is a positive, personal mission statement that all students make. As soon as I read it I was hooked!'

3. Student of the month award

This is given to a number of students and reflects effort and commitment rather than simply ability. 'We reward positive character traits,' Bob says, 'and we do so on a regular basis.'

4. Monthly gradings

Traditionally martial arts schools allow students to grade for their next belt only three or four times a year. Whilst Bob only allows such gradings every three months, he encourages students to grade for a tag – a step towards their next belt – every month. 'Short term goals motivate students,' he explains.

'Also the cost of the gradings are included in the monthly agreement. Which means I don't have to take money off my students when we meet. I can concentrate solely on teaching and their development.'

The Colne Valley Black Belt Academy was founded on EFC principles in 1999. It now has over 300 students and is growing rapidly. 'Actually, they're not just students, they're customers,' Bob says. 'I ask them for ways we can improve our service and facilities and I value their feedback.'

Bob and his team of instructors profile each 'customer' – often entire families become members – learning their names, individual needs, concerns and personal goals.

'The difference between the old days and now,' Bob admits, 'is that today I'm in the business of using martial arts to satisfy individual and community needs. In the past it was all about me: the instructor.'

And the future?

Bob's vision is precise. 'Every community will have a martial arts academy – or several depending on the size of the community. In five years we will be reaching 90% of people. We are the Youth Clubs, the Scouts, the cricket clubs of the future.'

Discussion question

2. What factors can prevent sport managers from developing a clear vision? How can these be overcome?

A vision must be clear, detailed and specific: it is a finished painting, not a general idea. On what is such a vision based? The foundation is recognition of the organisation's core competencies coupled with environmental analysis that leads not only to an understanding of the current situation, but also to an awareness of the most likely future(s) the organisation will encounter or can create. As previously discussed, this process incorporates:

- a commitment to strategic thinking as well as strategic planning;
- identification of key environments and their nature;
- analysis of influences, including competitors, operating within those environments: the relationships they share and their relative power;
- analysis of ones own strengths and weaknesses;
- a willingness to take action.

Identifying, understanding and analysing environments

There are essentially three environments the sport business strategist must understand. As shown in Figure 9.2 these are:

- global/social;
- industry;
- internal.

Although sport organisations exist to meet the needs of the environments within which they operate, it must be remembered that through this very process they also influence those environments. The relationship is interactive, a system, with 'arrows' of influence moving in all directions.

Sport management strategists aiming to turn a powerful, motivating vision into a valuable new reality need to apply methods of environmental analysis to enable and encourage their strategic thinking. A useful framework for analysing global and social environments is the PESTEL analysis.

PESTEL

This is a framework for identifying the:

- Political
- Economic

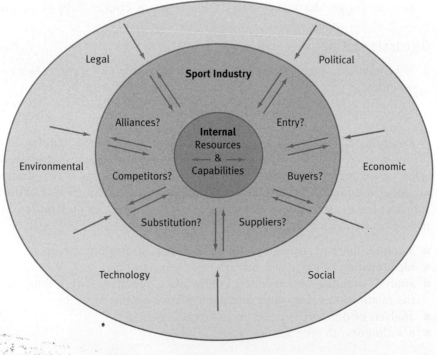

Figure 9.2 Strategic environments

- Sociological
- Technological
- Environmental
- Legal

influences on an industry and, by extension, on a specific business.

Political drivers are those driven by government initiatives. The political environment need not be limited to the country within which the business exists, but may extend to any country within which the business operates and/or the associated sport is played.

Economic drivers are those aspects of the economy that influence the industry. These aspects also tend to play a significant role in determining consumer behaviour. In times of recession for example, when disposable income diminishes, sport businesses might reasonably expect a decrease in turnover.

Social trends, attitudes and behaviours are influenced by many drivers, with education, health, changes in work patterns and demographics being amongst some of the more obvious influences on the sport industry. The impact of these drivers is reflected in both the workforce and consumers.

Whilst there are many who would not call fox hunting a sport, there are those who do. Whatever an individual's point of view, no one can deny the fact that changing social attitudes have fuelled a debate in the United Kingdom at the highest political levels about the appropriateness and value of this particular activity. Although at the time of writing the consequences of this debate are still unclear, what it does highlight is the relationship that exists between the various PESTEL factors and the potential influence they have for defining and shaping industry norms.

Technological drivers are recreating certain markets but, although their impact is clear within some elements of the sport industry, for some sport organisations it is their failure to keep up with technological advances that is even more significant. Triton Diving Ltd (Case 9.2) uses databases to profile customers, recording such information as contact details, purchases made and qualifications gained to determine how best they can meet individual customer's needs and when to offer new equipment or training. In contrast, few soccer clubs (even those with funds to invest) are currently applying technology to profile their fans and so develop the relationship between the club and its fan base.

Sondhi states: '... the key question to ask is "What advances in technology are driving change in your industry?"' (Sondhi, 1999: 36). When answering this question, as when determining other PESTEL drivers, sport management strategists need to be specific, ensuring they:

1. identify and focus on the essential drivers of change, not merely the symptoms of those drivers; and
2. be clear how these drivers affect the interrelationships between the business and the various environments it is influenced by.

According to Parker and Stone: 'To ignore the systemic nature of organisations, in terms of both the organisations' internal functions and their interaction with external environments and influences, is to risk: continual short-termism; costly, ineffective solutions; encouraging the language of blame; missed opportunities; organisational breakdown.' (Parker and Stone, 2003: 199)

WARWICKSHIRE COLLEGE LIBRARY

Increased awareness of, and interest in, *environmental* issues is such a significant social trend it is regarded as a driver of change in its own right. The debate regarding fox hunting (see above) is, for some, as much an environmental issue as it is a social and/or moral one.

Legal and regulatory factors are perhaps the easiest drivers for sport organisations to monitor as they are usually enforced. The strategist's skill lies in recognising and understanding the dynamics of the legal process, the political motives and, perhaps, the social demands that underpin it, in order to anticipate likely future regulation. Again, the key to successful application of a PESTEL analysis lies in a systemic, holistic approach geared towards increased understanding of the most likely future(s) the organisation will experience.

Discussion question

3. Select a sport with which you are at least familiar. Brainstorm all the ways the sport has changed in the last five years. You might consider, for example: the way the sport is produced; the way it is consumed; the involvement of media and technology. When your list is complete determine the:

- Political
- Economic
- Social
- Technological
- Environmental
- Legal

drivers of the changes you have identified. To what extent is the sport influenced by these PESTEL factors?

Porter's forces

Sport managers need to be strategic thinkers because these factors are constantly interacting and changing. So, too, are the six forces (Porter's forces) which, according to Michael Porter (1985), shape industry environments.

Michael Porter argues that the nature and, ultimately, the results of business competition are influenced by the following forces:

1. the threat of new entrants;
2. the power of buyers;
3. the power of suppliers;
4. the threat of substitutes;
5. the level of competitive rivalry;
6. the threat of internal strategic partnerships.

The threat of new entrants

> I teach my students that there is no defence against a surprise attack. If you're not strong enough to absorb the initial punishment, you've already lost. The only guaranteed way to overcome a surprise attack, is not to be taken by surprise in the first place. (Bob Sykes, see Case 9.1)

In rapidly-growing, dynamic and complex industry environments new entrants are inevitable and potentially dangerous. They are inevitable because there are always businesses looking to expand and develop into new arenas. They are dangerous because they can increase the level of competitive rivalry and, if they are not identified, monitored and responded to, they can deliver a surprise attack.

What influences the likely number of new entrants into a market segment? According to Porter it is primarily the existing barriers to entry and the expected response from current competitors. Barriers to entry are greatly determined by:

Economies of scale

If an organisation is unable at least to match the costs of current competitors, it is less likely to enter the industry.

Differentiation

To make an impact in an industry an organisation has to demonstrate such a significant meaningful product that it attracts sufficient custom. For 'new' sport organisations especially, the question of how to overcome existing customer or fan loyalty is a difficult one to answer.

Switching costs

These are simply the potential costs of switching from an existing player to a new player in an industry. The greater the cost, the less likely it is to happen and, therefore, the greater the barrier to entry.

Regulation

In some industries government policy can create obstacles to entry.

Capital investment and working capital requirement

If an organisation needs to invest large amounts in order to enter an industry, and/or if there are likely to be cash flow problems during the early stages, it might be deterred from entering.

Access to distribution channels

If an organisation cannot create partnerships that guarantee appropriate distribution of its product it might, again, refrain from entering an industry. Bob Sykes (Case 9.1) is aware that the Colne Valley Black Belt Academy is likely to face increasing direct competition within the next five years; the barriers to entry are not sufficient to deter newcomers in what appears to be a growth market. Although he welcomes this for the benefits he believes similar martial arts schools can offer the community, he is already making plans to respond to what, in this case, will not be a surprise attack. He argues: 'We will open a second Academy in the very near future. I cannot prevent other martial arts schools opening in our area – actually, I think it's essential that they do – but I can make sure we are the market leader.'

Buyer power

Buyers are customers. Buyer power, like Porter's other forces, can exist anywhere on a continuum from low to high. If buyer power is low it means that customers have minimal or no choice; the sport organisation they purchase from satisfies certain needs in an affordable and unique way. If buyer power is high, customers have extensive choice; they can select from an array of businesses all satisfying similar or the same needs in a similar or the same way. As mentioned previously, many sport organisations service fans – people with an intense, unswerving emotional commitment – rather than mere customers who will 'shop around' for the best deal. A family that supports Nottingham Panthers ice hockey team is unlikely, for example, to switch to supporting the Sheffield Steelers (Nottingham's great rivals) if there is a sudden change in the price of tickets. For this reason it could be argued that the buying power of Panthers' fans is low.

Supplier power

Suppliers are those businesses that supply the sport organisation with the resources it needs to operate. As with buyers, organisations aim to develop relationships in which the power distribution favours them rather than the supplier. As suppliers rarely, if ever, have the emotional commitment to a sport organisation that 'hard-core' fans do, the sport manager needs a level of negotiating skill if they are to create and maintain 'win–win' relationships.

The threat of substitution

If customers can switch easily from one organisation to another to gain benefit, the threat of substitution (and, therefore, buyer power) can be said to be high. Again, sport organisations, such as rugby clubs, whose operations focus on the provision of specific sporting events attract and keep a loyal following for whom even the thought of substitution is inconceivable. One of the challenges facing the sport management strategist, however, is how to ensure an increased customer base and how to turn an ever-increasing portion of that base into fans whose loyalty cannot be questioned. This requires, in part, an understanding of who potential customers are currently substituting 'our' organisation for, and why.

Of course, this cannot be achieved through strategic planning and thinking alone. The strategic plan is made manifest through the behaviours of the various business functions. The sport organisation's marketing plan, for example, must reflect and grow out of the overall strategic aim.

The level of competitive rivalry

Competitors fall into two categories: direct and indirect. Direct competitors are those who exist within the same industry segment and/or satisfy the same customer needs. In terms of the sport industry, indirect competitors are any businesses bidding for customers' leisure time and/or disposable income. Thus a local 'Showcase' cinema could be viewed by a rugby club as an indirect competitor.

The level of direct competition is determined by:

- the size and growth of the market;
- the number of competitors and their respective market share;
- levels of fixed costs;
- the degree of differentiation;
- barriers to exit.

Sport management strategists need to identify, analyse and understand their competitors as fully as possible.

The threat of internal strategic partnerships

Creating partnerships is one increasingly popular way in which sport organisations can create a meaningful difference and establish competitive advantage.

CASE 9.2 Triton Diving Ltd: creating partnership to develop competitive advantage

Opened in May 2002 by Nathan West and Chris Glen, Triton Diving Ltd is a dive centre and shop based in Islington, London, having previously been run for three years from Chris' home.

Triton's target is a clearly defined market segment: young professionals with a high level of disposable income. Islington is an area with a significant population of such people, being located next to the City and near to the Docklands – London's two main financial areas.

Although London is a substantial distance from any suitable open water, there is a large population of divers. The absence of open water has meant that Triton needs to diversify. Diving is one of the fastest growing recreation sports. The industry and, therefore, competition within it, is growing.

According to Nathan, 'All diving companies need to take responsibility for educating non-divers and bringing them into the world of diving. This will allow dive companies to sustain growth.'

In response to the above, Triton is creating partnerships with other businesses to provide added value for its customers. One example is the partnership established with the Virgin Active Health Club, also based in Islington. Triton runs an introductory diving programme called 'Discover Scuba' there. Virgin Active markets this programme at a reduced rate to its members on Triton's behalf. This reduction is perceived as a benefit by Virgin's members, and gives Nathan and Chris the opportunity to introduce non-divers to their sport.

Chris observes: 'We are currently facing a few challenges in the dive industry. If recession hits, it tends to be leisure and sporting activities that people pull back on first. Also, many dive businesses are finding it hard to compete with companies that are importing cheaper scuba kit from the continent and selling it at highlight competitive discounted prices on line. As the industry grows it will be essential to form partnerships with others in order to promote ourselves.'

Internal analysis

Whilst analysing external environments dispassionately and accurately is challenging, achieving an objective understanding of one's own organisational strengths and weaknesses can be even more so. How does the strategist decide the significance of specific strengths and weaknesses? In simple terms, by determining the extent to which they empower, or hinder, the organisation's ability to establish a meaningful difference – to create a valuable new reality – in the environments within which they are operating. Without the benefit of external analysis it is difficult to identify internal strengths and weaknesses, let alone the core competencies through which the organisation should aim for future growth.

Core competencies

An opportunity can only be realised if the organisation is capable of taking advantage of the opportunity. Therefore, prior to developing strategy an organisation needs to understand what its strengths and weaknesses are. More important, the organisation needs to be able to articulate its key strengths, the areas in which it is better than its competitors, that are difficult to replicate. These strengths are defined as the **core competencies** of the organisation. However, identifying the areas an organisation is good at, better than its competition, and that are difficult to replicate is not an easy task. (Sondhi, 1999: 154)

When considering the core competencies of many sport organisations, the unique nature and challenges of the sport management strategist's role is again highlighted. Is the core competency of Nottingham Panthers their ability to play ice hockey? Is the core competency of Leicester Tigers Rugby Football Club the team's skill on the pitch? Is the Colne Valley Black Belt Academy's core competency the fact that the chief instructor has the fastest side kick in Yorkshire? Or is the attention to detail paid when profiling the students? Or the regular grading structure? For those organisations whose *raison d'être* is the production of competitive sporting events, is the only competency the fans care passionately about the ability of their sporting heroes to perform at a high level? Is sporting performance more important to fans than business performance? Indeed, cannot the argument be made that the quality of the sporting performance directly influences, if not determines, the success of the business? And, if this is so, what role is there for the application of business strategy within such an organisation?

At the heart of the debate is the question: 'What exactly do competitive sport event organisations produce and sell?' Those involved with the business management of the organisation do not influence directly the quality or results of the sporting competition. However, in the words of Brandon Furse, marketing manager at Nottingham Forest Football Club, they can and should 'control the controllables'.

The unique nature of many sport organisations is not an excuse for not identifying and developing core competencies, but the very reason why it is essential to do so. The following analytical models and methods can be applied to help determine organisational strengths and weaknesses. The first is a powerful framework taken from the field of Neuro-Linguistic Programming (NLP).

The neurological levels model

The neurological levels model (Figure 9.3) is used primarily for evaluating and creating personal congruency and power; as organisations are essentially collections of individuals working to achieve specific, shared outcomes with usually limited resources and time, the model is equally applicable.

Internal organisational analysis seeks to determine the appropriateness and value of:

- the internal environment and resources within which, and with which, people are working;
- behaviours in all functions and the synergy between them;
- core skills and capabilities;
- corporate culture;
- corporate identity and the clarity with which it is presented in relation to expressed strategic intent and the known strategic means.

In NLP terms individuals who have these five levels in alignment are said to have 'personal power'. Sport organisations which have achieved the same in response to perceived environmental opportunities are likely to have 'commercial power'. A lack of

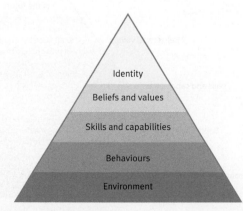

Figure 9.3 The neurological levels model

alignment weakens the organisation. A strategy that contradicts key organisational beliefs or assumes capabilities that cannot be achieved, for example, has only a limited chance of success. An analysis of the Colne Valley Black Belt Academy using the five levels model is shown in Figure 9.4.

The analysis highlights three important and interesting points:

- The five levels are in alignment: there is obvious synergy and cohesion from 'environment' through to 'identity'.
- There is cooperation between the Academy and other martial arts instructors and organisations even though they are essentially business competitors, reinforcing the value of strategic partnerships.
- The organisational beliefs – the culture – that underpins the business are passed on to the customers – the students. Indeed, in one sense the Academy actually **is** its customer base. Bob Sykes' students are at once the purpose and the product of his sport business.

These latter two points are common to many sport organisations. Triton Diving Ltd bases its strategy in part on partnerships with others in the sport and leisure industry; one of its measures of success is the number of non-divers who go on to become members of its dive club.

When sport businesses like the Colne Valley Black Belt Academy and Triton Diving Ltd have the five levels of their enterprise in alignment they create experiences for their customers/members that can be felt and shared, but which might be difficult to define or describe: a sense of being and belonging rather than simply buying. Committed sport fans will recognise and understand this state. Sport management strategists, needing to win the hearts and minds of colleagues in support of a new vision and required subsequent action, need to align the five levels so that those working within the business feel a similar powerful commitment. Strategists are ultimately dependent

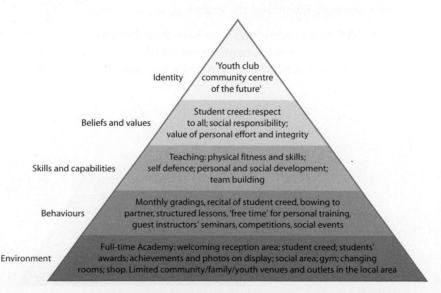

Figure 9.4 Analysis of Colne Valley Black Belt Academy

on the support and efforts of others; without significant stakeholder support strategic plans can flounder.

Stakeholder analysis

Some of a sport organisation's stakeholders will be external, while others will be internal. According to Parker and Stone (2003: 216), managers planning to introduce and 'sell' a new strategic initiative must:

- identify all stakeholders and the assumptions held by them;
- determine whether they will be supportive or resistant;
- assess the importance of the assumption (use a 0–10 scale);
- assess the degree of certainty attached to the assumption (use a 0-10 scale).

By plotting these key assumptions on a graph, the manager can determine the key factors that he or she needs to address and from there determine how to: 'best use the assumptions or forces that are supportive to overcome those that are resistant' (Parker and Stone, 2003: 216).

It is no surprise, given the special relationship that many sport organisations share with their customers, that this particular group of stakeholders can exert an obvious and powerful pressure when business decisions are not to their liking.

Life cycle analysis

The theory that organisations follow a life cycle, moving from birth to decline and eventual demise (see Figure 9.5) is not universally accepted. Proponents of the life cycle model argue that its value lies in the fact it enables strategists to:

- create strategies appropriate to the organisation's stage in its life cycle;
- evaluate the appropriateness of leadership style.

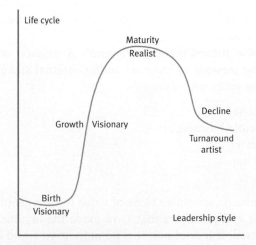

Figure 9.5 **Life cycle and leadership style**

Critics of the approach argue that it creates a self-fulfilling prophecy: believe your organisation has a limited lifespan and it will have.

The notion of determining appropriateness and, therefore, value is central to internal analysis. As each method of analysis provides additional insights into the organisation's resources, capabilities, structures, systems, etc., the question that must be asked consistently is: How appropriate is this internal factor in the light of our external analysis and likely future scenarios? The more appropriate the factor, the greater its value and strength. The less appropriate, the more of a weakness it is.

Both the Colne Valley Black Belt Academy and Triton Diving Ltd are in the growth stage of their life cycle.

According to Parker and Stone: 'As the organisation grows, the visionary leader becomes an information manager. He/she must also be able to balance the demands and challenges of growth and to act as a figurehead.' (Parker and Stone, 2003: 167) Bob Sykes (of Colne Valley), Nathan West and Chris Glen (of Triton) fulfil the role of visionary leader. They share information with customers, potential customers, media and other organisations. They seek to enhance and maintain growth through partnership development, internal initiatives and continual external analysis. They act as figureheads for their respective businesses and sports (Sykes performing this function most noticeably as editor of a leading sports magazine). It can be concluded, therefore, that their leadership style is appropriate for their business's current stage in its life cycle.

VMOST

VMOST analysis identifies and considers the synergy between an organisation's:

- Vision
- Mission
- Objectives
- Strategy
- Tactics

As vision and strategy have already been discussed, our focus here will be on the other three elements.

Mission means literally 'to send'. A mission statement should send a powerful, inspiring message to external and/or internal stakeholders. This statement will make clear the sport organisation's:

- purpose;
- principle business aims;
- identity;
- policies;
- values.

For a mission statement to be of value it must genuinely reflect the behaviours, beliefs, purpose and principles that have made the organisation successful and to which it is committed. If it does not, it is no more than a nod of the head in the direction of corporate political correctness.

A sport organisation's objectives, or goals, state precisely what has to be achieved, and by when, for the strategic intent to be implemented. Objectives need to be:

- Challenging
- Specific
- Measurable
- Achievable
- Relevant
- Time scaled

Tactics are the methods by which the objectives are reached. For example:

When we opened the Academy in 1999 I had a number of clearly defined objectives, the most challenging of which was to establish a membership of 150 students within the first year. We achieved this through a combination of formal advertising, events and demonstrations and word of mouth. (Bob Sykes)

McKinsey's 7S's framework

Every sport organisation is essentially the result of the interaction between the following McKinsey's 7S's:

- Strategy   (long-term plan)
- Structure   (organisational structure)
- Systems   (e.g. information technology and manual)
- Staff   (numbers; key members)
- Skills   (key skills; training)
- Style   (leadership)
- Shared values   (culture; values; beliefs)

These are the key elements of the organisational system, rather than stand-alone parts. Strategic change impacts on all seven elements to a greater or lesser degree, and the sport business strategist needs to be aware of, and manage, this interaction.

SWOT analysis

SWOT stands for:

- Strengths
- Weaknesses
- Opportunities
- Threats

A SWOT analysis is best used as a summary tool, bringing together the key evaluation from both external and internal analysis. Opportunities and threats exist in the external environments, whilst strengths and weaknesses belong to the organisation itself. Ideally, a strategy takes advantage of an opportunity (or opportunities) through the application of organisational strengths in such a way that it protects weaknesses and negates specific threats. The difficulties in achieving this ideal are caused by a number of interrelating factors:

Perception

Two cricket fans watching the same ball being hit to the boundary see two different things. The first sees a magnificent shot by the batsman. The second sees a poor delivery by the bowler and a misplaced field. The reason? Their individual perception, created by existing beliefs, value and past experiences.

Sport management strategists also bring their own perception to bear on the situations they are analysing and thinking about, which is why one strategist might view an external situation as an opportunity while another, in the same situation, might not. Strategists need to balance their ability to be passionately involved in the operational aspects of their business with the capacity to see the 'big picture' dispassionately and clearly. They need to be committed to their organisation without that commitment limiting their perception. It is a challenging requirement.

Flawed analysis

Analysis is flawed when strategists:

- fail to identify key environmental forces, behaviours and changes;
- misinterpret the significance of certain external forces, behaviours and changes;
- overestimate, or underestimate, their own organisation's resources and capabilities.

The mismanagement of time

This can be a cause of flawed analysis, with the process being rushed or left incomplete due to poor time management, and/or it can be a weakness in the implementation of the strategic plan itself. For a new reality to be perceived as valuable by internal and external stakeholders, it must come to fruition at the right time: too soon is as potentially valueless as too late.

A SWOT analysis can be regarded as a bridge leading from environmental analysis to organisational action; it enables the identification of the key issues the business needs to address and subsequent option creation, evaluation and implementation.

CASE 9.3 · The Football Association: developing the game through strategy and environmental analysis

Kelly Simmons became Head of Football Development at the Football Association (FA) towards the end of 2000. A sociology and social policy graduate of Warwick University and a keen soccer player in her own right, Kelly's interest in sport administration and development led to her joining the FA as a Regional Development Manager for Women's Football in 1991. Her focus was on:

- the development of girls teams;
- football in the community;
- the structure of the girls game.

At the time there were only three such managers in the country. Now, as a result of Kelly's strategy, there are ten regional managers and over one hundred football development officers.

'We needed local people to develop the game in their region – full-time professional people.'

In 1997 Kelly became National Coordinator for Women's Football. This gave her responsibility for international football, women's premier league and establishing a new programme of excellence. As a consequence of being, in her words, 'in at the deep end', she wrote a women's talent development plan, including plans to set up centres of excellence, coach mentoring programmes, sport science and medical support.

Kelly acknowledges that the driving force for the development of the women's game was a strong sense of social and ethical responsibility, and not market need(s) identified through research and environmental analysis. However, this was to change. Whilst Kelly's sense of social responsibility remained, she did recognise the need to research the environments she was aiming to influence.

Environmental analysis

The FA restructured and in 2000 Kelly became Head of Football Development, a position that encompassed both the men's and women's games. In 2001 Kelly commissioned the first major research ever conducted by the FA into the needs of 'grass-roots' football. Why did it happen then? As Kelly explains, 'I didn't want to invest millions of pounds into a hunch.'

Eight thousand questionnaires were sent to players, club managers, secretaries, and referees. A wide range of focus group meetings were established (which at the time of writing are ongoing). And the results of this research?

'The picture the results presented was bleak and it was essential that the FA took action to turn things around. Patterns of football were changing from the traditional 11-a-side to commercial 5-a-side. There were concerns over the quality of coaching and environments, child protection and poor behaviour of parents – none of which are conducive to positive learning experiences for children.'

Vision

The environmental analysis identified three key issues. These were the need for:

- investment in pitches and facilities;
- investment in club structures;
- supporting education to develop football.

Kelly consequently formulated her vision. It was to create:

- high participation across all social groups;
- well-qualified personnel and high standards of provision;
- improved pitches and facilities for clubs,

all supported by a comprehensive schools programme.

Strategy

Kelly set a five-year time-frame for her strategic plan. She acknowledges, 'Five years is a long time in rapidly changing environments like sport, but anything less would be just too short for the work needed.'

Her objectives focused on:

- people;
- money;
- partnerships.

Tactics to ensure club and community development included:

- club development programmes;
- facility development;
- training and development for coaches and volunteers;
- equity and inclusion work: players and clubs 'putting back' into communities to help with problems of crime for example.

Development initiatives in and through education encompassed primary, secondary and higher education.

Selling the strategy

Kelly wrote a consultation document which was distributed to all 'key partners', including the National Game Board, County Football Associations and Sport England. The 'sell' took approximately four months. The document received very positive feedback and, after some minor changes, it was approved; approximately one year after the research had been completed the strategy was ready to be launched.

In the summer of 2001 Kelly Simmons was awarded the MBE for her services to football.

The core skills of the sport management strategist

Strategists require a specific skill set and certain attitudes to perform their role well. Strategists need to be able to:

- analyse complex situations rigorously;
- identify the most likely future scenarios the organisation will encounter;
- construct a vision;
- identify possible ways for the organisation to achieve the vision;
- evaluate those options and determine the most appropriate;

- plan the implementation of that option;
- campaign and sell the vision and the associated plan to internal and external stakeholders;
- adapt the vision and the plan in response to unexpected external or internal changes.

Sport management strategists need to be able to think analytically, systemically, creatively, and pragmatically at different times of the process.

They must not only recognise what is happening in the environments that influence them, they must understand why it is happening. They must not only create options for future growth, they must evaluate them, select, 'sell' and implement those which seem most valuable.

Strategists are the creators of, and campaigners for, organisational change. Through the three key elements of the strategic process – analysis, choice and implementation – strategists influence organisational structure, systems and culture.

Conclusion

The strategic process is at the heart of the business of sport management. The main elements of business strategy formulation and implementation have much in common with the development and use of strategy in actual sporting competition. In the business of strategic sport management, however, environments are more far-reaching, complex and dynamic than their sporting equivalents, competitors can be far more difficult to identify and understand and the teams being managed can be great in number. Indeed, as has been noted, some writers argue that the very idea of being able to plan for the future is misguided. It is not simply a matter of semantics to question what is meant by 'future' in the context of sport. Strategy is a long-term plan, but in rapidly changing environments how far ahead is long term? For Bob Sykes of Colne Valley it can be one year. For Kelly Simmons of the FA it is five years. Sport business managers need to answer this question accurately for their own organisation and circumstance; in business, as in sport, timing is everything.

Environmental analysis is not performed simply to identify the current situation, but to encourage a consideration of the most likely future scenarios the sport organisation will face. In rapidly changing, complex environments this presents a significant challenge – particularly, perhaps, for those sport event organisations which have traditionally equated business success with sporting achievement and have, therefore, less experience in managing the business of sport than those organisations who focus on the production of sporting goods, clothing, equipment or facilities.

The strategic approach is not the reserve of those sport organisations which operate nationally or globally. Strategic planning and, more importantly, strategic thinking is an essential part of long-term business success, irrespective of organisational size or scope. Indeed, this chapter set out to argue that it is the driver of long-term success.

Of course, this requires an ongoing, daily commitment to the strategic process and role, and the question could be asked by many sport managers, 'When do I have the time to perform a continual strategic function? I'm too busy managing on a day-to-day basis to analyse environments and think in the long term.'

The response to which might simply be, 'In such a highly competitive market, can you afford not to?'

Bryson (1995) argues, however, that key decision makers should spend no more than ten per cent of their regular work-time on strategic thinking and planning.

It is not only managers, though, who can input successfully into the strategic process; valuable ideas and insights can originate from any source and every part of the sport organisation. Managers who encourage and access this support are not only maximising the use of resources available to them, but also increasing the likelihood of winning the 'hearts and minds' of colleagues when presenting a new strategic plan.

The sport industry and, therefore, the business of sport management will change – indeed is changing – as a result of environmental forces and organisational responses. Good sport management strategists will keep up with these changes. The very best will, in part at least, create them.

CASE 9.4　Tennis stars light way ahead for Argentina　FT

Sundays in Argentina are normally dominated by soccer but this week eyes will look towards Europe as Guillermo Coria and Mariano Zabaleta, two of a new crop of Argentine tennis players, do battle with each other for a quarter-final place at the French Open.

The fact that the two have to play each other in a grandslam tournament is not how they would have planned it. But with Argentine tennis at its best level since the days of Guillermo Vilas and Jose Luis Clerc 20 years ago, it is something they are likely to have to get used to. Coria, just 21, is one of two Argentine players in the world's top 10, and the country has 10 players in the top 100. By that measure, it is now the world's third strongest tennis nation.

Moreover, the country reached the semi-finals of the Davis Cup recently after beating Russia, the defending champions, 5–0. This month, all four semi-final places of the Hamburg Masters were filled by Argentines.

So what is behind the success? After all, the country has just passed through the worst economic crisis in its history, leaving almost 60 per cent of the population living below the poverty line. Gross domestic product in dollar terms has fallen about 70 per cent since 2001.

One simple explanation is raw talent: Argentines are simply good at sport. Soccer is one obvious example, but there are others such as volleyball, basketball and field hockey. Furthermore, sport occupies an important place in Argentine culture. Go to any of Buenos Aires's grand parks in the evening, and they will be full of people running, playing soccer and working out. In the provinces, sport is typically the main recreational activity.

Tennis, in particular, has become increasingly popular as the success of Vilas and Clerc inspired an entire generation. That was when – and why – most of the country's thousands of clay courts were built. In Buenos Aires alone, there are more than 260 registered clubs. Many of them have more than 20 courts each. As a result, tennis is both accessible and cheap, and it is played outdoors all year round.

Even today, Vilas continues to influence national tennis. He heads Argentina 2008, a programme sponsored by the government's department of sport, and he, together with a team of talent-spotters, scours the country in search of promising players aged between 10 and 12 with the aim of nurturing their talent.

But most of the current form is the result of the National Centre for High Achievement, a programme launched in 1996 by the Argentine Tennis Association (AAT). The initiative, which trains players between the ages of 13 and 18 and which has produced the likes of Coria and David Nalbandian, ranked eighth, had three aims: to raise the standard of tennis coaching; to increase the number of so-called future and satellite tournaments held in Argentina, enabling young players to compete for world ranking points without having to leave the country; and to give young players financial assistance to compete abroad.

'It has revolutionised Argentine tennis,' says Martin Rosenbaum, the AAT's secretary of sport. 'We are well on our way to having the strongest national team we have ever had.'

Jose Felippo, head of the AAT's youth activities, admits that progress in the girls' game has lagged behind the boys. But even here, there seems to be plenty of hope. Last month, for example, the under-16 girls team became South American champions. 'It is an area we have been working on for some time now and we are beginning to see the results,' says Felippo.

Still, there are some concerns about whether Argentina can continue to develop its talent. The economic upheaval of 2001 and last year has hit sponsorship hard and the number of future and satellite tournaments has fallen from about 20 in 1999 to just 12 this year. The result is fewer opportunities for players to win points at home, and many families are unable to finance costly trips abroad.

The AAT has been quick to react. In particular, it has decided to concentrate its limited funds on a handful of promising players aged between 15 and 16, such as Juan Martin del Potro and Emiliano Massa.

Luciano Benincasa, one of their trainers, is optimistic about the future in spite of the financial constraints. He believes that economic necessity acts as an additional incentive for young children to play sport and to see it as a potential solution to their financial problems.

'I used to train children in France and it was often difficult to motivate them because their lives were too comfortable and protected,' he says. 'There is never a problem motivating Argentine children.'

Source: Adam Thomson, *Financial Times*, 31 May 2003

Discussion questions

4. Using an established technique for examining the external and internal environment of an organisation, indicate what forces may have shaped the development of a strategy for Argentinian tennis.

5. In formulating a strategy for a sport such as tennis, what kind of time horizons should sport managers set, and to what extent do you think strategy should focus purely on the development of players?

Discussion questions

6. Consider the influence of Porter's forces on a sport organisation you know well. List the factors that determine the level of power or threat of each force. Use these to determine the levels of power or threat. Ask a friend or colleague with a similar knowledge of the same organisation to carry out the same analysis. Compare your results. How significant are the differences? What are the reasons for this? What are the lessons for sport business strategists?

7. Where would you place this organisation in its life cycle? Evaluate the appropriateness of the current leadership style and its vision, mission, objectives, strategy and tactics.

Guided reading

Westerbeek and Smith (2002) offer a global look at the business of sport from a political and economic perspective in the framework of global uncertainties and scenarios.

Slack (1997) provides an overview of the different levels of strategy available to sport organisations, and discusses strategy formulation and implementation and the relationship between strategy and organisational structure. His chapters on decision-making and managing change within sport organisations are also of particular relevance.

The need for sport business managers to be skilled at critical thinking, understanding research, problem solving and making informed decisions is discussed also by Parks and Quarterman (2003).

Wolsey and Abrams (2001) provide a useful look at the leisure and sport industry, Chapter 6 focusing on strategy.

The standard business texts on strategy are by Johnson and Scholes (2001) and Michael Porter (1980 and 1985). Sondhi (1999) offers a simplified text that provides a useful grounding in the three areas of strategic analysis, choice and implementation.

Richardson (2001) highlights the importance of building long-lasting relationships with internal and external stakeholders and the value of strategic partnerships, although this is, again, a standard business text lacking a sport bias.

Carling and Heller (1995) provide an interesting insight into the relationship between the use of strategy in the business arena and on the sports field, through a consideration of several sporting greats.

Recommended websites

The *Journal of Sport Management*: http://www.humankinetics.com/products/journals
The European Association of Sport Management: http://www.easm.org
The Center for Simplified Strategic Planning's eZine:
http://www.strategyletter.com

Visit www.booksites.net/chadwickbeech for links to these and other relevant websites.

Keywords

Life cycle; McKinsey's 7S's; mission statement; objectives; PESTEL; Porter's forces; strategy; SWOT analysis; tactics; vision; VMOST.

Bibliography

Bryson, J.M. (1995) *Strategic Planning for Public and Non-Profit Organizations*, Jossey-Bass, San Francisco, CA.

Carling, W. and Heller, R. (1995) *The Way To Win: Strategies for Success in Business and Sport*, Little Brown, London.

Gorman, K. (1997) *Lennox Lewis*, Faber and Faber, London.

Hamel, G. and Heene (1994) *Competence-Based Competition*, John Wiley, New York.

Johnson, G. and Scholes, K. (2001) Exploring Corporate Strategy, Financial Times, Prentice Hall, Harlow.

Mintzberg, H. (1994), 'The fall and rise of strategic planning', in *Harvard Business Review*, Jan–Feb, pp. 107–14.

Mintzberg, H. and Quinn, J.B. (eds) (1991) *The Strategy Process*, Prentice Hall International, Englewood Cliffs.

Parker, C. and Stone, B. (2003) *Developing Management Skills for Leadership*, Financial Times, Prentice Hall, Harlow.

Parks, J. and Quarterman, J. (eds) (2003) *Contemporary Sport Management*, Human Kinetics, Champaign, IL.

Porter, M.E. (1980) *Competitive Strategy: Techniques for Analyzing Industries and Competitors,* Free Press, New York.

Porter, M.E. (1985) *Competitive Advantage*, Free Press, New York.

Prahalad, C.K. (1997), 'Strategies for Growth', in *Rethinking the Future*, Gibson, R. (ed.), Nicholas Brealey, London.

Richardson, T. (2001) *Business is a Contact Sport*, Alpha Books, Fort Smith, Arkansas, USA.

Slack, T. (1997) *Understanding Sport Organizations*, Human Kinetics, Champaign, IL.

Sondhi, R. (1999) *Total Strategy*, Airworthy, Bury, Lancashire.

Westerbeek, H. and Smith, A. (2002) *Sport Business in the Global Marketplace*, Palgrave Macmillan, Basingstoke.

Wolsey, C. and Abrams, J. (eds) (2001) *Understanding the Leisure and Sport Industry*, Pearson Higher Education, Harlow.

Chapter 10

Managing sport operations, quality and performance

Terri Byers
Buckinghamshire Chilterns University College

Upon completion of this chapter the reader should be able to:

■ explain the nature of operations management in sports businesses;

■ discuss a variety of issues facing operations managers in sports businesses;

■ examine the nature of quality and customer satisfaction, and their relevance for sports businesses;

■ identify a range of performance measures that can be used by managers in sports organisations;

■ recognise a variety of issues for managers who are responsible for managing performance in sports organisations.

Overview

The purpose of this chapter is to introduce students to the concept of operations management in sports businesses. While there is an abundance of research in 'mainstream' operations management, there is considerably less known about the operations function within sports organisations. This chapter examines both mainstream literature and its application to sports businesses, and where appropriate, identifies research that has been conducted specifically in sport organisations.

The complexity of the 'operation management' concept, combined with the variety of contexts in which sport businesses are found, is reflected in the numerous examples and case studies presented throughout. Due to the increasing growth of the service sector in the sports industry, this chapter focuses on issues of importance to the 'service operations manager'. However, as a holistic approach to understanding operations, quality and performance in sports businesses is taken, some comparisons to manufacturing are made. Context is considered important when examining operational issues in sports businesses, hence the chapter discusses organisations of various sizes, and from the public, private and voluntary sectors. Key organisations found in the operational environment of sports businesses are also identified.

Consumers of sport-related goods and services are increasingly discerning and knowledgeable. Consequently, the concepts of quality and customer satisfaction are examined in this chapter. Finally, due to the rapid growth observed (Business in Sport and Leisure, 2002) and the increasingly competitive nature of the sports market, this chapter examines a range of performance measurement that can be used to help sport businesses monitor and evaluate their organisation's operations.

The nature of operations management

CASE 10.1   Gaelic Gear: innovation in service and manufacturing

Gaelic Gear is a young, vibrant, Irish-owned company, started in 1996 as a consequence of the troubles in Northern Ireland providing employment in a vacuum environment. The company quickly became successful, through fulfilling the needs of niche markets with quality and innovative products, delivered through an efficient operations system.

With extensive customisation techniques, particularly in printing and embroidery, the company continually updates technology to the highest and most recent specifications in order to meet consumer demand. Gaelic Gear has 150 embroidery heads at its disposal incorporating full design facilities. This ensures the capacity for the necessary expansion of the business and ensures that very large orders can be customised in the shortest possible time. Another unique feature of this company is that they have no minimum order. The company has built internal structures to ensure:

- innovative design and development;
- high product quality;
- competitive prices;
- efficient ordering systems;
- accurate customisation;
- efficient turn around times;
- worldwide express distribution.

Although Gaelic Gear has close business links with the largest international suppliers of corporate apparel, they have retained and expanded their capacity to manufacture, in both clothing and sports hardware, to ensure a quick response to specialist products and orders which cannot be purchased off the shelf. Gaelic Gear specialises in innovative presentation and packaging and recognises this as vital as well as value, quality and service, introducing new products on a regular basis. The motto is: If we don't supply it – we will!

What is operations management?

There are many different ways to define operations management. This section examines the meaning of operations management from three perspectives:

- operations management as a transformation process;
- operations management as a function of the organisation;
- operations management as a management activity.

■ A transformation process

> Operations management is concerned with creating, operating and controlling a transformation system that takes inputs of a variety of resources and produces outputs of goods and services needed by customers. (Naylor, 2002: 5)

> Operations management [is] the management of processes, people and resources in order to provide the required goods and services to a specified level of quality, doing so in the most cost-effective way. (Johnston and Clark, 2001: 4)

The definitions above reveal that 'operations management' is concerned with the *process* of ensuring a product/service is delivered or a product is manufactured according to some predefined specifications. Of course, many sports businesses provide both products and services. Paddle Sport in Warwickshire, England (see http://www.paddlesport.co.uk) is a specialist supplier of new and second-hand canoe/kayak clothing and equipment products. These products are brought to customers via a retail service and a worldwide mail-order service. In addition, Paddle Sport provides canoe and kayak courses to children and adults. As a process, operations management is concerned with the transformation of 'inputs' into 'outputs'. Therefore at Paddle Sport, 'operations' is the process of transforming the kayaks, the employees, the water into a service/activity desired by customers. The transformation process may be a manufacturing process or a service process. Figure 10.1 shows an example of operations management as a transformation process in a sports-equipment manufacturing business, Irish-owned company Gaelic Gear (see Case 10.1), supplier and manufacturer of sports clothing, equipment and other innovative products (see http://www.gaelic-gear.com).

Figure 10.2 illustrates operations management as a transformation process in a sports consultancy firm, Global Sports Management, an international sports business that offers a comprehensive range of management services for players and coaches, particularly in the sport of Rugby Union. Global Sports Management (see http://www.gsmworld.co.uk) offers services in contract negotiation, insurance cover, investment planning and tax advice for leading sports professionals.

The transformation perspective is useful in highlighting the important role of operations managers in producing goods and services. In general, sports businesses can transform either one or a combination of:

- materials (e.g. Spalding Sports UK Ltd, sports equipment manufacturer);
- information (e.g. Optima Sports International, consulting company);
- customers (e.g. JJB Sports, retail shops).

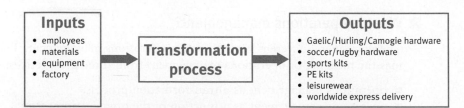

Figure 10.1 Operations as a transformation process – example: Gaelic Gear

Figure 10.2 **Operations as a transformation process – example: Global Sports Management**

However, operations management is more than a concern with efficiently transforming inputs into outputs (Russell and Taylor, 1998).

■ A function

Operations management can also be considered as one of the basic functions of an organisation, alongside marketing and finance. While marketing establishes demand for products and/or services and finance provides the necessary capital, operations is responsible for delivering the product and/or service to the customer, according to the specifications agreed with marketing and within the budget agreed with finance. The relationship between marketing and operations is particularly important to ensure that customers are satisfied with a product or service. That is, marketing efforts need to be consistent with what the operations function is actually producing so that customer experience is in harmony with or exceeds customer expectations. While the 'operations management as function' perspective provides another useful piece to the puzzle of 'What is Operations Management?', the final approach allows for a more detailed and specific examination of the concept.

■ A management activity

In some sports businesses, there is a designated 'operations manager'. For example, David Pomfret is the Operations Director at The Sports Industries Federation (TSIF; see http:/www.thesportslife.com), a non-profit trade organisation that represents the interests of businesses in the sports goods industry. Organisations that wish to join the federation benefit from a variety of free advertising offers, industry (and sector-specific) news, regular networking events and cost-saving packages on car hire, hotels cost and healthcare. In many instances in the sports industry, although the person may not be called the 'operations' manager, they perform many or all of the duties of an operations manager. When I asked Fred Moor, of Fredmoor Consultancy, a small business based in Lancashire, England, if his organisation had an operations manager, he replied 'no, as with many small businesses, you wear a lot of hats'.

As a management activity, Naylor (2002) suggests that operations management concerns the achievement of organisational goals through working with and through people, realising the greatest benefits from limited resources and balancing efficiency, effectiveness and equity. As indicated by this statement, the operations manager has many areas of responsibility. Slack, Chambers, Harland, Harrison and Johnston (1998) suggested that these responsibilities include:

Understanding the strategic orientation of the organisation

'An organisation without a strategy is like a motorist on a long journey without a map.' (Hope and Mühlemann, 1997: 40). Strategy represents the long-term plans or intentions of a business. The development of strategic plans can take place at different levels of an organisation. Corporate strategy (also known as business strategy) is the long-term plan for an entire organisation and is often represented by a mission statement. For example, the mission statement adopted by Nike is 'To bring innovation and inspiration to every athlete in the world' (Nike, 2003).

The intricacies of 'strategy development' are beyond the scope of this chapter. It is sufficient, for the purposes of understanding the operations function, to know that strategy essentially answers basic questions about the nature of a business and about its future direction. The mission statement of Nike conveys to employees and customers the commitment of the company to provide innovative products that inspire athletes (athletes are defined by Nike as any person with a body) to perform. It is this commitment to innovation that should inform the activities of the various departments of Nike, including research and development, marketing and operations, for example.

Developing an 'operations strategy'

Functional strategies indicate how each individual department of an organisation (i.e. operations, marketing, finance, etc.) contribute to the corporate strategy. Russell and Taylor (1998) suggested that strategic decisions in operations are concerned with:

■ products and services;
■ processes and technology;
■ capacity;
■ human resources;
■ quality;
■ facilities;
■ sourcing;
■ operating systems.

They also suggest that each of the above mentioned elements must fit together to complement one another. The products and/or services offered by a company determine its operations strategy. For example, products and services can be classified as 'make-to-order', such as sports management and marketing consultancy businesses where the service is offered in response to customer needs and according to their requirements. 'Make-to-stock' products and services are produced for a general market in anticipation of some demand. Examples include sports textbooks, equipment and clothing. A key operational issue is the forecasting of demand for these products. 'Assemble-to-order' products and services are produced as standard units with optional components, which are added according to customer requirements.

Processes can also be classified as projects, batch production, mass production and continuous production (see Figure 10.3). The process chosen should complement and enable the product or service being delivered. Therefore 'make-to-order' products, designed to customer specifications, would be impossible to produce using a mass production system. If the 'made-to-order' product is 'recommendations' from a sport

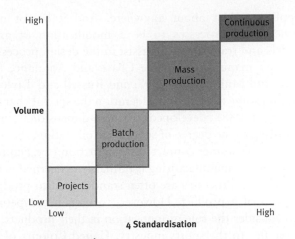

Figure 10.3 Product process matrix
Source: Russell and Taylor (1998: 44)

management consulting firm such as Global Sports, a project-based process would be more efficient and effective.

Operations strategy must consider the capacity and demand issue for the effective production of sports goods and services. Here there are a wide variety of questions to be addressed, within the specific context of the sports business. However, some possible questions may be:

- How much capacity is required – to meet average, potential and low demand?
- How will the company handle excess demand?
- What is the best size for a facility? Should demand be met with large facilities or many smaller facilities? Where should facilities be located?
- If international markets are part of the firm's overall strategy, should products be made and sold in other countries? What are the legal, ethical, cultural and organisation structure issues that may arise?

The issues associated with quality saturate every strategic decision. Operations managers must address target levels of quality, measurement systems, and the role of systems, processes and people in delivering quality and maintenance of quality standards. Few sport organisations are completely vertically integrated, making all parts and raw materials that are used in the production process. Therefore, strategic decisions are needed with regard to what items should be outsourced, how suppliers should be selected, how the quality and dependability of suppliers should be maintained and how many suppliers should be used, for example.

Finally, operating systems, such as the information technology system or the planning and control systems, facilitate strategic decisions on a daily basis. It is imperative that these systems are designed to support and enable the organisation's strategic vision.

Designing organisational products, services and processes

Designing a new product, service or organisational process begins with an 'idea'. Sports managers should realise that these invaluable 'ideas' may come from the organisation's research and development department, customers, competitors, marketing, suppliers – just about anywhere. And it is not uncommon for 'new' products, services and processes to be a modification of an existing phenomenon. Many models and frameworks to assist in the design process have been introduced for services and manufacturing (see Chase and Aquilano, 1995; Haywood-Farmer, 1988; Hope and Mühlemann, 1997; and Russell and Taylor, 1998). Some models are generic and some take into consideration the special characteristics of services. Haywood-Farmer (1988) developed a three-dimensional framework to classify services according to the degree of service customisation, the degree of labour intensity and the degree of customer contact and interaction (see Figure 10.4).

Design for manufacturing is primarily concerned with maximum efficiency and minimum costs. Processes are often standardised to produce consistent quality and specifications of a product. However, to remain competitive, sports manufacturers must also consider the role of innovation in their products, services and processes. Relative newcomer to the sports industry, United Colours of Bennetton, in their launch of a new line of 'sportswear', apply their innovative delayed-dying process to their sports clothing in order to produce contemporary colours as the market demands.

Manufacturing design processes may be modular (standardised parts to create a finished product) or designed for assembly (procedure for reducing parts in assembly, evaluating methods of assembly and examining assembly sequence). Increasingly, organisations are considering designing for environment (minimising material and energy use) and for quality (can be defined by organisation or by performance measurement standards). Technology is a central component of sports manufacturing businesses. Through CAD (Computer Aided Design), CAE (Computer Aided Engineering) and CAD/CAM systems, sports manufacturers can design and produce mass or bespoke products in relatively short time periods.

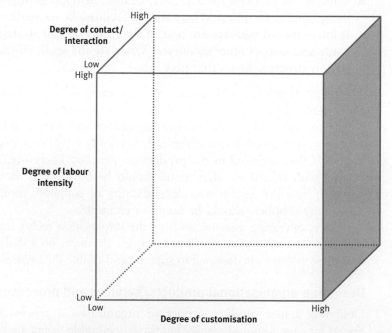

Figure 10.4 Three-dimensional classification scheme
Source: Adapted from Haywood-Farmer (1988: 25)

Boussabaine, Kirkham and Grew (1999) developed six models to assist professionals involved in feasibility studies at the design stage for sport centres. The models focus on modelling the total energy costs, related to providing safe and comfortable conditions in sport centres. More recent models, such as the 'Effective Product/Service Design' approach proposed by Verma, Thompson, Moore and Louviere (2001), have recognised the importance of integrating marketing and operations management decisions. The authors' models also highlight the importance of considering operational difficulty levels when designing products and services.

Service design begins with developing the 'service concept' (Desrumaux, Gemmel and Ossel, 1998). The service concept is a clear identification of the service's characteristics. Heskett (1987) suggested that identification of the service concept requires three questions to be answered:

- What are the important elements of the service(s) to be provided? (state in terms of results produced for the customer, employee and the company)
- How are these elements to be perceived by the target market segment? (also consider perception of employees, general public, other populations)
- What efforts does this suggest in terms of designing, delivering and marketing the service(s)?

It is important that the service concept addresses customer needs but not to the detriment of employee needs. In a service setting in particular, it is the employees who are in direct contact with customers. It is therefore essential that the service concept incorporates a common set of values that employees appreciate and support.

Controlling the product (delivery) of goods and/or services

Traditional conceptions of control in organisations are underpinned by assumptions of individuals as rational entities that can be directed towards organisationally legitimate behaviour by management systems. A variety of disciplines, including engineering (Gertosio, Mebarki and Dussauchoy, 2000), accounting (Anthony, 1965; Chua, Lowe and Puxty, 1989), cybernetics (Ashby, 1956), sociology (Johnson and Gill, 1993) and psychology (Salaman and Thompson, 1985) have examined control as a task to be performed by managers. To some extent this is true in that managers can employ administrative controls such as policies, formal procedures, job descriptions, accounting procedures and employee appraisals in order to monitor organisational and individual performance.

However, as suggested by Hopwood (1974), control in organisations is not limited to these administrative devices. These formal policies and procedures are 'controls' (external mechanisms such as disciplinary procedures) rather than 'control' (directing or influencing behaviour in a desired direction). Furthermore, controls can be implemented in direct and coercive manners or achieved more subtly through socialisation (Das and Teng, 1998), language (Boden, 1994), knowledge (Bourdieu, 1985), emotion (Fineman, 2000) and the manipulation of norms, values and culture. For a more in depth discussion of these subtle forms of control, see Mintzberg and Quinn (1998).

Measuring and improving organisational performance

It is important for sports managers to monitor and, where necessary, improve organisation systems, processes, and products/services. To do this, organisations must be customer focused and proactive in assessing aspects of the organisation and/or its staff. There are a wide variety of measures that can be used to assess organisation performance, including financial measures such as processing costs, total revenue, operating profit, and labour costs. However there are many more non-financial measures that may give managers a warning that financial performance is in danger, such as customer satisfaction, employee retention, customer loyalty, facility utilisation and waiting times. For example, if the manager of a sports performance laboratory regularly monitored customer satisfaction through a monthly survey, the results of which, over a six-month period, indicated a decline in customer satisfaction, the manager could take steps to improve the aspects of the service that people were dissatisfied with and prevent loss of business (and revenue).

The topic of performance measurement is discussed in greater detail later in this chapter. However, as a management activity it is important to emphasise that managers should focus on the 'improvement' of performance. Therefore, *measuring* customer satisfaction, as in the example of the laboratory manager, is insufficient to improve organisational performance. Rather, the manager must then take steps to address issues of failing performance. This may be in the form of a further survey to ascertain exactly the nature of dissatisfaction, or if it is clear why customers are not satisfied then to make changes and to inform customers that changes have been made.

Service operations management

Operations management is primarily concerned with the internal practices of organisations. 'Internal practices' constitutes an overwhelming number of different topics. There is a considerable body of generic literature (concerned with a wide variety of industries) devoted to the study of operations as a function of the organisation, as a process and as a management activity (see, for example, Hope and Mühlemann, 1997; Fitzsimmons and Fitzsimmons, 2001; and Johnston and Clark, 2001). Likewise, research into the internal operations of sports organisations (primarily commercial and public sector) has grown substantially in the last few decades (see Slack, 1997; De Martelaer, Van Hoecke, De Knop, Van Heddegem and Theeboom, 2002).

To discuss all of these is beyond the scope of this chapter. However, there are some key issues that are of interest to sports managers. There has been considerable research in sports businesses, focused upon operational issues of service quality (see, for example, Thwaites, 1999; De Knop, De Bosscher, Van Hoecke and Van Heddegem, 2001; Westerbeek and Shilbury, 2001) and customer satisfaction (see Kelly and Turley, 2001; Van Leeuwen, Quick and Daniel, 2001) with less interest being shown in performance measurement. There is, however, considerable practitioner and industry focus upon performance measurement in sports businesses. It is perhaps only a matter of time before academics begin to investigate this relatively uncharted terrain of sports organisations. The majority of operational research in sport (and in some cases, leisure or recreation) businesses has focused on the service sector. This is not surprising considering the considerable growth of services in the world economy and in the sport sector. Consumer spending on sport in the United Kingdom in 2000 was approximately £15.2 billion, an increase of 70 per cent in a single decade. However, an unexpected shift in the environment, namely foot and mouth disease, affected sport-related gambling, sport tourism and sport clothing suppliers as spending fell by 5 per cent (Business in Sport and Leisure, 2002). Of the 70 per cent increase in UK consumer spending in 2000, 64 per cent was spent on sport services (Business in Sport and Leisure, 2002). The next section examines the concept of services and the implications for operations managers of the unique attributes of managing a 'service'.

Services

There are four characteristics of 'services' that are not usually associated with manufacturing. As suggested by Hope and Mühlemann (1997), these characteristics are:

- intangibility;
- perishability (i.e. a service cannot be 'stored');
- heterogeneous (nature);
- simultaneity (of production and consumption).

These characteristics have important implications for the operations manager in a sports organisation. *Intangibility* refers to something that cannot be touched, which results in difficulties in measuring and defining the service. The *perishability* of a service refers to the urgent nature of service delivery in that there cannot be a surplus 'inventory' like there can be with tangible products. For example, if a Rugby League match only sells half of the available seats, those seats cannot be stored and sold again. Thus capacity management in the light of fluctuating demand for sport services becomes a key concern.

This highlights the fact that production and consumption of a service are *simultaneous*. Again, there is a sense of urgency about a 'product' that is both produced and consumed at the same time. It is difficult to ensure that the service is provided in a standardised manner, especially if several different people may be involved in service provision at different time periods. While staff training may remedy some of the problems presented by this service characteristic, we cannot train customers in the same way. Therefore clear signposting, layout and appropriate décor are considerations for operations managers.

Finally, the *heterogeneous* nature of services means that each time a service is performed, it is unique. That is, each customer may have different questions or requirements, the interaction between service staff may be different according to the customer and it is difficult and sometimes undesirable to standardise procedures to the extent that staff do not have the freedom to deal with customers' needs as they arise.

These characteristics are most evident in, for example, sport marketing and management firms such as Optima Sport Management International Ltd (http://www.optima-sports.com). This company provides 'advice' to clients on sponsorship negotiation, event creation and ambush marketing strategies. The services may be presented in a tangible form (e.g. a report or consultative document); however, the process of providing such a service is quite intangible, and may be unique for different customer requirements (heterogeneous). Likewise, the finished product is perishable in that the information is likely to be of some urgency for the client and not particularly useful after a certain deadline.

Customer satisfaction and quality

■ Defining quality and satisfaction

Garvin (1984) identified five approaches to defining quality:

- transcendent approach;
- the manufacturing-based approach;
- the user-based approach;
- the product-based approach;
- and the value-based approach.

The transcendent approach views quality as 'of the highest standard'. Here, quality is seen as innately excellent in nature, such as a newly-built sports stadium with the latest technological and architectural innovations, compared to a local community centre sports ground. According to this view, the stadium would be classed a 'quality' facility and the community centre does not represent a 'quality' facility.

The manufacturing-based approach views quality as conformance to some specification. Therefore a quality product is one which conforms precisely to its design specification. This view suggests that a novice gymnast who performs a simple floor routine with precision demonstrates a quality performance, whereas a senior gymnast performing more difficult skills but making a few mistakes and receiving a lower score than the novice, is classed as a lower quality performance.

The user-based approach deems quality to exist if a service/product meets the requirements of the customer/user. That is, the service/product is 'fit for purpose'. Therefore, an inexpensive tennis racket which allows an individual to enjoy the game on Saturday afternoons with friends, can be viewed as a quality product. However, a 'top of the line' carbon fibre racket can also be viewed as a quality product if it is required by its user for accuracy of play, minimal injury and speed/power of play. Arguably, this perspective confuses quality with satisfaction, where satisfaction exists when customer expectations are met (Hope and Mühlemann, 1997).

The product-based approach is a quantitatively defined approach where more equals better quality and measurable characteristics are of greatest importance. From this perspective, a golf club which produces a 300-metre shot is of higher quality than one which produces a 280-metre shot. Alternatively, less is sometimes deemed of a higher quality, such as the fastest 100-metre sprint time at the Olympics, or a sports marketing consultant who could produce a marketing plan for your new business in one day would be considered of a higher quality than the consultant who took one month!

Finally, the value-based approach takes 'cost' into consideration by viewing a product of quality as something that provides value for money. This is obviously a subjective judgement performed by a customer; for example, a £10 ticket (in regular seating) to watch the London Knights is seen as of higher quality than a £200 ticket in a corporate box.

Parasuraman, Zeithaml and Berry (1985) initiated much of the subsequent research into quality as an important construct in organisations, with their Gap Model which identified the ten determinants of 'service quality'. The determinants were later refined and reduced to five dimensions, namely reliability, responsiveness, empathy, assurance and tangibles (Parasuraman, Zeithaml and Berry, 1988). Perceived service quality was measured as the difference between customer comparisons of their expectations for what should happen and what actually happens in a service encounter, along the five dimensions named above. If a difference existed along one of the dimensions, it was characterised as a gap. To measure the gaps, the authors developed a 22-item questionnaire called SERVQUAL. This instrument is probably the most frequently adopted approach to measuring service quality (Haksever, Render, Russell and Murdick, 2000) but has been challenged by researchers on several bases (see Buttle, 1996; Robinson, 1999). Van Dyke, Prybutok and Kappelman (1999) cautioned on the use of SERVQUAL to measure quality of information services, adding to doubts of the effectiveness of the instrument in different contexts.

Not dissimilar to quality, satisfaction can be defined in a number of ways. However, Howat and Murray (2002) point out that satisfaction, as an affective state, occurs when an individual's needs and/or desires are met. In other words, when the needs of a customer are fulfilled, the customer feels satisfied.

Oliver (1997) referred to customer satisfaction as a subjective experience, a 'judgement' that a product and/or service has provided a certain level of fulfilment, or pleasure. According to Patterson and Spreng (1997), satisfied customers are more likely to use a service repeatedly and will relay positive information to potential customers (i.e. their family, friends, etc.). Satisfaction, therefore, may provide managers with a valuable indicator of future support for their organisation and service.

More importantly, Howat and Murray (2002) suggested that meeting customer expectations for key service quality dimensions should create satisfied customers who are loyal to a service and recommend it to others. In their study of a sports and leisure centre in Australia, these authors argued for an examination of the 'critical incidents' associated with sports services, in order to provide specific diagnostic information about quality and facilitate sport managers' ability to implement required improvements in quality.

Critical incidents were defined as 'specific moments-of-truth' (Wels-Lips, Ven and Pieters 1998: 286) and 'memorable in some way to the people involved' (Bitner, Booms and Tetreault, 1990: 72). Therefore, critical incidents can occur at any time while a customer is consuming a sports service, including interactions with personnel, physical features, other customers, and other visible aspects of the service. A well accepted premise of critical incidents is that they can evoke either extremely positive or extremely negative experiences for customers.

■ Measurements of quality in sport service settings

Several scales have been proposed for measuring service quality in sports businesses.

MacKay and Crompton (1990) developed REQUAL after examination of leisure and recreation services. This measure and subsequent versions developed by Wright, Duray and Goodale (1992) and Backman and Veldkamp (1995) were each developed in the context of public recreation services, the findings of which are arguably restricted in generalisability to this context, given that there are often significant differences in perceptions of quality in public versus private businesses (Crompton *et al.*, 1991).

Kim and Kim (1995), examining Korean sports clubs, developed QUESC, a scale including 11 dimensions of service quality. This measure was later translated into Greek by Papadimitriou and Karteliotis (2002) and found to have inconsistent conceptual validity and inconsistent internal consistency reliability. McDonald, Sutton and Milne (1995) developed TEAMQUAL to assess service quality in professional sports. The CERM developed by Howat, Crilley, Absher and Milne (1996) focused on Australian leisure clubs. Criticisms of this instrument include its lack of dimensions used to measure the service quality construct, as it only included three dimensions.

Although several models have been developed, the literature on service quality in the sports industry is relatively limited (Alexandris, Dimitriadis and Kasiara, 2001). Issues related with all service quality measurement instruments are concerned with the validity, reliability and contextual appropriateness of the measure. The suggestion has also been made that a more accurate measure of quality may be obtained by measuring perceptions only (Cronin and Taylor, 1992; Teas, 1993). Alexandris *et al.* (2001) have recently provided a valuable contribution to the service quality literature by focusing on perceptions of service quality (measured by using SERVQUAL) and the resultant behavioural consequences of those perceptions (measured using a model proposed by Zeithaml and Bitner, 1996).

◼ Quality standards

Quality standards are underpinned by the manufacturing-based approach to quality, in that they require businesses to 'conform to specified requirements' in order to achieve the recognised 'quality seal' (Kelemen, 2003). These standards are a mechanism that allows managers to measure and improve quality in their organisation. Some managers also believe that implementing quality standards helps to build a culture of excellence and achievement in their organisation. However, quality standards are also used as a marketing ploy by organisations or are adopted due to institutional pressures from customers, government and/or industry guidelines.

For the operations manager, quality standards help to ensure consistency in the way in which products and/or services are designed, manufactured and/or delivered as a service in their organisation. Historically, the development of standards has grown from manufacturers to be adopted by industry and finally to be developed into international standards such as the ISO9000 series (Conti, 1999). There are a wide variety of quality standards that organisations may choose from, including Investors in People, Chartermark, ISO 9000 and ISO 14000 (environmental variation). Sports facility managers have adopted quality initiatives such as the ISO series since the 1980s (Sport England, 2001); however, McAdam and Canning (2001) report that the service sector generally has been relatively slow in implementing ISOs. Reasons for the lack of acceptance may be due to the difficulties encountered by many firms including the resource implications of implementing, achieving and maintaining the standards, the lack of congruence between ISO and industry priorities and the relatively low importance that customers place on this registration (Ogden and Grigg, 2003).

In an attempt to resolve the disparity between international standards such as ISOs and the contextual demands of the sports industry, QUEST was developed in 1996 by Sport England as a sport-specific quality initiative (Sport England, 2001). As of January 2000, 650 Quest Manager's Guidance packs were sold with 119 sports facilities having achieved QUEST accreditation and 50 sport organisations actively engaged in the process (Sport England, 2001).

■ Sports events

Bitner (1992) discussed the importance of the 'servicescape' (the man-made physical attributes as opposed to the social environment) to satisfaction levels given the considerable amount of time a customer spends observing his or her surroundings at a sports event. Wakefield and Blodgett (1994) noted the significant impact of the perception of the sports facility upon satisfaction with the service experience. Research into sports events has shown the level of satisfaction experienced by sports fans is based on their comparison of their predictive expectations of the service encounter and what actually occurs (Zeithaml, Berry and Parasuraman, 1993).

Informed by the sports marketing and services literature, Kelley and Turley (2001) conducted an exploratory study that empirically assessed the importance of service attributes sports fans use when evaluating the quality of service and their levels of satisfaction with the sporting event. With 316 fans from four different basketball games in the south-east of the United States, the study included respondents of a variety of ages, education levels and incomes, and approximately 60 per cent males and 40 per cent females who took part in the survey. From a pool of 35 attributes, generated from existing literature and pre-test information, the perceived importance of each was ascertained through a seven-point scale with (1) as least important and (7) as most important. Results suggested that there are nine quality factors concerned with sports events and some of these are unique to the sports event context. For example, the 'game experience and showtime factors' were revealed in data analysis to be unique service quality dimensions for sports events (Kelly and Turley, 2001: 165). Interestingly, the data also highlighted that different categories of customers placed different weights on quality attributes. Therefore, operations managers may need to consider how to ensure that different homogeneous groups' needs are catered for and well managed, rather than assuming a crowd to be a single target market. Alternatively, some sports events may attract a more homogeneous crowd (i.e. dressage, polo matches, sheep-dog trials), making it easier for marketers and operations managers to address service quality perceptions.

CASE 10.2 Royal Yachting Association: Berth Holder Charter Award is the seal of approval

The Royal Yachting Association (RYA) was formed in 1875 under the name of the Yacht Racing Association, with the aim of harmonising the right-of-way and handicap rules for yacht racing. Today, the RYA is the National Association for all forms of sailing, windsurfing, cruising, sportboats, personal watercraft and powerboat racing. The purpose of the RYA is 'to develop yachting, under sail and power, in all its recreational and competitive forms' (http://www.rya.org.uk). As the governing body for yacht racing, the RYA takes responsibility for encouraging quality and safety in service provision from all its members. One of the specific goals of the RYA is to raise standards of proficiency and safety while also establishing and administering training programmes.

There are many organisations found within the operational environment of the RYA, such as the British Marine Industries Federation and the European Boating Association, which have an impact on the operational procedures at the RYA. These organisations in the external environment work closely with the RYA to expand the participation of boating and to develop boating in the UK consistent with standards in the European Union.

In their dedication to ensuring a high standard of service through members, the RYA has developed the Berth Holders Charter Award and encourages all marinas regardless of size or facilities, to adopt the standards advocated in the Award. The purpose of the Charter is to encourage and recognise good standards in customer service and value at all UK marinas. Using extensive survey data from berth holders and marina operators, the RYA identified the most important elements required by boat owners at any marina. Subsequently, these elements were developed into nine key requirements of the Charter Award. Hence, the Charter requires marinas to provide:

1. value for money;
2. security;
3. facilities;
4. maintenance;
5. suggestions and complaints procedures;
6. available, competent and helpful staff;
7. peaceful enjoyment;
8. communication, including advance notification of changes to facilities, conditions, services;
9. safety.

Many marinas are applying for and receiving the Charter plaque in recognition of the good work the marina managers and staff do for their berth holders. The Charter is granted on an annual basis and renewed following an inspection visit carried out by the local Berth Holder Association and the RYA's Berth Holder Association Coordinator. Specifically designed for and by the boating industry, the Charter is undoubtedly the mark of approval for marinas.

Performance measurements

Johnston and Clark (2001) suggest four main reasons why organisations should measure performance. These are:

- communication;
- motivation;
- control;
- improvement.

Performance measurements indicate to employees those aspects of the organisation's operations that are deemed important by managers. The measures inform employees what the organisation requires of them, within the context of the corporate strategy. For example, if a golf-club manager measures how many club memberships are sold by (designated) staff per week, this communicates to staff that the number of members is important to the organisation. However, if the golf-club manager measures too many aspects of an employee's performance, there may be confusion over what exactly is important. If performance measures are carefully chosen by managers and linked to a reward system, they can serve to motivate employees. Quite importantly, these measures should support the strategic aims of the organisation and may focus on, for example, speed of service delivery, quality of service, personal attention during service provision or standardisation of service offered.

Performance measures can serve as a formal mechanism of control in sports businesses. By measuring performance, managers are receiving feedback on how well organisational objectives are being met. For this information to be useful, there must also be a means of instituting appropriate action when targets are not being met. Finally, managers should measure performance in order to drive improvements in organisation processes, people and systems. Through performance measures, managers can identify those aspects of the organisation that enable and/or constrain reaching the objectives of the organisation.

Caton, Webb and Patterson (1999) suggested that performance measurements demonstrate, either qualitatively or quantitatively, the extent to which an organisation is achieving its aims and objectives. This definition is useful but limits the concept of performance to an 'organisational' level. A more comprehensive view is offered by Staw (1986), who recognises that performance measures can be taken at the individual, group or organisational level. Therefore, 'performance' of each of these factions can be measured in relation to how well they are progressing towards achieving organisational objectives. Furthermore, the implications of any differences in these levels of performance measures have been referred to by Edgar (1996) as a 'strategic gap', where an organisation cannot meet long-term objectives until individual, group and organisational performances are consistent in working toward organisational goals. There are several measures of performance discussed in the literature, including benchmarks and service blueprints.

Measures of performance

Organisations need to evaluate their performance on a variety of dimensions. Traditionally, measures of organisation performance have been through financial figures alone. However, there are many useful non-financial data that may be obtained and explain performance in a more detailed and in-depth manner. The most advantageous use of performance measures for sports managers would be a balance of financial and non-financial measures. Financial measures include, for example, share price, return on capital employed, and ratios. Non-financial measure include customer feedback, staff turnover, staff satisfaction, quantity and type of complaints and facility utilisation.

■ Benchmarking

Hope and Mühlemann (1997: 244) describe benchmarking as 'the process of continuous improvement'. Benchmarking is the measurement of an aspect of an organisation's performance against an internal or external target. Benchmarks are used widely throughout the sports industry in public, private and voluntary organisations. The process of benchmarking can help managers assess performance, set performance targets, realise new methods of working, stimulate creativity and innovation in performance and make considerable improvements throughout an organisation.

Internal benchmarking is the comparison of operational units within an organisation and often takes place in large firms. For example, JJB sports retail outlets may benchmark across retail outlets, in terms of sales, turnover, customer satisfaction or staff satisfaction. Organisations can benchmark their performance against that of their strongest competitor, in an attempt to establish 'best practice'.

Two organisations that currently provide a benchmarking service for local authorities in UK sport are Sport England, which operates a national benchmarking service for sports halls and swimming pools and the Association of Public Service Excellence, which provides a service for sport and leisure facilities as part of their Performance Networks.

■ Performance measurement systems

There are a wide variety of frameworks which act as performance measurement systems that can be used by sports managers. These include the Balanced Scorecard, Customer Value Chain, EFQM Award, Investors in People (UK), Charter Mark (UK), the Speyer Award (Germany, Austria, Switzerland), New Public Management, ISO Certification and country/industry-specific quality assurance and certification systems. This section examines two of the most well known, the Balanced Scorecard and the EFQM Award, as they aim to provide a comprehensive measure of organisation performance, and are not just focused on one aspect of organisations, such as people.

Balanced Scorecard

The Balanced Scorecard was developed by Kaplan and Norton (1992) and encourages a variety of measures of performance with the overall aim of revealing the important links between strategy and operational performance. In fact, this method has been embraced by a rapidly growing number of large corporations as a vehicle to help effectively manage corporate performance and strategy. Anthony and Govindarajan (1998) stated that the Balanced Scorecard is a tool that can be used by managers to focus, improve communication, set objectives and provide feedback. There are four key 'cards' within this approach, each requiring managers to ask some fundamental questions about their operations:

■ financial perspective (how do we perceive our shareholders?);
■ customer perspective (how do we perceive our customers?);
■ process perspective (in what processes should we excel to succeed?);
■ learning and innovation perspective (how will we sustain our ability to change and improve?).

Each of the above perspectives should be considered in consultation with the organisation's vision and strategy. An entire industry of consulting, computer software and independent organisations has grown out of the work of Kaplan and Norton. This is perhaps due to the fact that each organisation should have its own version of the Balanced Scorecard (Gautreau and Kleiner, 2001). That is, an organisation must develop measures within each of the perspectives, which fits its own strategy and goals.

EFQM

For more than ten years, the European Foundation for Quality Management (EFQM) Excellence Model has continuously helped to improve business results. The performance measurement system aims to give employees a better working environment and provide customers with the best possible value and quality. Introduced at the beginning of 1992, the model was used as a framework for assessing applications for The European Quality Award. It is the most widely-used organisational framework in Europe and has become the basis for the majority of national and regional Quality Awards, including the sports-specific QUEST.

The key principles of the model are as follows:

- results Orientation – attempt to delight all organisation stakeholders;
- customer focus – sustaining customer value;
- leadership and constancy of purpose;
- management by processes and facts;
- people development and involvement;
- continuous learning, innovation and improvement;
- partnership development;
- corporate social responsibility.

The EFQM model was designed to suit all sectors, public, private and voluntary. However, a public and voluntary-sector version has been produced, in order to demonstrate some of the slight differences between the private and other sectors. In the public and voluntary sectors, self-assessment and improvement needs to address the management role and how it interfaces with the political role. Therefore, the EFQM Excellence Model does not seek to assess the quality or excellence of political policies, but rather the management of excellence within organisations. Recognising the importance of contextual variables upon the management of business operations, there is also a version of the EFQM model for small firms.

The sports management literature on performance measurement is rather limited (Caton, Webb and Patterson, 1999). However, it is only a matter of time before the academic community focuses on the many recent developments in performance measurement in sports businesses. Public-sector sport has been increasingly conscious of the need to compete with private and voluntary-sector provision of sport opportunities.

CASE 10.3   The Australian sport system: performance measurement a priority

As with many countries throughout the world, sport management in Australia is undergoing a period of change. The changes that sport systems in developed countries such as Canada, the United Kingdom and Australia have been experiencing include professionalisation of the administration and delivery of sport by national and local sports bodies, increasing competition from a wide variety of sports and other cultural and leisure activities and increasing pressure to adopt technology in the management of sports organisations. With these changes in the external environment have come changes to the internal operations of sports organisations in the public, private and voluntary sectors. These internal changes include a focus on customer needs, service quality and creative approaches to delivery.

Caton, Webb and Patterson (1999) published a study with recommendations for the appropriate measurement of performance in state and nation sport organisations. Through consultations with an expert panel, consisting of two academics, representatives from three national sports organisations and two state sports organisations and a representative from the Confederation of Australian Sport and the Australian Council, the research firstly identified sport development actions that the panel considered essential to the development of the sports organisations. Next, the panel identified performance indicators that would measure and evaluate the development actions. The result of this consultation was 66 sport development actions and 10 areas of competency, essential to the performance of national and state sport organisations. This research was then compiled into a questionnaire and presented to 500 Australian national and state sports organisations, resulting in 15 leading sport development actions, ranked by mean score indicating level of priority and importance.

Today, many facets of the Australian sport system are recognising the value of performance measurement, such as Australian Institute of Sport (AIS). In particular, the Technical Direction Division of the AIS aims to lead in innovation and quality assurance of athlete and coach services, in part by advocating the use of benchmarking. The division has released a benchmarking report for Sport Psychology, after interviewing Australian and international sport psychologists to determine 'what is best practice for delivery of psychological services to athletes and coaches at the AIS'. It was concluded that best practice related to knowledge, ethical/lawful conduct and empathy. It was recommended that measurements of service provision must be derived from evidence-based methods and through athlete and coach feedback. Australia's national organisation for softball has also publicised its mission statement, goals and strategies, together with performance indicators used to measure their achievement. Indeed, academic and practical interest in performance measurement in Australian sport (and leisure) is growing, as evidenced by Gary Howat's project on performance indicators for public sports and leisure centres and the Hillary Commission project titled 'Performance Indicators – A Guide for Leisure Managers' (http://www.ausport.gov.au/ausfc/afc-perf.html).

The operational environment: sports industry business

The operational environment for sports business is to some extent unique to the specific sport or industry sector. However, there are a number of organisations that offer important services to businesses operating in the sport industry. While this list is in no way conclusive, some of the key organisations include:

- The Sports Industries Federation (TSIF), which plays a vital role in coordinating the sports industry in the United Kingdom and provides a strong voice to government and the media.
- Business in Sport and Leisure (BISL), which is an umbrella organisation representing the interests of over 100 private-sector sport, hospitality and leisure businesses. BISL acts as a lobbyist to government and the media.
- The National Association for Sports Development, which provides support, advocacy and professional development for companies involved in the development of sport.
- Institute of Sport and Recreation Management, which aims to improve the management and operation of sport and recreation services through standards, training, information and consultancy services.
- European Operations Management Association, the leading professional association for those involved in operations management. This is a European based network devoted to bridging the gap between research and practice.
- International Association for Sports Information, which provides information forums on the sports industry and advises on planning, operations and development of sports information.

Issues in operations management

There are a number of challenges facing operations managers in today's competitive industry. This section briefly highlights some of these challenges. They may not be unique to the sports industry but do affect the industry in a specific way, simply because of the different context in which sports businesses exist. This context is characterised by continuous change (markets, trends, customer expectations), technological innovation, increasing regulation and governmental pressures. Consistent with the main focus of this chapter, we will examine operational challenges relevant to service organisations.

Challenges facing operations managers in sport can be grouped into broad and specific categories. Broad operational issues include:

Globalisation

Sport is a global concept, as are many sports products and services. Technological innovations allow sport managers to offer products and services to customers all over the world rather than only to a local market. This expansion of marketplace presents the manager with logistical difficulties of communication, purchasing and customer care. There are also social and political implications of the globalisation of sports businesses, such as the exploitation and corruption of workers in developing countries.

Culture

A key challenge of globalisation is for the operations manager to offer products and services to different cultures, with different values and norms or basic assumptions. Dimensions of cultural differences include the individual versus collective nature of people, affective versus affective-neutral tendencies and reliance on present/past in life versus reliance on the future to guide behaviours.

Social responsibility

Increasingly, organisations are under pressure to demonstrate social responsibility. This has translated into greater attention by operations managers to customer safety, social impact of products and services, staff safety, pollution and disabled access/ issues.

Environmental responsibility

Most pollution and environmental disasters are the result of some operational failure. Environmentally-friendly materials, processes and services are increasingly found in such sport sectors as golf (impact of golf courses, environmental management of turf), equestrian sport (European grants for construction of environmental facilities), packaging and distribution of sport equipment and risk and environmental impact assessments by local sports clubs offering competitive and recreational opportunities.

Managing complexity

These broad pressures coupled with specific contextual demands (size, structure, nature of the service) of each business means that sports operation managers are expected to coordinate and control many interrelated components.

Specific operational concerns are nearly endless and should be identified by operations managers for their own organisation. Examples of specific challenges include:

- knowing the customer;
- understanding what the organisation is selling;
- managing customer experiences;
- understanding, implementing and adapting organisational corporate strategy;
- improving the organisation through performance measures;
- capacity demands.

Conclusion

The subject of operations management is a complex and intricate weave of concepts, research findings and organisational contexts. In this chapter, we have looked at the public, private and voluntary sectors of the sports industry. Increasingly, while these sectors have unique characteristics, they are under similar pressures and compete directly with one another for custom and human/financial resources. Operations management is a function of sports businesses, it is an activity engaged in by sports managers (formally or informally) and it is a process integral to the sustainment of competitive business practices.

Traditional operational issues have not been fully explored by sport management academics. However, there have been some admirable attempts to begin investigating this important aspect of the sports industry. Most notably have been the studies into quality in sports/leisure centres as well as in professional sport. Other progress is being made in examining customer satisfaction in sport businesses and in service provision in the sports industry. Greater attention needs to be paid to the issue of performance measurement in sport organisations. A number of sector-specific measures of quality and performance such as the RYA Berth Holders Charter, and QUEST for public sport/leisure centres have been examined in this chapter. However, there is a vast selection of other performance measurement systems available to sports managers such as EFQM, the Balanced Scorecard and Investors in People. The key to the successful adoption and utilisation of these systems is to consider their fit with the particular context of the sport organisation in question.

While there are many responsibilities of an operations managers (developing operations strategy, designing products and service, measuring performance, etc.), there are also broader issues that have an impact on the role of the manager. These issues, including globalisation and pressures of social and environmental responsibility, mean that the operations function is a complex and intricate part of organisation success.

CASE 10.4 Hired to be fired   FT

A week ago Tuesday, 48 hours after the final out was recorded in a thoroughly miserable season for the New York Mets, the guillotine fell on the team's manager of the past six years, Bobby Valentine. Three days later, a Mets fan called the Mike and the Mad Dog Show, New York's most popular sports radio programme, hoping to discuss Valentine's dismissal. But as soon as the caller announced his intention, he was interrupted by Mike Francesca, one of the co-hosts.

'Bobby Valentine?' Francesca bellowed, his dismay echoing across the airwaves. Before the hapless caller could fashion a response, he was cut off. Valentine, you see, was already ancient history.

This was not the first time Valentine has been consigned to baseball's managerial dustbin – he was sacked by the Texas Rangers in 1992; the news was broken to him by the team's president, an oilman and aspiring politician named George W. Bush. Nor was he the only Major League skipper to lose his job that week; five of his peers were also let go. This is on top of the four who were replaced at the start of the season in April.

The bloodletting is nothing out of the ordinary, of course. 'Managers are hired to be fired,' as the saying goes. But while heads have always rolled in baseball, they seem to be rolling a lot more frequently these days. What is driving this trend? What else but money.

That impression is not universally held: A decade ago, two American economists, Kenneth Chapman and Lawrence Southwick, concluded that the job insecurity among Major League Baseball managers – at the time, the average tenure was 2.7 years, compared with three years for NBA coaches and 4.6 for National Football League field marshals – was caused by the dizzying frequency with which players changed teams. A newly arrived manager, they argued, might be an excellent match for a franchise, but a year or two later its composition was likely to have been so substantially altered that he would no longer be an appropriate fit.

Now this might well be a plausible theory, but away from the academic grottoes, in the less rarified atmosphere of the local tavern, the more cynical view is that it is all just about the bottom line. Take Valentine. To be sure, few tears were shed for him. True, he led the Mets to the 2000 World Series, where they were dispatched in five games by their cross-town rivals, the defending champions, New York Yankees. After a disappointing 2001 campaign, the Mets, who already had baseball's fifth-highest payroll (the Yankees boast the highest), went on a shopping spree that added several marquee names – Roberto Alomar, Mo Vaughn, Roger Cedeno – to their line-up. The results, however, were even worse, with the team finishing in last place in its division this season, with a record of 75–86.

The reversal of fortune was bad enough; Valentine made the situation infinitely worse by habitually questioning personnel decisions taken by his bosses; by occasionally knocking players in public; and by generally being his acerbic, off-centre self (though it must be noted that his image problems were greatly compounded by the fact that he was coaching in the same city as the Sainted One, Yankee manager Joe Torre, a venerated figure in New York).

On the other hand, Valentine is one of baseball's shrewdest tacticians; it is generally acknowledged, for instance, that his strategies were what really catapulted the underdog Mets to the World Series in 2000. And while he did not bring out the best in his players over the past two seasons, he was not fielding a squad of his own choosing – it was the handiwork of general manager Steve Phillips – and it was a team clearly incapable of acting like one. The real problem with the Mets this year was that they were a group of overpaid, underachieving individualists incapable of generating any *esprit de corps*. Which prompts the question: why did Valentine take the fall?

Simply put, because someone had to pay for the team's woeful performance this year, and Valentine was the most vulnerable, expendable asset. All the wheeling-and-dealing during the off-season had pushed New York's payroll to $95 million (£60 million), and ownership naturally expected an immediate and very generous return on that investment (read: a title run). So did the fans. For the Mets, the easiest and cheapest move was simply to swallow the $2.7 million remaining on Valentine's contract and show him the door.

Nor is the trigger-happiness limited to rich franchises; teams with modest payrolls are not especially forgiving of losing managers, either. The Tampa Bay Devil Rays, with a payroll of $34.38 million, play in the same division as the Yankees, a team that doles out roughly $90 million more in annual salaries. Not surprisingly, the Devil Rays were no match for the Yankees; in fact, they finished 48 games behind the Bronx Bombers this year, no small achievement in a 162-game season. But despite the fact that his hands were so obviously tied, no mercy was shown manager Hal McRae; he was relieved of his duties the same week as Valentine.

Even Torre's future is hardly guaranteed. True, with seven years at the helm of the Yankees, he has endured longer than any other manager under owner George Steinbrenner (in 29 years, Steinbrenner has gone through 18 managers). And the fact that in those seven years the Yankees have won four titles offers Torre some measure of security. But New York's early exit from this year's playoffs – it was bounced out in the first round by the Anaheim Angels – has left Steinbrenner seething. If the Yankees are not en route to another World Series this time next year, Torre, beloved though he is, will have reason to be looking over his shoulder.

So what, besides luck, is required to survive as a manager? The immortal Casey Stengel (famously known as 'The Old Perfessor'), who led the Yankees to seven world titles between 1949 and 1960 and then managed the Mets from 1962–1965, boiled it down to the bare essentials.

His advice? 'The secret of managing is to keep the guys who hate you away from the guys who are undecided.'

Source: Michael Steinberger, *Financial Times*, 12 October 2002

Discussion questions

1. To what extent do you think, as in the case of the New York Mets, the performance of a team on the field of play and the performance of the sport business off it are inextricably linked?

2. Assuming there is a link between team performance and the performance of a sport business, what should be the nature of performance targets that sport business owners apply to players, coaches, team managers and commercial/marketing managers, and how should these be implemented?

Discussion questions

3. Why is it important to study 'operations management' in sports businesses?
4. Choose a sports manufacturing company and a service-oriented sports business and compare the 'transformation process' inherent in each. How does transformation in a manufacturing context differ from transformation in a service context?
5. Compare and contrast the EFQM Model with the Balanced Scorecard. Choose a sports organisation in the service sector and discuss any difficulties in applying each of the models in the sports context.
6. Discuss the disadvantages of having two different bodies providing benchmarks for sports facilities in the United Kingdom.
7. What is the difference between customer satisfaction and service quality?

Guided Reading

Kelley, S.W. and Turley, L.W. (2001) 'Consumer perceptions of service quality attributes at sporting events', *Journal of Business Research*, 54, pp. 161–6.

Bitner, M.J. (1992) 'Servicescapes: the impact of physical surroundings on customers and employees', *Journal of Marketing*, 56(2), pp. 57–71.

Recommended websites

The Sports Industries Federation: http://www.thesportslife.com
The Australian Sports Commission's Australian Sports Web:
http://www.ausport.gov.au
The European Foundation for Quality Management: http://www.efqm.org

Visit www.booksites.net/chadwickbeech for links to these and other relevant websites.

Keywords

Benchmarks; customer satisfaction; operations; performance measurement system; quality; quality standards; service.

Bibliography

Alexandris, K., Dimitriadis, N. and Kasiara, A. (2001) 'The behavioural consequences of perceived service quality: an exploratory study in the context of private fitness clubs in Greece', *European Sport Management Quarterly*, 1(4), pp. 280–99.

Anthony, R.N. (1965) *Planning and Control Systems: A Framework for Analysis*, Harvard, Boston.

Anthony, R.N. and Govindarajan, V. (1998) *Management Control Systems*, McGraw Hill.

Ashby, W.R. (1956) *An Introduction to Cybernetics*, Chapman and Hall, London.

Backman, S.J. and Veldkamp, C. (1995) 'Examination of the relationship between service quality and user loyalty', *Journal of Park and Recreation Administration*, 13(2), pp. 29–41.

Bitner, M.J. (1992) 'Serviscapes; the impact of physical surroundings on customer and employees', *Journal of Marketing*, 56(21), pp. 57–72.

Bitner, M.J., Booms, B.H. and Tetreault, M.S. (1990) 'The service encounter: diagnosing favourable and unfavourable incidents, *Journal of Marketing*, 54, pp. 71–84.

Boden, C. (1994) *The Business of Talk*, Polity Press, Blackwell Publishers, Oxford.

Bourdieu, P. (1985) 'The social space and the genesis of groups', *Theory and Society*, 14: pp. 723–44.

Boussabaine, A.H., Kirkham, R.J. and Grew, R.J. (1999) 'Modelling total energy costs of sport centres', *Facilities*, 17(12/13), pp. 452–61.

Business in Sport and Leisure (2002) *The Active Annual: Business in Sport and Leisure 2002 Handbook*, Business in Sport and Leisure (BISL), Surrey.

Buttle, F. (1996) 'SERVQUAL: Review, critique, research agenda', *European Journal of Marketing*, 30, pp. 8–32.

Caton, M.A., Webb, P. and Patterson, J. (1999), 'Using performance indicators within Australian national and state sporting organisations', *The Sport Educator*, 11(2), pp. 30–3.

Chase, R.B. and Aquilano, N.J. (1995) *Production and Operations Management: A Life Cycle Approach*, 4th edn, Irwin, Homewood, IL.

Chua, W.F., Lowe, T. and Puxty, T. (1989) *Critical Perspectives in Management Control*, Macmillan, London.

Conti, T. (1999) 'Quality standards development in a hypercompetitive scenario', *The TQM Magazine*, 11(6), pp. 402–8.

Crompton, J.L., MacKay, K.J. and Fesenmaier, D.R. (1991) 'Identifying dimensions of service quality in public recreation', *Journal of Park and Recreation Administration*, 9(3), pp. 15–27.

Cronin, J.J. and Taylor, S.A. (1992) 'Measuring service quality: a reexamination of extension', *Journal of Marketing*, 56, pp. 55–68.

Das, T.K. and Teng, B.S. (1998) 'Between trust and control: developing confidence in partner cooperation in alliances', *Academy of Management Review*, 23(3), pp. 491–512.

De Knop, P., De Bosscher, V., Van Hoecke, J. and Van Heddegem, L. (2001) 'Quality control in youth sports clubs: a project of the government of Flanders', *Book of Proceedings*, 9th Congress European Association of Sport Management, Victoria-Gasteiz, Spain.

De Martelaer, K., Van Hoecke, J., De Knop, P., Van Heddegem, L. and Theeboom, M. (2002) 'Marketing in organised sport: participation, expectations and experiences of children', *European Sport Management Quarterly*, 2(2), pp. 113–34.

Desrumaux, P., Gemmel, P. and Van Ossel, G. (1998) *Defining the Service Concept, in Services Management: an Integrated Approach*, Financial Times Pitman Publishing, London.

Edgar, D.A. (1996) 'The strategic gap: a multi-site, short break perspective', in Johns, N., (ed.) *Productivity Management in Hospitality and Tourism*, Cassell, London, pp. 38–54.

Fineman, S. (ed.) (2000) *Emotion in Organizations*, Sage, London.

Fitzsimmons, J.A. and Fitzsimmons, M.J. (2001) *Service Management: Operations, Strategy, and Information Technology*, McGraw Hill, New York.

Garvin, D. (1984) 'What does "product quality" really mean?', *Sloan Management Review*, Fall, pp. 22–44.

Gautreau, A. and Kleiner, B.H. (2001) 'Recent trends in performance measurement systems: the Balanced Scorecard approach', *Management Research News*, 24(3/4), pp. 153–6.

Gertosio, C., Mebarki, N. and Dussauchoy, A. (2000) 'Modeling and simulation of the control framework on a flexible manufacturing system', *International Journal of Production Economics*, 64(1–3), pp. 285–93.

Haksever, C., Render, B., Russell, R.S. and Murdick, R.G. (2000), *Service Management and Operations*, Prentice-Hall, New Jersey.

Haywood-Farmer, J. (1988) 'A conceptual model of service quality', *International Journal of Operations and Production Management*, 8(6), pp. 36–44.

Heskett, J.L. (1987) 'Lessons in the service sector', *Harvard Business Review*, Mar/Apr, pp. 118–26.

Hope, C. and Mühlemann, A. (1997) *Service Operations Management*, Prentice Hall Europe, London.

Hopwood, A. (1974) *Accounting and Human Behaviour*, Prentice Hall, London.

Howat, G. and Murray, D. (2002) 'The role of critical incidents to complement service quality information for a sports and leisure centre', *European Sport Management Quarterly*, 2(1), pp. 23–46.

Howat, G., Crilley, G. Absher, J. and Milne, I. (1996) 'Measuring customer service quality in recreation and parks', *Australian Parks and Recreation*, Summer, pp. 77–89.

Johnson, P. and Gill, J. (1993) *Management Control and Organizational Behaviour*, Paul Chapman Publishing, London.

Johnston, R. and Clark, G. (2001) *Service Operations Management*, Financial Times Prentice Hall, Harlow.

Kaplan, R.S. and Norton, D.P. (1992) 'The balanced scorecard: measure that drive performance', *Harvard Business Review*, Jan/Feb, 70 (1), pp. 71–9.

Kelemen, M.L. (2003) *Managing Quality*, Sage Publications, London.

Kelly, S.W. and Turley, L.W. (2001) 'Consumer perceptions of service quality attributes at sporting events', *Journal of Business Research*, 54(2), pp. 161–6.

Kim, D. and Kim, S.Y. (1995) 'QUESC: an instrument for assessing the service quality of sport centres in Korea', *Journal of Sport Management*, 9, pp. 208–20.

McAdam, R. and Canning, N. (2001) 'ISO in the service sector: perceptions of small professional firms', *Managing Service Quality*, 11(2), pp. 80–92.

McDonald, M., Sutton, W.A. and Milne, G.R. (1995) 'TEAMQUAL™: measuring service quality in professional team sports', *Sport Marketing Quarterly*, 4(2), pp. 9–15.

MacKay, K.J. and Crompton, J.L. (1990) 'Measuring the quality of recreation services', *Journal of Park and Recreation Administration*, 8, pp. 47–56.

Mintzberg, H. and Quinn, J.B. (1998) *Readings in the Strategy Process*, Prentice Hall, London.

Naylor, J. (2002) *Introduction to Operations Management*, 2nd edn, Financial Times Prentice Hall, Harlow.

Nike (2003) www.nike.com retrieved 01/04/03

Ogden, S.M. and Grigg, N.P. (2003) 'The development of sector based quality assurance standards in the UK: diverging or dovetailing?', *The TQM Magazine*, 15(1), pp. 7–13.

Oliva, T.A., Oliver, R.L. and MacMillan, I.C. (1992) 'A catastrophe model for developing service satisfaction strategies', *Journal of Marketing*, 56(3), pp. 83–95.

Oliver, R.L. (1997) *Satisfaction: A Behavioural Perspective on the Consumer*, McGraw Hill, Boston, MA.

Papadimitriou, D. and Karteliotis, K. (2000) 'The service quality expectations in private sport and fitness centres: A re-examination of the factor structure', *Sport Marketing Quarterly*, 9, pp. 157–64.

Parasuraman, A., Zeithaml, V.A. and Berry, L.L. (1985) 'A conceptual model of service quality and its implications for future research', *Journal of Marketing*, 49(4), pp. 41–50.

Parasuraman, A., Zeithaml, V.A. and Berry, L.L. (1988) 'SERVQUAL: a multiple item scale for measuring consumer perceptions of service quality', *Journal of Retailing*, 64(1), pp. 14–40.

Patterson, P.G. and Spreng, R.A. (1997) 'Modelling the relationship between perceived value, satisfaction and repurchase intentions in business-to-business, service context: an empirical examination', *International Journal of Service Industry Management*, 8(5), pp. 414–34.

Robinson, S. (1999) 'Measuring service quality: current thinking and future requirements, *Marketing Intelligence and Planning*, 17(1), pp. 21–32.

Russell, R.S. and Taylor, III, B.W. (1998) *Operations Management: Focusing on Quality and Competitiveness*, Prentice Hall, New Jersey.

Salaman, G. and Thompson, K. (1985) *Control and Ideology in Organizations*, The Open University Press, Milton Keynes.

Slack, T. (1997) *Understanding Sport Organisations*, Human Kinetics, London.

Slack, N., Chambers, S., Harland, C., Harrison, A. and Johnston, R. (1998) *Operations Management*, FT Prentice Hall, Harlow.

Sport England (2001) *Quality Management: Putting the Facility To Work for Sport*, www.sportengland.org/whatwedo/place/quest.htm, retrieved 19/02/03

Staw, B.M. (1986) 'Organizational psychology and the pursuit of the happy/productive worker', *California Management Review*, Summer 4, pp. 40–53.

Teas, R.K. (1993) 'Expectations, performance evaluation, and consumers' perception of quality', *Journal of Marketing*, 57(4), pp. 18–34.

Thwaites, D. (1999) 'Closing the gaps: service quality in sport tourism', *Journal of Services Marketing*, 13(6), pp. 500–16.

Van Dyke, T.P., Prybutok, V.R. and Kappelman, L.A. (1999) 'Cautions on the use of the SERQUAL measure to assess the quality of information systems services', *Decision Sciences*, 30(3), pp. 877–91.

Van Leeuwen, L., Quick, S. and Daniel, K. (2001) 'Determinants of customer satisfaction with the season ticket service of professional sports clubs', *Book of Proceedings*, 9th Congress European Association of Sport Management, Victoria-Gasteiz, Spain.

Verma, R., Thompson, G.M., Moore, W.L. and Louviere, J.J. (2001) 'Effective design of products/services: an approach based on integration of marketing and operations management decisions', *Decision Sciences*, 32(1), pp. 165–93.

Wakefield, K.L. and Blodgett, J.G. (1994) 'The importance of servicescapes in leisure service settings', *Journal of Services Marketing*, 8(3): pp. 66–76.

Wels-Lips, I., van der Ven, M. and Pieters, R. (1998) 'Critical services dimension: an empirical investigation across six industries', *International Journal of Service Industry Management*, 9(3), pp. 286–389.

Westerbeek, H. and Shilbury, D. (2001) 'An empirical holistic framework for service quality research in the sport entertainment industry, 9th Congress European Association for Sport Management Conference Proceedings: 361.

Wright, B.A., Duray, N. and Goodale, T. (1992) 'Assessing perceptions of recreation center service quality: an application of recent advancements in service quality research', *Journal of Park and Recreation Administration*, 10(3), pp. 33–47.

Zeithaml, V.A. and Bitner, M.J. (1996) *Services Marketing*, McGraw Hill, New York.

Zeithaml, V.A., Berry, L.L. and Parasuraman, A. (1993) 'The nature and determinants of customer expectations of service', *Journal of the Academy of Marketing Science*, 21, pp. 1–12.

Chapter 11

Information technology and management information systems in sport

Cameron O'Beirne and Susan Stoney
Edith Cowan University

Upon completion of this chapter the reader should be able to:

- identify the various forms of information technology that are used by sports businesses;

- specify a range of management issues relating to the use of information technology by sports businesses;

- discuss how the development of eBusiness systems will impact upon sports businesses;

- outline the strategic eBusiness management requirements of sports businesses;

- demonstrate how sports businesses use eBusiness to meet these requirements;

- explore how changing technology will continue to impact upon the sports eBusiness.

Overview

In a changing world, the innovation of information communication technologies (ICT) provides opportunities for sport business to grow. The rapid adoption of the internet as a commercial medium, coupled with experimentation in eBusiness strategy, eMarkets and eCommerce systems, has led to the creation of what can be termed 'sport eBusiness'. Included in this mix is a variety of sport organisations, such as sports information services, retail sports merchandisers, as well as various international leagues and teams, and national, state and local sport associations that are using the internet and associated technologies to help develop a presence for consumers and members alike in order to grow the business of sport.

Since the internet has transformed markets and industries within a short span of time, it is inevitable that a level of uncertainty exists within sport organisations as to how it can be utilised. These uncertainties can include a lack of knowledge of internet technologies, resources required to develop and implement websites, specific business objectives, website features and the value of website features to the organisation in delivering business outcomes.

It is now widely accepted that the internet has become the most significant business instrument in the post-industrial age (Allen Consulting Group, 2002; Chen, 2001), and the use of sport as a means of driving business growth within traditional corporate structures through sponsorships and customer relationship management (discussed in Chapter 16), and more recently the use of enabling technologies by sport businesses, have become widespread. This chapter focuses on providing an understanding of the internet and the role of management information systems (MIS) in the transformation of sport eBusiness through a variety of information and case studies in this emerging area. The role of eBusiness processes, digital convergence and disintermediation in supply chain management, and key components of information systems for the successful sport eBusiness are discussed.

Introduction

Advances in the use of information communications technology (ICT) and, in particular, the use of the internet have changed the way that sport services can be delivered to consumers and clients. Today's sport business has access to a wide range of technologies that can assist in developing and delivering business efficiency. These include highly-efficient networked computers, digital television services, mobile telephony, personal digital assistants, and intelligent appliances in the home and office.

Although it discusses traditional uses of information technology, for example, the use of computers and associated networks to provide desktop applications such as word processing, spreadsheet analysis and database management, this chapter focuses specifically on business that is conducted over networks that use non proprietary protocols (open to everyone) such as the internet.

The reason for this is the increasing dependence on the use of the internet to facilitate the functions of management information systems and eBusiness, which is in part driven by the facility for everyone to access the internet's vast global network at a relatively low cost using existing telecommunications infrastructure. Some of the reasons that the internet has proved so popular and transformed markets so quickly are:

- Low cost of access compared to other proprietary networks. Most people can afford access at home or have internet access through their employment.
- Ease with which connection to the internet by the average person can be obtained.
- New technologies that allow one-to-many and many-to-many communication and the transfer of information across a variety of devices.

Defining eBusiness

The concept of eBusiness, or eCommerce, can be described in various ways; however it can be broadly interpreted as:

> every type of business transaction or interaction in which the participants prepare or conduct business electronically.

This may be as simple as sending an email to a colleague requesting information about an upcoming event, to purchasing tickets for a sports event online or watching live sporting events 'streamed' directly into your home via a broadband connection. The basic components to operate such a system are shown in Table 11.1.

Some people distinguish between eBusiness and eCommerce as two separate functions. The former focuses mainly on business activities that include communicating with clients and partners, and utilising technology to enable business processes. The latter, can include all forms of financial and commercial transactions such as electronic data interchange (EDI), electronic funds transfer (EFT) and debit and credit card activities.

There are four main types of eBusiness based upon the type of transaction that occurs (Table 11.2).

The key to eBusiness: the rise of the internet

The internet is a worldwide connection of many thousands of computer networks. These networks use a common language, called Transmission Control Protocol/Internet Protocol (TCP/IP) to communicate. The networks are connected to one another through communications channels, many of which remain permanently open. The standardised organisation and structure of the networks that form the internet enable the instantaneous transmission and reception of digital data in many forms between computer systems across the globe. The internet is a cooperative community of networks. No particular body owns the internet. It is made up of many small parts in many different countries. Within each country, there is an organisation that supports the internet and provides the main communication channels. Within the world, there is a group that coordinates the overall network. It is a facility which anyone can use. People often comment that the internet belongs to everyone and to no one.

The internet is structured in a hierarchical form. At the top, each country has at least one major backbone network that carries internet data between its main cities

Table 11.1 eSelling and eBuying

Selling	Buying
Content production (word processing, video and still cameras)	Link to an electronic network (usually the internet)
Digitisation of content (editing software)	Search and locate content (goods and services) through search engines, directories or specific websites
Storage of digitised content (either online on remote servers or locally in hard drives and portable storage devices such as CDs)	Retrieve and display information from network
Link to an electronic network (usually the internet)	Place order through web browser interface
Link to an electronic payment system (usually through the internet utilising a PC with a web browser)	Link to an electronic payment system (usually through the internet utilising a PC with a web browser)
Link to physical distribution systems (when there is an exchange of goods)	

Table 11.2 eBusiness classifications

eBusiness classification	Description
Business to Consumer B2C	Online store or shopping sites providing an additional sales channel for existing companies or for new 'pure play' internet companies to have direct access 24/7 to consumers. Examples include nike.com (see Case 11.1) and, in book retailing, amazon.com. Other examples include online banking and sharetrading facilities and informational sites for niche markets such as sporting events, team information and fan sites.
Business to business B2B	B2B websites act to create 'virtual supply chains' in linking suppliers, distributors, resellers, consultants and contractors electronically to facilitate the flow of information. The main reason to use B2B practices in dealing with other companies is to streamline business processes, so creating efficiencies in the business and reducing costs. Sport examples include sportnet (see Case 11.3).
Consumer to consumer C2C	C2C websites provide a means by which consumers can directly interact with one another to exchange information, services and products. Examples include online classified advertisement sites, auction sites such as ebay.com and memorabilia sites for sports fans.
Consumer to business C2B	C2B websites are characterised by individuals offering professional services to others, such as lawyers, accountants and consultants. As well, C2B allows the consumer to control transactions through processes such as a reverse auction whereby the bidder sets the price for services or goods, and requesting quotations for goods and services. Other examples include paying government charges and taxes online.

and centres. These networks consist of high-speed communication channels that carry the digital data. There are then many smaller networks that connect homes, schools, universities and commercial users to the backbone networks. A network of channels is then used for connections between countries and continents.

Part of this network is the graphical user interface called the World Wide Web (WWW). The WWW supports interactive multimedia, including photographs, images, video and sound clips. Whilst the WWW and its accompanying browser interface through a personal computer provide the predominant platform for accessing the internet at the moment, changes in technology such as computer speeds, and most importantly bandwidth (the size, speed and ability of the network to carry information), will alter the way that information is accessed through the internet in the future.

Categorisation of information communication systems in sport business

As explained in the introduction, this chapter focuses specifically on sport business that is conducted over the internet, and the associated technologies that enable and facilitate business processes. However, it would be remiss not to provide a brief description of traditional forms of IT that the sport business uses in day-to-day operations. This includes the technology that drives core business functions, such as personal computers for word processing and database management, software for event scheduling and other operational activities, and facsimile, printers and other peripheral devices that store and manage data.

Needless to say, the increasing reliance on the internet by sport business has led to a wide range of sport organisations using the internet to leverage their business. Whether they be professional sport businesses with large financial capital and concomitant member and supporter bases, or the small local sport team that has a website, each organisation can benefit from utilising eBusiness processes.

Typically, the internet is utilised by sport businesses to offer a wide range of experiences for the fan, member or consumer. From the post-match results or fixture times, they offer the whole experience, to buying team merchandise in the online shop, and to watching the events through the site itself. For sports goods manufacturers, retailers and marketers, the internet is another part of their global brand strategy, and for advertisers, sports websites represent a proposition with definite future potential.

Sport websites can be classified into various categories depending upon the sport business they deliver. Various commentators have suggested a number of ways the use of the internet by sport organisations or associated groups can be categorised (Caskey and Delpy, 1999; Delpy and Bosetti, 1999; Duncan and Campbell, 1999; Intille, 1996; Haggerty, 1999; Kahle and Meeske, 1999). For our purposes (see Table 11.3), we can identify three major categories of sport eBusiness:

- content delivery of commercial sport and eMarketing of sport by organisations with a specific profit focus;
- educational, coaching and training applications within sport organisations, including tools for managing team performance;
- delivery of services and content to members and stakeholders in non-profit sport organisations.

Commercial sport

Of the categories of sport eBusiness, by far the most widely used and accepted are the sites that provide content and services to a wide market with a global reach. These sites are usually called portals, which means the sites act as a gateway for supporters or other users to access information and services. The goal of the portal is to be designated as the sports fan's startup web page. Portals usually offer free services such as a search engine; local, national and worldwide sporting news, plus general news; email and chat rooms; weather, and of course, up-to-date sporting results. Many portals can be personalised so that the fan only receives information about his or her favourite sports or teams. An example of a specialised portal is adventure-sports.com, which is a one-stop shop for anyone interested in outdoor activities. It also services the travel and tourism industry, and provides members with access to like-minded people through its various special interest groups. Portal sites have proved very popular in deriving revenue through advertising, subscriptions, and merchandising.

Governments are now investing heavily in sporting portals and gateways. For example, Sport England (sportengland.org) is a Government initiative with a mission

Table 11.3 **Sport eBusiness type**

Sport eBusiness type	Function	Example
Commercial sport sites	Content delivery Entertainment alternative to other media Profit focus with various revenue models such as advertising, ticket sales and merchandise sales Information source, with a focus on aggregating services around a portal	Sportal.com Sportbusiness.com Olympics.com Nike.com Athletics-weekly.com
Education sport sites	Education, training and coaching applications Alternative to traditional delivery methods	ausportgov.au (Australian Sports Commission) swimming.about.com Cadability.com.au
Service-focus sport sites	Provides services to members and other stakeholders Content delivery Timetabling and results Information focus Community focus Virtual communities	sportengland.org surfingaustralia.com wasa.asn.au (Western Australian Swimming Asssociation) surfingclubs.org

to develop sport 'by influencing and serving the public, commercial and voluntary sectors' (sportengland.org/about/about_1.htm).

CASE 11.1   B2C@nike.com: something for everyone

Nike.com went live in 1996 at a time when the future of B2C services was largely unknown. The site had no eCommerce facilities and was really an online brochure for the company. This was reflected by the style and design layout of the site. Branding was predominant and was split into separate pages and themes based upon the wide range of apparel and sports Nike was involved with. The site encouraged visitors to come back by providing changing content in the form of athlete interviews and news on sport events, as well as technical information on the apparel and goods that Nike produced.

In 2003, nike.com has morphed into a global eBusiness and eMarketing channel. Multiple sites now exist from the main site based upon country of origin, with the user having the choice to select a language of preference. Alternatively users can visit nike.com by sport or activity. Branding is reflected in the style and design of the sites and makes heavy use of the multimedia application Macromedia Flash to deliver interactive elements, online games and dynamic experiences.

Discussion questions

1. Try to purchase a pair of shoes from nike.com. Is it easy or difficult?

2. Importantly, ask yourself: would you buy a pair of shoes online? What are some of the barriers to purchasing 'look and feel' goods (like shoes) on the internet?

3. If you buy the shoes online would you expect them to be cheaper or not as opposed to buying them at the store?

4. What do you think are the main reasons that nike.com exists?

For further information visit nike.com

It can be said that virtually no professional sports teams in the United States does not have a website, and most are linked together through networks of websites coordinated through the various league offices that the teams compete in. These relationships and linkages between competitor teams are driven in part by agreements between the league teams on activities, such as revenue sharing for media broadcasting, as well as merchandise sales. Portals have also emerged through a common interest and driven in part by advances in communications technology. This is exemplified by the site at Worldsport.com, which brings together the 88 members of the General Association of International Sport Federations (GAIF) that represent all of the sports played at the Olympics. Features of the Worldsport site include general technological support through activities such as promotional information and marketing, administrative information for athletes and administrators in secure areas of their sites, educational programming such as certification and logistical support such as a global email communication system.

CASE 11.2 Can sport sites make money on the internet?

In the late-1990s, sport portals such as Quokka.com and Sportal.com relied almost solely on a business model that focused on advertising revenues through traditional TV marketing mechanisms, either by rights syndication of events or paid advertising on the site by event sponsors.

Quokka sports (quokkadev.com) provided a barrage of free sport content to subscribers as did other companies such as UltimateBid.com, MVP.com and Broadband Sports, all of which have burned through millions of dollars in an effort to attract users to their sites.

As well as advertising on site, some sites have also used sports stars in an attempt to grow business opportunities. This has included online media companies, such as Liberty One, keen to promote celebrities' digital rights on a profit-share basis. Sites such as shark.com, a golfing lifestyle site with golfing star Greg Norman as the public face, provides golfing tips, information on Greg Norman, and opportunities to buy branded clothing and other goods through the website. Liberty One, the company behind shark.com, argued that the principal factors that would affect the success of shark.com included the ability to build a substantial database of repeat visitors; create content that leveraged Greg Norman's golf insight, knowledge and skills; attract and retain support from major advertisers and sponsors; and integrate eCommerce shopping opportunities.

In 2000, Liberty One, which was the first publicly listed Australian internet company, was in receivership after burning millions of dollars in less than a year (Needham, 2000). Shark.com is still live on the internet.

Sportal, one of Europe's largest content sites, has been another recent casualty. Sportal operated websites for Juventus and AC Milan, the Italian football clubs, and owns Scrum.com, a large rugby union portal website.

So what went wrong? Possibly the focus on advertising as the key revenue source coupled with a lack of strategic direction may be the reason that sites such as these fail. Some analysts have suggested that the online sports market is over-supplied (Gapper, 2001) and will be 'devastated' within the next five years and that those with unique content, strong user communities, interactive features, sports personalities and online rights will be best placed to survive. In retrospect, it is almost as if the first 'wave' of large portal sites dominating sport on the internet is over. The inability of companies to raise revenue through sites has been a major problem, with a focus on advertising and eyeball herding predominant as opposed to building rich communities that have ownership of information. Perhaps the second wave of 'web-sport' is about the people and communities that are actually involved in the sport, game or club – not the spectator base which is a mass media toll of consumption.

Discussion questions

5. Visit two large sport portals. What do you think their revenue models are?

6. Do you think they are sustainable?

7. What are some of the issues that confront commercial sport websites in making money?

Whilst the nature of large sport portals appears to be in demise, the use of sport as a vehicle by some commercial organisations to leverage their internet business has been successful. Perhaps the largest instance of sport being used as a vehicle to drive strategic business growth is the Olympic Games. The major technology provider for the Sydney 2000 Olympic Games, IBM, spent millions of dollars providing the online infrastructure for the Games. Accordingly IBM's eBusiness strategy was based around showcasing the services that IBM provided for the Olympic Games as the vehicle for that. IBM presented and hosted the official Olympic Games website that provided event schedules, ticketing procedures, merchandising and other interactive services.

Quite clearly, the amount of information and content made available by IBM on the internet highlights the relevance of these online communication channels. Importantly, IBM catered for all levels of web users and provided a model that was accessible to most people around the globe. The Olympic website had to be accessible to most of the technologically poor countries involved in the Games. Therefore the use of large amounts of graphics and cutting-edge technology had to be restricted in favour of providing the information in a smarter way by combining established methods. This has huge implications for all designers of websites and website strategies for sporting and recreational organisations and indeed for businesses as well.

Sport educational, coaching and training information

Other uses of the internet such as online teaching and training have begun to be used by researchers in sport science (Pankey and Henrich, 1999) and those teaching sport coaching (Taylor, 1999) as well as distance education (Rushall, 1999) and web-based learning (Chappelet, 2001). Sport coaches use the internet for a variety of reasons including information searches on trends and new topics, communication with colleagues and athletes, background on competitors' teams, players, coaches and competition locations, weather, transport, and accommodation. The internet makes it possible for coaches and athletes to analyse and integrate information and resources in order to improve training, decision-making and development. An example of the use of technology to manage team performance is DSV Capture. This is a digital video capture and playback system used by international cricket teams, where stored data can be analysed in real time as the game is being played. Data is accessible to both coaches and players anywhere on the ground. Reports can be produced instantly and data can be archived for later retrieval. An example of a report (Figure 11.1) shows many different features in graphic format for easy reading.

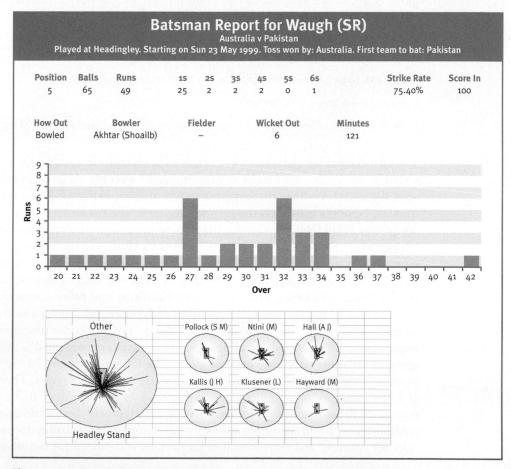

Figure 11.1a Examples of reports generated by DSV capture software

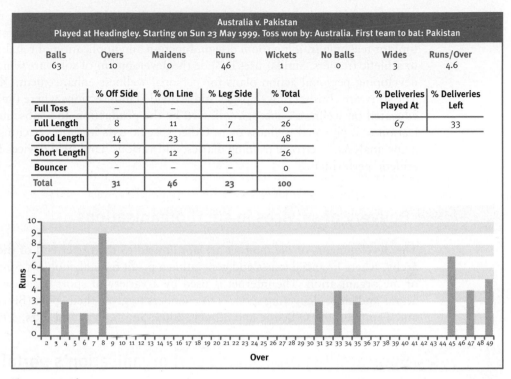

Australia v. Pakistan							
Played at Headingley. Starting on Sun 23 May 1999. Toss won by: Australia. First team to bat: Pakistan							
Balls	Overs	Maidens	Runs	Wickets	No Balls	Wides	Runs/Over
63	10	0	46	1	0	3	4.6

	% Off Side	% On Line	% Leg Side	% Total	% Deliveries Played At	% Deliveries Left
Full Toss	–	–	–	0	67	33
Full Length	8	11	7	26		
Good Length	14	23	11	48		
Short Length	9	12	5	26		
Bouncer	–	–	–	0		
Total	31	46	23	100		

Figure 11.1b

Source: Reprinted with permission of Cadability Pty Ltd

Technology can impact broad-based participation in sport and promote social inclusion. Data management tools and systems are extremely useful for the sports administrator, especially in the area of event management as exemplified in Table 11.4.

Other applications include the use of flexible teaching models within tertiary institutions to assist learning in the sport management and science field that allow students to utilise online bulletin boards, upload assignments and download course notes and other resources.

Other applications such as that considered by Holcomb (1997) used virtual reality modelling language (VRML) to illustrate a virtual athletic training room as an adjunct

Table 11.4 Use of electronic data in sport

Sport function	Database content
1. Teams and individual athletes	Demographic information: name, age, sex, contact information, medical details, performance history
2. Coaching	Training and conditioning, timetabling
3. Administration	Rosters of volunteers, officials, timekeepers, equipment and inventory lists, facility maintenance software packages, marketing information such as ticket sales, accounting and business records, employee directories
4. Marketing	Donors or potential donors whether this be for money or in-kind services, source of their motivation or affiliation, frequency of participation

to training of athletic trainers. Trainers are educated on appropriate modalities of treatment for the real world. The model has been found to be a beneficial educational tool for teaching training room design, function and application of rehabilitative tools to athletic trainers. Similar uses include the development of software which is used for developing personal action plans for personal wellness enhancement (Xiong, 1998). The software consists of web pages and is divided into sections where the user is firstly educated on wellness concepts, followed by the production and subsequent administration of a personal wellness plan. Other specific uses in sport coaching can include game analysis, electronic training diaries, and various hand-held devices for recording athletic performance.

Delivery of services in sport organisations

The developments of the internet are not limited to the upper end of the sports hierarchy, where financial issues and generating a profit for stakeholders control the focus of the organisation. The internet is used by a variety of sport organisations, associations and clubs delivering services to members to grow their sport (Beech, Chadwick and Tapp, 2000a; O'Beirne and Stoney, 2001; Smith, Pent and Pitts, 1999).

CASE 11.3 Sportnet: the Australian sport organisation's portal

Australia has a strong sporting culture, and Australian sporting organisations of all types receive significant financial support from the Australian Federal Government for the development of strategic management. Australia is a vast country (Europe would fit into Australia and there would still be room to spare) and providing sport services to regional areas can sometimes be difficult.

A review of the services provided by and for regional sports organisations in Australia suggested that sport services would be enhanced by the adoption of appropriate online information structures, together with the development of specific technology applications. Specific efficiencies in service provision were also identified that could be made in the context of online delivery. These included data collection and data maintenance for various groups in the sports and recreation industries, as well as for government agencies and departments. The benefits would facilitate more efficient administrative services, including reporting to and by governments for various stakeholders.

Sportnet has been developed by the Australian Sports Commission (ASC) in partnership with Telstra to provide a fully integrated eBusiness package for sports organisations. The Sportnet package includes email accounts, internet access, and web templates for use in constructing intranet and internet sites. As well as communication tools, Sportnet features include registration and membership management through online databases, and eCommerce facilities.

Sportnet can be described as a 'virtual reception desk' for sporting clubs and associations, as well as supplying an efficient way to service a club's membership and facilitate communication. The fundamental aim of Sportnet is to expedite communication. Whether a visitor uses email to query the organisation's grading standards, or a member uses the bulletin board to initiate a social discussion concerning last week's thrashing, the website encourages communication and builds a strong bond between its members.

Visit Sportnet.com.au

Indeed it has been suggested that a presence on the internet is an important part of any sport organisations strategic mix (Beech *et al.*, 2000a). There is a wide-ranging scope of internet use by sport organisations of varying sophistication, and organisational structure. Sites vary in professionalism, content, features and serve a number of purposes. A variety of strategies or online models are available, usually through web hosting or design companies, who provide basic websites that typically provide information on players, merchandising, press releases, photo galleries and sport statistical information.

Various authors (Pope and Forrest, 1997; O'Beirne and Stoney, 2001) suggest that although sport organisation websites may serve a variety of purposes, the integration of offline and online strategies to maximise community involvement in the sport, and the creation of efficiencies in the sport business may be lacking. This 'vacuum' concept is driven in part by general internet issues of access to the web, internet clutter, security and privacy, that affect sport organisations utilising the internet as an effective business tool (Duncan and Campbell, 1999).

So how do sport organisations address these issues and create sustainable online resources for members and fans? Beech *et al.* (2000a) suggest there are four key areas that sport organisations need to address in building compelling web content. Based on research in the English Premier League, areas important to success included:

■ the ability to address supporter access in the context of different communities, each of whom have different needs from the site;
■ the need for the site to adapt in order to attract a global audience;
■ the need for organisations to take better advantage of emerging online technologies such as streaming audio, online chat and discussions and the use of cookies;
■ attracting and keeping fans and members at the site by engaging or promoting fan rituals and culture.

It is also clear that strategic preparedness is essential in developing online resources for sport organisations that deliver services to members, and that the relative sophistication and maturity of sport organisations' websites is an indicator of this. Figure 11.2 demonstrates a relationship between the strategic capability of the organisation and the sophistication of the website and subsequent use based upon the results of the evaluation of websites and research questions.

The model suggests that as strategic capability develops in sport organisations, that is, as strategies change from an emergent form to a deliberate form, a concomitant change in website sophistication should ensue. Importantly, as the strategic imperatives are managed within the organisation, the consequence would be a movement of the sport organisation to the innovation quadrant of the model, which would be measured

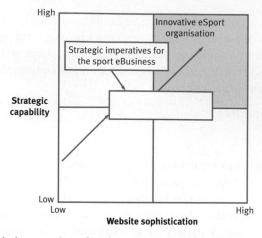

Figure 11.2 Strategic imperatives for the eSport organisation

by the adoption and use of strategic imperatives within a sport management framework that grows the organisation.

CASE 11.4 **Sharing information: Swanbourne Nedlands Surf Life Saving Club**

Surf Life Saving in Australia is a national icon. Part sport, part community service, the organisation has over 265 clubs and 80,000 members, spread across the breadth of Australia. Not surprisingly, communicating with clubs and members has provided a challenge to the Association. Importantly at a club level, information needs to be timely and concise and delivered to the appropriate officer in the club so that they can then take action. Because Surf Life Saving is a multifaceted organisation, a number of channels can be used to deliver information on competitions, changes to equipment specifications, life-saving procedures and administrative functions.

One club in Western Australia, the Swanbourne Nedlands Surf Life Saving Club (swannysurfclub.iinet.net.au) is using the internet to facilitate this communication with its membership. The club uses two methods, a website, and an e-newsletter to keep members informed. As well as providing news and information for members, the website serves other functions: it is a living record of the club history; it provides camera images of the beach on a streaming live basis; it is a promotional tool for sponsors and the like; and it serves as an archive for committee minutes and decisions, and lists of teams and rosters. An added bonus of the website has been in providing information to external stakeholders. The surf club conducts an open water swim every February, with over 800 people competing in the race. Previously, entry forms were mailed to each individual, and race statistics and placings were not available until a week after the race. These were then mailed to each competitor, which was costly, both in terms of financial resources and physical resources – having someone print out the information, put it in an envelope and post it in the mailbox, let alone having to lick 800 stamps! The website facilitated interaction between the club and competitors by allowing the competitor to pull the information off the website in their own time, at their own cost. Entry forms and race results were placed in a portable document format (PDF) which can be downloaded and opened by most web browsers and computers.

Concurrent with information the website provides, the e-newsletter provides a weekly update that is sent to members who have email. The e-newsletter is formatted in such a way that members can skim the information. The use of short paragraphs with hyperlinks to the website assists the reader, and, should they wish to, they can access information that is of interest to them by clicking on the link and going to the website.

Discussion questions

8. What are the benefits to a local sporting club such as the example outlined in using the internet as a communication channel?

9. What are some of the issues and problems concerning the use of the internet as a communication channel?

10. What other areas of the club business could be leveraged using the internet?

The impact of eBusiness and competitive strategy for the sport business

With the advent of eBusiness a wide range of areas that constitute the sport business market – products, services, events, trade and distribution, manufacturing and goods, regulations and laws – are being redefined.

Consequently a number of issues become apparent for the sport business to remain competitive. For example, how will wider changes in business on the internet affect sport business; how can sport business compete in the new marketplace and what parts of their current business translate to an online environment; and how is this new business channel integrated and marketed into the existing business? It is vitally important then that the changes that the online environment brings have implicit implications which managers must understand.

CASE 11.5 Cadability: using sport information and technology

Cadability was established in 1990 as a specialist graphics company focusing on applications for clients in the video broadcasting industry. Since 1993 Cadability – under the direction of Managing Director and Chief Designer, Arun Khanna – has been focusing on value-added products in the multimedia field.

In 1995 the company became involved with sporting multimedia content by negotiating a licence with the Australian Football League (AFL). This was seen as a branding exercise as the AFL had icon status in Australia, with a strong sports culture, and a large club membership and fan base. Since 1995 Cadability has developed a strong base of systems and solutions for some of the most followed sports around the globe.

The driving forces of sports and technology have influenced Cadability's growth in the sporting world. Cadability develops innovative applications for the sporting world, providing interactive and smart real-time information on premier sports.

Cadability has been successful in this field by customising its core competencies of capture, analysis, organisation, storage and retrieval in developing innovative technologies and high-quality sports products. With technology evolving and becoming more affordable, Cadability continues to develop innovative interactive sports datacasting content for the internet, interactive TV and emerging multimedia technologies.

Management

Cadability's organisational structure is simple and flat so that they remain lean and flexible to respond to change instantly. Cadability has a core team of six innovative and sports-oriented professionals employed at their head office, and uses contract staff worldwide. Originally, the management of Cadability were quite traditional in their thinking, but have now reached the conclusion that bricks and mortar are not the way to build their business. They now do most of their work with information management methods and customer relationship management (CRM). They have not met face-to-face with a client in three years, and they have never met their contractors – they hire them online and train them online. Their contractors work online and get paid electronically.

Project management and high-level management are now critical to the company. Every project is carefully monitored, and the company's customers have realised that they need partners rather than suppliers, with the focus of the company now helping customers achieve results.

Products

Amongst the diverse array of products and services Cadability has developed over the years, the most successful and highly publicised have been in the sporting arena. They have three main products: Sportsflash Datafeeds, which give live coverage of nine major international sports; Matchlets™, which 'enable users to keep track of a game as it happens, to review a game on an elapsed time or event-by-event basis, and to "drill down" into the database of team and player profiles, statistics, records, scorecards and highlights' (http://www.cadability.com.au); and DSV, which allows for the capture of a game or activity and provides the ability to analyse data across multiple matches or games. DSV is a cutting-edge integrated solution for managing and enhancing team performance.

Cricketer International, the most popular cricketing magazine in the United Kingdom, uses Sportsflash to add content to its website (see http://www.cricketer.com and Figure 11.3).

Completed Matches

England v. Namibia World Cup Match 17

St Georges Park

England won by 55 runs

Go to Matchlet™
Go to Scorecard
Head to Head stats
Last 5 Encounters
Series Points Table
Series Stats

Figure 11.3 **An example of the way cricketer.com uses Sportsflash to analyse a cricket match**

Source: Reprinted by permission of Cadability Pty Ltd

Business-to-business (B2B) is still the main source of income for Cadability, with businesses such as AOL and Yahoo paying licence fees for the software. However, they do have B2C (business-to-consumer) applications, where anyone who buys a sports DVD can log on to the Cadability site and run their software in parallel with the DVD. This allows the sports fan to interrogate the DVD in a unique way – analysing the play, choosing a specific player and looking at their individual performances, and pulling out particular activities. Cadability creates a front end to allow the user to navigate the content. This is seen as a way of exploiting computers that have DVD players, as about six times as many people have DVD players in their computers as have them attached to their televisions. Many DVDs have a fee for this service built in to the purchase price, but older DVDs may not, in which case a subscription fee needs to be paid.

One of the major selling points for the Matchlets™ is the fact that an entire five-day cricket test can be watched in one hour. Technology can help manage performance and players, and it compresses information to usable levels. Australian cricket teams can pull out anything they need to review within a five-minute meeting, without having to scroll through eight hours of video tapes.

Obstacles

Business peaked in 1996/97, however, income is now halved, mostly due to the downturn in IT-related businesses. Internet billing is ten per cent of what it was in 1998. One of the main obstacles to Cadability's online business is the fact that consumers need to pay small amounts of money for some of the services, and very few of them have access to micro-money accounts.

Future

The current focus of Cadability is forming alliances overseas. They have grown their overseas business to thirty per cent of the total local business, and hope to bring it to the same level.

By building on their existing sports products, Cadability will be able to move into eTourism, medicine and health, and education. This enables the company to grow in a sustainable and scalable manner, whilst maintaining its core competencies of interactive multimedia content.

Discussion questions

11. How would Cadability use its existing products to move into health and medicine, tourism or education? Choose one and discuss.

12. Review http://games.sportsflash.com.au and explore how Cadability has created a unique model for looking at the Olympic Games' results.

13. Take a sporting activity not currently covered by Cadability and discuss how its technology could enhance the business of that particular sport.

Changing technology and the sports eBusiness

As technology advances, its impact on the business of sport is growing daily. For technology to be truly useful it needs to be ubiquitous and this is true for both business and sport. The following are a few of the issues that are now impacting on sport and will further advance the way in which sport is pervading everyday life.

Wireless channels

Wireless technology is the new growth area in sports. For example, fans may go to a sports ground with their mobile phone and receive SMS messages on player statistics and match statistics. This is already happening for Cadability customers. Cadability has initiated a system whereby a cricket fan may receive real-time statistics via his or her mobile phone within a cricket ground.

There are some issues with this of course, privacy being the main concern. However the sports fans will be alerted to a privacy policy and will agree to terms and conditions, much as already happens when they access websites.

Interactive television

The advent of interactive television is going to have many interesting benefits for both sports businesses and sports fans. For example, Cadability has produced CD-ROMs for training umpires. By using existing materials and videos, they have put together a product called 'interactive umpiring'. By using the internet in conjunction with the CD or video they can access an online agent in the form of a genie which asks questions and talks to the user, making the CD engaging and interesting to use. The CDs contain self-assessment methods, the results get posted to the sports association and an online certificate is issued.

In the US, sports fans are able to use a PVR (personalised video recorder). A match or sporting activity is recorded on hard disk, and the content can be manipulated in the same way as for the DVD described in Case 11.5 on Cadability.

Micropayments and eCash

The use of micropayments will become an essential facet of eBusiness, where users will be able to buy small amounts of information for small amounts of money. There is no doubt that eCash will be one of the next killer applications and that it will not only revolutionise the internet, but it will change the global economy.

One of the fastest growing methods of internet payment is eGold. This is a virtual gold currency, and is seen as an easy and secure way to make payments and receive payments. eGold type transactions eliminate the issue of currency exchange as the value is based upon secured holdings of gold metal.

Users get a gold account number and a password, which means they do not have to provide their credit card and bank account details online. The advantage for business is that transactions are instantaneous, and the currency is standard globally. There are no charge backs, which often add to the costs of the transaction for the vendor, and security is assured.

However, both the vendor and the customer must have accounts with the same specific gold currency system, which is a major drawback. It is now common to see gold currency being used with Yahoo and eBay auctions.

ePublishing

Although not something that is readily associated with sports business, ePublishing has the potential to add value to the dissemination of results, as well as being of enormous benefit to the sports fans.

ePublishing comes in many forms, one of which is eInk. This is an electronic ink technology aimed at mobile applications such as Personal Digital Assistants, mobile communication devices and electronic readers.

Electronic inks allow highly portable devices to offer a paper-like look with exceptionally low power consumption, and an extremely thin, light form. eInk devices are six times brighter than normal LCDs and are more easily read because of high contrast and good visibility in even low ambient light. The image is retained on the screen after the power source is terminated, meaning that users can read articles, scores, and data analysis without using battery power.

Another contributor to the growing demand for ePublishing is electronic paper. ePaper is really a very thin, flexible electronic display, a bit like a computer monitor, but one which can be rolled up and carried around in a brief case. One major commercial application has been the development of electronic signs connected via a wireless link. This is an application that could be expanded from retail stores to the sporting arena, allowing more information to be displayed around the grounds. It is also possible that each spectator has his or her own piece of electronic paper, to which statistics, scores, advertising material, and anything else the sports promoters feel appropriate are sent. The text remains on the ePaper until the next update, meaning that the need to print documents such as programs can be eliminated.

Conclusion

This chapter has emphasised the importance of the internet as a vital communications tool for the sport business and sport organisation at every level of sophistication. The use of the internet and incorporation of technology into the sport business brings many challenges that include types of eBusiness models that work for sport business, the use of technology, and the application of resources to gain efficiencies from the use of the internet.

CASE 11.6 Clubs get smart by marking fans' cards   FT

British football clubs are better known for their disastrous media deals and overblown player salaries than for their customer service, but the industry is beginning to see returns from customer relationship management (CRM) schemes – more and more of which are integrated with smartcard-based season tickets.

After turbulent beginnings when they struggled to sell tickets on under-used web portals and experimented with unsuccessful entry systems, the UK's football clubs have begun to introduce smartcard season tickets. The aim is to cut ticketing costs, control security and reward the fans' attendance and spending with partner businesses inside and outside the ground.

Currently about 200,000 fans are swiping smartcards in turnstiles at British football grounds each week. About 40 per cent of these cards are provided by Scottish-based Scotcomms, with software supplied by London-based Computer Software in an IBM-backed partnership called Talent sport.

Chelsea FC recently unveiled the latest and most integrated Talent sport CRM project at its Stamford Bridge home in south-west London, where it has been installed on a new dedicated network around the ground. 'We've been looking at the idea for years' says Elaine Clark, IT manager at Chelsea FC, 'but after only three games with the new system we can already see the top spenders emerging and know where they are spending money.'

The Chelsea scheme includes partnerships with local car dealers in west London as well as selected local Safeway supermarkets and Alders department stores. Purchases in participating outlets charge the smartcard with loyalty points that can subsequently be spent at the Chelsea Village store or used to reduce the price of a season ticket.

A similar scheme is in operation at Bolton Wanderers, another Premier League Club, in north-west England. Randall McLister, chief executive of Scotcomms, says the Daewoo dealership in Bolton has so far sold 15 cars to Wanderers card holders who each receive £300 off their next season ticket.

'Electronic ticketing is the easiest way for fans to prove entitlement' says Mr McLister. 'It says: "I'm the guy who supports the club, I'm the guy who buys the most replica kit and you'll know I'm the best fan when the time comes to allocate cup tickets".'

But while premiership clubs such as Bolton, Manchester United and Chelsea, with a high percentage of season-ticket holders, can expect to cash in on smartcard CRM schemes, first and second division clubs in the lower Nationwide League have more limited local followings and are struggling.

These smaller clubs often have little ability to adapt to technological change, and implementing loyalty programmes can be a minefield.

'I may think that Manchester United is commercially exploitative but at least they are doing a good job on making offers to me and my son,' says Richard Sheahan of Round, the London-based CRM consultancy. 'But my local county cricket club continues to send me what I know are non-exclusive offers for discounts on double-glazing. Football clubs start at a point that most businesses would love to begin from – they have the strongest affinity (with their supporters). The difficulty is capitalising on that without making uncompetitive offers and wrecking the relationship', says Mr Sheahan.

Another big club, Rangers, has the UK's oldest established football club CRM scheme. James McGlynn, managing director of Carnegie Information Systems, which implemented the Glasgow club's system, says working with smaller clubs is fraught with difficulties.

'These businesses have enormous loyalties but they think all they have to do is open the doors, heat up the pies and turn on the lights' he says. 'They have a product but they have no idea what the market is and no idea why people are spending money or not. The smaller clubs are like family-run hotels. Obviously they need to fight for repeat business but they have a serious skills shortage and need to see enough [extra revenue] coming back to pay a salary before they implement anything new.'

Frequently small clubs which begin CRM systems find that within months they have accumulated a database that exceeds their stadium capacity and then surpasses their selling abilities.

Peter Cox, chief executive officer of ID Data, the UK's leading retail smartcard provider, argues that fan data may be most useful in the hands of sponsors. 'When football teams don't have the money, the introduction of integrated CRM will be driven by sponsors who want to identify exactly who is there looking at their perimeter boards,' he says.

Cash-strapped Leicester City, which was forced into administration last month, rejected a smartcard system last year for its new Walker Stadium, and Norwich City has pursued a non-smartcard CRM strategy since relegation from the Premiership in 1999.

'We suffered a customer relationship breakdown when [we] were relegated to the first division,' says Mario Zambas, information systems manager at the East Anglia club. 'And we had to develop strategies to come back from that. Now 20 per cent of our turnover comes from corporate sponsorship and banqueting and the stadium gets used more.' The club has created affiliations with banks and insurance companies and arranges discounts for fans with Q8 petrol stations and local super-markets as well as joint ticketing with other businesses in the city.

'When we build the new south stand we may have smartcard access readers but we won't rip out what we have elsewhere – it's going to depend on hardware costs,' says Mr Zambas.

In the meantime leading smartcard companies such as ID Data and Scotcomms are looking beyond football fans to golfers, who need a standardised way of proving their handicaps and are notoriously affluent consumers. Scotcomms has recently issued 250,000 cards to Scottish club golfers on which handicaps can be recorded and purchases rewarded.

But as Mr Sheahan at Round notes: 'A lot will depend on the extent to which rewards are offered. Golf clubs may offer executive boxes, but these people know they're attractive. They may drive a Jag [Jaguar car] to the golf club, but they are also the most resistant to being sold to.'

Source: Andrew Gelately, *Financial Times*, 6 November 2002

Discussion questions

14. The intrinsic appeal of sport on the field of play, allied to the reputation of a club or team, and the undying loyalty of many sports fans to their sport, means that customer relationship management is little more than a current fad that will disappear. Discuss this view of CRM, commenting specifically on whether the costs of acquiring and managing an electronic CRM system are warranted.

15. Assume you are the commercial manager for an internationally well-known football team that is considering the acquisition of an electronic CRM system. Develop a plan that highlights the stages you will go through in acquiring, organizing and implementing the system, indicting the key challenges you are likely to face.

Discussion questions

16. Which key administrative aspects of a sport business could be made more efficient with use of information communications technology?
17. The global IT company, IBM has made a continued commitment to providing IT solutions to a range of major sporting events usually as some type of sponsorship arrangement. What might the company's objectives be in supporting these types of events?
18. The role of ICT continues to change at a fast rate. What sort of services could be provided utilising new ICT technologies that could benefit consumers of sport?

Guided Reading

Further information on technical aspects of the internet and associated technologies is available in the book *How the Internet Works* (1999) by Preston Galla. Using simple illustrations and graphic representations, this book provides a comprehensive guide to online management information systems.

An alternative view from a holistic perspective to strategic management of information systems is available in the book *Funky Business* (2000) by Kjell Nordstrøm and Joan Riderstråle. In particular, Chapter 4 details the strategic economics of eBusiness and analyses the industry impacts of eBusiness.

For further information on specific case studies that have investigated the use of the internet by a variety of sport organisations see Beech, Chadwick and Tapp (2000a, 2000b), O'Beirne and Stoney (2001), and Turner (2000).

Recommended websites

The following websites may provide useful starting points for further knowledge on the use of information technology and eBusiness within sport business management.

Jakob Nielsen's website http://www.useit.com provides information on principles of best practice in web design and how people actually use the WWW. This can be supplemented by information from Macromedia.com: http://www.macromedia.com/macromedia/accessibility/whitepapers/ on the need for accessibility as an issue and how accessibility guidelines can improve websites for everyone.

The IBM website at http://www.ibm.com highlights case studies and the company's involvement with sport organisations and the solutions that have been provided. Using the search function and entering 'sport' links to pages of case studies of various sport organisations IBM has been involved with including the US Open Tennis, The Olympics, Wimbledon, The Ryder Cup Golf Championship, and the US national Hockey League.

Visit www.booksites.net/chadwickbeech for links to these and other relevant websites.

Keywords

Broadband; digital convergence; disintermediation; internet; MIS; world wide web (WWW).

Bibliography

Allen Consulting Group (2002) *Australia's Information Economy: The Big Picture*. Available: http://www.noie.gov.au/Projects/information_economy/research&analysis/IE_Aust/start.htm.

Beech, J., Chadwick, S. and Tapp, A. (2000a) 'Towards a schema for football clubs seeking an effective presence on the internet'. *European Journal for Sport Management*, special issue, pp. 31–51.

Beech, J., Chadwick, S. and Tapp, A. (2000b) 'Emerging trends in the use of the internet – lessons from the football sector', *Qualitative Market Research: An International Journal*, 3(1), pp. 38–46.

Caskey, R.L. and Delpy, L.A. (1999) 'An examination of sport websites and the opinion of web employees toward the use and viability of the World Wide Web as a profitable sports marketing tool', *Sport Marketing Quarterly*, 8(2), pp. 13–24.

Chappelet, J. (2001) 'Web-based learning for sport administrators. The example of the SOMIT project, Proceedings of the 11th IASI World Congress: Sports Information in the Third Millennium. Available: http://www.museum.olympic.org/e/studies_center/iasi_e.html.

Chen, S. (2001) *Strategic Management of eBusiness*. John Wiley & Sons, Chichester.

Delpy, L. and Bosetti, H. (1999) 'Sport management and marketing via the world wide web', *Sport Marketing Quarterly*, 7(1), pp. 21–7.

Duncan, M. and Campbell, R. (1999) 'Internet users: how to reach them and how to integrate the internet into the marketing strategy of sport businesses', *Sport Marketing Quarterly*, 8(2), pp. 35–41.

Galla, P. (1999) *How the Internet Works*, Que Publishing, Indianapolis, IN.

Gapper, J. (2001) *Online Sports Market to be Decimated*, Net Imperative.com. Available: http://www.netimperative.com/media/newsarticle.asp?ArticleID=10360&ChannelID=2&ArticleType=1.

Haggerty, T.R. (1999) 'Computer based information technologies and sport administration'. Available: http://www.unb.ca/sportmanagement/haggerty/chapter00.htm.

Holcomb, B.E. (1997) 'The virtual athletic training room', unpublished MA thesis, San José University.

Intille, S. (1996) *Sport Online*. Available: http://www-white.media.mit.edu/~intille/st/sp.html.

Kahle, L.R. and Meeske, L. (1999) 'Sport marketing and the Internet: it's a whole new ball game', *Sport Marketing Quarterly*, 8(2), pp. 9–12.

Needham, K. (2000) 'Liberty One rescuer pulls out, administrator called in', *Sydney Morning Herald*. Available: http://www.smh.com.au/news/0012/07/bizcom/bizcom7.html.

Nordstrøm, K. and Riderstråle, J. (2000) *Funky Business*, Bookhouse Publishing, Stockholm.

O'Beirne, C. and Stoney, S. (2001) 'Scoring goals: strategic application of the internet by Western Australian sport organisations', Proceedings of the 2nd International We-B Conference, November, 2001, Western Australia.

Pankey, R. and Henrich, T.W. (1999) 'Piloting exercise physiology in the web-based environment'. Available: http://thesportjournal.org/journal/vol2no3/HENRICH2.HTM.

Pope, N. and Forrest, E. (1997) 'A proposed format for the management of sport marketing websites', *The Cyber Journal of Sport Marketing*, 1(2). Available: http://www.cjsm.com/Vol128.

Rushall, B. (1999) 'The internet and coaching education', International Coach Education Conference Proceedings, Canberra.

Smith, R.L., Pent, A.K. and Pitts, B.G. (1999) 'The world wide web as an advertising medium for sports facilities: an analysis of current use', *Sport Marketing Quarterly*, 8(1), pp. 31–4.

Taylor, J. (1999) 'Coach education in the 21st century: challenges and opportunities', International Coach Education Conference Proceedings, Canberra.

Turner, M. (2000) 'Content analysis of branded Australian Football league websites on the World Wide Web', Proceedings of the 3rd International Sport Management Alliance Conference, Sydney, p. 44.

Xiong, D.C. (1998) '*The development of software for the wellness development process, La Crosse Wellness Project*', unpublished thesis, University of Wisconsin-La Crosse.

Part III

Sport management issues

■ This section considers some of the current issues facing sport business managers. Readers should be aware that the content of this section, more than any other, is likely to change rapidly. Changes in technology, developments in the law and general shifts in sport management practice are likely to be such that readers will need to remain vigilant of the impact these may have for the chapters in this section.

■ The first purpose of the section is to highlight key factors currently facing sport businesses. In particular, broadcasting, sponsorship and the importance of fans are considered, primarily because the three in total represent the largest proportion of income in many sports. Secondly, practices common to most organisations, but which have a particular resonance in the sport sector, are then considered: the law, risk management and event and stadia management (more likely to be physical resource or property management in other sectors). Thirdly, the section considers the future for sport businesses and reflects upon many of the observations made in this book as the basis for making predictions about what might happen over the next five years in sport.

■ The section contains chapters on sports and the law, event and facility management, sponsorship and endorsements, sport broadcasting, eManaging sport customers, risk management, the betting industry and the future for sport businesses.

■ Some of the cases included in this section are trademark infringements in sport, managing cycling events, the sponsorship of cricket, the European television rights market, loyalty amongst sports fans, crisis management in soccer, and branding in wrestling.

Chapter 12

Sports and the law

Karen Bill
University College Worcester

Upon completion of this chapter the reader should be able to:

■ examine a number of general legal principles of contract law and their application to a sport problem and understand the legal principles governing professional sports-persons' contracts;

■ develop problem-solving skills and acquire an understanding of how to interpret and analyse legal cases;

■ understand the legal principles of intellectual property rights governing sport;

■ identify and distinguish the various defences and remedies in cases where sport is subject to litigation;

■ define a number of the concepts that are central to both intentional and unintentional tort law from the perspective of sports participant, referee/governing body and spectator/occupier;

■ identify professional practice and sources of legal advice and support by means of alternative dispute resolutions (ADRs) used in sport.

Overview

This chapter provides a basic understanding and application of aspects of a number of principles of contract, tort and intellectual property law, which are pertinent to those students studying sports law from a general perspective. Readers are directed to the guided reading section in order to familiarise themselves with the structure and the role of institutions within the legal system in England and Wales and the European Union.

Although this chapter refers to European Union Law, it is written from a UK perspective. Legal systems and precedents will vary within the European Union within the jurisdictions of member countries, and in countries outside the European Union.

Problem solving, as a mode of assessment, is applied extensively within the domain and the chapter provides a practical case study along with study skills. Other legal cases are presented, with discussion questions, in order to promote the interpretation and analysis of case law.

The chapter concludes by looking at how a team of sports lawyers from James Chapman & Co handle sport disputes. It discusses the mechanisms for legal advice and support to sports businesses.

The chapter should not be treated as a source of definitive legal advice and as such the author, the editors and the publishers do not accept responsibility for any advice inferred.

Introduction – what is sports law?

This is an area of academic debate. Although Beloff's book, *Sports Law* (2000), refers to the purpose of the Court of Arbitration for Sport (CAS) and how this may facilitate a 'sports law' jurisprudence, Woodhouse states that 'there is no such thing as sports law. Instead it is the application to sport situations of disciplines such as contract law, administrative law (disciplinary procedures), competition law, intellectual property law, defamation and employment law' (1996). Similarly Grayson notes, 'there is no subject that exists which jurisprudentially can be called sports law' (1994, p. xxxvii).

'Sport is not above, or outside, the national legal system' (Grayson, 2003). In 2002 numerous cases hit the headlines demonstrating sport's engagement with a variety of branches of the law. For instance, *Flitcroft* v *The Sunday People (B & C v A (2002) H.R.L.R. 25)* over allegations of his private life, *Vowles* v *Evans and the Welsh Rugby Union and Others (2002) EWHC 2612* over a negligence injury and more recently the contractual issues surrounding both Mark Bosnich and Chelsea FC and Shane Warne and the International Cricket Council (ICC). According to Thomas, 'the game itself is merely a warm-up for the real contest at some future date in the law courts' (2002) and to Grayson that 'foul play and sport are no different from road rage and transport negligence as high risk litigation areas' (Grayson, 2003).

Parallel to this has been the increase in lawyers specialising in sport (*Sport and Law Journal*, 2002) and the formation of specialist panels to deal with the increased volume of sporting disputes as more and more money is at stake within sport. This growing professional interest has been matched by academic interest, with a proliferation of sports law texts such as those by Lewis and Taylor (2003), Kevan, Adamson and Cottrell (2002), Parrish (2003) and Blanpain (2003).

Law of tort and sport

It is difficult to formulate a meaningful definition of tort because tort deals with so many different situations. Essentially tort is a civil wrong. The main area of tort, as applied to sport, is negligence to which courts have considered many analogous situations. Negligence is a tort that imposes a duty on one person to take care not to injure another person.

Table 12.1 depicts all the main cases in sport that have involved a duty of care from the position of sports participant, referee/governing body and spectator/occupier. The cases are presented in chronological order with a brief narrative for each case indicating the decision and what evidential tests were used to establish a duty of care. A number of articles are mentioned at the end of the chapter to broaden the reader's understanding of the legal issues presented in the cases.

Table 12.1 **Standards of care applied in sporting situations**

Case citation (see section on legal research)	Evidential test for liability
Donoghue v *Stevenson (1932) AC 562* Miss Donoghue drank from a bottle of ginger beer to find the decomposed remains of a snail. Her companion had paid for the bottle. [NB Non-sport case]	'You must take reasonable care to avoid acts or omissions which you can reasonably foresee would be likely to injure your neighbour' (at 580). (Lord Atkin) *Held*: Liable
Hall v *Brooklands Auto Racing Club (1933) 1 KB 205* Spectators injured when 2 racing cars crashed and left the track, and tried to claim damages from the organisers.	'there is no obligation to protect against a danger incident to the entertainment which any reasonable spectator foresees and of which he takes the risk' (at 217). (Scrutton L J) *Held*: No liability
Rootes v *Shelton (1968) ALR 33* A water skier sued the driver of his boat who caused him to collide with another boat in the course of a water skiing display.	'the conclusion to be reached must necessarily depend according to the concepts of the common law, upon the reasonableness, in relation to the special circumstances, of the conduct which caused the plaintiff's injury' (at 37). (Kitto J) *Held*: No liability
Wooldridge v *Sumner (1963) 2 QB 43* A horse competing in a show bolted from the arena and into 2 spectators. One of them, a photographer, was injured.	'If the conduct is deliberately intended to injure someone whose presence is known, or is reckless and in disregard of all safety of others so that a departure from the standards which might reasonably be expected in anyone pursuing the competition or game, then the performer might well be held liable for injury his act caused' (at 56). (Sellers L J) *Held*: No liability
Wilks v *Cheltenham Homeguard Motor Cycle and Light Car Club (1971) 1 W.L.R. 668* A motorcycling scrambler lost control of his machine, which left the course and injured 2 spectators.	'the proper test is whether injury to a spectator has been caused by an error of judgment that a reasonable competitor being a "reasonable man of the sporting world" would not have made' (at 674). (Edmund Davies L J) *Held*: No liability
Harrison v *Vincent (1982) RTR 8* A competitor in a motorcycle and sidecar race was injured when the brakes on his cycle failed and he crashed into a vehicle, which was obstructing the emergency slip road.	'the injuries sustained by the Plaintiff were not the result of any risk which was inherent in the sport which the Plaintiff should be taken to have accepted' (at 19). (Watkins L J) *Held*: Motorcycle rider and race organiser liable

Condon v *Basi (1985) 1 WLR 866*
Amateur footballer sued an opponent who broke his leg as a result of a late tackle.

'there will of course be a higher degree of care required of a player in a First Division football match than a player in a local league football match' (at 868).
'reckless disregard of the Plaintiff's safety and which fell far below the standards which might reasonably be expected in anyone pursuing a game' (at 869).
(Sir John Donaldson M R)
Held: Damages for negligence £4,900

Elliott v *Saunders & Liverpool F.C. (1994) QB transcript 10 June 1994*
A case against Dean Saunders from Liverpool FC who had tackled Paul Elliott from Chelsea FC resulting in the severance of his cruciate ligaments in the process.

'an intentional foul or mistake, or an error of judgment may be enough to give rise to liability on the part of the defendant, but whether or not it does so depends on the facts and circumstances of each individual case'
'did not agree with the obiter dictum from *Condon* v. *Basi* in that there might be a higher standard of care required of a player in say, the Premier League ... The standard of care required in each case was the same'
(Drake J)
Held: No liability

McCord v *Swansea City AFC. QBD 1996*
A case against John Cornforth who challenged Brian McCord for a loose ball and broke his opponent's leg. It was judged to be an intentional foul.

'the error was inconsistent with the defendant's duty of care towards his fellow player' (at 1).
(Ian Kennedy J)
Held: Player was liable

Smoldon v *Whitworth (1997) ELR 249, CA*
Referee in under 19 colts match held liable for injuries to Smoldon who broke his neck after a rugby scrum collapsed.

'The level of care required is that which is appropriate in all circumstances, and the circumstances are of crucial importance. Full account must be taken of the factual context in which a referee exercises his functions, and he could not be properly held liable for errors of judgment, oversights or lapses of which any referee might be guilty in the context of a fast-moving and vigorous contest. The threshold is a high one; it will not easily be crossed' (at 55)
(Lord Bingham C J)
Held: Referee liable

Watson v *Bradford City AFC* v. *Gray & Huddersfield Town AFC (Quantum) QBD 7 May 1999*
A claim against a professional footballer as a result of a tackle by an opponent during a First Division league match.

'it must be proved on the balance of probabilities that a reasonable professional player would have known that there was a significant risk that what Kevin Gray did would result in a serious injury to Watson' (at 1).
'a forceful, high challenge, particularly when carried out when there is a good chance that the ball had moved on, was one that a reasonable, professional player would have known carried with it a significant risk of serious injury'
(Judge Michael Taylor)
Held: General damages £25,000. Past lost earnings £152,461. Future loss of earnings £700,500. Lost tax relief pensions benefit £30,000. Loss of bonuses awards £8,265. Medical expenses £12,168

Caldwell v *Maguire and Fitzgerald (2001) PIQR 45* Professional jockey was seriously injured whilst riding a 2-mile novice hurdle race at Hexham.	Woolf L C J extracted five propositions as guidance for duty of care: '1) Each contestant in a lawful sporting contest owes a duty of care to each and all other contestants. 2) That duty is to exercise in the course of the contest all care that is objectively reasonable in the prevailing circumstances for the avoidance of infliction of injury to such fellow contestants. 3) The prevailing circumstances are . . . its rules, conventions and customs, and the standards of skills and judgments reasonably to be expected of that of a contestant. 4) The threshold of liability is in practice inevitably high; the breach of a duty will not flow from proof of no more than an error of judgment . . . or momentary lapse in skill . . . when subject to the stresses of a race. Such are no more than incidents inherent in the nature of the sport. 5) In practice it may therefore be difficult to prove any such breach of duty absent proof or conduct that in point of fact amounts to reckless disregard for the fellow contestant's safety' (at 2). (Woolf L C J) *Held*: No liability
Pitcher v *Huddersfield Town Football Club (2001) QBD 5953* A claim for personal injury suffered as a result of a late tackle in a Division One match resulting in the premature ending of Darren Pitcher's career.	'It was a foul but I am not satisfied it was more. It was an error of judgment in the context of a fast moving game . . . has not in my judgment succeeded in crossing the threshold, the high threshold' (at 19). (Hallett J) *Held*: No liability
Watson v *British Boxing Board of Control Ltd and Another (2001) Q.B. 1134* Negligence case against the British Boxing Board of Control for the inadequacy of medical support when during a middleweight fight Eubank v. Watson, Watson was knocked out and suffered serious head injuries.	'The three-stage test in Caparo industries *PLC* v. *Dickman (1990) 2 AC 605* is applicable in determining whether in making (or failing to make) rules to regulate professional boxing the board owes a duty of care to individual boxers. The first test, foreseeability of injury. The second test is proximity. The third test, whether it is first, just and reasonable to impose a duty of care' (at 4). (Lord Phillips of Worth Matravers M R) *Held*: British Boxing Board of Control was liable
Vowles v *Evans and the Welsh Rugby Union and Others (2002) EWHC 2612.* The referee in an adult rugby match was held liable for injuries sustained to a player due to repeated set scrums, which left him paralysed.	Morland J. was referred to the threefold test enunciated in *Caparo Industries PLC* v. *Dickman (1990) 2 AC 605* of 'foreseeability, proximity and whether it was just, fair and reasonable that there should be a duty of care' (at 2). The evidential test in Smoldon was also applied (at 5). *Held*: Liable

Source: Based on Westlaw UK (2003)

Before any liability in negligence can be established, a duty of care must be proved. The three main elements to tortuous liability are conduct, fault and damage. Butler first found the concept of a duty in 1768. The more modern concept is that defined by Lord Atkin in 'the neighbourhood test' in the famous negligence case of the decomposed snail in the ginger beer, (*Donoghue* v *Stevenson (1932) AC 562*). According to this concept everyone must take reasonable care to avoid acts or omissions, which they can reasonably foresee and which would be likely to injure their neighbour.

Hall v *Brooklands Auto Racing Club (1933) 1 KB 205* applied the 'reasonable man test' where according to Alderson B:

> Negligence is the omission to do something which a reasonable man, guided upon those considerations which ordinarily regulate the conduct of human affairs, would do, or doing something which a prudent and reasonable man would not do. (*Blythe* v *Birmingham Waterworks Co (1856) 11 Exch 781 at 784*)

Duty of care by sports personnel

Sport participants owe a duty or standard of care to one another when competing: 'Those who take part in a competitive sport owe a duty of care to other participants and may be liable in negligence for conduct to which another participant may be expected not to have consented' (*Condon* v *Basi (1985) WL 312199*). *Condon* v *Basi* is still regarded as the leading authority on sports participants owing a duty of care to one another.

Sport occupiers owe a duty of care to its spectators. *Woolridge* v *Sumner (1963) 2 QB 43*, is perhaps the most cited authority, with respect to a duty of care to sport spectators, creating the issue of liability being based on 'reckless disregard'. However, they also owe a statutory duty of care under the Occupiers Liability Act (OLA) 1957. This applies to lawful visitors, i.e. those with permission, such as seasonal ticket holders. They also owe a duty to unlawful visitors under the Occupiers Liability Act 1984. Furthermore, a special responsibility applies to minors (S 2 (3) (a) of the OLA Act 1957): 'An occupier must be prepared for children to be less careful than adults.'

Governing bodies owe a duty of care to their sports players. The *Watson* v *British Boxing Board of Control Ltd (2001) Q.B. 1134* was a significant case in that it established negligence against the British Board of Boxing in terms of inadequate medical facilities, which left the board bankrupt despite policy considerations with respect to it being a non-profit making organisation which did not carry any insurance. The evidential test applied was based on that laid down by Lord Bridge in *Caparo Industries* v *Dickman (1990) 1 All ER 568*.

A referee who oversees a match may also owe a duty of care to the players to ensure no injuries (*Smoldon* v *Whitworth (1997) E.L.R. 249*). This was a judicial precedent case in that it held that the referee was liable in an amateur context to young players. The more recent case of *Vowles* v *Evans* (see Case 12.1) illustrates a similar judgment, although this time to an adult amateur team.

CASE 12.1   *Vowles* v *Evans*

Richard Vowles, aged 29, received a dislocated neck, with consequential permanent incomplete tetraplegia, during a local match between Llanharan and Tondu in 1998 after collapsing after a number of repeated set scrums. During the game Llanharan loose-head prop went off with a dislocated shoulder leaving Llanharan with a substitute with no experience or any training as a front-row forward.

Mr Leighton Williams Q.C. held that as a matter of policy or decision, no such duty exists that a referee owes a duty to take reasonable care for the safety of adults playing in a rugby match. *Smolden* v *Whitworth [22002] PIQR 137* was distinguishable because there the existence of a duty of care in a colt's game was conceded. Mr Leighton Williams submitted that whether it was fair, just and reasonable to impose a duty upon a referee would depend upon a number of factors including the interests of rugby as a game and the overall public interest. He stressed that such an imposition would discourage participation in rugby. However, Mr Justice Morland did not consider it logical to draw a distinction between amateur and professional rugby. He asserted that it is open to a player to protect his own interests by insurance cover.

In Mr Justice Morland's judgment the first defendant was in breach of his duty to take reasonable care for the safety of the front-row forwards in failing to order non-contested scrums. According to Law 3(5) 'Any team must include suitably trained/experienced players' and Law 3(12), 'In the event of a front-row forward being ordered off or injured or both, the referee, in the interests of safety, will confer with the captain of his team ... When there is no other front row forward available ... then the game will continue with non-contestable scrummages'. Mr Justice Morland in deciding, applied the evidential test of liability from that of *Smoldon* v *Whitworth (1997) E.L.R. 249* in that a full account should be taken of the circumstances of the game and that due to the fast-moving and vigorous contest, the threshold of liability would be high and not easily crossed.

Mr Justice Morland concluded that the lack of technique and experience as a prop was a significant contributory cause. Even if the first defendant may have been entitled to give a trial as loose-head prop as law 3(12) seems to envisage, he should have kept such a trial under constant review, having regard to the history of repeated and increasingly numerous bad set scrummages.

The claimant succeeded on liability against the first defendant and liability was accepted by the Welsh Rugby Union (WRU). It is a landmark case which could open the floodgates.

Source: Based on Westlaw UK (2003)

Discussion questions

1. What evidential test was applied to construct an argument for liability?

2. What is the standard of care expected of a referee?

3. What other cases could one refer to in order to provide guidance?

4. What impact does this case have for sport, in particular contact sports?

5. Discuss the requirements of 'proximity', 'foreseeability' and 'reasonability' and applying the facts of this case, establish why a duty of care is owed to the claimant? Explain the legal basis for your answer.

(For the full case see: *Vowles* v *Evans and the Welsh Rugby Union and Others (2002) EWHC 2612*)

■ Damages as a remedy in tort

The aim of damages in tort, as in contract, are to put the plaintiff back in the position s/he would have been if the tort had not been committed.

■ Defences to negligence:

The main ones are as follows:

1. *Volenti Non Fit Injura* (Voluntary assumption of risk) i.e. those participating in sports assume that there are risks involved in participating. The incident of Gary Walsh (Ipswich Town FC and Bradford City AFC) found that such a defence was dismissed as spectators only assume a risk when the ball is in play.
2. Contributory negligence i.e. where a sport player has contributed to his or her own injury, perhaps through engaging in horseplay. One could cite the case of *Grinstead* v *Lywood (2002) WL 31397573*, where an owner of a speedway track sought the defence of contributory negligence from the stewards.
3. Vicarious liability i.e. where a third party, often an employer, can be accused of negligence either because the illegal act is authorised by the employer, or because, if unauthorised, it is within the scope of employment. In the case of *Vowles* v *Evans* (see Case 12.1) the RFU were liable for the lack of duty of care of the referee.

■ Intentional Tort

Intentional torts are those wrongs which, when committed, intend to produce harm. They cover a wide range of sporting situations from assault to corruption, defamation and privacy, some of which may become criminal acts.

Defamation imposes a duty on one person not to injure the reputation of another. It can be either libel or slander, as in the case of *McVicar* v *United Kingdom (2002) 35 E.H.R.R. 22*. It is governed by the Defamation Act 1996, which applies to both unintentional defamation and innocent defamation.

There are three elements to defamation:

1. the statement is defamatory and lowers the public's estimation of the sporting celebrity;
2. the statement actually refers to the sportsperson;
3. the statement was published.

Since the Human Rights Act (1998) there has been an increase in the number of actions sought to protect claimants from the publication of newspaper articles carrying allegedly defamatory statements infringing their privacy.

Human Rights Act (1998)

It incorporates the rights contained within the European Convention on Human Rights and Fundamental Freedoms. The jurisprudence of this Act is one of the fundamental pieces of legislation in the United Kingdom, providing directly enforceable rights which people can now exercise against public authorities and which the UK courts are bound to 'take into account' (*Sec 2. HRA 1998*).

The Human Rights Act affects all areas of sports-related law and litigation, in particular:

- Article 2 – the right to life (e.g. the lack of provision of adequate medical facilities in the case of *Watson* v *British Boxing Board of Control Ltd (2001) Q.B. 1134*).
- Article 5 – the right to liberty and security of the person (e.g. player transfers and restraint of trade).
- Article 6 – right to a fair trial (e.g. *McVicar* v *United Kingdom (2002) 35 E.H.R.R. 22.* McVicar, a journalist, used this as a defence against Linford Christie who filed a case against McVicar for defamation*).
- Article 8 – the respect for private and family life (e.g. *Flitcroft* v *The Sunday People (B & C v A (2002) H.R.L.R. 25*, in terms of the publishing of Garry Flitcroft's affairs (see Case 12.2).
- Article 10 – freedom of expression (e.g. newspaper allegations regarding the behaviour of sporting celebrities).

A new category of 'quasi-public bodies', established by the Act, has been subject to judicial review, e.g. the recent controversy over the exposure of corruption in the Jockey Club.

There have been successful libel cases, e.g., Clive Everton, a snooker commentator, who secured an out-of-court libel settlement in April 2002 against the World Professional Billiards and Snooker Association (WPBSA).

However, some cases have not been quite so successful, for instance, the precedent case of *Grobbelaar* v *News Group Newspapers Ltd and Another (2001) 2 ALL ER 437*, whereby the jury's original decisions in favour of Grobbelaar, with respect to the allegations of taking bribes for matches, was overruled by the judge.

There is no general privacy law in England, which presents a controversial and increasingly rare gap in the law. It is often described as a patchwork of rights and given the predisposition of many celebrities to attract publicity, the task of balancing competing issues like the freedom of expression, public interest and the individual's right to privacy and a private life, is an extremely difficult one.

The piecemeal and uncertain form of a privacy law has been judicially recognised by Lord Glidewell in *Kaye and Robertson and Another (1991) FSR62*:

> It is well known that in English law there is no right to privacy, and accordingly there is no right of action for breach of a person's privacy ... in the absence of such a right, the plaintiff's advisors have sought to base their claim to injunctions upon other well-established rights of action.

There are a number of defences to defamation which have been used in sport cases:

1. Justification – to determine that it was the truth (*McVicar* v *United Kingdom (2002) 35 E.H.R.R. 22*). The journalist used this as a defence but could not prove the allegations.
2. Fair – that the comment was in the public interest and honest (*Flitcroft* v *The Sunday People (B & C v A (2002) H.R.L.R. 25*). The newspaper stated that its comment was in the public interest. See Case 12.2.

3. Privilege – of which there are two types: absolute and qualified. (*Flitcroft* v *The Sunday People (B & C v A (2002) H.R.L.R. 25*). The newspaper relied upon qualified privilege in order to expose information about the footballer's sexual life.

CASE 12.2 *Garry Flitcroft* v *Sunday People*

'A', who it emerged when the case went to appeal was Gary Flitcroft, the captain of Blackburn Rovers, a Premiership soccer team, sought an injunction which was granted against a national newspaper in order to prevent publication of his private sexual life involving adulterous relationships which could prejudice his marriage and also indirectly harm his children. Mr Justice Jack ruled that the laws of confidentiality protected details of relationships outside marriage and that there was no public interest in publishing the details.

Both sides had used the European Convention of Human Rights to argue their case. The newspaper invoked its rights of freedom of expression in Article 10, whilst the footballer invoked Article 8, which assures the right to privacy.

Newspaper headlines on BBC News Online on 6 November 2001 entitled 'Kiss and tell ban raises privacy fears' illustrate the concerns of the Newspaper Society and the Society of Editors in that the courts seem to be developing a law of privacy or threatening the freedom of speech. In a landmark Court of Appeal decision (March 2002) Lord Woolf, the Lord Chief Justice, backed the newspaper's view that the story was in the public interest. Along with other appeal court judges he overturned the injunction ruling, saying it had been an 'unjustified interference with the freedom of the press' which was also referred to in the case of *Theakston* v. *MGM LTD [2002] EWHC 137, QB*. Lord Woolf said the footballer was 'inevitably a figure in whom a section of the public and the media would be interested' and that 'footballers are role models for young people and undesirable behaviour on their part can set an unfortunate example'.

Source: Based on Westlaw UK (2003)

Discussion questions

6. Why did the *Sunday People* fight so hard to publish the conventional kiss-and-tell revelations of a footballer most people had not heard of?

7. Why is this a landmark case? Give your reasons.

For the full case see: *Flitcroft* v *The Sunday People (B & C v A (2002) H.R.L.R. 25*

Contract law and sport

A contract is a legally-binding agreement between two parties enforceable in law. It consists of various terms, including both implied and expressed, which can be both written and oral. *White* v *Bristol Rugby Ltd (2002) I.R.L.R. 204* illustrates issues around the expressed terms in a contract. An express term is that which is expressly articulated and agreed such as the administration of rights to endorsements. An implied term is that which is necessary or obvious, custom and practice.

Within a contract, external standards may apply, for example, the purchase of sports equipment would imply the terms of the Sales of Goods Act 1979. Attempts to exclude liability for personal injury or death caused by negligence is prevented under Section 2 of the Unfair Contract Terms Act 1977 and other terms apply where an element in a contract is deemed unfair, for example, the membership agreement stipulating six-months notice in David Lloyd Leisure Ltd (health and fitness clubs) (OFT, 2002) was deemed unfair and subsequently amended to three months.

CASE 12.3 *Snell* v *Sporting History*

Sporting History is a small retail sports shop in Worcestershire. In May 2002 the owner, Mr Lane, placed the following notice in his shop window:

> Come along to the great summer sale with some fabulous bargains for you sports enthusiasts. For the first person to enter the store this Saturday and present a voucher (which is to be found in the local evening paper this evening) a mountain bike worth £350 could be yours for only £30!

Tom Snell happened to see this notice in the window on the Thursday evening. It so happened that he was a mountain bike enthusiast. He rushed to the newsagent to buy the evening paper, which contained an identical notice to the shop window, including the voucher and then camped out for two nights by the front entrance of the sports shop in order to ensure that he would be the first customer.

During Friday passing shoppers commented on how keen Tom must be to want the bike. On Friday night Mr Lane locked up the sports shop and said goodnight to Tom commenting that he would no doubt see him first thing in the morning for the bike.

Early Saturday morning the queue outside the shop started to form and Mr Lane arrived at 8.30am to open up. To Tom's dismay, five minutes later he noticed that one of the shop employees was removing the notice out of the window along with the bike. At 9am Tom was first into the shop and went to the cashier and presented his voucher and his £30 cash and asked for the bike. The cashier informed Tom that it was no longer for sale.

Tom was so annoyed that he commenced proceedings against Mr Lane for breach of contract.

Discussion questions

8. Determine whether Tom had made a contract with Mr Lane.

9. What would be Mr Lane's defence?

10. Assuming that a contract was made, what remedy would be available?

Developing problem-solving skills

The following section is intended to advise the reader upon the technique of tackling 'problem' questions, and will help when answering the discussion questions given with the case studies.

A problem question is a factually-based scenario, which demonstrates legal issues and tries to give appropriate advice and solutions whilst adopting the following techniques:

- Ensure the case is read through thoroughly a few times and the main issues are highlighted. (A missed issue may affect the whole structure/outcome of the answer.)
- Draw a visual map of the case if it is quite complicated and a number of people are involved, illustrating the facts and nature of their relationships, e.g. referee/player.

The answer should be structured in the following manner:

- Identify the *issues* involved by analysing the facts.
- State the *rules* of the law which are pertinent to the issues (be selective). Explain the meaning of the law (provide any relevant law, citing relevant cases and statutory provision and discuss any grey areas or controversial matters).
- The law should be *applied* to the nature of the problem.
- Draw a *conclusion*. (Consider all relevant aspects of the law and facts before reaching any conclusion.)

Remember – Issues, Rules, Application and Conclusion.

Types of contract

Contracts can be classified into two broad types, bilateral and unilateral. A bilateral contract involves an exchange of promises. A unilateral contract is a promise in exchange for an act. It is made to the whole world, for example, the offer of the bike.

Phases of a contract

Under English law, a legally-binding contract is generally dependent upon there being offer and acceptance, consideration, intention to create legal relations and a lack of vitiating factors.

Intention to create legal relations

The courts differentiate between social/domestic and business agreements. There is a presumption that family and social arrangements do not intend to create legal relations (see *Balfour* v *Balfour (1919) 2 KB 571*).

An offer

It is important to distinguish between what is an offer and 'an invitation to treat'. The latter normally appears in shop windows, displays (*Fisher* v. *Bell (1960) 3 All ER 731*) and advertisements (*Partridge* v *Crittenden (1968) 1 QB 256*). These are sometimes referred to as a 'mere puff'. However, advertisements offered to the whole world, for example 'a mountain bike ... could be yours', can be an offer as in the infamous case of *Carlill* v *Carbolic Smoke Ball Co (1893) 1 QB 256*. In this case, the proprietors of a medical preparation called the 'Carbolic Smoke Ball', issued an advertisement in which they promised to pay £100 compensation to any person who contracted influenza after having used one of their smoke balls in a specified manner and for a specified period (for two weeks, three times a day). Ms Carlill, on the basis of her faith in the advertisement, bought one of the balls and used it as specified, but nevertheless contracted the influenza.

Acceptance

Acceptance has to be communicated in order to bind a contract with the exception of a unilateral contract, where performance constitutes acceptance (*Carlill* v *Carbolic Smoke Ball Co (1893) 1 QB 256*). In this case collecting the voucher would be the start of the performance. Silence, i.e. not responding, is generally not sufficient as in the case of *Felthouse* v *Bindley (1862) 11 CBNS 869*.

Revocation

A contract can be revoked up to the point prior to acceptance but not if the offeree has commenced the task (*Daulia* v *Four Millbank Nominees (1978) 2 All ER 557*). In the case of a unilateral contract, the same methods for both the communication and revocation of an offer should be used (*Shuey* v *United States (1875) 92 US 73*). In the example of Case 12.3, the revocation should also appear in the newspaper. A contract can also be revoked if the offeree rejects the offer or where a 'counter-offer' arises and the original contract is rejected (*Hyde* v *Wrench (1840) 3 Beav 334*).

Consideration

Consideration is where each party promises to do something or give something to the other party. For example, a professional sportsperson may contract to play exclusively for one club and receive a signing-on fee as consideration. Consideration does not have to be of equal value but must have some value or be sufficient (*Chappell & Co Ltd* v *Nestle Co Ltd (1959) 2 All ER 701*). 'The bike worth £350 could be yours for only £30!' would indicate some value.

Vitiating factors

Some people have only a restricted capacity to enter into a contract, for example minors and people of unsound mind. The general rule is that 'a contract made by a minor with an adult is binding on the adult but not on the minor' (Smith, 1992: 608). Both parties must be eligible to enter into a contract and consent to a lawful agreement, without any economic duress, for a contract to be legal.

■ Remedies for breach of contract

A contract can be discharged by agreement, performance, breach or frustration. A long-term sporting injury could terminate the contract through frustration, in which case there would be no dismissal or statutory rights. The right not to be unfairly dismissed is a statutory right under the Employment Rights Act (ERA) 1996. Dismissal in sport would be under incapability and misconduct.

Enforcement of contracts involves an action for damages or performance. The remedies of equity, which are discretionary, include:

1. recission of contract;
2. rectification;
3. specific performance;
4. injunction.

The current case of Mark Bosnich, challenging the rights of Chelsea FC over the termination of his contract, for alleged 'gross misconduct' on a drugs charge for taking cocaine, illustrates that the courts are prepared to allow an interlocutory injunction to players who are distressed by disciplinary sanctions by the sporting governing body.

In order to succeed in damages, there are two legal issues. Firstly, remoteness of damage. Here the plaintiff must show that the loss was due to the breach of contract. If the loss is too remote then it cannot be recovered (*Hadley* v *Baxendale (1849) 9 Exch 341*). Secondly, quantum of damages (sum). The principle of remedy involves placing the injured party in the position they would have been in had the contract been properly carried out. Damages can be awarded for the incurring of expenses and non-pecuniary loss (i.e. that which is not financial such as for disappointment and discomfort (*Jarvis* v *Swan Tours (1973) 2 QB 233*). One could argue in Case 12.3 that there is both disappointment and the potential loss of a bargain. Other types include inconvenience (*Bailey* v *Bullock (1950) 2 All ER 1167*), a lessening of future prospects (*Dunk* v *George Waller (1970) 2 QB 163*) and also speculative, expectational and consequential loss. However, the concept of 'mitigation of loss' places an important restriction on claims as a duty to minimise losses exists.

Sport contracts

Professional sports players have the same common statutory rights as other employees under employment law. Their contracts are often termed 'standard contracts' which provide a variety of duties and rights to both parties.

The case of *Carlton Communications* v *The Football League (2002) EWHC 1650* highlights a number of issues surrounding the formation of sports contracts. The Football League lost its case because the contractual documentation was unenforceable due to the reliance on a short-form contract, which had included neither prior guarantees nor the correct signatures.

Grievance and disciplinary procedures are formalised in a contract. FA contracts, for example, ensure that the players are subject to:

■ club rules and the terms of their contract with a club
■ rules and regulations of the competitions in which they play

- the laws of the game
- rules and regulations of FIFA and the FA

and the types of punishments for offences committed are set out in Table 12.2.

Table 12.2 Types of punishments for offences committed where players are guilty of specific breaches of rules

Types of offence	Punishment
Striking/assaulting a match official	Minimum (for jostling, pushing) of a 12-match suspension for a player or club official and a fine equivalent to 4 weeks' salary to a greater penalty for pushing and serious/bodily harm to a Match Official.
Conduct of players (Intimidation/harassment by 3 or more players from one club of match officials)	A fine for the club of up to: £250,000 FA Premier League £50,000 Football League Division 1 £25,000 Football League Division 2 £10,000 Football League Division 3 £2,500 Football Conference £1,000 Isthmian, Northern Premier & Southern Leagues (in very serious cases a 2-point deduction and any separate action against individual players).
Conduct of players (Mass confrontations between players)	As above
Conduct of players (Cautions/sending off)	Where in one match 6 or more players have received cautions/been dismissed, a fine for the club of: £25,000 FA Premier League £5,000 Football League Division 1 £2,500 Football League Division 2 £1,000 Football League Division 3 £500 Football Conference £250 Isthmian, Northern Premier & Southern Leagues (repeat offences may incur heavier penalties).

Source: www.TheFA.com reproduced by kind permission of The Football Association.

Restraint of trade

The doctrine of restraint of trade is aimed at protecting the right of the individual to work and to promote free and competitive economic conditions. In this respect EU law impacts upon domestic contract law through Articles 81 and 82 of the EU and the UK Competition Act 1998.

There have been a number of cases where clubs and players have been successful in suing their sports governing body over issues of restraint of trade and anti-competitive practices (*Eastham* v *Newcastle United Football Club Ltd (1964) Ch 413*). Here Newcastle United was held in restraint of trade over the FA's transfer rules holding players at the end of their contracts. See also (*Newport Association Football Club Ltd and Others* v *Football Association of Wales Ltd (1995) 2 All ER 87*). In cricket (*Greig v Insole (1978) 1 WLR 302*) presents a similar conclusion to that of Eastham whilst in horse racing (*Nagle v Feilden (1966) 2 QB 63*) it was held that the Jockey Club were unreasonable in granting a licence to a woman horse trainer. In rugby (*Williams v Pugh; Russell v Pugh (1997) unreported*) Popplewell J granted injunctive relief to two Welsh Rugby Union clubs against the Rugby Union, restraining the Union from restricting the clubs' activities. Finally, snooker provides a more recent case (*Stephen Gordon Hendry and Others* v *The World Professional Billiards and Snooker Association Limited (WPBSA) (2002) E.C.C.8*).

■ Bosman ruling

The Bosman Case (*Union Royale Belge de Societés de Football* v *Jean Marc Bosman (1995) ECR 1–4921*) represents a milestone in the freedom of movement despite the fact that similar cases had been heard for some twenty years. This is the case of a Belgian soccer player who took his employers, Standard Liege, to the European Court of Justice in order to claim for damages for breach of contract and by virtue disputed the transfer system and received £312,000 in damages. As a consequence, UEFA (the European Football governing body) abolished all financial conditions and restrictions on the flow of players linked to the transfer of players at the end of their contracts between clubs in European Union member states.

■ Bosman ruling 2

In March 2001, FIFA reached agreement with the European Commission on the main principles for the amendment of FIFA's rules regarding international transfers. All players who had reached the end of their contracts were free to move internationally throughout the world, subject to the provisions of paragraph 2 concerning training compensation. 'Solidarity mechanisms' were also introduced in order for clubs to have a financial incentive to train young players.

Intellectual property rights

Intellectual property rights (IPRs) are legally enforceable rights which 'give the creator a degree of exclusivity in respect to the use and exploitation of his or her creation' (Lewis and Taylor, 2003). By endorsing products or services, the players can increase their potential earnings. Beckham's earnings on the pitch are dwarfed by multimillion pound deals to endorse brands such as Pepsi, Vodafone and Marks & Spencer – 'a footballing superstar who earns over £20,000-a-week for his image rights alone' (Gallagher, 2003).

Nowadays proportionately more time is spent protecting and exploiting IPRs in order to maximise commercial value, such as is evident in the recent sale of Manchester United's merchandising business to Nike. This is done through merchandising, sponsorship, broadcasting rights and the use of trademarks, designs and copyright material to reinforce distinctiveness. In *The Rugby Football Union and Nike European Operations Netherlands BV* v *Cotton Traders Ltd (2002)*, the RFU was unsuccessful in defending the distinctiveness of the 'classic rose'.

'Saving face is all a matter of image for the famous' (Michalos, 2002) as the judgment in favour of racing driver Eddie Irvine demonstrates (*Edmund Irvine, Tidswell Limited* v *TalkSport Ltd 2002 WL 1876169*). Mr Irvine contended that the use of a doctored image of himself holding what appeared to be a radio to his ear was actionable in passing off as a misrepresentation by TalkSport Limited that he was endorsing Talk Radio (now TalkSport).

'Passing off' arises where a trader makes misrepresentations that damage the reputation of someone else (see Lord Oliver's summary in his judgment on *Reckitt & Colman Products Ltd* v *Borden Inc (1990) RPC 341 at 406*). Passing-off actions have frequently failed on the basis that there was no common field of activity in which both parties were engaged. In the Irvine case the judge recognised that it is now common practice for famous people to exploit their name and reputation by endorsement of a wide variety of products or services way beyond their own field of activity, in contrast to the narrow approach taken in *McCullock* v *May (1947) 65 R.P.C. 58*.

However, other countries have jurisprudence protecting celebrities' images, for example 'In Canada and America, there is "the right of publicity". This is an individual's right to control commercial use and exploitation of his persona including image, voice and likeness' (Michalos, 2002).

The Irvine case raised the distinction between endorsement and merchandising. Endorsement involves the exploitation of goods whereas merchandising involves the exploitation of images. More recently *Arsenal Football Club* v *Reed* (see Case 12.4) has been an important registered trademark case for sport businesses.

CASE 12.4   *Arsenal Football Club* v *Reed*

Arsenal Football Club (AFC) brought an action against Mr Matthew Reed for passing off and trademark infringements after the defendant sold scarves, from a stall outside the ground, which were not officially authorised by the club and which bore signs referring to the club. AFC's complaint was that the sale of such products bearing its name and logos constitutes passing off and infringes one or more of its four registered trademarks, each of which consists of or includes the prominent use of the word 'Arsenal'. The court held that there had been no passing off committed by the defendant. In relation to trademark infringement the essential function of a trademark was to guarantee origin and hence act as a control for quality. Article 5(1) of First Directive 89/104 on trademarks provides 'The proprietor (of a registered trade mark) shall be entitled to prevent all third parties not having his consent from using in the course of trade: a) any sign which is identical with the trademark in relation to goods or services which are identical with those for which the trademark is registered ...'. In the circumstance of the case the defendant's use of the signs constituted a link between the proprietor and was likely to jeopardise the guarantee of origin. In Mr Reed's defence he asserted that the name and badges on the replica kits did not function as trademarks as they did not tell people where the goods originated. Rather, the Arsenal marks served merely as 'badges of support, loyalty or affiliation'.

The court felt that it was necessary to make a preliminary ruling (Article 234) to the Court of European Justice concerning the interpretation of the Trademarks

Directive 89/104 in relation to infringement under Article 5(1) (a). The question referred to the Court was whether or not non-trademark use can represent a violation of registered trademark rights.

The European Court argued that 'in the circumstances' of this case, Arsenal should succeed, thus appearing to indicate that Mr Reed was infringing Arsenal's registered trademarks, in part due to the material link between his replica goods and Arsenal, despite the sign above his stall indicating that the merchandise was unofficial. The Court queried the purchase of the goods away from the stall and the perception of customers then as to the origin. The Court of Justice had exceeded its jurisdiction in determining issues of fact and the judge was not, therefore, bound by its final conclusions. Mr Reed appealed over the jurisdiction of the European Court decisions. Mr Justice Laddie stated 'it was the Court of Appeal which had jurisdiction to overturn or make alternative or supplementary findings of fact'.

Source: Based on Westlaw UK (2003)

Discussion questions

11. Are there any courses of action left open to Arsenal and if so what are they and how effective do you think they will be?

12. What messages does this send to the replica sports kit industry and to major sponsors like Adidas, Nike etc.?

For the full case see *Arsenal Football Club Plc v Reed (2003)* 1 C.M.L.R. 13.

Professional practice – the sports lawyer

CASE 12.5 James Chapman & Co., Solicitors, Manchester

James Chapman & Co. is a specialist insurance litigation firm, which has been based in Manchester for over 100 years. It is also highly regarded for its specialist sports law department, which was established over 25 years ago.

A specialised team of sports lawyers advises individuals, governing bodies and clubs in all areas of commercial rights, governing rules and regulations in domestic, European and other jurisdictions. Maurice Watkins, senior partner at James Chapman & Co., played a key role in the negotiations surrounding the successful re-appointment of Sir Alex Ferguson as manager of Manchester United FC and is a member of the FIFA Dispute Resolution Chamber, which adjudicates on issues arising from player transfers.

The company boasts a high calibre of clients that it represents in areas such as football, cricket, rugby, swimming, motor sports, boxing and speed cycling. Major clients are Manchester United plc, Manchester United FC Limited and the FA Premier League, to whom they offer the full range of legal services. The firm advised on the sale of the club's merchandising business to sportswear manufacturer and retailer Nike in a record-breaking deal worth over £300 million. The firm has also advised on a number of high-profile football transfers including MUFC's acquisitions of Juan Sebastian Veron and Rio Ferdinand. The firm also represented Roy Keane in his recent disciplinary hearing before the Football Association.

James Chapman & Co. advises both individual sports practitioners and elite performers in a range of sports. For instance, they represent a substantial number of professional Rugby Union players and advise the SCA (Swimmers Competitors Association), a body representing elite athletes in the aquatic disciplines. They represented the British Swimming Team prior to the Sydney Olympics in the negotiations involving the British Olympic Association for the swimmers to wear the new Speedo Fastskin swimsuit rather than the official sponsor's swimwear.

Specialist contracts have been negotiated on behalf of Formula 1 racing drivers, boxers and sponsorship and endorsement deals for golf players. The firm has also advised Jason Queally, Olympic Gold Medal speed cyclist.

The firm's sports law department draws a distinction between the traditional litigation services offered to its insurance clients and the services offered to its sporting clients, including the resolution of disputes for sporting clients. Approximately two-thirds of its business concerns non-contentious areas such as drafting contracts and exploiting intellectual property rights, with the remainder focused upon contentious business including the protection of intellectual property, defamation and regulatory issues. Many of the disputes the firm advises upon involve the interpretation of governing body statutes and regulations and following procedural mechanisms outside the civil procedure rules. Most sports tend to deal with legal disputes internally, avoiding civil litigation.

But what sort of advice is given to players or clubs when in dispute?

According to the sports lawyers a number of practical questions have to be asked to the player or club client:

- What is the nature of the sporting competition you are involved in?
- Who organises and regulates the competition?
- Are there procedural rules governing resolution of disputes?
- Who has jurisdiction over these procedural rules?

In soccer, for example, the clubs involved in any particular match may come from different leagues and different national associations if the match is in a European club competition. Consequently, in the event of a dispute or breach of the rules by any participant club, the appropriate competition rules will be applicable in the determination of the dispute. The questions above help to discover which disciplinary or arbitration procedures must be followed. The framework for resolving international disputes within football can be seen below.

Soccer – A framework for dispute resolution

A hypothetical example involving a contractual dispute between a soccer club and player from the same national association where the player wishes to move internationally to a 'foreign' club. The dispute may move up the chain if not resolved at each level.

CAS (Court of Arbitration for Sport)*

↑

FIFA Dispute Resolution Chamber

↑

National Association/League dispute procedures

*FIFA is currently in the process of incorporating CAS into its Statutes

Note: The contents of this section are the efforts of the author's own work and do not express the views or legal opinions of James Chapman & Co., nor do they constitute legal advice and are a general guide to the particular subjects referred to.

Source: An interview with Sports Lawyers Jason Smith, Matthew Bennett and Edward Canty with respect to highlighting sources of legal advice and help available to sport organisations engaged in dispute resolution.

Sport dispute resolution

The FIFA Dispute Resolution Chamber (DRC) contains an equal representation of players and clubs from different national associations. The DRC's remit includes resolving contractual disputes between clubs and players and determining disputes over training compensation fees. The DRC can impose disciplinary measures and sanctions to attempt to curb breaches of the FIFA Regulations. DRC rulings can be appealed against by either party to CAS (Court of Arbitration for Sport) although its exact jurisdictional parameters have not yet been finalised.

CAS was created in 1984 and is an independent institution providing services in order to facilitate the settlement of sports-related disputes through arbitration or mediation by means of procedural rules adapted to the specific needs of the sports world. The process aims to create an accessible, cost effective and speedy resolution to sports disputes. These are of two types: commercial disputes, for example contracts, sponsorship, sale of TV rights, etc. and disciplinary disputes, for example doping cases. There is also a division, set up for major sports events such as the 1996 Olympics in Atlanta and the 1988 Commonwealth Games in Kuala Lumpur. In 2001 it had 42 requests for arbitration to be filed. One of the most recent cases to be heard involves that of Alain Baxter and the use of the Vic Vapour Rub in the men's alpine skiing slalom event at the XIX Olympic Winter Games at Salt Lake City in February 2002 (*CAS 2002/A/376 BAXTER v / IOC*).

Sports associations and regulatory bodies generally incorporate some form of dispute resolution clause within their rules as a means of resolving disputes internally. Most also make provision for an appropriate sports-based forum for the dispute to be heard. For instance, the statutes of both FINA (international governing body for swimming) and the IAAF (international governing body for athletics) provide for the jurisdiction of CAS within their disciplinary procedures. In addition there are a number of other 'alternative dispute resolution panels' (ADRs) available offering facilities to resolve sports disputes like the British Sports Dispute Resolution Panel.

Conclusion

This chapter has introduced a number of relevant legal principles in the study of sports law. The contemporary nature of the material together with the inclusion of a comprehensive reading list, case citations and relevant websites broadens the chapter's appeal. The theoretical principles are balanced by the more practical requirements of problem solving, which will assist in developing legal skills in interpreting case law, and its professional practice in a variety of case studies. Sports law is both contentious and progressive. At the time of writing there are many cases still being challenged. For instance, the recent announcement of Naomi Campbell that she is now taking her privacy battle to the House of Lords begs the question, are we any clearer about where the law stands on privacy? Furthermore, the case of *Vowles* v *Evans (2003)*, at the time of writing, was due to go to the Court of Appeal.

It is hoped that this chapter has demonstrated sport's engagement with the law in a variety of areas and served to whet one's appetite on what is a truly captivating area of academic study.

CASE 12.6 A middleman on top of his game   FT

When not scoring extravagant goals, David Beckham has lately been weighing up the offer of a new contract from Manchester United. The possibility that he may be tempted away from the world's richest football club by a money-spinning transfer to a top Italian or Spanish rival has become an obsession of the European sports press – and with good reason. Beckham is one of the most bankable names in world football.

The advice and negotiating skills of Jon Holmes will play a crucial part in what happens. The managing director of SFX Sports Group Europe, a subsidiary of Clear Channel Communications, represents Beckham. He has also just forged an unlikely alliance between Beckham, one of the biggest personalities in British sport, and Marks & Spencer, the purveyor of slippers and dressing gowns to the British middle classes.

If Beckham signs for United, the deal is sure to set a new benchmark – reports suggest the club's offer could be worth more than £80,000 per week. Any team trying to lure him away may have to pay his current club more than £40million.

Mr Holmes will not be drawn on the negotiations, but says: 'It is extraordinary. We are into new territory with Beckham, for a number of reasons.' First, football has a new, higher profile. Second, there is the money Beckham is earning from his endorsement deals. Beckham's marriage to former Spice Girl Victoria has only increased his media allure, while Manchester United's status as a quoted company 'means that even papers like the FT are interested in him'.

Mr Holmes' role in the contract negotiations and the Marks & Spencer deal is also evidence of the growing power of sports agents.

Agencies such as SFX have to cater to the demands of stars with rising expectations of how much they should be earning, while avoiding over-exposure.

They must also strike a balance between securing the most established – and profitable – stars and building a stable of younger names who have yet to reach their full earnings potential.

SFX's portfolio ranges from Michael Owen, winner of the European Player of the Year award, to Darius Vassell, the promising Aston Villa striker who last month made his debut for England.

The strength of SFX's football client list has made it the leading player in the UK sports representation market, which has grown following the decision by a number of agencies to list on the stock market. Jerome Anderson's Sport, Entertainment and Media Group, which acts for the boxer Lennox Lewis, and First Artist Corporation, are among those that have gone to the market.

The sector has been fuelled by the rapid growth in sports stars' earnings, with agents sharing in their clients' increased wealth. The escalation of footballers' salaries has also encouraged agencies to offer more sophisticated services, such as financial advice. The move to the market has also introduced the issue of corporate governance to an industry long associated with questionable transfer deals done in smoke-filled boardrooms.

Despite this trend, Mr Holmes says sports agencies are better served as private groups or, like SFX, as part of larger companies.

'Most sports agencies are too small to be proper public companies,' he says, adding that as the sector is still in its infancy, listed agencies' shares tend to be illiquid.

While there are performance expectations at Clear Channel, there is no short-term shareholder pressure on SFX, he says. Such pressure would reduce the agency's flexibility to attract and motivate the best agents – and therefore damage its ability to retain the biggest clients, he argues. 'Our profits are strong, but I am not under the cosh to produce ludicrous growth targets to satisfy investors. What I have to do is make sure that the people who have the relationships with the clients are well enough compensated. That does not necessarily link to the quick profit growth that is required (of quoted companies) and the margins are subsequently not as strong.'

Low margins or not, the attractions of his business have led to a series of deals. Mr Holmes ran Park Associates, his own agency, for 17 years, representing the likes of Gary Lineker, the England footballer who became a pitch-man for Walkers crisps, and cricketer David Gower. The business was bought by Marquee, a US-based sports management group, in 1998. While at Marquee, Mr Holmes engineered the purchase of TSA, an agency managed by Tony Stephens, whose clients included

Beckham. Marquee was bought by SFX in 1999, which merged with Clear Channel in 2000.

The SFX deal brought Mr Holmes into a global group that represents, among others, the basketball phenomenon Michael Jordan, and André Agassi, the tennis player, while Clear Channel's leisure division recently promoted a sell-out US tour by U2, the rock band.

Whether there are substantial synergies from being part of a broader group is open to question. 'There are occasions when it feels like a better fit than others,' Mr Holmes admits. 'It is a media company, and sport is about the media.' Mr Holmes does not believe sport will ever form as large a part of Clear Channel as other parts of the business, such as its radio or television divisions. 'It is a sexy part of the business, it is visible and has a high profile – sometimes it is quite nice to have that,' he says. 'If you went out into the street and asked somebody: "Who are Clear Channel?" most people would not have a clue. But if you asked them who David Beckham was, it would be a completely different story.'

With Gary Lineker, and, latterly Michael Owen and Beckham, Mr Holmes has managed to turn stardom on the pitch into significant revenue generating opportunities. He admits to borrowing the model from Mark McCormack, the founder of International Management Group (IMG), the world's largest sports agency. 'When I was at university, I read Mark McCormack's book about Arnold Palmer. Palmer was one of my idols, and the way McCormack talked about managing a sports star was new,' says Mr Holmes.

> The interesting thing about him was that he understood the value of TV. The big three sports stars at that time were Gary Player, Arnold Palmer and Jack Nicklaus, and he got them all. He used them to make TV programmes, and he worked on the principle that if you look after the game, the game will look after you.

There are problems with this model, however. Forty years after the creation of IMG, sports management has become a competitive industry. 'You are only as good as your clients,' says Mr Holmes, well aware that covetous rival companies will, if given the chance, lure his best clients away. Tony Stephens continues to work closely with Beckham since his business became part of SFX but there have been whispers that he may retire this year, leaving Beckham free to go elsewhere. This is strenuously denied by Mr Holmes. 'Tony is not retiring. He is not packing up, that is the opposition trying to spread misinformation.'

Footballers – and the agents that represent them – have certainly benefited from the soaring value of sports media rights. British Sky Broadcasting's successive investments in the English Premier League culminated in a £1.1 billion bid for the current TV contract, which expires in two years.

But the media rights market is collapsing and the outlook for future rights deals looks bleak, with broadcasters realising they overpaid – ITV Digital, one of the biggest spenders in this market faces administration unless it can renegotiate its contracts.

Mr Holmes accepts players will have to start tightening their belts. 'There has been phenomenal growth in football over the last 10 years but the growth in wages is going to be slow and become much more steady,' he says. 'Are the players aware that the gravy train is running out? I would suspect they are not aware – they don't tend to be avid readers of the financial pages.'

Source: Matthew Garrahan, *Financial Times*, 25 March 2002

Discussion questions

13. Using concepts and principles from the chapter, discuss the legal issues that arise given the relationships between a sports agent, his/her client, the team/club the client plays for, the team/club's owners and managers, and the commercial partners with whom the client may be involved.

14. In the context of Question 13, and the increasing role of sports agents, what legal advice would you give to sport managers about how they should handle their relationships with agents?

Legal research – case citations

The law which is valid in England is established in either:

- EU Law
- Statutes
- Cases
- Statutory Instruments

Law Reports – case law

There are various diverse Law Reports and often cases are reported in more than one of these. The cases are referred to by their name, for example *Wooldridge* v *Sumner*. Some of the main reports for example are:

All England Law Reports	(All ER)
Appeal Cases	(AC)
Kings Bench Division	(KB)
Panastadia International Quarterly Report	(PIQR)
Queens Bench Division	(QB)
Weekly Law Reports	(WLR)

How to cite cases correctly

Cases are referred to by the names of parties to the action. In addition, because there may be several versions of a case reported, the case name is followed by a sequence of numbers and letters which identify where the report is published.

Cases contain 5 elements:

1. The names of the parties.
2. The date – the year in which the case was reported.
3. The number of the volume of the law report.
4. The abbreviation of the category of law report (help in expanding fully the abbreviation of the title of the law report is available in publications such as:
   Current Law Case Citator (any issue)
   Legal Journals Index (any issue)
5. The page number where the case is located.

Here is an example of how a case would be cited:

1	2	3	4	5
Condon v *Basi*	*(1985)*	*1*	*WLR*	*866*

The case is to be found in Volume 1 of the *Weekly Law Reports* for 1985 at page 866.

Guided reading

Slapper and Kelly (2001) provide a useful insight and the necessary legal knowledge of the essential institutions, practices and principles of the English Legal System. At http://www.parliament.uk/index.cfm a brief guide to the history and procedure of the UK Parliament with links illustrating how legislation is made is available. For a basic text on the Institutions of the European Union and the Community law-making process, read Douglas-Scott, S. (2002). Craig and de Búrca, G. (2002) is a more challenging book that combines textual commentary with extracts from judgments and other academic literature. There are also a large number of websites devoted to EC Law, for example http://europa.eu.int/, which provides up-to-date coverage of European Union affairs and essential information on European integration.

There is an increasing array of resources on tort and duty of care in relation to sport. One can refer to the full citation of each particular case but also look at the case commentaries for discussion around the issues within a particular case. Kevan (2001) provides a review of the legal principles involved in sports injuries and the liability of sports personnel, whilst two articles produced by Duff (1999, 2002) discuss the issue of duty of care and reckless disregard. Dovey (2000), focuses on some of the earlier cases in sport around issues of breach of duty and discusses single or variable standards of care. Moore (2002) discusses vicarious liability and level of care of sport officials in sporting events, whilst James (2003) looks more specifically at rugby and discusses the liability of rugby drawing on analysis from cases such as *Smoldon (1968)*, *Caldwell Maguire and Fitzgerald (2001)* case, the recent case of *Vowles* v *Evans and the Welsh Rugby Union and others (2002)* in order to ascertain the evidential test and player's duty of care.

For further information on the impact of the Human Rights Act 1998 on sport and a case commentary about Flitcroft (Case 12.2) see Boyes (2002b). For a discussion on the protection of sports stars and whether the HRA 1998 will help improve the situation of sporting celebrities, see Boyd (2002).

Koffman and Macdonald (2001) is a general textbook on the area of contract law; however a more palatable book in terms of relating to sport would be that by

Griffith-Jones (1997). For help with legal skills see Lane (2002) and http://www.lawteacher.net/Study.htm, which has a study skills page on problem solving. For further reading on the operation of the transfer market for footballers along with a comparative analysis of cricket, see Morrison (2002).

For those seeking a more detailed commentary on the case of *Arsenal* v. *Reed* and the issues of Intellectual Property Rights, Misquitta (2003) is a useful article.

Information on the Sport Dispute Resolution Panel can be gleaned from Kate Hoey's commentary (2002), which charts the development and operation and progress of the SDRP, but see also Siddall (2002) for a review of the first two years. Kevan, Adamson and Cottrell (2002) is the first book dedicated to the topic of sports injury law. It is a useful guide to organisers and clubs who have a possible liability and for those sports participants who may injure themselves in the sporting environment. The book is aimed at a wide cross-section of people involved in litigation namely personal injury practitioners to unqualified claim assessors.

Parrish (2003) delves into the issues of commercialisation of sport from both the legal and political analysis and raises questions concerning regulation at the EU level. Lewis and Taylor (2003) provides widespread coverage on such aspects as the commercialisation of sports events, the legal control of sport and the aspects of self-regulation. It also examines the impact of EC law on sport and the nature of contracts in relation to intellectual property rights.

Blanpain (2003) reviews the present transfer system imposed by the International Foundation of Football Associations (FIFA). He incorporates the issues of sportsmen and sportswomen as 'workers', the status of players' agents, disciplinary rules and dispute resolution and the disagreements with competition law.

Finally, any of the sports law texts within the bibliography would be a useful resource for all of the different aspects of legal principles discussed within this chapter.

Recommended websites

Altis: http://ww.altis.ac.uk
Consilio on-line magazine: http://www.spr-consilio.com
Daily legal update: law@lexisnexis-alerter.co.uk
Europa – the portal site for the EU: http://europa.eu.int
The Institute of Legal Executives' Journal: http://www.ilexjournal.com
InfoLaw – useful links to legal resources: http://www.infolaw.co.uk
Law Student on-line magazine: http://www.lawstudents.org.uk. Use this link to access a UK-based legal dictionary: *Dictionary of Law* – Peter Collin Publishing.
LawTeacher.net by Asif Tufal: http://www.lawteacher.net
Legal Subject Index, Index to Law School, Academic Law Journals: http://www.FINDLAW.com
Mondaq article service: www.mondaq.com/articles/asp
Panstadia: http://www.panstadia.com
The Social Science Information Gateway: www.sosig.ac.uk/law
Sports Law Centre at King's College London: www.kclsportslaw.co.uk
The British Association for Sport and Law: www.basl.org

UK Parliament: http://www.parliament.uk
Villanova Sports and Entertainment Law Journal: http://vls.law.vill.edu/students/orgs/sports
Web Journal of current legal issues: http://www.webcli.ncl.ac.uk

NB: for recent guides to legal resources on the internet see Epstein, R. (2003) 'Law on the Web', *The Legal Executive Journal*, February 2003'; Bill, K. (2003) 'Sports Law on the Web', *The Legal Executive Journal*, May 2003.

Visit www.booksites.net/chadwickbeech for links to these and other relevant websites.

Keywords

Arbitration; defendant; interlocutory injunction; judicial precedent; jurisprudence; libel; mediation; *obiter dicter*; plaintiff; qualified privilege; slander.

Bibliography

BBC News Online (2001) 'Kiss and tell ban raises privacy fears'.
Beloff, M. (2000) *Sports Law*, 3rd edn, Butterworth, London.
Blanpain, R. (2003) *The Legal Status of Sportsmen and Sportswomen under International, European and Belgian National and Regional Law*, Kluwer Law International, New York.
Boyd, S. (2002) 'Does English law recognise the concept of an image or personality right?' *Entertainment Law Review*, 13(1), pp. 1–7.
Boyes, S. (2002a) 'Sports policy', *Sports Law Bulletin*, 5(2), pp. 6–7.
Boyes, S. (2002b) 'The regulation of sport and the impact of the Human Relations Act 1988', 6(4) *EPL* 517.
Butler in Lunney, M. and Oliphant, K. (2000) *Tort Law, Text and Materials*, Oxford University Press, Oxford.
Craig, P. and de Búrca, G., (2002) EU Law – *Text, Cases And Material*, 3rd edn, Oxford University Press, Oxford.
Douglas-Scott, S., (2002) *Constitutional Law of the European Union*, Longman, Harlow.
Dovey, D. (2000) 'Tort and contact', *The Legal Executive*, pp. 18–19.
Duff, A. (1999) 'Reasonable care v. reckless disregard', *Sport and Law Journal*, 7(1), p. 44–54.
Duff, A. (2002) 'Reasonable care v. reckless disregard revisited', *Sport and Law Journal*, 10(1), pp. 156–9.
Gallagher, P. (2003) 'Beckham's injury a freak accident, says Alex', *The Scotsman*, 18 February.
Gardiner, S., Felix, A., O'Leary, J., James, M. and Welch, R. (1998) *Sports Law*, Cavendish Publishing Limited, London.
Grayson, E. (1994) *Sport and the Law*, 2nd edn (1994), Cavendish Publishing Limited, London.
Grayson, E. (2003) 'Don't fight the law. Law 4 today – Online legal issues for the UK public and profession'. (Accessed on 03/02/2003) <http://www.law4today.com/sport/sport1.htm>
Griffith-Jones, D. (1997) *Law and the Business of Sport*, Butterworths, London.
Hoey, K. (2002) *Daily Telegraph*, 20 May 2002, p. S7.
James, M. (2003) 'Referees, scrums and spinal injuries', *New Law Journal*, February 7, pp. 166–7.

Kevan, T. (2001) 'Sport injury cases: footballers, referees and schools', *Journal of Personal Injury Law*, 2, pp. 138–48.

Kevan, T., Adamson, D. and Cottrell, S. (2002) *Sports Personal Injury*, Thomson: Sweet & Maxwell, London.

Koffman, L. and Macdonald, E. (2001) *The Law of Contract*, 4th edn, Tolley, Surrey.

Lane, K. (2002) *Skills to be Acquired by Undergraduate Law Students*, London Metropolitan University.

Lewis, A. and Taylor, J. (2003) *Sport: Law and Practice*, LexisNexis Butterworths Tolley, London.

Michalos, C. (2002) 'Saving face is all a matter of image for the famous', *The Times*, 26 March 2002.

Misquitta, A. (2003) *The Legal Practitioner*, Farrer & Co. (Mondaq's article service).

Moore, C. (2002) 'Sports related injuries: negligence on the field of play', *Personal Injury Law Journal*, 8(Aug), pp. 22–4.

Morrison, M. (2002) 'A good catch: a transfer system for cricket?', *Sports Law Administration & Practice*, 9(2), pp. 1–3.

OFT (2002) *OFT Bulletin* 17 March, p. 16.

Parrish, R. (2003) *Sports Law and Policy in the European Union*, European Policy Research Unit Series, Manchester University Press, Manchester.

Siddall, J. (2002) 'The UK Sports Dispute Resolution Panel – Report on the first two years' 5(4) *Sports Law Bulletin* 15.

Slapper, G. and Kelly, D. (2001) *The English Legal System*, 5th edn, Cavendish Publishing, London.

Smith, J.C. (1992) *A Casebook on Contract*, 9th edn, Sweet and Maxwell, London.

Sport and Law Journal (2002) 10(2).

Thomas, B. (2002) 'Sued rather than bruised', *Journal of the Institute of Legal Executives*, February 2002, pp. 38–9.

Westlaw UK (2003), various case citations, Sweet & Maxwell, London.

Woodhouse, C. (1996) 'The lawyer in sport: some reflections', *Sport and the Law Journal*, 14, 4(3).

Chapter 13

Sport event and facility management

Dave Arthur[1]
Southern Cross University, New South Wales, Australia

Upon completion of this chapter the reader should be able to:

- define 'special event' and have an appreciation of the scope of the event industry;

- demonstrate a broad knowledge of the major processes, plans and skills required of the successful event manager;

- demonstrate a broad knowledge of the major processes, plans and skills required of the successful facility manager; and

- apply aspects of the theoretical knowledge gained in both event and facility management to real-life situations in a practical and usable manner.

Overview

In recent years, and in particular since the 1984 Olympic Games were held in Los Angeles, the staging of special events has become increasingly significant to the sporting organisations concerned and to the cities and countries in which the events take place. Many sporting organisations, and indeed other stakeholders associated with the sporting industry, are utilising special events as a means of establishing and strengthening relationships with their respective target markets and customers. As a result, management principles embodied in planning, human resource management, financial management, marketing, risk management and evaluation have all been applied to the event industry that has evolved. The first section of this chapter examines the phenomenon of events and looks briefly at the relevant aspects of event management. Similarly, significant growth in sport and recreation facilities has also been experienced since the 1970s, as the various levels of government have given a higher priority to the provision of such facilities. Indeed in some cases such facilities have been constructed as a means of procuring events. This increase in facility planning, design and management has seen an increased complexity of skills required by staff involved in

[1] Dave Arthur acknowledges the help of Terry Woods, Ray Booker and Jak Carroll of the School of Exercise Science and Sport Management, Southern Cross University, in the preparation of this chapter.

the planning and management of those facilities. The latter section of this chapter looks at some of the key issues and skills associated with stadia management.

The chapter is not designed as a complete 'how to' manual of event and facility management but more as an introduction to each subject. To facilitate comprehension and to broaden the skill base in certain areas, a number of case studies and related exercises are introduced throughout. These are complemented by suggestions for further reading that reinforce the basic knowledge gained from this chapter.

Event management

Definition of special events

An all-encompassing definition of a special event has proved difficult to achieve, largely due to the vast scope of events in existence. Indeed Getz (1997) questioned the very need for a concise definition mainly because meanings evolve from event to event. In a sporting sense special events can range from 'mega events' such as Olympic Games and the respective World Cups of football, rugby union and cricket through to events that, although they are small by comparison, have a significant impact on their respective host communities. Somewhere in between lie the myriad organised events that form a major facet of the sport industry. From horse racing at Longchamps to a Rugby League grand final in outback Australia the term 'special event' has been coined to describe what happens. Allen, O'Toole, McDonnell and Harris (2002: 11) define 'special events' as the 'specific rituals, presentations, performances or celebrations that are consciously planned and created to mark special occasions or to achieve particular social, cultural or corporate goals and objectives'. This is the definition utilised throughout this chapter.

The impact of special events

There are a number of impacts that are a direct or indirect result of *any* special event. Whilst the scale of these impacts will change according to the type, duration, importance and popularity of the event there is a need for all impacts to be considered by the event organiser. Such impacts, which may be negative or positive or a combination of the two, could include those related to:

- social and cultural aspects (e.g. the building of civic pride and increased prevalence of performance-enhancing drugs);
- physical and environmental aspects (e.g. a legacy of infrastructure and environmental loss);
- political aspects (e.g. the refinement of administration skills and event failure);
- touristic and economic aspects (e.g. the creation of jobs and inflated prices).

One of the often-touted benefits of special events is the economic impact that accrues to the host community as a result of conducting a special event. For example the Commonwealth Department of Industry, Science and Resources has estimated that major Australian events generate tourism expenditure in the region of AUS$ 3 billion per annum (2000). Generally, money spent as a result of a special event is divided into three areas:

- direct expenditure – e.g. where a person purchases a beer at an event;
- indirect expenditure – e.g. the beer is supplied by a third party; and
- induced expenditure – e.g. a person is employed by event organisers to serve the beer.

Economic impact studies are often used by organisers of the event as a basis for its promotion. In some cases they are even used to convince, for example, local government authorities, lobby groups and similar organisations to get behind the event in question. However, when representing the estimated economic impact of an event it is vital that such results are accurate. A number of methods of estimating economic impact are available but where possible any estimations should be undertaken by an independent body to avoid the potential for perceived or real conflicts of interest.

CASE 13.1 Surfing the wave of special events

The proliferation of special events worldwide has encompassed many different sports. Surfing is one such sport that, as a result of the growth of events and other factors such as increased corporate sponsorship and the commercialisation of sport in general, now has an acknowledged and highly professional world championship. Formerly the surfing tour was based around a number of loosely-connected events staged on an ad hoc basis. This evolved into a more structured series of events conducted largely at metropolitan beaches, close to crowds and at times more suited to spectators than the prevailing surf conditions. Nowadays the Association of Surfing Professionals (ASP), which has governed the sport of professional surfing since 1976, conducts the World Championship Tour (WCT). The tour, which caters for both male and female professional surfers and an increasing number of niche markets, encompasses venues in places as geographically diverse as Sunset Beach (Hawaii), Bell's Beach (Australia), Figueira da Foz (Portugal), Teahupoo (Tahiti), Nijiima Island (Japan), Santa Catarina (Brazil) and Jeffery's Bay (South Africa). Locations are selected for their status as legendary surfing hotspots and competitions are scheduled at appropriate times with generous waiting periods to ensure optimum conditions. Multinational companies such as Billabong, Rip Curl and Quiksilver compete for naming rights sponsorship of these events and prize-money has increased markedly from meagre beginnings. In short the WCT has become an inextricably linked series of special events that brings with it a number of impacts to the host community.

Discussion questions

1. What is the scope of the potential positive and negative impacts associated with the conduct of surfing events in such legendary locations?

2. Do you think the various impacts have changed in line with the change in venue from largely metropolitan to the current locations? If so, how have they changed.

3. Given similar numbers of participants and event management staff will the economic impact of an ASP event in Tahiti be similar to that for an ASP event in Australia (give details)?

For full details of the WCT, the other events conducted worldwide under their auspices and other aspects of the organisation readers should access the official site of the ASP at: http://www.aspworldtour.com/.

Event planning

Events do not simply just happen and are usually the result of complex planning and research. As Smith and Stewart (1999: 250) stated quite categorically, 'a sporting event is only as good as the planning that goes into it'. On the proactive side an understanding of the intricacies of the special event product and the customers who intend utilising it allows the event organiser to ascertain the feasibility or otherwise of the event. On the reactive side, however, many sporting organisations find themselves with the opportunity to bid for the hosting rights to a special event. At the highest level the process can be complicated and involve long timespans. For example, the 2007 Rugby World Cup was awarded to France in 2003 and a bid to stage a summer Olympiad is better measured in decades and years rather than months and days. Even at a lower level the need to comprehensively plan and understand lead times is paramount.

The planning function

The planning of any special event requires an assessment of the current position of the organisation as well as a determination of the desired position of the organisation post event. As such, effective and efficient planning is essential for the conduct of any event. Allen *et al.* (2002) feel that the planning process can be broken down into two processes – strategic and operational planning. The strategic plan should set the scene for the operational plan to follow. That is, the strategic plan focuses on long-term, directional strategies whilst the operational plan is usually more specific and related to the detailed 'abc' of how to conduct the event.

The strategic plan

The strategic plan for an event is really little different from that of any sporting organisation. It should encompass the following four key elements which are generally undertaken consecutively:

1. Vision and mission

The vision and mission of the event – these can be expressed as a single statement. A good mission statement is usually derived from the input of many people and is a great tool for giving direction to the event organisers.

2. Objectives

Good objectives are essential. In particular objectives should conform to the SMART acronym (Specific, Measurable, Achievable, Relevant and Time-bound) developed by Hersey and Blanchard (1993). If objectives are not SMART then they tend to be immeasurable, 'pie in the sky' ideals that will do little for the event in the long term.

3. SWOT analysis

Following the compilation of vision/mission statements and the stating of SMART objectives the event organiser can then perform an analysis of the event's internal and external environments. This is referred to as a SWOT (Strengths, Weaknesses, Opportunities and Threats) analysis where S and W are internal (physical, financial and human resources) and O and T external (outside factors that may have an effect on the event).

4. Strategy selection

Following the SWOT analysis, strategies that build upon the strengths and opportunities and attempt to negate the weaknesses and threats are developed. Although such strategies should be dependent on the previous analysis they could include any of the following (Allen *et al.*, 2002):

- Growth strategy – whereby the event grows via, for example, having more people attend, obtaining greater sponsorship revenue or adding certain facets to the core product.
- Consolidation strategy – where organisers decide not to expand the event – this of course may be due to the size of the stadium utilised or another reason.
- Retrenchment strategy – here organisers may decide to pare back certain aspects of the event to focus on the core product. For example, a Masters Games may decide to cut the number of individual sports to concentrate on team sports.
- Combination strategy – this is where aspects of each generic strategy are utilised for the good of the event.

The operational plan

Once the strategic direction of the event has been decided there is a requirement for the development of operational plans. Even here there are separate categorisations – either:

- single-use, where non-recurring activities are concerned; or
- standing plans for activities that take place frequently.

The former are used to achieve a particular objective and comprise the programmes (and any constituent projects) required to achieve them. For example, a key single-use plan for any event is a budget. A budget should show all anticipated income expenditure and may also act as a control mechanism as the event takes place and is evaluated. A standing plan comprises three key elements. *Policies* give event managers boundaries on which to base their decision-making, *rules* define exactly what they can and cannot do whilst *standard procedures* are used to guide management when confronted with common occurrences (Allen *et al.*, 2002). Obviously different events will require emphasis to be placed on different operational planning aspects and the event manager should be involved in deciding which are required.

Organisational structure

A major task of the event manager is to decide upon a suitable structure that maximises the effectiveness and efficiency of the organisation. Hanlon (2002) termed organisations that conduct special events in the sporting sphere as 'pulsating organisations' (p. 20). Essentially this means that they comprise few full-time staff for the majority of the time but immediately prior to and during the event this is supplemented by paid and volunteer labour. Organisations that stage events such as the Olympic Games, the annual Melbourne Cup Carnival or the British Motor Racing Grand Prix are good examples of such pulsating organisations. Obviously this will have a major effect on the type of organisational structure that is employed. Robbins and Barnwell (1994) felt that there were three dimensions to organisational structure – the degree of differentiation, formalisation and centralisation. That said, according to Allen *et al.* (2002) a range of structures can be used. These include:

- Simple structures – such a structure is characterised by centralised decision-making and multi-skilled employees and is most commonly found in smaller event organisations.
- Functional structures – such a structure is characterised by specialised managers and areas of responsibility that can be added to at any time.
- Network structures – such a structure is characterised by the addition of outside consultants on a needs basis.

CASE 13.2 Mastering the games

Masters Games are acknowledged generally as festivals of sport that attract a wide variety of competitors aged from around 25 to over 100 years of age. The last World Masters Games was held in Melbourne in 2002 and attracted nearly 25,000 competitors to the various sports. Over and above certain age categorisations there are no qualification criteria for most sports – everyone is welcome to compete with the emphasis on having fun in a friendly and inclusive environment. Given the success of major Masters events a variety of smaller events have been established. Catering for similar target groups such Games range in participant numbers from under a hundred to thousands. The Rainbow Region Masters Games are an example of just such an event:

It is anticipated that competitors for the Games will be drawn from a New South Wales catchment area extending from Tweed Heads in the north to Port Macquarie in the south and to Tenterfield and Glen Innes in the west. In keeping with other Masters Games however there is a strong likelihood that other competitors will be enticed from other areas such as south-east Queensland and from south of the area mentioned above. The range in ages will be as significant as the geographical area, with competitors expected to rank from just over 30 years of age in some sports, allowing it, to in excess of 80 in some others. Whatever their age and place of residence they do have one major facet in common – an ability to impact economically in the region in which they are accommodated and participating. Conservative estimates put the value to the local community of such spending throughout the Games at some AUS$500,000. A total of sixteen sports will be conducted over the three days of competition with various social functions scheduled for every evening and a race day scheduled for the Saturday afternoon.

Discussion question

4. Imagine you have been appointed as the event manager for this event. As an initial consideration you wish to form a committee to run the event and also provide prospective members with your view of how the event will proceed. In order to do this you are required to undertake a SWOT analysis specifically for the event.

Further details regarding Masters Games can be accessed through the International Masters Games Association website at: http://www.imga-masters.com/. In addition information regarding the actual event referred to in this case study can be found at: http://www.liscity.nsw.gov.au/article.asp?ArticleID=415

Human resource management

Once a strategic and an operational plan for the event are agreed upon and put in place, it is then possible to determine the number and types of human resources required to conduct the event. Getz (1997: 186) suggested a three-step approach to facilitate this:

1. Breaking down the programme into separate tasks;
2. Determining how many people are needed to complete these tasks; and
3. Making a list of the numbers of people, the supervisors and skills needed to form the best possible 'crew'.

Of course, the particular strategies for human resource management developed for an event will depend largely on the type of event envisaged. Hanlon (2002) identified that when managing personnel in a special event, various specialised human resource stages emerge. Whatever the focus of the event, staff, be they full time or part time, paid or volunteers, should:

- be carefully chosen according to specifically developed criteria;
- receive appropriate training for the position;
- be given some direction as to organisational goals and objectives;
- be shown how their efforts will contribute to the overall conduct of the event;
- be motivated to achieve the goals set for them.

This is of particular importance to volunteers, as many events will rely on the recruitment and use of volunteers. The Sydney 2000 Olympics required about 55,000 of them – including 47,000 in official multi-coloured uniforms, 6,000 ceremony performers, and hundreds of others from various sources. Even small-scale events such as 'fun runs' require many volunteers to ensure the conduct of a safe event. The management of volunteers is therefore crucial to the success of any event.

Managing and motivating staff and volunteers

Motivation commits people to the event, enthuses and energises them, and enables them to achieve goals. Your ability as an event manager to motivate people is a fundamental component in your repertoire of skills. For without this ability, paid employees and, in particular, volunteers can lack enthusiasm for achieving your organisation's goals and can even show a lack of concern for the success of the event.

This is likely to be reflected in a poorly perceived event. Auld (1994) felt that a good approach to managing and motivating staff as well as alleviating any conflicts that may arise could be achieved through fostering cooperation, establishing relationships and properly defining volunteer roles.

Event administration

To assist the event in becoming successful you will need to address some key financial and marketing issues. These include the ability of the event manager to:

- Generate sufficient revenues and reduce costs. Correct financial planning techniques will allow the event manager to recognise revenue sources and costs.
- Secure sponsorship for the event. Most events conducted nowadays, be they international, national, state or local, rely on the assistance of sponsorship.
- Market and promote your event. The conduct of special events can become a profitable activity in terms of dollars, awareness and entertainment when professionally marketed and promoted.

Financial management

The main purpose of financial management in a special event setting is to ensure that any financial objectives set are met. Such objectives could include operating at a defined profit, breaking even or operating at a pre-determined loss. The event manager needs to think creatively about potential revenue-generating aspects of the event along with an assessment of the financial risks involved. Proper financial management will also assist greatly in the identification of potential sponsors by identifying those areas where expenditure will be required. For example, the budget could identify that $10,000 is required for telecommunications, making a telecommunications company a logical target for in-kind sponsorship. In-kind sponsorship means supplying materials or services as opposed to the direct input of monies. Just as event planning is important, financial management will allow the event manager to recognise probable revenues and costs. Although estimating costs can be a somewhat difficult task and, of course, projecting expected revenues can be inaccurate, they can be still be planned for.

Sponsorship management

Sponsorship is entrenched as a valid and successful way for companies to promote their goods and services (see Chapter 14 for a more detailed analysis of sponsorship in general). However, companies will be interested in the event only if it is professionally packaged and presented. This requires a complete and thorough understanding of both the event in question and the needs and requirements of potential sponsors. It is essential therefore to match the event with the sponsor's needs (Ferrand and Pages, 1996).

The event manager needs to understand the concept of sponsorship and the reasons for the growth of sponsorship at special events. Catherwood and Van Kirk state that 'in its simplest form, sponsors provide funds or "in-kind" contributions to promoters of events and receive consideration in the form of logo usage and identity with the event' (1992: 101). Whatever the benefits sought, the event manager must realise that sponsorship is no longer charity or patronage but is a business exchange transaction where the sponsor gets a return on investment for the sponsorship contribution (Crompton, 1993).

Once the type of sponsor has been clearly identified it is important then to match sponsors with your event by selecting those sponsors who will have a similar target market to you.

Marketing and promotion

The marketing and promotion of an event must become a part of the overall philosophy and public relations campaign of your particular sporting organisation. You will need to plan for the major steps of the campaign, namely:

- setting SMART objectives;
- planning and budgeting;
- implementing;
- evaluating.

These steps should be used whether you are conducting a small event that only requires the production of a newsletter or whether you are developing a multi-media campaign that may surround a major event. Along with the public relations campaign and the marketing of a special event, the importance of advertising should not be underestimated. Regardless of your type of event, you will most probably be required to spend money on paid advertising since if no one knows the event is on, then no one will be there!

Advertising the event

The frequency and format of advertising will be dependent on the type of event and the budget available. An advertising plan must be formulated early in the planning cycle to maximise the advertising dollar. A thorough understanding of the target market/s will ensure that the message is reaching your chosen audience. An event advertising plan could include these considerations:

- the SMART objectives of the advertising campaign;
- the advertising budget;
- the desired outcomes;
- the target market;
- the aspects of the event which will be advertised;
- the advertising media to be used;
- the length of the advertising campaign, i.e. a long gradual campaign or a short intensive one; and
- systems of measuring and monitoring the effectiveness of each advertising medium used.

Remember also that there are other stakeholders with an interest in your event that could be expected to help with advertising the event. These include sponsors, the facility where your event is to be conducted, government agencies and local community groups.

Event logistics

Setting up basic operations

When setting up basic operations, consideration needs to be given by the event manager to the negotiations that will need to take place with the public- and private-sector bodies that control venues, security factors, insurance factors, ticket sales, communications and the use of volunteers.

Risk management

Despite undertaking risk management and insurance, you may still find yourself involved in litigation should something go wrong at the event. It has been shown over the past few years that sports litigation is growing. With this in mind it will be valuable for you to develop approaches that will systematically manage liability risks. Risk identification and treatment measures must be undertaken.

A risk management analysis is an essential component of event planning, with a risk management plan for the event an obvious end product. The analysis should determine the appropriate level of insurance required and will minimise any risks to organisers, participants, spectators and the general community from your event. Of course, many of the issues identified will be the responsibility of the facility hosting the event, and will be clarified during contractual negotiations. Remember, however, that the event manager is responsible for all participants in the event.

Risk identification needs to be practical, systematic and realistic. Risk assessment follows risk identification, where risks are assembled and dealt with in priority order. Once risks have been identified and assessed, event managers must implement an appropriate risk-reduction campaign. Reduction of risks will generally reduce the number and likelihood of accidents and help maintain or even reduce insurance premiums payable.

Even the best risk management programme, however, will not totally prevent accidents from occurring. This means that insurance is an important aspect of the risk equation and is in itself an important method of minimising risk.

See Chapter 17 for a more detailed coverage of risk assessment.

Communication

Communication is another important aspect of any event and can make or break it. Consider the following points when assessing the communication needs of the event. How will you:

- communicate with the other organisers on the day of the event;
- communicate with off-site persons on the day;
- communicate with facility staff;
- communicate with the media and they with you;
- get results distributed interstate or overseas if necessary;
- get urgent messages to those involved in your event;
- arrange for all staff to communicate with each other?

After contemplating each question a simple strategy can then be derived to answer each pertinent aspect. For example, to communicate to other organisers it may simply be enough to provide a list of mobile telephone numbers or set up a walkie-talkie network. Similarly communication with the media may involve facsimile or email.

Techniques of logistics management

Many of the tools used in project management can be successfully adapted to satisfy event logistical requirements. These tools include:

- scheduling – the use of bar charts, time charts, GANTT charts;
- contingency charts – detailing back-up plans if things go wrong;
- network analysis – use of critical paths; and
- site and venue maps.

Event evaluation

Event evaluation is essentially a simple process of observation, measurement and monitoring of the event as a whole or in its constituent parts. Perhaps the most important result of any event evaluation is that, if done correctly, it can act as a tool for analysis and will improve future events – in short the event manager will be left with an operations manual. According to Smith and Stewart (1999) this manual should comprise the original event plan, any modifications made to this plan, and a schedule as well as a contingency chart. It should also be noted that evaluation is an ongoing process that should occur through all stages of the event, the literature, in particular Getz (1997) and Allen *et al.* (2002), points to three key periods when event evaluation may prove useful:

1. Prior to the event – sometimes taking the form of a feasibility study, the pre-event evaluation will usually involve market research as well as the establishment of performance benchmarks for measurement of success or otherwise of the event.
2. Event monitoring – this is the process of tracking how the event is progressing through its various stages. Monitoring of, for example, the budget may result in a reallocation of resources from one cost centre to another, whilst monitoring of media may require further print advertisements to be produced.
3. Post-event evaluation – this can involve numerous types of data collection from simple verbal surveys regarding event enjoyment to complex analyses of consumer expenditure. The scope of post-event evaluation relates closely to the size of the event and its key objectives.

Event debrief and report

A final debrief is an important part of any event as clear, concise and accurate documentation will provide information and may form a 'blueprint' for the committee that organises the next event. The debrief can be as comprehensive as the event manager chooses; however, whatever the event, a report as a formal document, should be produced. The purpose of the report must be decided early in the debriefing process. Will the report merely be a description of the event just completed, will it be a blueprint for future events or will it be a combination of both? The report can include visuals, such as a video of the event, a video of the television exposure generated, clippings from newspapers, photographs of the event, copies of programmes, etc. The debrief and report could cover the following areas but will largely depend on the size of your particular event:

- Financial performance – a full financial overview including profit/loss statements, balance sheets (including accounts receivable and any outstanding liabilities), budget comparisons.
- Plan review – a review of the effectiveness of any operational, marketing or human resource plans used throughout the event. This could be achieved through an environmental scan (market research) before and after the event.
- Infrastructure review – a review of all aspects of the venue's infrastructure, for example catering arrangements, parking, transport, equipment, security, presentation of facilities.
- Economic impact assessment – a calculation of the benefit of hosting the event for the local community, i.e. financial impact, number of people coming into the community, exposure that the event generated for the community.
- Critical incident report – a review of any incidents (minor or major) that may have occurred or that could involve an insurance claim against the event organisation.
- Sponsor report – a report detailing such items as media gained, sponsor recognition, photographs, attitude of spectators to sponsors.

Summary

The first part of this chapter discussed some of the basic aspects of event management. This included the impact of events, planning considerations, structure, human resource, financial, marketing and risk management as well as event evaluation. The second part of the chapter moves on to similar issues associated with the management of the facility.

Facility management

Introduction

Sports facilities, from the Olympic Stadium in Sydney to the Stadium of Light and from the Melbourne Cricket Ground to Lord's in London, are essentially not new concepts. In fact, as long as 2,500 years ago, sport facilities were developed and utilised for the health and well being of the people. Although the primary purpose at that time may have been to maintain military readiness and entertainment for nobility, these facilities led the way to today's sports complexes. The first part of this section of the chapter will focus upon the planning, design and construction of sport facilities.

Over the last two decades demands on the provision of leisure services has increased with a consequent increase in demand for the provision of sport and recreation facilities. Along with this growth has been the need for facility providers to become more effective and efficient in their operations than ever before. In their quest for effectiveness and efficiency, it is imperative that facility managers have knowledge of the factors that may contribute to the success of a facility even from the time its construction is first considered.

Issues and trends in planning a facility

The number of sporting facilities throughout the world has increased significantly, as have the cost of building, managing and maintaining such facilities. It is therefore essential that those sporting facilities that are planned and designed are done so in a cost-effective manner and are responsive to the changing needs of the community. Previously many facilities were single-purpose, with little thought being given to multiple usage, social requirements or even effective management. Communities are finding it more and more difficult to support these single-purpose facilities. A number of current issues need consideration in the planning stages of sport facility development. These include the manner in which sport is now played (e.g. some sports traditionally played outdoors can now be played and viewed indoors), the range of sports, which is greater now than at any other time in history, as well as increased awareness of the need for multipurpose, flexible facilities.

The process of planning and designing facilities

As discussed so far, the need for and the design of facilities is not new. The quality of the management of these facilities can often determine their effectiveness and viability. It has been recognised that facility management plans must be prepared in conjunction with the design plans, because once the facility has been erected many management options may be lost. However, the success of any facility is often aligned to its design not just its management. It is important therefore to have knowledge of the planning and design process for sporting facilities.

The preparation of planning documents

If any facility is to operate successfully in the medium to long term the designer must meet clearly defined needs by developing a planning document. The community/sporting groups involved in the development of the facility must ask themselves a number of very important and specific questions before commencing such a document. Extensive market research is required very early in the planning process to enable all stakeholders to have a consistent understanding of why the facility is being developed and what its role will be.

Unfortunately, in the past major facilities were constructed with the aim of hosting a major sporting event, for example the Commonwealth Games or an Olympic Games. Yet events like this barely last two weeks. In today's economic climate, however, all facilities should now be constructed as multi-purpose and flexible venues capable of long-term economic viability. As Shilbury, Quick and Westerbeek (1998) opined:

> Planning of facilities for mega events like the Olympic Games, or facilities for a professional basketball club, or facilities for the local sports club, all should involve a long-term perspective in terms of the prospective usage of the facility. With production and

consumption of the sport taking place in the facility, not only current provision but also future provision needs to be taken into consideration. (pp. 267–8)

The same principles apply when designing smaller community facilities. Venues should be multi-purpose and flexible, and prior extensive market research is vitally important. One valuable research tool is consultation with the community.

The consultation process

The consultation process in designing a community sporting/recreation facility can encompass many stakeholder groups. These may range from politicians, local business people and their respective organisations, sporting/recreation associations, school groups/educational bodies, and various other target markets as well as the general public. The consultation process must be structured, planned and orderly, allowing input from all the stakeholders to be considered. In building ownership of the facility among stakeholders in this way, ongoing operation will be improved as a result. Involving these individuals and groups in the original design of the facility is a great start. Some of the technical tools used to determine the structure and make-up of the facility may vary, but the need to consult will not.

As for other aspects of management there is an essential requirement to set SMART objectives (Hersey and Blanchard, 1993) for the facility to allow for its long-term viability, both financially and in its usage by community groups. The stakeholders will be able to help develop the objectives for the facility.

This consultation process becomes an essential part of the feasibility study. The feasibility study should determine:

- if the construction of the facility is justified;
- whether the facility will be financially viable (remembering some facilities operate at or below break-even);
- if sufficient capital can be raised and interest payments met;
- who will use the facility; and
- what type of activities will occur.

Once the decision has been made to proceed, the project planning team will need to develop a project brief.

Project briefs

The project brief is an instruction to the design team of what the project planning team expects from the facility. This document can also be used as a checklist of issues and concerns for the design team to discuss with the planning team. Essentially the project brief contains the criteria on which the preliminary design, final design, finished building and operational procedures will be evaluated.

The physical design of the facility

In the physical design of the facility, the various components within the facility need to be considered. These components include the specific spaces that are utilised throughout the facility. The Victorian Department of Youth, Sport and Recreation issued guidelines (1988) outlining how these spaces could be considered in the three major components of functional, technical and aesthetic.

- Functional components – relate to (for example): the types of spaces and number of users, circulation/movement patterns through the building from one space to another, visual relationships, control, cost implications, vertical movement, availability and emergency provisions.
- Technical components – relate to (for example): the choice of artificial or natural light, environmental conditions inside and outside the facility, electrical lighting, plumbing, mechanical services, acoustics, ceiling heights, floor surfaces and choice of construction materials.
- Aesthetic components – relate to (for example): the image and three-dimensional effect externally, the desired atmosphere, the varying requirements of sport versus non-sport spaces, ease of finding one's way through the facility and how to make the facility inviting and comfortable.

Building the facility

The three control areas of cost, energy and quality are also applicable to the building of any type of facility.

Cost is critical to any facility, as with any project; budgets must be set and followed. The design will be greatly affected by the funds available for the project.

Energy control is an important long-term consideration. Through careful planning and research, ongoing maintenance, heating, lighting, cleaning and material costs can be reduced.

Quality design relates to customer service, so understanding the needs and wants of your market will assist you in this area. Safety considerations must also be noted because errors or oversights in this area could lead to expensive litigation or modifications in the long term.

The building process

The construction of major facilities in particular is usually more than a twelve-month proposition depending upon variables such as weather, labour conditions and supply of materials. The selection of a contractor to build the facility over such a length of time becomes a major decision in the planning process.

Facility modification

Not all communities can afford or have the need to construct new facilities. Many facilities are suitable for refurbishment. One of the more recent facility design issues being witnessed is that of facility modification, where existing facilities are altered to meet current needs. This is particularly noticeable within aquatic facilities. During the 1950s and 1960s swimming pools worldwide were constructed as oblong boxes designed for competitive swimming. In the 2000s, however, the pool consumer demands more of a leisure or recreational experience. Shilbury *et al.* (1998: 267), observed that relatively new revenue streams had become increasingly important to a facility's viability yet older facilities are not equipped, for example, to host corporate guests in specifically designed suites. Hence facility modification to alleviate this problem may occur.

Joint use of facilities

Constructing new facilities adjacent to existing similar facilities and the joint use of community facilities have also proved successful in recent times. The obvious advantages of this approach include:

- utilising existing facilities, i.e. parking areas, changing rooms, etc.;
- not having target markets with different leisure needs in conflict with each other. For example, at an aquatic centre, children could use the water slides allowing aquarobic classes or older groups to use the 25-metre pool;
- the more efficient use of facilities;
- more extensive range of equipment.

An example in Australia was the conversion of the Adelaide Aquatic Centre. Originally the complex consisted of a 50-metre, 8-lane pool and a diving pool. Additional facilities were added to this to incorporate leisure aquatic facilities (i.e. water slides, free-form pools, rapids, etc.). Elite sports are still catered for in the original facilities but a whole new market was created for the Centre through the provision of the additional facilities.

Management

One reason many facilities have difficulty in fulfilling their potential is that they have inadequate or inexperienced management. In relation to new facilities, the development of suitable management plans commences long before the decision is made to construct the facility, while, in relation to existing facilities, the implementation of suitable management plans and management options is also vital to their successful operation.

Poor quality management can lessen the facility's chance of meeting its own objectives or the objectives set by the managing authority. In many instances poor management will lead to the facility being under utilised by the community. Just as in the formulation of any business enterprise, it is evident that good management begins with a well-developed and well-written management plan. In the case of new facilities this plan is written in the early stages of development along with the physical planning of the facility.

Management options

During the development of a management plan, the management team will look at the various facility management options available to them. These could include leasing, contract management, a management committee or self-management.

Leasing is a traditional management system that has been used particularly by local government authorities. In most cases leasing only covers the operational aspects of providing the facility. In more recent times, contract management has been undertaken by organisations (commercial and community) that specialise in facility management. A management system that may be adopted by local government and community groups is a management committee which oversees the management of the facility and whose members are usually drawn from elected members and appointments. A self-management system allows the facility to manage its own affairs once an appropriate staff has been recruited. The aims, objectives and expectations relating to the facility and described earlier in this chapter will dictate the most effective management option for your facility.

Tower (1993) believed that facility providers should consider a number of criteria before they determine which management option they will select as their management system. Such criteria include planning, people and systems (comprising finance, service delivery and human resource management).

Compulsory competitive tendering

Previous discussion has related to a range of management options available to facility managers. These could be considered as the traditional management options that have been successfully used. However, a management option known as compulsory competitive tendering (CCT) is becoming increasingly popular worldwide.

Emanating from Britain in January 1992 the compulsory competitive tendering process requires local authorities to call for public tenders on the management and operations of the majority of their leisure facilities. These facilities include swimming pools, indoor sports halls, golf courses, squash courts, tennis courts, etc. The underlying rationale for its introduction was the belief that governments, in their role as managers of sporting/leisure facilities, would operate more effectively if exposed to competition from the private sector.

Probably the main advantage of CCT is that competition invariably results in an improved service to the customer. Organisations tend to become more customer focused rather than systems or internally focused, especially if they operate in a competitive market. The main disadvantage that is likely to arise is when conflict exists between client and contractor. In many instances the local government authority may not trust private enterprise, whilst on the other hand private enterprise may not trust the local government authority due to conflicting values and goals.

Regardless of which option is preferred for the overall management of a facility there will be many instances whereby leases and sub-contracts for operations/services will be undertaken within the facility, for example catering, cleaning. The greatest advantage in leasing or sub-contracting these operations/services is that it allows the manager to introduce a greater level of expertise than the present staff may have. In addition, performance indicators play an important part in the contract. Performance indicators for a facility can include expenditure, revenue, number of users, labour costs and so on. You must be able to ensure that both parties are continuing to meet the conditions as stated in the original agreement. Performance indicators also allow facility managers to compare their performance with those of similar types of facility.

■ Staffing within the facility

The great majority of facilities will involve more than a single employee, therefore the facility manager will need to devote some time to recruiting, orientating, training and supervising employees. Staff members are a special kind of resource within the facility, because the importance of a professionally committed staff is essential in all service industries. The success of most sport and recreation facilities is dependent upon the interaction of its personnel with the public and the relationship of employers and employees with each other. In many instances customers of the facility will judge its effectiveness on the friendliness, alertness and performance of the staff. It is therefore imperative that a facility manager fully understands staffing issues.

■ Staffing culture

Having the 'right' staff for the 'right job' is essential to the successful operation of any facility. The facilities may be immaculate but if the staff do not have the skills or personality to meet and exceed customers' expectations then the facility may not succeed.
  Three specific staffing issues need to be addressed.

1. organisational culture within the facility;
2. the importance of training and developing human resources; and
3. communication.

Organisational culture

Organisational culture plays a powerful role in determining how staff members respond to the customers, to their work colleagues and to management. Consequently, it is important to recognise all aspects of the culture of the facility, so that positive elements can be encouraged and potential conflicts and problems can be avoided. Many organisational cultures reflect values that were prevalent decades ago. The need for facilities to have a culture reflecting the values of the day is obvious. Increased competition for the consumer's leisure dollar along with a more sophisticated, more demanding and better-educated customer, ensures that those facilities that do not see themselves as part of a service industry or are not customer focused, will suffer. Many service organisations, particularly those in the sport and recreation industry, are striving to improve their level of quality service through the performance of their employees.

Training and developing human resources

Training and developing staff must play an important role in all service industries – as Shilbury *et al.* (1998: 272) relate: 'The level of training, skills and abilities of potential employees of the sporting organisation become "people variables" that will make the difference between mediocre and excellent service provision.' People do not magically develop skills and must first be taught the skills then given the opportunity to practise and develop them. With the pace of change affecting facility management, the need for ongoing training is obvious. Again as with any process, facility managers must have a clear idea of the aims and objectives to be achieved through the training and development of their staff.

Communication

As with any staff-related matter, a key issue is communication. Communication must start at the top and executives must be committed to this process. When faced with change, many employees experience discomfort, and consequently resist any new changes, thus the reasons, the benefits, the process, and expectations regarding the change must be clearly communicated to all staff.

The area of human resources within facilities is a large and important aspect of management. Human resource management often determines the success or otherwise of a facility. The interaction of staff with the public, with each other and with management will contribute to this success considerably. Understanding the impact of staff relationships, competencies for staff, organisational culture and the training needs of staff will help equip the facility manager with skills that lead to the successful management of the facility.

Financial management of the facility

As previously stated the financial viability of any facility relates back to design and management issues. If adequate market analysis was undertaken in the design stage of the facility there is every possibility that the facility should meet its financial objectives. However, if correct analysis was not undertaken then the facility might struggle financially. Once constructed the facility must be managed efficiently and effectively to allow its financial objectives to be met.

Efficient management of a facility implies that management is accomplished with an economy of resources for a maximum of results. For example, the recreation and sporting programmes developed within the facility are done so with the least possible expense; all money spent promoting the programmes reaches the largest possible target market and the programmes are offered at a price to maximise participation by the community.

Effective management of a facility implies that the right actions are put into place to further the objectives of the facility. For example, the sport and recreation programmes offered would be exactly what the community wanted, at a price they could pay, and employees would give the type of service that would make participants want to return.

Facility managers should strive for a combination of the two. Financial management relates to establishing financial objectives, determining pricing strategies and maintaining financial records.

Financial objectives

One of the first steps in financial management is the development of clear objectives. These objectives will help the facility manager determine if the facility is achieving, or moving towards, financial success. Two of the major objectives at the heart of financial management relate to liquidity and profitability.

Liquidity is the ability to generate enough cash to pay the bills when they fall due. Short-term liquidity may be the first part of a facility's objective; however, long-term profitability must be achieved in order for the facility to succeed, particularly in the case of commercially owned and operated facilities. Non-profit facilities (usually government owned and managed) may not have profit as an objective, but may strive for a break-even scenario or even a small loss.

Pricing

The financial objectives of the facility will assist when determining the pricing structure under which the facility will operate. Arriving at an appropriate pricing structure is never easy, but is a core responsibility of any facility manager. Marriott felt that the pricing of leisure services 'pops up regularly because there is a worry about the cost of recreation provision and the major or perceived inequities are identified by one group and there is no apparent set of strategies for either dealing with or resolving these' (1993: 42). Marriott emphasised the fact that pricing has a number of purposes that may include:

- philosophical – to improve fairness and equity or to maximise the opportunity to use facilities;
- managerial – to ration and regularise use within an individual facility or across a group of facilities or to encourage positive consumer attitudes;
- entrepreneurial – to encourage commercial investment or to provide one basis for programme and staff accountability;
- financial – to contribute to cost recovery or to help ensure the efficient use of financial resources.

Pricing methods

The facility manager must be aware of all the reasons for introducing a price structure into the facility. The pricing strategy must be consistent with the facility's objectives. Such fees can be determined via:

- an agreed amount – reached after discussions with all relevant stakeholders;
- a going rate – examines what similar facilities are charging and introduces prices that reflect such charges;
- an ability to pay – reflects an opinion on how much the various target markets are able to pay for the use of the facility;
- a cost-based fee – set as a result of the calculation of fixed and variable costs.

Each pricing method has advantages and disadvantages and the facility manager may need to use a combination of all four methods. For example, a cost-based method may be used when programming where minimum costs to be recovered are set (for example, instructors fees, consumable equipment). Similarly an agreed amount may be used with regular season users such as sporting associations.

Price discounting

Discounting can also play an important part in a facility's pricing policy. Discounting may provide a means whereby the facility can access unrealised revenue from those target markets that may be incapable or unwilling to pay the full fee for using the facility or attending one of the programmes offered. For example, conditions may be introduced on the service (only available from 10.00 am to 3.00 pm) to maximise revenue through attempting to eliminate quiet times in the facility's activities. Similarly many facilities provide opportunities for customers to purchase two or more services in a single package for a discounted price.

Financial records and planning

As with any business the maintenance of accurate financial records is imperative to allow informed management decisions to be made. Poor record-keeping leads to poor decision-making. Facility managers must understand why financial record-keeping is important as well as knowing what records to keep and having an understanding of the accounting process. The type of records that should be kept include income, expense, tax record, payroll records, mortgage and debt records, regular financial statements, accounting records, personnel records, facility and equipment records, legal records and administrative records.

Risk management

Risk and safety management is essentially the process of controlling potential risks and minimising potential losses or damage that may occur in the facility. Facilities have a high exposure to potential risk issues and as such it is difficult to operate any facility in a risk-free environment. Therefore risk management and safety issues must always remain a top priority for the facility manager.

By their very nature, facilities are high-risk areas. Such risks can be due to the wide array of activities that can be conducted (particularly aquatic activities), the difficulty associated with full-time supervision of areas within the facility (changing rooms etc.) and the depreciation of the equipment used in the facility. If risks are not managed properly and planning not undertaken, then losses may occur.

Risk management plans

Crossley and Jamieson state that there is 'a tremendous need for commercial recreation managers to develop a risk management plan' (1988: 141). As most recreation managers are facility managers then this statement is just as true in the facility management arena. Although written fifteen years ago Crossley and Jamieson's three-step model for a risk management plan is just as useful today. The model has three major components:

Step 1 – Identify all risks by analysing past accident records, the facility and its programmes and by encouraging staff input.

Step 2 – Analyse and classify every risk according to the Risk Management Strategy Grid shown in Figure 13.1. Use this grid to classify each risk according to its frequency of occurrence and severity of injury should it occur.

Step 3 – Implement risk strategies according to the Risk Management Strategy Grid.

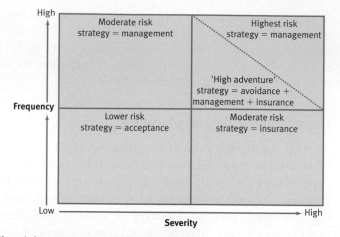

Figure 13.1 The risk management strategy grid
Source: Crossley and Jamieson (1988: 142) from Nilson and Edginton (1982)

Lower risk/acceptance

Certain accidents happen infrequently and with minor injury. For example, a participant may strain a muscle whilst engaging in an aerobics class. Such injuries are very difficult to anticipate or prevent. Many organisations and their participants accept these minor risks as a natural part of engaging in the activity. Typically, the cost of any accident falls below the deductible limits of the organisation's insurance policy. Therefore, if there is any expense involved, it is picked up directly by the organisation or the participant.

Moderate risk/insurance

On rare occasions, there are accidents with major injury and/or property loss. Usually these occurrences are also very difficult to anticipate or prevent. An example would be water damage from a burst pipe or tank. In such instances, adequate insurance cover is the best remedy.

Moderate risk/management

There are many recreation activities in which minor injuries are relatively common: slipping on the deck of a water theme park, sprained ankles and broken bones in sports competition and so on. While insurance is advised to back up the organisation in these instances, the best strategy is to manage the activity better. This means providing safety-conscious supervisors for the young age-group competition and training lifeguards to prevent situations where injury may occur.

Highest risk/avoidance

There are some recreation activities that have relatively frequent accidents, sometimes with severe consequences. Examples include competitive boxing or hang gliding. Risk management is essentially a systematic plan that can be utilised by facility managers not only to identify particular risks associated with an activity but also to allow them to devise strategies that will minimise the potential risk of injury to their patrons.

CASE 13.3 Managing the risk – The Getbigquik Fitness Studio

The Getbigquik Fitness Studio is a major fitness and recreation facility located in a regional centre. The Studio was opened fifteen years ago and during that time has undergone a major renovation with the result that the facility is now divided into separate areas:

1. a state-of-the-art aerobics studio;
2. a weight-training area; and
3. three indoor cricket pitches which can be reformatted for other indoor sports such as soccer, netball, volleyball and boxing.

Unfortunately, the facility was recently closed down for six months due to an unfortunate accident when a client was crushed and subsequently died whilst performing an unsupervised maximal bench press. The staff member on duty was dismissed and the manager left her position following the accident. Due to a downturn in business following the accident the centre shut down. However, apart from this accident no other claims have been made against the facility owners or management. A similar centre across town has recently also closed down, which has led the facility owners to reopen the Getbigquik Studio. You have recently been appointed to manage the facility on behalf of the owners, and as a graduate manager with over ten years experience in the industry, you must formulate a plan to manage risk.

Discussion Questions

5. Identify the general types of risk facing the facility through its activities.

6. Analyse and assess the severity and anticipated frequency of the risks.

7. Identify a plan to implement risk strategies.

Use Crossley and Jamieson's three-step model and their risk management strategy grid to achieve these tasks.

■ Facility marketing

Effectively marketing any facility in the 2000s has never been more important as more and more facilities and other forms of entertainment enter the marketplace. Facilities can no longer be seen merely as a product; they are now in the service industry and as such need to develop communications with their customers. Competition for the leisure dollar is more intense than ever and consequently marketing has taken on a greater role in facility management. Consumers nowadays are more discerning and more demanding in their expectations of leisure/recreation providers.

■ Marketing a service

The difference between marketing a good and marketing a service is significant. Issues that you need to consider when marketing a service include these:

- Whereas goods are tangible, produced prior to consumption and can be stored, services are intangible and are, in effect, produced and consumed simultaneously.
- People contacts are the most important aspect of marketing a service. Therefore, having well-trained staff is essential for those in service industries.

Service marketing relies on the relationship between the customer and the service being marketed. Relationships are developed that can be continuous and strong. Accordingly, there exists a real need for motivated and well-trained staff, as they are a valuable asset in the management of the facility.

Communication tools

Within the facility the following communication tools can be of assistance:

- Personal selling obviously requires well-trained staff who are familiar with the facility's goals and objectives.
- Direct response via telephone, mail or email is a powerful marketing tool in facility management that, if correctly undertaken, can result in high levels of customer retention.
- Television, radio and press advertising are all well-known and well-utilised communication tools in facility management, with each method having differing pros and cons.
- Trade publications are often a useful medium in which to advertise.
- Newsletters, brochures and fliers are used extensively by facility managers, with this form of communication playing a similar role to that played by packaging when marketing a good.
- Public relations and promotions are two tools also used frequently in the marketing of facilities and events and should be considered as part of your communications mix.
- Word of mouth. Within a facility environment it is vital to strive for positive word of mouth as this is indicative of satisfied customers. Customers expect to receive consistently good service, but when they do not they rarely tell management or staff – they tend to tell friends, family and neighbours.
- Direct marketing allows the facility manager to access target markets cheaply and quickly and should play an important role in the facility's marketing mix.

The marketing plan

There are a number of benefits of having a facility marketing plan. Such a plan should act as a road map for the development of the facility. Some facilities may look 5–10 years ahead with short- and long-term marketing goals, while others may only plan 1–2 years ahead. It may also ensure that the appropriate marketing activity takes place along with the assignment and responsibility of tasks. Obviously with the myriad of communication tools available (described above) it is essential that resources be used in the most effective and efficient manner. A marketing plan also sets performance standards by monitoring the marketing activities of the facility. These can then be checked against the objectives and changes made to ensure particular marketing objectives are met. In short, such a plan is essential for the facility manager.

Programming within the facility

There are very few facilities where there are not peaks and troughs in usage patterns. Consequently, to maximise the use of facilities, managers should develop skills in the delivery of recreation programmes within the facility. The effective delivery of these recreation programmes is dependent upon two essential components, programming and scheduling. Programming is essentially the provision of services or events to meet the needs of a segment of the facility's market, whilst scheduling is ensuring that all your bookings and hiring groups have access to the facilities.

Programming

Because most facilities experience peaks and troughs in their usage patterns, programming should aim to increase usage during those troughs and maximise the financial return during peak times. Programmes are therefore vital to the success of any community facility. Effective programming results in the needs and wants of target markets being met. This results in increased usage of the facility and an improved positive financial position. Meeting these needs may require a proactive rather than reactive approach. This proactive approach means creating a service or programme that can be offered to the target group to satisfy its needs.

Being proactive also means being entrepreneurial and this may result in the creation and marketing of events specifically designed to meet the needs of the facility and its stakeholders.

Scheduling

One of the main reasons for having scheduling skills is that all facilities are built to service the needs of many different clubs, associations, individuals and special interest groups and all these needs must be met. For example, a typical community centre may service the needs of many groups including sporting groups, students, library users, the general public and staff members – all of whom have different needs and expectations.

Most facilities cater for more than one usage or tenant and, as the majority of facilities are government funded or subsidised by the ratepayers, scheduling within multifunctional facilities is very necessary.

A facility manager should at the very least ensure that a policy exists to determine scheduling priorities if different groups require the same resources at the same time. As with any policy the aim is to make decision-making easier and reduce the risk of potential conflict.

CASE 13.4 Swimming with the sharks

You have been appointed the facility manager of the Deepwater Indoor Olympic Swimming Complex. The facility is ten years old and comprises both a 50-metre pool and a 25-metre pool and operates between 5.00 am and 9.00 pm, seven days a week. The previous facility manager retired six weeks ago but in the changeover period he related that the pools always seemed overcrowded at peak times (especially between 6.00 am and 8.00 am and between 5.00 pm and 7.00 pm, Monday to Saturday). Due to the overcrowding, three swimming organisations (the Old Salts – a Masters swimming organisation of 130 people; the Aquanuts – an aquarobics group of 50; and the local triathlon club of 20 people) became disenchanted and no longer use the facility. You decide to attract these important groups back to the Deepwater facility and have decided to formulate a usage policy and a schedule designed to incorporate programmes for all existing, past and potential user groups. Such groups are as follows:

■ Learn to swim (including babies, children and adults);
■ Elite squad swimmers;
■ Triathletes;
■ Masters swimming;
■ Aquarobics; and
■ General swimming.

Discussion questions

8. Explain when and why you would schedule each activity at certain times during the week.

9. Explain how you would attract the three disenchanted groups back to the facility.

Conclusion

The first part of this chapter discussed some of the basic aspects of event management including the impact of events, planning considerations, structure, financial, marketing, human resource and risk management as well as event evaluation. Similarly, the second part of the chapter examined the importance of management involvement throughout the planning and construction of the facility, available management options, human resource management within the facility, financial management and pricing, risk management, marketing and finally programming. It is hoped that the chapter has provided students with a broad appreciation of both event and facility management and facilitated this through case studies and related discussion.

CASE 13.5 A great race goes steadily downhill   FT

How a great sporting event loses its lustre is a mysterious thing. Racegoers today can barely imagine a time when the Ascot Gold Cup was the most esteemed race in the calendar after the Derby, while it is not so long since the annual match between England and Scotland was one of the highlights of the football year. And although international rugby obviously has a future, it is by no means so obvious that the Six Nations championship has. The Anglo-Scottish Calcutta Cup might one day be as much of a relic as its football equivalent.

For many years, the Giro d'Italia was one of the great three-week bike races of Europe, the Italian equivalent of the Tour de France, which it precedes, and of the

Spanish Vuelta. It is still a marvellous race, but the Giro – which finishes its first week today with a stage from Maddaloni to Avezzano in the Appenines – is seemingly in decline, buffeted by doping scandals.

If that were the only reason for the Giro's eclipse, it might logically apply to the Tour as well. But then the Giro, if it has never had a single shock as qualitatively horrendous as the Festina affair, has been deluged by a sheer quantity of drugs busts.

The Italian race also has the air increasingly of a domestic competition: 11 out of the 19 teams competing this year are Italian, as were 3 of the first 4 riders in Wednesday's general classification. (Yesterday was a rest day.)

Some of the riders are fairly obscure, although that's scarcely the word for Mario Cipollini, for whom Margaret Thatcher's description of Jeffrey Archer as 'the extrovert's extrovert' might be borrowed.

After his all-too characteristic recent ejection from a Belgian race for throwing his bidons at an official, Cipollini has been hoping to equal the record for 41-stage wins in the Giro, and was only just pipped on Wednesday by Alessandro Petacchi wearing the maglia rosa, the Giro's equivalent of the yellow jersey.

But many of the leading riders and teams now ignore the Giro, or treat it with something like contempt. Lance Armstrong and his US Postal Team are preparing ferociously for the centennial Tour in July (where he will be favourite to win a record-equalling fifth consecutive victory) but are nowhere to be seen in Italy.

Even those serious contenders for the Tour who do enter the Giro don't all do so in a very flattering spirit. Robbie McEwen won the 'points' or sprinters' prize in last year's Tour, and the Australian has his eyes on this year's French race, by desultory way of the Giro.

After having won the second stage on Sunday, McEwen was disqualified for dangerous riding at the finish. The stage was awarded to Fabio Baldato, whom he had knocked out of the lead (or, 'I only closed the door on Baldato, as we say in cycling'). Then on Tuesday, McEwen had his revenge, showing race-winning form in taking the stage from Terme Luigiane to Vibo Valentia.

And yet he isn't riding in the Giro with the intention of so much as finishing, let alone winning. He has said he will ride for less than two weeks, 'and then go home to get ready for the Tour'. It is hard to think of any other sport where a great event would be treated like this.

It was not ever thus. Even if the Giro belongs especially to tifosi (as the Italians call cycling fans), and even though it has never quite threatened the pre-eminence of the Tour, it has historically been a race the stars want to win. The Giro–Tour double used to have a glory of its own, and was won by Jacques Anquetil in 1964, by Eddy Merckx in 1970, and by Miguel Indurain in 1993: three of the greatest riders ever. Where are the riders with the capability of succeeding them? Otherwise engaged, intent on the French race, for which anything else is mere practise.

What makes it worse is that this year's Giro has been designed to be as competitive as possible, with a series of exhilarating climbs and what could be a decisive final time trial into the cathedral square in Milan. It surely deserves a worthy winner, and I hope, looking a little nervously at some of the riders and their previous drugs transgressions, that it finds one.

Source: Geoffrey Wheatcroft, *Financial Times*, 16 May 2003

Discussion questions

10. If a sporting event such as the Giro d'Italia appears to be in decline, particularly when drugs scandals and rival events pose a threat to it, what contribution can a more professional approach to event management play in resurrecting it?

11. In your view, what should organizers and managers of the Giro d'Italia do to ensure the race has a future?

Guided reading

An interesting discussion of the various definitions of special events as well as the positive and negative impacts derived from events generally is provided in the first two chapters of Allen *et al.* (2002).

For further guidance on risk analysis students are directed to Crossley and Jamieson (1988: 142).

A fuller description of these criteria can be found in Tower (1993: 55–61).

To understand compulsory competitive tendering students are directed to Sparrow and Bolt (1988).

An interesting perspective on the place of the facility in the marketing mix can be found in Chapter 13 of Shilbury *et al.* (1998).

Recommended websites

The official website of the Association of Surfing Professionals (ASP) can be found at: http://www.aspworldtour.com
The official website of the International Masters Games Association can be found at: http://www.imga-masters.com
The following website http://www.panstadia.com provides a good resource for students interested in sport facility management.

Visit www.booksites.net/chadwickbeech for links to these and other relevant websites.

Keywords

GANTT chart; project brief; SMART objectives; special events; SWOT analysis.

Bibliography

Allen, J., O'Toole, W., McDonnell, I. and Harris, R. (2002) *Festival and Special Event Management*, John Wiley and Sons, Sydney, Australia.

Auld, C. (1994) 'Changes in professional and volunteer administrator relationships: implications for managers in the leisure industry', *Australian Journal of Leisure and Recreation*, 4(2), pp. 14–22.

Catherwood, D.W. and Van Kirk, R.L. (1992) *The Complete Guide to Special Event Management*, John Wiley and Sons, New York.

Commonwealth Department of Industry, Science and Resources (2000) 'Towards a National Sports Tourism Strategy', Working Paper, Commonwealth of Australia, Canberra.

Crompton, J.L. (1993) 'Understanding a business organisation's approach to entering a sponsorship partnership, *Festival Management and Event Tourism*, 1, pp. 98–109.

Crossley, J. and Jamieson, L. (1988) *Introduction to Commercial and Entrepreneurial Recreation*, Sagamore, Champaign, Illinois.

Department of Sport and Recreation (1988) *Community Recreation Centres: A Planning and Design Manual*, Department of Sport and Recreation, Melbourne, Victoria.

Ferrand, A. and Pages, M. (1996) 'Image sponsoring: a methodology to match event and sponsor, *Journal of Sport Management*, 10(3), pp. 250–61.

Getz, D. (1997) *Event Management and Event Tourism*, Cognizant Communication Corporation, New York.

Hanlon, C. (2002) 'Managing the Pulsating Effect in Major Sport Event Organisations', Unpublished doctoral dissertation, Victoria University, Australia.

Hersey, P. and Blanchard, K.H. (1993) *Management of Organizational Behavior – Utilizing Human Resources*, 6th edn, Prentice-Hall International, New Jersey.

Nilson, R. and Edginton, C. (1982) 'Risk management: a tool for park and recreation administrators'. *Parks and Recreation*, August, pp. 34–7.

Robbins, S.P. and Barnwell, N.S. (1994) *Organisation Theory: Concepts and Cases*, 3rd edn, Prentice-Hall, Sydney.

Shilbury, D., Quick, S. and Westerbeek, H. (1998) *Strategic Sport Marketing*, Allen and Unwin, Sydney.

Smith, A. and Stewart, B. (1999) *Sports Management. A Guide to Professional Practice*, Allen and Unwin, Sydney, Australia.

Sparrow, C. and Bolt, A. (1988) 'Compulsory competition: it's here'. *Leisure Management*, 8, pp. 7, 26–7, 29.

Tower, J. (1993) 'Management options for facility providers', Conference Proceedings, NSW Department of Sport and Recreation, pp. 55–61.

Chapter 14

Sport sponsorship and endorsements

Des Thwaites and Simon Chadwick
Leeds University Business School

Upon completion of this chapter the reader should be able to:

- define the terms sport sponsorship and endorsement, and appreciate the nature of these activities;

- explain the importance of sport sponsorship and endorsement from both a sponsor and sponsee perspective;

- identify the wide range of corporate and brand objectives that can be achieved through sponsorship and endorsement;

- appreciate the major stages in the development of an effective sport sponsorship or endorsement programme;

- highlight important issues relating to sport sponsorship and endorsement activity, such as ambush marketing and legal regulation.

Overview

The chapter begins with a definition and explanation of the terms sponsorship and endorsement and relates these to the sporting context. Distinctions between advertising and sponsorship are drawn at this point. The importance of sponsorship and endorsement are then discussed by reference to growth rates over previous time-periods. The focus then turns to the provision of a systematic framework for the development and management of an effective sport sponsorship or endorsement programme. Major issues include: functional location, objective setting, selection, evaluation and control. The discussion then addresses the growth of ambush marketing in the area of sport sponsorship and looks at some of the legal issues that relate to these forms of activity.

A number of case studies, based on the practical experiences of well-known companies, are introduced at regular intervals to illustrate core aspects of sport sponsorship and endorsement. Several leading sporting organisations and athletes also form the basis of case material. Important learning points are reinforced by the use of discussion questions that draw on case material or other issues and topics raised in the chapter.

Introduction

Despite the current interest in sponsorship and endorsement, these activities are not of recent origin. Evidence exists for their use at the time of Caesar's gladiators and in support of artists, musicians and composers in Shakespearean times. The Howell Report (1983) cites Spears and Pond, a firm of Australian caterers, as the sponsors of the England cricket tour of Australia in 1861–2. Over the years, sponsorship has developed into a highly versatile and adaptable medium that has, in part, contributed to the difficulties of creating an enduring definition. Head (1981) described the exercise as 'like trying to harpoon a butterfly in a gale'. There is however, general agreement that sponsorship represents a business transaction rather than patronage or philanthropy. The commercial dimension is covered in many definitions of sponsorship, for example, Otker (1988) suggests it represents 'buying and exploiting an association with an event, team etc. for specific marketing purposes'. Meenaghan (1991b) adopts a similar view and identifies sponsorship as 'an investment in cash or kind, in an activity, in return for access to the exploitable commercial potential associated with that activity'. These definitions highlight that the primary justification for involvement lies in the material benefit available to the sponsor. In summary, the features of sponsorship are:

- an exchange between two parties: the sponsee receives cash and/or benefits in kind while the sponsor secures a right of association with an activity or event;
- the sponsor seeks to achieve a range of marketing objectives through the exploitation of the relationship;
- it is a business relationship rather than corporate philanthropy.

Endorsement is commonly associated with sponsorship and has some similar characteristics. In essence, a company provides an individual with financial or material benefit in return for her/his use, promotion or support of their products. The amounts involved can be considerable. For example, during 2000 Nike Golf signed a five-year extension to their contract with Tiger Woods, worth about £62 million, which includes endorsement of the Nike golf ball and apparel. In 1998, Michael Owen, the 18-year-old England soccer player, had an excellent World Cup and was courted by many household names such as Pepsi, Coca-Cola, McDonald's, Marks & Spencers and Tesco, all of whom wished to be associated with this emerging talent. It is reported that contracts totalling £35 million were available to Owen but not taken up.

Is sponsorship another form of advertising?

A view sometimes expressed is that sponsorship is another form of advertising. Hastings (1984) takes issue with this statement, as does Meenaghan (1991a), who distinguishes the two forms of communication in relation to issues of control, message, implementation, motivation and audience reaction. Jones and Dearsley (1989) suggest that sponsorship can deliver additional benefits in the minds of consumers who can see tangible benefits for sport, the arts, the community, etc.

Marshall (1993) believes that sponsorship can provide a sponsor's communications with valuable elements that would be difficult, if not, impossible, to achieve through mainstream advertising. These elements are summarised below:

- *Credibility* – provides validity for product claims.
- *Imitation* – relates good credentials of the event/athlete to prospects/customers.
- *Image transference* – links product with a set of positive image qualities.
- *Bonding* – gains involvement of prospects/customers.
- *Retention* – generates enduring awareness and exposure.

However, Marshall cautions that the attitudes of the public to sponsorship may vary across international borders. His research revealed that German consumers were much more inclined to see sponsorship as another form of advertising, compared to French and UK consumers. The belief that sponsorship could promote a good image for the sponsor and its products was particularly strong in Spain, but much less so in France. These are just two examples of the distinctions identified by Marshall, which have implications for those companies who may conduct sponsorship in a variety of geographic locations. One of the reasons why consumers identify sponsorship as another form of advertising may stem from the fact that companies do not fully understand sponsorship and fail to manage it properly in a way that exploits its full potential. Some of these issues are developed later in the chapter.

Growth and development

Establishing an accurate figure for the amounts spent on sponsorship has proved difficult as many small-scale initiatives go unreported, for example, support for a village soccer or rugby team. In addition, the methods for collecting data may vary across countries and institutions. For example, are the reported figures merely rights fees or do they include the costs of exploiting the relationship with other communications media? Are the costs of player endorsements included or excluded? Given these difficulties it is reasonable to assume that many of the published estimates may be understated.

There is some consensus that global sponsorship expenditure was in the region of £15.7 billion during 2002, an increase of £12.6 billion in the last 10 years. North America accounted for approximately 40 per cent of the total and Europe 33 per cent. Several reasons are put forward for this dramatic growth, for example:

- Escalating costs of media advertising.
- New opportunities generated by increased leisure time.
- Greater media coverage of sponsored events.
- Inefficiencies of existing media, for example, clutter.
- Prohibition of advertising by tobacco companies in some countries.
- Proven benefits of sponsorship.

Early entrants into the sponsorship market were drawn from industries such as brewing, tobacco and motor manufacturers. Their success has now encouraged entry by companies from a much broader range of industry sectors such as financial institutions, computer and electronics firms, mobile-phone companies and high-street retailers.

The provision of support (in cash or kind) for sports events, teams, performers, stadia etc. has proved the most popular investment vehicle for companies, accounting for approximately two-thirds of worldwide sponsorship expenditure. The particular attraction of sport derives from its high visibility and its capacity to attract a broad cross-section of the community. It can be used to target mass markets or specific niches and offers a means of transcending national boundaries and breaking down cultural barriers. It also generates high levels of television coverage through the provision of all-round family entertainment.

Another significant cause of the dramatic increase in sport sponsorship activity stems from the inability of governments to continue to fund sport to the levels necessary to maintain its development. Consequently, sports organisations have turned to the corporate sector to make up the shortfall. Indeed, media and sponsorship activities are now such an important element in the funding of sport that many sporting bodies and events would find it difficult to continue to operate in their current form without these sources of cash injection. As an example, during 2002, 36 per cent of the turnover of Manchester United plc came from media and 18 per cent from commercial activities, of which sponsorship contributed 90 per cent. The club's annual report for 2002 (Manchester United, 2002) emphasises the importance of relationships with the corporate sector.

■ On 1 August a new kit sponsorship and merchandising deal with Nike began, including a 13-year guarantee of £303 million in return for the right to produce all Manchester United branded products worldwide.
■ The relationship with sponsors, Vodaphone, continues to grow as both parties seek to develop revenue-generating services.
■ Budweiser has signed up as the official beer of Manchester United, while also agreeing stadium 'pouring rights'.
■ Pepsi has renewed as the Club's official supplier of soft drinks.
■ Ladbrokes has become the Club's official betting partner in the stadium and its interactive gaming partner worldwide.
■ Dimension Data has joined up as the Club's business services provider while also redesigning the website. It has also become a partner in the development of a long-term Customer Relationship Management initiative.
■ Terra Lycos has taken responsibility for the development of a Chinese website and acts as sales agent for the English language site. Lycos UK has become a club sponsor.
■ Fuji has agreed to become the Club's official imaging partner and a sponsor, helping pursue new business-to-business (B2B) and business-to-consumer (B2C) services.
■ Century Radio renewed its existing sponsorship.
■ Wilkinson Sword became the Club's official male-grooming partner.

Early sponsorship initiatives in the United Kingdom focused on sport and, to a much lesser extent, arts and community projects. Mintel (2000) reported that sport accounted for £30 million in 1980, £223 million in 1990 and an estimated £404 million by 2000. This represented 85, 75 and 48 per cent respectively of total sponsorship expenditure. The significant change over the last decade has been the dramatic growth in broadcast sponsorship. From a zero base in 1989, this form of sponsorship was estimated to have grown to £176 million by 2000, accounting for 21 per cent of the UK market. Arts sponsorships also increased in popularity, rising from 12 per cent in 1990 to 21 per cent in 2000 while community projects also gained momentum, rising from 5 per cent of the market in 1990 to 9 per cent by 2000 (Mintel, 2000).

The amount relating specifically to endorsement is difficult to establish, as companies do not always wish to disclose the sums involved. Nevertheless, this does appear to be an increasingly popular form of marketing activity involving substantial financial commitment. For example, sportbusiness.com reported that in 2001 David Duval signed a contract with Nike Golf believed to be valued at £17.6 million over 4 years, including incentives. Former Brazilian soccer star, Pele, is thought to earn in the region of £12.5 million per annum from endorsement contracts with a range of companies, including, MasterCard, Pfizer, the manufacturers of Viagra, Coca-Cola, Petrobras, Nokia and Samsung.

CASE 14.1   The costs of sport sponsorship

The rights fees that allow companies to associate with particular properties have continued to grow over recent years. While inexpensive properties may still be available, the more prominent teams, competitions or events command significant sums of money. For example, the 3-year Emirates Airline deal with Chelsea FC was for £22 million. Vodaphone's 5-year deal with the English Cricket Board was reported to be £13 million. Lloyds TSB's 3-year deal to sponsor the Rugby Union Five Nations Competition cost £12 million, while Embassy paid £5.4 million for their 4-year involvement in the Snooker World Championships.

Although sport sponsorship expenditure has continued to grow, both in the United Kingdom and worldwide, there are some concerns on the horizon. Recent reports suggest that some Formula 1 motor-racing teams have been obliged to cut their asking prices significantly in order to attract sponsors for the 2003 season. It is alleged that some middle-order teams have been particularly hard hit and that the demise of both Prost and Arrows has been hastened by the withdrawal of commercial support. Reported prices for the 2003 season are significantly down on 2000. Signage on a front/rear wing and sidepod that would have cost £7 million in 2000 was available for £4 million in 2003. Likewise, the cost of wing mirror signage had fallen from £750 thousand to £500 thousand.

Sources include *The Times, Evening Standard* and sportbusiness.com

Discussion questions

1. Do you feel that the situation described above relates purely to Formula 1 or is the concern a more general one?

2. What are the factors that may contribute to a decline in the value of sport sponsorship properties or limit a company's willingness to be involved in this form of activity?

CASE 14.2 The benefits of sport sponsorship

Sponsorship does different things for different companies. Some spend huge amounts of money and achieve little more than the satisfaction of knowing they are associated with a particular player, team or event. Others may be more strategic in their selection of sponsorships, and in their evaluation of their success. But irrespective of the company, or of the sport, sponsorship does get results. Here is an example:

Green Flag's sponsorship of the England football team

Approximate cost of sponsorship per year:	£1mllion.
Increase in customer awareness levels of the Green Flag brand:	21%
Largest increases in awareness:	
Scotland	25%
London and the South-East of England	25%
UK respondents who thought the company was a 1998 World Cup sponsor (even though they were not):	11%
UK respondents who thought the sponsorship was an effective way of raising brand awareness:	43%
Proportion of people who thought they would be more likely to buy the company's products:	32%
Proportion of people who perceived the company's products more favourably:	27%
Proportion of people who changed their attitude towards the brand:	28%

(Adapted from Miles, 2001)

An effective framework for sponsorship management

A feature of the sponsorship literature over recent years has been the reference to greater accountability. Many early sponsorship initiatives were seen as cavalier with limited thought or strategic rationale. This gave rise to the term 'chairman's wife syndrome' suggesting that particular sports were chosen for sponsorship because they appealed to the family members of senior staff within the company. The early literature also suggests that some initiatives that were intended to bestow commercial benefits on the sponsor degenerated into philanthropy because of a failure to manage the process effectively. The recent trend towards greater accountability suggests that both parties to the sponsorship contract should manage the process as effectively as possible to create mutual benefits.

In order that sponsorship can make an effective contribution to a company's communication objectives it is important to develop an effective framework for its management. The adoption of a structured and systematic approach will overcome many of the problems identified in earlier research. Irwin and Asimakopoulos (1992) offer a simple conceptualisation of the main stages in the sponsorship management process, shown in Exhibit 14.1. These issues are discussed briefly in the following section.

Exhibit 14.1	The main stages in sponsorship management
Step 1	Review of corporate marketing plan and objectives
Step 2	Identification and prioritisation of specific sponsorship objectives (corporate and product/brand related)
Step 3	Identification of evaluation criteria and assignment of relative weighting based on the prioritisation from Step 2
Step 4	Screening and selection of sponsorship proposals
Step 5	Implementation of selected sponsorship proposals
Step 6	Evaluation of sponsorship's effectiveness in achieving prescribed objectives

The need to consider the corporate marketing plan during the initial step serves to emphasise that sponsorship is one element among a number of promotional activities that need to be coordinated following an evaluation of their strengths and weaknesses. Meenaghan (1991a) uses the analogy of an orchestra where the various instruments combine to create the performance. There is general agreement in the literature that the use of sponsorship or endorsement in a manner that is unhinged from these broader considerations will limit its contribution to the company's overall objectives. It should also be noted that the sponsorship activity should complement other elements of the marketing mix. In this respect, it is important at an early stage to identify the functional responsibility for sponsorship to avoid what has been termed 'the illegitimate child syndrome', where everyone shows an interest but nobody accepts responsibility.

Following a review of corporate marketing objectives, communication strategy and budget implications, attention turns to the role of sponsorship in the communication mix. Rigorous research into potential sponsorship opportunities will allow the development of clear, concise and focused objectives. This is an important stage in the process as a failure to develop and prioritise sponsorship objectives and to investigate the strengths and weaknesses of particular sponsorship platforms will limit the effectiveness of the programme and militate against subsequent evaluation. One of the positive features of sponsorship is its ability to contribute to a broad range of objectives at both corporate and brand level. Although there are overlaps between the characteristics of brand and corporate sponsorships, the former tend to be shorter term, brand-led and decided at brand level. Pay-back tends to be tightly quantified and activities are aimed at users of the brand and potential users. In comparison, corporate sponsorship tends to be longer term, corporate affairs-led and decided at board level. Activities are more speculative and aimed at opinion formers. In terms of objectives, at brand level the focus is commonly on factors such as media coverage, sales leads, sales/market share, and target market awareness. Corporate objectives tend to emphasise community involvement, public awareness, increasing/changing public perception of the company or its image, building goodwill and trade relations or staff relations.

Although sponsorship can be used to fulfil a wide range of objectives, there is some evidence to suggest that specific forms of sponsorship are more appropriate to particular objectives. For example, Witcher *et al.* (1991) suggest that both sport and the arts are useful platforms for promoting corporate image, but sport offers an advantage in generating brand awareness, media exposure and sales generation.

A feature of sponsorship is its ability to appeal to a broad range of internal and external audiences, for example:

- Potential customers
- Existing customers
- General public
- Local community
- Business community

- Workforce
- Distributors
- Suppliers
- Shareholders
- Government

While the attraction and retention of business will be important and give emphasis to potential and existing customers, sponsorship also allows messages to be delivered to other groups who are specifically involved with the company or affected by its conduct or success. Case 14.3, drawn from Barclays Bank plc, illustrates a major positive aspect of sponsorship, namely the ability to achieve a number of objectives and target a range of constituencies through a single programme.

CASE 14.3 Barclays Bank plc

During the period between 1987 and 1993 Barclays Bank plc were the sponsors of the major English soccer competition, The Football League Championship. Through this sponsorship, Barclays were able to fulfil a range of objectives and target a number of different audiences.

- Soccer interests a wide range of age and sociological groups allowing specific target groups to be identified.
- Opportunity to secure national coverage – the home base of every league club had at least one Barclays' branch.
- Soccer gains a high level of media coverage, particularly television.
- Scope for corporate hospitality – agreement provides for complimentary tickets to all home games.
- Availability of other communications media – programme advertising, perimeter boards, Barclays' logo on Football League materials etc.
- Soccer appeals to the youth market which is a prime recruitment area.
- Links with the community – competitions for the National Association of Boys' Clubs.

The increasing costs of staging sporting competitions has led to a corresponding increase in the number of unsolicited requests for support that companies receive. Against this background it is important to have an effective screening process that can discriminate between the good and bad proposals. Choosing to support an inappropriate proposal is likely to prove expensive given the cost of the initial rights fee and the subsequent expenditure necessary to exploit the relationship. Companies appear to show various levels of sophistication in selecting between proposals. At one extreme are companies that rely largely on intuition and 'gut feel' while at the opposite end of the spectrum are those who use complex evaluation criteria. A range of factors may be influential in the decision. For example, Irwin *et al.* (1994) suggest 42 factors, which fall within 11 generic categories:

- budget considerations;
- event-management issues;
- positioning/image (issues of fit);
- targeting of market (media coverage and immediate audience issues);
- extended audience profile;
- public relations;
- promotional opportunities, e.g. licensing, signage;
- competitive considerations, e.g. ambush;
- sponsorship status, e.g. level, exclusivity;
- alternative sponsorship (co-sponsor, in-kind supplier); and
- sponsorship type (event, competition, team).

The factors identified above can be assessed and subsequently weighted depending on their importance to a particular sponsor. Each sponsorship proposal will then gain a total score that forms a basis for decisions about selection or rejection.

Although there are numerous factors that a potential sponsor may wish to consider in coming to a decision on a particular sponsorship opportunity, the issue of fit has received considerable attention in the literature (see for example Speed and Thompson, 2000). There is general support for the view that consumer attitudes towards a particular sponsorship are more positive when they perceive there is a degree of fit between sponsor and sponsee. This fit may take a variety of forms, such as a logical connection between event and sponsor. An energy drinks manufacturer sponsoring an endurance-based sports event would be an example. The fit may also operate at an image level, where both organisations have a similar image or where they have a similar ethos. These issues are explored in the Tetley Bitter case (Case 14.4).

Earlier in the chapter, a distinction was drawn between advertising and sponsorship. At this point, it is appropriate to extend the discussion to include the issue of leverage. In essence, this means optimising the value of the association that has been created through the payment of the rights fee. A review of the literature indicates that, in particular, companies who are new to sponsorship may assume that this is the total level of their commitment. In the belief that sponsorship works in a similar manner to advertising, they pay a fee and sit back waiting for a positive response. Sadly, this is unlikely to be effective. The rights fee merely allows the company to be associated with the property. Subsequently, it is necessary to exploit the relationship through other media. The specific nature of the contract, in terms of what is included in the initial cost of association, will clearly influence the amount spent on leveraging. However, figures of up to three times the original sum are suggested in the literature.

One of the sponsorship issues that has raised considerable and ongoing debate is the question of evaluation. On the one hand there are those who argue that the effects of sponsorship cannot be measured or at best are difficult to measure. On the other hand there are those who advocate a range of techniques to measure the effectiveness of sponsorship initiatives. The nature of the company's objectives and the extent to which these objectives are framed in a manner capable of evaluation will influence the choice of method. Several approaches have been adopted, for example:

- measure media coverage/exposure;
- monitor guest feedback;

- measure communication effectiveness (prompted/unprompted awareness);
- monitor sales leads;
- measure actual sales;
- monitor staff feedback; and
- measure awareness by trade contacts.

The measurement of media coverage appears to be a very popular approach, although its value has been questioned in certain situations. It is important to appreciate that this represents 'an opportunity to see' and as such relates to exposure, not necessarily awareness. Furthermore, there is evidence that companies involved in sport sponsorship have noted the length of time their logo has been displayed during a televised event and translated this into the equivalent cost of rate card advertising. This comparison is flawed, not least because several glimpses of a logo as a backdrop to more compelling action are unlikely to be as effective as a tailor-made advertisement appropriately placed in a suitable medium.

CASE 14.4   Cricket sponsorship

The Joshua Tetley Brewery in Leeds (part of Carlsberg-Tetley) is famous for its leading beer brand, Tetley Bitter. This is one of the most popular bitter brands in the Yorkshire region and exhibits values relating to quality and tradition. Commencing in 1987 the company undertook a number of sponsorship initiatives focused on cricket. This proved successful and in 1991 a further £1 million was allocated. This investment included a renewal of the sponsorship agreements with Yorkshire County Cricket Club and the Scarborough and Harrogate Cricket Festivals and broadcast sponsorship of major international matches shown by BSkyB. An evaluation of these activities suggested that awareness of the brand was strengthening in its northern heartland, where the majority of its distribution outlets were located, but also increasing nationally. The market share for Tetley Bitter was growing and two thousand three hundred new distribution outlets were established, following approaches by retailers. These gains were attributed to the complete integration of promotions, perimeter advertising, media coverage, competitions, indirect player product endorsement and sustained press activity.

The company appreciated that in order to build Tetley Bitter into a national brand, it would need to increase awareness, particularly in the Midlands and South of the country. This was achieved through a three-year, £3 million sponsorship of the England cricket teams. The benefits accruing from the agreement included:

- Title of Official Sponsor for New Zealand and the World Cup;
- Tetley Bitter name on shirts/track suits of England and England A teams;
- supplier of beer;
- team photographs twice yearly;
- full-page colour advertisement in all UK international match programmes;
- a maximum of 3 players for corporate work on 6 occasions per annum;
- 10 players per year for individual branded photo stories;
- 20 large and 20 small autographed bats;

- 25 signed photos of the team for both home and away series;
- 3 board perimeter advertising package;
- County Challenge sponsorship.

In addition to the initial cost of association, the company allocated £500,000 for media sponsorship, PR and promotional activity and advertising. This was intended to assist in building awareness of the brand, not only among cricket supporters but also across all bitter drinkers and those who purchase beer on behalf of their families for home consumption.

Early research carried out before the sponsorship agreement was formalised suggested the link with English cricket would be well received by the target audience. When asked if it was good for the England teams to be sponsored, 44 per cent replied that it was a very good idea, while the same percentage felt it was quite a good idea. When asked how they felt about Tetley Bitter becoming a sponsor, only 7 per cent indicated they were not in favour. Later research highlighted that members of the target audience had been reached through the cricket sponsorship activities. On 6 November 1991, only 4 per cent associated Tetley Bitter with cricket sponsorship but by 1 April 1992 this had risen to 24 per cent. Similarly, unprompted awareness of Tetley Bitter as the sponsor of the England teams rose from 2 to 28 per cent during the period, and prompted awareness from 8 to 39 per cent.

Source: Thwaites and Eastwood (1995)

Discussion questions:

3. What were the objectives that Carlsberg-Tetley set out to achieve through their sponsorship of the England cricket teams?

4. The notion of fit is discussed earlier in the chapter. Is there a fit between Tetley Bitter and English cricket?

Ambush marketing

Although the amounts spent on commercial sponsorship have continued to grow during the last two decades, this trend will only continue if sponsors are able to see tangible benefits from their involvement with particular properties. For example, sponsors of the Winter Olympic Games at Salt Lake City paid between £3 million and £35 million depending on their level of involvement. These sums can only be justified if the anticipated benefits of the association are realised. As sponsorship activity has grown, so too has the practice of ambush marketing (sometimes known as parasitic marketing). This has been particularly prevalent in the sports area. There are various forms of ambush marketing, which limits the scope for developing a comprehensive definition. Initially it was viewed as a practice by which a company, usually a competitor, attempted to secure a benefit by attaching itself to an event without paying a rights fee. In so doing it could generate a positive image for itself while reducing the benefits to the rightful sponsor by creating confusion in the mind of the consumer. For example, at the Atlanta Olympic Games, billboards showing the Nike name and 'swoosh' logo were erected on a building specifically constructed by Nike close to Atlanta's Olympic Park. Reebok was the official sponsor of the sports goods category.

The high cost of association with major events (Coca-Cola is reputed to have paid approximately £30 million to be associated with the 1996 Olympic Games) category exclusivity may have encouraged some companies to seek alternative approaches. Legitimate responses to these problems include, for example, the sponsorship of the television broadcasts relating to the event or the sponsorship of national teams who will compete at the event. Although included under a generic definition of ambush marketing these activities are clearly different to the activities of Nike described earlier, as no attempt is made to avoid payment.

Some definitions of ambush marketing include reference to the degree of confusion created among the public. As an example, during the soccer World Cup of 1990 only two of the ten official sponsors of the event (which included companies such as Coca-Cola and Mars) achieved greater recognition than National Power, who only sponsored some of the broadcasts. Likewise, at the 1992 Olympic Games non-sponsors such as Federal Express and Sears outperformed Express Mail and J.C. Penney, the official sponsors of the same categories. The growth of ambush marketing posed a potential threat to the viability of corporate sponsorship and, accordingly, both rights owners and potential sponsors have considered ways in which sponsorship rights can be protected. A number of activities are now undertaken to reduce the scope for ambush strategies. For example, event organisers could adopt some of the following approaches:

- Provide category exclusivity, for example only one soft drink company and publicise the name of the official sponsor.
- Control photographic and broadcast images to prevent unauthorised use.
- Control licensed souvenirs and merchandise to limit scope for counterfeiting.
- Offer official sponsors the first option on other promotional activities.
- Seek to purchase poster sites near the major event locations and stadia. These can then be offered to official sponsors.
- Publicise sanctions for unofficial use of copyright material.
- Publicise details of companies who are seeking to misrepresent their relationship.
- Establish a group responsible for 'policing' venues etc. and monitoring breaches.
- Package certain rights thereby giving major sponsors the option to gain priority in relation to media opportunities that could be used by competitors as a basis for ambush activities.

Sponsors cannot rely totally on organisers putting in place all the measures necessary to prevent ambush marketing. They must also take responsibility for maximising their relationship with a particular event and minimising the opportunities for competitors to adopt ambush strategies. This will require a detailed assessment of all aspects of the event where opportunities to ambush may occur and subsequent implementation of a number of counter-ambush strategies. Invariably this will involve additional expenditure. Through early and heavy leverage of their investment, sponsors should seek to develop a position in the mind of their target audience that will be difficult for an ambusher to usurp.

CASE 14.5 Illegal, immoral or legitimate competitive practice?

Nike, who were not official sponsors of the 1984 Olympic Games held in Los Angeles, launched a marketing campaign revolving around the theme 'I love LA'.

In 1988, American Express discontinued its sponsorship of the Olympic Games at which point Visa took over the category of official credit card sponsor. American Express subsequently launched an advertising campaign featuring former Olympic athletes. Visa's response was to advertise the fact that American Express cards were not accepted at the Games. American Express then retaliated by suggesting that it was possible to purchase items with their card and there was no necessity to have a 'visa' to enjoy the Games.

The battle continued in 1992 when American Express purchased advertising space on the room key tags at the Hotel Princess Sophia in Barcelona. This was the official hotel of members of the International Olympic Committee. Visa was the official credit card category sponsor.

Federal Express promoted its sponsorship of the United States men's basketball team although UPS was the official Olympic sponsor in the overnight mail category.

PepsiCo developed an advertisement that used famous soccer players wearing shirts with a Pepsi logo and the word PEPSI on the front. The phrase 'Tokyo 2002' was included in the advertisement, together with football images. PepsiCo was not a sponsor of the 2002 World Cup held in Japan and Korea.

At the Commonwealth Games 2002 in Manchester, David Beckham appeared at the opening ceremony in a tracksuit, emblazoned with the word 'Adidas' in what was presumed to be a 'clean' stadium.

Visa ran a competition on its Brazilian website that displayed the FIFA World Cup trophy. No authorisation for this activity had been granted by FIFA.

BAE Systems, a defence and aerospace company, used advertising that included a number of footballing metaphors and photographs of soccer shirts bearing the number '6'. The strap line read 'Who do you think spends this much on defence every season?'. The advertising coincided with Manchester United's purchase of the England defender, Rio Ferdinand for more than £30 million. Ferdinand plays at number six.

Source: Thwaites (1998), sportbusiness.com

Discussion question

5. Use the examples above as a basis for a discussion of the legality and morality of ambush marketing. Following this discussion, develop your own definition of ambush marketing.

As sponsorship and endorsement activity has grown, so too has the complexity of these relationships. This is illustrated by reference to the Cricket World Cup held in South Africa during February 2003. Prior to the competition, sponsorship agreements were put in place with leading companies such as PepsiCo, LG Electronics, South African Airlines and Hero Honda. To protect these companies from ambush marketing the International Cricket Council (ICC) required players to sign a contract that prevented them promoting rival brands to the main sponsors for a period of 30 days each side of the event. As a number of Indian players had lucrative contracts with rival brands they were unable to sign the contract. The matter was eventually resolved through mediation, although during the competition Samsung ran advertising featuring Indian players, requiring stern action from the International Cricket Council in response to what they viewed as blatant ambush marketing. This situation is not an isolated example and further conflict between endorsed athletes and rights holders of major events appears inevitable.

Conclusion

The increasing costs of staging sporting events and the limited support that governmental bodies are able to offer will maintain, if not increase, the demand for corporate sponsorship. During its early years, sponsorship was often undertaken in a somewhat casual manner with little concern for measurement and accountability. The rigorous evaluation methods used to assess the effectiveness of other promotional tools, such as advertising, were rarely used. Over the years, this situation has changed, perhaps in part due to greater experience with the medium, a tighter economic climate and the increasing costs of association. There is now a general trend in the literature that suggests companies are seeking measurable and tangible benefits from their sponsorship activity. Where this is not apparent there is a willingness to seek alternative ways of achieving their communication objectives.

To contribute to the delivery of tangible benefits there is an onus on the company to develop an effective framework for the management of its sponsorship initiatives. This will ensure that the right properties are selected in the first place and that the opportunities that the relationship offers can be realised. In addition, there is an onus on the owners of the sponsored property to contribute to the development of the relationship. One major criticism of sports organisations has been their tendency to 'take the money and run', which has left sponsors feeling that their rights fee has disappeared into a black hole. To develop a win-win situation rather than a give-take relationship there is a need for greater understanding of the needs of both parties to the agreement. As the 2002 Annual Report of Manchester United plc states 'The purpose behind our partnerships with leading consumer brands is to create mutual commercial advantage.' It is important for the continued growth of sport sponsorship that sporting bodies genuinely adopt this approach and avoid paying lip-service to it.

CASE 14.6 Charting a course to fraternité   FT

The sight of thousands of spectators perched on rocks, clad in sodden anoraks against the November wind and rain and staring out to sea from the cliffs of Brittany, is enough to warm the heart of many a French marketing manager.

An estimated one million people – remarkable for an activity not usually considered a spectator sport – braved foul autumn weather this year in St Malo to gawp at the high-technology boats being prepared for the Route du Rhum, a single-handed sailing race across the Atlantic to Guadeloupe that is held once every four years.

France's love affair with sailing, especially single-handed ocean racing, is attracting growing interest from companies eager to exploit advertising opportunities that barely exist in other countries – even in the British Isles, where the start of the transatlantic Ostar race draws only a fraction of the number of spectators watching the Route du Rhum.

The benefits of sail sponsorship in France fall into two categories: first, it can publicise a brand in a way that many marketing managers believe is highly cost-effective; and second, it can be used to promote team spirit among employees within a large company.

Fujifilm, the Japanese photographic company that began expanding overseas in the late 1970s, has sponsored sailing for the past 15 years. With only 350 staff in France, it spends EUR1.5 million (£960,000) a year on the sport. This is primarily to advertise its name to customers and to add a bit of passion to the company's image – sailing and the sea have long aroused the emotions of the French – rather than for any internal corporate reasons.

Football was the group's first sponsorship operation. 'But in France we realised it wasn't enough,' says Marc Heraud, communications director of Fujifilm France. 'In the 1980s we realised we were seen as a technological Japanese brand and thus a little cold. 'In France, sailing gets lots of media coverage. And although it represents 15 per cent of our sponsorship spending, when we ask consumers what they remember, it's the sailing. Sailing isn't expensive compared to football.'

For retail and distribution groups such as Geant of France and the UK's Kingfisher – both are prominent in the Route du Rhum through their sponsorship of skippers Michel Desjoyeaux and Ellen MacArthur respectively – a sailing race serves a dual purpose: it advertises the company name and acts as a rallying point for tens of thousands of employees.

Like Fujifilm, the hypermarket group Geant, part of Casino, started with football, in this case with teams in central France. But the number of players involved made the teams unwieldy sponsorship tools – when visiting supermarkets, for instance.

'It hadn't worked as well as we would have liked,' says Daniel Sicard, Geant's managing director. 'So we thought about the possibility of another project. We made a cold analysis of our advertising investments and sponsorships and we arrived at the choice of a man on a boat.' Sailing, Mr Sicard adds, offers 'by the far the best price-to-quality ratio'.

The reality for a good racing skipper is that he or she must learn to live with very little sleep, eat badly and grapple with advanced computer technology handling information on weather, boat performance and routing. But sailing, notes Mr

Sicard, 'has an aesthetic and healthy image – and what child does not dream of seeing the sea?'.

A crucial aim of the decision to build Mr Desjoyeaux the trimaran named Geant was to promote team spirit among the company's 23,000 employees and help them to 'dream'.

The choice of skipper is perhaps the most difficult decision of all. The idea is to have a lone hero(ine) battling against the elements – but preferably one who can work closely with the necessary technical and marketing experts and not be so distant from ordinary people that staff cannot identify with him or her.

Being a winner helps, too. Mr Sicard says the soft-spoken Mr Desjoyeaux – who last year won the gruelling Vendee Globe, a single-handed, non-stop, around-the-world race – is 'honest, approachable and simple'.

Kingfisher has an equally potent marketing weapon in the form of the bilingual Ms MacArthur, the diminutive and determined 26-year-old British sailor famous for being more famous in France than in her own country. She came second in the Vendee Globe and is now leading in the 60 ft monohull class in the Route du Rhum.

In France, Kingfisher controls Castorama, the home-improvement chain, and Darty, the electrical stores. Overall it has 30,000 French employees. As at Geant, the parent company's managers regard the internal corporate benefits of the sail sponsorship as vital.

'Very few Castorama employees knew what Kingfisher was,' says Mr Fairbank. 'Four years ago people asked, "What is this company that owns Darty?" There was no respect or understanding about Kingfisher and it probably went all the way up to middle management. Now an employee will say, "I work for Darty, part of Kingfisher, you know – Ellen MacArthur!" It's given a human face to Kingfisher.'

Stephen Robertson, who heads Kingfisher's internal communications, says both staff and customers are keen to meet and support a sailing celebrity in a country where yachting is beaten only by football and cycling in annual hours of television sports coverage.

During this year's Route du Rhum, a controversy has erupted over the fragility of the fast multihulls in the race and the problems of having a single person in control of such delicate and dangerous machines 24 hours a day. Ms MacArthur's current Kingfisher is a monohull but several of the carbon-fibre trimarans – including Fujifilm's – have broken up in heavy seas, forcing their skippers to abandon ship and pull out of the race.

Sail sponsorship as a French marketing tool, however, seems well entrenched. As Ms MacArthur remarks, it is a symbiotic relationship. 'People invest in sport for two marketing reasons – internal and external,' she says. 'With Kingfisher, both of these have worked remarkably well. And this sport cannot exist without sponsorship.'

Source: Victor Mallet, *Financial Times*, 20 November 2002

Discussion questions

6. To what extent do you agree that sponsorship of French sailing is little more than a form of advertising intended to raise awareness of brands and, ultimately, to increase product sales; can sponsorship ever really about anything else other than boosting sales?

7. When deciding to sponsor a property in another country, as the English company Kingfisher has done in France with sailing, what considerations will sponsorship managers have to address if the sponsorship is to be a success?

Discussion questions

8. Discuss, with examples, how sponsorship may enhance advertising through the five elements of credibility, imitation, image transference, bonding and retention.
9. What difficulties may arise in the use of player endorsements?
10. Why do you think some people argue that sponsorship effects are difficult to measure?

Guided reading

Sport sponsorship issues may be investigated through a range of sources. Sport-specific academic journals such as *Journal of Sport Management*, *International Journal of Sports Marketing and Sponsorship*, *Sport Marketing Quarterly*, *Sport Management Review* and the *European Sport Management Quarterly* provide a rich source of information.

Sport sponsorship is also addressed in mainstream management and marketing journals, for example Meenaghan (1996) in *Sloan Management Review* provides a useful introduction to ambush marketing and Speed and Thompson (2000) provide valuable insights into the sponsor-event fit in the *Journal of the Academy of Marketing Science*. A number of journals also provide special issues relating to sport marketing/sponsorship, for example *European Journal of Marketing* and *International Journal of Advertising*.

A further source of valuable information is publications by companies such as Mintel, who provide in-depth reports on a variety of markets. The sponsorship report covers a range of issues including current trends and growth patterns, influences on the market and data relating to different sponsorship options, for example sport, arts, broadcast. The sport section then addresses a number of different sports.

Recommended websites

Sport Business International: www.sportbusiness.com

Visit www.booksites.net/chadwickbeech for a link to this and other relevant websites.

Keywords

Ambush marketing; leverage; rights fee; sport sponsorship.

Bibliography

Hastings, G. (1984) 'Sponsorship works differently from advertising', *International Journal of Advertising*, 3(2), pp. 171–6.

Head, V. (1981) *Sponsorship – The Newest Marketing Skill*, Woodhead-Faulkner, Cookham.

Irwin, R.L. and Asimakopoulos, M.K. (1992) 'An approach to the evaluation and selection of sport sponsorship proposals', *Sport Marketing Quarterly*, 1(2), pp. 43 –51.

Irwin, R.L., Asimakopoulos, M.K. and Sutton, W.A. (1994) 'A model for screening sport sponsorship opportunities', *Journal of Promotion Management*, 2(3/4), pp. 53–69.

Jones, M. and Dearsley, T. (1989) 'Understanding sponsorship', in 'How to Increase the Efficiency of Marketing in a Changing Europe', Esomar Conference, (Turin), p. 257.

Manchester United PLC (2002) 'Not just a football club', Annual Report.

Marshall, D. (1993) 'Does sponsorship always talk the same language?', Text of a paper given at the Sponsorship Europe Conference, Monte Carlo. 1993.

Meenaghan, T. (1991a) 'The role of sponsorship in the marketing communication mix', *International Journal of Advertising*, 10(1), pp. 35–47.

Meenaghan, T. (1991b) 'Sponsorship – legitimising the medium', *European Journal of Marketing*, 25(11), pp. 5–10.

Meenaghan, T. (1996) 'Ambush marketing – a threat to corporate sponsorship', *Sloan Management Review*, 38(1), pp. 103–14

Miles, L. (2001) 'Successful sport sponsorship: lessons from association football – the role of research', *International Journal of Sports Marketing and Sponsorship*, 2(4), pp. 357–69.

Mintel (2000) *Sponsorship 2000*, Mintel International Group Limited, July.

Otker,T. (1988) 'Exploitation – the key to sponsorship success', *European Research*, May, pp. 77–86.

Speed, R. and Thompson, P. (2000) 'Determinants of sport sponsorship response', *Journal of the Academy of Marketing Science*, 28(2), pp. 226–38.

The Howell Report (1983) 'Committee of Enquiry into Sports Sponsorship', Central Council for Physical Recreation.

Thwaites, D. (1994) 'Corporate sponsorship by the financial services industry', *Journal of Marketing Management*, 10(8), pp. 743–63.

Thwaites, D. (1995) 'Professional soccer club sponsorship-profitable or profligate', *International Journal of Advertising*, 12(2), pp. 149–64.

Thwaites, D. (1998) 'Kuala Lumpur 98 The XVI Commonwealth Games', in Jobber, D. (ed.), *Principles and Practice of Marketing*, McGraw Hill, London, pp. 438–40.

Thwaites, D. and Eastwood, N. (1995) 'Tetley Bitter', in Jobber, D. (ed.), *Principles and Practice of Marketing*, McGraw Hill, London, pp. 461–4.

Witcher, B., Craigen, J.G., Culligan, D. and Harvey, A. (1991) 'The Links between Objectives and Function in Organisational Sponsorship', *International Journal of Advertising*, 10, pp. 13–33.

Chapter 15

Sport broadcasting

Harry Arne Solberg
Trondheim Business School, Sør-Trøndelag University College

Upon completion of this chapter the reader should be able to:

■ understand a range of influences on sport broadcasting;

■ highlight the monetary values of television (TV) sports rights fees;

■ explain the profitability of acquiring sports rights deals;

■ illustrate the distribution of sports rights among the various categories of channels;

■ indicate how the revenues from the sales of sports rights are distributed between sports associations and local organisers of sporting events – for example clubs.

Overview

This chapter focuses on economic aspects related to sport broadcasting. Special attention is paid to Europe after the deregulation of European broadcasting, which began in the mid-1980s. It concentrates particularly on analysing issues such as:

■ the price of sports rights fees;
■ the profitability of sports rights deals;
■ the distribution of sales revenues – both among the various sports and also between sports associations and local organisers of sporting events;
■ collective sales versus individual sales;
■ the motives of TV channels for acquiring sports rights;
■ the export of sports programmes.

The chapter also analyses the consequences of the regulations that still remain in European broadcasting, partly in a comparison with the unregulated North American markets. These regulations, which are founded on a welfare economic rationale, influence the market values as well as the distribution of sports rights among the various categories of TV channels. One part of this regulation policy is the public service broadcasters, which still play an important part in European broadcasting, although their market position is weaker than some few years ago. In addition there are general regulations on TV advertising.

Finally the chapter also gives attention to the Listed Events regulation, which is intended to prevent sporting events of major importance to society migrating to TV channels with limited penetration. It first presents the background that has paved the way for this regulation. This is followed by a discussion of its rationale from a perspective of welfare economic theory.

Introduction

The most significant change in the sport industry since early in the 1990s has been the increasing importance of broadcast demand for sport. This has led to massive escalation in the prices of broadcasting rights for professional team sports and major sporting events – as seen in Exhibit 15.1. In Europe an important event took place in 1992 when the Rupert Murdoch-owned BSkyB acquired the rights for live matches from the English Premier League for the first time ever, at a price that was three times the existing deal held by ITV. When BSkyB later renewed the deals, the annual value quadrupled in 1997 and tripled in 2001. In Italy, the Serie A clubs earned around €550 million annually from selling domestic TV rights for the 2001/02 season, which was more than ten times the value of the rights ten years earlier (Soccer Investor, 2001 and 2002a). A similar development has also taken place in other European countries, most notably in Germany, Spain and France.

These strong price increases have made broadcasting revenues the single most important source of income in all the 'big five' European soccer nations (England, Italy, Spain, Germany and France). For the 2000/01 season, sale of TV rights accounted for 54 per cent of the total revenues for the Italian Serie A clubs, while the proportion was 51 per cent in France and Spain, and 45 and 39 per cent in Germany and England. This picture was different in the smaller nations. In Scotland and Portugal, TV rights accounted for 23 and 20 per cent of the total revenues for the premier league clubs and only 4 per cent in Denmark and Norway (Boon, 2002).

It is worth noting that the strong price escalation during the 1990s brought the value of the most expensive European TV rights, which is the English Premier League (EPL), above the level of the North American Football League (NFL), when the prices are adjusted for differences in population, as seen from Table 15.1. The EPL rights escalated by more than 3,000 per cent from 1990 to 2002, while the NFL rights increased by 145 per cent. The NFL rights are the most expensive TV products on the North American market, and their value has equalled the combined value of Major League Baseball (MLB), North American Basketball Association (NBA) and National Hockey League (NHL) in recent years. The values of international soccer tournaments also increased considerably from the early 1990s onwards. The World Cup finals took a giant leap from 1998 to 2002, and the European soccer finals for national teams from 2000 to 2004.

Such high values are not typical for the entire range of soccer products. Indeed, clubs in the lower divisions have not even come near the value of the TV rights on the most attractive products. The same applies to female soccer products – even in

Table 15.1 Per capita price of TV rights ($US)

	1990	1994	1998	2002
English Premier League	0.4	1.1	4.1	11.0
North American Football League	3.3	4.0	8.0	8.0

Source: Solberg (2002a)
Notes: Only including domestic deals. All calculations are based on the 1999 populations, which were 276.2 million in the US and 58.7 million in the UK. NFL only including the $17.6 billion deal between the NFL and ABC, ESPN, FOX and CBS.

Exhibit 15.1	Values of television rights

FIFA World Cup soccer rights fees – $US million

1982 – Spain	23	24 teams
1986 – Mexico	29	24 teams
1990 – Italy	57	24 teams
1994 – USA	67	24 teams
1998 – France	97	32 teams
2002 – Japan/Korea	789	32 teams
2006 – Germany	910	32 teams

UEFA Euro soccer rights fees – $US million

1980 – Italy	3.2	8 teams
1984 – France	4.1	8 teams
1988 – Germany	5.2	8 teams
1992 – Sweden	17.0	8 teams
1996 – England	64.0	16 teams
2000 – Belgium/Netherlands	83.0	16 teams
2004 – Portugal	476.0	16 teams

Champions' League clubs TV revenue (£ million)

Season	1993/94	1997/98	2000/01
Revenue of two finalists	9.2	16.7	46.5
Revenue of eight highest earners	22.8	51.5	140.6

Summer Olympic TV rights ($US million)

	USA	Europe
1980 – Moscow	72	7
1984 – Los Angeles	226	22
1988 – Seoul	300	30
1992 – Barcelona	401	95
1996 – Atlanta	456	248
2000 – Sydney	705	350
2004 – Athens	793	394
2008 – Beijing	894	443

Winter Olympic TV rights ($US million)

	USA	Europe
1980 – Lace Placid	16	4
1984 – Sarajevo	92	6
1988 – Calgary	309	7

1992 – Alberville	243	20
1994 – Lillehammer	295	26
1998 – Nagano	375	72
2002 – Salt Lake city	545	120
2006 – Turin	613	135

Domestic TV rights English Premier League

	Channels	Annual fee (£ million)
1983–4	BBC/ITV	2.6
1985	BBC/ITV	1.3
1986–7	BBC/ITV	3.1
1988–91	ITV	11.0
1992–6	BSkyB/BBC	60.0
1997–2001	BSkyB/BBC	185.0
2001–4	BSkyB/ITV	450.0

Sources: FIFA, UEFA, IOC, FA, interview with Rolf Rustad, former chief of the sport department in the Norwegian Broadcasting Corporation, Solberg and Gratton (2004)

countries which have been considerably more successful in female soccer than in male soccer on an international level.

The values of Olympic rights have also increased substantially since the mid-1980s. Unlike most valuable soccer products, however, the Olympics are considerably cheaper in Europe than in the US. It must also be borne in mind that the European population is 250 per cent of the US population. The relative price gaps between the two continents, however, have narrowed considerably in recent years. Until the 1990s, the European Summer Olympic prices averaged approximately 10 per cent of the US prices, while the proportion had increased to 50 per cent for the years 1996–2008. The gaps have diminished less for the Winter Olympics, with the 2000–2008 European prices only equivalent to 20 per cent of the US level.

It is important to bear in mind that the values of soccer rights are not representative of the majority of sports. One example which illustrates the different conditions is the current broadcasting deal between the Norwegian Ice Hockey Association and the Norwegian Broadcasting Corporation (NRK). The deal started in 2001 and gave NRK the rights to (or, more precisely, obliged them to) broadcast 25 matches per season. Contrary to the pattern which is common when the commodity is soccer rights, it was the ice hockey federation that had to pay the costs. NRK received Nkr 5 million (€650,000) per season, which covered the production costs as well at the costs for the sponsoring of the programmes (source: Terje Jørgensen, General Secretary of the Norwegian Ice Hockey Association).

The European markets can roughly be subdivided into three different levels, in terms of rights. Soccer has the number one position everywhere and even absorbs more than 50 per cent of total revenues in many countries, as seen in Table 15.2. At the next level follow three to five sports competing for the number two position. Which sport that happens to be varies from one country to another, depending on historical factors and how successful national competitors have been on an international level.

On the third level follow the majority of sports, which are living under financial conditions that are comparable neither to soccer nor to any other sports that are mentioned

Table 15.2 Top five earning sports – 1998

	Germany	UK	Italy	Netherlands	Denmark	Austria
Total (€-million)	732	679	430	94	37	30
Percentage	42	52	65	55	45	32
Sport	Soccer	Soccer	Soccer	Soccer	Soccer	Soccer
Percentage	7	12	8	9	13	11
Sport	Tennis	Rugby	Motor Racing	Motor Racing	Handball	Skiing
Percentage	6	8	5	7	12	6
Sport	Motor racing	Cricket	Basketball	Tennis	Cycling	Motor Racing
Percentage	4	4	2	4	4	4
Sport	Boxing	Motor Racing	Cycling	Cycling	Motor Racing	Tennis
Percentage	4	2	1	3	3	3
Sport	Basketball	Tennis	Skiing	Athletics	Boxing	Ice Hockey

in Table 15.2. Archery and fencing, for example, do not attain high-rating figures when screened on television. Therefore these sports hardly receive any TV revenues at all.

It is worth noting that soccer has earned the highest TV revenues even in countries that have been considerably more successful in other sports. As an example, alpine skiing has historically been a very popular sport in Austria. National competitors have won a large number of medals over the years. Nevertheless, skiing only received one-third of the revenues of soccer, even though Austrian teams have not achieved any successes on an international level. A similar picture characterises Denmark, which has also won medals in international handball championships on several occasions. Nevertheless, handball earned less than one-third of the revenues that soccer did.

One reason for soccer's superiority in terms of rights values has been its ability to attract TV viewers. As an illustration, a soccer match topped the TV rating lists in 75 per cent of 50 countries in 1998. In Germany, 86 of the top 100 programmes were soccer related (Kagan, 1999), and in France the equivalent number was 73. In the United Kingdom, 6 of the top 10 TV programmes were soccer matches from the World Cup finals (Solberg, 2002b). Club matches from domestic leagues have also been attractive TV programmes. However, since a large proportion of these matches have been screened on pay-TV channels with restricted penetration, the rating figures have not been particularly impressive.

The strong price increases were also associated with developments in the markets. It was the liberalisation of European Broadcasting in the mid-1980s that paved the way for astronomical price rises for the most attractive products. Since then a growing number of channels have acquired sports rights in order to strengthen their market position. In addition, the sellers of sports rights have gradually learned to take advantage of the increased competition by staging auctions. When FIFA sold the 2002 and 2006 World Cup soccer rights, the European Broadcasting

Union[1] (EBU) was informed of Prisma's higher bid and encouraged to increase its own offer, but declined to do so (source: Anthony Bunn, EBU). Similar procedures have characterised the auctions of the English Premier League and other TV rights.

However, it takes time to learn how to benefit from market transactions, and the markets for sports rights are no exception. Joint bids from more than one channel have not been uncommon in Europe. Such cooperation, which reduces competition and thus also the market value of the rights, is banned in the US unless the channels belong to the same parent company.

The organisers of a sporting event will also earn revenues other than TV rights fees, such as gate receipts, stadium advertising and sponsorship support. These revenues are not independent of each other. Sponsor revenues will increase if the events are broadcast on TV, and will also be positively correlated with the number of viewers. On the other hand, people living in the region may prefer to watch the event on TV instead of at the arenas, particularly when the programmes are broadcast on free-to-air channels. Hence, the gate receipts can be reduced, unless the demand for tickets exceeds the capacity at the arena.

The broadcasting of TV sport – some characteristics

In order to analyse these issues more deeply we first have to look at some characteristics of TV broadcasting in general, and also of TV sport programmes as commercial products. Firstly, the receiving of TV signals partly satisfies the criterion of public goods. Pure public goods are characterised by non-rivalling and non-exclusive criteria (Olson, 1971), and the reception of TV signals satisfies the former criterion completely. One television viewer's consumption of a sport programme neither reduces the amount of this programme, nor its quality, that is available for other viewers. Moreover, once the programmes are being transmitted there are no variable costs related to the consumption of them. Thus, the costs will be unaffected by the number of viewers. Contrary to this, the inputs used in the production and the transmission of the programmes are private goods, which can not be applied in more than one production process simultaneously. This applies to cameras, the staff and frequency, which can be used in one (and only one) process at the same time.

Profit-maximising channels will be motivated to offer programmes as long as the marginal revenues exceed the marginal costs related to these programmes. The point where the marginal revenues equal the marginal costs is also the pont where the profit is maximised. In addition, it is also necessary that the marginal revenues from each and every programme are equal. Otherwise changing the mixture of programmes can increase the profit. Thus it is important to bear in mind that the resources used on sports programmes alternatively can be used on other programme activities, e.g. on a 'soap' or a news programme. For commercial channels the values of the forgone revenues from such alternative actions represent an alternative cost.

---

[1]   EBU included a total of 69 active members in 50 countries (Europe from east to west, North Africa, and the Middle East), and 49 associate members in 30 countries in 1999. It is operated on a non-profit basis, and most of the European public service broadcasting (PSB) channels are active members. 'Pure' commercial channels, such as pay-TV channels are not members.

The distinction between fixed costs and variable costs is essential in production theory. Broadly, variable costs are the costs which change as output changes, whilst fixed costs are the costs which do not vary with output. The difference between the two categories, however, also relies on the time perspective. The longer the time perspective, the more possible it is to vary the level of production, and thus the higher is the proportion of variable costs. Some of the fixed costs are conditional on production. These costs are brought about by production itself and disappear when production closes. The level of these costs, however, remains constant irrespective of production level. In addition, there are the costs which relate to the use of facilities. These costs do not depend on whether the firm is producing or not. It is only when the facilities are closed down that this cost element will vanish. The last category is sunk costs, which are totally irretrievable. When they have been paid there is no economic regain for the producer from closing down production and going out of business. This money will be lost unless the firm manages to resell the sunk cost element to some other producer. Hence when sunk costs are paid for, they should not influence later decisions taken by the firm (Johnsen, 2001).

For a TV channel, the variable costs relate both to the broadcasting and the production of the programmes. An example of the first is renting a frequency to transmit the programme. In addition there will be variable costs for the individual production. The better the production is, other things being equal, the better is the quality of the programme. The more cameras used to screen the competition, the better the overall production will become (Johnsen, 2001). With its high level of fixed costs and relatively low level of variable costs, TV broadcasting is a typical 'economies of scale' production. The production and transmission of TV programmes usually require considerable 'startup' costs. The fixed costs include franchising a cable, installing the cable or buying an existing operator, and the lease of a satellite transponder, as well as other overheads, which together can be exceedingly costly. In such cases only producers with access to a large amount of financial resources are able to enter the market. On the other hand, those that can afford to enter the market will usually enjoy economies of scale and scope by spreading overhead costs, applying common managerial techniques, spreading risks, and enjoying large-scale advantages such as discounts from programme suppliers.

The cost structure directly related to sport broadcasting will depend on the value of the rights and also the terms in the contracts. If the prices are expensive and fixed, then a large proportion of the total costs will be sunk costs. Hence, the purchasing channel will have to bear the entire risk if there is a negative shift in demand from viewers and/or advertisers.

The profitability of sports rights deals

The high proportion of sunk costs can make investments in expensive sports rights very risky. The purchasing channels have no guarantees of stable market conditions during a contract period, particularly in the case of long-term deals. If sport broadcasting yields profit above the average rate, this can attract new entrants to the market. New channels can establish themselves, and in addition the existing channels may be tempted to broadcast more sport. This can spread the viewers across more programmes, which is the same as leftward (negative) shifts in the established programmes' demand curves. In addition, the viewers of sports programmes can also be tempted to watch other programmes.

Such fragmentation creates an incentive for all profit-maximising channels to lower their programme costs. Due to the large proportion of sunk costs, however, the channel will find it difficult to reduce the costs. However, since the receiving of TV signals is a public good, neither reducing the number of programmes nor broadcasting them to a lower number of viewers helps. If the result is an abundance of TV sport, few channels will be able to cover costs at any level of output. A recession in the economy can have similar effects. When firms reduce their spending on advertising, or the number of subscribers declines, the incomes of the channels will be reduced.

Therefore it is no coincidence that there have been a number of unprofitable deals. Two such examples are the collapse of the TV deal between the Nationwide League and ITV Digital in England and the financial problems of Kirch Media in Germany (in 2001/02). Similar problems have hit the two Italian channels (Telepiu and Stream) which have held the broadcasting rights for the Italian Serie A since the end of the 1990s.

Problems have occurred regularly in the North American markets, where sports rights have a longer history of being a commercial good than in Europe. CBS, one of the four American broadcasting networks, almost went bankrupt in the early 1990s after having overestimated the value of Major League Baseball (MLB) (Quirk and Fort, 1999). In 2002, News Corp took a write-down of $909 million on unprofitable sports deals shortly after NBC, another network, reported losses on their deal with the National Basketball Association (NBA) at $300 million (Gould Media, 2002).

If the risk is extremely unevenly distributed this can prevent the trade of deals that could have been profitable both for the seller and the buyer, a phenomenon which is well known from principal-agent theory. One way of solving such problems is to implement contract clauses that tie the rights fees to rating figures, thereby letting seller and buyer share the risk. To what degree this will be enforced is also a matter of how the market power is shared between the supply and the demand sides. For the seller, the best situation is being a monopolist, whilst there is tough competition among buyers. Such a situation developed during the 1990s in Europe when a number of channels regarded attractive soccer rights as effective tools for strengthening their market position. One consequence was that the markets developed into a 'sellers market'. This development left the sellers in a position where they could dictate the terms of the contracts. Consequently the channels had to accept fixed prices, which forced them the bear the burden of the risk alone.

However, it is important to bear in mind that the acquisition of sports rights also generates indirect revenues for the TV channel, for example by providing more subscribers, which also increases the advertising revenues from other programmes. In North-America the broadcasting networks need attractive programmes to uphold good relations with their affiliates and thereby their overall penetration rate. An equivalent system of broadcasting networks and affiliates is not found within European broadcasting. Moreover, it is common knowledge that a proportion of the viewers of a sports programme tend to 'stay with the channel' and continue watching the next programme(s). Such lag effects increase the overall rating figures and thereby the advertising revenue. Thus, the profitability of sports rights deals cannot be judged entirely on the basis of their direct revenues and costs.

TV sports represent a content category where the products are more heterogeneous than other goods and services. Many sports programmes are unique to the viewers and thus are difficult to copy or substitute, at least compared with other forms of television programming (Gaustad, 2000). This makes it difficult to replace them with other programmes without losing many viewers. Therefore the rating figures in tournaments with knock-out procedures are often subject to strong fluctuations. Many supporters do not continue to watch when their favourite team has been eliminated. This was well illustrated during the 2002 World Cup soccer finals, when the Italian and French channels which held the broadcasting rights lost substantial amounts of money, due to the lack of success for their national teams (see Case 15.1). In addition, some events are of a character that makes it impossible to replace them. As an example, a World Heavyweight championship match in boxing cannot be substituted by just another boxing match. If it is, the commercial value of the match will drop considerably.

CASE 15.1   Early exits of Italy and France from World Cup soccer finals hit TV channels

Italy's national broadcaster RAI considered taking legal action for financial damages against world football body FIFA, blaming dubious refereeing for Italy's early exit from the World Cup. Italy had a golden-goal 'winner' by mid-fielder Damiano Tommasi disallowed for offside when television replays showed the goal was legitimate.

RAI had paid €80 million for the rights to broadcast World Cup matches in Italy. The national team's matches regularly drew audiences in excess of 20 million, a figure which dropped considerably for the remainder of the games, thereby reducing the channel's advertising revenue. Advertisers and sponsors had invested more than €140 million into Italy's World Cup effort, and the value of this investment was considerably reduced after Italy was sent home.

In France, TF1, the commercial channel which bought the exclusive French rights to broadcast the World Cup for €60 million plus production costs of €8.7 million (Desbordes, 2003), suffered similar experiences. The channel was hoping to recoup its costs through advertising revenues, but advertisers were only contracted to pay the higher fees if the French team got into the quarterfinals and beyond.

France had to win the final match against Denmark by at least two goals to progress into the next round, but goals from Danes Dennis Rommedahl and Jon Dahl Tomasson sent the defending champions home earlier than what was expected.

In fact, France secured only one point from its three games in the tournament.

About 10.6 million people watched the France-Uruguay match, giving the channel an audience share of 75.5 per cent. Such figures were impossible to achieve after the national team was out of the finals.

The early exit of the French team was estimated as costing TF1 €12 million.

Sports programmes as export goods

Normally a TV programme which is broadcast both within and outside its home market will, if all other things are equal, attract less lower interest outside the home market than within, due to cultural differences. The 'loss' created when a media product is exported outside its home market is known as the cultural discount (Wildman and Siwek, 1987). The degree of cultural discount depends on the cultural distance between the home market and the export market. The monetary value of the cultural distance of a TV programme depends on the nature of the product in question (Gaustad, 2000). Sporting events are, however, of a nature where the television content is less dependent on language than most other categories of programmes (Cowie, Campbell and Williams, 1997).

This does not mean that TV sports are exempt from cultural discount effects, but, compared to other genres, they have a unique opportunity to cross linguistic barriers. Television programme producers will benefit from selling programmes to external markets as long as the additional revenues exceed the transmission costs. The cost to the original producer is independent of the number of channels which acquire the rights for its rebroadcast. Moreover, the programme-related costs are also independent of the number of viewers, once the programme is being broadcast, as is typical for public goods (Throsby, 1994; Brown, 1996).

Thus, it is no coincidence that many sports programmes are also broadcast on international markets, outside their own domestic market. As an example, the English Premier League, the Italian Serie A and the Spanish Premier leagues enjoy tremendous popularity even outside their domestic markets. One reason for this is that these leagues are of better quality than the leagues in the smaller nations. In addition some international championships and other prestigious events are attractive TV programmes worldwide, even in countries which do not have any participants.

The local and traditional compositions of sport interest are probably among the strongest elements determining cultural discount for sports programming. These elements include viewers' awareness and knowledge about different sports. Moreover, the viewers' knowledge of and interest in the athletes in each sport is also important for cultural discount, in addition to the quality aspects. The proliferation of multinational teams has further stimulated such international interest. As an example, the success of Ole Gunnar Solskjær and Sami Hypia at Manchester United and Liverpool has enhanced the popularity of the English Premier League among Norwegian and Finnish soccer fans. This, however, also represents a leakage which reduces the income potential of the domestic leagues in the smaller nations if the viewers prefer to watch matches from foreign leagues instead of their own. Sports enthusiasts and advertisers, like anybody else, have limited amounts of money and time. On the other hand, geographical differences combined with differences in time zone can increase the cultural discount and thus reduce the demand for sports programmes on external markets. As an example, the North American National Hockey League (NHL) has a large number of European players. However, the difference in time zone between Europe and North America (from 6–11 hours) reduces Europeans' abilities to watch live matches. Since live sport programmes are known as instantly perishable goods, the time aspect is essential for the valuation of most sports programming. Even minor shifts in the transmission time from the time when the event is actually taking place may result in a substantial loss of value. This time sensitivity has to do with *the uncertainty-of-outcome* element in sports. After the competition is finished and the result known, the excitement is lost, and with it, much of the value of the programme (Cowie, Campbell and Williams, 1997).

There will, however, be variations between sports regarding the importance of time-sensitivity. Elements other than the uncertainty of outcome also contribute to the overall valuation of the sports broadcast. Such elements may include the aesthetic performance, the general interest in the athlete, etc. How dependent the valuation of the programme is on time sensitivity varies with the relative weight each of these factors is given in the evaluation. The value of a soccer match will rest heavily on the uncertainty-of-outcome element. Thus the demand for this programme will decline rapidly after the match is finished and the result is known. In sports such as gymnastics and figure-skating, the aesthetic performance is given relatively more weight in the evaluation, and hence these programmes are less time sensitive (Gaustad, 2000).

Collective versus individual sale of sports rights

Sports rights are defined as the rights to broadcast from a sporting event, most commonly within specific geographical areas. The rights can be split up in different products, such as live broadcasting and highlight programmes. Each sport has a so-called '*lowest meaningful level*'. Below this level it is technically impossible to film in a meaningful way (Cowie and Williams, 1997). The general TV audience wants to have an overview over the developments in the competition. It does not make sense to film only one competitor in a race, or only the players in one of the teams in a football match. Each sporting competition will have a basic unit, which in general will be a match or a race.

There have been various practices regarding the ownership and sales procedures of sports rights. In team sports the owner can be the home club, which sells the rights individually and hence receives the entire revenues alone. When the competition is part of a tournament, the owner can also be a sport association or a similar representative body (e.g. the International Olympic Committee (IOC)).

Tables 15.3 and 15.4 illustrate some examples from various sports where the competitions are part of a larger event or tournament. As an example, a 100-metres race is only one of several competitions at the Bislet Games, while the Bislet Games are included in the International Association of Athletics Federations (IAAF) Golden League events. Likewise, a soccer match can be part of a league or a cup tournament.

The sale procedure that is chosen can influence the value of the TV rights as well as the distribution of the revenues. This becomes evident by comparing the two most valuable European soccer leagues, the English Premier League and the Italian Serie A,

Table 15.3 Team sports

Sport	Player	Team	Match	League
Soccer	Michael Owen	Liverpool	Liverpool v. Leeds	English Premier League
Ice Hockey	Wayne Gretsky	New York Rangers	New York Rangers v. Dallas Stars	National Hockey League

Table 15.4 Individual sports

Sport	Competitor	Competition	Event/Tournament
Golf	Tiger Woods	Round 1	US-Open/UPGA-Tournament
Tennis	Andrei Agassi	Agassi v. Sampras	Wimbledon/Grand Slam tournament
Motor Racing	Michael Schumacher	Belgian Grand Prix	Formula 1 Championship
Athletics	Carl Lewis	100-metres race	Bislet Games/Golden League

which have practised different sale procedures since the 1999 season. The English Premier League, which has been the highest earning European league since the mid-1990s, has always sold the rights collectively. In the 2001/02 season 47 per cent of the total revenues were shared equally among the clubs. The remaining revenues were distributed on the basis of sporting achievement and on the number of appearances that the clubs had on TV. Contrary to this, the Italian Serie A clubs have sold the rights for live matches individually since the start of the 1999 season. This means that the clubs have the total income from their home matches at their disposal.

CASE 15.2 Sport broadcasting in the European Union   FT

Members of the European Parliament on Thursday [24 May 2001] warned the European Union's competition authorities that if they broke up the centralised way soccer broadcasting rights are sold it could favour the sport's biggest clubs and hurt smaller ones. But the European Commission indicated that it had concerns with the current system. Glyn Ford, a UK Labour MEP, said that so much money could be diverted to the biggest clubs that European soccer could end up 'like the Harlem Globetrotters [basketball team] systematically thrashing its rivals in front of an audience of tourists'. In February (2001), Mario Monti, competition commissioner, said that Brussels would investigate the collective selling of broadcasting rights to sports events in several pending cases and would use the opportunity to set out the rules for the issue.

In particular, the Commission is looking into the collective selling arrangement of the UEFA Champions League and the marketing of games by the German football association, after being notified by both organisations. At the moment the rules governing collective sales of rights differ across the different jurisdictions of the EU, but the Commission has responsibility for cross-border issues. The parliament has no formal role in the execution of competition policy. Speaking at a public hearing in the European parliament, Mr Ford said that he was 'not trying to prescribe an outcome, (but) just trying to start a debate'. But he said that if the bloc-sales system was broken, the cost of screening some games at big, popular clubs could increase by two or three times, while smaller clubs could see their revenues fall.

Media companies recently paid more than £1.6 billion for the rights to screen top-flight football in the UK over the next three years. Jürgen Mensching, a Commission official, said that the Commission would take into account how the current system helped smaller clubs, but would also look to see if such clubs could be helped by other means. He added that where the sale of rights was expensive, long term and exclusive it could help a dominant television operator and freeze out new operators. He said such a situation was 'difficult to accept, particularly from the point of view of a consumer whose choice is limited'. Earlier this year, the Commission finally agreed a deal with soccer authorities to introduce limited changes to the player transfer system, which it had also investigated on competition grounds.

Source: D. Dombey, *Financial Times*, 1 June 2001

Individual sale of sports rights gives the most attractive clubs higher revenues compared to collective sale, while the poorest clubs will be worse off. This is confirmed by the figures in Table 15.5, which reveal that the Italian top clubs earned more than the English top clubs, whilst the poorest Italian clubs earned considerably less than the poorest English clubs. Bear in mind that the Italian Serie A figures only include the revenues from selling the live matches, not the highlight packages as for the English Premier League. Thus, the revenue gap between the top English and Italian clubs is even wider than the table reveals. When the highlight packages are included the gaps between the poorest Italian and English clubs will be somewhat reduced.

The main reason for selling the TV rights collectively is to uphold the competitive balance. If the best clubs become too dominant, this may reduce the interest for the matches and consequently also the league itself. This phenomenon is well treated in the sport literature, first known as the 'Louis-Schmelling paradox' (Neale, 1964), named after Joe Louis and Max Schmelling, boxers who dominated the ring during the inter-war years in a way that perhaps only Mohammed Ali has subsequently. Its importance was illustrated by the delayed start of the 2002/03 season in Serie A. The poorest clubs rejected the new offer from the TV channels and this delay also hit the wealthiest clubs. The dispute was solved when the richest clubs offered to pay the remaining amount. This incident illustrated how the best clubs depend on the other clubs that do not achieve the same success as themselves. It takes two teams to stage a soccer match and many more than that to establish an interesting league.

The distribution of the TV revenues

History shows various patterns regarding the distribution of TV revenues, as Table 15.6 reveals. These large variations are mainly due to the different levels of competition on the demand and supply side. In sports markets, as anywhere else, the actors on the supply side will benefit the tougher the competition is on the demand side, and vice versa.

This becomes particularly evident when comparing the distribution of TV revenues between the European soccer championship for national teams and the Champions League. In both cases the initial owner of the rights is UEFA. However, while UEFA keeps 90 per cent of the revenues from the sale of the national team championship, they only keep 25 per cent of the Champions League rights.

Since the 1990s there have been several applicants that have competed for hosting the championship for national teams. This competition has put UEFA in a position

Table 15.5 Distribution of TV rights

English Premier League – 2001/02 season		Italian Serie A – 2002/03 season	
Club	Revenues (€ million)	Club	Revenues (€ million)
Manchester United	40.4	Juventus	54.0
Liverpool	40.4	Inter Milan	49.0
Arsenal	40.1	AC Milan	49.0
Leeds	35.3	Rome	37.2
Newcastle	32.6	Lazio	32.0
Chelsea	31.0	Parma	24.8
Tottenham	28.9	Bologna	13.4
Aston Villa	28.2	Udinese	12.9
West Ham	26.6	Atlanta	8.3
Blackburn	25.5	Brescia	8.3
Fulham	24.4	Torino	8.0
Southampton	23.8	Chievo	7.2
Middlesbrough	23.3	Reggina	7.0
Everton	22.7	Perugia	6.2
Ipswich	22.2	Como	5.7
Sunderland	22.0	Empoli	5.7
Bolton	21.8	Modena	5.7
Charlton	21.7	Piacenca	5.7
Derby	17.9		
Leicester	16.9		
Total	**545.7**	**Total**	**340.1**

Source: Based on data from *Soccer Invester* and Kagan European Sports
Note: UK figures calculated on the basis of exchange rate from 31 May 2002. €1 = £0.63917.

where it can dictate the terms for how the revenues are distributed. However, for the Champions League, the situation has been totally different since it is UEFA that has been challenged. Mediapartner, the Italian media company (amongst others), has tempted the clubs (see Appendix 1) with higher TV revenues if they start playing in a European Super League instead of the domestic premier leagues and the tournaments run by UEFA (the Champions League and the UEFA cup). So far the clubs have turned down the offer and continued their relationship with the national soccer federations

Table 15.6 Distribution of revenues between the local organiser and the international governing body

Events	Distribution of TV rights
Olympic Games	The local organiser receives 49% while the IOC receives 51%. The distribution was 60/40 in favour of the local organisers until the Sydney games in 2000.
World Championship Skiing	The local organiser receives 60% while the International Skiing Federation (FIS) receives 40%.
World Championship Ice Hockey	The International Ice Hockey Federation (IIHF) receives the entire revenues alone. Nothing goes to the local organiser.
European Soccer Championship – national teams	UEFA receives 90%, while the local organiser receives 10%.
UEFA's Champions League	For income up to 800 million Swiss Francs, the 32 clubs which qualify for the tournament receive 75% of the income, while UEFA receives 25%. For additional income the clubs receive 82%, while UEFA receives 18%.

and UEFA. To keep the clubs, however, UEFA has been forced to increase the disbursements to the clubs (Solberg and Gratton, 2004).

Due to the high amounts of money involved it is no surprise that there have been legal disputes between the clubs and soccer federations regarding the ownership of sports rights. Some have even ended up in courts. The German Soccer Federation demanded to have the exclusive TV rights for German teams playing in European matches, but the German federal court decided that TV rights belonged to the teams (Baskerville Communication Corps, 1999). In the Netherlands, the competition authorities upheld an argument by Feyenord that they should be able to negotiate their own television deals (Downward and Dawson, 2000).

The collective sale of broadcasting rights also violates the general anti-competitive rules. Therefore the UK Office of Fair Trading (OFT) accused the English Premier League of illegal cartel behaviour. The Premier League won this case and was allowed to continue the collective sale. The main reason for this decision was concerns for the competitive balance. This outcome, however, might not be the final decision since the European Commission has declared that it will investigate whether such sale procedures contravene European Union competition rules (Soccer Investor, 2002b).

The distribution of sports rights among the channels

In recent years the distribution of sports rights has been dramatically altered in Europe. Most noticeable is the migration of popular soccer rights to pay-TV channels. To analyse this phenomenon, we must consider some characteristics of the various categories of TV channels that are involved in the trade of sports rights – and of their objectives. Figure 15.1 gives an overview of the European TV landscape, and from which sources the channels earn their revenues.

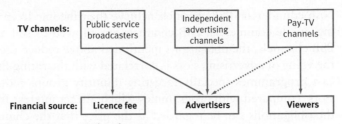

Figure 15.1 **The European TV landscape**

Public service broadcasters (PSB channels) still play an important role in European broadcasting, although their market position is weaker than two decades ago when they were monopolies in most countries. Such channels have objectives other than the entertainment of viewers and the profitability of private broadcasting firms. According to welfare economic theory, their aim should be to maximise the welfare of the society, subject to financial restrictions that are set by politicians (Brown, 1996). One example is their duty of providing to the public so-called 'merit goods' programmes. Musgrave (1959) developed the concept of merit goods to commodities that ought to be provided even if members of society do not demand them. Certain programmes can be considered to be merit goods, and by using TV channels with a high penetration these externalities are provided to a large audience. This is based on the paternalistic philosophy that governments know better what is good for the general public than people do themselves. This includes concerns for national identity and culture; catering for all interests and tastes (including minorities); providing programmes that are specially targeting children; a 'local content' provision requiring domestic production of specified proportions and categories of programming.

The obligation to provide programmes that fulfil these requirements also reduce what PSB channels can spend on sports rights. The production of TV programmes is characterised by high 'first copy' costs; it is more expensive to produce in-house programmes than to purchase the programmes from other channels. Selling the programmes to other channels contains an element of cost sharing. The BBC has an objective of producing 80 per cent of its programmes in-house. Therefore it would be impossible for the BBC to fulfil its role as a public service broadcaster if it were spending the same amount of money on sports rights as BSkyB. PSB channels have access to terrestrial transmission which gives them a penetration of almost 100 per cent of the TV households in their respective countries. This high penetration represents an advantage when competing for sports rights. It was the main reason why the IOC sold the complete 2000–2008 Olympic rights to the European Broadcasting Union (EBU) for $1.4 billion, instead of to Rupert Murdoch's News Corporation, whose bid was $2 billion. The IOC feared Murdoch would re-sell (at least some of) the Games to pay-service channels. This would have challenged the long-term relations between the IOC and its sponsors, who prefer TV channels with maximum penetration (Preuss, 2000). In addition the IOC has a charter of upholding the image of universal games, which corresponds to the objectives of non-commercial PSB channels of maintaining diversity in their menu of programmes. It is important to bear in mind that the Olympic Games also encompass a large number of moderately popular sports, which are not attractive to commercial channels, which tend to give priority to the most attractive sports and competitions (Preuss, 2000).

Non-commercial PSB channels achieve their income from licence fees or public funding, while commercial PSB channels are allowed to sell advertising. For commercial PSB channels, the obligations mentioned above reduce their income (potential). Since the value of advertising slots is correlated with the rating figures, obligations to broadcast programmes specially targeting minority groups reduce the value of advertising slots, compared with programmes which attract interest from a mass audience. Thus, the obligations can be regarded as the price that the channels have to pay to achieve high penetration.

Other independent advertising channels are free to construct a menu of programmes that is mainly based on commercial considerations. However, since these channels do not have admittance to terrestrial frequencies, they cannot charge the same prices for advertising slots as commercial public service broadcasters which reach close to 100 per cent of the TV households in their respective countries. Independent advertising channels have a penetration of 50–70 per cent of TV households in many countries.

Advertisers seek to shift the demand curve for their product or make it more inelastic, permitting an increase in price. Profit-maximising advertisers will continue to supply advertising up to the point where the marginal cost of advertising equals the marginal revenue from advertising for them (Kaldor, 1950). Since they want to reach as many potential consumers as possible, the amount of revenue received by the broadcaster will broadly be positively correlated to audience size. Thus, profit-maximising, advertiser-financed broadcasters will always have the incentive to provide programmes that attract larger audiences. However, to advertisers, not all viewers are alike. The greater the spending power of viewers and/or the greater their attractiveness to the advertisers, the more the advertiser will pay to reach them. This creates an incentive to discriminate in favour of households with a high income and to offer programmes to which they can relate.

Europe has general regulations on advertising which are considerably stricter than in the US, as seen from Exhibit 15.2. In Europe, the channels are obliged to follow the regulations in the country from which the programmes are being broadcast. Thus, some channels choose to broadcast from the countries that have the most liberal rules. In addition some European countries do not allow commercials connected to programmes that are aimed at children.

Pay-TV channels receive their main revenues from the consumer surplus that the viewers would have received if the programmes had been broadcast on free-to-air channels. Usually the charges are split into a two-tariff system. Firstly, there is a subscription fee, which is often split between a one-time (lump sum) fee paid when signing the subscription, and also a current fee paid at regular stages. The latter allows for adjustments if the fixed costs increase as market conditions change. In addition, pay-TV channels can also charge pay-per-view fees. Unlike advertiser-supported broadcasting, pay-TV may take account of the intensity of viewers' preferences expressed in financial terms. By doing so, subscriber-supported broadcasting has the potential to broadcast additional programmes that attract interest from audiences which are too small to be profitable on advertising channels. This assumes that a sufficient number of viewers are willing to pay for watching the programmes. In addition, this is contingent upon the channel finding a way of extracting a sufficient proportion of the viewer's willingness to pay, to make the programme profitable.

Exhibit 15.2	Amount of advertising allowed on TV channels
USA	No federal law limits the amount of commercial matter that may be broadcast at any given time. The exception is television programmes aimed at children 12 years and below, where advertising may not exceed 10.5 minutes per hour on weekends and 12 minutes per hour on weekdays.
UK	The BBC is not allowed to air advertising. Channel 4 and ITV are limited to 7.5 minutes per hour, while BSkyB is limited to 9 minutes per hour.
Germany	Public Service channels are limited to 20 minutes per day, while private channels are limited to 12 minutes of advertising per hour.
Italy	The public service channel, RAI, is restricted to 7.2 minutes per hour (a daily average of 2.4 minutes per hour). Private national channels are limited to 10.8 minutes per hour (a daily average of 9 minutes per hour). Private local channels are limited to 12 minutes per hour.
France	Private TV channels are limited to 12 minutes per hour (a daily average of 6 minutes per hour), while Canal Plus is limited to 9 minutes per hour (a daily average of 6 minutes per hour).
Spain	Private TV channels are limited to 12 minutes per hour, while Canal Plus is restricted to 2.3 minutes per hour.

Source: Solberg, 2002a; based on Kagan World Media Ltd (1996) and the Federal Communication Commission website (www.fcc.gov)

The consequences of these differences in purchasing policy between advertising channels and pay-TV channels are illustrated in Figure 15.2. A sport programme which is represented by the inelastic D_1 demand curve might be profitable on a pay-TV channel. A number of viewers are willing to pay a high price for watching this programme. On the other hand, many people will be uninterested in watching, even if the programme is broadcast free on air. Thus, advertising channels may not find this kind of programme profitable.

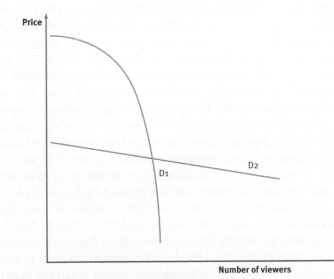

Figure 15.2 The demand for sport programmes

This is different for the programme which is represented by the D_2 demand curve. A large number of viewers may tune in to this programme. Therefore, advertisers would be interested in – and hence willing to pay for – being connected to it. However, since the viewers are unwilling to pay high amounts for watching, pay-TV channels would not be interested in this programme. On the other hand, since viewers are not strongly committed to the programme, this may also indicate that the demand is unstable and thus readily subject to negative shifts. European pay-TV channels have mainly based their activity on acquiring sports rights and popular films. Such a policy is risky, compared with offering the viewers a broad spectrum of programmes. In addition some pay-TV channels are part of bundles which include channels that are available on cable or by terrestrial transmission. This particularly applies to pay-TV channels that are only broadcast by satellite platforms, for example BSkyB. However, since the other channels in such bundles are also available by alternative transmission, it is the pay-TV channels and their content that make the difference, and hence they represent the main motive to subscribe to the satellite platforms.

According to BSkyB's own surveys, more than 50 per cent of its own viewers would have cancelled their subscription if the channel lost its soccer rights. Thus, the alternative to continuing to acquire such rights is probably going out of business. Pay-TV channels have been the most successful when holding exclusive rights to a tournament or a league. It is more difficult to recruit (and retain) the number of subscribers if some of the matches are screened on free-to-air channels. Thus, the market position of pay-TV channels may be threatened if the sellers are forced to split the leagues between various channels, as has been proposed by the European Commission (Solberg, 2002b).

The listed events regulation

In Europe, market forces are not the only factors that influence the distribution of TV rights. In 1996 Rupert Murdoch's News Corporation almost acquired the European rights to broadcast the Olympics for the period 2000–08. Two years later, his rival in Germany, Kirch, was more successful and bid away from EBU the rights for the World Cup soccer finals in 2002 and 2006. These two episodes sent shock waves through the whole European system of sport broadcasting. One consequence was the initiative of the Listed Events regulation. It was first introduced in the United Kingdom, and later the European Commission adopted the idea. Its objective is to prevent sporting events of major importance to society from migrating to TV channels with restricted penetration (European Commission, 1997). The phrase 'major importance for society' indicates concerns for impacts that are stronger than, for example, from an ordinary soccer match. The objective is not to protect sports fans from having to pay for watching sport. The UK regulation, for example, requires that the event has 'a special national resonance', and that it serves to unite the nation, a shared point in the national calendar. The Italian regulation requires that the events must have a particular cultural significance and strengthen Italian cultural identity.

The impacts that the Listed Events regulation aims to protect are what economists refer to as *externalities*. Externalities appear when the activity of one entity (a person or a firm) directly affects the welfare of another in a way that is not transmitted by market prices; one entity directly affects the welfare of another entity that is 'external' to it. Unregulated markets tend to undersupply the output of goods and services which generate positive externalities, and oversupply in cases when there are negative externalities. The Listed Events are concerned with the undersupply of goods which generate positive externalities, for example feeling pride from domestic competitors' successes in international sport competitions, strengthening of national identity and similar impacts. In addition, such externalities also satisfy the non-rivalling criteria as is typical for public goods. If one person feels pride at what national sporting heroes have achieved, he or she does not prevent others from enjoying the same. In fact, many people will regard it as a value in itself to have someone to share the pleasure with. In other words, having a party completely alone is not worth much. It is difficult to imagine a state of 'national celebration' if very few people are interested in the sport – or if the majority are prohibited from watching the event on TV. Hence providing the general audience with access to the same sport programmes strengthens the externalities absolutely. This is where the Listed Events regulation comes in, the purpose of which is to guarantee that most people have this possibility.

The actors that are involved in trading sports rights will maximise their own object functions and not the welfare impacts. Profit-maximising TV channels will neither take into account whether the programmes generate externalities, nor consider the public good aspect. Ideally, PSB channels are supposed to maximise the welfare for the whole society, which also involves externalities and the public good aspects. However, due to the extremely expensive prices of the most attractive sports rights, the licence-financed, PSB channels in particular have found their possibilities limited.

Sports associations generally use TV sporting events in order to promote the sport and hence stimulate recruitment to it. Thus, they will prefer selling the rights to channels which maximise the number of viewers, other things being equal. However, it is well known that many sports associations suffer from a permanent lack of financial resources. Thus, it is sometimes difficult to reject offers from pay-TV channels, particularly if the values of the other bids are considerably lower.

The switch of popular sporting events from free-to-air channels to pay channels represents a disadvantage for those who cannot afford to subscribe to pay channels since cost is obviously a barrier to subscription for pay channels. Thus a concern with equity could provide a motive for government intervention (Boardman and Hargreaves-Heap, 1999). However, the equity argument applies to whatever programmes are being broadcast, not only to sporting programmes. Thus, concerns about equity do not make sense as a single argument in this case, as unequal income distribution influences people's ability to purchase all sorts of goods (Solberg, 2002b). Since the Listed Events regulation reduces the number of channels that are allowed to submit bids, it also reduces the value of the rights fees of the events in question.

Conclusion

This chapter has focused on how the markets for sports rights have developed since early in the 1990s, with most attention on Europe. It analysed factors that have led to strong price increases in sports rights fees, particularly in soccer rights.

Even though commercial channels have been (and still are) willing to spend enormous amounts of money on acquiring attractive sports rights deals, there are several examples of unprofitable deals. A number of European TV channels have been hit by the so-called 'winners' curse' and lost enormous amounts of money from deals, which originally looked promising. Therefore the chapter analysed factors that are influential for the profitability of sports rights deals. In addition it also focused on characteristics which are essential for sports programmes as commodity goods.

The final section provided the background for the migration of attractive sports rights to pay-TV channels with low penetration. This development has paved the way for the Listed Events regulation, the rationale of which was discussed from a welfare economic perspective.

CASE 15.3 Football's TV-run gravy train grinds to a sharp halt **FT**

The end is nigh for football's golden era of TV-fuelled dosh.

With media groups from Germany's Kirch to NTL, the cable company, struggling for survival, it has begun to dawn on football club chairmen that the days of regular sharp increases in the sums of TV money sloshing into club coffers are now firmly behind them.

The plight of such companies threatens to reduce competition for the sports TV rights whose value has increased exponentially over the past decade, spurring rapid rises in the turnover – though often not profits – of football clubs in the main European markets.

Bob Murray, chairman of Sunderland, one of three Premiership clubs in north-east England, now reckons that the amount of money raised by live, pay-per-view and overseas rights to England's top league stand to increase only by 'about the rate of inflation' when the next TV contract comes to be agreed.

Under the present three-year deal, which kicked off at the start of this season, these rights fetched close to £1.5 billion.

This could have serious implications for clubs that have allowed their cost base and debt levels to swell in an era when TV-related income was climbing both regularly and rapidly.

'We are very concerned about giving players contracts beyond the next review date,' Mr Murray says. 'We are in a changing market. Football clubs have got used to a life of luxury.'

About 50 per cent of the turnover of Sunderland, a mid-ranking Premiership club, is media-related.

In a further symptom of the returning sense of realism among broadcasters hit by the worst advertising recession in recent memory, media companies – once dazzled by the idea of clubs as gold mines – are writing off the value of their investments in Britain's national sport.

British Sky Broadcasting, controlled by Rupert Murdoch's News Corporation, last month wrote off £60 million of goodwill associated with investments in clubs.

That figure represents roughly half the value of Sky's football equity portfolio, the most expensive of which was a 9.9 per cent stake in Manchester United, bought for £60 million before an attempted takeover of the club.

Granada too has reduced the book value of its football investments, which saw it pay £47 million for a 5 per cent stake in Arsenal and £20 million for a 10 per cent stake in Liverpool.

Last year it wrote off £65 million of its £135 million portfolio of assets including football clubs, dotcoms and subsidiary channels such as Wellbeing and ITV2.

The breakdown was not disclosed, but football investments, including their media assets, were worth £90 million before the impairment charge. It is likely their book value would now be about half that.

But if England's top clubs at least have the cushion of a further two seasons of their current highly lucrative TV contracts, those lower down the pecking order may have no such luxury.

ITV Digital, the lossmaking digital television platform, is expected to start trying to renegotiate its £315 million rights deal with the 72 clubs in the Nationwide League, English football's three lower divisions, as soon as next week.

The platform, jointly owned by Granada and Carlton Communications, has already paid £136 million to the league under the deal, agreed at the height of media rights valuations, but is seeking to reduce the £178 million still owed.

Its virtual admission that it paid too much for the rights to screen Nationwide League and Worthington Cup matches comes at a time when the squeeze on marketing budgets caused by a slowdown in the economy has hit ITV the hardest.

On advice from Deloitte & Touche, the accountancy firm brought in last week to oversee a 'fundamental restructuring of ITV Digital's cost base', ITV executives are expected to argue that the terms are unsustainable.

Granada and Carlton want to cut the operating costs of the platform, which needs a further £300 million of investment to break even. The ITV companies have already spent £800 million on the way to 1.2 million subscribers.

But the Football League, which represents the lower division clubs, has hired a QC in anticipation of a legal fight and believes it has a 'very robust position' to hold ITV Digital's shareholders accountable for the money still owed under the existing contract.

The dispute between the two sides is likely to centre on whether a 'short form' contract contains a financial guarantee from the parent companies to honour the £178 million payment should ITV Digital fold.

ITV believes it has 'sound' advice from its in-house lawyers that 'the buck stops with ITV Digital' and that no such parent guarantees exist.

The League on the other hand, advised by lawyers Hammonds Suddards Edge, media rights specialist Active Rights Management and auditors Andersen, is confident it does.

Obtaining a parent guarantee when dealing with a subsidiary company is a 'basic thing to do', according to sports rights experts.

A 'long form' contract, fleshing out the agreed terms, was never drawn up. But there is no doubt the preliminary contract is legally enforceable.

The League asked all bidders for the rights to offer parent guarantees and this demand is said to be set out in its tender document.

Football executives, mindful of the fate of scores of lower league clubs should the rest of the money not come through, are thought to be determined to sue Granada and Carlton on this basis.

Any reduction of the sums paid under the current contract would add significantly to the problems of the lesser lights of the English leagues, many of which are battling for survival in spite of pocketing the £136 million already paid.

According to one league insider: 'It's not even the fact that these clubs have budgeted for the TV money to come in – they have already spent it.'

Ironically, many of the clubs which appear most at risk are in the First Division, which takes 75 to 80 per cent of the TV revenues from the ITV deal.

Speaking before the start of the season, Jez Moxey, chief executive of Wolverhampton Wanderers, the Midlands club that has a benefactor in the shape of Sir Jack Hayward and now looks destined for the Premiership, said he believed it was 'virtually impossible to make a profit if you are going to invest in buying players'.

Mr Moxey estimated that Wolves would get about £1.9 million more than last season from central funds as a result of the TV deal – £3 million as against £1.1 million.

Moreover, with the situation at NTL remaining precarious, football league club chairmen also worry about the security of an internet rights deal with the cable operator that offers them each income of about £300,000 a year.

A change of management at Premium TV, the subsidiary that manages NTL's football interests, has unsettled the industry. Stephen Carter, NTL UK & Ireland chief executive, denied Premium TV was closing. 'There has been a change of leadership but not change in commitment,' he said.

As so often, then, in the harsh commercial world of modern-day professional football, it looks as though the sport's comparatively poor relations are set to feel the backlash from the media sector's present crisis before their richer cousins.

With the best games still capable of attracting massive television audiences, some top clubs indeed still envisage a hugely lucrative future as part of some, for now, imaginary European Superleague.

Whether there are big-name casualties in the scrap for a place at this top table will be one of the compelling stories of the coming decade in the world's biggest sport.

Source: Ashling O'Connor and David Owen, *Financial Times*, 9 March 2002

Discussion questions

1. Following developments noted in the case, what are likely to be the short- and long-term implications for businesses such as Sunderland Football Club, as well as those businesses involved in other sports?

2. In response to current turbulence in the television market, explore a range of strategies that sport businesses such as Sunderland Football Club could implement to address opportunities or weaknesses this turbulence may bring.

Discussion questions

3. Make a list of the five most valuable sports rights deals in your own country. The list should include the values and also the name of the sellers and buyers. Categorise the TV channels according to the categorisation in this chapter. Discuss the motives of the channels for acquiring these sports rights.

4. What are the main differences between European and North American markets for sports rights? Discuss the main reasons for these differences?

5. Discuss why the acquisition of sports rights can be a risky affair for the purchasing channel.

Guided reading

Some of the issues that received attention in this chapter have been analysed more profoundly in the following articles and books: Boardman, A.E. and Hargreaves-Heap, S.P. (1999); Cave, Martin and Crandall, Robert W. (2001); Cowie, Campbell and Williams, Mark (1997); Dunnett, P. (1990); Fort, Rodney (2003); Gaustad, Terje (2000); Solberg, Harry Arne (2002a, 2000b); and Solberg, Harry Arne and Gratton, Chris (2000). See the Bibliography for full details.

You will find data about previous and current sports rights fees in the reports listed below. These reports also describe how the major sports rights markets have developed since early in the 1990s.

■ Books and reports

Baskerville Communication Corporations (1999) *Global TV Sports Rights*, 2nd edn, London.
Baskerville Communication Corporations (1997) *Global TV Sports Rights*, London.
Kagan World Media Ltd (2003) *European Sports Rights Agencies*, London.
Kagan World Media Ltd (2000) *European TV Sports 2000 Databook*, London.
Kagan World Media Ltd (1999) *European Media Sports Rights*, London.

Recommended websites

The following newsletters and web-pages will keep you updated with some of the developments in the sports rights markets:

Financial Times – http://www.ft.com

Kagan's Media Sport Business – http://www.kagan.com/sports

Soccer Investor – http://www.soccerinvestor.com

TV sports markets – http://www.tvsportsmarkets.com

Sportcal.com – http://www.sportcal.co.uk

Visit www.booksites.net/chadwickbeech for links to these and other relevant websites.

Keywords

Collective sale of sports rights; cultural discount; European Broadcasting Union (EBU); individual sale of sports rights; pay-TV channels; public service broadcasting (PSB) channels; sports rights.

Bibliography

Baskerville Communication Corporations (1999) *Global TV Sports Rights*, 2nd edn, London.

Boardman, A.E. and Hargreaves-Heap, S.P. (1999) 'Network externalities and government restrictions on satellite broadcasting of key sporting events', *Journal of Cultural Economics*, 23(3), pp. 167–81.

Boon, Gerry (2002) *Deloitte & Touche Annual Review of Football Finance*, Manchester.

Brown, A. (1996) 'Economics, public service broadcasting, and social values', *The Journal of Media Economics*, 9(1), pp. 3–15.

Brown, A. and Cave, M. (1992) 'The economics of television regulation: a survey with application to Australia', *The Economic Record*, 68(202), pp. 377–94.

Cave, Martin and Crandall, Robert W. (2001) 'Sports Rights and the Broadcast Industry', *Economic Journal*, 111(469), pp. F4–F26, February.

Cowie and Williams, Mark (1997) 'The economics of sports rights', *Telecommunications Policy*, 21(7), pp. 619–34.

Desbordes, Michael (2003) *The Relationship between Sport and Television: the Case of the French Network TF1 and the World Cup 2002*, paper presented at the fifth IACE Conference in Neuchatél, Switzerland, May 2003.

Downward, Paul and Dawson, Allistair (2000) *The Economics of Professional Team Sports*, Routledge, London.

Dunnett, P. (1990) *The World Television Industry – An Economic Analysis*, Routledge, London and New York.

European Commission (1997) *Television Without Frontiers Directive*, 89/552/EEC, Article 3a (2).

Fort, Rodney (2003) *Sports Economics*, Prentice Hall, Upper Saddle River, New Jersey.

Gaustad, Terje (2000) 'The economics of sports programming', *Nordicom Review*, 21, pp. 101–13.

Gould Media (2002): http://www.gouldmedia.com.

Johnsen, Hallvard W. (2001) 'A cost perspective on televised sport – the optimal economic utilisation of sport's media rights, paper presented at *The 15th Nordic Conference on Media and Communication Research*, Reykjavik, Iceland 2001.

Kagan World Media Ltd (1999) *European Media Sports Rights*, London.

Kagan World Media Ltd (1996) *European Television Channels and Country Profiles*, London.

Kaldor, N. (1950) 'The Economics of Advertising', *Review of Economic Studies*, June 1950, p. 87.

Musgrave, Richard (1959) *The Theory of Public Finance*, McGraw-Hill, New York.

Neale, W.C. (1964) 'The peculiar economics of professional sports', *Quarterly Journal of Economics*, 78(1), pp. 1–14.

O'Keffe, Lisa (2002) *Tradition to Technology – Rugby League and the Road to Murdochisation*, paper presented at the *10th European Sport Management Congress*, 4–7 September 2002, Jyväskylä, Finland.

Olson, Mancur (1971) *The Logic of Collective Action: Public Goods and the Theory of Groups*, Harvard University Press, Cambridge, Mass.

Preuss, Holger (2000) *Economics of the Olympic Games. Hosting the Games 1972–2000*, Walla Wall Press in conjunction with the Centre for Olympic Studies, The University of New South Wales.

Quirk, James and Fort, Rodney (1999) *Hard Ball: The Abuse of Power in Pro Team Sports*, Princeton University Press, Princeton, New Jersey.

Samuelson, Paul A. (1954) 'The Pure Theory Of Public Expenditure, *Review of Economics and Statistics*, 36, pp. 387–9.

Soccer Investor (2001) *Kagan European Sports Rights*, 27 November.

Soccer Investor (2002a) *Kagan European Sports Rights*, 23 July.

Soccer Investor (2002b) *Kagan European Sports Rights*, 24 December.

Solberg, Harry Arne (2002a) 'The economics of television sports rights. Europe and the US – a comparative analysis', *Norsk Medietidsskrift*, 9(2), pp. 57–80.

Solberg, Harry Arne (2002b) 'The European Commission's Listed Events Regulation – over reaction?', *Culture, Sport, Society*, 5(2), pp. 1–28.

Solberg, Harry Arne and Gratton, Chris (2000) 'The economics of TV sports rights – with special attention on European soccer', *European Journal for Sport Management*, 7, special issue, pp. 68–98.

Solberg, Harry Arne and Gratton, Chris (2004) 'Would European soccer clubs benefit from playing in a super league?', *Soccer and Society*, 5(1).

Throsby, David (1994) 'The production and consumption of the arts: a view of cultural economics', *Journal of Economic Literature*, 32(1), pp. 1–29

Wildman, S.S. and Siwek, Stephen (1987) 'The privatisation of European television: effects on international markets for programs', *Columbia Journal of World Business*, Fall, pp. 71–6.

Chapter 16

eManaging sport customers

Alan Tapp
Bristol Business School, University of the West of England

Upon completion of this chapter the reader should be able to:

- understand the importance of managing customers in the sports sector;
- apply the necessary underpinning theory to explain customer management;
- assess the impact of the internet on sports organisations;
- see how sports brands can be leveraged for income;
- understand the practical implications of all these issues.

Overview

In this chapter we will examine how the world of professional sport is slowly being changed by commercial management practices. The new trends towards managing customers have been driven by the Customer Relationship Management movement, itself a development of direct marketing practice. This chapter studies how these strategies are deployed in the sports sector. Later in this chapter, we also highlight two important developments in sports marketing: firstly, the use of the internet, and secondly, the use of promotional methods for merchandising. The key issue of sports brands will be discussed.

Supporter management

The importance of supporter management

The very idea of managing one's customers is new in the world of sport.

It is not unfair to suggest that until very recently most sports organisations have been product led with supporters largely ignored. The typical sports club marketing mix – if it existed at all – perhaps consisted of sponsorship, perimeter advertising, media management, and some small-scale selling of merchandise – strips, scarves, etc. – all very traditional. Clubs did not worry about *supporters*, they worried about *tickets*. This landscape, it has to be said, still dominates many big and smaller sports alike.

Soccer provides a case in point. Work by Tapp and Clowes (1999) suggests that soccer clubs in the United Kingdom are still in a developmental phase of marketing orientation, with the main functions concentrating on ticketing and selling specialist products such as conference and corporate entertainment facilities. There is a relative lack of 'marketing-led' activity. For example, there is still little or no market research, database marketing in many clubs is still in its infancy, and the idea of relationship marketing with loyal supporters has not really sunk in. The separate operations of 'ticketing' and 'commercial' departments mean that in many clubs marketing functions are isolated from supporters.

Although Mullin, Hardy and Sutton (2000) similarly criticise sports marketing in the USA as suffering from marketing myopia, the Americans remain considerably ahead of most European sports. Their influence has gradually filtered over the Atlantic, leading to a movement towards supporter-led marketing. This marketing evolution has to some extent been led by smaller, newer (to the United Kingdom) sports such as ice hockey and basketball. Athletics has also made serious efforts in Europe to provide an attractive, spectator experience, and indeed leads the US in this regard. Overall however the picture remains patchy, with sports executive knowledge and skills in customer management varying enormously between different organisations.

However, let us take a step back. The first task is to explain the principles behind customer management and see how they apply to sports. So, we will investigate how the Customer Relationship Management approach that is sweeping through commercial sectors can impact on sports marketing. The debate that follows assumes a working knowledge of the basics of relationship and transaction marketing theory. The customer management ideas that follow originate from Ted Levitt's famous assertion that 'The purpose of business is to get and keep a customer'. Hence much of customer management is organised around these two activities: acquisition is 'getting' customers, while retention is 'keeping' them. With a nod to the economics of supporter management, the aim is to show how professional sports clubs can attract supporters, make money from their support, and keep their fans loyal when times are bad.

Principles of supporter management

As has already been mentioned, the marketing myopia of sports managers – 'if we play, they will come' – is slowly being replaced by an attention to supporters that was hitherto lacking. Sport is waking up to the importance of using supporter management to court the source of its income – their customers. This is because:

- sport can no longer take supporters for granted. People have a variety of options for their leisure time;
- a closer focus on supporters leads to opportunities for more income from cross-selling;
- competition forces clubs to copycat customer friendly strategies. 'Me-too-ism' is rife in sport management.

So, what exactly is supporter management? Managing supporters is done using individual data held about each fan. Sports marketers would systematically gather information about their individual supporters' attendance, purchases and personal details.

Supporters' behaviour is tracked over time, and action taken to maximise both club revenue and fan satisfaction. An excellent way of picturing this activity is to imagine the 'ladder of loyalty'.

The ladder of loyalty – segmentation of supporters by value

A key facet of customer management is the strategy of organising supporters into different groups according to how much they spend with the club. Typically, clubs will have season-ticket holders, members, and possibly other groups such as casual fans or even 'armchair fans' who watch their club on TV but not through live attendance. These groups represent a hierarchy of supporters according to what they are worth to the club. See Figure 16.1. Each circle highlights the key activities that the sports marketer should consider for each group of supporters. There are two very important aims: firstly to migrate casual supporters up the 'staircase' so that their behavioural loyalty increases; secondly, to keep those loyal fans happy, hence reducing dissatisfaction and defection rates.

Making it happen – the data

The more valuable the supporter is, the easier it tends to be to gather and update data on them. Season-ticket membership is relatively straightforward to manage, with its annual renewal cycles: a basic renewal request once a year is all that many clubs will do. The floating army of more casual fans is more difficult to identify; here close liaison is needed between the marketing department and customer service delivery in the ticketing section. Casual fans may be identified by asking how many games they have attended that season, then asking for permission to contact them in the future. New

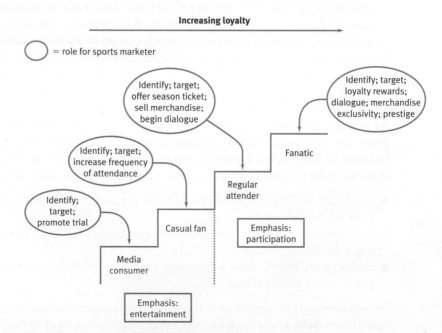

Figure 16.1 The loyalty ladder

technology is expected to further transform the marketer's life. Automatic swipe card entry will be introduced as standard in bigger, richer sports in the next decade (for example baseball in the US, soccer in Europe). With these swipe cards will also come the power to record supporter behaviour automatically – and this is the key to successful direct marketing in other sectors.

Another key technology for data gathering is the internet. Often, websites ask for initial registration requiring users to set a password and/or user name. Sports enterprises can then track the access, use and length of time that their customers are engaged in using club net facilities (McCarthy, 1999, highlights the growing use of 'cookies' by sports clubs as part of this process). This allows businesses to construct a database of users containing large amounts of detailed customer and market information.

We will now take a closer look at supporter acquisition and retention.

Acquisition

All commercial enterprises have to attract new custom, and sports events are no exception. The majority of sports clubs will rely on predominantly local support, with research suggesting that those who live more than one hour's drive from the club are unlikely to attend. (Exceptions to this are those clubs or events that can attract a national or international following, for instance the Tour de France, the Weltklasse athletics meet, and so on.) The importance of socio-geography in the appeal of sport means that the attraction of new fans should begin in the local community, with local media a potentially vital driving force.

The trigger for new attendance will often be fathers taking sons for the first time, or friends introducing friends. The club itself may not have to significantly intervene to attract custom if it is successful: the media will do the work for it. Relying on such local 'buzz' is dangerous however – what happens when the media lose interest? Here, the club's local links can be vital: football clubs may do local PR work themselves; for example, local training sessions for community schools will help. More astute sports marketers will also operate acquisition marketing campaigns. These could be untargeted – a 'kids for a quid' day; or targeted – identify possible new supporters based on profiles of existing support, and approach them with offers of discount. Research by Tapp and Clowes (2002) found that discounts may not be necessary or desirable however. In fact, potential supporters are often put off by the misplaced belief that there may be serious limits on ticket availability; even more simply, they may not know about fixtures, times, dates. Such problems are easily rectified by an alert marketing department.

■ Use of the internet as an acquisition tool

Most users of sports websites are highly-involved existing supporters. Nevertheless websites do provide sports organisations with a cost-effective way of reaching out to large numbers of casual supporters who may then be tempted onto the 'ladder' of more permanent support. Websites offer a number of mechanisms to draw in casual fans. Tickets may be bought without having to personally be at the ticket office.

Merchandise may be purchased from the comfort of one's own home. Fans can be drawn into the daily diet of news and stories that will both feed local press and react to press stories. A casual supporter may find him or herself attracted to visiting the site more often; this increased interest may lead to more tangible support.

■ Retention – keeping supporters loyal

The importance of retention

Retention of existing customers is the key economic driver behind customer management. Workers at Bain & Co (Reichheld, 1996) found that resources allocated to keeping customers who would otherwise leave pays off very handsomely. Their research findings held true for an impressive variety of sectors. They found that an increase in loyalty by 5 per cent could lead to profit increases of up to 125 per cent depending on the sector. However, it has to be said that practitioners have not exactly leapt out of the blocks in implementing retention strategies. One study found that about 90 per cent of marketing directors described customer loyalty as 'very important', but to illustrate the lack of action on this front, only 58 per cent claimed to even measure retention (let alone do anything about it) (Aspinall *et al.*, 2001). This reflects the difficulty in shifting the old habit of focusing on short-term sales and monthly product market-share statistics.

There is every reason to believe that sports marketers would enjoy great success from retention marketing strategies aimed at their supporter base. Firstly, and most importantly, the underlying concepts of *loyalty* and *relationships* between club and supporter have a great deal of meaning in sport. This contrasts with their dubious merit in commercial sectors – no one chants 'loyal customers' walking down the aisle of Tesco! Secondly, supporters spend sufficient money on their interest that the economics of supporter management make sense, as we can see in Case 16.1.

CASE 16.1 Crunching the numbers: the economics of acquisition and retention in sport

Here are some typical costs and revenues on a per supporter basis.

Acquisition

Let's say we run a large sports club and want to attract new fans for the forthcoming season. Each supporter is worth, say, £100 per annum to us.

Acquisition marketing activities:

Press ads	£25,000
Radio	£25,000
Open day	£20,000
Total	**£70,000**

Number of new fans recruited 1,000
Marketing cost per new supporter = £70,000/1,000 = £70

Each new supporter is worth £100, so total new revenue = 1,000 × £100 = £100,000
Margin from acquisition activity = £100,000 − £70,000 = £30,000

Retention

We also want to retain as many of last season's supporters as possible:

Direct mail to last year's 20,000 season-ticket holders offering ticket for this year	£20,000
Relationship building activities through the year	£80,000
Total retention costs	£100,000

We achieve 95% retention of season-ticket holders. Without the above retention activity, studies suggest we would have retained 85% of supporters (i.e. lost 3,000 fans from the base of 20,000).

So, 95% retention means we lose 1,000 supporters from last year, so we have retained 2,000 fans that would otherwise have been lost.

Total saved revenue that is otherwise lost: 2,000 fans at £100 per fan = £200,000

Hence margin from retention activities = £100,000

CASE 16.2 Loyalty is complex

Some very interesting research across different sports (Tapp, 2003; Bristow and Sebastian, 2001) suggests supporter loyalty is multi-faceted. Different supporters exhibit different levels of behavioural and attitudinal loyalty. Tapp and Clowes's (2002) research identified the following:

Fanatics

Traditional hard-core fans who will be fanatically devoted to one club and may not take a wider interest in the sport as a whole.

Repertoire fans

These fans will be heavy attenders of matches but will also attend other matches not involving teams they say they support.

Committed casuals

Partisan fans who nevertheless do not regularly attend games. Perhaps leading complex lifestyles.

Carefree casuals

Uncommitted fans with relaxed attitudes to support; see the game as purely entertainment; neither attitudinally nor behaviourally loyal.

Champ followers

May be heavily involved with the sport, but not loyal to one team, serially switching from one club to another.

The advice to the sports marketer is to identify these different groups, then segment their offerings accordingly. For instance carefree casuals could be targeted with entertainment-led messages, whilst committed casuals could be approached with a call to their loyalty in the team's hour of need.

To understand the importance of retention marketing further let us go back to Reichheld's original findings (Reichheld, 1996). The reasons why existing customers are more profitable than new customers are:

- Acquisition costs are more expensive than the costs of retention of existing customers.
  In sports organisations this is likely to hold true. There is ample opportunity for sports clubs to hold details of their existing customers on a database, making it easy to contact them. In future, e-mail will make this even more cost effective.
- Cross-selling and up-selling of goods and services to existing customers.
  Sports clubs have opportunities to cross- and up-sell tickets, merchandise, media services, and corporate services to what is often a willing audience of existing supporters.
- Existing customers will do your recruiting for you.
  In football, the traditional mechanism of fathers bringing sons to games is now increasingly mirrored with mother–daughter links, although interestingly it is sometimes the daughter introducing the mother to live spectating.

Implementing retention strategies

As we have seen, an important part of the sports marketer's job is to ask him or herself – what would keep supporters with us? The most obvious answer is team success, but as this is outside our control, there needs to be recognition of the importance of treating sport as a leisure product or service. That way, even if the team does not do well, the fan is at least partly satisfied with the experience. Some examples of key areas follow.

Service delivery

Good sports clubs do what they can to make the service excellent. The key to this is the match-day experience, from the drive there, to the ticketing, to pre-match entertainment, half-time entertainment and provision of refreshments, and post-game convenient exiting of the ground. If this good service can be enhanced for loyal fans, then so much the better. In English soccer, Charlton makes available free coach travel for their most loyal fans for the last match of the season. Gestures such as these are appreciated and remembered.

Loyalty schemes

Loyalty schemes in the guise of volume related discounts go back to the early 1900s with the UK Co-operative organisation's famous 'divi' (dividend) – a refund given to shoppers who spent regularly. This is effectively a reward for loyalty. Given the fanatical devotion of many supporters one would envisage such schemes enjoying popularity in sport, and indeed some clubs do make use of them. In English soccer, Chelsea runs a points scheme designed to reward regular attendance at less attractive games. Fans are rewarded with a place higher up the pecking order when applying for tickets to high-demand games. Cross-sector schemes are also being considered. For example, clubs could link with superstores looking to drive traffic into their stores. Points gained at the store could be redeemed for sports-related rewards. Schemes such as these do require significant management time and effort however, so smaller organisations would be unlikely to resource such ideas.

Collectors

Many sports consumers share a long established hobby of collecting sports memorabilia (Tapp, Beech and Chadwick, 1999). Whilst some consumers purchase goods and services as a statement of team affiliation or fashion, a hard-core of consumers gathers memorabilia as part of an ongoing collection. This culture of collecting is one that has existed for many years and stimulates a large number of people to gather artefacts including match programmes and tickets, replica shirts and club pennants. Indeed, these collectors not only indulge in the purchase of current products that may ultimately become football memorabilia, but also increasingly in a range of more historical items (Jenkins, 1998). The collection of sports-related products is thus an established activity and effectively exists at two levels: collections motivated by club brand loyalty which is born out of team affiliation, and those arising from a wider interest in football specifically and collecting generally. The acquisition of a scarf or a car sticker allows purchasers to make a public statement about their affiliation to a particular team. The more ardent supporters may take this one step further and use the display of such items to assert their credentials as serious supporters of, or authorities on, 'their' team. In both cases, people may attempt to derive benefits from the sense of 'group belongingness' or tribalism that the mass purchase of football club products can bring. As an extension of this a replica strip or a team poster may provide an opportunity for certain individuals to perceive an indirect participation in 'their' club.

Whilst the social contact or tribalism of collecting can be significant, the activity can equally be seen as a private affair. As hunters and gatherers, sport provides people with ample opportunities for the accumulation of artefacts and items. This may perform a self-actualising function and allow the collector to establish an identity or sense of inner direction. There may also be an element of territorialism as the collector seeks to lay claim to a piece of the sport that he or she supports. The tag of 'subject expert' is one that is often applied to collectors and this may give the individual a heightened sense of self-esteem or social superiority.

Having examined the subject of supporter management, we will now move to two related subjects. First we will examine the burgeoning use of the internet in sports marketing; then to finish the chapter we take a more in-depth look at sports sales promotion techniques.

The internet in sport

■ Introduction

Hoffman and Novak were correct when they predicted in 1996 that the internet would change a firm's relationship with its customers, and sports franchises have been at the leading edge of such change. With its attractions as an entertainment-based medium, sport is ideally placed to attract browsers with entertainment and then entice them into business transactions.

As with other business sectors, there has been a dramatic growth in the number of sports websites in recent years. The quality of the sites run by clubs is quite impressive bearing in mind that at best these are no more than medium-sized businesses. However, in spite of recent progress in European sports, the level of sophistication achieved by these websites pales in comparison to the sites of major North American professional sports clubs (for example, see websites of the Houston Astros and Los Angeles Lakers). The main difference would appear to be in the way that the web is used to gain an advantage over rival teams or sites, and in the way that it adds value to existing activities such as ticketing. The notions of 'competitive advantage' or 'value-added' that perhaps should underpin site development are sometimes missing, particularly with smaller less well-developed sports.

The internet allows clubs to make large amounts of standardised information widely available. The provision of club 'facts and figures' and merchandising are the most obvious examples of how this facility is being exploited. Club provision of chat facilities, both delayed and live online, has been appreciated by keen supporters and is widely used. Suggestions, complaints and feedback – in short, dialogue – are all encouraged.

The much vaunted 'multi-sensory experience' has been largely absent in European sports websites to date, limited mainly to live match audio commentaries, and perhaps downloads of historical videos. This is set to change with the sale of internet rights for live viewing of events, led inevitably perhaps, by the richest sport, soccer. A significant barrier to this remains the deployment of broadband cable, without which live video feeds through the internet are very slow. It is broadband that is the key to the next stage of growth of this remarkable medium.

The use of the internet in the sport sector presents us with a number of significant strategic implications to consider.

■ Using the internet for acquisition and retention

Strauss and Frost (1999) point out that both transaction (4Ps: product, price, place, promotion) marketing and relationship marketing are enabled by the internet. Internet technology offers clubs the opportunity to enhance their marketing activities by establishing a more direct method of communication with supporters and customers (Thomas, 1998). At one level, net technology enables secure transactions between buyers and sellers to take place. Thus, activities such as ticketing services and sales of club merchandise can most obviously take place electronically. Alba *et al.* (1997) and Ody (1999) suggest that the net is a particularly good medium for merchandising. This can be further enhanced by the use of graphics and images which, in the case of ticketing for example, can be used to show the view that a supporter might get from a particular part of a stadium.

Meanwhile, according to Berry (1983), relationships are enhanced through the following:

- tracking buying patterns;
- customising services to customers' specific requirements;
- providing 2-way communication channels;
- augmenting core service offerings with valued extras;
- personalising service encounters as appropriate.

Internet enabled services

The plethora of sports-related websites reflects the structural set up of each sport. In addition to club sites, you will encounter individual player sites, supporter sites, league sites, sponsors, pressure groups, and other stakeholder sites.

A sophisticated club site (see, for example, the soccer club site www.chelseafc.com) may offer the following:

- information: club history, club structure, player profiles, virtual tours, forthcoming matches, etc.;
- supporter interaction: chat rooms, supporter feedback to club, surveys, games, competitions, etc.;
- services: betting, travel, etc.;
- ticketing including online buying;
- merchandise: extensive opportunities for virtual purchasing online;
- video and audio clips.

In less developed sports the lack of sophistication in websites is clear. For example, if a cricket fan wants to buy a ticket online, most sites duplicate information that is more readily available elsewhere. Apart from the biggest soccer clubs or for major events, tickets are generally not available to purchase online and priority bookings cannot therefore be given to those who purchase tickets in this way. Compared to the North American sports sites, this side of club activity is still poorly developed. For example, the Boston Red Sox site allows the user to access a view from each part of their stadium, then to reserve and pay for a ticket (choosing an acceptable payment method) and then have it delivered (using a chosen delivery method).

The internet levels the playing field

Most sports clubs are small-, or at the most medium-, sized businesses. For small businesses, the internet can be a great leveller (Strauss and Frost, 1999). Unlike conventional advertising, set-up and entry costs are low. Hence it is difficult for the internet site of one sports organisation to drown out that of another. This has any number of ramifications. The speed of new business entry for new sports or clubs is increased. The advantages of economies of scale and high market share are much reduced. However, having a web presence may not be enough on its own. The need to integrate web and conventional marketing is clear – website access is led by consumers not marketers, and they need a reason to access a site, as well as knowing that such a site exists.

Consumer behaviour on the internet

The sheer *convenience* of sports websites has allowed many fans who live a long way from the club to more actively engage and involve themselves. For events like the Tour de France or the Commonwealth Games, websites allow supporters to organise themselves, to gather information about hotels, travel, ticketing and so on. Sports clubs with overseas appeal can use websites to foster international fan clubs; at the very least such activities are likely to increase merchandise sales.

Successful websites will actively engage browsers as well as merely passing on information. The internet encourages behaviour as well as information swapping: interactive games or competitions are one facet; another may be devices like on-line auctions or betting. All of these things will draw the fans in to involve themselves more with the club.

Belk, Sherry and Wallendorf (1988) suggest that the internet is analogous to a flea market. That is, those individuals who access sports information on the net will generally range from passive browsers through to those who are actively searching and seeking to buy. This implies that the 'market' for the net-based facilities offered by sports enterprises is likely to be fragmented and so highly segmented (Armstrong and Hagel III, 1996). Some users may simply want to access and gather information whilst others may be keen to transact for both goods and services on a regular basis.

Internet information flows are different to traditional markets

In traditional markets, information is passed 'down' to customers from companies taking advantage of their control of the act of going to market. However, the internet's low cost of access allows customers (or agents acting on their behalf) to take control of going to market. In addition, the internet caters for easy 'sideways' information flows, allowing customers to talk to each other, forming communities of interest extremely quickly (Mitchell, 2000). Instead of one type of marketplace where companies tell customers what they have to sell and customers react or choose as a result, Mitchell suggests we now have three marketplaces:

- the sellers' marketplace – the traditional model;
- the neutral marketplace – for example an online auction house;
- the customers' marketplace – for example a buying club.

In the sports sector, the high involvement of the product generates huge interest in sites run by fans for other fans, swapping information, news and opinions, or more seriously, organising themselves to exert pressure on clubs or structures. The *Economist* predicted in 1997 that 'the most important effect of the internet is the shift in power from the merchant to the consumer'. One aspect of this shift in power is illustrated by the rise in protest groups that use websites to orchestrate collective behaviour. Supporters are realising that, collectively, they have immense power: they can remove managers or even owners that they do not like; they can lobby for structural changes within the sport.

The plethora of unofficial club sites provides an impressive array of facilities which, taken in totality, offer the user a more interactive experience than most of the official club sites. Some offer live radio broadcasts of games, some send regular e-mail updates of team news to site subscribers, others provide more than enough to satisfy the information and statistical needs of the most ardent fan. Whilst it is unlikely that all sites can provide everything to everybody, the unofficial sites are often an indication of what official sites could achieve.

■ Internet connectivity

Websites themselves do not represent the true character of the internet. The most important feature of the internet is its connectivity – everything is connected to everything else, and devices like click-through banners allow us to easily move from one to another. Hence the internet is acting as a catalyst for partnership building, helping build relationships between the sports organisation and its stakeholders such as sponsors, affinity partners like banks or holiday companies, and the media.

The final section of this chapter examines sales promotions in sports sectors.

Sales promotions in sport

If you are one of those people with an eye to a bargain as you push your trolley round the store, then sales promotions are for you. Defined as short-term incentives to turn desire into action, the mechanisms vary from the straightforward, say, 50 per cent off, to the complex, say, save points with a variety of suppliers and exchange for air miles. Sports clubs can offer a wide variety of sales promotions, at least in theory.

We will briefly examine price and non-price promotions before turning our attention to the merchandising of sports' brands.

■ Price promotions

Price promotions should be particularly useful in increasing attendance and maximising revenue. First, clubs could deploy variable pricing depending on the demand for a fixture. Soccer clubs will sometimes do this – the visit of, say, Arsenal costing fans £40 while the match with Aston Villa costs £30. Second, clubs could deploy time-based pricing to regulate demand. This typically works well in sectors that have high fixed costs and low variable costs, such as airline travel, telecommunications or restaurants. Each extra customer does not add significantly to the costs of the operations – costs are dominated by land, fixed purchases, salaries. The sport sector certainly fits into this category when considering attendance at events.

As Figure 16.2 shows, after the break-even point of supporters paying full price, the marketing team has the option of discounting the remaining tickets, in a profitable manner. However there are at least two difficulties with implementing this idea:

■ In many sports, spectators arrive to purchase tickets just before the game begins. Hence, it is difficult to know when to discount.

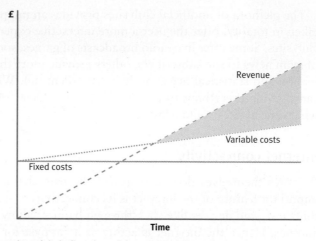

Figure 16.2 Sport is a high fixed and low variable cost business

- In some sports there is a perception amongst managers that spectators who find their neighbour has received a discounted ticket will not be happy.

To counter these problems, direct marketing may be used to provide extra control over the price discounting process. Discounts can be offered directly to casual fans who otherwise would not attend. Good information is at the heart of the success or failure of such an operation – how do we spot casual fans? We could examine previous purchase history, or more speculatively target local people who fit the profile of supporters but who currently do not attend.

Price bundling may also be used as a mechanism. Season tickets are a common example of price bundling of a series of games under one price. This guarantees income for the club in advance, and may smooth demand over the season. Alternatively, the club may bundle together the purchase of a high-profile attractive cup game with a run-of-the-mill league fixture.

Extend beyond the core product

In general, sports promotions should be used with caution. Fans may 'cherry pick', that is attend games only when there is a promotion. Discounting impacts directly and heavily on the bottom line, and with overuse fans will see it as a bribe, not a loyalty reward. Non-price promotions are better, perhaps linked to theme or event evenings at the stadium. Newport Rugby Club in South Wales has transformed its attendances by deploying family entertainment, bouncy castles, fireworks, entertainers, and so on. Good marketers recognise the need to extend the leisure product beyond the game itself. One of the defining features of sport is that the marketer has no control over the product – we cannot guarantee a winning team. Winning, however, in marketing terms, is not the only thing. If the supporters are entertained, they are more likely to be loyal, more likely to return, and entertainment may be consumed from off-field as well as on-field activities. Open days may also be popular, introducing the club to curious casual fans who may not have hitherto visited. Behind-the-scenes visits are also popular, maybe incorporating the chance to try out the sport – how far can you kick a rugby penalty over the posts?

Based on their extensive experience of US sport, Mullin, Hardy and Sutton (2000) suggest the following further devices for promotional marketing:

■ **Coupons**
These should be used with caution, as they can be perceived as a move that cheapens the organisation's image. However, used as 'member get member' devices introducing friends to the club, coupons may be a sensible deployment.

■ **Product samples**
The club may link up with a sports product such as Lucozade Sport that is launching a new product. Golf club manufacturers may hold a special trial at the club.

■ **Contests**
These add glamour and pizzazz, and sit well with an audience that may be fanatically involved with the product – sport. Supporters often pride themselves on their knowledge of their sport and will test themselves enthusiastically.

■ The sports brand

Following the success of branded sports goods in the US, European sports franchises have copied their American counterparts with some success. The concept of building a brand as a way of differentiating one's goods goes back to the industrial revolution, though branding techniques were refined by FMCG companies from the 1930s onwards. The merchandising of sports goods also stretches back to pre-war times with Chicago Bears merchandise on sale in the 1930s.

A sports brand can be defined as that complete set of images associated with the club in the mind of the supporter. The stronger and more numerous the images are, the stronger the link. These images may be complex and multi-faceted, but ultimately will be *represented* by the name, the logo, and the 'packaging' of the team – its colours, for instance. A sports brand may be the club, the team as a whole, or individuals.

Such brand images are at the heart of what makes sports figures attractive to supporters. There is only one Tiger Woods. He is the pre-eminent golfer in the world today, though his brand extends beyond the bedrock of his performances. His brand also consists of his personal history, his personality and that of the people around him, and the sheer intensity, drive and will to win that sets him apart. Contrast this 'brand' with that of 'Long' John Daly. Here is a man who can drive the ball further than just about all his peers, a skill that is breathtaking to the average golfer. However there is more to the 'brand' of John Daly. Famous for his colourful personality and demeanour on the golf course, he is a recovering alcoholic who has fought his way up from a tough working-class upbringing.

CASE 16.3   The brand of Manchester United FC – from Busby's babes to the Champions League

Aside from the tragic loss of life, the implications for football in the aftermath of the Munich air disaster were all too clear. It was the end of an era for a team that was hailed as one of the greatest ever. The long-term implications, decades later, could surely not have been foreseen. The unique nature of the tragedy was perversely instrumental in building, overnight, awareness and interest in Manchester United FC in countries thousands of miles away. It may be stretching the point, but it can be argued there is a direct link between the tragic drama of that icy runway in Munich and, forty years on, the gigantic Manchester United Megastore in Kuala Lumpur.

What is the Manchester United brand? Strictly speaking, you'd have to ask each fan. They'd each tell you about their favourite player, a game they will always remember, or a sublime piece of skill from Ryan Giggs that they have tried, and failed, to copy at home. All of these things make up the brand. Go deeper, and they would probably agree on the legacy of United being the first English club to win the European Cup, the 'holy trinity' of Best, Law and Charlton, and more recently the huge success of the team built by Sir Alex Ferguson.

The bottom line? Manchester United is the world's biggest sports franchise, bigger even than the Dallas Cowboys or Real Madrid (the latter's spending power is at least partly due to its £300 million overdraft underwritten by the city). In 2002, United's revenue was over £150 million, much of this made from TV and merchandise revenues that rely on its estimated 5 million fans worldwide.

The point about such brands is that they are valuable. Firstly, fans want to identify with such brands. Sports brands are primarily symbolic, allowing fans to present their own personality in terms of that of the team or individual they support. 'Who am I? I am a Llanelli fan' a rugby supporter from South Wales might say. Cialdini *et al.* (1976) coined the idea of BIRGing – basking in reflected glory. When the team does well, there is a high social cachet in announcing oneself as a supporter. Supporters may go as far as actually defining themselves in terms of their support for their team. This is also true of participation: a cyclist who presents himself as such to his friends may have a high likelihood of purchasing, say, Tour de France related merchandise. As well as building personal esteem, products also build social communities by transmitting affiliations to others who also share them. Formula 1 fans of Ferrari are apt to wear copious amounts of Ferrari branded goods. This is the bottom line of brand management for sports marketers: they can make money from strong sports brands. Buying a licensed or affinity product allows the fan to 'take the experience home' after an event, or at the extreme to substitute for actually being there (Mullin *et al.* 2000). Brands based on teams or individuals are hard or even impossible to copy. The bond between the club and its fans is stronger than that between customers and commercial firms in mainstream sectors. Sports managers have recognised that this link can be exploited (not a term that fans would welcome) through sales of branded goods, and through affinity links to partners allowing sales of non-sport-related services that will accrue revenue to the club.

CASE 16.4 The wonderful world of sports brands

It's consumer paradise! Come on sports fans! Pick up your Leeds United Duvet. Get your Ireland Rugby team wallpaper here. What's that – going on holiday? Pick up your England Cricket–Lunn Poly branded trip to Australia. Worried about your credit card bills? Well at least you'd have the satisfaction of supporting your team with our Beneficial Bank–Liverpool FC affinity card. And so on it goes.

Discussion questions

1. What other affinity goods are used in sports branding? Identify them within the three broad categories given in the text.

2. Are there limits to which the brand can be stretched with affinity goods?

Affinity goods like these can be divided up into three broad categories:

- branded goods linked directly to the sport – for example, a cricket bat;
- branded goods not linked to the sport – for example, a duvet cover;
- branded services – for example, holiday agency, credit cards, and so on.

Branded sports goods are not a one-way bet however. What is hot stuff today can easily be yesterday's news tomorrow. While highly successful clubs can expect lasting demand, some sports suffer from 'fad' boom and bust. The fate of American Football in the United Kingdom is one example, with fan clubs for the Dallas Cowboys springing up in the late 1980s, only to sink without trace just a few years later. How many warehouses were left full of un-sellable Dallas Cowboys' products?

Conclusion

In this chapter we have seen how the sportscape is changing for sports marketers. Sports clubs are becoming less myopic, focusing more on supporters than ever before. Part of this focus involves better supporter management, with direct and database marketing techniques helping the marketer in getting and keeping supporters. Other developments have grown out of increased use of the internet. Here, sports websites have been at the leading edge of change compared to other sectors. The internet is now an established and important part of the sports marketing mix. Finally we considered sales promotions in sport, focusing particularly on brand affinity marketing – an area of considerable growth potential in Europe and beyond.

CASE 16.5 Pukka chukkas out of Africa   FT

Eight years ago South Africa's polo clubs could count their members on the fingers of one hand. Now, the sport's supporters are ready to take on the world.

The polo field at the Inanda Club in Johannesburg is clearly visible from the board-rooms of the city's new financial district of Sandton. Equestrian enthusiasts among South Africa's investment banking community chose their offices for the town–country view they afford of the club's stables and the ball-chasing horsemen beyond.

The club was not always so popular. Eight years ago, interest in polo had dwindled. The club had only four polo-playing members. Then, its expansive grounds were seen to belong to retired British cavalry officers and a fast-fading era of empire. Property developers eyed the grounds jealously.

But numbers have begun growing again, and today Gauteng province alone has 85 active polo players.

Investment bankers, telecommunications entrepreneurs, eye surgeons and senior legal counsel have joined KwaZulu-Natal sugar farmers and Free State maize grow-ers in their enthusiasm for the game.

Leo Baxter, chief executive of information technology company MB Technologies, has built his own polo field and stables at Sunninghill, to the north of Johannesburg.

Not far away, Jonty Sandler, the former finance director of black empowerment company New Africa Investments, has established the Ngwenya polo-training school.

'Over the past four years there has been a huge revival in polo,' says Walter Grindrod, head of Inanda's polo division and heir to a South African shipping line.

'Having people coming into polo who have wealth has been good for the game. They have come with enthusiasm and brought with them spending power and investment in horses and jobs. They have created new facilities and new expecta-tions.'

Some of the fastest expansion has taken place in the Eastern Cape province at Plettenberg Bay, the Johannesburg-based business community's premier beach resort.

Polo fields cost between R300,000 and R1 million (£55,000 and £183,500) each. Plettenberg Bay has six polo fields. Another three fields are planned by the end of this year and the town's polo fraternity has ambitions to host a regular international fixture on New Year's day. A match against England is planned for the beginning of next year.

One of the most celebrated polo grounds in Plettenberg Bay is Kurland. Its owner, Clifford Elphick, a De Beers director and the former personal assistant to the late South African industrialist Harry Oppenheimer, took up polo three years ago. He hopes to put Plettenberg Bay on the international polo circuit, competing with Argentina by offering first-class hospitality to the European market.

He says a week or two's holiday, including tuition and tournaments and a few days at a Cape winery and a game farm, can be provided at a fraction of the costs of a similar break in, for example, Spain, Florida or Argentina.

Polo is not a difficult game to play: Elphick estimates that a horse-riding novice can be swinging a mallet after two weeks, while someone with equestrian experience can learn to 'enjoy the game' even quicker.

Ngwenya, though in rather less-alluring Johannesburg, is already registering international interest. The 2½-year-old school has trained about 30 players from the UK – from novices to accomplished sportsmen and women. It offers coaching and full board for a group of four players and their partners for a total of £1,000 a day.

Buster Mackenzie, captain of the South African polo team and a coach at Ngwenya, says: 'In the past five years, South Africa has almost reached international standards. I always felt Australia and New Zealand were a step ahead. But a lot of international players are coming through. It's no longer good, amateur bush polo (in South Africa).'

Playing good polo depends largely on the quality of the mount. South Africa has an abundant supply of thoroughbred horses that fall short of winners at the races, but can make good polo ponies. The opening price for a thoroughbred racehorse lies between R2,000 and R5,000. A high-goal polo pony costs between R20,000 and R70,000. In the UK, the equivalent costs about £15,000.

Transport costs, vet bills, grooming and feeding all add to the high costs of playing polo. But Mackenzie, a Natal farmer, insists that the costs of polo playing are on a par with competitive mountain-biking.

'I'm a little anti the big-name polo trip. It's done more harm for the sport than good,' he says.

Source: James Lamont, *Financial Times*, 18 May 2002

Discussion questions

3. What distinctive customer management, promotions and branding challenges do the managers of polo face? Discuss each of these issues, particularly in relation to the view that polo is elitist and an anachronism.

4. If you were responsible for building the polo brand, promoting the sport and managing customers in South Africa (or another country of your choice), how would you do it?

Discussion questions

5. Watch some TV adverts and ask yourself what sort of brands are being built and maintained. Why are sports brands so strong compared to those in most other sectors?

6. Make a visit to a sports club megastore and examine the goods on offer. What sort of brand extensions are being considered by the sports enterprise? Is there anything that you think they should not consider? Why?

7. What are the key principles that underpin supporter management? Explain the difference between the loyalty of a sports consumer to his club and that of a bank consumer to his bank.

8. Access five English Premier League soccer websites and five from lower leagues. What differences do you notice in: appearance; products on offer; services; information provision?

9. Why do some supporters collect memorabilia? Explain what the underlying psychological traits of a collector are.

Guided reading

If you need more detailed information, you will find *Sports Marketing* by Mullin *et al.* (see Bibliography) very rewarding. This book is packed with detailed explanations of every aspect of sports marketing, and is clearly written. You should note that the book is entirely based on US perspectives, and all its examples come from sports that are popular in that country.

A detailed bank of academic research is available on sports marketing in *Sport Marketing Quarterly*. This journal, again, is US dominated, and its papers are heavily scientific in nature. You may be better off looking up the abstracts of conference papers from The European Association of Sports Management (EASM), which not surprisingly concentrates on European perspectives.

Recommended websites

I would recommend English Premier League sites as providing well thought through entertainment/sales sites. The key to a good site is its ability to attract traffic in the first instance, and then to facilitate commercial sales once the supporter is interested. Of course, the best club sites worldwide probably reside in the US – check out Dallas Cowboys, Boston Red Sox, New York Yankees, and so on.

Boston Red Sox: http://boston.redsox.mlb.com
New York Yankees: http://newyork.yankees.mlb.com
Dallas Cowboys: http://www.dallascowboys.com
Manchester United: http://www.manutd.com

Visit www.booksites.net/chadwickbeech for links to these and other relevant websites.

Keywords

Customer management; sports brand; sports promotions.

Bibliography

Alba, J., Lynch, J., Weitz, B., Janiszewski, C., Lutz, R., Sawyer, A. and Wood, S. (1997) 'Interactive home shopping: consumer, retailer and manufacturer incentives to participate in electronic marketplaces', *Journal of Marketing*, 61, July, pp. 1–18.

Armstrong, A. and Hagel III, J. (1996) 'The real value of on-line communities', *Harvard Business Review*, May/June, pp. 54–69.

Aspinall, E., Nancarrow, C. and Stone, M. (2001) 'The meaning and measurement of customer retention' *Journal of Targeting, Measurement and Analysis for Marketing*, 10(1), pp. 79–87.

Belk, R.W., Sherry, J.F. and Wallendorf, M.A. (1988) 'Naturalistic inquiry into buyer and seller behaviour at a swap meet', *Journal of Consumer Research*, 14(4), pp. 235–51.

Berry, L.L. (1983) 'Relationship marketing' in Berry, L.L., Shostack, G.L. and Upah, G.D. (eds) *Emerging Perspectives on Services Marketing*, American Marketing Association, Chicago, pp. 25–8.

Bristow, D. and Sebastian, R. (2001) 'Holy cow! Wait 'til next year! A closer look at the brand loyalty of Chicago Cubs baseball fans', *Journal of Consumer Marketing*, 18(3), pp. 77–91.

Cialdini, R.B., Borden, R.J., Thorne, A., Walker, M.R., Freeman, S. and Sloan, R. (1976) 'Basking in reflected glory: three football field studies', *Journal of Personality and Social Psychology*, 343(2), 366–75.

Hoffman, D.L. and Novak, T.P. (1996) 'Marketing in hypermedia computer-mediated environments: conceptual foundations', *Journal of Marketing*, 60, July, pp. 455–68.

Jenkins, R. (1998) 'Soccer trivia bids reach fever pitch', *The Times*, 11 April, p. 19.

McCarthy, L. (1999) 'Information technologies for sport micro-marketing: one-to-one marketing with browser cookies', Proceedings of the 7th Congress of the European Association of Sport Management, Thessoloniki, Greece, 16–19 September.

Mitchell, A. (2000) 'In one to one marketing, which one comes first?', *Interactive Marketing*, 3(1), pp. 354–68.

Mullin, B., Hardy, S. and Sutton, W. (2000) *Sport Marketing*, Human Kinetics, Baltimore.

Ody, P. (1999) 'On the verge of a retail revolution', Financial Times Electronic Business Survey, 24 March.

Reichheld, F.F. (1996) *The Loyalty Effect*, Bain & Co., Boston.

Strauss, J. and Frost, R. (1999) *Marketing on the Internet*, Prentice Hall, New Jersey.

Tapp, A. (2003) 'Blowing bubbles forever – or just till next season? The West Ham Syndrome revisited', Academy of Marketing Conference, Aston, UK, July.

Tapp, A., Beech, J.G. and Chadwick, S. (1999) 'The culture of collecting: an opportunity for database marketers in the sport sector', *Journal of Database Marketing*, 6(3), pp. 38–51.

Tapp, A. and Clowes, J. (1999) 'The role of database marketing in football clubs: a case study of Coventry City FC', *Journal of Database Marketing*, 6(4), pp. 670–88.

Tapp, A. and Clowes, J. (2002, 'From carefree casuals to football anoraks: segmentation possibilities for football supporters', *European Journal of Marketing*, 36(11).

Thomas, J.W. (1998) 'The brave new world of internet marketing', *Direct Marketing*, 60(9).

Chapter 17

Risk management in sport

Dominic Elliott
University of Liverpool Management School

Upon completion of this chapter the reader should be able to:

- define the scope of risk for a sports organisation;

- explain the importance of risk and crisis management for sports businesses;

- understand that organisations may incubate the potential for failure themselves;

- identify the range of threats and hazards faced by sports organisations;

- understand the key components of effective crisis incident management.

Overview

On surviving the horrific weather conditions which wreaked havoc upon the 1998 Sydney to Hobart boat race, Larry Ellison, CEO of Oracle, a participant, commented, in a choking voice, 'this is not what racing is supposed to be. Difficult, yes. Dangerous, no. Life-threatening, definitely not ... the seas were enormous, and the wind made noises we'd never heard before' (Knecht, 2002). Yet risk and sport are inseparable and the casual observer may consider that ocean sailing carries many of the risks associated with deep-sea fishing, long acknowledged as one of the most hazardous of occupations.

An understanding of risk has much significance for the sports person as well as for the sports manager, although it is the latter with whom we are primarily concerned. As other chapters have demonstrated, sport is big business (for example, FIFA estimates that soccer generates a turnover of $250 billion per annum, Tomlinson, 2002), although with some distinctive features, and as other organisations grapple with issues of risk and crisis management, so too must sports businesses and organisations. Sporting events often involve large, excitable crowds within confined spaces and safety management must be a primary concern of event organisers. The process, which is outlined below, is generic in that it applies to organisations of all types. The guided reading identified at the end of this chapter provides guidance to more detailed approaches to risk management.

Sports organisations may be distinguished from others in a variety of ways, including the peculiar relationships between them and their spectators (fans) and participants, and the high level of media interest in sporting events and clubs at local and national level. These reflect the less tangible areas of risk and crisis management, yet, as Coca-Cola found when they abandoned their original formula for their soft drink, public pressure in the United States, forced an expensive turnaround. More tangible are those threats associated with managing a business, poor decision-making and strategies, health and safety and legal compliance.

The amateur origins of many sports, and their organisations, was reflected in a make-do approach to management in which a small group or an individual was responsible for a wide range of activities, such as ticket sales, contract negotiations, match arrangements, health and safety; as one football club secretary commented, 'Ashes to ashes, dust to dust, what the others won't do the secretary must.' (Elliott, 1998). Another chief executive reported:

> Unfortunately, football being what it is, most people do two or three jobs ... Everybody has more roles than they should have, you just do not have the time, it's not an excuse, it's a fact, football clubs can't afford to pay that number of people because the financial structure of clubs is wrong ... In football it is impossible to do a cash flow for the next month, there are so many unforeseen things that can happen and it is all down to kicking a football on the pitch or drawing a number out of a bag. (Elliott, 1998: 160)

Effective risk management, within such a context, is unlikely to receive the attention required. A particular problem is that the necessary skills set are likely to be missing. However, risk management is a simple process that should be a part of effective management. The chapter begins by identifying a number of assumptions which underpin this chapter's approach to risk and crisis management, before proceeding to a consideration of the scope of risk and introducing tools for assessing the types of threats and hazards which organisations may be faced with.

Individuals make judgements about risk every day of their lives, from deciding what to eat and drink to deciding when to cross the road. In playing sport it might be the decision when to change tyres in Formula 1 or whether a player should pass the ball or attempt to score the try in Rugby. In most cases the probabilities are uncertain and the range of outcomes unclear. Perceptions will be shaped by a host of subjective factors – our mood, interactions with those around us, our view of our competitors, familiarity with the situation; all these combine to influence the final decision. Thus, although the risk management process may be aided by the use of scientific tools and frameworks, it is not a science, and it will be shaped by the perceptions of those conducting the analysis and interpreting the results.

A crisis management approach

Underpinning this chapter is a crisis management (CM) approach which is defined here as one that:

- acknowledges the impact, potential or realised, of interruptions upon a wide range of stakeholders;
- recognises that hazards and threats possess both social and technical characteristics;

- recognises that, if managed properly, hazards and threats do not inevitably result in crises;
- assumes that organisations themselves may play a major role in 'incubating the potential for failure';
- assumes that managers may build resilience to business interruptions through processes and changes to operating norms and practices.

The discipline of crisis management recognises a minimum of three distinct phases of crisis, as depicted in Figure 17.1 (see, for example, Smith, 1990; Pauchant and Mitroff, 1992). These phases can be conceived of as the before, during and after phases. The pre-crisis stage refers to the period in which the potential for failure is incubated. In the years and months before an incident occurs, decisions will be made that make the organisation more or less vulnerable to crises. Such decisions might include (in)appropriate staffing levels, the discrediting or ignoring of internal and external safety reviews, or a focus upon profit to the detriment of safe working practices. Pauchant and Mitroff (1992) argue that people and groups within organisations may employ a range of reasons and strategies to resist change, even when events highlight inadequacies in systems, procedures and beliefs. For example, the 1971 Ibrox Stadium disaster was the fourth incident to involve fatalities or hundreds of injuries on Stairway 13 within a 10-year period (see Elliott and Smith, 1993).

The second stage refers to the immediate organisational handling of an incident and includes the immediate period of the crisis, between the crisis taking place and the resumption of operations or activities. Clearly, this period will vary according to the nature of the crisis itself and the ability of the organisation to respond. A distinction must also be drawn between the crisis and the trigger. The cancellation of the ITV digital contract with the Football League in 2002 triggered crises for a number of clubs, especially those recently relegated who retained Premier League cost structures. The impact of this trigger was determined by the existing financial state of the clubs. Those that had taken such events into account within their planning scenarios were better placed to deal with the contract's cancellation than those who had not undertaken any such scenario planning. Similarly, effective crisis management may exacerbate or reduce the impact of a trigger event. Fitzgerald (1995) describes the period following the advent of a crisis as a 'glide path'. Aircraft will vary in their ability to glide based on environmental conditions, design, load and pilot skills; similarly, organisations

Figure 17.1 Stages of crisis model
Source: Adapted from Smith (1990)

may, following an interruption to their operations, be able to continue their operations albeit for a short period of time. In general terms, the so-called 'glide path' connotes the manner and speed with which operations are recovered.

The third, and final, stage refers to the period in which an organisation seeks to consolidate and then reposition itself. Of course, stage three feeds back into stage one as organisations may or may not learn from their experiences.

A crisis management approach has evolved from considering how to manage crisis incidents (i.e. phases two and three), to considering how the potential for crisis may be incubated by organisations themselves (see Pauchant and Mitroff, 1992, and Elliott and Smith, 1993 for a detailed sports industry case study). Thus, although risk management describes the process as undertaken by organisations, a crisis management approach denotes a frame of reference in which incidents occur in three stages and in which organisations, themselves, incubate the potential for failure.

Although risk management is a process undertaken by organisations, crises usually affect a wide group of stakeholders. Brazil's 160 million population mourned, officially, for three days when Ayrton Senna died competing in the San Marino Grand Prix, in 1994. The investigations into the causes of the crash indicated a range of socio-technical factors with a number of allegations being made: that the steering column of Senna's vehicle had been cut to satisfy the driver's demand for more space in the cockpit, but that it had been poorly re-welded; that the maintenance of the track was another significant cause. Lovell (2003) suggests that charges against the organisers of the event and the owners of the vehicle were either dropped or 'eased' because of the political connections of key Formula 1 personnel with senior Italian politicians. These political connections and the economic importance of Formula 1 to Italy were key factors, demonstrating both the wide range of stakeholders involved but also the particular influence of sport.

Without wishing to consider the ethical dimensions of this case, it illustrates: the range of stakeholders who may become involved; the social and technical dimensions of failure (from the politics to the technicalities of the course and vehicle); that effective management resolved the incident; and that the organisations involved probably played a major role in incubating the potential for failure. Although Senna bore the physical risk, Williams the financial risk of a lost vehicle and lost points in the championship, Formula 1 faced a threat to its viability and reputation. Such a case illustrates some of the facets of risk management.

■ Managing risk

From a practical perspective there are a number of steps required to manage risk effectively:

- Step 1 concerns *identifying hazards and threats*.
- Step 2 concerns *assessing the impact* of such hazards upon business activities.
- Step 3 concerns *measuring the risk, assessing its probability and deciding upon priorities*.
- Step 4 concerns *considering alternative options*, ranging from avoidance (withdrawing from an activity), deferment (wait and see), reduction (improve prevention and control measures, for example, through a continuity plan) or transfer (via insurance).

The scope of risk: identifying threats and hazards

Imagine you are invited by an acquaintance to watch a professional soccer match in England. Asked to identify possible threats to your safety, it is probable that hooliganism would feature high on your list. Think a little harder and you may remember the deaths of 96 people, crushed to death at Hillsborough in 1989, or 56 people who died in the fire at the Bradford Stadium in 1985, or 39 killed in the Heysel Stadium in Brussels, or the 66 crushed on the Ibrox Stadium's Stairway 13. These are the most obvious threats, most easily recalled given the extensive media coverage of hooliganism or disaster. Yet our perceptions of risk rarely fit with the true probabilities. Individuals are more likely to die or be injured as they drive to a soccer match than suffer as victims of either hooliganism or of a major disaster. Within the stadium itself spectators are more likely to get either food poisoning or be scalded by hot drinks. The scope of health and safety type operational risks are broad indeed and the frame of reference for hazard or threat identification provides an important first step in the process of risk management.

■ Categorising risk

The scope of risk management can be narrow or broad, reflecting the managerial mindset of an organisation. Jones and Sutherland's (1999) guidance notes supporting the Turnbull Report (1999) identify four broad areas of risk (see Table 17.1).

Their particular concern was with identifying risks for publicly-listed companies, although it provides a useful overview of risks for organisations of all types. As the sports industry has shifted towards professionalism, business and financial risks have become more pertinent. For example, the revenue streams associated with playing in the UEFA Champions League are vitally important to leading clubs such as Barcelona, Real Madrid and Manchester United – so much so that Manchester United reportedly was insured against the threat of failure to secure a place in the Champions League.

The football stadia disasters of the past thirty years and the deaths of spectators and drivers in Formula 1 highlight the threats associated with sport which go beyond those faced by participants. These are the most tangible of hazards. However, as the sports industry has become more professional, the threats from other categories of risk have become more obvious, as Manchester United's insurance policy indicates. Within the football industry the growing separation of coaching from business management is a response to this. Fynn and Guest (1994) report of a dispute between Terry Venables, then manager at Tottenham Hotspur and Frank McClintock, then acting as a player's agent; the dispute centred around the charging of Value Added Tax (VAT), and the fact that such a dispute arose indicated the lack of business knowledge of the two parties. This highlights the dangers of former sports professionals assuming business management positions without the necessary training or support.

Risk management in business and finance is concerned with strategic management. Organisations such as Easyjet, GE, IBM and Microsoft have sustained success through ongoing market research, competitor analysis and sound understanding of how their competences fit with their environments. Although understanding does not guarantee success it provides a sound basis for it. The introduction of new formats (for example,

Table 17.1 **Risk management**

Category of risk	Example	Sports Illustration
Business	Wrong business strategy	In early 1970s Adidas dominated the running shoe industry. It underestimated the growth in demand for running shoes and the aggression of new rivals Nike. With relatively low barriers to entry, stronger promotion, sharper pricing and ongoing research and development might have built barriers to entry (Hartley, 1995).
	Industry in decline	Reflecting the decline of County Cricket in the UK, English clubs offer free admission to some matches to encourage spectators (Birley, 1999).
	Too slow to innovate	English Rugby Union resists pressures for professionalism.
Financial	Liquidity risk	FIFA cyclical business leads to negative cash flow in non-World Cup years.
	Credit risk	Leicester City borrow £50 m to build new stadium and are relegated, losing key revenue stream.
	Misuse of financial resources	Players' agents. Bribery.
Compliance	Tax penalties	Silvio Berlusconi subjected to ongoing enquiries concerning tax evasion. Horse-racing jockey Lester Piggot imprisoned for tax evasion.
	Breaches of Companies Act	
Operational and other	Succession problems	Inspirational coaches move on with no obvious successor.
	Health and safety	Stadia management, disasters in Johannesburg (2001), Bastia (1992), Hillsborough (1989). Spread of SARS virus threatens World Badminton championships to be held in Birmingham, UK, 2003.
	Reputation risk	Allegations of racist behaviour or drug taking may affect individual sports stars and their clubs.

one-day cricket, a change of season for Rugby League) reflects changes in the environment; as spectators' lives change so must the services offered by the sports industry.

Shrivastava and Mitroff (1987) have developed a framework for classifying types of resources according to where the crisis is generated (internal/external) and which systems (technical versus social) are the primary causes (see Table 17.2).

The benefit of using such a matrix is that it can be used as the starting point for a brainstorming session for any organisation that wishes to identify the range of interruptions that it might experience. Developing contingency for every eventuality may be impractical, given the wide variety of potential failures. This matrix provides the basis for clustering 'families' of crises together and preparing for these rather than for each individual incident. For example, in terms of impact, illegal drug taking amongst key personnel, evidence of bribery and match fixing, and the identification of key staff

Table 17.2 Crisis typology for sports businesses

	Internal	*External*
Technical/Economic	Temporary seating collapses Fire **Faulty maintenance of key equipment**	Key sponsor defaults TV rights monies cease suddenly Stadium collapses due to earthquake Adverse weather conditions **SARS virus threatens travel of sportspeople**
Human/Social/Organisational	Crowd crushing disaster Players industrial action Drug taking Bribery and corruption Lose key personnel **Accusations of child abuse**	Adverse media coverage Leading players labelled as racist Legislative change Hooligan behaviour **Failure of key supplier**

Source: Adapted from Shrivastava and Mitroff (1987)

as racist would all combine both legal and reputational dimensions. Although the precise details would differ, an organisational response, common to the three, might be appropriate. Planners are limited in terms of time and resources and cannot account for all eventualities. Each sport would develop a matrix for its own sector, thus adverse weather might have very different connotations for yachting and cricket. Within each sport there may also be scope for threats and hazards to be identified relating to different levels within the sport as illustrated by Case 17.1.

CASE 17.1 The world's most popular sport is a mess of a business

In the week before the 2002 World Cup kicked off in Japan and South Korea the following reports appeared in the business weekly, *Fortune*. The article introduced an investigation of FIFA, which reported that it was run like a dictatorship in a way which might constitute criminal offences under the Swiss penal code. With soccer's popularity never higher the sport had been beset by bankruptcy, financial scandals and power plays. The FIFA president, Joseph 'Sepp' Blatter, was alleged to have awarded $100,000 between 1998–2000 to a Russian, Kolosokov, for his work on the executive, a position he no longer held. Blatter was also accused of paying a referee from Niger to discredit the head of the Somalian FA, who had reported that Blatter supporters had sought to bribe him. Blatter admitted that the payment to Kolosokov was 'irregular' and admitted to giving the referee $25,000 as an act of personal charity. Estimates of FIFA's accrued losses for the 1998–2002 period range from between $31.9 million and $115.6 million.

Despite this, blue chip sponsors (e.g. Coca-Cola, Gillette, Hyundai, Mastercard) paid an average of $20 million each for exclusive marketing deals with the 2002 World Cup. Such sponsors are attracted by the prospect of viewing figures in the region of 40 billion in nearly 200 countries. Broadcasting rights had been sold to ISSM group, a Swiss sports marketing firm which crashed in May 2001. Its collaborator Kirsch assumed control of these rights. ISSM group had also been responsible for all non-broadcast commercial rights for the World Cup too (from sponsorship through to replicas of the mascot). Immediately following the collapse FIFA, under the instruction of Blatter, allegedly, brought this all in-house, although continuing to employ the same personnel. Michel Zen-Ruffinen, general secretary of FIFA, expressed surprise that FIFA had chosen not to pursue criminal investigations against the former managers of ISSM.

FIFA's finances are predicted by its auditor KPMG to reach negative equity of $142 million by the end of 2004. A key problem for FIFA is that its cash flow is cyclical and flows in during World Cup years but not at other times.

Source: Adapted from Tomlinson (2002)

CASE 17.2 Death in British stadia

In 1985 56 died when a fire swept through the main stand at the Bradford Stadium. Although the Health and Safety Executive (HSE) had expressed concerns about the stand, the stadium was not then covered by the Safety at Sports Ground Act. There was little pressure upon such football clubs to raise standards of safety because of their 'difficult' financial circumstances and an ongoing decline in attendances. In July 1984 the local authority informed the club and the local fire service that:

'The timber construction [of the main stand] is a fire hazard, and in particular there is a build up of combustible materials in the voids beneath the seats. A carelessly discarded cigarette could give rise to a fire risk.'

On 11 May 1985, with some 11,000 spectators squeezed into this part of the stadium a fire was ignited when a cigarette-end fell amongst some old papers and sweet wrappers. The fire quickly took hold and within less than 2.5 minutes the entire main stand was in flames. Lack of exits and systems to communicate with the crowd prevented a quick evacuation. Spectators fleeing from the fire encountered unattended, locked gates.

In 1989, the deaths of 96 people at Sheffield's Hillsborough Stadium placed crowd safety high on the agenda across Britain and Europe. The tragedy occurred when standing areas became overcrowded. The pens in which the deaths occurred had been created by walls of steel, some of which had been installed for crowd control purposes and others which had been installed for crowd safety, a subtle but vital difference. There was no system for controlling the numbers of people in these enclosures and a strong mindset prevailed amongst football club, police and local authority regulators that the primary problem was of hooligan behaviour. The underlying causes of the disaster were a combination of the technical layout of the stadium and the management of spectators within it.

Source: Elliott and Smith (1993, 1997)

As the Case Studies 17.1 and 17.2 illustrate, sports industries may contain a number of distinct levels with particular threats and hazards. The hazards and threats associated with FIFA, of business risks, low liquidity, cyclical cash flow, and weak corporate governance will equally apply to other governing bodies as well as to the small and large sports businesses. Similarly, the hazards and threats associated with the Bradford and Hillsborough disasters apply equally to other sports where thousands of spectators are brought together for short periods of time. The collapse of a temporary spectator stand at Bastia in Corsica, in 1992, should provide a warning for all users of such structures, whether in basketball, Formula 1, golf, rugby or tennis.

The aim of this section has been to consider the wide range of threats and hazards which may affect sports organisations. The frameworks provide a focus for considering the broad scope of risk. However, as the examples illustrate, hazards and threats rarely impact on one organisation alone; the nature of risk and crisis is that they encompass multiple stakeholders and sporting organisations are as reliant upon suppliers and distributors as other types of business, as the collapse of the British broadcaster ITV Digital ($447 million for broadcasting second-tier soccer) illustrates.

Assessing the risk

Two broad approaches to risk assessment have emerged, the heuristic and scientific approaches. The heuristic (rule-of-thumb approach) is qualitative and based upon judgement. The scientific approach utilises statistical modelling. Toft (1993) has argued that all risk assessment, no matter how sophisticated the modelling, remains inherently value laden.

Elliott *et al.* (2002) offer a framework for risk assessment. The framework emphasises the interdependence of organisations and the importance of a full stakeholder analysis. Key questions and issues to be examined include:

- What is the nature of the hazards with which we are faced?
- What is the potential impact upon our business and other stakeholders?
- What is the probability of a failure occurring?
- Key business and operational objectives.
- Descriptions of key processes (flowcharts etc.).
- Resource needs.
- Linkages and dependencies within the sports organisation.
- Linkages and dependencies with suppliers, agents, customers and other agencies.
- Legal issues.
- Consequences of the threats identified.
- Prioritisation of core and other activities.
- Minimum resources required to restore key activities.
- Seasonal trends or critical timing issues.
- Is the risk acceptable to our stakeholders and us?
- What should be done to manage risk?
- What could we do?

These headings (which lead to related questions) should be adapted to meet the needs of the organisation and would certainly differ, for example, between an industry association and an individual sports club. The purpose of such questions is to stimulate data gatherers and managers to consider risk and how change in any of these broad categories might affect business processes. Elliott *et al.*'s (2002) framework emphasises the importance of understanding an organisation's internal and external environment. For example, Table 17.3 highlights functional dependencies both within an organisation and its supply chain. Sporting events may be interrupted by failures or difficulties experienced by suppliers or by the failure of backroom activities. An observation of Elliott *et al.* (2002) was described as the 'soccer star syndrome'. Within the finance sector certain primary activities, such as the dealing rooms, are elevated to a high status with remuneration packages to match for the 'star dealers'. This resembles the football industry because greater management attention is focused upon the playing field than on the unglamorous, but very necessary, backroom and stadium management support activities. Defenders and goalkeepers rarely attract the large transfer fees of top strikers, yet their functions are as vital to achieving the overall objectives of the football team. Identifying the functional dependencies provides an opportunity for examining the linkages between the exciting and the humdrum that deliver customer value.

The aim of the risk assessment stage is to identify the range of risks and provide some estimation of the degree of threat in terms of severity of impact and probability of occurrence, as depicted in Figure 17.2. Categorisation may occur from a simple ranking exercise, ensuring that high-threat events that are likely to occur receive the highest possible attention.

Table 17.3 Functional dependencies

Dependencies	Examples
Operations management and production	Sporting events require crowd management, facilities management
Information and communication technologies (ICT)	Growing reliance upon automated ticketing systems Automated crowd control systems CCTV
Marketing (shared brands, marketing and promotion)	Leeds United drawn into negative media coverage when players were accused of racist attacks
Distribution channels (type, number and mix of wholesalers/retailers)	Increasing concentration of power in media companies with TV rights
Purchasing and procurement (raw materials and components from suppliers)	Collective bargaining from professional players' unions Providers of key sporting venues
Logistics (whether in house or otherwise)	Direct ticket sales dependent upon postal services for delivery
Organisational support activities (such as legal, finance, etc.)	Lawyers give advice on key contractual issues

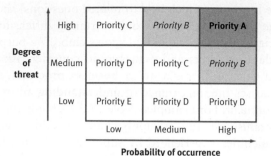

Figure 17.2 Risk assessment matrix

Although risk analysis and assessment may be aided by complex mathematical modelling these can only aid judgement as they are based upon many subjective assumptions. The aim of such tools is to help managers arrive at a considered understanding of the hazards and threats their organisations face together with an understanding of the potential impact upon operational and strategic objectives. The tools are, perhaps, best used, to frame the discussion of hazards and risk management and ensure that such issues are not ignored. Resulting from analysis and discussion a strategy for risk management should be developed.

Implementing risk strategies

The hazards of Formula 1 are obvious, and not surprisingly safety issues receive detailed consideration. In 1982 the Brabham team introduced pit stops; it enabled cars to run with lighter fuel loads and softer tyres and provided an opportunity for sponsors to publicise their logos. There are, however, hazards associated with blasting fuel into tanks via pressure hoses, as illustrated by the spillage of fuel over Keke Rosberg's car during the 1982 Brazilian Grand Prix. Such pit stops were banned until 1994 when Bernie Ecclestone, aware of the dramatic impact on television, successfully advocated their reintroduction – the risk was considered worth the television entertainment value (Lovell, 2003). Risk practice results from a trade-off; in this case driver safety versus revenue streams. Despite other accidents, pit stops quickly became part of the Formula 1 mix.

Another example from Formula 1 highlights the role of judgement in putting risk management into practice. The use of a safety car to slow cars down in the event of an accident, whilst the track is cleared, reduces the need for lengthy restarts. There was a fear that long waits for restarts would encourage bored television viewers to switch channels. Drivers' concerns that the slowness of the safety car could cause the tyre pressure to drop and seriously reduce handling capability were ignored.

These two examples illustrate the balance that managers need to strike between conflicting objectives. The purpose of risk assessment and analysis is that such decisions are grounded in a critical evaluation of the evidence. In this way risk management permeates all areas of the sports business. Risk strategies may also be evident in preparations for managing the crisis, the subject of the next section, and in the preparation of business continuity plans.

Simply explained, a business continuity plan (BCP) is the outcome of a thorough process in which the links between an organisation's objectives, resources, environmental context and dependencies are critically examined. The resulting plan identifies how an organisation will re-establish itself in the event of an interruption. It may include a blueprint of key personnel, contact details, equipment, activities, key deadlines etc. in order that any business recovery can be achieved quickly (see Elliott *et al.*, 2002 for a full discussion of business continuity management). The objective of a BCP is to ensure that recovery occurs in an orderly manner in a way that supports the strategic objectives of the organisation.

Managing the crisis

Even well-run organisations may experience a crisis and proper preparation will result in a greater probability of survival.

■ Handling events

Major sporting events bring together thousands of people. From boxing, the Olympics to soccer they may be characterised by dynamism, excitement and the unfamiliarity of many spectators with their temporary surroundings. The deaths of spectators watching motor racing or attending soccer matches has encouraged the expectation that sports venues should develop the capability to manage a crisis incident. Time is likely to be of the essence in incidents where there are deaths, injury or serious threats to property, although a longer time frame may be more important where there is a significant threat to an organisation's reputation.

A key component of effective incident management is the crisis management team. In addition to the day-to-day structures required to implement risk management, a command and control structure for managing crisis incidents is needed. A commonly used format is a three-tier structure, as advocated by the Home Office (1997a, 1997b), mimicking the structure used by the British Police Service, who label the three levels bronze, silver and gold system (respectively tactical, operational and strategic). This structure emerged from an attempt to encourage consistency between the emergency services and thereby minimise confusion when dealing with an incident (Flin, 1996).

The purpose of the three levels is to ensure that an organisation's response to an incident is effectively coordinated. Bronze (operational) corresponds to the normal operational response provided by the emergency services where the management is of routine tasks. The immediate response to an incident is likely to be managed at this level. When the emergency services deal with a major incident, the 'Bronze commander' is likely to lead a front-line team. Silver (tactical) refers to the command level, which seeks to identify priorities and allocate resources accordingly. During a major incident, it is likely that the silver commander will take charge of managing the incident itself. The role of the Gold (strategic) group and commander is to take an overview, to arbitrate between any conflicts at silver level and to assume responsibility for liaising with the media and key stakeholder groups. The 'Gold commander' is not expected to participate in the detailed management of an incident (adapted from the Home Office 1997a, 1997b). There is no one best way and organisations should plan to use structures that best fit their needs and resources. The three levels identify a minimum of three roles to be undertaken when managing an incident. In smaller organisations one team or individual may perform these distinct roles. Sport abounds with examples of task specialisation – fielders, bowlers and wicket keepers in cricket, forwards and backs in rugby, strikers, midfielders, defenders and goalkeepers in soccer, to name but three. Individuals may switch from defence to attack depending upon need and revert as necessary. This is an apt metaphor for the crisis team. The same individual may fulfil different roles as necessary.

Teams are important because, generally, they outperform individuals although, as Janis and Mann's (1977) groundbreaking work identified, teams may be fallible. Errors may arise from the poor quality of information available, a lack of monitoring key indicators (e.g. accident statistics, budgetary controls), the cognitive abilities of the group and political differences within a group. Sport provokes high emotion, as can be seen from the battle to take Rugby Union from amateurism to professionalism (Jones, 2000), or the media coverage of Bernie Ecclestone (for example Lovell, 2003). Inevitably political manoeuvring may reduce team effectiveness. Smart and Vertinsky (1977) identify a range of remedies for the potential difficulties of fallible teams, including the inclusion of independent experts, encouraging alternative viewpoints, protecting minority perspectives and holding crisis simulations. Implicit in Smart and Vertinsky's analysis is the development of the critical team that continually questions decisions and information whilst possessing the mechanisms, personnel and communication channels to support quick and effective action.

Conclusion

Management of professional sport needs to reflect up-to-date business practice, rather than the historical context of many sporting organisations. Effective risk and crisis management are increasingly required by organisations of all types. The volatility of many sporting organisations' environments, reflecting the links between performance and revenue streams, in addition to the more tangible health and safety type operational risks, highlights the relevance of risk and crisis management to this industry. It has been argued that crises impact upon a wide group of stakeholders, not simply the host organisation. A multiple-stakeholder perspective is thus the starting point for effective risk management and should flow through subsequent analysis.

A four-stage process has been outlined, briefly, above. It provides a basic blueprint for risk management. The process is only constrained by the imagination of the analyst and it is argued that stage one should consider the widest range of possible failures in all of the areas of risk identified. The second stage is concerned with assessing the impact of a failure upon the sports organisation. A clear understanding of the organisation's objectives is a vital prerequisite to this. The third stage is concerned with calculating the probability of failure. The fourth step involves managers considering alternative options for action ranging from avoidance (withdrawing from an activity), deferment (wait and see), reduction (improve prevention and control measures, for example, through a continuity plan) or transfer (via insurance).

CASE 17.3   Cricket World Cup a mere rehearsal for football   FT

Something peculiar happened at the cricket World Cup: nothing went wrong in South Africa. Add this to other evidence and it is time to start revising opinions about the country.

Admittedly most people will be relieved when the cup ends tomorrow. It has been disfigured by the matches played in Robert Mugabe's Zimbabwe, fear of terrorism in Kenya, crucial games being rained off and never replayed, the Iraq issue and the hosts South Africa getting knocked out in the first round.

But in South Africa, two dogs did not bark: no fan or player seems to have suffered crime and there were no great organisational blunders. Fans got their tickets on time, the television broadcasts were good, the pitches sound, the opening ceremony as tedious as anywhere else and there were no power blackouts, accidents at grounds or ambush marketing stunts. When New Zealand played a warm-up game in Soweto, the worst thing that happened was that almost all the watching children became bored and went home.

It is true that the organisation would have shamed a serious company, but then all sports events I have been to, except the 1994 football World Cup in the US, have been organised appallingly. This is because they are staffed largely by student and pensioner volunteers who are not told what to do. But when things went wrong in South Africa the volunteers smiled and tried to help, whereas in countries like France or the Netherlands they acted as if it were just what you deserved.

The smooth hosting could be dismissed as a fluke, except that in recent years South Africa has also hosted the rugby World Cup smoothly, football's African Nations Cup and the World Summit on sustainable development. In May 2004 the country will probably be named host of the football World Cup of 2010, and quite rightly too. People's perceptions of other countries generally being years out of date, foreigners still tend to use the word 'crime' after any mention of South Africa. Their fear has some justification but it has ballooned into hysteria. Just before this World Cup began, one of the tournament's security officials was sacked for advising tourists to shoot any assailants with bleach-filled water pistols. In fact, South Africa seems to be becoming safer. It is not yet Luxembourg but nor is it as dangerous as Colombia. The country's murder rate, which is the most reliable crime statistic, has dropped by more than 25 per cent since the transition to black rule in 1994. This may come as a surprise given the prevailing belief that crime soared after the African National Congress took office. It's true that reports of other kinds of crime have risen in the period, but that may simply be a function of people in black neighbourhoods starting to tell police about crimes. The decline of murder in South Africa is seeping into local consciousness. Visiting during the cricket World Cup, I found that white conversation is no longer solely about crime, and on Friday and Saturday nights in the Johannesburg neighbourhood of Melville, hundreds of blacks and whites sit drinking and chatting in pavement cafés without a security guard in sight. Tour operators have also noticed the change: last year, a bad time for global tourism, the number of tourists arriving in South Africa rose 20 per cent to more than 6.4 million.

Tourism is crucial to this cheap country with mountains, deserts, game parks, oceans and millions of unemployed. South Africa's economy used to float on gold, but the metal has had a bad two decades and will doubtless fade again when the war in Iraq ends.

Tourists will come to South Africa if they know it is safe, and the only chance most of them get to find out these days is when watching sport on television. (If war is God's way of teaching Americans geography, international sport is how He teaches it to the rest of us.) The ideal advertisement for South Africa would be hosting the football World Cup. The country lost the 2006 tournament by one vote to Germany when Charles Dempsey, the New Zealander, ignored his instructions to vote for South Africa and abstained in the last round. FIFA, football's governing body, has since said the 2010 Cup will be played in Africa.

Five other countries – Egypt, Libya, Morocco, Nigeria and Tunisia – have joined the bidding, but at least two of them have no chance and Egypt and Tunisia almost none. When I asked Danny Jordaan, head of South Africa's bid committee, about the rivals he chuckled: 'There is no other African country with the record of event management of South Africa. In fact practically no other African country has hosted major events.' South Africa should win, and if it is allowed to sell match tickets cheaply the country's grounds will be packed with people who will never get another chance in their lives to see a World Cup match.

Nine football World Cups have been held in Europe, seven in the Americas, one in Asia, and guess how many in Africa? 'One can't talk about a world event if it has never been held in Africa,' says Jordaan.

South Africans care deeply about this issue. Getting the World Cup is a favourite item on radio talk shows, and when the country was turned down for 2006, tearful callers blamed racism and colonialism. Of all the snubs the world hands Africa, this one is the most easily remedied.

Source: Simon Kuper, *Financial Times*, 22 March 2003

Discussion questions

1. To what extent do you think a developing nation would make a good host nation for a future soccer World Cup, and what risks do you think might be associated with holding the event in a developing nation?

2. In the context of the above, what strategies and techniques might be available to FIFA in order to minimise, if not eliminate, the risks that you have identified?

Discussion questions

3. Imagine that you are a consultant briefed to prepare a report dealing with risk management across the soccer industry. Prepare a matrix for FIFA and for a professional soccer club. How might these be clustered?

4. What is a crisis management approach?

Guided Reading

Although obviously biased, Elliott *et al.*'s (2002) text dealing with business continuity management provides a practical guide to preparing a business continuity management plan and crisis incident handling. It includes a range of short case studies from a range of industries. Waring and Glendon's (1998) book provides arguably the best introduction to risk management, including a range of detailed case studies, although none are sports related. The Financial Times' *Mastering Risk*, Volumes 1 and 2 (Pickford, 2001) provide a useful overview of current thinking, particularly on business and market risk (Fenton-O'Creevey and Soane, 2001), although these volumes are primarily concerned with the finance sector. It is my view that many business and financial risks can be dealt with through effective strategic management and there are many solid textbooks dealing with this. As an introduction to crisis management Elliott and Smith's (1993) analysis of the football stadia disasters is a readable, applied study that highlights, through case studies, how the potential for crisis is incubated and how organisations respond more or less effectively. This latter is picked up more forcefully in Elliott *et al.* (2002) and although it deals primarily with the soccer industry it has a generic relevance. Bernstein (1996) provides the most comprehensive history of risk management to date.

Recommended websites

The Register www.theregister.co.uk – a seminal website which deals with a wide range of risk mitigation issues.
UK's Health and Safety Executive: http://www.hse.gov.uk – a clearly signposted website dealing with many health and safety type risks.

Visit www.booksites.net/chadwickbeech for links to these and other relevant websites.

Keywords

Business continuity planning; crisis; crisis management; hazard; incident management; risk; risk management.

Bibliography

Bernstein, P. (1996) *Against the Gods: The Remarkable Story of Risk*, John Wiley, New York.

Birley, D. (1999) *A Social History of English Cricket*, Aurum Press, Gloucester.

Elliott, D. (1998) 'Learning from crisis', unpublished Ph.D. thesis, University of Durham.

Elliott, D. and Smith, D. (1993) 'Learning from tragedy: sports stadia disasters in the UK', *Industrial and Environmental Crisis Quarterly*, 7(3), pp. 205 – 30.

Elliott, D. and Smith, D. (1997) 'Waiting for the next one', in Frosdick, S. and Walley, L. (eds), *Sport and Safety Management*, Butterworth Heinemann, London.

Elliott, D., Swartz, E. and Herbane, B. (2002) *Business Continuity Management: A Crisis Management Approach*, Routledge, London.

Fenton-O'Creevey, M. and Soane, E. (2001) 'The subjective perception of risk', in Pickford, J. (ed.), *Mastering Risk*, Financial Times–Prentice Hall, London.

Fitzgerald, K.J. (1995) 'Establishing an effective continuity strategy', *Information Management and Computer Security*, 3(3), pp. 20–4.

Flin, R. (1996) *Sitting in the Hot Seat*, John Wiley, London.

Fynn, A. and Guest, L. (1994) *Out of Time*, Simon and Schuster, London.

Hartley, R.F. (1995) *Marketing Mistakes*, 6th edn, John Wiley, New York.

Home Office (1997a) *Business as Usual: Maximising Business Resilience to Terrorist Bombing*, Home Office, London.

Home Office (1997b) *Bombs, Protecting People and Property*, Home Office, London.

Janis, I. and Mann, L. (1977) *Decision Making*, Free Press, New York.

Jones, S. (2000) *Midnight Rugby*, Headline Publishing, London.

Jones, M.E. and Sutherland, G. (1999) *Implementing Turnbull: A Boardroom Briefing*, Institute of Chartered Accountants of England and Wales, London.

Knecht, G.B. (2002) *The Proving Ground*, Fourth Estate, London.

Lovell, T. (2003) *Bernie's Game*, Metro Publishing, London.

Pauchant, T. and Mitroff, I. (1992) *Transforming the Crisis-prone Organisation'*, Jossey-Bass, San Francisco, California.

Pickford, J. (2001) *Mastering Risk*, Financial Times–Prentice Hall, London.

Shrivastava, P. and Mitroff, I. (1987) 'Strategic management of corporate crises', *Colombia Journal of World Business*, 22(1), pp. 5–11.

Smart, C. and Vertinsky, I. (1977) 'Designs for crisis decision units', *Administrative Science Quarterly*, 22(4), pp. 640–57.

Smith, D. (1990) 'Beyond contingency planning: towards a model of crisis management', *Industrial Crisis Quarterly*, 4(4), pp. 263–75.

Toft, B. (1993) 'The failure of hindsight', *Disaster Management and Prevention*, 1(3), pp. 48–60.

Tomlinson, R. (2002) 'The world's most popular sport is a mess of a business', *Fortune*, 27 May, pp. 28–34.

Turnbull, N. (1999) *Internal Control: Guidance for Directors on the Combined Code* [The Turnbull Report], The Institute of Chartered Accountants in England and Wales, London.

Waring, A. and Glendon, I. (1998) *Managing Risk*, Thomson Learning, London.

Chapter 18

The sports betting industry

David Morris
Coventry Business School

Upon completion of this chapter the reader should be able to:

- understand the nature and scope of the sports betting industry;

- identify the major sectors of the industry and analyse the differences and similarities between them;

- understand the major ways in which sports betting is undertaken;

- analyse the major drivers for change in the industry;

- appreciate the major avenues for future development of the industry.

Overview

The chapter begins with an overview of the main sectors of the gambling industry and the place of sports betting within it. A section on types of sports betting has been included to help readers who have never placed a bet to understand the nature of betting transactions. We then move on to consider whether or not sports betting markets are 'fair' and whether it matters or not. The chapter continues by looking at the available market research data to see who bets and consider some of the motivations of sports betting consumers. The chapter concludes by considering two major drivers of change in the industry – technology and deregulation. This is summarised in terms of looking at a possible new business model for the industry. Two case studies based on particular betting events are used to illustrate the major themes of the chapter. The case study questions are designed to reinforce important learning points.

The sports betting industry

Sports betting is part of the wider gambling industry. Gambling encompasses games of chance or chance and skill played at casinos including those played on machines for large prizes in outlets licensed for the purpose (a sector usually known as gaming), bingo halls and the like, lottery games, playing machines for small prizes in pubs and clubs (known as Amusement With Prizes or AWP machines) and sports betting itself.

Sports betting can be further divided into betting on animal racing (predominantly racehorses but also greyhounds and in some countries ponies and even camels), football pools and betting on other sports. It is difficult to give an accurate estimate of current UK household expenditure on gambling but the figure is likely to be in the region of £seven to eight billion in net terms (that is stakes less winnings) excluding illegal betting and gaming. The overall structure of the market can be seen in Table 18.1.

A major trend over time in the United Kingdom has been the displacement of football pools by the National Lottery as the favoured means of gambling regular small amounts in the hope of very high returns and the emergence of other forms of betting on football than just the pools. For example, the UK football pools market declined by two-thirds in the 1990s. A similar fall in popularity occurred in the Italian football pools market despite the introduction of a new product where punters were asked to select the six matches with the highest aggregate score from a selection of thirty. Such a game could give payouts of lottery jackpot proportions. It is not hard to see why football pools have declined in popularity. Essentially they were fairly clumsy to use and sometimes difficult to understand, the average returns poor and the distribution system (often through an army of agents each handling very small volumes) expensive and inconvenient. The National Lottery has none of these drawbacks. Even the poor rate of return on winnings is offset by the feel-good factor of contributing to good causes. The second shift through time has been the gradual decline of horseracing as the major medium for sports betting *per se*. Fixed-odds betting on football has become popular; in Italy it now has a larger share of the bookmaking market than horseracing. Up until the early 1990s animal racing (racehorses plus greyhounds) accounted for about 97 per cent of bookmakers' turnover. The share of horseracing has fallen to under 70 per cent and greyhound racing to around 17 per cent. Betting on football and other sports has filled the gap.

Table 18.1 **Expenditure on gambling in the UK: estimates for 2003**

Sector	Amount bet (£million)	Amount returned to punters as winnings (£million)	Net expenditure (stakes less winnings) (£million)
National Lottery	5,000	2,500 (50 per cent)	2,500
Bingo	1,200	900 (75 per cent)	300
Casinos	2,700	2,200 (82 per cent)	500
Gaming machines	9,000	7,300 (81 per cent)	1,700
Football pools	320	81 (25 per cent)	239
Horseracing	7,000	5,600 (77 per cent)	1,400
Greyhound racing	1,900	1,520 (77 per cent)	380
Other sports (mainly football)	600	510 (80 per cent)	90
Total	**27,720**	**20,611 (74 per cent)**	**7,109**

Sources: Various Mintel and Datamonitor reports; author's estimates

Forms of sports betting

There are three major forms of sports betting apart from the football pools:

- wagering;
- pool betting;
- bookmaking.

Wagering is perhaps the oldest form of betting. A wager is simply an agreement to pay out an amount of money based on the outcome of an unsettled matter. In sports betting the unsettled matter is the outcome of some sports activity, for example a match or penalty kick or race or whatever. Wagers are still most frequently made on the outcome of a match (a contest between two participants or teams), itself the oldest form of sporting event. For example, betting on horseracing in the United Kingdom began to be organised as it was realised (in the 1770s) that it was important to record the results of match races and the wagers made on them. James Weatherby, a lawyer, was recruited to take on this role and that of holding the amounts wagered on each horse (the stakes) for future payout to the winners. The role of 'stakeholder' was thus born and has its influence today in the idea of a stakeholder economy. A wager is therefore a contract between a small number of individuals, often two. Wagers are bets between individuals and it is here that there is an important distinction between wagering, pool betting (betting against anonymous other betters) and bookmaking (betting against a bookmaker). Parties to a wager set their own odds. Whilst the terms betting and wagering are often used to mean the same thing it is worthwhile making the distinction because it has been revitalised by the emergence of internet betting exchanges (sometimes called betting brokerages) such as Betfair. These employ the internet to put people who wish to wager in touch with each other and perform the role of stakeholder. In addition much wagering takes place in the informal economy whereas both pool betting and (legal) bookmaking take place in a highly regulated economic environment. A frequent example of a wager is betting on a round of golf among the players.

Pool betting, for example the Tote in the United Kingdom or the Pari-Mutuel in France, operates like a lottery. Betters (or punters in common parlance) buy stakes on certain events. All the stakes are pooled. At the close of betting the number of stakes is added up, a deduction made to cover operating expenses, profits, taxes and any other costs, and the total remaining divided up amongst the winning tickets and the pool distributed to the winning ticket holders as a dividend. The important distinction here is that pool betters bet against each other; the operator of the pool betting system does not take a position on the outcome of any event but simply runs the system. In many countries only pool betting is legal; bookmaking is illegal. Football pools are a particular form of pool betting. Once the mainstay of the regular weekly 'flutter' (that is, betting a small stake on the very small chance of winning a huge return), football pools work by asking punters to forecast the results of football matches. The best-known version of this is to select eight games from those played on a Saturday afternoon (in the United Kingdom) which the punter expects to end in a draw where goals are actually scored (i.e. other than a 0–0 result). As such they are also an early example of what are now called 'complex' or 'exotic' bets since they rely on forecasting the results of a number of matches.

In bookmaking the punter bets against the bookmaker. Bookmakers operate from shops, via telephone, from 'pitches' or shops at sporting venues and, increasingly, via the internet. The bookmaker displays a list of prices (known as 'odds') at which he is willing to take bets. For example, suppose we are interested in backing (i.e. placing a bet on) a particular football team winning the European Champions League. The bookmaker will offer various prices on the different teams; for instance, he may offer Manchester United at 3/1 to win. This means that if we bet one euro on Manchester United and they win we will receive three euros winnings plus our one euro stake (less any deductions for taxes). If Manchester United do not win we lose our one euro. The 3/1 ('three-to-one') price says that Manchester United has an expected chance of winning of one in four or 25 per cent. The bookmaker has taken a 'position' on Manchester United by giving punters a price and accepting bets at that price. Of course, the bookmaker is taking bets on the different teams in the competition, so if we are lucky enough to win then others will have lost. Whether or not the bookmaker wins or loses overall depends on the distribution of bets he has taken on the event. This collection of bets is known as 'the book' (literally because they were always written down in a book kept for the purpose) and the bookmaker 'makes a book' on the event. This can be a complex and skilled business since there may be many possible outcomes, bookmakers will be competing with each other and other sports betting outlets for business, and the book is made in real time. This latter point means that bookmakers may offer different odds on the same outcome at different points in time depending on how much money is bet on different eventualities and the information available at any point of time. For example, the transfer of a star player may be seen as lessening a team's chances and the bookmaker may need to offer a more attractive (known as 'longer' odds) price to attract further bets on that team.

In an ideal world most bookmakers will attempt to make a book which will give them some profit no matter what the outcome of the event is. Take a very simple example of a football match where the three possibilities are (see Table 18.2):

- team A wins;
- team B wins;
- the match ends in a draw.

Consider Scenario X. In this case each outcome is judged equally likely having a probability of 33 per cent. If Team A wins the bookmaker pays out 300 to punters who have backed A and nothing to those who have backed Team B or the draw. A similar

Table 18.2 Scenarios, odds and stakes

Scenario	Team A wins	Team B wins	Draw
X: odds	2/1	2/1	2/1
X: stakes	100	100	100
Y: odds	6/4	6/4	2/1
Y: stakes	100	100	100
Z: odds	6/4	6/4	2/1
Z: stakes	100	100	80

picture holds if B wins or the draw occurs. Given that the bookmaker has taken in 300 in stakes no matter what happens the bookmaker will neither win nor lose. In Scenario Y he has set the odds so that there is the chance he can win. Notice the odds on the win by either team are not so generous ('shorter') as they are in Scenario X. A winning punter will now only get one-and-a-half times his stake back in winnings plus the original stake itself. Thus if Team A wins, the bookmaker pays out 250 and makes a profit of 50. The same overall distribution occurs if Team B wins. But look what happens if the draw occurs. In this case the bookmaker ends up even. Indeed, if he had taken more than 100 in bets on the draw he would have ended up losing money. Scenario Z shows an ideal book from the bookmaker's perspective. In this case the bookmaker will end up in profit no matter what the outcome of the match. This occurs for two reasons. Firstly, the odds on the different outcomes have been set in such a way that the percentage chances add up to more than 100 per cent (40 per cent on Team A winning plus 40 per cent on Team B winning plus 33 per cent on the draw) and secondly, through ensuring that not too much money is taken on any one outcome.

Where there are a large number of possibilities, for example in a horserace or who will win a league, bookmakers will attempt to 'lay the favourite'. That is they will ensure that they do not lose if the most favoured outcome occurs. They will then vary prices on less favoured possibilities ('outsiders') to attract bets on them to cover any payouts on favoured possibilities. So whilst some bookmakers may speculate on particular outcomes of sporting events by making books which leave them exposed to losses if their guesses are wrong, most bookmakers will attempt to make books which have the desirable property (for them) that they cannot lose. Whilst this may seem unfair to punters we should remember that bookmaking is a retail service and the question is not whether bookmakers make profits but whether or not those profits are reasonable given the service they provide.

Types of bet

It is also helpful briefly to consider the types of sports bet that can be made. The staple bet in the United Kingdom is a fairly simple affair. The punter will bet on who they think will be the winner of an event, match or a race. A variant on this is where there are several participants, as in a horserace or a golf tournament for example, when the punter may bet 'each way'. This gives a smaller return if the horse, golfer or whatever finishes in the first few places. The exact number of places that will win in this way depends on the number of participants. Much of this betting is at fixed odds, that is the odds are determined at the time of the bet. In horseracing, however, the bet may be struck at the starting price (SP), that is the odds which rule in the market at the time the betting closes just before a race starts ('the off'). Sometimes bookmakers will only accept bets at the SP. This pattern of straightforward win only and each way betting has, in the past, accounted for over 90 per cent of bookmakers' turnover in the United Kingdom. The SP is determined by the market at the racecourse even though this usually accounts for less than 10 per cent of total betting turnover on a race. The other 90 per cent is accounted for by punters visiting betting shops (Licensed Betting Offices, or LBOs, to give them their correct name).

Complex bets, or multiple or exotic bets, are ones where punters bet on a series of outcomes all of which have to occur in order for the bet to be won. The total odds are the multiple of all the odds on each outcome. The simplest example is a 'double' where the punter chooses two events and attempts to predict the winner of both. Suppose that the punter bets ten euros on Tiger Woods to win the (British) Open at 2/1 and Andrei Agassi to win Wimbledon at 5/1. If Agassi wins, the punter has 60 euros 'running on' to the Woods bet. If Woods then wins the punter will receive 180 euros back in total. This is equivalent to odds of 17/1 on the double. Nowadays information technology makes it possible for bookmakers to keep track of very complex bets, for example naming the first five horses home in a race in any order. A common football bet is to name the winning team, the final score and the scorer of the first goal. These bets are becoming much more popular especially amongst many younger sports betters. In many other countries where sports betting is a major industry, for example Hong Kong and Japan, exotic bets are the norm.

Spread betting is perhaps the most sophisticated type of sports betting and enables more interesting bets to be placed on many events. It has not been very exciting, at least in the recent past, to bet on the winner of the Formula 1 motor racing championship. However, betting on the margin of victory may be of more interest. At the time of writing one spread betting company is quoting Michael Schumacher to finish the Formula 1 season with between 108 and 111 points (the spread). If I think he will do worse than this I sell points to the bookmaker. For example, I choose to bet £5 per point that Schumacher will not reach 108 points. Suppose he only manages 100 points. In this case I win £5 per point for every point he is below the lower end of the spread (108), that is I win £35. If Schumacher has a good season I lose. So if he gets 120 points I lose 120 minus 108 points times £5, that is £60. The opposite of selling is buying and I would choose to do this if I thought Schumacher would have a good season. Obviously you need to have an account with a spread bookmaker in order to participate. You might also consider limiting your losses and winnings to a particular amount before you bet. One consequence of spread betting is that it is quite possible to win (and lose) large amounts of money on events where the odds on the obvious outcomes are not interesting enough to whet the appetite of many punters.

CASE 18.1 A day in the life

On the morning of 28 September 1996 Peter Meadows (not his real name, but everything else in this case is true), the Trading Director (that is Chief Bookmaker) of one of the UK's larger gambling businesses, decides that he can safely leave handling the day's trading to his deputy. The famous jockey, Frankie Dettori, has a relatively straightforward day with seven rides at Ascot, one in each race. At least he will not need to rush from one course to another. Meanwhile somewhere in England a punter puts £1 on an accumulator bet on Dettori winning all seven races. The bet is accepted at starting prices, SP.

In the morning racing press Meadows' firm is offering the following odds on Dettori's rides:

Wall Street	3/1
Diffident	10/1

Mark of Esteem	9/4
Decorated Hero	14/1
Fatefully	10/3
Lochangel	No odds given
Fujiyama Crest	12/1

Meadows telephones his deputy. In early trading the book on the afternoon looks good. The company would make a profit of £4,650. If the pattern of betting continues the company will do quite well as more bets are struck. However, no one knows, at this stage, how many small exotic or multiple bets have been placed by punters wanting to get some excitement out of the afternoon's racing. By now early prices are showing on all runners at Ascot, and if these prices become the SPs, the £1 bet on Dettori winning all seven races would net one lucky punter £234,928.

During the morning there is a run of bets on Wall Street and the price is cut to 5/2. There is no particular reason to change the odds on any of the other Dettori rides. The meeting starts and Dettori wins the first three races. Wall Street started as the 2/1 favourite, Diffident at 12/1 and Mark of Esteem at 10/3. Overall the prices are not far different from those quoted in the early morning when the racing papers went on sale.

By now many punters are beginning to think Dettori can do no wrong and Decorated Hero is backed down to a 7/1 SP. Meadows' deputy is telephoned by a LBO who gives him the news that there is a punter holding a £1 bet on Dettori to win all seven races; he telephones Meadows, who is tidying up his garden. With this punter's bet and other multiple bets there is now £400,000 running on to Fatefully, Dettori's fifth ride. Fatefully is still at 10/3 in the betting and the potential losses are in excess of £1.7 million if Dettori wins again. Meadows instructs his staff on-course at Ascot to start betting with other bookmakers on Fatefully. This is known as hedging and has two effects. Firstly, if Fatefully wins Meadows will win some money back for his company and secondly it will drive the SP down thus limiting potential losses. Fatefully is backed down from 10/3 to 7/4 favourite in under ten minutes. Meadows' staff bet £75,000 on Fatefully. Fatefully wins. Their winnings are £140,000 but more importantly they have reduced the payout to other punters by £200,000.

Meadows arrives at the trading room. In the morning press Dettori's ride, Lochangel, was given so little chance of winning that none of the major bookmakers even advertised a price. However, there is now a feeling (or a worry if you are a bookmaker) that Dettori would be the first ever jockey to win seven races at one meeting. Lochangel is now in the market at 13/8. Even so the money running on to the sixth race is £600,000 and Meadows' company stands to lose over £1.5 million. Meadows instructs his staff to hedge as much as they can. They manage to place £82,000 on bets on Lochangel to win and the SP is driven down to 5/4. Lochangel wins; the hedging has won Meadows £106,000 and reduced his liability to punters by £225,000.

The seventh and final race is due to start at 5.00 pm. Fujiyama Crest had been quoted at 12/1 in the morning. After Lochangel's win Meadows now has

£1.03 million running on to Fujiyama Crest. At 4.35 pm, just after the end of the sixth race, Fujiyama Crest is still being quoted at 4/1. With just twenty-five minutes to go Meadows stands to lose over £5 million if Dettori does the seemingly impossible. Meadows' staff hedge £195,000 with fifteen different bookmakers. Even so the starting price of Fujiyama Crest only drops to 2/1. History is made as Dettori wins. Meadows wins £365,000 on his Fujiyama Crest bets and reduces the company's liabilities to other winners by £220,000. Even so they are just over £4 million down on the day. Overall the large bookmakers lose an estimated £23 million on the day.

Meadows goes home and reflects that if he had not taken any hedging action the losses would have been much greater. (Other bookmakers did not hedge their bets on the last race.) Frankie Dettori goes down in history. And somewhere a punter picks up £25,096 for a £1 bet at starting prices that Dettori will win all seven races at Ascot.

Discussion questions

1. Should bookmakers be allowed to influence the odds in their favour by hedging?

2. Would it be better to have upper limits on payouts to accumulator bets so that they do not exercise a disproportionate influence in bookmakers' calculations?

3. Given that only the bookmakers know how much money is running on to races from accumulator bets is hedging a form of insider trading?

Why gamble on sports?

The reasons why people gamble on the outcome of sports events are, in general, the same as those for participating in many other forms of gambling. The first of these is financial gain, whereby the key feature of placing a bet is the hope of future profit. Most gamblers would state that this is their reason for betting. However, this is not an entirely rational position as only around a quarter of bets actually make a positive return. This may mean that gamblers who say that their motive is financial profit are over-optimistic to the extent of suppressing a response which indicates that they are motivated by other factors.

The second factor is that of intellectual challenge. Here, the idea is that predicting the outcome of a sports event presents a complex problem which requires significant and developed decision-making skills. As a result, a successful or winning bet reinforces the individual's belief in his or her own decision-making ability. Some spread betters may well fall into this category.

Thirdly, gamblers bet for excitement. Sports offer the build-up to the event, the event itself and the finish. As such, losing can be good value for money, in perhaps the same way that an arcade game, which offers no financial return, can also be good value. Televised coverage of sport, slow motion replays and so on can obviously add to the excitement. Betting can add a dimension of excitement either to participating in sport, as in wagering amongst friends playing golf, or in being more active spectators. Gamblers who bet for excitement are often attracted by exotic bets where quite large potential winnings can be gained for small initial stakes.

Fourthly, we can identify social interaction as a motivation for betting. This is clearly not always the case and there are many gamblers who are solitary and private. However, an interest in sports betting can clearly be used to meet others with similar interests. Alternatively some groups with common interests may have a high tendency to gamble. For example nearly half of all male US college athletes (a term taken to mean participants in all sports) gamble on sports. As a possible piece of counter-evidence only 10 per cent of regular sports betters do most of their gambling as part of a syndicate.

These four motivations for betting may form a more productive basis for market segmentation than what betting products there are or what groups of people bet, since there are clear differences in the promotional approaches and marketing communications which might work for different types of punters.

Some evidence for the idea that some gamblers consume betting, that is treat it as entertainment rather than as a form of financial investment, can be found in the existence of 'favourite-longshot bias' in most sports betting markets (an exception seems to be major league baseball in the US where the opposite tendency has been found). This is the tendency for punters to overbet outsiders and underbet short-odds outcomes and favourites in particular. A number of explanations have been suggested. The best known are that some people enjoy a 'flutter' and that punters like to gamble. Sports betters enjoying a flutter tend to bet for the fun of it; they restrict their activity to major events such as the Derby or the Grand National horseraces and rely mainly on luck to generate wins. Here sports betting is a form of occasional entertainment for which people are willing to pay. In the case of liking to gamble, regular punters are more likely to put on a smallish stake with an outside chance of winning a large sum of money than to bet to win small sums of money. This would lead to favourites being underbet. Gamblers who are consuming the activity, that is gambling for reasons other than to make a profit, are often liquidity traders. Such gamblers may have a fixed sum which they are willing to stake and will continue to bet until the stake is exhausted or the time period over which they are active has come to an end or they emerge without having exhausted their stake.

Who gambles?

Nearly half of all betting consumers in the United Kingdom spend an average of less than £5 per month. This includes National Lottery customers (by far the largest category) and occasional punters on big events such as major horseraces. Only about 5 per cent of the adult population spends more than £30 per week on gambling activities. About 20 per cent of the adult population does not gamble at all. Only 11 per cent of the adult population can be classified as regular sports betters, that is those placing a bet more often than once a month. This is a low level of involvement with gambling compared to Australia, where the average weekly spend across the population as a whole is around £3. Comparative figures for the US are complicated by estimates of the level of illegal gambling activity, which range anywhere from $80 billion to $380 billion annually compared to a legal turnover of around $50 billion. With an adult population of 209 million this equates to an annual average expenditure per head of anywhere between $622 and $2,057. At the conservative end of the scale this gives an average weekly expenditure of about £8.50. Even allowing for the fact that the gambling industry is a mainstay of some regional economies in the US, notably Nevada, and that a significant proportion of gambling turnover may be attributable to non-domestic tourists, the comparative data hardly justifies the idea that the British are a nation of gamblers.

The traditional UK regular sports better has been male (well over twice as many men as women bet regularly), aged over 45, works in a manual or semi-manual occupation and probably lives in the north of England or Scotland. The children have left home (empty nesters) or he has had no children. He places fairly straightforward bets on horseracing usually at a betting shop but sometimes on-course, that is at the racecourse. Such people are not from the higher income groups. The only upside to this customer profile is that this age group is still increasing in size and that such punters are inherently conservative in their betting behaviour. The traditional off-course punter still bets predominantly in betting shops at the same times as he has always done. For such punters there is a betting shop culture into which they have become socialised and which gives them a sense of familiarity and stability. The downsides are clear, at least if you happen to be a bookmaker. However, the pattern is different for newer forms of sports betting such as online betting.

The internet sports better still tends to be male but there the comparison ends. In a 2001 Mintel survey of online betting more people in the 18–24 age bracket said that the thought of being able to gamble from home was appealing than in any other age group. Two-thirds of actual or potential online betters are aged between 18 and 44. The reasons would appear to be fairly obvious, greater awareness of online technology (mainly the internet and iDTV, interactive digital television) and the generally poor image of betting shops. The higher socio-economic groups are also more comfortable with carrying out financial transactions online and those in full-time employment with less time for leisure activities find online betting a useful option. However, the overall market share of online betting is still small, probably under 10 per cent, but is growing rapidly as punters become more familiar with the technology and because the proportion of stakes returned to punters as winnings tends to be higher. This is for two reasons. Firstly, the operating costs of suppliers in the online betting industry are lower than those for conventional operators and, secondly, online betting often gives opportunities for tax avoidance (and possibly evasion) since the punter may be placing bets with an off-shore operator who can legitimately operate from a location where the total tax burden is lowest.

An interesting but unresearched and therefore unanswered question is whether or not sports betters are also participants in, or spectators of, sports *per se*. At one end of the scale there will be those who are gamblers first and foremost but for whom sports betting is the preferred vehicle for gambling. Such punters will only attend sporting events either because the tax regime for on-course (or at-event) gambling is more favourable, as has been the case in the United Kingdom and still is in many other countries, or there is useful information to be gained, for example the look of a horse just before a race. At the other end of the scale there will be sports fans for whom a casual bet is part of the entertainment package. In between there will be a range of other possibilities. Overall, however, there does not seem to be any convincing evidence to support the hypothesis that sports betting and paying to watch sports events, whether in person or on pay-TV, are strong complementary goods.

Betting markets

Betting markets are a particular form of financial markets. In all financial markets, for example those for stocks and shares, there is concern to ensure that they operate fairly, openly and efficiently. Where stock markets are concerned it is easy to see why this should be the case. There would clearly be little incentive for investors to make their savings available to markets, and take financial risks in so doing, if they thought that markets were not fair. When we remember that very large numbers of people are indirect investors via pension funds, life insurance policies and the like we can see the importance of markets operating fairly, openly and efficiently. If they did not do so small investors would not make the funds available to markets and firms would not be able to raise funds to expand. The same is true in sports betting markets. Punters will not bet if they believe that markets are 'rigged' in some way so that some group of people 'in the know' has an unfair advantage and will end up winning more than their fair share of the money. We can understand how sports betting markets operate by considering Figure 18.1.

Figure 18.1 shows the system for bookmaking. The important feature to note is that money flows around the system in one direction whilst information flows in the opposite direction. We are here taking bets as a source of information since the bet consists of the particular eventuality being bet upon as well as the amount of money staked. It is this which the bookmaker records and forms one source of information to allow him to conduct his business. Clearly if we remove the information flows, or they are distorted in any way, the market can no longer function or will function unfairly.

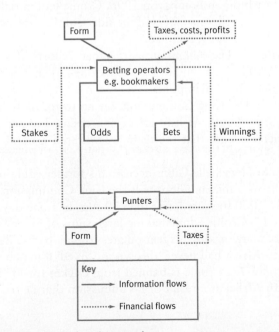

Figure 18.1 **Flows in the sports betting market**

CASE 18.2   The Hansie Cronje scandal

April 2000: Delhi Police reveal they have a recording of a conversation on a mobile phone during the one-day series between India and South Africa in March. It is alleged that the taped voices are of South Africa captain Hansie Cronje and a representative of an Indian betting syndicate.

The voice alleged to be Cronje's divulges information about the team, including a suggestion that off-spinner Derek Crookes would open the bowling later in the series. The two individuals also agree Herschelle Gibbs should not score more than 20 runs.

Cronje brought himself on first change and bowled 10 overs for 69 and Gibbs scored 19 in the third match in Faridabad. Crookes opened the bowling in the final match.

Crookes later admitted his astonishment at being asked to open. He conceded 53 runs in six overs.

Cronje strenuously denies all allegations on April 7 and 9.

April 11: Cronje calls Ali Bacher (head of the South African cricket board) at 0300 to inform him he had not been 'entirely honest' about his comments of two days ago.

He admits to having accepted between US$10,000 to US$15,000 from a London-based bookmaker, for 'forecasting' results, not match-fixing.

April 15: Doubts now surround England's victory in the last Test at Centurion, where Cronje took the unexpected step of forfeiting an innings.

April 16: It is revealed that South Africa came closer than originally believed to accepting a $250,000 bribe to 'throw' (i.e. intentionally lose) a one-off international against India in Bombay in 1996. Cronje had initially said the team 'laughed it off'. However, other members of the side said the offer was discussed in three team meetings before being declined.

April 17: The *Guardian* newspaper reports that Cronje allegedly accepted an £85,000 bribe as an advance to fix one-day matches in India, according to evidence obtained by Indian police.

June 7: The King Commission, set up to formally investigate allegations of match-fixing by South African cricketers, opens. Former South African Test spinner Pat Symcox alleges that the team was offered around $250,000 (£150,000) to lose a one-day game.

June 8: Herschelle Gibbs accuses his former captain Cronje of offering him a bribe to throw a match. Gibbs tells the King Commission he had agreed to Cronje's offer of $15,000 to score fewer than 20 runs in a one-day match in India earlier this year.

June 15: Cronje admits taking large sums of money for giving information to bookmakers and asking his team-mates to play badly. But he tells the King Commission South Africa had never 'thrown' or 'fixed' a match under his captaincy.

October 11: Cronje is banned from cricket for life by the United Cricket Board of South Africa as a result of his admission that he received money from bookmakers.

Discussion questions

4. How do instances such as this damage the sports betting industry?

5. What steps would you recommend might be taken to eliminate such practices?

6. Should the cricket authorities ban betting on cricket?

Are sports betting markets fair and efficient?

So what do we mean by saying that betting markets are fair and efficient? The efficient market hypothesis (EMH) states that:

Prices fully and instantaneously reflect all available and relevant information.

Thus betting odds are correct signals in the sense that they fully and instantaneously reflect all relevant information and direct the flow of funds from punters to bets yielding the highest returns. Intermediaries (for example bookmakers) performing the service of channelling funds from punters to 'bets' do so at the minimum cost, which provides a fair return for their services, that is, there is what economists call operational efficiency in the market.

What do we mean by 'all prices fully and instantaneously reflect all relevant information'? Is there some rule or set of tests we could follow?

It is conventional to lay down three alternative criteria.

1. *Weak-form efficiency*
   No punter can earn excess returns from betting rules based on historical price or returns information, e.g. computerised results services.
2. *Semi-strong efficiency*
   No punter can earn excess returns from betting rules based on any publicly available information, e.g. form guides, betting systems sold on the internet, etc.
3. *Strong-form efficiency*
   No punter can earn excess returns using any information whether publicly available or not, e.g. insider information.

The words 'excess returns' are important here. These do not imply that a punter cannot make any return but it is limited to a fair return to:

- exercise of skill;
- risk taken;
- capital employed;
- effort put into obtaining information.

So professional punters might still be able to make a living through their efforts by developing skill in interpreting form and other information, undertaking research and maintaining substantial cash floats (working capital) to enable them to withstand runs of losses. The question is whether or not the amount they make by undertaking betting effectively as a job makes them any more money than using their talents and resources in some other way.

If betting markets are weak-form efficient then punters who exploit their (hard-gained) knowledge should make a reasonable living. If betting markets are semi-strong-form efficient there are only profits to be made from insider dealing, that is by exploiting information that is not made public and that only close insiders have access to. Examples of inside information might be that a particular player was not 100 per cent fit or about to be traded or, indeed, that a certain bowler will feature more strongly than normal in a cricket match. If strong-form efficiency holds then only normal returns can ever be made but note that big money moving fast would still result in large (but not excessive) profits and short-term gains are possible (via luck for example).

There are, in general terms, two types of analysis which punters can undertake in order to improve their chances of winning. Fundamental analysis seeks to forecast outcomes by studying playing systems, strengths and weaknesses of participants, skill gaps, etc. Technical analysis attempts to forecast the return by searching for patterns in past performance. Even weak-form efficiency rules out success via technical analysis. Semi-strong efficiency rules out success via studying form and undertaking other types of fundamental analysis.

So can some punters beat the market? This is not just a matter of testing an elegant theory for it is obviously important that betting is seen to be a 'fair game'. If it were widely known that a few professional gamblers or insiders were creaming off the market then it would be very difficult to persuade average punters to bet. In this case the market would only consist of 'professionals' and insiders and the advantages of being one would disappear. Of course, if everyone (or everyone who is interested and cares to find out) has inside knowledge then that information is public and hence no longer 'inside'. At first this sounds odd but inside information really only is inside information if the general public does not believe such information exists or that, if it exists, it is of any use. There are major problems with testing the EMH. The most obvious one is that if anyone could beat the market then they would have no incentive to give away or even sell the secret to anyone else. If the market is semi-strong-form efficient then it would be possible to exploit insider information to make a profit. But insider information, by definition, is a secret shared by the few. On the other hand if it was possible to make money out of the analysis of past results, that is the betting market was not even weak-form efficient, the formula would soon become known.

The future

In this final section we look at three broad influences on the future of the sports betting industry: technological change, deregulation and globalisation. Whilst it is helpful for the purposes of presentation to distinguish the three they are intimately intertwined in their effects on the industry.

Technological change has had two broad effects on sports betting. Firstly, it has gradually allowed greater and greater spatial separation of the better from the other party to the betting transaction (the bookmaker or fellow wagerer or pool operator), and secondly, it has reduced the time necessary to complete the complex calculations needed to operate the business.

Recall James Weatherby holding the stake for two rivals wagering on the result of a horseracing match around 1770. In this situation the only available technology probably required that all three parties to the business were present at the location of the match when it took place. Indeed in the United Kingdom only on-course betting was legal before 1961. The development of television and, in particular, televised sports events made much more sense of off-course betting since it was no longer essential to attend the event to see what had happened for yourself. Somewhat strangely, however, televisions were not allowed into LBOs until 1986. The next major step forward was probably the use of the telephone for placing bets. Whilst the telephone is a far from new invention it is only relatively recently that credit card transactions could be authorised quickly over the telephone. This opened up telephone betting to the majority of punters who bet small amounts and for whom, on both sides, it was not worthwhile opening a credit account. The emergence of freephone numbers and the rapidly falling costs of making international calls allowed bookmakers to move their telephone betting operations overseas thus avoiding domestic taxes on gambling such as the UK's General Betting Duty. At one stage off-shore telephone bookmakers were offering to take bets and deduct as little as 3 per cent from winnings to cover costs and profits. Telephone bookmaking rapidly became the preferred option for regular sports betters for simple economic reasons. The development of WAP phones allows punters to access the latest odds and place a bet in a very short space of time; 3G telephones will provide even greater functionality for gamblers. The internet and iDTV have allowed even greater physical separation of the elements of sports betting yet have combined them in one virtual environment. I can now access the latest odds, place a bet, watch an event and verify the winnings being credited to my account at a keystroke or push of a few buttons on my remote control. With split-screen and information streaming technology I can potentially see all three (the odds, the event and the state of my account) at the same time. I can even place spontaneous bets during an event, for example who will win a tie-break during a tennis match or whether a penalty kick will result in a goal. And, of course, I can bet on any sporting event anywhere in the world. Put succinctly the development of digital technologies has expanded the available channels of distribution for betting and the range of products on offer. Indeed betting may be the ideal eCommerce product because there is no physical distribution requirement. Datamonitor estimates that the western European online betting market will be worth approximately six billion euros by 2005. A Merrill Lynch report is even more upbeat, suggesting that the UK market alone could be worth £10 billion by 2005.

The invention of the first totalisator machine in Australia in 1913 is a somewhat understated event in the development of sports betting. Firstly, it made pool betting a reality and, secondly, it was the start of the trend to ever faster calculation of returns to gambling, transactions handling and management of very complex bets. The application of the modern Tote to greyhound racing in the United Kingdom is a good example. Modern greyhound racing stadia are predominantly dining and entertainment venues. The product, for the occasional consumer, is the opportunity to watch live greyhound racing from the comfort of a restaurant whilst being able to place small, often multiple bets. Races occur with sufficient frequency (every twenty minutes is common) to retain the interest. It is also important that all bets can be placed and all winnings paid out in this twenty-minute gap without either rushing the customers or making them wait too long. This has only been made possible with the development of affordable, reliable, high-speed but localised computing. A more futuristic idea has iDTV viewers around the world placing bets on a sporting jackpot worldwide. This could be on a set of horseraces occurring in different countries in the same time period, a few hours say, or on a set of major events across the world over a long time period.

Deregulation has, in part, been pushed along by technological changes. However, ethical and social influences have also played their part. In broad terms pool betting, including lotteries, has been generally socially acceptable in many countries, though not, of course in the Islamic world. For example, bookmaking is still only allowed on-course in Australia, but their version of pool betting, known as the TAB, has wider distribution than the Tote in the United Kingdom with TAB machines placed in bars and clubs. In the United Kingdom off-course bookmaking was widespread but illegal before 1961, when the government of the day decided to legalise betting shops and, unsurprisingly perhaps, tax off-course bets. Since 1961 there have been successive tranches of deregulation of LBOs although the United Kingdom has not yet reached the point of permitting sports betting entertainment complexes of the type common in Japan. Even so, social acceptability of gambling in general has been improved by the National Lottery.

Deregulation was again forced on the UK government when technological change allowed betting to take place off-shore. This made taxes on gambling avoidable and prompted UK bookmakers to move the non-traditional elements of their business to low-tax overseas locations such as Gibraltar and Malta. The eventual response was to shift the tax base from an excise duty collected when the bet was struck to a gross profits tax. This brought all business struck with UK-owned bookmakers back into the tax base. However, it also amounted to a very significant reduction in the tax rate. The legalisation of off-course betting and the abolition of General Betting Duty are both examples of governments deciding that it is better to regulate and benefit from gambling than outlaw or tax it too heavily.

An inevitable result of applying a borderless technology within a successively deregulated environment is to create a globalised industry. The only real inhibitor to this trend where sports betting is concerned would seem to be the nature of sport itself. There are relatively few global sports on which betting can take place. Baseball and American football are not widely exported; soccer is not a major sport in North America. Formula 1 motor racing does have global coverage but has not excited a great deal of betting interest. Horseracing seems to be the most universal of sports and in many ways is an ideal betting vehicle. It also occurs sufficiently frequently and in great enough volume to provide a constant stream of events on which bets can be taken, books made and pools operated. However, horseracing is not a sport of choice of many young consumers.

Conclusion

Table 18.3 provides a comparison of the characteristics of traditional and online sports betting markets. As such it serves as a summary of this chapter. However, the final row of the table still leaves some important questions open. How are the links between sports betting and the sports industry in general changing as the sports betting business model changes from traditional to online? In the past the relationship was often dominated by that between the bookmakers and horseracing. In countries

Table 18.3 Characteristics of traditional and online sports betting industry

Market characteristic	Traditional sports betting	Online sports betting
Products	Simple bets mainly win only and each way.	Complex and varied. Accumulators and exotic bets common.
Production system	Labour intensive, low technology.	Capital intensive, high technology.
Customers	Male, older, lower-income groups. Tend to be conservative in their betting habits.	Male, younger, higher-income groups. More willing to try new products.
Distribution	On-course betting. Physical retailing via LBOs.	Internet, iDTV, telephone.
Betting vehicles	Predominantly horseracing and football via the Pools.	Horseracing has largest share but a much wider range of sports available for betting. Football betting rapidly growing.
Payment means	Mainly cash with some credit bookmaking for approved customers.	Credit cards and other forms of electronic payment.
Industry structure	Highly concentrated with a long tail of small independent bookmakers. Statutory monopoly of pool betting in many countries.	Traditional bookmakers still major force (brick and click model) but successful new entrants emerging among online pure plays. A long tail of small traditional and internet operators.
Markets	Mainly regional (as in US) or national (as in UK).	Most major operators are global.
Location of operators	Close to markets.	Can be anywhere so countries with most favourable tax and regulatory regimes serious contenders even if they have no domestic betting market.
Regulatory regime	Generally strict, betting tolerated and usually heavily taxed.	Has to be more liberal as operators and customers are both footloose.
Links to sports	Some cooperation required to ensure flow of betting vehicles, for example links between football leagues and pools operators and horseracing and bookmakers.	Market driven; excess supply of betting opportunities.

where off-course betting was allowed, such as the United Kingdom and Ireland, the bookmaking industry needed a constant flow of betting-friendly races in order to feed the LBOs. In general this required racecourses to put on meetings which were unprofitable since there was not the volume of on-course customer demand to sustain them. The solution to this problem was for bookmakers to subsidise horseracing. The mechanism for this was the Levy, effectively a hypothecated tax on betting which was distributed in the interests of racing by a statutory body, the Horseracing Betting Levy

Board. Similar arrangements operate in some other parts of the world. In some other countries the horseracing and betting industries are operated in a much more integrated way; Japan is an example.

In the online world betting operators can source their betting vehicles from anywhere. If there is not enough UK racing available, and that which was put on specifically to feed the bookmakers was of fairly low quality on occasion, then why not use US or South African racing? Both are broadcast in English so language problems are not at issue. Indeed the dedicated iDTV channel 'attheraces' does rely heavily on US product. Clearly there still needs to be some kind of relationship between betting and sports. However, this is much more likely to be driven by individual cooperation based on mutual gain rather than collective arrangements whether backed up by law or not. Thus in the United Kingdom the relationship between horseracing and bookmakers is shifting towards bilateral agreements between bookmakers and racecourses.

CASE 18.3 Betting on internet exchanges   FT

Ten minutes before the first race at the 2002 Cheltenham national hunt festival in March, a punter wanted to put £80,000 on a horse at better odds than those displayed. Even at the biggest betting meeting of the year the most resilient of on-course bookmakers would balk at such a risk. But the bet was quickly matched; not by a bookie but by 109 people who had signed into Betfair, an internet-based 'betting exchange'.

Why is this significant for the future of the internet and indeed for commerce as a whole? Because the people who picked up the risk were – for the most part – not professional bookmakers but individuals who had been brought together for this one-off project of 'laying', or taking, the bet – that is, backing their judgement that the horse would lose.

Betfair, by far the most successful betting exchange, is sending violent tremors through the UK bookmaking industry (restrictions in other countries make this a predominantly British and Irish phenomenon). Traditional bookmakers are increasingly insistent that such exchanges be controlled, while most punters and racing commentators and at least some bookies see them as a new source of entertainment and liquidity. Betfair has gone from start-up in mid-2000 to a turnover of £50 million a week in matched bets; next month it expects its turnover to outstrip that of Coral, one of the 'big three' UK bookmakers. It has been profitable since early 2002.

But its significance goes well beyond its own industry. Betfair is a post-bubble dotcom that is demonstrating that the internet can be used to create profitable new business models when imagination is combined with rigorous execution. It also shows that a commercial peer-to-peer model – where people do business with one another rather than through an intermediary – has great potential.

The auction site eBay created a whole new breed of hobby traders; now the betting exchanges are busy breeding hobby bookmakers. Andrew Black, co-founder of Betfair, has conceived a commodity trading system based on the same platform. The question now is how much further the model can be taken.

Mr Black, a former derivatives pricing modeller and professional gambler, started work on his platform in 1998. The bookmakers, led by William Hill and Ladbrokes, had already grasped the importance of the internet but they used it as an extra channel, not to change their business model. Mr Black was one of several people who believed that the eBay model could be adapted to betting; what set him apart was the rigour he brought to it.

The concept of an exchange is simple. The horses in a race are listed on a website (though other sports are covered, horseracing dominates). Registered users deposit funds and bet for or against a horse at a price they fancy. The site matches the betters and layers: if one person wants to bet on Slow Trotter at 20:1 and another wants to bet against it – by taking a bet at that price – they are paired off. This is much like eBay but with bets replacing trombones and the other merchandise found there.

Betfair missed the eCommerce funding frenzy and had to launch on a scraped-together £1 million budget. This was partly because funds had been committed to Flutter.com, which also launched in summer 2000.

Yet in December 2001 Betfair bought Flutter. The reason, says Betfair's communications director Mark Davies, was that Mr Black had spotted a crucial difference between bets and trombones.

Where Flutter insisted on a one-to-one match between punters and layers, Betfair aggregated bets to create pools of liquidity: betters and layers could dip into that pool without having to find an exact counterparty. Mr Davies says its software is similar to that of SETS, the London Stock Exchange system that also allows partial matching.

Betfair has attracted sophisticated punters, who like the fact that they can often get better odds than they can at a bookmakers. This, though, is where Betfair runs into trouble with the established industry. Betfair takes between 2 per cent and 5 per cent commission on every bet but its members are often prepared to lay bets at a price bookies cannot match. There are peripheral reasons for this: the layer will not pay tax unless he is a professional and has negligible overheads. But the main reason, Mr Davies says, is that Betfair layers 'will express a view and take a risk'. They do not need, as a bookie does, to run a book on the whole field and add a 15 to 20 per cent margin. 'We are squeezing margins,' he says. 'But that's good for the punter.'

The big bookmakers have a series of complaints about exchanges such as Betfair but their central argument is that anyone who lays a bet without being licensed is, under the 1963 Betting Act, breaking the law.

'I would like the Department for Culture, Media and Sport to inform Betfair that layers should have to have permits and if necessary there should be a prosecution,' says Tom Kelly, director-general of the Betting Office Licensees Association. John Brown, executive chairman of William Hill, last month accused the government of a 'dereliction of duty' in failing to come down hard on exchanges.

In other words, the majors are attacking exchanges for their main selling point, their ability to convert 'ordinary people' into 'business people'. Mr Davies disputes the illegality on a point of the Act's wording but acknowledges that it is good wallet-fattening fare for lawyers. 'Our barristers say we are right; their barristers say they are right,' he says.

More important, he says, is that most of the protection the Betting Act seeks to give punters is built into Betfair's *modus operandi*. It is impossible to lay a bet without having sufficient funds, deposited in a third-party trust account, to cover maximum liability. It is also impossible to bet without a credit card, which creates an audit trail that cash betting cannot match. As for crooked trainers or owners betting against their own horses – well, yes, but they have always been able to do that; and they are more likely to be identified through the audit trail.

Mr Kelly says he does not want to close exchanges down: 'I take my hats off to the guys who thought of them.' But he insists that the law would make it possible to restrict laying to licensed bookmakers.

The essence of all these arguments lies in Betfair's belief that technology has out-grown current legal structures and that it is therefore better to wait until a new regime, expected to include a new gambling commission, comes into force in 2004. They also reflect the industry's belief that even this period of assault from the exchanges would be too long. 'I'm not looking two or three years ahead on this one,' Mr Kelly says. 'My concern is the interim period.'

The big bookmakers are certainly worried about the threat to their margins. But while the argument is more complex than that of David taking on self-serving Goliath, they do have a big public relations problem: letters to the *Racing Post* run at least 10 to one in favour of betting exchanges. Established bookmakers could take legal action against Betfair (as the music industry did against another new internet model, the file-sharing site Napster). But they would be brave to risk the derision of much of the sporting world – almost as brave as the government would be if it decided to take action against a popular and disruptive newcomer.

Source: David Bowen, *Financial Times*, 26 September 2002

Discussion questions

7. What role do online exchanges such as Betfair play in the sports industry, and what management issues does this imply for the successful operation of such a site?

8. Companies such as Betfair currently represent a major threat to conventional forms of sports betting. Evaluate the various strategies and tactics a company like Betfair could employ to ensure they maintain a competitive advantage over their rivals.

Discussion questions

9. Should sports betting companies pay sports event owners for the right to offer odds on the outcomes of events?

10. Why should governments be concerned about the rise of internet sports betting?

11. Can the sports betting market ever be global if sports themselves are not global?

Guided reading

Probably the best way to keep up with market trends in sports betting is to read the regular Mintel Reports on gambling and betting. These occur under a number of titles but the most obvious ones are 'Sports Betting' and 'Online Betting'. Datamonitor also provides regular reports and forecasts of trends.

Journal articles on gambling have tended to concentrate on three major areas, the social consequences of gambling (including addiction), whether or not gambling markets exhibit fairness under the EMH definitions and the consequences of regulation and taxation. Sports betting is often only mentioned as a small component of the gambling industry. The majority of journal articles are of American origin. However, Williams (1999) provides a useful summary of the debate on efficiency in betting markets and deregulation is accessibly discussed by Neal (1999).

Other useful sources are Bruce and Johnson (1992) and Sauer (2001). For online betting see Jones et al. (2000) and Paton et al. (2002).

Recommended websites

Spread Betting Guide: http://www.spread-betting-guide.co.uk
University of Nevada Gaming Internet Resources:
http://library.nevada.edu/subjects/gaming_internet.html
Betfair: http://www.betfair.com

Visit www.booksites.net/chadwickbeech for links to these and other relevant websites.

Keywords

Betting exchange; bookmaking; complex bet; efficient market hypothesis (EMH); pool betting; spread betting; staple bet; wagering.

Bibliography

Bruce, A.C. and Johnson, J.E.V. (1992) 'Toward an explanation of betting as a leisure pursuit', *Leisure Studies*, 11(11), pp. 201–18.

Jones, Peter, Clarke-Hill, Colin M. and Hillier, David (2000) 'Viewpoint: back street to high street to e-street: sporting betting on the internet', *International Journal of Retail & Distribution Management*, 28(6), 222–7.

Neal, Mark (1999) 'The ongoing effects of deregulation on betting shop customer profile and behaviour', *Managing Leisure*, 4, pp. 168–84.

Paton, David, Siegel, Donald S. and Williams, Leighton Vaughan (2002) 'A policy response to the e-commerce revolution: the case of betting taxation in the UK', *The Economic Journal*, 112 (June), F296–F314.

Sauer, Raymond D. (2001) 'The political economy of gambling regulation', *Managerial and Decision Economics*, 22(1), 5–15.

Williams, Leighton Vaughan (1999) 'Information efficiency in betting markets: a survey', *Bulletin of Economic Research*, 51(1), 1–30.

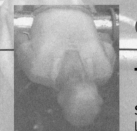

Chapter 19

The future for sport businesses

Simon Chadwick
Leeds University Business School

'Taking the TV concept of I'm a Celebrity Get Me Out of Here! *to its logical conclusion, [former featherweight boxing champion Ruben Olivares] is selling the broadcasting rights to his own funeral.'*

Mitchell, 2002

Upon completion of this chapter the reader should be able to:

■ explain the nature of a variety of techniques sport businesses can use to predict the future;

■ identify sources of information available to sport businesses seeking to predict the future;

■ identify emerging trends and challenges facing sport businesses;

■ indicate what strategies sport businesses could implement in the light of emerging trends and challenges;

■ highlight the potential implications for students, academics and practitioners who read this book.

Overview

The chapter is intended to serve three main purposes: it examines a variety of techniques sport businesses can use to forecast the future, it considers emerging trends and challenges that are impacting upon sport businesses, and it subsequently addresses some of the ways in which sport businesses could respond. The success of such responses is often based upon an ability to predict the future. The chapter therefore begins by examining the techniques that are available to sport managers seeking to identify a range of possible futures facing their businesses. An important dimension in the credibility of these techniques is the quality of the information used. Hence, the chapter goes on to highlight several key sources available to sport managers. A number of key generic emerging trends and challenges are then considered from the perspective of four groups:

- sport businesses;
- participants;
- resource providers and business partners;
- fans and customers.

In turn, a general examination of the responses sport businesses could take, and are taking, in response to the trends and challenges is provided. To illustrate some of these, the chapter considers three cases: the global expansion of the World Wrestling Entertainment brand, Ericsson's sponsorship of the America's Cup yacht race, and the growth of sports stars claiming payment for the use of their image rights. The chapter concludes with a commentary upon the likely impact of the book *The Business of Sport Management*.

Introduction

It seems strange that goalkeepers once had to pick up coins thrown at them during football matches because they were so poorly paid. In the same vein, the distinctions between professionals and amateurs in rugby and 'gentlemen' and 'players' in cricket, and the notion that sport is confined simply to on-field competition, are anathema to many of those involved in sport businesses today. When football clubs are more like leisure businesses selling their shares on the stock market, when motor racing drivers can earn upwards of £30 million per season, when 500 million people or more can watch a sporting event on television and the internet, when boxers sell the television rights to their own funerals, you know sport is changing.

Just as those involved in sport one hundred years ago would probably struggle to come to terms with what has happened, it is just as difficult for us to imagine what might happen in the next one hundred, fifty, ten, even five, years. Yet such are the on-field and off-field commercial pressures now facing sport businesses that ignoring the future is not an option. If a sport business is to be successful, it must address the challenges it faces and implement appropriate strategies in response. The question is, in a rapidly changing environment where sport businesses need to think about team performance on the field and financial performance off it, and where there is a natural tendency towards short-term thinking about the next game or the next season, how do you predict the long-term future?

Predicting the future

The English economist John Maynard Keynes once said that, in the long run, we are all dead. In this respect, the future is both inevitable and predictable. However, the practice of predicting what might happen in the meantime is rather less precise. When Delpy and Bosetti (1998) anticipated a growth in the use of the internet by sport businesses, they probably did not realise how important the medium would become. Alternatively, when Chris Akers – then Executive Director of Leeds United Football Club – (1997) announced at a sport conference that he anticipated the massive growth of digital television, he did not know that things would not quite work out as he anticipated.

Trying to predict the future would therefore appear to be a difficult task, although choosing not to think about it potentially stores up problems. Indeed, Glendinning (2001) points out that sport businesses that fail to consider what might happen at a later date are left exposed to all kinds of problems. Not least of these are financial difficulty and, potentially, ultimate closure. As such, sport managers need to consider how they can use a range of business forecasting techniques to help them predict the future. Finlay (2000) distinguishes between two types of predictive technique: forecasting and scenarios. The former focuses on the near and middle future, when existing information can be used as the basis for identifying possible trends and developments. The latter is more frequently used when identifying the long-term future, for which there is no information and no precise indication of what might happen.

A *forecast* can be described as a statement containing projections about the future, and may be undertaken in a number of ways. These include:

- Time-series forecasting, which primarily involves collecting past and current data, and then extrapolating it into the future. For example, if we identify that the salaries of basketball players have increased by 2, 4 and 6 per cent in each of the last three years, we may forecast next year's salary rise to be somewhere in the region of 8 per cent. This form of forecasting is often used, primarily because it utilises existing data and is relatively easy to use as a basis for projection. The biggest problem with the approach is the extent to which the past can help to form an accurate picture of the future.
- Causal forecasting, which takes a similar approach to time-series forecasting by using past and current data as the basis for predicting the future. The main difference is that it uses observations about cause and effect relationships between two or more variables to highlight what might happen in the future when a similar relationship is evident. For example, in the past, when unemployment in a town rose by 5 per cent, it may have been observed that attendances at local rugby matches fell by 2 per cent. In which case, the sport manager might conclude that predictions about rising unemployment over the next year will have a similar impact on match day attendances. As with time-series forecasting, this approach is useful because it is based upon existing data, but it adds elements of previous experience, particularly in relation to the impact that two variables can have on each other. The two main problems with this are the extent to which a past relationship ever really existed between the variables, and whether a continuing association can be assumed to exist in the future.
- Judgemental forecasting is often used where the data needed for a time-series forecast is unavailable, or where there is little experience of a specific set of circumstances. In such cases, experts make judgements based upon their knowledge and experiences. For example, the growing interest in English football in China is such that we might expect the country to become a major export market for branded football club merchandise because the Chinese population is both large and fanatical about football. This is a good technique for building on the competences and specialised knowledge of many sport managers. Many of them will know 'their' sport well, and most will have network contacts who keep them informed about important developments. The main concern is that the technique is largely subjective and, as such, predictions may be inaccurate or biased.

Scenarios are pictures of the future developed by those with an understanding of a business or an industry, and are often used to predict the longer term, that is, a time in the future when past or current data may not be applicable. In such a case, the precise nature of what might happen to a sport business becomes incredibly difficult to pin-point. Scenarios can therefore be used to develop logical and coherent views of the future, where sport managers attempt to establish the way things might turn out. In the case of motor sport, given that tobacco advertising in Europe is due to become illegal, teams are already thinking about likely scenarios: lose revenue and cease to operate; seek alternative forms of sponsorship; continue to be sponsored by a tobacco company, display the name and logo outside Europe, but think creatively about the sponsorship and advertising inside Europe. In this respect, scenarios force sport managers to think about the long term. In turn, this enables them to begin thinking about the likely ramifications of their observations. Nevertheless, although scenarios can be methodically and professionally developed, what will happen in five or ten years time can never really be accurately identified.

There are a number of other techniques that can also be used for generating information about the future, and for making predictions. The former include brainstorming and the Delphi technique, whilst the latter embrace practices such as model building and impact analysis. Brainstorming is a well-established technique involving groups of creative or insightful people meeting to assess future trends. Extending beyond this rather unstructured practice, the Delphi technique is more systematic, where, through an iterative process of discussion, managers reach a consensus about the future. Both techniques are likely to generate qualitative information and may involve observations being made about issues such as the likely future use of the internet by sport managers, or proposals for reforms in sport governance.

This is in contrast to modelling, which often uses sophisticated computer software to generate hard quantitative data. Modelling primarily focuses on identifying trends and patterns, and involves making predictions based upon the influence of a number of key variables that are input into the software by managers. For example, when planning a service delivery process, sport managers should be able to generate a computer-based model of the process which can identify the impact of, say, a rise in the cost of producing merchandise, a fall in demand for tickets, maybe even the impact of rain on an event or competition. *Impact analysis* may also use computer software, but may equally rely on qualitative data analysis. For events such as the Olympic Games or the Rally of Great Britain, forecasters regularly attempt to identify the impact these events will have on local and national economies.

Sources of information

The techniques noted above are never going to generate a completely accurate picture of the future. Yet the sport manager will still need to ensure that forecasts are as close as possible to what, ultimately, might actually happen. Clearly, the use of a technique such as modelling demands a high level of statistical competence on the part of those using it. Similarly, whilst Delphi is widely used by managers across industry, it nevertheless requires them to have a detailed understanding of their industrial sector. A consideration common to all forecasting techniques therefore is the quality of information fed into the forecasting process. Unless sport managers have accurate information about trends and patterns, they can never convincingly construct a time-series analysis. Nor, if they work uninformed, can they expect to make authoritative judgements about the future state of their sport. The way in which information is gathered and analysed is therefore fundamental not only to forecasting, but also to a general understanding of how different sports are changing.

There are two types of information that can be used to assist in the forecasting process: that gathered from primary sources (information collected specifically for the purpose of the forecast), and that from secondary sources (information collected for another reason but which may be used for the purposes of forecasting). Saunders *et al.* (2003) provide a good overview of the differences between the two sources of information, and discuss some of the advantages associated with each. For a more detailed commentary on the specific sources of information available to sport managers, Scarrott (1999) is an excellent resource.

Emerging trends and challenges

Illustrating what the emerging trends and challenges for sport businesses will be over the next five to ten years is an immense task. Some of the trends and challenges are already becoming evident, the consideration of others will require reflection on the part of the reader. It is hoped this chapter enables readers to undertake the latter in a more structured and focused way. In doing this, readers should remember that the book deals with a range of issues in a highly discrete way: a marketing chapter, an operations chapter, an ethics chapter, and so on. The reality of managing a sport business is rather more complicated. Hence, the emerging challenges and trends noted in Table 19.1 are expected to transcend business functions and impinge upon all aspects of sport businesses' operations. For example, if there are changes in customer service expectations, this has obvious implications for sport marketing. But it can also influence human resource management by imposing the need to recruit the right staff, to train and develop them, and to motivate them to provide excellent customer service.

Ultimately, the reader will have to distinguish the relevant from the irrelevant, and this presumably will be driven by the nature of the sport business in which the reader works. A good illustration of this is the increase in legal actions taken by sports participants affected by 'on-field' incidents. Clearly, this is potentially a huge challenge for the managers of businesses involved in contact sports like rugby and wrestling. But it is likely to be of less concern for those involved in tennis and darts. In this context, the reader is expected to use Table 19.1 as a resource, a decision-making tool or a guide to the future. The table is split into four sections – sport businesses, participants, resource providers and sport business partners, fans and customers – with a range of potential developments being noted in each case. To support these observations, a number of examples and cases are provided. A range of strategic responses to these trends and challenges is presented in the next section.

Table 19.1 Emerging trends and challenges in sport

Group	Developments	Related examples
Sport businesses e.g. ice hockey club, speedway event	**Changing nature of the sport product** Is the sport product something which is related only to on-field activity? To what extent are sport businesses becoming multi-product leisure brands? What part will broadcasting play in augmenting and promoting the sport product? **Globalisation** Are globalisation and industrial concentration inextricably linked? Will globalisation inevitably lead to the homogenisation of the sport product? What are the management implications for sport businesses moving towards global operations? **Commercial development of sports businesses** To what extent will profit and the exploitation of revenue streams conflict with the needs of supporters? Will governing bodies and governments step in to regulate the commercial development of sports businesses?	Case 19.1 (see also Benz, 2001). Following its flotation on the London Stock Exchange in 1996, Chelsea football club has engaged in developing its product portfolio and extending the club brand. The club now consists of businesses including a travel company, hotel and night-club. Chelsea also sells around 3,000 product lines in its club shops.
Participants e.g. tennis player, football team	**Image rights** How can participants exploit the commercial value of their images? How can participants protect the exploitation of their image rights from organisations to which they are not contracted? What protection is offered under the terms of the human rights legislation? **Role of agents and representatives** What role does an agent or representative fulfil? To what extent do they distract a player from their on-field activities? To what extent do they ensure that participants receive an appropriate share of revenues generated by sport businesses? **Litigation** If a participant is injured during a game, what might the impact be on his or her earnings potential? What legal redress will the participant have under domestic and international law? Is there a need to draw additional protection from insurance companies, unions and sport businesses?	Case 19.2 (see also Wheatley, 2002). In the run-up to the 2003 ICC trophy, cricketers were asked to sign a contract with the organisers agreeing to hand over the rights to use their images. The organisers felt the players' personal sponsorship deals might conflict with tournament sponsorship deals. A number of top players, most notably those playing for the Indian team, refused, claiming individual freedom to control the use of their images. At one stage, it was suggested several players would boycott the tournament and take legal action (Dickson, 2002).
Resource providers and sport business partners e.g. sponsor, kit supplier	**Strategic considerations** How can an involvement in sport, such as through sponsorship or technical partnering, add value to a business? To what extent can the benefits of such relationships go beyond marketing and brand association? How should	Case 19.3 (see also Dickson, 1999). In November 2002, Ford signed an agreement to market and promote the CART motor racing series in America. As well as the obvious marketing benefits associated with the deal, the sponsorship has enabled Ford to establish

such relationships be managed to ensure the mutual achievement of maximum benefit?

Cost of securing sports property rights

If the market for sports property rights continues to concentrate, how should resource providers compete for the relatively small number of attractive properties? What can they do to ensure the rights to attractive properties are secured? How should companies measure the cost-effectiveness of securing the rights to exclusive properties?

Exclusivity and control

How can a partner, such as a sponsor or official supplier, ensure exclusivity? What should a partner do to ensure he or she is able to leverage the maximum value from an association with a sport business? In cases where a number of organisations may be seeking to partner with a sport business, what can a company do to build loyalty and long-term durable relationships?

exclusive control over the engines used in the series. Moreover, the company will benefit from a technical partnering arrangement attached to the sponsorship (Barrand, 2002).

Fans and customers
e.g. match day customers, merchandise purchasers

Changing social and leisure trends

To what extent will sport remain popular in the context of proliferating expenditure choices? How will expectations about the sport product change? Will customers come to perceive sport as a virtual experience or will the live experience have an enduring appeal?

Service expectations

With customers placing a growing emphasis on service quality, will sport businesses/ should sport businesses be able to resist the trend? If sport businesses are to develop a service culture, what measures will need to be applied to their operations? Should sport businesses fail to respond to expectations about service quality, will the appeal of sport be undermined?

Market fragmentation

With the fragmentation of markets and the onset of tailored services, will those sport businesses that succeed be more flexible and responsive to the needs of specific groups of customers? Should sport businesses acknowledge the relevance of market segmentation, and work to tailor their products in response? To what extent will the need to tailor services, accompanied by the potential homogenisation of provision that has become evident in other industrial sectors, create tensions for sport businesses?

Tapp (Tapp and Clowes, 2002) indicates football clubs can no longer view their customers as a homogenised mass, and they should begin to tailor services and products. This is based on a view that the sport market place consists of a number of different customer segments. These segments will differ according to, for example, the number of times customers attend a game, how much they spend in a club store, whether they prefer entertainment before, during or after a game, and the information a customer will demand from a club.

The move towards satisfying service and quality expectations is already becoming evident in European football. Glendinning (2002) reports on a new licensing system currently being put in place to support the Euro 2004 and 2008 football championships. The standards are intended to improve the internal organisation and structure of football, whilst ensuring tournaments meet the needs of local communities and global customers.

Strategies and responses

The emerging challenges mentioned in the last section may ultimately revolutionise the sport industry, they may become part of the day-to-day activities of every sport business across the world, or they may simply be fads and fashions that disappear without trace. Just as it is difficult to know how they will develop, it is equally unclear how sport businesses should respond to them. There will be a range of strategies that emerge for dealing with the trends becoming evident over the next five to ten years. The information presented in Table 19.2 provides an indication of strategies through which each of the four groupings mentioned above might be able to manage the challenges they face. These are based on practices becoming evident in a number of sport businesses that could be said to be creating precedents. But what might be relevant to one sport business may be wholly inappropriate for another; what gives direction and focus to one sport business may complicate things for another. It is therefore left to the reader to read this book, consider the content of this chapter, address the review questions at the end of the chapter, and then decide how to manage the business within which they might work.

Table 19.2 Responses to future challenges and scenarios

Group	Potential strategies	Possible scenarios
Sport businesses	Sport businesses will increasingly engage in the diversification and development of product portfolios; this will embrace brand building and brand extension, and the extension of sport business franchises; there will be a greater need to engage in the assessment of new market opportunities; in turn, sport businesses will have to address how to stimulate market development and gain access to new markets; sport businesses will move from being single-product sports clubs to multi-product sport and leisure businesses. Strategic collaboration with business partners and customers will be the vehicle through which business and market development will take place; this will involve identifying opportunities for working with business partners for reasons including cost minimisation, resource acquisition and strategic gain. For reasons of exclusivity and commercial value, sport businesses will seek to control the commercial activities of players; they will need to develop systems for rewarding/compensating participants when they cede control of commercial properties associated with their names. Developing managerial competence in activities such as operations	In order to increase their market share in the growing sport leisure business sector, Team X (the recently crowned rugby world champions) announce a 'Champions Tour' holiday and entertainment package. Using their database of supporters who have previously bought a branded Team X product or service (such as Team X perfume or Team X Cola), the business ventures to sell exclusive fourteen-day breaks in each of the global venues at which the team plays over the next twelve months. Using partnerships with an international airline, tour operator and hotel chain, Team X guarantees to provide customers with a high-quality holiday and leisure experience of a lifetime. Amongst the package's features are exclusive access to players. In return for an image rights payment by Team X, players agree to accompany customers on personal shopping tours, training sessions and evening meals. Customers get to select a player of their choice to accompany them.

and human resource management will become essential; sport businesses will need management expertise to reconcile the competing demands of customers and elite performers.

Managing ethical and governance concerns, both in relation to on-field and off-field performance, will increasingly impinge on sport businesses; there will be a need to balance equality and fairness with a need for sporting and business excellence; there will be growing public and media scrutiny of business operations, not just playing performance.

Implementing risk management techniques will become necessary; given the potential cost and revenue implications of sport business ventures, decisions will have to be taken and implemented in the context of identified risks; where perceived risks outweigh the attractions (sporting, commercial or otherwise) of e.g. stadium relocations, appropriate decisions will need to be made.

Participants

The need to consider legal rights and responsibilities more carefully and, where appropriate, to explore protective measures such as enhanced insurance cover; need for legal affairs to be taken more seriously in relation to both on-field and off-field activities. In an era of freedom of movement, rising salaries and the proliferation of commercial opportunity, sport businesses may seek to tie participants to teams, clubs and events; in an attempt to guarantee exclusivity, participants may be able to negotiate shareholdings in sport businesses and rights to payment for use of their image and intellectual property; need to address the legal and ethical ramifications of such arrangements.

Given the importance of top performers to the on-field playing and off-field commercial performance of sport businesses, need to address the implications of conduct and behaviour on and off the field of play; also need to address the relevance of information to the relationship with a club e.g. in the case of a long-term injury, if a participant chooses to remain silent about this when signing for a team or club, what are the implications should this information subsequently become public knowledge?

Captain K is one of the old school – football is a contact sport and should be played with commitment, passion and spirit. In an end of season game, Captain K goes for a ball but, in so doing, injures Captain S. Captain S is injured and carried off with serious injuries to his head and foot. The transfer value of Captain S immediately falls, and the bonuses he will receive from a proposed transfer during the summer are slashed. A lucrative contract endorsing running shoes and hair care products also becomes endangered. Captain S therefore takes legal action against Captain K, claiming commercial loss as a result of his challenge. Captain K makes a counter-claim against Captain S when S suggests that K is a 'thug'. Captain K indicates this will impact upon his market value as a commercial property. Captain K also takes a daily newspaper to court as a result of its reporting of the incident. In particular, Captain K wants to be compensated for the alleged damage their report has done to the 'Captain K' branded sportswear range.

In the context of the above, participants will have to consider how to reconcile on-field and off-field pressures; participant training and development needs may become evident, particularly in relation to educational background; need to consider whether traditional agents can continue to provide an appropriate service or whether professional business managers fulfil a more useful role.

Resource providers and sport business partners	Strategic collaboration will become increasingly prevalent; resource providers and sport business partners will expect a reciprocal relationship; in return for providing e.g. sponsorship funding, organisations will demand that sport businesses contribute to the strategic development of their businesses e.g. through brand association and development, development of new technology, products and services; sport businesses will therefore need to view such relationships as more than revenue generators, in which case there will be organisational and management issues. In such relationships, the contractual detail of the arrangement will be important; this will identify the rights and responsibilities of each party, and clarify the role the sport business plays in any such arrangement; in particular, issues relating to image rights, ambush protection and leverage expenditure will be of paramount importance. Given proliferation in the sports rights market, sport business will need to be aware of the opportunities available elsewhere to resource providers and sport business partners; sport businesses will need to address the financial value of such arrangements, particularly in the context of other market opportunities; consideration will need to be given to defection of partners to rivals, allied to issues of loyalty and commitment to partnership arrangements.	'Tone and Flex' (TAF) in conjunction with 'Active Male' (AM) announces a major commercial partnership with athlete Jack X. It's not a sponsorship, it's a collaborative relationship. 'Tone and Flex' is a leading body image and cosmetic treatment company, whilst AM is a lifestyle media group. TAF is using their association as a test-bed for male cosmetics, and is targeting 'the active man'. During races, Jack is expected to wear their latest cosmetics – it is stipulated in the contract, he must be groomed to perfection for every race. Meanwhile, AM has contracted Jack to appear in their monthly magazine and on their weekly digital television programme. With a reputation for being a trailblazer, Jack is a valuable endorsement property for them, and they pay him well for the use of his image. The contractual relationship between TAF and AM is an interesting one; Jack is contractually bound only to grant interviews with AM reporters. He must also mention TAF products at least three times in any interview. TAF and AM have also agreed that, when Jack races, they will use virtual signage technology to place TAF and AM logos onto Jack's torso and legs – to prevent ambushing, the whole of Jack's body is contracted to the two companies.
Fans and customers	Sport businesses will need to address how to gather and analyse data about customers, or how to develop other mechanisms through which information about the behaviour and preferences of customers can be gathered; issues of direct and database marketing will become important, which in turn will impact upon the segmentation of the sport market-place and the subsequent development of product and service offerings.	Thomas and Barbara love Josephine Yi, the latest snooker sensation from China. Following a major drive to exploit the global commercial value of the World Snooker Association brand, markets such as China have become a major source of revenue, and the sport is hugely popular. Thomas and Barbara don't really like snooker; they are more interested in Josephine and collect all of her merchandise. They particularly like her website. For a small

There will be a need to question the extent to which fans and customers stay loyal to a particular sport business brand, especially as sport comes to be dominated by a small number of global brands; given the proliferation of products and services, customers may associate with a sport business for reasons other than sport; in both cases – and in the context of a pervading loyalty scheme culture – sport businesses will need to examine the need for loyalty schemes, especially where stadium or event capacity is not fully utilised.

The growth of a service culture in other sectors will begin to impact on sport businesses; sport businesses will need to consider how they meet customer's expectations of off-field service and performance; this will impact upon operations management; the relevance of quality and performance standards will need to be examined; fans and customers who are not loyal to a particular brand or who buy from a broad portfolio of products maybe make purchase decisions based on, e.g. use of service promises or customer charters; in this context, there will need to be a greater emphasis on managing the service experience. The need to track customers and manage quality (whilst at the same time sourcing appropriate supplies from business partners) will necessitate the increased use of information technology and management information systems.

subscription, they get exclusive access to the site, where they can use the latest viewcam technology to watch every aspect of Josephine's life. During matches, they can choose from over 50 different camera angles, including 'cue cam'. They also have web access to Josephine's home and enjoy looking at her furniture and clothing. Josephine doesn't mind; she is able to track what they have looked at and is using this to target product offerings at them via direct marketing. She hopes her latest range of home furnishings will sell well. In turn, Thomas and Barbara also don't mind; whenever they buy from Yi Home Furnishings, they do so with confidence. The company was recently awarded the ISO 12000 quality measure for excellence in customer service.

Implications of the book

The Business of Sport Management is one of the first British academic textbooks to consider the growth and development of sport businesses, and the challenges facing sport managers. Many of the issues raised by the book, and covered in the case material, are nevertheless variously relevant to continental European, Oceanic, American, Asian and African sport managers. It is therefore anticipated that the book will have a broad appeal amongst students and academics alike. It is also hoped the extensive use of case material will appeal to practitioners. This is not just intended to be an academic textbook; it is envisaged sport business managers too can also benefit from reading it.

There are a number of reasons why the book should have such a broad appeal: sport is like never before. Although one can refer back to historical claims of payment and professionalism in relation to the first Olympics, sport is now dominated by commercial practice more than ever before. Naturally, some sport businesses have resisted the growth of professionalism and the pressures of the market. But the question is: for how long?

Just as businesses in other industrial sectors have to address how social trends, technological developments and globalisation will influence them, sport businesses must also consider the challenges they face. Moreover, sport faces its own unique challenges, including rising player costs, the status of its star performers and regulatory intervention by governing bodies. Until now, sport organisations have been able to satisfy themselves that the intrinsic appeal of sport will be sufficient to sustain them in the face of a multitude of challenges. However, the reality is somewhat different and sport managers need to know about the challenges they face. This might sound somewhat negative, but sport managers equally need to be acutely aware of the commercial opportunities available to their businesses. They cannot all be Manchester United or the Dallas Cowboys. But the better a sport business is managed, the more capable it will be of developing products and services which serve the needs of customers, its operations will be more efficient and, ultimately, the more profit it will make. The book is therefore intended to help current and prospective sport managers understand that the world is increasingly complex. Rather than perceive this as a threat, hopefully the book demonstrates that sport is uniquely appealing and can benefit from developments in management practice.

The mention of profit or commerce in connection with sport induces many critics of current developments to accuse sport business managers of exploitation and unethical behaviour. In some ways, this is a valid observation that is being addressed in a number of ways. The case of English soccer is one example of this, where the Football Task Force and football supporter trusts have been set up to ensure that the best interests of supporters continue to be served in a commercialising sport (Supporters Direct, 2002). Yet managing a sport business (and reading this book) is not simply about making profit. Rather, it is also about utilising and managing resources in an efficient way, and about developing products and services that add value to the customer experience. One need think no further than horse racing tracks where, for large parts of the year, huge expanses of land lay largely unused. Sport business management is about using this land effectively so that sufficient revenue can be generated to ensure its continued existence. Whether sport purists like it or not, if sport businesses do not at least break even, they go bankrupt – ask the owners of, say, the Arrows Formula 1 team.

If this book enables students and practitioners to build successful sport businesses that are both efficient and profitable, it will have achieved its main objective. In so doing, the authors will hopefully have helped sport managers to think in a different way about their organisations. Traditionally, many sport businesses have tended to operate like small firms, with a few people employed to look after stadium management, ticket sales and sponsorship. As the sport business environment has changed, so has the way in which some of these businesses are managed. Sport business managers may still question why they need to know about, for example, risk management or ethical business practices. But if a rugby league team decides to move to a new £20 million stadium, knowing how to identify and manage risks associated with the move is imperative. In the same way, a decision to produce and sell replica team strips is not simply about making money. Fan loyalty dictates that there is an ethical dimension to this kind of decision. The authors of this book believe the commentary and cases presented in the text suitably illustrate why these, and each of the other areas covered in the book, are essential reading for intending and current managers of a modern sport business.

The main problem in compiling a book of this nature is that things change. Ten years ago it was difficult to envisage that sportsmen and sportswomen would readily litigate for injuries sustained during a sporting contest. In the same way, the internet was little more than a government information network. It is now a major sport business phenomenon – a way to promote merchandise, sell tickets and communicate with supporters. Clearly, the authors of the book hope that much of the content has an enduring relevance, although such developments may not always be easy to predict. Therein lie two further challenges for the sport manager: how to apply the observations about management made in the book, and how to keep abreast of changes taking place in sport. Although the book cannot be an automatic recipe for success, nor a panacea for all ills, it is hoped sport managers will at least feel more informed, if not enthused, by reading it.

CASE 19.1 World Wrestling Entertainment: from American phenomenon to global brand

Some people think it is a joke, others believe it is a fix, but wrestling is a serious business. Based in the USA, World Wrestling Entertainment (formerly the World Wrestling Federation) is at the forefront of globally promoting wrestling.

Until the late 1990s, the WWF was a distinctly American phenomenon. In the financial year ending in 1999, the corporation made US$33 million profit from its US operations, attracted 5 million pay-TV viewers and sold 2.3 million tickets to live events in America.

Wrestling was a big hit with the American public. So much so, that the WWF began selling shares on the New York Stock Exchange in 1999. Managers at the newly floated corporation immediately began to build upon the success of what they had to offer, taking the decision to extend the WWF brand outside the USA.

Initially, this involved selling television rights overseas to countries such as Great Britain, where WWF wrestling was shown on Channel 5. This was an important element in the development of the brand, creating both awareness of the WWF and intense excitement about the product on offer.

To satisfy growing European interest which the television coverage had created, the WWF announced plans in 2001 for a European tour. This represented a major commitment to diversifying the corporation's activities, and an opportunity to pursue growth by penetrating new international markets.

The WWF implemented measures to reinforce this strategy, most notably setting up an international programming network (consisting of offices in cities such as London) to be responsible for organising and managing the global development of the brand. The corporation also introduced its 'Think Again' initiative to encourage potential global advertisers and marketing partners to work with them. By mid-2001, they had recruited 150 partners.

In 2002, the WWF suffered what appeared to be a major blow to its plans. Following a successful legal action by the World Wide Fund for Nature, the corporation lost the right to call itself WWF (becoming World Wrestling Entertainment instead). Directors of WWE nevertheless saw this as an opportunity. It established a unique and distinct global identity for the brand, and demonstrated that the corporation had become more than an American sport business. It had progressed to become a global phenomenon delivering branded entertainment products.

WWE now has plans to expand into Asia and Oceania, and to license its name to themed attractions at amusement parks.

CASE 19.2 Never mind the football, just don't spoil my hairstyle

For a time during the 2001–02 English soccer season, Manchester United fans feared the worst. Rumours abounded that contract negotiations with David Beckham had broken down and he would therefore seek a transfer to another club. In reality, the negotiations had reportedly stalled because of disagreements over image rights.

Beckham is not just a hot property on the field. Amongst his reported off-field deals with companies, he is thought to earn £3 million from a contract with Adidas, £1 million from Police sunglasses, £1 million from Brylcreem hair products and £600,000 from Pepsi. As part of a proposed new contract, Beckham apparently wanted to keep control of these deals. He was also thought to have demanded that United pay him for the use of his image. In May 2002, the club capitulated and Beckham signed a new contract. It is believed the club agreed to pay him £20,000 per week for use of his image.

The debate about image rights in English soccer emanates from the 1995 transfers of Dennis Bergkamp and David Platt to Arsenal. Constrained by a strict wages policy, the club apparently struggled to persuade the players to join them. To secure their services, Arsenal supposedly agreed to indirectly boost their salaries by signing additional deals with companies owned by the two players. This involved the club making payments for the use of each player's image rights and the time they spent working for the club on promotional activities.

The growth of image rights payments is not specific to English soccer. In Spain, Luis Figo (the Real Madrid midfield player) is thought to earn US$50 million each year from image rights deals, a figure similar to that reportedly earned by Michael Schumacher (the racing driver). Interestingly, Schumacher is understood to earn only US$20 million from his contract with the Ferrari Formula 1 team. It is estimated that Anna Kournikova (the Russian tennis player) wins around US$500,000 in prize money each year, although she has yet to win a major Grand Slam title. She is nevertheless believed to earn more than US$8 million per year from her image rights contracts.

CASE 19.3 Keeping the business afloat: Ericsson's sponsorship of the 2000 America's Cup

Arguably the most prestigious event in the yacht-racing calendar, the America's Cup was first run as the Hundred Guineas Cup in 1851. Today, it is at the pinnacle of the sport, attracting entrants from across the world.

The costs of participating in the event have spiralled upwards. Some estimates have suggested that a team intent on winning the Cup currently needs to spend more than US$40 million over the four years between each event. For the host venue, the costs are equally significant. When Auckland, New Zealand, hosted the event in 2000, it was suggested that an investment of up to US$400 million had been needed to prepare the city.

To offset these costs, yacht racing has increasingly sought to attract commercial sponsorship. This typically has involved businesses buying space on yachts and in harbours in full view of spectators. But the 2000 event was notable for changes in the involvement of sponsors. Businesses were more strategic in the way they collaborated closely with both event organisers and participating teams.

Ericsson, the communications solutions company, was especially keen to secure more than brand association and product recognition when it agreed to sponsor the Cup. Rather, the company wanted to contribute to the development of the event. This not only served to demonstrate a commitment to yacht racing, it also provided a platform for testing its latest communications technology that, in turn, helped to showcase company products.

Working with event organisers and teams, Ericsson was able to place a number of its products on participating yachts. This included the use of wireless IP technology that enabled organisers and competitors to electronically monitor position data, course information and weather conditions. The system had an added benefit in that, having developed it in collaboration with Animation Research and Telecom New Zealand, Ericsson and ESPN were able to broadcast this information direct to television and the internet, reaching a potential audience of 600 million people.

Conclusion

This chapter has focused on the future: how sport businesses can try to predict what might happen, where they can get information from that will help them to do this, what the emerging challenges facing them could be, and how they might attempt to deal with these challenges. As such, the chapter will represent a radical agenda for those sport businesses that concentrate more on the present than on the future, especially where current on-field performance is seen to be of paramount importance.

But sport businesses need to begin thinking more carefully about the next five to ten years. What they do now can have a huge impact upon what happens at a later date. Ask the managers of Formula 1 motor racing teams or English Premier League football teams, where the boom years of the 1990s have been replaced by a harsher commercial reality. Alternatively, sport businesses need to realise they cannot sit and wait for things to happen. If they are to perform well on the field, they need to be well managed off it (whether we like it or not, the two seem to have become inextricably linked). Hence, sport business managers have to face the reality that they need to forecast and plan if they are to gain both a playing and a commercial advantage. Moreover, they need to recognise that they will be doing this in an increasingly uncertain world.

The chapter has therefore considered the techniques available for forecasting the future. It has also identified where sport businesses can access information about the environments in which they operate. Knowing how to collect and analyse such information is a massive task alone, but to use information about the future is vital if sport businesses are to respond to the challenges they face. The chapter has not only detailed some of these challenges, it has also highlighted some of the responses sport businesses could take (and are taking!). It is therefore intended that the chapter serves as a useful resource for sport businesses seeking to remain competitive, to gain an advantage over their rivals, to make themselves different/attractive/more appealing to customers, and to ensure that commercial success is paralleled by on-the-field performance.

CASE 19.4 Power, but not enough glory   FT

Edoardo Polli proclaims to the ensemble of promoters, politicians and media executives in a Trieste restaurant that he is 'the most famous playboy in the world'.

A regular face on the society pages, the 54-year-old Italian textiles multi-millionaire is often seen with a beautiful young woman on his arm. So it is no surprise that a guest at this dinner in northern Italy recognises him from *Hello!* magazine.

But it is not just his beautiful girlfriends or his wealth, amassed through Legler, his Milan-based clothing company, that attract press attention.

For 10 weekends a year, Polli is a powerboat racer. The dinner in Trieste has been arranged to mark the inaugural race of the 2001 Class 1 (C1) World Offshore Championship held in Plymouth last weekend.

Offshore racing, established as a sport in 1964 by the Union Internationale Motonautique, the governing body for motorised water sports, is undergoing a transformation.

The sport has made little real progress since Sam Griffith won the inaugural Miami-to-Nassau race on May 6 1956 in a 215hp wooden Chris Craft. The greatest developments have been driven by technology, which has altered the aesthetics but little else.

Powerboat racing has struggled to be more than a hobby for the rich. But a new promoter is seeking to lessen the playboy image that has held back its commercial development. The task for Television Corporation, the London-based media group with the TV rights for the next 55 years, has parallels with that once faced by

Formula 1 motor racing and its boss Bernie Ecclestone. It took Ecclestone 15 years to turn F1 into a multi-million-pound franchise; TV Corp has a three-year plan for C1.

'This circuit has made little headway in the public consciousness,' says Terry Bate, TV Corp chairman. The reason for this, he says, is 'television, television, television. Beginning and end'.

The realisation of C1's financial potential is growing at TV Corp's Sackville Street offices. Chris Rowlands, chief executive, is making a point of containing his excitement. 'I don't want to over-hype this. Obviously it is never going to be as popular as F1,' he stresses. 'But it need only be 1 per cent as popular to make a reasonable profit. It will take three years and then we will make serious money.'

Dresdner Kleinwort Wasserstein, the investment bank, estimates that Offshore Sport Promotion, the C1 promoter acquired by TV Corp for £15 million in January, will be worth £21 million by 2005.

'We believe (this) is conservative – especially given TV Corp's ability to professionalise the sport,' it said. 'To put this value into context, it represents only the annual amount that Germany alone pays for F1 TV rights.'

Rowlands says 2001 will be a year of transition for C1, as it builds on its existing fan base. More than 1 million people, for example, watched a race from the banks of the Bosphorus in Turkey last year. The trick is how to make money from this audience.

TV Corp is planning to invest £1 million this year to build TV and sponsorship sales. A distribution deal has been struck with Channel 4, which will show the first series of races from September.

Global TV revenues in 2005 are forecast to reach £6 million. Dresdner Kleinwort Wasserstein expects £2 million of annual sponsorship for C1 from 2003. But these figures are still small compared with the amount companies pay to advertise on the side of a F1 car.

'It has all the elements of F1. In respect of the locations it rivals F1, because the dramatic coastal scenery in each country differs so much,' says Martin McDonald, business development manager at All Ways Forward, a provider of support services for F1.

Racing these boats is an expensive business and the lack of sponsorship is the main reason the sport has stayed the domain of the rich.

'Earlier in this sport, if you had enough money, you won,' says Helge Otto Mathisen, of Color Line, the Norwegian shipping company backing the team run by Bjørn Gjelsten, owner of Wimbledon Football Club and one of Norway's richest men.

Indications of the wealth needed come in the shape of the articulated lorries that transport the boats. There were plenty parked around the port in Trieste, which in June played host to the Italian Grand Prix. Even bigger trucks house elaborate headquarters for teams, their managers, mechanics, and a raft of support staff. Hospitality tents, crammed with people enjoying VIP privileges, dot the water's edge.

The most impressive set-up belongs to the Victory Team, financially assisted by the Dubai government. State-of-the-art technology and a professionalism that observers say rivals any F1 team has put it ahead of the pack.

Race entrants will have spent about $1 million each on their boats alone to get to the start line. The carbon-fibre hulls can cost $450,000; the two engines – 12-cylinder Lamborghini petrol or 10.3-litre Seatek diesel – are $80,000 each.

Polli, who has never won the world title, has pumped at least $15 million into this pursuit since 1985. He says it costs him $1 million a year to maintain Highlander, his boat emblazoned with a snarling, cigar-chomping cartoon bear.

This is probably a conservative estimate and pales in comparison with the budgets of rivals. Spirit of Norway, Gjelsten's boat, has at least Nkr20 million ($2m) a year at its disposal. It is said that Victory, which has won the world championship for the past two years, spends $15 million a year running its three teams.

Yet Polli claims C1 is a 'relatively inexpensive sport'.

'It costs Ferrari $500,000 a year to run a medium (motor-racing) team and you can spend $300m to $400m on go-karting,' he says, lighting up his ubiquitous Cuban cigar (he even takes one with him during a race).

Polli, a charismatic character, is chairman of the International Offshore Team Association, which represents the circuit's teams. He is one of those trying to reshape the sport and is courted by the sport's men in suits. But he also embodies the past.

As Rowlands says: 'It has been very much a way of life rather than a sport or a way of making any money.'

Rowlands sees TV Corp's production expertise as vital. The company sharpened TV coverage of cricket on Channel 4 and presentation of C1 will feature far more than sun-drenched backdrops, bikini-clad groupies and flashy boats. Helicopters, for example, can fly close to the boats – during the Italian Grand Prix, the Victory helicopter flew at more than 100mph touching its boat's spray.

Explanatory graphics and statistics – about engine performance, for example – are also likely to enhance the viewing experience. And TV Corp is keen on personalities – creating heroes and villains.

To this end, the quest is on for new blood. Even the younger drivers have been around for some time: Steve Curtis, the 36-year-old three-times champion, has 58 races under his belt.

And while the cost of entry is high, prize money is paltry. Sponsorship, it is hoped, will help attract younger, less-affluent drivers.

Steps have also been taken by the regulatory bodies to get the sport into better shape, most importantly with a long-negotiated change in the rules regarding technical specifications, which should make the sport more accessible by reducing costs.

Another change is a ban on visible exhaust fumes, an important PR move. Environmentalists say the sport is dirty and destructive to wildlife and in Trieste, 20 campaigners swam out to the starting line, delaying the race for an hour.

The governing bodies are making moves to address concerns. Noise tests, for example, have measured the impact on fish and nesting birds in the fjords in Norway. The effect was negligible, according to Richard Ridout, president of Cominoff, the commission which enforces the sport's rules.

Another stain on the sport's image is its association during the 1970s and 1980s with drug smugglers, using speedboats to outrun the US coastguard. A decade later, the sport was tarnished by allegations of tax evasion by Italian participants.

'Respectability has started to creep in with the arrival of the Dubai and Norwegian teams,' says Ridout.

Mismanagement has been another concern. 'The sport has been fantastically mis-managed,' says Rowlands. 'Bureaucracy has held it back. It's incompetence rather than corruption.'

At least safety has been improved in recent years, following the death in 1990 of Stephano Casiraghi, husband of Princess Caroline of Monaco, as he defended his world title in front of a home crowd.

The championship was abandoned that year but since then open-style cockpits, such as the one Casiraghi was in, have been replaced by canopies borrowed from the aerospace industry. The two-strong team – a driver and throttleman – wear fireproof overalls, thick suede boots and helmets fitted with a radio. They are also strapped into special seats.

However, the memory of Casiraghi runs deep and dramatic crashes keep fears alive. Earlier this month at the German Grand Prix in Lübeck, Polli destroyed his boat.

Joking about being a Highlander and therefore immortal, as was the namesake in the film, he promptly bought another one.

If TV Corp is to marry this cavalier spirit with a serious business ethos, and make the leap from rich man's plaything to serious brand, it has to act swiftly. The time for winning over an audience may be short.

'If it is not cracked by the third year, it never will be,' says Ridout.

Source: Ashling O'Connor, *Financial Times*, 4 August 2001

Discussion questions

1. To what extent do you think the unpopularity of powerboat racing is due to the industrial concentration currently taking place in the sport industry? Is it due to the failure of managers to market the sport properly? Or, does the sport simply lack intrinsic appeal?

2. What is the range of potential scenarios facing powerboat racing, and what strategies do each one of them imply that the sport's managers should implement?

Discussion questions

3. Select one of the following examples of a sport business: a professional football club such as Manchester United, a venue such as Cardiff's Millennium Stadium or a motor racing event such as the British Grand Prix at Silverstone. For your chosen example, develop three scenarios which detail what might happen to the business over the next ten years. For each scenario, provide an indication of any actions the business should take in response to the changes you have noted.

4. Using the information presented in Tables 19.1 and 19.2, explain how a sport business such as the Once pro-cycling team, the Wigan Warriors rugby league team or the Doncaster Belles women's football team might respond to the challenges it could face in the future. In particular, note what you think might be the specific operational implications for each business, referring directly to chapters in this book in support of your answer.

5. Assess the impact that broader changes in customer service expectations have had upon sport. Examine whether sport businesses are in a position to respond to these expectations, noting any internal or external changes you feel a sport business of your choice will need to make to enhance the service it provides in the future.

6. To what extent do you think the internet will continue to be important for sport businesses in the future? Using a sport business of your choice, explain how the business has thus far utilised the internet, the benefits this has brought, and how you envisage the business using the internet in the future.

7. What do you understand by the term strategic collaboration? In the case of the collaborative relationships between the Olympic Games and companies such as Heineken, the Williams Formula 1 motor racing team and companies such as Compaq, and the England cricket team and companies such as Admiral, explain what forms collaboration has taken, what the motives for it are in each case, and whether or not the strategy will continue to help the businesses concerned in the future.

Guided reading

For students wanting to familiarise themselves with business forecasting techniques, a standard textbook on strategic management, such as Lynch (2003), should be sufficient as an introduction. For those seeking a more detailed commentary, Finlay's book on strategic management (2000) examines a range of forecasting techniques and highlights key issues for those who intend to use the techniques mentioned. In cases where students require a more quantitative approach to forecasting, Waters (2001) contains information about the statistical procedures underpinning some of the techniques mentioned in this chapter. The area of business forecasting is also well served by journals such as the *Journal of Business Forecasting Methods and Systems*. This is a good source of information on current forecasting practices and students might find articles by Chase (1998) and Lapide (2002) an interesting overview of recent developments in forecasting.

Further resources relating to business forecasting can be found on the Institute of Business Forecasting website, which, in turn, provides links to other forecasting resources. Journals in the area of strategy and planning, including *Long Range Planning*, can also prove to be useful reading and are sometimes a good source of information about potential future developments in the business world.

There is an increasing array of sport business-related information available including journals, websites and current issues publications. A number of relevant websites are listed below, although students will find that the *Journal of Sport Management* and *European Sport Management Quarterly* are good academic sources of information, whilst news services such as Sport Business International, ESPN Sports Business and Sports Business Daily offer a more practical perspective of business developments in sport. Students may also find it useful to monitor developments associated with the European Association for Sport Management, the Sport Management Association of Australia and New Zealand and the North American Association of Sport Management. Each of these organisations holds an annual conference at which academics and practitioners present papers of current interest. Their websites are also good sources of information about current and potential future developments in sport.

Recommended websites

ESPN Sports Business: http://espn.go.com/sportsbusiness
European Association for Sport Management: http://www.easm.org
European Sport Management Quarterly: http://www.meyer-meyer-sports.com
Institute of Business Forecasting: http://www.ibforecast.com
John Beech's Sport Management Information Gateway:
http://www.stile.coventry.ac.uk/cbs/staff/beech/sport/index.htm
Journal of Sport Management: http://www.humankinetics.com/products/journals
Long Range Planning: http://www.lrp.ac
North American Association of Sport Management: http://www.nassm.com
Sport Business International: http://www.sportbusiness.com
Sport Management Association of Australia and New Zealand:
http://www.gu.edu.au/school/lst/scrvices/smaanz
SportQuest: http://www.sportquest.com
Sports Business and Industry Online: http://www.sportsvueinc.com
Sports Business Daily: http://www.sportsbusinessdaily.com
Sports Business Journal: http://www.sportsbusinessjournal.com
Sports Business News: http://www.sportsbusinessnews.com
The Sport Journal: http://www.thesportjournal.org

Visit www.booksites.net/chadwickbeech for links to these and other relevant websites.

Keywords

Brainstorming; causal forecast; Delphi technique; image rights; judgemental forecast; modelling; primary data; scenario; secondary data; strategic collaboration; time-series forecast.

Bibliography

Akers, C. (1997) 'Case Study: Caspian's move to Leeds United', SMi Football Conference, London, March.

Barrand, D. (2002) 'Ford signs CART marketing deal', *Sport Business International*, 22 November, accessed from http://www.sportbusiness.com

Benz, M. (2001) 'WWF may body slam its way across the globe', *Amusement Business*, 3 December, p. 48.

Chase, C.W. (1998) 'The role of life cycles and forecast horizons in a forecasting system: Reebok's perspective', *Journal of Business Forecasting Methods and Systems*, vol. 17(1), pp. 23–9.

Delpy, L. and Bosetti, H.A. (1998) 'Sport management and marketing via the World Wide Web', *Sport Marketing Quarterly*, 7(1), pp. 21–7.

Dickson, G. (1999) 'America's Cup goes digital', *Broadcasting and Cable*, 5 July, p. 27.

Dickson, M. (2002) 'Nasser men backing the ICC Rebels', *Daily Mail*, 22 August, p. 87.

Finlay, P. (2000) *Strategic Management: An Introduction to Business and Corporate Strategy*, FT Prentice Hall, Harlow, pp. 54–80.

Glendinning, M. (2001) 'Preparing for trouble in paradise', *Sport Business International*, 1 July, p. 6.

Glendinning, M. (2002) 'UEFA sets new agenda', *Sport Business International*, 10 July, accessed from http://www.sportbusiness.com

Lapide, L. (2002) 'New developments in business forecasting', *Journal of Business Forecasting Methods and Systems*, 21(2), pp. 11–14.

Lynch, R. (2003) *Corporate Strategy*, 3rd edn, FT Prentice Hall, Harlow.

Mitchell, K. (2002) 'Last rights for Ruben', *The Observer*, 8 September, p. 15.

Saunders, M., Lewis, P. and Thornhill, A. (2003) *Research Methods for Business Students*, FT Prentice Hall, Harlow.

Scarrott, M. (ed.) (1999) *Sports, Leisure and Tourism Information Sources*, Butterworth Heinemann, Oxford.

Supporters Direct (2002) *The Supporters Direct Initiative*, accessed 3 December from http://www.supporters-direct.org/

Tapp, A. and Clowes, J. (2002) 'From "Carefree Casuals" to "Professional Wanderers": segmentation possibilities for football supporters', *European Journal of Marketing*, 36(11), pp. 34–46.

Waters, D. (2001) *Quantitative Methods for Business*, FT Prentice Hall, Harlow, pp. 262–99.

Wheatley, C. (2002) 'When a face is worth a fortune', *Sunday Business*, 30 June, p. 1.

G14 clubs

G14 describes itself as 'the outcome of the determination of the chairmen of the leading football clubs in Europe to join forces' and brands itself as 'the voice of the clubs'. Beginning as a group of six clubs, it grew incrementally to a membership of fourteen, the grouping from which it took its name. More recently four further clubs have joined without a change of the group's name.

Current members are:

Club	Country
AFC Ajax	Netherlands
Arsenal FC	England, UK
FC Barcelona	Spain
Borussia Dortmund	Germany
Bayer 04 Leverkusen	Germany
PSV (Eindhoven)	Netherlands
Juventus FC	Italy
Liverpool FC	England, UK
Olympique Lyonnais	France
Real Madrid	Spain
Manchester United FC	England, UK
Olympique de Marseille	France
AC Milan	Italy
FC Internazionale Milano	Italy
FC Bayern München	Germany
Paris Saint Germain	France
Futebol Clube do Porto	Portugal
Valencia CF	Spain

Membership by country: England 3; France 3; Germany 3; Italy 3; Netherlands 2; Portugal 1; Spain 3.

Source: Based on information available at http://www.g14.com

Glossary

Ambush marketing: A tactic whereby a company attempts to ambush or undermine the sponsorship activities of a rival that owns the legal rights to sponsor an event; often involves creating the sense that they, and not the actual sponsor, are associated with the owners of the event or activity.

Amenity services: Provided largely to locally-determined standards to meet the needs of a local community.

Anthropomaximology: Abbreviated as *AML* in Russian and derived from the Greek word, *anthropos*, which means human being, the Latin, *maximum*, and the Greek, *logos*, which was interpreted to mean study. *AML* is the science investigating the reserve potential of the healthy employee and the way to realise such potential fully under maximum effort.

Arbitration: Settling of a dispute by an outside person or persons, chosen by both sides.

Behavioural factors: Those relating to the individual, to how that individual lives or has lived and to how that individual actually behaves.

Benchmarks: Targets for performance.

Benefits: What the sport product or service offers the person.

Betting exchange: An online exchange where people deposit funds in order to make a bet. The exchange then matches people betting for and against, for example, a horse and they are paired off. Exchanges allow betting to take place up until the end of a sporting contest, providing people betting for and against an outcome can be found.

Bookmaking: In bookmaking the punter bets against the bookmaker. Bookmakers operate from shops, via telephone, from 'pitches' or shops at sporting venues and, increasingly, via the internet. The bookmaker displays a list of prices (known as 'odds') at which he is willing to take bets.

Brainstorming: A technique for generating, refining and developing ideas that can be undertaken by individuals, but is more effective when undertaken by a group of people.

Broadband: Technology that allows a high rate of electronic data transmission.

Bureaucracy: An organisation typified by formal processes, standardisation, hierarchic procedures, and written communication.

Business: An organisation that operates in order to make a profit; also the collective word for the activities in which they engage.

Business continuity planning: Identifies an organisation's exposure to internal and external threats and synthesises hard and soft assets to provide effective prevention and recovery for the organisation, whilst maintaining competitive advantage and value system integrity.

Capital asset price model (CAPM): The rate of return on any asset consists of two components – the pure time value of money and the risk premium reflecting the sensitivity of the asset to changes in market returns. The beta value of an asset measures its sensitivity to general market movements.

Causal forecast: Forecasting technique used to identify the relationship between two or more variables whereby a change in one variable causes a change in one or more of the other variables.

Central Council for Recreation and Training: Formed in 1935 to improve physical and mental health.

Collective sale of sports rights: When a league sells the broadcasting rights for the entire (or a large number of) matches in the league.

Commercialisation: The process increasingly found in sport where a business or businesses from outside the sport have become significant stakeholders in the sport in order to make a direct or indirect profit.

Complex bet: Punters bet on a series of outcomes all of which have to occur in order for the bet to be won.

Control: Monitoring and if necessary adjusting the performance of the organisation and its members.

Crisis: An incident or event with consequences which pose a significant threat to the strategic objectives of an organisation.

Crisis management: A term that refers to a three-stage process from the incubation of crisis potential through incident management to post-incident media management and brand repositioning.

Cultural discount: The reduction in value of a TV programme when it is being sold on an external market.

Culture: A shared psychological framework for ordering and interpreting experiences, and for determining responses to them.

Customer management: A technique based on direct marketing that attempts to manage customers (supporters) over time.

Customer satisfaction: Comparison of expectations versus perception of experience.

Debt irrelevance proposition: Under ideal conditions of perfect capital markets, no taxes and no bankruptcy or financial distress costs, the market value of a company is unaffected by its capital gearing (i.e. the proportion of debt in the capital structure). At a practical level, the debt irrelevance proposition implies that the value of a company depends primarily on its business model not its financial structure.

Defendant: Person who starts an action against someone in the civil courts. (Note: since the introduction of the new Civil Procedure Rules in April 1999, claimant has replaced this term).

Delphi technique: A technique for generating information about the future involving a number of iterative stages through which managers establish a consensual view of what might happen to a business.

Demographic factors: Those relating to personal characteristics such as age, gender, social class, level of education, occupation and family status.

Devoted fan: Has a strong association with a team, a personality or possibly a sport.

Digital convergence: The technological trend whereby a variety of different digital devices such as televisions, mobile telephones, and now refrigerators are merging into a multi-use communications appliance employing common software to communicate through the internet.

Discounted cash flow (DCF) analysis: The present value of any individual asset or portfolio of assets equals the discounted value of expected net future cash flows. The discount factor should reflect the cost of waiting (i.e. the pure time value of money), the risk of the asset and expected future inflation. DCF analysis is applied to investment project appraisal and corporate valuation.

Disintermediation: The process of doing away with middlemen from business transactions.

Dividend discount model (DDM): The market value of a company's equity equals the present value of expected future dividend payments. The DDM assumes that either dividend payments are fixed or grow at a constant rate so that the company's equity can be treated as a perpetuity.

Dysfunctional fan: Exhibits extreme loyalty and often obsessive behaviour.

Efficient market hypothesis (EMH): An asset market is information-efficient if asset prices fully reflect all currently available information on future asset returns. New information is incorporated quickly and correctly into asset prices through market trading.

Equality and equity: Whereas equality may mean equality of opportunity, of resource allocation, of objective outcome, of subjective outcome (that is taking into account different needs or just desserts), equity is taken to mean equality relative to individual contributions.

Equivalence proposition: The market value of a company can be measured by three theoretically-equivalent methods – the present value of expected future free cash flows (i.e. cash flows generated by operating activities net of taxes and asset purchases/sales), the current market value of debt and equity, and the current going-concern value of the company's assets.

Ethics: The principles or assumptions underpinning the way individuals or organisations ought to conduct themselves.

European Broadcasting Union (EBU): An organisation of 69 TV channels in 50 countries, mainly European, which is driven on a non-profit basis. Its members are mainly public service broadcasters.

Facility services: Services for people to draw upon if they wish.

Fanatical fan: Exhibits quite addictive but controlled behaviour.

Financial ratio analysis: The analysis of a company's financial performance using selected summary ratios calculated using the accounting information provided in financial statements. Financial ratios are categorised typically into five groups covering profitability, asset efficiency (or activity), liquidity, financing and market value (or shareholder returns).

Financial statement: The report provided by a company on its financial performance using accounting standards. A company's financial statement consists of a profit and loss account, a balance sheet (i.e. assets and liabilities) and a cash flow statement.

GANTT chart: A bar chart used to illustrate both the sequence and expected duration of activities within an event.

Geographic factors: Those relating to the place or environment where that individual spends, or has spent, a proportion of their time.

Governance: The management of a system, usually political or organisational, involving mutual adjustment, negotiation and accommodation between the parties involved rather than direct control.

Group norms: Informal standards of behaviour and performance that develop from the interaction of the group.

Hazard: A physical entity, condition, activity, substance or behaviour that is capable of doing harm.

Image rights: The legal rights associated with using the image of a sports person in marketing and promotional activities.

Impact of expectancy: From a western perspective, the 'impact of expectancy' can be explained from the angle of seeing another individual's behaviour being affected by (a) what a person wants to happen; (b) his/her estimate of the probability that an event will become manifest; (c) his/her belief that the event will satisfy a particular need.

Incident management: The process of managing a crisis event.

Individual sale of sports rights: When the home club sells the broadcasting rights for all their matches – or separately.

Interlocutory injunction: Injunction which is granted for the period until a case comes to court.

Internet: A global system of interconnected networks providing links to millions of computers that allow access to billions of web pages on a huge number of topics.

It relies on a system of computer protocols to allow information to be exchanged between networks.

Judgemental forecast: Forecasting technique involving the use of opinion, experience and judgement; often used when there is little information about a specific set of circumstances.

Judicial precedent: Precedent set by a court decision, which can be reversed only by a higher court.

Jurisprudence: Study of the law and the legal system.

Leadership: Influencing and directing the performance of group members towards the achievement of organisational goals.

Leverage: The methods and techniques used to ensure a sponsorship is managed in such a way that it generates the maximum possible value for the sponsor.

Libel: Written and published or broadcast statement which damages someone's character (in a permanent form).

Life cycle: A method of analysing industries and/or specific organisations based on the premise that all business has a lifespan, moving from birth to eventual demise.

Local fan: Identifies with particular geographic area.

Management: The process of planning, leading, organising and controlling people within a group in order to achieve goals; also used to mean the group of people who do this.

McKinsey's 7S framework: A framework for analysing the seven interrelating framework elements of an organisational system.

Mediation: Attempt by a third party to make the two sides in an argument agree.

MIS: Management information system.

Mission statement: A statement that makes clear the sport organisation's purpose, principle business aims, identity, policies and values.

Modelling: Forecasting technique normally involving the use of computer software; software is used to identify the nature and strength of relationships between variables contained in sets of data.

Motivation: A psychological concept with no single universally accepted definition, but which organisational sociologists aver concerns the determinants of *intent*, *effort* and *tenacity*, factors that push or pull us as individuals to behave in a particular manner.

Multiple intelligences: Howard Gardner argues that his intelligence does not stop at his skin and moves both intrinsically to his bio-psychological make-up and extrinsically to his social and natural environment. Thus, the term encompasses seven intelligences that encompass the biological, psychological, social, naturalist and spiritual dimensions of our life.

National Recreation Centres: Elite residential centres created after the Second World War.

Need services: Services provided for all, regardless of means.

Needs: The reasons why people buy/consume sport products.

Not-for-profit organisation: An organisation whose primary purpose is other than making a profit. To survive, a not-for-profit organisation must at least break even financially. Hence: Not-for-Profit Sport Organisation (NPSO).

Obiter dicta (singular is obiter dictum): Latin phrase meaning 'things which are said in passing': part of a judgment, which is not essential to the decision of the judge and does not create a precedent.

Objectives: The organisational goals that must be achieved if the strategic intent is to be implemented.

Operational sport marketing: The execution of sport marketing involving research, analysis, planning, implementation and control.

Operations: A transformation process; a function of an organisation and a management activity.

Organisation: Used collectively to describe a group of people acting to achieve a common goal.

Pay-TV channels: TV channels which receive their revenues mainly from charging the viewers subscription fees and/or pay-per-views. Non-commercial PSB channels receive their entire incomes from public funding and/or licence fees. Commercial PSB channels receive their main revenues from selling advertising.

Performance measurement system: Financial and non-financial comprehensive manner to monitor organisational progress.

PESTEL: A framework for social/global analysis enabling a strategist to identify the key influences on his/her industry.

Plaintiff: Person who is sued in a civil case.

Pool betting: Betters buy stakes on certain events. All the stakes are pooled. At the close of betting the number of stakes is added up, a deduction made to cover operating expenses, profits, taxes and any other costs, and the total remaining divided up amongst the winning tickets and the pool distributed to the winning ticket holders as a dividend.

Porter's forces: The five forces which, according to Michael Porter, shape competition within an industry.

Primary data: Data collected specifically for a purpose; sources may include questionnaires, interviews and focus groups.

Professional: Being paid to do an activity as the significant portion of one's income.

Project brief: The project brief is an instruction to the design team of what the project planning team expects from the facility.

Protective services: Provided for the security of the population; run according to national guidelines.

Public service broadcasting (PSB) channels: TV channels which have objectives other than the entertainment of viewers and the profitability of private broadcasting firms.

Qualified privilege: Protection from being sued for defamation given to someone only if it can be proved that the statements were made without malice.

Quality: The customer's perception of the degree to which a product or service is fit for purpose.

Quality standards: Benchmarks of levels of service or design specification.

Return on capital employed (ROCE): A key financial ratio that measures profit before interest and tax as a return on capital employed (i.e. debt and equity). ROCE can be decomposed into two constituent ratios – asset turnover (measuring the marketing efficiency with which sales revenue is generated from the asset base) and the net profit margin (measuring the operating cost efficiency with which profits are earned from sales revenue).

Rights fee: The payment made in cash or in kind by the sponsor to the sponsee in order to secure the legal rights of association with an activity or an event.

Risk: The probability that a specified hazard will result in an undesired event.

Risk management: The overall process of ensuring that risks are managed in the most cost-efficient and cost-effective way.

Scenario: Pictures of the future developed by those with an understanding of a business or an industry, which are often used to predict the longer term, that is, a time in the future when past or current data may not be applicable.

Secondary data: Data collected for a purpose other than the one a forecaster may use it for; sources may include newspapers, press releases, market research reports.

Service: Unique characteristics of heterogeneity, simultaneous, intangible and perishable offering.

Shareholder value: The present value of the future dividend stream expected to be generated by a company.

Slander: Untrue spoken statement which damages someone's character.

Small- to medium-size enterprise (SME): A variety of definitions exist, the most widely accepted one being 'a business employing fewer than 250 people'.

SMART objectives: SMART acronym (Specific, Measurable, Achievable, Relevant and Timebound) – if objectives are not SMART it is hard to ascertain if they have been achieved or not.

Special events: The specific rituals, presentations, performances or celebrations that are planned and created to mark special occasions or to achieve particular social, cultural or corporate goals and objectives.

Sport marketing plan: Formal written statement of marketing intent that summarises the key points of the operational sport marketing process.

Sport sponsorship: An exchange between two parties whereby the sponsee receives cash and/or benefits in kind while the sponsor secures a right of association with an activity or event.

Sports brand: The complete set of images about the sport organisation held in the mind of the supporter.

Sports Council: Created in 1971 to help develop elite performers and increase overall participation.

Sports promotions: Short-term devices that convert the hesitant buyer into action.

Sports rights (also called broadcasting rights): The rights to broadcast from a sporting event on TV or another media within a specific region, most commonly a nation.

Spread betting: The most sophisticated type of sports betting that enables more interesting bets to be placed on many events and contests such as a bet on the margin of victory.

Stakeholder: Individual or group which holds an interest in, has made a contribution to, or is significantly affected by an entity such as a business, community or political organisation. The contribution to, or impact of, the organisation may be financial or a contribution in kind such as voluntary effort, or may be intangible such as an emotional commitment/impact. Stakeholder analysis has come to mean that the interests of all affected by a company or political decision should be considered, not simply those with a direct financial interest.

Staple bet: The punter will bet on who they think will be the winner of an event, match or a race.

Strategic collaboration: Strategy through which one organisation works or combines with another organisation in order to achieve goals that would otherwise be unattainable; includes joint ventures, strategic alliances and partnerships.

Strategy: A long-term plan that influences and directs all business functions.

SWOT analysis: Refers to an analysis of the strengths, weaknesses, opportunities and threats of an organisation or an event.

Tactics: The behaviours through which objectives and, ultimately, the strategic intent are achieved.

Temporary fan: Shows only a limited engagement that will not lead to high levels of loyalty or particularly fan-like behaviour.

Time-series forecast: Forecasting technique which utilises past and current data as a basis for extrapolating about the future.

Vision: A clear, detailed picture of what should be achieved.

VMOST: A framework for internal analysis.

Wagering: An agreement to pay out an amount of money based on the outcome of an unsettled matter.

Weighted average cost of capital (WACC): The overall cost of a company's financing calculated as the average of the after-tax interest rate on the company's debt and required rate of return on the company's equity weighted by the respective proportion of debt and equity in the company's capital structure. The WACC represents the capital market's overall assessment of the rate of return that should be earned by the company to cover the pure time value of money, the risk premium and expected future inflation. The WACC provides the company with the benchmark discount rate for evaluating average-risk projects.

Wolfenden Committee: Established in 1957 to suggest how statutory bodies could assist in promoting the general welfare of the community in sport and leisure.

WWW: World wide web is the graphical user interface supported by HTML that displays web pages on the internet and is accessed using computer software called a browser.

Yenza: A Zulu word which means taking small steps, exploring the risks as a dynamic collective or team and starting 'to do' the job so as to accumulate a holistic understanding of the human capital development process. This results-centred bottom-up approach translates strategic HR planning and design efforts into 'action' that can be measured in human terms.

Index